CONTENTS

v

vi

i.m.

Jacqueline Bardolph

1936-1999

ACKNOWLEDGMENTS

The editor and publisher of this book of essays are very grateful to the following individuals and institutions for permission to reprint formerly published materials or materials to which they hold or administer copyrights. All reasonable effort has been made to trace other copyright holders; any responses or relevant information will be welcomed.

Nuruddin Farah and the *Third World Quarterly* for "Why I Write."

Nuruddin Farah and *World Literature Today* for "Celebrating Differences: The 1998 Neustadt Lecture."

Reed Way Dasenbrock and *World Literature Today* for "Nuruddin Farah: A Tale of Two Trilogies."

Charles Sugnet and *World Literature Today* for permission to publish a revised and expanded version of "Nuruddin Farah's Maps: Deterritorialization and the Postmodern."

Michael Eldridge and *World Literature Today* for permission to publish a revised version of "Out of the Closet."

John C. Hawley and *Ultimate Reality and Meaning* for permission to reprint a revised version of "Nuruddin Farah: Tribalism, Orality and Postcolonial Ultimate Reality and Meaning in Contemporary Somalia."

Barbara Turfan and the *Journal of Commonwealth Literature* for "Opposing Dictatorship: Nuruddin Farah's *Variations on the Theme of an African Dictatorship*."

Jacqueline Bardolph and the *Journal of Commonwealth Literature* for "Time and History in Nuruddin Farah's *Close Sesame*."

The *Journal of Commonwealth Literature* for permission to reprint material from Derek Wright's "Going to Meet the General: "Deeriye's Death in *Close Sesame*."

Kirsten Holst Petersen and *ARIEL* and the Board of Governors, University of Calgary, for "The Personal and the Political: The Case of Nuruddin Farah."

ARIEL and the Board of Governors, University of Calgary, for permission to reprint material from Derek Wright's "Zero Zones: Nuruddin Farah's Fiction."

Ian Adam and *World Literature Written in English* for "The Murder of Soyaan Keynaan."

Florence Stratton and *World Literature Written in English* for "The Novels of Nuruddin Farah."

Gerald Moore and the *International Fiction Review* for "Nomads and Feminists: The Novels of Nuruddin Farah."

Felix Mnthali and *Ufahamu* for "Autocracy and the Limits of Identity: A Reading of the Novels of Nuruddin Farah."

Peter Schraeder and *Northeast African Studies* for "The Novels of Nuruddin Farah: The Sociopolitical Evolution of a Somali Writer."

Ali Jimale Ahmed and *The Red Sea Press, Inc.* for permission to reprint "Nuruddin Farah and the (Re)Writing of Somali Historiography: Narrative as a Politically Symbolic Act" from Ali

Jimale Ahmed's *Daybreak is Near: Literature, Clans, and the Nation-State in Somalia* (1996).

Dubravka Juraga and *Critique* for "Nuruddin Farah's *Variations on the Theme of an African Dictatorship*: Patriarchy, Gender and Political Oppression in Somalia" originally published in *Critique* 38, 3 (Spring 1997), pp.205-220. Reprinted with permission of the Helen Dwight Reid Educational Foundation. Published by Heldref Publications, 1319 18th Street, NW, Washington, DC 20036-1802. Copyright © 1997.

Critique for material from Derek Wright's "Nations as Fictions: Postmodernism in the Novels of Nuruddin Farah," originally published in *Critique* 38, 3 (Spring 1997), pp.193-204. Reprinted with permission of the Helen Dwight Reid Educational Foundation. Published by Heldref Publications, 1319 18th Street, NW, Washington, D.C. 20036-1802. Copyright © 1997.

Eckhard Breitinger for material in Derek Wright's essay, "Mapping Farah's Fiction: The Postmodern Landscapes," which appeared in different form in the author's *The Novels of Nuruddin Farah* (Bayreuth African Studies, 1994).

Patricia Alden and *Matatu* for permission to reprint a revised and expanded version of "New Women and Old Myths: Chinua Achebe's *Anthills of the Savannah* and Nuruddin Farah's *Sardines*."

Francesca Kazan and *NOVEL* for "Recalling the Other Third World: Nuruddin Farah's *Maps*." *NOVEL: A Forum on Fiction*, vol.26, no.3, Spring 1993. Copyright *NOVEL* Corp. © 1993. Reprinted with permission.

Francis Ngaboh-Smart, *Research in African Literatures*, and Indiana University Press for "Dimensions of Gift-Giving in Nuruddin Farah's *Gifts*."

Abdulrazak Gurnah and the *CRNLE Reviews Journal* for "Nuruddin Farah's *Gifts*."

Simon Gikandi for "The Politics and Poetics of National Formation: Recent African Writing."

Rossana Ruggiero and Bulzoni Editore for "Nuruddin Farah's *Maps*: The Faint Borderland of a Warrior of Words."

William Riggan and *World Literature Today* for photographs from the Neustadt International Prize for Literature Ceremony at the University of Oklahoma, October 1998.

Eckhard Breitinger and Helen Tiffin for the other photographs in the anthology.

INTRODUCTION

Nuruddin Farah is one of Africa's most multilingual and multi-literate writers. At the age of ten he knew, in addition to spoken Somali, four language-scripts: the Amharic script of his school in the Ogaden; the Arabic script of the Koranic academy; the Roman script of the two colonial languages, English and Italian (thus English, his chosen medium of expression, is his fourth tongue); and Cusmanniya, the future basis of Somali orthography but then an underground script learned secretly because of the disapproval of the Ogaden's Ethiopian and European colonial authorities. At thirteen he had read Dostoevsky and Victor Hugo in Arabic and English translations. "We moved from one language universe to another," he has written, "with the disquiet of a tenant on a temporary lease."[1]

It is with equal disquiet that Farah, as man and writer, has become, quite literally, a wanderer across worlds, a global nomad who is at once both more and less free than the traditional nomadic pastoralists of his native culture. While the herdsman's movements are tied narrowly to a single microcosmic group, Farah's travels and tenancies—in Europe, North America, India, and (since 1981) seven African countries—have given him access to many diverse communities, cultures and ideas. But the territorial borders that collapse to allow the herdsman the freedom of movement that is crucial to his survival do not come down so readily for the international migrant. Since the fortuitous 1976 phone call from Rome to his brother in Mogadiscio, in which he was warned that it was not safe for him to return to Somalia, Farah has lived in permanent exile, revisiting his homeland only once (in 1996), and he has had to endure all of the trials and traumas of the homeless person which are harrowingly documented in his recent book on Somali refugees: the endless anxieties over permits and visas, harassment and humiliation at the hands of immigration and embassy officials, the insecurity and upheaval of temporary residencies, and the strain of living in a "country of the imagination," a "country-as-a-hypothesis"[2] whose relationship to its prototype is made increasingly problematic by distance and time. Since his Ogadenese childhood, in which Somali speakers were taught from Amharic, Arabic and English textbooks borrowed from neighboring colonies, the dislocative and unsynchronized have been standard features of Farah's life, and his novels, most of them begun in one country and finished in another, have about them an appropriate air of displacement and culture-lag. Yet, as Farah has acknowledged, it is the very displacement of exile, and his ability to "domesticate," refine and exploit it ("Distance distils and makes ideas worth pursuing"), that feeds the neurosis upon which his artistic creativity flourishes—a creativity which has, moreover, been sparked by his eclectic interaction with other cultures and discourses and which would, by his own admission, have been impoverished by his remaining in Somalia: "Even if I returned, I would still be in exile because Somalia can't contain the experiences that I have been exposed to through living in so many different countries and continents."[3]

Farah has also been a wanderer through the world's literatures: accordingly, his literary and intellectual sources and influences are legion, though many of them were active or accessible within his own culture. These include, albeit indirectly, Somali oral poetry, with its baroque verbal ornamentation and intricate use of parallelism and allusion, to which the imagistic richness of the fiction is distantly indebted; Arabic literature, particularly *The Arabian Nights*, which is a possible source for Farah's labyrinthine narrative structures, multilayered analogical play, and encyclopediac combination of genres (witness the blending of political thriller, detective novel, and metaphysical inquiry in *Sweet and Sour Milk*); and the Koran, always a pervasive influence, reference source and touchstone, most especially in *Close Sesame*, which is structured around the pattern of the Suras and saturated with Islamic lore and Caliphate history. But no less important than these is Farah's wide reading in Western literature, notably avant-garde Modernism and its successors, as instanced in the abundance of epigraphs and quotations from European authors, the extravagant networks of leit-motifs, his fondness for fragmented, composite characterization and inconclusive narrative models, and (in *Maps*) his destabilization of national, gender and ontological boundaries. In this writing Africa and the West, the pre- and the postmodern join hands.

Nuruddin Farah is thus a man of many parts, drawing upon many languages, cultures and literatures which react in combination to produce an exciting fictional chemistry. He comes, appropriately, from a complex, many-voiced culture, famous for its volatile temperament and a rich heritage of contradictions which is notoriously unstable of definition and classification. An African people neither of the Maghrib nor of sub-Saharan Africa, the Somalis, in their wayward post-independence history, have been of uncertain political orientation and alignment, shifting from British and Italian colonial overlordship to Soviet and then American patronage and, under Siyad Barre's twenty-two-year dictatorship, subjected to a strange confection of Marxism, Islam and tribalism which carried the nation from democracy and socialist revolution to clan dynasty and patriarchal despotism. Though culturally unified, as Africa's only ethnically and linguistically homogeneous nation, the Somalis have been politically atomized, firstly by pastoralist political traditions which proved too anarchically ultra-egalitarian to be incorporated into any viable democratic system of government, and secondly by parochial tribalisms of clan and lineage which were ruthlessly exploited by the dictator and finally plunged the nation into the chaos of warlord gangsterism. Though fragmented by diaspora both in and (since the catastrophe) beyond the Horn of Africa, they remain inveterately irredentist in their sense of a Pan-Somali identity.

Farah's writing is itself the locus of many of these clashing currents and shifting paradoxes, and it is, in consequence, a relativist minefield through which it is impossible to plot absolute judgments. In the early *A Naked Needle*, set after Barre's 1969 coup, all of the manifold voices of Somalia's postcolonial turmoil—tribal and international, democratic and totalitarian, revolutionary and traditional— are loud in contention, clamoring equally to be heard. In the following trilogy, *Variations on the Theme of an African Dictatorship*, an unworkably corrupt, vote- buying democracy has long given way to the efficient evil of military dictatorship, replacing the despicable with the detestable, and the underground group of ineffectual liberal dissidents who fight a forlorn rearguard action against "the General" present no viable alternative to his patriarchal rule. In *Close Sesame* and *Maps* Pan-Somali irredentism is represented first positively, in the anti-colonial veteran Deeriye, and then negatively, in the ethnocentric Askar, and is at odds, respectively, with parochial clan fanaticism at home and with the broad multicultural reality of Greater Somalia. The oral tradition is also, in the first trilogy, a double-edged sword: on the one hand, a tool ripe for abuse by an obscurantist dictator whose repressive surveillance techniques exploit illiteracy and, on the other, a potentially empowering, revolutionary weapon in the form of the Sayyid's poetry and subversive cassettes recorded direct from the singer Dulman's mouth and smuggled abroad for unscripted performance. The same is true of the Somali diaspora which, in the non-fictional *Yesterday, Tomorrow*, renders the women refugees resiliently adaptable to their new lives abroad but only entrenches and intensifies the narrow patriarchal values of their men. In Farah's writing these and other conflicts—between men and women, parents and children, family and state, the repressive and liberating aspects of Islam, the malign and benign faces of patriarchy—are presented in alternative lights and from different positions; they are examined from the perspectives of both traditional and modern ideas, indigenous and Western influences, and liberal and conservative sympathies, making any final judgment or absolute evaluation impossible. Meanwhile, in his own life and career, in his diverse residencies and employments, Farah has performed a similar balancing act with multifarious and often conflicting roles, managing to be at once both nomad and cosmopolitan, native and exile, African-based Somali and international celebrity and laureate (of the 1998 Neustadt Prize), a writer who lives everywhere except in the place he writes about. To add two further ambivalences, he is also—an oddity on both counts—a male African author from a patriarchal culture who expresses a deep sympathy for women and a fiction-writer from a family tradition of oral poets, a tradition with which he has disavowed any direct connection[4] even as he has been elusively, imponderably influenced by it.

Farah's is thus a multivocal vision, expressed in many conflicting voices and styles. There is, however, nothing random, anarchic or indifferent about it. On the contrary, it is a deeply committed vision, informed by certain moral and political constants and touchstones. Implicit in its underlying aesthetic is, in essence, a spirit of democratic pluralism:

> A writer...is in a sense everybody. He is a woman, he is a man. He is as many other selves as those whose shadows reflect his ghostly images; he is as many other selves as the ones whose tongues he employs to articulate his thoughts; he is as many other selves as there are minds and hearts he dwells in.[5]

Farah's novels are forums of debate which "allow very many different competing views to be heard,"[6] in the hope that truth will issue from the collision of opposing ideas; for truth in this fiction is relative, elusive, ambiguous, and is to be found in open-ended narratives and multiple viewpoints which he associates with freedom and tolerance, as he associates closure and the single omniscient view with tyranny (dictators insist that there is only one way of looking at things).[7] There is no unqualified commitment to any single point of view, only a succession of narrative voices and outlooks: young and old, African and Western, Somali and Pan-Somali, male and female, or, as in *Maps*, a combination of these ("the woman's self in the man, the man's self in the woman").[8] In his intellectual pursuit of reality Farah, like each of his protagonists from Ebla and Koschin to Askar and Kalaman, crosses boundaries and migrates between zones. Underlying this shifting, many-voiced discourse, and fuelling its author's literary challenge to Barre's dictatorship, is an overriding, desperate commitment to individual human freedom and autonomy on a continent where, as he has put it, "If you write something condemnatory of the regime in power they pass the death sentence on your head."[9] This commitment has—importantly, in the light of its totalitarian adversary—always been a balanced and discriminating one, a non-partisan, non-aligned engagement that has challenged the orthodoxies of both Right and Left: "The only thing one can do is to be aware and to struggle harder and harder against repression in whatever form it comes—whether traditionally in the form of a patriarch, religiously or in wearing the masks of an alien ideology."[10] Oppression in Farah's fiction is traced to many culprits and collusions—of family and state authoritarianisms, Islam and Marxism, government and clan—and each of them is regarded with the same fair-minded vigilance and impartiality. In this broad and balanced vision no easy options are offered, nothing is rejected outright, no party exonerated or blamed; rather, every position is tested for whatever support it lends to independence of thought and unfudged moral judgement, a process which involves giving equal voice to opponents: "I like to give even the people whom I disapprove of a chance for their words to be heard."[11]

Always, great care is taken to preserve this balance. For example, in his *Dictatorship* trilogy, Farah does not look to the communal ethics and group- economics of the traditional past for sanctuary from contemporary post-colonial evils; rather, he reveals how traditional communal values have become props for familial and tribal parasitism and have been implicated in the trials and terrors of clan tyranny in the present. The General is seen, at the political level, to answer to and to represent something authentic in the Somali experience: his totalitarian tribal oligarchy is but the old patriarchal despotism of the Somali family writ large. Yet Farah does not wholly reject these corporate values in favor of an exclusive and isolationist Western individualism. The Western nuclearized family that displaces the extended kinship group in this sequence of novels is shown to develop subtle new tyrannies of its own, and its principal champion, Medina in *Sardines*, wonders whether her education in foreign ideologies and cosmopolitan values has not rendered her a guest in her own country, unqualified to criticize what she sees. After Farah's scrupulously fair-minded fashion, the patriarchal and matriarchal dragons of these books are allowed to have their say. Even the terrible Idil, who in *Sardines* asserts the passive powers of the matriarch—the right to be listened to and obeyed, to profit from her son's prosperity and not be evicted from his house—scores telling points in her response to the Western challenge to her mode of civilization. Idil, who refuses to accept a son who cooks and lives off his wife's wealth in his wife's house, accuses Medina's generation of failing to develop "an alternative cultural philosophy" to replace what it has rejected: "I am what and who I am. I am the product of a tradition with a given coherence and solidity; you, of confusion and indecision."[12] As for Idil, so for her patriarchal counterpart in *Sweet and Sour Milk*, Keynaan, who tells his son Loyaan: "You have no common ideology and no principles. You work for the interests of the countries in which you received your academic training."[13] There is at least some truth in the first part of his statement: the new generation of dissidents which looks to Western liberal humanism for its inspiration has little of its own to put in the place of the coherent tribal heritage which the General's Soviet-backed ideologues are careful to keep intact and to appropriate for their own uses.

In the novel as a whole, of course, there is little to redeem Keynaan or to be said in his defence. Farah relentlessly pinpoints his patriarchal bigotry as a principal source of political authoritarianism and police-state terrorism, demonstrating how he combines the roles of family head and ex-policeman-cum-informer to the regime and, by conniving at the death and defamation of his other son Soyaan, stamps out subversion, simultaneously, at both state and familial levels. In one sense he is, in Ibrahim's words, "worse than evil." Yet the reader is made painfully aware that Keynaan's decision to collude with the General's regime in the oppression of his family and countrymen is made in the context of a society that poses only a choice of inescapable humiliations. The first and preferred option is the humiliation of compromise and sell-out through collusion, taken "in order to eke out an indecent living for the weaker members of the family, for mother, for sister and for the children."[14] The alternative is the worse humiliation of the dawn raid, detention, and the betrayal of colleagues under torture. The above words about the protection of families are Soyaan's and it is surely significant that, before Soyaan's death, Keynaan found out in advance about the car sent to arrest him and interceded for him with the General, winning an amnesty for his son on the condition that he would, at his father's persuasion, desist from further subversive activity. We have only Keynaan's word for this but Loyaan appears to believe him and, though the brief reconciliation on the penultimate page of the book is perhaps less than convincing, Loyaan does, finally, turn to his wretched father for counsel and declares a temporary truce: "Who would have thought that Keynaan and I would ever speak to each other with respect, that we could listen to each other and reason together? *After a storm, the calm; after a fight, a reconciliation!*"[15] In a culture of humiliation and betrayal which poses only evil, impossible choices, but where the family remains paramount and is the reason for all actions, there are no easily identifiable culprits and the rhetoric of blame is best avoided. The destinies of father, son and all family members, whether good or evil, are inseparable: each is part of a chain of oppression, passing on the regime's violence to those beneath and around them. Mindful of this, Farah hedges his condemnation of Keynaan with cautious qualifications and doubts.

In the trilogy's complex profile of dissident and reactionary elements, ranging from the youthful Koschin to the aging Deeriye, from the despised Keynaan to the appalling parricidal Xaji Ibrahim, no one—whether Westernized or "traditional"—has a monopoly on either virtuous opposition to or cowardly support for the General's rule. They are each investigated, in a spirit of sceptical inquiry and creative doubt, for all of the positive and negative capabilities that they present. As Farah has said in interview: "I usually doubt almost everything, and therefore, because I doubt, I would look at different possibilities of looking at the same thing."[16] Or, as Deeriye puts it in *Close Sesame*: "It is the prerogative of God alone to be sure of anything. I am only a human. And I am therefore in doubt."[17] At times this sceptical agnosticism has extended even to the author's own creative powers, questioning, for example, his knowledge and ability to go on creating humanly believable Somali characters from the distance of exile: "Of late...I've failed in raising in them an instinct of humanity."[18]

Farah's many voices have produced many readings and there are almost as many Farahs as there are readers. As Patricia Alden and Louis Tremaine remark in their recent book on the author, "he becomes many different kinds of writer, depending on the reader and the context in which he is read. There is Farah the feminist,...Farah the innovative prose-poet and stylist, Farah the social scientist, Farah the committed activist, Farah the paradoxical postmodernist, and so forth."[19] This is not surprising, given that all of the novels are different and that each one, moreover, has its own peculiar kind of multidimensionality to suit different reader agendas, featuring material as heterogeneous as detective fiction and Orwellian dystopias (*Sweet and Sour Milk*), national allegory and surrealist fantasy (*Maps*), or Caliphate history, oral legend, and Koranic eschatology (*Close Sesame*). For justice to be done to Farah's versatility, each of his voices must be heard. Hence the very large and varied collection of essays in this anthology, ranging across subjects as diverse as Farah's feminism, sociopolitical evolution, and historical vision; his use of allegory and symbolism; his treatment of family, clan and tribe, patriarchy and dictatorship; and his relation to the oral tradition and postmodernism. (The contributors are as varied as their subjects, hailing from a total of fifteen nationalities over four continents and from many occupational backgrounds, including writers, librarians, historians, political scientists, educationalists, publishers, and dance specialists as well as literary critics). Also included are essays on the author's non-fiction (including his plays), a new interview, and the text of his Neustadt Prize acceptance speech. The list is not exhaustive and, of course, no anthology of criticism on a prolific contemporary novelist writing at the peak of his powers can presume to have said the last word. But the collection is ample, I hope, for a first critical anthology on Farah and sufficient to open a few windows into his work. It aims, broadly, to represent the developing debate about the author's achievement by featuring a variety of interpretive approaches and critical opinions, giving due emphasis, as any critical anthology should, to those areas and aspects of his work about which opinion is divided. I have tried to give equal or at least proportionate space to all of Farah's critics—African, European, North American, and Australian—and to coverage of both the early and the late writing, the two trilogies (albeit with a heavy concentration on *Maps*), and successive as well as individual works.

On a cautionary note, I should make it clear at the outset that not everything in this anthology is new; indeed, about half of what follows is made up of previously published material. I make no apology for this and no concession to the current academic vogue for the freshly-minted. Novelists, however the accidents of history may have restricted their work to minority readerships, do not write solely or even primarily for academic researchers who have privileged subsidized access, in print and on-line, to the journals and periodicals in which most literary criticism is published. Their audience is anyone who reads them and their work is public property, not the preserve of academic monopolies (the most endearingly enthusiastic response to Farah's work I encountered was in a letter from the manager of an Albuquerque department store). I offer this anthology in the belief that there is still a place, and a strong case, for compilations from far-flung, often remote and obscure sources, some of them foreign language publications, of the best criticism that has been published on an author over a period of twenty years and the presentation of this in a single, easily accessible and affordable volume. Only in this way can readers—all readers—read about Farah as freely and readily as they can read Farah. If this collection of essays makes even a modest addition to his growing readership it will have served its purpose.

I am grateful to each of the contributors to this anthology and to Kassahun Checole of the Africa World Press for his encouragement of the work and for its timely publication. Thanks are also due to the English department of the University of Queensland for a two-year teaching position which provided me with a resource-base from which to recruit contributors for the volume and for helpful secretarial and technical staff who expedited the book.

I regret to end on a sad note. The present anthology was to have included a new essay on Farah's most recent novel, *Secrets*, by Jacqueline Bardolph, who died in July of last year. As Farah's French translator, prolific critic, and tireless promoter, Jacqueline did more than anyone to bring his work to the world's attention. I include an earlier essay by her on Farah's own favorite among his novels, *Close Sesame*, and respectfully dedicate this volume to her memory.

Brisbane
July 2000

NOTES

1. Nuruddin Farah, "Childhood of My Schizophrenia," *The Times Literary Supplement*, 23-29 November 1990, 1264.

2. Nuruddin Farah, *Yesterday, Tomorrow: Voices from the Somali Diaspora* (London: Cassell, 2000), pp.48-49.

3. Maggie Jonas, "Living in a Country of the Mind," *New African* (December 1987), 60-61; Farah, *Yesterday, Tomorrow*, pp.192-93.

4. Feroza Jussawalla and Reed Way Dasenbrock, *Interviews with Writers of the Post-Colonial World* (Jackson: University of Mississippi Press, 1992), pp.49-50.

5. Nuruddin Farah, "The Life and Death of Words," *South* (April 1984), 54.

6. Armando Pajalich, "Nuruddin Farah Interviewed by Armando Pajalich," *Kunapipi* 15, 1 (1993), 63.

7. Pajalich, 63.

8. Robert Moss, "Mapping the Psyche" (interview with Farah) *West Africa*, 1 September 1986, 1828.

9. Moss, 1827.

10. Moss, 1828.

11. Pajalich, 64.

12. Nuruddin Farah, *Sardines* (London: Heinemann, 1982) p.77.

13. Nuruddin Farah, *Sweet and Sour Milk* (London: Heinemann, 1980), p.93.

14. Farah, *Sweet and Sour Milk*, p.74.

15. Farah, *Sweet and Sour Milk*, p.235.

16. Pajalich, 63.

17. Nuruddin Farah, *Close Sesame* (London: Allison & Busby, 1983), p.202.

18. Nuruddin Farah, "Savaging the Soul of a Nation," *In These Times*, 28 December 1992, 17.

19. Patricia Alden and Louis Tremaine, *Nuruddin Farah* (New York: Twayne, 1999), p.vii.

PART ONE

Farah on Farah

WHY I WRITE

Nuruddin Farah

I cannot remember precisely when I began writing: perhaps the day, aged four, when I traced the Aleph (in Arabic) under the censorious stare of a Quranic teacher. I recall holding a copy of the Quran, bound in leather, a few years later, and wondering if I dared scribble my own name in it—and what would happen. The book was my family's (I have never owned one to this day, except in English translation and, in any case, it is said, you never "own" a Quran: you pay to have access to its contents). On this occasion I did not dare defile the family copy, and had to wait a little while yet before seeing my name on a book.

Around the age of ten I remember thinking I was luckier than most of my contemporaries because I shared a name with a famous prince in *A Thousand and One Nights*. With a discarded razor-blade, I cut out the name Nuruddin and glued it to my exercise book, with its arithmetical tables on the back. Then I would boastfully tell my friends, "See, see my name is in print!" I wonder if my writing dates back to that moment when I appropriated the spirit of the prince and stepped from a culture belonging to the oral tradition to the written one.

More realistically, perhaps, I can point to the day when, while reading a story of mice and cats, an ingenious thought crossed my

1

mind. A couple of mice reminded me of my classmates and the cats of my teachers. I set about cross-matching the names of classmates, teachers and character traits. Naturally I had to alter some of the speeches. I made some of the protagonists use their favourite phrases so as to develop their characters a bit. It was great fun. I would show this to close friends, particularly those to whom I had given good speeches, those whom I had depicted as courageous, brave, generous and good.

It is important that I mention here that all the text-books we used in our schools in the Somali-speaking areas of the Horn of Africa were meant for other people: the Arabic books for the Arabic-speaking child; the Amharic books (if you happened to be going to school in the Ogaden, say) for the Amharic-speaking child in Upper Ethiopia; and the English for the British East African colonies. Not only did we feel alienated from the texts we read, but the universe which these portrayed had nothing familiar to offer to a Somali child like myself in a Somali-speaking Ogaden. Ethiopia did not have enough currency of its own to circulate in its own Empire. (We used the British East Africa shilling notes and coins and hardly set eyes on the Ethiopian *birr*, although the portrait of the Emperor was everywhere.) Similarly, the Ethiopian school curriculum was not sufficiently developed, so we used the same English-language text-books as the British colonies in East Africa. The cosmos the schools presented me with was inordinately varied—but alienated and alienating, too, so I suppose that one thought ran through my head almost all the time: that to live in the world of which I was part, I had to make it my own. As I have already said: the Quran could not be mine because it was God's and no human could "own" it, but at least I could make a small claim in other areas, recreating the cosmos as I knew it in the hope that I would see the world and my friends in it, the way one sees a mirror's reflection in another mirror.

When I was thirteen or fourteen, our English teacher, an American, asked that we enter an essay competition for her. She said we could write on any subject we liked. I chose something to do with a journey into the mind of a traveller pitching a tent in a country he had not been to. Because I had been reading Ernest Hemingway, I lifted a couple of longish passages from one of his travelogues, a world already familiar to me from the Oxford English Reader Series that we used as our English text-books. The essay was returned to me, almost all of it marked with red. My teacher did not discover that I had "appropriated" Hemingway's material and universe, rather she marked the essay so rigorously that she gave it a 'C' grade. When I pointed out, my finger resting on the plagiarised portions, that there was nothing wrong in a phrase I had employed, my teacher turned round and spoke summarily, "We don't express ourselves in this manner, in English." But what did she mean by "we"? She meant "we native-speakers of English"—a "we" which had no room for me. After much hesitation, I told her that the phrase was not mine but Hemingway's. Later, I regretted having given away that part of Hemingway which I had taken as my own, for the teacher requested that I return the essay for regrading, and this time gave it a 'D'.

It is a very perverse world, the one in which a Somali child in the Ogaden reads a Russian novel such as Fyodor Dostoevski's *Crime and Punishment*, in Arabic at the age of thirteen: or Victor Hugo's *Les Misérables* in classical Arabic with an introduction translated from English. I do not think I read books in those days. Rather, I ploughed through them with the tedious slowness of one who has learnt the alphabet of a foreign tongue the previous day. If I were to underline the words I did not understand, nearly every paragraph would have appeared as though it were the favourite passage of somebody's quotation book. But I did not underline any word, no, I dared not do that. For the books belonged to others, they were not mine. They were my elder brother's, and so was Bertrand Russell's *History of Western Philosophy*, which I read with the careful pace of a thoughtful man, half understanding every phrase and in the end not comprehending anything. If I am trying to make a point, it is this: that the text-books we were taught from belonged in the mind and culture of other people; and that the books I, as a child, read for the acquisition of knowledge, belonged in the world of adults. I must hasten to add that neither of my parents owned books (my mother is a poet—but from the oral tradition; and my father speaks a little English and a little "market" Arabic). Our house was nevertheless thought of as "learned," I suppose because there were more books, journals, and magazines than one saw in any other house in the Kallafo of my childhood.

My eldest brother encouraged me to read a lot and to go to him for guidance. He would draw me in pencil as I concentrated wholeheartedly on unravelling the mysteries of a Dostoevskian cosmos. And I: I whose name occurred in a lullaby song my mother had composed for me (my mother had composed a praise-song for her first four sons and over the years added a line here or there, but I suspect gave up the idea of a praise-song for every one of her ten children); I: who watched a mother pace up and down, a mother who was fully engaged in the act of poetic composition; I: who was constantly reminded of a great poet who was a relation! Consequently the future I foresaw for myself involved one in which I composed poems like my mother in Somali, poems praising the Somali, poems propagating the supremacy of the Somali mind and culture over any other. What I did not consider for one single moment was that the more I read books pertaining to other cultures and other languages, the more I would find "Somali" to be inadequate for self-expression.

At times, I think, it is all a matter of names. Have you noticed how one's first publication appears under an eponymy of a kind? Very often, students finishing their degrees at higher institutions of learning, where one of the requirements is to present a publishable work of research, spend a great deal of time and thought before they settle for a name which they feel will suit their newly cultivated personality. You read a flourish of first, middle and last names decorating the right-hand bottom of prefaces to a thesis, opposite copyright notices and so on. It is as if one were taking possession of the produce, first privately and then publicly, leaving no one in doubt as to whom its soul belongs. I, too, employed a lustre of formal and informal names, under which I published my first longish short story in (I believe?) July 1965. I wrote it when in hospital, in pain and certain I would not survive the operation I was to undergo. I wrote *Why Dead So Soon?* so feverishly I can only remember a close friend of mine calling at the hospital, taking away pages of it in longhand and returning a few days later with the typed manuscript. I was convalescing when it came out in the now-defunct *Somali News*, a fortnight from the day I had submitted it. The story was received well. I became a celebrity overnight. Friends and acquaintances asked what I was working on, whenever we met anywhere. I only wished I had published it under another name. I might have written the first story because I was afraid of dying. And, I thought, it would have been proper had I either published it under another name and then returned to my own; or, having released *Why Dead So Soon?* under my own, it might have agreed with the becalmed spirits if I employed a pseudonym from then on. I reminded myself of a wisdom commonly circulated among Somalis: that the Amhara (the dominant ethnic community in Ethiopia) change their names after a long and serious illness in the hope that this will bring along better luck in future. Ought I not to have done that, I asked myself. But surely I did not write *Why Dead So Soon?* because I was conscious or afraid of death or did I? And in any case, it was not my first. Why then did I write? Why do I write?

My second short story earned the praise of a novelist whom I happened to meet in Somalia. Among other respected works about her place of origin, Canada, Margaret Laurence had written a travelogue about Somalia, and a collection of stories set in Ghana, but I had not read any of them. I had heard of her name, had seen her book about Somalis—*The Prophet's Camel Bell*—and was very pleased when I was introduced to her by somebody who believed I might gain something from the encounter. Anxious, inexperienced, I had little or nothing to say to her, and later in the evening I sat by her, watching a dance performance at the National Theatre meant for visiting delegates who had arrived to celebrate the country's sixth anniversary of independence. When she returned to her, then, base in Britain, she wrote a letter full (I thought so then) of an older writer's preoccupations, something to do with an artist's portrayal of reality, sense of aesthetic trust and faith in the mind-grown truths. Her 300-word letter ended by saying that if I were willing to cut the last paragraph in the second story which she liked very much, then she was confident that she would be able to publish it somewhere. I wrote to say: no, I did not want the paragraph cut or a word omitted, but I also told her of a novel I had begun working on and hinted that I might send it to her. In fact, a year and a half later, in 1967, when studying at university in India, I dropped her a line informing her that I had finished the novel. Ms Laurence's reply was inordinately hostile, giving, in a postscript, the address of Heinemann African Writers, Series, Ibadan, Nigeria. I put the manuscript in the mail and while waiting, re-read Ms Laurence's first letter which I had kept as an item to be treasured. I decided, in the light of what had transpired, that I was not writing "in defence of truth and a sense of faith in the aesthetic sort of writing as art." I was not. But why was I writing then, I asked myself.

In the meantime, I got a response, in short a rejection letter from Heinemann. Looking back on it now, I believe it was the most arrogant missive a young writer had ever received from the editor of a reputable publisher. Aig-Higo, the Nigerian Editor of the Heinemann African Writers Series told me that I had no right submitting a worthless manuscript to a house of their name and high reputation, and he suggested that, since I had no talent whatsoever (these are his words and the letter is there for anyone to read), I had better consider what I wished to do with my life. This so upset me that I nearly wrote to request Knopf, who had been reading another manuscript, to return it. In the event, Knopf turned down the one I had submitted to them. In their rejection letter, Knopf were gentle, suggesting that I send them any subsequent work (the manuscript Knopf had seen was part-pastiche, part-parody of Camus's *The Stranger*, set in Mogadiscio, with a young woman as its protagonist, a woman who refuses to be a woman: to marry, have children, cook, in short a woman who refused to please "men" or, she thought, God; and who feels at odds with society in general, and with her own status in particular). Then one day, after several depressive months, I sat down and in less than a month-and-a-half wrote *From a Crooked Rib*. Within a week of each other, I received three letters: one was reprimanding me for not having taken my studies very seriously, because I had to repeat two papers; the second was from a Longman's fiction editor and she was full of praise for the work but suggested I rewrite the final part of the novel; the third letter was from Mr James Currey, the then editor of the Heinemann African Writers Series, London. In his letter, Mr Currey asked: was I a woman or a man? And could I send them a photograph? How curious! I thought. However, if anybody had put to me the question "Why do you write?" then, my answer might have been, "I write because I wish to prove to others that I can do it as well as anybody else."

Crooked Rib was in page-proof when I returned home. This also coincided with a change of style of government in the country, for the army toppled the civilian regime and the years 1970-73 were tumultuous. I remember them as "noisy": in those days, one's ears were filled with badly-sung choruses praising the Generalissimo, the man who headed the army takeover. I had come from India pregnant with a novel and a play: neither had anything to do with politics. In point of fact, my favourite authors during that period were James Joyce, Samuel Beckett and Virginia Woolf—and in my naivety I thought of their writings as apolitical. Mornings were vibrant with surprises and shocking news: you heard that so-and-so was arrested on suspicion of anti-revolutionary sentiments; nights were frightening since the sinister National Security Service made dawn arrests without warrants. People sought one another's company and comfort, and in order not to be arrested they formed large gatherings during the brightest hours of the day, singing sycophantic songs of the Generalissimo, certain of only one thing: that the NSS would not sweep them away into detention centres but would wait until one was alone, or in bed at home, wait, at any rate, until nightfall. As the cliche has it, you were for or against the regime of Mohamed Siyad

Barre, the self-declared Messiah of the Somali nation. Those for as well as those against courted my pen: after all, fortune or misfortune conferred upon me the honour of being the first Somali national ever to publish a work of fiction. The then Minister of Higher Education and Culture (now in detention) and the President of the National University (now Somalia's Ambassador to Britain) were most frightening in their insistence that it was for my own good that I write something favourable about the revolution. The camp against was equally convincing, filling me with horror stories, after-midnight tales of detention, torture and terror. In short, both camps asked, "Why don't you write about the revolution?"—please choose yourself whether or not to put inverted commas around the word "revolution." At any rate, they asked not "Why do you write?" but "Why don't you write?"

Because I did not want to allow either camp to penetrate my awareness, I began writing the sort of things which were as apolitical as I could make them. I wrote a three-hour-long play, in the vein of Edward Albee's *Who's Afraid of Virginia Woolf?* and committed a perfidy, providing words for Beckett's *Act Without Words*. At a friend's place, we had the four parts in *A Dagger in Vacuum* read. The question was whether or not we would be allowed the licence to stage it. In retrospect, I am glad the censors rejected it, although not for the reasons they gave—that it was "scandalously un-revolutionary." The censors' verdict was if anything in keeping with the jargon of the period. In retrospect, I would say that the play was very naive, and although it might have worked on the stage, it certainly did have flaws in its author's grasp of social reality. For a while, agitated like a restless butterfly, I hopped from one flowering tree to another as aromatic as an eucalyptene. To the question, "What are you writing?", my answer was truthful: "I feel inadequate and haven't the experience nor the talent to write intelligently about the events and the interesting debates taking place right in front of me. How can I write about such a grand subject? I haven't the ability." Keen-eared, I listed to the debates; also I watched peoples' features, conscious of their

8

psychological and bodily behaviour as fear began spreading on their faces, as though it were melting butter. Yes, the days were noisy as violent tides; and the nights were filled with frightened whispers of people listening for the footsteps of the NSS men who were sure to come at dawn to arrest them, to humiliate them, to take away the husband from the wife, the son from his parents, the bread from the breadwinner. Mine was a mind in great disorder. I knew that a novel like *A Naked Needle* was not the answer to the tremendous challenge the tyrannical regime posed, but I was tired of holding my pen in mid-air—and I thought in any case that I should get it out of my way while I gave serious consideration to how best to rise to the summons. I did not know at this stage if I would do one or a series of books; nor could I tell what genre I would choose. It was coincidentally at this period (the manuscript of *A Naked Needle* had by then gone to my publishers in London with the strict instructions not to release it) that, in the month of October 1972, Somalia officially became a language with an orthography. Now the nature of the challenge altered slightly but substantially. Very often in those days, I heard the question, "Why don't you write in Somali?" And so I published in serialised form a few chapters from the first novel in Somali ever written. It was 1973. Publication of my novel in Somali was discontinued because the censors found a particular chapter suspicious, to say the least. I happened to be out of the country, in the Soviet Union, when the censors' letter reached the editor of the daily. And that was the end of that.

I think it was after a trip which took me to the Soviet Union, Hungary, Greece (of the Colonels) and Sadat's Egypt that I returned to Somalia thinking about the novels that were to take shape in my mind years later as *Sweet and Sour Milk*, *Sardines*, and *Close Sesame*. I did not come home laden with gifts. Rather, an idea, a generalised notion of an idea, had come to me during this sojourn abroad: that dictatorial regimes, wherever they were, invested power more in their own variety of truths, each of which had a fictive truth to support its validity, than in the plain home-grown truth you and I grow in

9

our (fertile?) imagination. I had lived in India where there had been a plurality of truths, that is views; in India, you couldn't help feeling there was a corporate truth, packaged in a manner not totally alien to the original concept of the sub-continent's corporate name. The Soviet Union, too, had a body of opinion concomitant with ideological principles pulsating in the core of its being. Not Africa, I had thought; definitely not in Somalia. The body politic whose sinewed muscles, strong as pillars, embodied the collective strength to which every member of the community contributed: in Africa this was sadly absent. And so was the "groomed" truth, the nursed truth so to speak, a truth mended as though it were a broken pot, a truth plastered with a "cured" cloth.

Somalia was a badly written play, I had thought, and Siyad Barre was its author. To our chagrin, he was also the play's main actor, its centre and theme; as an actor-producer, he played all the available roles. He did not think anyone was as good as he, so he was its stage-designer and light technician, as well as the audience. You can imagine how Siyad-Barre-as-subject oppressed and obsessed me. I was in awe of it, afraid that I was not up to it, that I would mess it all up for future authors dealing with the same material even if from a detached, historical angle. In short, I felt more inadequate than ever. What does a writer do when he or she cannot write? I was very depressed—and I read and read and read the writing of others. I had come away from these authors' wells thirstier than I had been before. Then I did a rough draft of *Sweet and Sour Milk*. I was not happy with what I had done and so dropped into the severest depression. This did not lift until after I had done a readable version in Denmark in March 1975. As a matter of fact, it was in 1976 when answering the question of a journalist after the publication of *A Naked Needle*, that I said, "I write the way I do because my writing is an alternative to the propaganda Siyad Barre's oligarchy released to the world's press as the unchallengeable truth."

No doubt, you have noticed that "truth" is the operative word here—but it is a kind of truth that bears a vague resemblance to the "aesthetic truth" of which Margaret Laurence wrote, in her letter to me in 1966. Somalia is incestuously clannish, it is a country peopled by a race of men and women who are decidedly united in their unmitigated arrogance and pride in being unique, the only country in Africa that qualifies to be called a nation. The common popular wisdom often circulated in Somalia is that Siyad Barre taught the Somalis who "in truth" they are, something the colonialists never managed to teach them. This has been unsettling to the Somalis who generally lack a centrally organised form of opposition, of resistance. The "truth" that there is nothing unique about them has upset them greatly. In consequence, they have scattered themselves to the winds, making a study of their character difficult, cumbersome, almost impossible. When in exile, they long to get back home: home to a notion of Somalia, commonly accepted to be the guiding principle of its people; when at home, they are eager to get away from the promiscuity of the-Somali-idea, the particularity of the Somalis' world view. Recently, at a conference held under the auspices of the University of Hamburg and the International Somali Studies Forum, a highly placed Somali dignitary, who poses as a scholar and a diplomat, said in English, to an audience half of which was non-Somali, that "We Somalis present here, must not speak openly and with a view to thwarting the unity of our nation, we must not say anything which might give the sad impression to the foreigners present here that we, Somalis, wherever we are, do not hold the leader of our nation in the highest regard possible." And when someone asked him if one must not utter the truth, the diplomat-cum-scholar replied, "It's not the truth which matters. What is paramount is the unity of the Somali nation." The diplomat continued, "but you cannot invent a nation as unique as ours. That's the truth that matters."

The "truth" that matters, indeed! What if I argue that truth must be "spoken" whether in the privacy of one's chambers or in the presence of others? What if I argue that it must be given a body, a physical existence, that truth must be clothed in the bodied concepts of words, of motions—so that others may share it, challenge it or

11

accept it? My writings have been summarily described in Somali government jargon as "a selection of untruths," because I have not been to Somalia for years but have written books which challenge the propaganda which the official media give as "the truth." My books, say the anti-Siyadists, give a true picture of the state of affairs. To both camps it is not truth that matters but to whom it is given. "Tell the world how things are," the anti-Siyadists say to me, "since you are our only writer." I respond that I cannot tell others how things are, I can only tell them how I perceive things to be. But the pro-Siyadists accuse me of paying more attention to the perforative nature of their "truth," a lattice-work of half-truths whose principal frames are painted prominently so as to give the pattern a veri-similar appearance. "You see only the holes," they say, "and pay no attention to the overall design we have in mind." Each group belonging to either camp sees itself portrayed in the writing: the anti-Siyadists are of the opinion that they are truthfully represented; the pro-Siyadists dispute the impartiality of my vision. Which is why they classify my writing as forming part of "fantastic literature," a genre related not to the Latin American form of *One Hundred Years of Solitude*, but to the mode of *A Thousand and One Nights* or *Kalila and Dimna*. Also, they exploit a "weakness" of sorts, the fact that I write in English. They say, "Is it not true that African writers writing in European languages tend to pander to a 'world audience', not to a local one?" I say: "Don't African politicians who embrace socialist, Marxist-Leninist, Maoist or even capitalist ideologies pander to foreign ideologies?" And I add: "writing in Somali and living in the country would enable the regime to silence me easily." I remind them of our brothers and sisters living in South Africa who insist on writing not in their native tongues but in English, so they can feel part of a wider world, one that cannot be totally stifled by the tyrannical regime in their country. "But why write," they say, "if your people cannot read your books?" Your people? My people? Their people? Whose people? "Truth never turns tail like a disinterested cat: it purrs, it winks its feline eyes, it sees, it envisions; truth is the breath in the air, the breath that someone some-

12

where in the world will inhale, and then speak, in the end," I say.

Despite everything, I managed to write four books on Siyad Barre's dictatorship from 1971 to 1980. For almost a decade, therefore, writing these books was my primary occupation, novels whose overall theme is "Truth versus Untruth." During this period, whenever anyone asked me why I wrote the kind of books I did, I answered that I wrote to put down on paper, for posterity's sake, the true history of a nation. To complete the picture, I must also add that I wrote plays, short stories and other commissioned pieces to earn money. But directly I finished the trilogy on dictatorship, I moved to Africa and have since written a full-length play, *Yussuf and His Brothers* (set in the Horn of Africa in the period following the Second World War), a novel, *Maps* (set in the aftermath of the 1977 war for the Ogaden), and another novel set in present-day Somalia, about foreign aid, entitled *Gifts*. At present, I am at work on the third in a sequence of novels, tentatively entitled *Letters*. In other words, there has been a change of emphasis and of thematic concern: I could attribute this change to the fact that I feel I have acquired a new pageboard on which I keep the keys giving one access to my universe. Also, I have since moved to the African continent—a move which has enriched my experience and allowed me to enter into a debate with my fellow-Africans. So why do I write nowadays? I write because a theme has chosen me: the theme of Africa's upheaval and societal disorganisation. And I write in order to recover my missing half.

CELEBRATING DIFFERENCES:
The 1998 Neustadt Lecture
Nuruddin Farah

I was born into a difference at a time in my continent's history when the power of speech lay elsewhere, in other people's tongues. In those days we, as colonials and as Somalia, existed more in reference to whom we were made into as colonial subjects than whom we presumed ourselves to be, or who we ought to have been. Ours was a language divested of authority. Moreover, I was born into a difference with its own specificity: of a mother and a father who were not wholly literate in Somali. I say "not wholly literate," because even though my father had mastered the rudimentaries of reading and writing in at least three languages and my mother was an oral poet, the truth is that they were seldom engaged in activities I would associate with the fully literate.

At the age of four and a half, my three elders brothers and I were sent to school by our parents. I doubt that my parents could articulate what must have been a disturbing ambivalence in their minds; I doubt that they meant to pay hefty fees they could ill afford with a view to imposing philosophical discontinuities between their worldview and ours. We became literate in the foreign tongues in which we received our formal education. It would dawn on me before my tenth year, once I became aware of my potential, that there were immense benefits to being literate in foreign tongues. For not only could I read the Koran as a professional reciter might—by then I had earned the honorific "Haafizul Qur'an," a title given to those who have obtained the formidable distinction of committing the entire Scripture to memory—but I could read Dostoevsky and Victor Hugo in Arabic, or struggle my way through Bertrand Russell's *History of Western Philosophy* in English. Not that I understood much of what I read. But one thing was very obvious: I had gained access to a larger and more varied world than the ones my parents ever anticipated, a world more dangerous but at the same time more rewarding than that which my age mates had known. And what a different world it was, with some of the distances made smaller, no bigger than a book, and new distances amplified. Reading these books helped me to reach out, as though I was meant to touch the frontiers of this immense world. I was touched by what I read, I was moved, I was changed too. In those faraway days, a particular piece of wisdom from the Prophet Mohammed was frequently on everyone's lips: "To acquire knowledge, one must travel very, very far, even to China, if need be." I had no idea where China was. However, I sensed it as if I were more than prepared to travel there or even beyond it. We valued knowledge for what it was worth, and were ready to seek it wherever we might. Because of our peculiar circumstances as colonial subjects and especially as Somalis, it mattered little where we found it, in foreign tongues or in books written by others and published in other lands. We got used to the inconveniences with which we associated these alien languages. We might have been the proverbial hunchback who makes do with his daily discomforts, but who continues to live his life most fully regardless.

Out of love, and because they wanted the best for us, our parents did not stand in the way of our acquisition of knowledge, well aware of the fact that we were growing into alien children, not wholly of their making. My father was instrumental in the establishment of a community school in our town. He travelled far in his search for a teacher willing to come and live in Kallafo. Of the many whom he interviewed, the one whom he liked best proved to be demanding, insisting that he be given free lodging in addition to his monthly salary, conditions which my father ultimately accepted. Once he arrived, the teacher lived in our own compound, and until he got married he was fed out of the same kitchen as ourselves, his guests more ours than his, as we had more space in our part of the compound.

Later, when a Christian missionary group established its own school, my brothers and I were all sent there. The school was run by evangelists, eager to win converts to their faith. But not if you paid a school fee, because then you were treated differently. As it turned out, it was not obligatory for us to attend the special Bible classes in the after-school hours, since our parents had the wherewithal to foot the bills. Not so the boys from poorer families, a handful of whom converted to Christianity out of convenience. We all knew who these were. One of them used to lend me his Bible, which boasted the marked passages thought to be relevant to one's redemption. From our perspective, it was as though we were doing a course in comparative religion, something I am sure our parents were aware of. As Somalis, we all had an extremely robust confidence in our faith then, and were convinced that we were equal to any challenges posed by other religions. We had no qualms in quoting to the missionaries the verse from the Koran, "To each his religion, you [keep to] yours and we to our own!" Our society was so self-confidently tolerant in those days, so accepting of the differences in character and mental acumen between ourselves and the Christian missionaries, whom we accused of taking advantage of those with no means to fight them off.

As residents of Kallafo, a town with a population of fifteen to twenty thousand, we were accommodating of others who were different from ourselves. The Lord knows there was a wide variety of other peoples from different parts of the world for a town in the backwaters of the Shebelle river in the Somali-speaking Ogaden. We

had Yemeni Arabs in our midst, we had a small community of farmers originally from East Africa, a wide array of Somalis from other
corners of the peninsula, plus a couple of Palestinian families,
refugees really, who were on their way elsewhere for resettlement.
Ours was a tolerant Islam. You lived your life as you saw fit, not
according to self-appointed Mullahs threatening you with fire and
brimstone if, in their opinion, you strayed from the righteousness of
the faith, as they decreed it. We were who we were, self-confidently
proud of who we perceived ourselves to be, in spite of our status as
colonial subjects. With our minds open, our hearts likewise, we
received the world, and along with it the knowledge that made the
world larger and more varied too.

There is something forward-looking about knowing other languages, something outward-looking about studying the cultures of
other peoples: not only do you enrich your understanding of your
own culture, but it makes you appreciate yours all the more. I remember my first encounter with *A Thousand and One Nights* and how, reading it in the original, I felt suddenly whole. In fact, the more I read and
got to know about other people's cultures, even if cursorily, the more
confident I became about my own. I became more convinced than
ever that I needed to create a universe familiar enough to Somalis, and
which might inspire a sense of mission in themselves. Not that I could
do much about the language in which I ought to write. When I started
writing, no standardized system of spelling or of writing existed in
Somali; none was established until October of 1972.

Despite this, writing in foreign languages was as much fun as
reading had been entertaining and edifying too. I felt encouraged by
what I read, stories whose cunning and sophistication enabled me to
get in touch with the narrative genius that is the African folktale.
Literature of the written and oral variety became a mansion in which
I moved with self-edifying ease, reading books in foreign tongues and
listening to the oral wisdom transmitted in Somali. Meanwhile I
enjoyed going from *Kalila and Dimna* to Ernest Hemingway, to Mark
Twain, to Agatha Christie, to a Somali poem recited under the shade

of a tree. I was elated by this multicultural encounter, the world now unitary, and now boasting of a wealth of differences, each expressive of a human need: the need to gain more knowledge about myself and about the lives of others, in order to be fulfilled.

It was easy for me to make the journey from the Arabic culture of *A Thousand and One Nights* to the translation of *Kalila and Dimna* from Sanskrit. With a bit of help from my eldest brother, who encouraged me, I was able to tackle Dostoevsky and Hugo in Arabic too. The quirkiness of my reading could be explained in part by the fact that, because of the oral nature of our society, books in any tongue were seldom available. But what a pleasure they were to me when I had them, and what a delight to lose my bearings in the multi-storied mansion of a writer's imagined universe. Sadly, I admit to having become more fascinated by the written variety of literature, perhaps because, as with all new converts, I was attracted to the barely familiar in preference to the oral tradition which was everywhere around me. There was a freshness to the stories in the books every time I read them. I was a child apart, my parents two wordsmiths, in their different ways, each forging out of the smithy of their souls a creative reckoning of an oral universe. It was in deference to their efforts that I lent a new lease on life later to the tales told to me orally, tales that I worked into my own, all the more to appreciate them.

In addition to the powers associated with being literate in foreign tongues, there were economic benefits too. As a child, I lived in a part of the world where a large segment of the population do not read and write. So whenever I was short of cash, I hired out my services to an illiterate adult in need of a letter to be written. It occurred to me too that perhaps I had more power than did my father as an interpreter, whose oral rendering of what the Englishman said in Swahili had something short-lived about it. As a scribe, I had more power, giving flesh to ideas orally delivered and therefore transient, and which, by dint of being written down in another language, became more real. In written form, the letter could be read and reread, and its message could travel farther than an oral one, travel through space and time, unaltered.

19

There was something else. I had at my mercy grown men, my father's age, some humouring me so I might write a letter for them without pay, or at a discount. On occasion, my parents interceded on behalf of some of our relations. I was always paid the compliment of being a very lucky boy, some providing me with a chair and a table, some with a drink. Deferent silence attended my every intervention, respect for my status accompanied the order of the moment. I was lavishly pampered. I was so adept at what I set out to do that, in my eleventh year, I delivered a speech I helped write to the visiting emperor, Haile Selassie, an honour accorded to me after two grown men, both of them my teachers, felt too intimidated by the prospect of standing before His Majesty. My photographs decorated many a royal wall in Addis Abeba for a while as a result of delivering it.

I grew more confident the more I read. The more I got to know about the injustices perpetrated by men against the womenfolk, the more conscious I grew of my powers. I had not yet completed my twelfth year when an elderly man, a friend of my father's, required that I write a letter for him to his estranged wife—estranged, because he had the frequent habit of beating her. Apparently the woman had gone to another town where she had taken refuge amongst her kin, refusing to return in spite of their pleas and despite the assurances the husband had given to her elder brother, now sitting close by. The elder brother kept nodding his head, as if in agreement with the wife-beater, who was adamantly insistent that he had done no wrong. I also gathered that, in a message orally delivered to the husband and her elder brother, the woman had filed for divorce, a request neither the husband nor her elder brother was prepared to consider. "I will not divorce you," he instructed me to write, "and if you do not come back within a couple of days of receiving this letter, I will have you brought back forcibly and will beat you until all your bones are broken."

Unbeknownst to him, I did what was within my power to do: I sabotaged the intent of the man's message by a deliberate omission, supported by an intentional mishearing of his statements. In the letter I made him say that if she did not come back within a few days of

20

receiving the letter, or if she continued raising objections against being beaten by her legal husband, then there was nothing left for him but to divorce her, as she had requested. It was perhaps with a view to giving myself legal cover that I demanded the husband put the authority of his thumb to the bottom right-hand side of the letter.

Six months later I learnt of what had inevitably come to pass: the estranged wife, assuming that she was divorced, remarried another man of her choice, a man who was more tender toward her. The case went to court, and the letter I had written for the husband was produced. The Islamic Qadi decreed that the woman was now legally the wife of her current husband, by whom she had a son. I could not determine from the expression on my father's face if he were proud of me or ashamed. But he was clearly disturbed by "my wily ways," as he put it, forbidding me henceforth to write letters on behalf of others.

* * *

A question I've often asked myself is: are my parents continued in me? One was a translator communicating in Swahili to the Englishman and then transmitting the response in Somali. My father learnt Swahili as a child because he was brought up in Nairobi, in the very city—then a small town—in which the Englishman came to acquire the language, perhaps with the assistance of a native instructor. It is safe to assume that the colonialist's register of Swahili was different from my father's. Even so, almost all the transactions being oral, my father, and his boss the Governor, spoke as if in twinship with each other, the one employing Swahili, the other rendering it into Somali. I wonder if there was a point when my father ceased to be the Englishman's sidekick and became an agent in his own right, with a new authority to his agency?

Was there a point when my father's relationship to the truth of the Englishman's authority took on its own energy, through the agency generated by his own truth and authority as a colonial? No doubt there was a world's distance between the moment my father heard the Englishman say something in Swahili and the moment he interpreted this into Somali. Did my father, by interpreting, insinuate himself into the ideas he worked with, ideas to which he gave a new lease of life? How much, if any, did he transform these ideas? And did he take vengeance on the colonial master who originated the ideas? In short, was my father ever an anti-colonialist?

Being a poet, my mother helped me gain access to hidden, creative energies within me, even in so young a child. I remember the placidity of her moods, as she paced back and forth in a bedroom with the door locked from inside. A family poet, she composed *buraanbur* lyrics in praise of the bride or bridegroom, or made up a special lullaby for one of her many children. Unlike my father, she had the self-confident vitality to reinvent the world daily by singing about it. There was a self-assuredness to all her doings. I thought she was more articulate than my father, who, patriarch that he was, talked in certainties, never doubting that he might be wrong. She was a great one to help one confront one's quotidian uncertainties.

Born into a difference: I lived in a world different from that of my parents. Not that I always had their permission to be different from them. All the same, we met, my parents and I, as though we were travellers meeting in a transit lounge. As children raised apart, we were, in essentials, journeymen of the future, hybrids of a new sort. In an effort to get closer to my mother, or perhaps to bridge a chasm, I learnt as much of the oral tradition as I possibly could. It was maybe in imitation of the poet in her that I tried my hand at making up my own lyrics in Somali to tunes borrowed from the songs that were popular in those days.

As a youth I was as inventive as children who speak the correct language to the correct parent, to each parent his or her own, in a world with its own value systems, where the calendars are not the same, where people do not worship the same deities. For me, as a child, the most prominent distances were those between temperaments, my mother's and my father's. I am alluding to the fact that language, and what uses we make of it, *is* the longest distance between two persons, the one a poet, sensitive, committed to ideas larger than herself, the other despondently despotic, a patriarch willing to submit the world to the authority of his whim. My mother once described another man who was equally deficient in sensibilities as rather like a three-legged stool with one leg missing. She demonstrated what she meant, her head exaggeratedly tilted to one side, one of her arms bent at the elbow, hanging down as though broken.

She was interested in what I wrote, my mother was, often requesting that I tell her the stories as I developed them in my head. Generous to me, she accommodated my eccentricities and provided me with as much space as I required (We spoke once of how she might have become a major poet if she hadn't spent all her time looking after her numerous children). Interested in where the story was headed, she put me right when I got the spirit of the tale wrong. Not my father. He would've been happier, he told me, if I had become a clerk at the bank and brought home all my earnings. And yet it was he who had sought out "knowledge" in the shape of teachers, he who had helped establish the first school in our town. My mother died sixteen years after we last met, whilst I was still in exile. But my father and I met more recently in a hospital in Mombasa, Kenya, where he was recovering from an injury to his head. I found him intolerant of my views. We had a set-to about my choice of dress, of habits, of friends. He was at his friendliest when showing me off to his cronies, when he chose to be praiseful of my achievements as a writer.

On my way to the airport, I called on him to make peace with him, and to say my farewell. The two of us alone, I reminded him of how I had been impressed with his contributions in terms of our secular education, which hadn't until then been available in our town; how, in fact, it was he who had made it possible for me to become a writer. He looked restless, a man wanting to get something off his chest. And he spoke regretfully about "knowledge." Pronouncing the Somali word for knowledge, *aqoon*, as though it were synonymous with venom, he accused me of betraying all his aspirations, and of being treacherous to his and everyone's expectations of me. I do not know

23

why, but I reminded him of the dialogue between Knowledge and Everyman in the English morality play *Everyman*, when Knowledge says, "Everyman, I will go with thee and be thy guide, In thy most need to go by thy side." Maybe I hoped he would be supportive of my efforts as a writer the way my mother had been. Would he not agree, I wondered, that I had continued where he and my mother left off as a professional interpreter, and a poet, considering that I had turned out to be a wordsmith with a difference.

He said, "No one trusts subversives."

I said I was not sure what he meant.

In his reply he quoted a Somali folktale in which a boy, born to a single mother, reaches the mature age of nine before uttering a word. The woman prays daily, appealing to God to make her son speak. At the age of ten, he does so. To his mother, he says, "Shall we fornicate, Mother, you and I?" Shocked, the mother then prays to the Almighty to make him mute once again.

I asked myself if, in the opinion of my father, I was subversive because I wrote in foreign tongues, or because, in my writings, I challenged the authoritarian tendencies of Somali tradition? I could say, in self-defence (but did not), that writing in cosmopolitan settings, in foreign tongues, is, to my mind, more forward-looking, ultimately more outward-looking, than much of the writing done in the indigenous languages in Africa and elsewhere; that a great body of these literatures is remarkable for its nationalistic bent, and its jingoism too; and that much of Somali oral poetry and prose is reactionary, inward-looking in a clannish sort of way.

Instead I said, "I was born into a difference, born into a world not of my own making. I wish the two of us could be sufficiently tolerant of each other so as to celebrate our differences. It is time we got to know ourselves better, time we celebrated the differences in our world views."

Norman, Oklahoma, 29 October 1998

HOW CAN WE TALK OF DEMOCRACY?:
An Interview with Nuruddin Farah by
PATRICIA ALDEN and LOUIS TREMAINE

In April and May of 1996, Nuruddin Farah returned for the first time in 22 years to Somalia, the land of his birth and the setting of all his novels. His purpose, in part, was to gather material for a non-fiction work in progress on Somali refugees. Leaving Somalia, he traveled to Oxford, England, where he was to spend a term writing and offering public lectures. We met with him there, just after his arrival, to discuss questions related to a study of his work that we had recently undertaken. Brief excerpts from that interview, conducted on May 17th and 18th, appear in the completed book (*Nuruddin Farah*, Twayne, 1999). He has agreed to allow longer portions to be published in the present volume. In what follows we have adhered to our original understanding that the portions of our conversation bearing on Farah's experience of return from exile and on current political conditions in Somalia were to be off the record. At the time we spoke his most recent novel, *Secrets*, was still in manuscript.

Alden and Tremaine: *Media accounts of political struggle in Somalia commonly represent those who have been tortured or killed as victims of clan warfare that has been going on for centuries. Your books, however, have consistently ignored or dismissed the claims of clan identity. Why is that?*

Farah: In 1975 I met with a man who worked for Amnesty International as a Somali specialist. I told him at the time that victims have no clan names. When someone is detained, tortured, dealt with rather savagely by dictatorial regimes, you do not belittle that person by giving the name of the clan from which they come. And the reason is that it is not the clan that is getting this terrible treatment, it is *this* person for *his* idea. And I said to him, "You are playing into the hands of Siyad Barre. Siyad Barre continually isolates people by saying, 'They are opposing me because of the clan to which they belong.' But I'm saying to you that these people oppose Siyad Barre on grounds of ideology."

He gave me a long lecture. Then he invited one or two people and said, "These are Somalis. They are the ones who brought this information to me, and they are the ones who say that so-and-so from that clan is being tortured." I told him, "I don't care what they say. I say, what I want you to do is simply to say that a person who is against dictatorship was tortured. That person, with a name, remains unclassified as belonging to a family. He doesn't belong to a family."

Subsequently Amnesty used more and more of the same technique, to the extent where I could not say, whenever anybody was tortured, that this person and I belonged to the same ideology because we were fighting against Siyad Barre. And the reason is that I continued calling myself Somali and they continued calling these people by their clan names, which obviously means that they were separating me from both Siyad Barre and the people whom he was torturing.

Now, I think I was either a visionary or insane, one of the two, probably both, because I was seeing into the future to a time in which other people would read about somebody in the paper and say, "You know,

26

he's not one of ours. I have nothing to do with this man. He's from that clan, I'm not from that clan." You know that poem that goes, when they came for the Jew I didn't speak, because I wasn't a Jew, and so on, and when they came for me there was nobody left to say anything. The point is that the moment that somebody becomes a Jew and you're not a Jew, there is something in you that says, "Why should I risk my life, since the definition 'Jew' doesn't apply to me, but applies to him or her?" And then, you see, the rest of the world accepted it, the Amnesty International interpretation, which coincided with Siyad Barre's interpretation, and which didn't agree with mine.

I continued saying, and even now I continue saying, a victim has no clan name. A victim is a victim, and let's talk about him or her and find out why they've been victimized, why they're fighting. I mean, you don't risk your life for the sake of a clan. You don't. Now, at no time in my writing have I ever mentioned the names of clans, and the reason is because I always knew that the moment you play clan name games, you're talking about something completely different from Somalia and that you are actually talking about things in colonial terms, [or] if you want, postcolonial terms, but never, never in traditional Somali terms. The simple fact is that no two clans who did not occupy lands, territories, that were contiguous with each other ever fought a battle in the history of the nation. You see, people do not fight in the name of a clan. They do so for something bigger than themselves, something bigger than the definition that clan gives them.

So I kept saying to Amnesty International and to my Somali friends, let's not forget what we're speaking of. We're speaking of a day in which people will be divided into clans, and people who are not taking up arms against each other now will be taking up arms against each other on the basis of clans. You will not have gotten anywhere nearer an understanding of who a person is by defining them according to a clan name, because you have two million persons sharing a clan name and any individual's ideology is obviously going to be very different from as many of the two million as possible. If you read this fantastic book by Benedict Anderson, *Imagined*

Communities, instead of "nation" just take "clan." A clan comprises hundreds, thousands, millions of people who do not know each other and who claim to belong to the same myth—mythical nonsense. People from the same clan may be fellow travelers for half a day, because they're interested in the same thing and fighting sometimes for the same reason, but they are different individuals, so you cannot lock them together. It's no form of definition.

You've compared the logic of clan identity to the logic of nationality as Benedict Anderson describes it and said you can substitute one for the other. But Anderson also says that those for whom such identities are invented do, in fact, take them on, contrived as they are, in their own subjectivities. And there's that very powerful question that he begins the book with: why is it that people are willing to fight and die for these invented categories? Is it not the case that there are many people in Somalia who do, in fact, accept the category of clan as meaningful?

No, you see, I have compared it to a working hypothesis. When you have a working hypothesis, working because it's functioning for you, you are going to die for it. A clan, a nation, is a working hypothesis. It doesn't work when it's not working for you. I met a person in Kismayo who said that he was my cousin. He then said that he wanted some money. I said, "I don't have money." And so he said, "Do you know who I am?" He told me again who he was, and I explained that I had only two hundred dollars, which I needed for my plane ticket and visa. So he said, "Give me the two hundred dollars. I want you to stay with us." I asked him what I would do. He said, "Well, we suffer here. You must suffer with us." So I said to him, "You told me you were my cousin. Now I know you're not," and I sent him away empty-handed. If you saw that man today and said to him, "Nuruddin is a clansman of yours," he would tell you, "No, he's not." And the reason is that it didn't work for him, that I didn't give him the two hundred dollars that I had in my pocket. If you landed in Mogadiscio today and you were driving a car and there was one white man in town, he would expect you to give him a lift. But the whiteness is what you share. There are certain things that are taken for granted but that work only for a short period of time.

Clan is not a definer. Clan is not an organizer of people. These are a disparate group of persons who are brought together by circumstances, like a rain shower. We are all standing together under a jetty, you know, you and I, and we could become friends for a few minutes because there is a thunderstorm and we are all seeking shelter under the jetty from the thunderstorm. We share as many things, features, as clanspeople do. And yet we are there temporarily, for fifteen minutes, when the downpour makes us stay there. That's how clans work: for a very short period of time. When people get to know each other, they become individuals. I'm saying to you that this is no way of defining a person. You cannot say, as people do, "In this cabinet, in this government, there is no one from our clan." No one represents a clan. Neither does anyone represent a nation.

Do you think of gender in the same way as clan and nationality, as analogous to a bond that is created by, but does not outlast, sharing shelter from the elements?

Gender would have more things in common, because women have been subjected to more torture for a much longer period of time [than a given clan or nation], and therefore there are more things shared. But the moment women become powerful, then the story changes.

You said that you never use clan names in your books, because that would be playing into the hands of Siyad Barre. But Siyad Barre's own name is also notably absent from your novels, despite their specific and contemporary Somali setting. It appears in A Naked Needle, *written just after the revolution—and before Siyad had fully shown his hand—but then you never use it again so long as he is in power, that is, not until* Secrets.

For the same reason I say that a victim has no clan name, I would also say that a tyrant has no name. A tyrant is a tyrant. When you say "tyrant," lots of different names come to people's minds. Some people think of Hitler, some people think of Hussein, some think of Siyad Barre, some of Stalin, some of Joe McCarthy. Different people think differently, depending on what their situations are. In other words, a tyrant becomes, for his victims, an historical moment of terror and that moment may come through your life, or mine, at different times and different periods of history, but the name is insignificant.

You see, I'm not one of those who fights a regime. If I did not make this clear [in the Dictatorship Trilogy] I think I should have failed in my duty as a writer: that Siyad Barre was not a target for me. No dictator is born out of a vacuum. A dictatorship comes out of a society and therefore one must stand in that society and one must see it as part of an authoritarian program. And my worry is that more and more writers, and Africans in particular, concentrate on the regime that is in power and work very hard at destroying it, felling it, without due regard for the society from which the dictators come. When the dictator goes, another dictator is going to come. What I used to say was, Siyad Barre is not the problem. The problem is Somali society. Somali society is authoritarian. Let's change our ways and let's start with the family. Let's start with the father, the son, and the mother. Let's start from the man in the kitchen. Let's start from sharing duty, sharing responsibility, whatever it is. However the family works out this particular sharing of responsibility is none of my business. But I will not be interested in talking about a dictatorship, a regime, because no matter what you do, when you get rid of Numeiry, in the Sudan, and you have Sadiq Al-Mahdi democratically elected Prime Minister in the Sudan, there is no *democracy* in the Sudan, because Sudanese society is undemocratic. The wife doesn't have rights, the child has no rights, they can't walk in the street. And if none of these things is possible, then we can't talk of democracy.

How do you, then, as a political writer, "talk of democracy"?

Politics usually means a concentrated effort on engineering society through elections, through free expression, journalism, something called democracy. This is not what I consider myself to be part of. What I am interested in is to be able to work within the family as a unit, and if there is no democracy in the house, there can certainly be no democracy in the capital. There is no democracy in India, for example. They keep telling me India is the largest democracy. There is no bloody democracy. How could there be when you have around 125 million untouchables? And I'm not talking about ideals. I'm just saying society will have to work from within and to reform itself so that the woman is fine where she is, loved, and the child and the animal have their rights. It might sound utopian, but it isn't. It's just starting with the small and moving towards the big. If I were interested in politics and somehow became Minister of Politics, then I could dictate from higher up, saying, "Right, people, you must be democratic." No, this is not what's going to be, and therefore my job is much more difficult. And the reason is that, first of all, I'm not talking of a regime. I'm talking of the totality of society, the whole thing.

Though you are not "one of those who fights a regime," it's clear from your books that you have been familiar with those who do fight regimes, with the Somali dissident community, for example, that was active in Italy while you were there. Did you think of yourself as part of that community?

I knew them. You see, I have an aversion to joining movements, and the reason is that movements have no center to them. What happens is that, although people are working for a cause, they're also working against one another. There is loss of temper, there is a great deal of anger on personal matters. The vote is usually taken on the basis of "I don't like what this man is saying although I agree that we should get rid of Siyad Barre." And therefore I would have been an associate

31

member of some of these movements in the sense that I would be able to meet some of them on a regular basis, but I have never been a member of any movement, because I was known to be a dissident and therefore I didn't need my presence to justify who I was. The majority of these people made "movementing" into a business, because they weren't doing anything else. They were "in politics," they were fighting against the dictatorship in the only way they could, and therefore they met regularly, they wrote letters, they organized themselves along either clan lines or friendship ones. With me it was a bit different. I could fight better not being a member of them, because the moment I became a member of them, some of them would not want to openly associate themselves with me because of my well-known views.

I was also against many of the things that these very people were doing. They were dealing terribly with their own wives. They were not people I wanted to associate myself with. I did not like what they were doing *outside* the movement time. Because dictatorship for me is not simply that political thing. Dictatorship for me is part and parcel of the way we live. And if someone is away from his wife the whole day and the whole night and never accounts for his time, I would say, I don't want to have anything to do with you. Because before you fight against Siyad Barre you must run a clean house. There must be a healthy relationship between you and your family before you can actually talk about authoritarian regimes. When I raised questions of a familial nature, the reaction often was "This is not the time to talk about these things. Let's get rid of Siyad Barre first and then we will deal with everything else." And I was saying that before you get rid of Siyad Barre or the regime of Siyad Barre you have to straighten these things within your own household. And that's where the difference was.

Somalia is now rid of Siyad Barre, but perhaps not of the more fundamental issues you've been talking about. Under these conditions, what sort of political role, apart from your writing, might you see for yourself once you are able to return permanently to Somalia?

I would love, for example, to be able to have a radio program once a week to talk about some of these things in a free-for-all kind of discussion. I would love to be able to take part in a reconstruction of Somali society in such a way that nobody feels left out. This is what I consider to be democracy. What I'm saying is that I would not be able to hold any position in any structure. My position, if there is any, is among the ordinary persons. If I were able, I would probably give lectures and talk to people and go to the schools and have a column in the newspaper—you know, participate in the reconstruction *that* way, so that it's not seen as running for office or president or wanting to be made ambassador here or there. That's not what I want to do.

Who or what do you think first started you thinking in these ways about rights and relationships, about democracy in the way you've been describing it?

Perhaps my mother—her cynical attitudes toward power. She was often more generous than most people and wanted me to be magnanimous. I was always full of rebellion and she was always magnanimous. She would always say, "Most people do not know what they're doing, so you cannot hold them responsible," whereas I always, even today, hold people responsible for being late for an appointment, for letting me down, for doing all kinds of things.

Did her attitudes toward power extend to her own sons and daughters?

I'm the fourth son of a family of ten—five boys and five girls. There were three boys ahead of me and I was the border mark from then on with the girls, but I was always discouraged from playing with the girls, because I was a boy, and was sent on to school, because I was a boy. And my sister was not sent to school, because she was a girl. My mother said she was happy there were two girls immediately after me so that the house would be run efficiently. But she was obviously aware of it, because later on, when the opportunity arose, she worked

33

harder to give the girls the same opportunity as the boys—to the extent where, in fact, in our family the girls have far better educations, in terms of certificates from university and so on, than the boys.

She was an oral poet, too, wasn't she?

She would have been a *buraambur*. There is a classical type of women's poetry. It's called *buraambur*. I think she would have become a major poet had she not had so many children.

What were your other sources of exposure, as a child, to poetry?

People quoted poems all the time, proverbs, parables. You couldn't hear someone speak long without their quoting a poem or a proverb. We were brought up slightly differently in the sense that, in addition to the oral literature, we were also exposed to Arabic poetry and English poetry. So it was a richer world, I think, because it gave us access simultaneously to different cultures and poetries.

Your parents obviously had a special concern about education. What sorts of schools did they send you to?

When the Ogaden was handed over to Ethiopia in 1948 my father lost his job [as an interpreter for the British in Kallafo]. And so, since a section of his family owned property in the Kallafo area, he became a farmer and a businessman. And then he helped set up the school, because the Ethiopian government wasn't keen on the idea of having schools there. It was a kind of an informal educational system. There were no certifications as such, because it wasn't recognized by the Ethiopian government. And so you went to school for as long as the teachers knew how to teach you and then you went to take exams somewhere else. Then, soon after we had done what could be done at the mainly Arabic-language school, the Sudan Interior Mission—a Christian, missionary, evangelical organization—came and set up a school. And then we just went over. Sometimes simultaneously we went to one school in the morning and the other one in the afternoon, and you had enough from both the Qur'an and the Bible by the end of the day.

We eventually left for Somalia after the 1964 skirmish between Ethiopia and Somalia. By then almost everything was half-finished and on hold. I would have been a third-year secondary-school student by that time, but I had no school certificate. I was working as a clerk-typist for the Ministry of Education and using English, Arabic, and Italian simultaneously, having picked up Italian quite fast also through trips—my eldest brother used to go to school in Mogadiscio. I then registered to finish secondary school in a teacher-training college. If you had enough of everything, you took a month off from work and you had an intensive course in one or another of the areas of weakness and then you took the exam. A year and a half after getting to Mogadiscio I had the secondary-school certificate.

And then you left to study English literature at Punjab University in India?

I can't remember what I studied. [Laughs.] All I remember is that I didn't think I learned much from the university. I enjoyed being in the library, and there was a lot to learn, and not the kinds of things that they were teaching us: somebody else's poems, and so on and so forth. But the only other thing I remember from university is that I was doing English literature at one point and taking a novel exam—there was a course under the pretentious title, "The English Novel"—and I came to take the exam on that day, and I was on a bicycle, cycling to the university to take the exam. I met the postman, who was a friend of mine, and he waves to me an envelope, saying there's a letter for me. And there was a letter, a rejection slip, from Heinemann African Writers Series, Nigeria, which had seen the second novel. This was before *Crooked Rib*—I can't recall the title. In it the editor said, "Dear Mr. Farah, If your father is a farmer, please continue in that line; if your father raises chickens, please continue in

35

that profession, because you have no talent as a writer." I turned around. I didn't take the exam. I refused to take the exam, saying, if I can't do my own why should I learn somebody else's? And then it was after that that I wrote *From a Crooked Rib*, and then quit the university altogether. My eldest brother then wrote a letter to me, saying that if I thought that I was good enough as a novelist, I should be able, in addition to writing novels, to take a degree, and it would be best to continue both things rather than just drop out. So I went back to the university.

Was anyone showing support for your writing in those days?

At the time that I was working on my first novel I met three writers who were very different, and all of them successful. One was Anita Desai. Another was Ruth Jhabvala. And Margaret Laurence. And I learned from the three of them that if you're a writer you're on your own. Ruth Jhabvala lent me the first book by an African writer that I read, Achebe's *No Longer at Ease*, and then said to me, "If you're interested in writing, that's it." This would have been 1968 when I first read a novel by an African south of the Sahara. And then I met Anita Desai, whose book, *Cry of the Peacock*, I love very much. They were all kind to me. It was very good for me to learn early on in my life that I had to continue doing the thing, and no one would do it for me. From that time on I have never had fellowship with writers. I've had them as friends. Sometimes the friendship and the writing overlapped, but the fact that they were writers didn't matter. Most of my friends now actually are not writers.

From a Crooked Rib did find a publisher and, unlike later books, was not banned in Somalia. What response did it receive there?

No, it was not banned, but someone called Walter Rodney, who wrote *How Europe Underdeveloped Africa*, came to Somalia and attacked *Crooked Rib* savagely for being a novel about some stupid young woman thinking about her own freedom, and so forth, when the nation is in chains. So it was seen as a bourgeois kind of novel, and so I was taken in, actually, when Walter Rodney was there, and I was interrogated by the Security for being bourgeois. And Leroi Jones [Amiri Baraka], who also came at the time, saved me from being detained by insisting on dining with me, he and his wife, on the day that I had an appointment with the Security. He gave me a meal and talked to me, whereas Walter Rodney ran me into the ground. They thought that *From a Crooked Rib* was about the petty bourgeois aspirations of a young woman, and if every Somali woman was to think about her own freedom, said Walter Rodney, where are we going to end up?

So that was the more-or-less official response. What about the reading public?

Crooked Rib has far more friends than any of my other novels has ever had. It is the novel that almost everybody seemed to have read when I was in Mogadiscio this time. It was also an easy kind of novel for them. One of the reasons why so many Somalis loved *From a Crooked Rib* was because it was easy for them to read, and because everybody knew someone similar to Ebla. There was, in fact, the now famous story of a woman coming and saying her name was Ebla and wanting to share royalties. If they liked it, it was also because it said things in a very clear way. Because after that the novels become more and more difficult, until *Gifts*. And now with *Gifts* it's possible again for them to read it and enjoy it. *Gifts* is going back to the same story as Ebla's, with only one difference, and that is, she stays with the man: you know, the same age, same kind of background, but one of them stays, the other one goes. So what happens to the one who goes, and what happens to the one who stays? Because she will eventually go too, you see.

37

You said that, with Gifts, *it's possible again for Somalis to read and enjoy your work. But that's only possible, of course, if they can obtain it, and your books have not been freely available in Somalia for many years. Do you still see yourself, nonetheless, as writing for a Somali readership?*

Well, you must also remember that nowadays the continents are so intermixed that a Somali readership, for example, in America, is far more likely than a Somali readership in Mogadiscio, because the majority of people who are able to read and write have all gone out of the country. And then readership—now, what is a readership? I mean, it's a very funny concept. When I was in Mogadiscio, people there listened to radios and read newspaper articles far more than they read novels, as such, but they are far more familiar with the ideas which I try and write into my books than I had imagined. They were able to read *From a Crooked Rib* when it was in existence, they were able to read articles and to cope with them, and they were able to listen to the voice message which one gave to them. If you gave these people books, how long would it take them to read a book, no matter how complicated or uncomplicated it is?

You have in fact given them, not only books, but stage plays. When did you first become interested in writing for theater?

While I was in India, I wrote a program for family planning in India. When I came back to Mogadiscio one of the first things that I did was to see if I could put on a play, called *A Dagger in Vacuum.* And a year into Siyad Barre's regime the censors wouldn't allow the play to be put on. There is one Somali character in the play who is drunk, and so they said it would show the moral weakness of the Somali people. "This is not the kind of thing that we're interested in." And so it was not allowed to be performed.I could have been more interested in theater if there were openings in theater, but there didn't seem to be. Somali theater was really one-track minded, musical comedies, and I wasn't interested in that. I was interested in bringing hard-edged philosophy and real social issues, and so on, and they weren't interested in that kind of theater—the authorities were not. And every play had to go through a censorship board. When it became apparent that it was not possible for me to do theater, I then started writing a novel, *A Naked Needle*. The whole of 1971 and '72 I worked on *A Naked Needle*.

A Naked Needle *was published in 1976 but is no longer in print. You have given the impression that you prefer that it remain out of print. Is that correct?*

Yes. I thought at the time that I was being satirical about misogynists, in addition to many other things, and people misunderstood the sarcasm and the satirical nature of the book and took it literally to heart. I didn't want to add one more misogynist to world literature. It's not an easy book to read if you're prone to not seeing beyond the surface. It's a playful kind of book.

The thinking about it was also contemporaneous with a novel I published in Somali, which is where the germ for *Maps* is actually located. It is, in fact, my first attempt at writing in "I-you-and-he." In 1972, December, *A Naked Needle* was finished, and by that time Somali had been provided with an orthography. I remember somebody at the university saying something to the effect that this Nuruddin writes novels in English, why can't he write a novel in Somali? So to prove a point I wrote a novel in Somali, which was to be serialized in the newspaper. There was a lot to do with generational differences in culture, and how much of one's life one is responsible for and how much your family is responsible for. There's a young fellow who comes out in all manner of clothes. His parents say that they feel ashamed to walk in the streets of the area where they live, because people say, "Look at your son, look at him." They want him to behave, to act and to dress in the normal way. He's quite rebellious, and says, "I refuse not only you and what you stand for, but I refuse all the things you espouse in life." So there is a dialogue between them.

It continued to be published way into the summer of 1973 and then was discontinued by the censors, because they didn't like one of the chapters. I could not speak in defense of the text, because I was in the Soviet Union. When I came back and discovered the discontinuation of the novel, I went to inquire the reason why. They said that they wouldn't even return the chapters that they still had, and so all the chapters that I had done vanished. They had the only copy.

And then the first idea of the Dictatorship Trilogy came into being. I remember writing the outline for the series of books sometime before I left Somalia.

And when you left Somalia again it was to study for a master's degree in theater?

I left Somalia for Britain to be, first, at the University of London from 1974 to '75 and then from there to go to the University of Essex from '75 to '76. While I was a student at Essex I was commuting from where I lived in London, because I was also attached to the Royal Court Theatre, training as a director. There was no teaching as such and therefore "attached to" meant that I could sit in on productions, on rehearsals. Back stage was opened to me, front stage was opened to me, I could do what I wanted, and I had no responsibilities. And someone paid me.

I wrote *The Offering* for the University of Essex, for my M.A. thesis, and it was produced by an assistant lecturer in drama, or something like that. I did all the things I was required except a 100-word essay, which I was supposed to submit. And on the day that I was to submit it I had a conflict, an open, theatrical clash with one of my lecturers, and I used bad language, or she used bad language. And then I walked out and never went back to collect the degree.

Also, I was realizing that, because I was working at the time on *Sweet and Sour Milk*, doing and redoing the book, I was quite certain that I would not be able to go back to Somalia. But I was hoping against hope that I might do the mad thing of publishing the book and then going back to Somalia. *A Naked Needle* was still not published. And then in some kind of fever of creativity I went and locked myself up somewhere in Denmark, in an apartment owned by a friend, and wrote the whole of the first draft of *Sweet and Sour Milk* in eighteen days, and then came back and forgot completely about the novel, and did whatever else I had to do.

And then, "hoping against hope," you set out for home?

I left for Rome, and then eventually, I was hoping, to Somalia, with *Sweet and Sour Milk* having gone through two drafts. And then I put it on hold on the assumption that I would go to Somalia and finish it in Somalia, in other words, with some authenticity. But this was not to happen, because, in July of 1976, having just come from Paris to Rome on my way to Mogadiscio, I was told, "We advise you not to come back." By then *A Naked Needle* had come out.

So what did you do?

I house-sat in Trieste—somebody wanted their cat fed. Trilogies are difficult to write and the reason is because you can't finish the first or the second before you actually know what's going to go into the third. And so I worked on those books, back and forth, all the time that I was in Italy. And I was in Italy from 1976 until October or November, 1979, working on the trilogy and earning bread by translating from various languages into various languages and working also as an English-language teacher, that kind of thing, mainly in Rome and Milan.

You had already written two drafts of Sweet and Sour Milk *when this period of work in Italy began. Did you revise it further before sending it to the eventual publisher, Allison and Busby?*

The book that they bought, the *Sweet and Sour Milk* that they bought, was very, very different from the one that they published, because I changed nearly every single word, tightening it, revising the language and the imagery that goes into the making of the story. Almost everything was changed. There are novels that go through many drafts, because either I can't find the voice or, in the first draft, the novel reads like the one just before. And because I generally go from a novel in which there is a central female consciousness followed by one of male consciousness, often followed by a third that is neither totally male nor wholly female, where you couldn't actually determine who is the main impetus. And therefore it is in fact the search for the voice that takes a long, long time. Stories are not very difficult to make up. It's usually the voice, it's the ambience. You can see how different *A Naked Needle* is from *Sweet and Sour Milk*. The reason is that there is a gap of years that I spent moving away from *A Naked Needle*. And the same with *Naked Needle* and *Crooked Rib*.

Do you keep the earlier drafts of your books or a record of the revisions?

Every book has along with it a companion text that is written in longhand. Every book. [He holds out a notebook.] This is the refugee book. This is what I'm trying to make sense of—notes and interviews and such. Everything that I write, even the shortest article, will have a companion text. And then there is the manuscript, and when the manuscript undergoes change the sweeper sometimes comes and sweeps away some of the pages that I changed. But from about *A Naked Needle* on there is in existence a notebook that has every major change in the text.

Did the other two books in the first trilogy go through as many revisions as Sweet and Sour Milk *did?*

I didn't do many changes [to *Close Sesame*]. *Sardines* underwent a great deal of change. At one point, one of the versions was wholly set in Milan. As a matter of fact, if you studied the structures of the novel, you could see that you could have done it in just two rooms. Because it's the ideas that generate the novel, and it's the situations. Like a lot of the other novels, it requires people to make it work, but almost all these people are the kind of persons who could have been plucked out of anywhere—Somalis, intellectuals, daughters of intellectuals, and so on.

You said that you outlined the entire first trilogy before beginning to write and that you were thinking about all three books together while writing each book. It seems that the novels of the second trilogy gestated more individually—certainly more slowly—that you did not have the same strong sense of the whole.

I think that's because I like my books to be a commentary on Somalia and the history of Somalia, and I like them to follow it to a certain degree—not to dictate, but to follow. And it was turning out that Somalia was undergoing far more changes than one could explain, and I didn't like the changes when I hadn't predicted them. So that's why it took a long time, because things were progressing in directions that I was very uneasy about. And I was always afraid that it would tumble into some kind of civil war. So I was holding myself back, because the Siyad Barre dictatorship was easy to find as a theme, whereas it was very difficult nowadays, you couldn't actually tell. Hence the indecision on my part.

Has that indecision been of particular concern in writing Secrets? *You've used different titles over the past few years, for example, to refer to the work in progress, and described different emphases.*

Well, there were all kinds of mutations. At one stage it was *Letters* and at another stage it was *Motives*. It's the same book. The basic story

43

remained the same, the skeletal framework, but maybe they were telling different stories. I think that what did happen was that from about 1983 I wasn't quite certain that Somalia would not explode sooner than it did. I did not want to be caught unawares, and so I prepared a draft of a book set in a civil war, which I had no intention of publishing if no civil war occurred. And so at different stages I went back and forth between the idea of a novel set in a civil war and the idea of a novel set in normal times. Eventually I aborted it when the civil war did take place, and I was at that time at work on a book about the civil war in 1990. And I have now gone back to it. I've just done a first draft—a book after *Secrets* and after the refugee book, directly set in civil war. But it exists only in skeletal shape.

Secrets *may have originated in indecision, but it doesn't seem, compared to* Maps *and* Gifts, *to be about indecision.*

No, most characters state their positions quite clearly in *Secrets*. In *Maps* you see everything through the eyes of Askar and therefore he can do any number of tricks and then disown everything towards the end of the book and say it's all made up or it doesn't matter. *Gifts* has been missed by practically every reader whom I have met, not thinking, even for a moment, that there is no story, that this is a story that a woman tells herself from the beginning to the end. It doesn't happen. It happens inside her head when she goes from home to work. She's narrating the story to herself and imagining what would happen if her luck turned.

It's interesting, in any case, that there is a certain openness about lots of taboo material in *Secrets*, more than in much of African fiction, where there is a certain prudishness about it. And my view is if the members of a society can do unto each other such savageries, then who are they to remain prudish? Who are they to say there are no longer virgins, there is no honesty, there is no truth, there is no trust, nothing, and therefore it's a world in which every acceptable truth can be challenged? Because truth has also several dimensions, and the old man does certain things that he doesn't want anyone else to know. Some people would see the exposure of what an old man like Nonno is doing—in the bathroom masturbating, for example—to be the most heinous thing for Somali decency and gentlemanliness. They say, "Why would you talk about this stuff?" But then it's also the same kind of people who talked about my being highly indecent at first when I published *From a Crooked Rib*. They said, "Why are you telling all our terrible things to others?"

Whatever he may be hiding, this old man in Secrets, *Nonno, is a figure of almost mythic proportions, comparable in this sense to Deeriye in* Close Sesame. *One can't help noting that the deaths of these revered patriarchs are the culminating events in both trilogies.*

There are different stages in the nation's history. These two stages are different in the sense that there is still a decency at the time that Deeriye dies, kills himself, gets killed—whether he's committed suicide or not is a question. There is still decency because the Qur'an is still playing an important part and because there are still intellectual questions: honesty, violence, how do you solve an unresolvable crisis? But once the gentleman—and Deeriye is a gentleman, honest, truthful—dies, then after that the beginnings of the civil war, in fact, start with *Maps*. However much it's masked, it's downhill from then on. Almost everything that happens in *Maps* is a prelude to more crises, personal, existential, philosophical, historical. And then it's also the "disintegration" of the family as we know it. Because there is suspicion that Askar's uncle did rape his mother, so there is in fact incest of the lowest degree, barbaric. And so the clan as such is dead, and the reason is because the patriarch has dishonored it. This is the beginning of the book, of *Maps*. The boy is born, and the boy then wants to fight, not for a clan, but for a nation, because he wants to start all over again. In *Maps* nothing is straight. No line is drawn straight, because every line goes through mined territory of information, of truth, of philosophy. Everything is a debris and therefore you go through the enthusiasms of nationality and then the death of nationalism, because with the end of the novel the question is, is there something called Somalia? Who am I? Who is Somalia? Who is Askar? Who is Misra? And therefore *Secrets*, in fact, terminates the process with which *Maps* begins. *Secrets* ends with the internal civil war. The external combustion of the civil war was external because Somalia, Somalis, invaded Ethiopia. With the defeat, when they return, there is an implosion. There was an explosion, because it went outward, out of Somalia into Ethiopia, and then there is the implosion. The signs of the implosion are there already in *Gifts* and also when a person dishonors his mother, which is what Askar does to Misra. No more honor is left. There are many, many folk tales and stories that are told in *Maps* about sons who are disloyal to their mothers.

The issue of sons dishonoring their mothers arises in the Dictatorship Trilogy as well—for example, in Samater's throwing Idil out of the house. Is the difference that, at the earlier historical stage, the principle that sons do not dishonor mothers—the principle of decency—is intact, even if it is violated, whereas the principle itself is no longer present in the world of the later novel?

Yes, in other words, even if people were to distance themselves from what Samater does, some people would say it's understandable. It's also part of a plot in which matriarchy has no more space than it used to be given traditionally, whereas the lack of decency on the part of Askar is something that is unpardonable. Or at least the whole concept [of decency] is questionable. Because there's a brother-in-law raping a sister-in-law. There are families doing things to each other. And it's the same thing repeated, time and time again, in what should have been the *third* trilogy—because the first trilogy in fact was *From a Crooked Rib*, *A Naked Needle*, and the play that never was published, *A Dagger in Vacuum*. And now I'm working on another trilogy, which may not, all three, be novels, but may include the refugee book.

PART TWO

General Essays

NURUDDIN FARAH:
A Tale of Two Trilogies
Reed Way Dasenbrock

Nuruddin Farah attracted attention as a writer less through his first two novels, *From a Crooked Rib* and *A Naked Needle,* as impressive as these are as novelistic debuts, than from the next three, *Sweet and Sour Milk, Sardines,* and *Close Sesame,* which form a trilogy Farah has named *Variations on the Theme of an African Dictatorship.*[1] These three novels were published in relatively quick succession, appearing between 1979 and 1983. The pace of Farah's production as a novelist has slowed: *Maps,* the first installment of a second trilogy, appeared in 1986, but its successor novels, *Gifts* and *Secrets,* were published in 1993 and 1998 respectively.[2] Although contemporary African writers have linked their works together in a number of ways *(Things Fall Apart* and *No Longer at Ease* coming to mind as one example), Farah is unique in anglophone African writing and in postcolonial anglophone fiction in general in utilizing the trilogy as a form, not just once but twice.

A number of questions are posed by the centrality of these two trilogies to Farah's oeuvre. What attracts him to the form of the trilogy? How do these novels work together to form a trilogy? Do the two trilogies work the same way? What continuities are there between them, what resemblances, what departures? These questions take on a fresh form with the completion of the second, as yet unnamed trilogy which coincided with the awarding of the 1998 Neustadt Prize to this fascinating and unique writer.

Variations on the Theme of an African Dictatorship is a very different kind of title from the striking titles of the individual books which constitute the first trilogy. The novels have short, brilliantly evocative titles which nevertheless give little clue to what one may encounter in them, whereas the trilogy's title at first glance evokes a landscape of abstract political concepts. Yet one's initial sense that the novels have literary titles and the trilogy a political one is undercut slightly in two ways: first, the term *Variations,* which hints of a musical form to the trilogy, and the variation of definite and indefinite articles which echoes *A Portrait of the Artist as a Young Man.* The titles in fact work well together to describe the novels and how they fit together: each novel in the trilogy involves a struggle against the General (Siyad Barre, the dictator who ruled Somalia from 1969 to 1991) led by a group of idealistic, young, privileged, European-educated Somalis, but the links among them in terms of plot are loose and casual, consisting primarily of references in the later novels to the failed efforts of characters in the earlier novels to overthrow the General's regime. The free-standing nature of the novels is well suggested by the striking variance of the titles, and in fact each novel works extremely well on its own; yet there is a common cluster of themes around which the three novels circulate and to which they consistently return.

But what finally creates the unity of the first trilogy above all is the homogeneity of the characters, particularly the important protagonists. (Deeriye from *Close Sesame* is a partial exception here, to whom I shall return.) The protagonists of the first trilogy are all young, oriented toward European culture and languages, and generally European-educated: they speak Italian as well as Somali and converse in Italian as a kind of secret language their children don't understand and as an intellectual lingua franca in which certain concepts are more easily expressed. There is an overlap between their Italian/European frame of reference and the English language in which the novels are written which identifies Farah with these protagonists as cosmopolitan, multilingual Somalis necessarily at some remove from the *mentalitè* of the average Somali. These characters are aware that the languages in which they have been educated give them access to aspects of international culture which would otherwise not have been open to them: they assume a familiarity with Pablo Neruda and John Coltrane which the average Somali (or American, for that matter) does not have. What the course of events in each novel makes the readers aware of is that this access comes at a price, that though they identify intensely with Somalia, what these idealistic young Somalis have gained access to separates them from the culture which surrounds them. Deeriye, the only protagonist in these novels not of this class and age cohort, is the exception which illustrates the general rule: though fully literate in Italian and undeniably sophisticated intellectually, he is oriented more toward oral Somali culture and the culture of Islam. He prefers listening to poetry and prayers on cassette and to the Arabic-language services of the BBC, and for these reasons and others, he is far more rooted in the culture of the nation than are his children and the other young revolutionaries in the other novels. This of course does not make him any more successful than the others in overthrowing the General, who still rules at the end of *Variations,* but it does make him less isolated.

However, what Deeriye shares with his children and the others may be more important than what he does not share, and I would like to call this a settled identity of opposition. I mean by this to point to two things at once: first, the characters with whom we come to identify know who they are in *Variations.* Despite their international/cosmopolitan frame of reference, they have a strong sense of themselves as Somali, resisting the attempts of others to label them as non- or quasi-Somali because of their broader frame of cultural reference, and in that sense their identity is quite stable. It is also oppositional, and by that I mean first of all that it is primarily constituted by opposition to the General's rule and to the status quo in Somalia and indeed in all of Africa. That is a tremendous strength, and these characters are immensely appealing in their heroic and ultimately self-sacrificing attempts to undo the rule of the General. But with the distance which fifteen years and the new trilogy brings, it can also be seen that they have a certain narrowness to their vision. If the problem is the General, then fixing the problem ought to be simple: get rid of the General. Their analysis isn't that simple, of course: there is a good deal of sophisticated analysis about how Somali family and clan structure reinforces the General's rule and creates the conditions in which it can operate. But nevertheless, that analysis remains limited in the sense that it operates with a clear and precisely defined sense of the problem, which is defined as caused by other people. We are not the problem; we are the solution, because the problem is represented by those people over there.

What this means is that there is an enormous psychic dividing line in the middle of each of the novels in *Variations* between those who represent the problem and those who represent the solution. In *Sweet and Sour Milk* and *Sardines* the divide is essentially cultural and generational: the young, cosmopolitan revolutionaries are in sharp contrast to their parents, more caught in traditional Somali modes of being and acting, who are seen to be complicit with the oppressive Somali regime. Deeriye in *Close Sesame* is such an important character because he breaks through this way of putting the divide: he is a father who declines to play the authoritarian role of the Grand Patriarch which sustains the despotism of the General; he is the traditional Somali and devout Muslim who shows that one can be these things and act non-despotically. Moreover, his reminiscences about Italian colonialism and the discussions he and his son Mursal have about Shi'a ways of theorizing revolt should serve to remind us (in case we need reminding) that the European frame of reference of the young revolutionaries has a despotic element and that Islam has a revolutionary component. Until this point in the trilogy, Italy comes in as a frame of reference largely vis-à-vis the politics of the Italian Left: several of the characters in *Sardines* were involved in leftist politics while students in Italy, and their journalist friend Sandra enters the novel as a representation of the naive, pro-General policy of the PCI (the Italian Communist Party) at the time. The longer historical perspective Deeriye introduces complicates the idealization of European culture in which the younger characters participate.

This is an important complication, yet it does not change the sense in which all these characters are confident that they are the "good guys." Moreover, we share that confidence as we come to identify with these characters. I do not wish to undermine that confidence retroactively as much as describe it, as a way of indicating one aspect of the second trilogy which seems conspicuously different: namely, the fact that the latter is set in a landscape in which the settled and bordered identities of *Variations* are no longer readily obtainable. We should infer this from the differences in the titles alone. With *Close Sesame,* we are placed immediately in an Islamic frame of reference, even though the familiar "Open Sesame" of the *1001 Nights* is replaced by a "Close" which suggests that the magical possibility and openness to change of the tales may not obtain in the world of the novel. *Maps, Gifts*, and *Secrets* work very differently: each title is one word, a plural abstract English noun which is strikingly heedless of place. In Farah's earlier plans for the trilogy, the final novel was to be called *Letters,*[3] indicating that Farah's general idea about what kind of titles he wanted came before all the actual titles themselves. These are thematic titles, in a long-standing tradition in English-language fiction *(Persuasion* comes to mind as one example). The themes—particularly *Maps* and *Gifts*—put us in a European colonial frame of reference, a frame reinforced by the novels themselves in references to the maps created by European colonialism and the problematic gifts given countries like Somalia which, whatever the givers' motives, help perpetuate the tradition of neo-colonial dependency. Hence, the differences between the two trilogies are indicated quite accurately by the differences in the titles. Although at first glance *Variations* seems more explicitly political than the second trilogy, in the sense that political struggle is rarely absent from the action of the novels, the second trilogy is just as political if in a deeper sense, since it focuses on a searching reflection on what created the landscape of the first trilogy.

Maps moves us into this reflection from the very beginning. Not least among the problems which the newly independent African states inherited upon independence was the problem of the borders created by European imperialism. The lines between and among British, French, Portuguese, Belgian, German, Spanish, and Italian colonies in Africa only occasionally corresponded to the differences between nations and peoples in place before European contact, and this has meant that every state in postcolonial Africa has had a very complex and problematic relation to the nations which constituted them. The European powers, though aware of the problems they had bequeathed to their former colonies, by and large opposed and continue to oppose any changes in borders, on the theory that if any border were to be revised anywhere, then full-scale chaos would result. Because all borders in Africa are equally problematic and arbitrary, allowing the revision of any single border opens them all to question and to possible revision in the same way. Indeed, the recognition of the independence of Eritrea is the only real revision in the colonial map of Africa which has taken place in the postcolonial era. Moreover, ironically, even that revision in a sense merely returns the map to the colonial period between 1896 and 1935, between Adowa and Mussolini, when Eritrea was an Italian colony but Ethiopia as a whole retained its independence.

Somalia stands in a unique relationship to the postcolonial mapping of Africa, a relationship which is at once favorable and unfavorable: favorable in the sense that the country of Somalia is unique among African countries of any size in being made up of speakers of the same language—Somali—who share a cultural identity. Thus, in this respect at least, Somalia has the potential to be a coherent nation-

54

state along familiar European lines (even if it can hardly be said to have fulfilled this potential). However, Somalis and citizens of Somalia do not exist in anything like a one-to-one relationship: what was Italian Somaliland and British Somaliland may have been united as Somalia, but French Somaliland remains the separate country of Djibouti, while both Kenya and Ethiopia have substantial Somali-speaking populations in the areas of these countries contiguous with Somalia.

The first section of *Maps* is set in the Ogaden, the Somali section of Ethiopia, and the second section takes place in Mogadiscio, the capital of Somalia, at the height of Somalia's ill-fated but initially successful attempt to reclaim the Ogaden in 1977-78. The novel's protagonist, Askar, is a young orphan of Somali extraction who grows up (as Farah himself did) in Kallafo in the Ogaden but then moves to Mogadiscio to live with his aunt and uncle. But as important in the novel is his foster mother, Misra, who is Ethiopian or at least non-Somali (she is Amharic-speaking but of Oromo descent). Misra joins the refugee exodus from the Ogaden following the defeat of the pro-Somali Western Somalia Liberation Front (WSLF) forces, but after a complex reunion with Askar she is tortured and killed in somewhat unclear circumstances. The novel ends with the police taking Askar off for questioning about Misra's death.

This bald plot summary is even less helpful than in the case of Farah's other novels: the essence of the novel is not in what happens but in the sense the characters and the readers make of what happens. Askar as a young child in the Ogaden has no clear sense of who he is: "Who is Askar?" is a question he himself asks. When he grows to adolescence in Somalia, he attempts to answer this question by embracing the cause of the WSLF and contemplating enrolling in the "liberation army." But in indirect response to this growing militancy, his uncle, Hilaal, asks a question to which Askar does not have an answer: "The point is, who's an Ethiopian?" This is a profound and subtle question, since it asks about the very basis of the Somali claim to the Ogaden, which is to say the basis of Askar's claim to be Somali. For Askar and the Ogaden alike to belong to Somalia and not to

Ethiopia, one must be able to distinguish between Somalis and Ethiopians. But this is what no one can really do. As we see from the first part of *Maps,* set in Ethiopia, Ethiopia is not a nation-state made up of ethnic Ethiopians (not a possible category), but rather is a polyglot, multi-ethnic, imperial state with an Amharic-speaking elite dominating a mèlange of different peoples. In an important sense, Askar is as Ethiopian as Misra, even though for him Ethiopians are "other." He dreams early in the novel of a world where "most people they met along the way had their bodies tattooed with their identities: that is name, nationality and address. Some had engraved on their skins the reason why they had become who they were when living and others had printed on their foreheads or backs their national flags or insignia."[4] But this dreamworld is the land of the dead precisely because identities are not neatly discrete in the way Askar dreams. This condition does not obtain in the real world in which Askar and Misra live. One image of this is that there are a number of variations on Misra's name, each one of which establishes a different ethnicity for her. Who is Askar? Who is an Ethiopian? These are good questions in the world of *Maps.*

They are also very concrete ones, not abstractions as they might seem to readers but bitter, concrete realities: though no one can clearly say who and what they are, people are killed because of who and what they are. It is not until Somali liberation of the Ogaden becomes a possibility that the differences between Misra and Askar become apparent to him, since he grows up thinking of her as his mother and speaking a Somali influenced by her less-than-perfect pronunciation of the language. Askar and Misra begin talking about these matters only when the villagers grow hostile to her.

> I asked: hasn't Misra chosen to be one of us? Hasn't she chosen to share with us our pain and our pleasure? Now she was undecided whether to leave us or share our bitter destiny with us. She spoke of this too, although I do not think I understood it at the time. '*I*

am an Ethiopian,' she said. But how was I to know what species an 'Ethiopian' is? I asked the appropriate questions and got the appropriate answers. The image which has remained with me, is that of a country made up of patchworks—like a poor man's mantle. She wasn't decided whether to go back to the Highlands or stay, she repeated. Although she no longer spoke or understood the language of the area of Ethiopia in which she was born.

I said, 'I'll come with you.'

She greatly belied her pleasure by saying, after a long, long silence, during which she wiped away the tears which had stained her cheeks, 'I will not want you to come with me.'

'Why not?' I asked.

She turned towards me, her eyes aflame with hot tears. 'Because it's not safe for you. They will kill you, my people will, without asking questions, without wanting to know your name or what our relationship is.'

I asked, 'Your people, my people—what or who are these?'

'One day,' she said, speaking of a future in which we would meet, 'one day, you will understand the distinction, you'll know who your people are and who mine are. One day,' she prophesied, speaking into that void of a future in which she hoped we would meet again, 'you will identify yourself with your people and identify me out of your community. Who knows, you might even kill me to make your people's dream become a tangible reality.' (94-95)

This passage anticipates the narrative movement and the denouement of the novel: by leaving Misra in Kallafo, Askar attempts to escape the complex and confused landscape of identity in which he has necessarily dwelt until this point. Somalia for him is a sign of an untroubled singular identity, and living in Somalia, he comes to understand himself as Somali. This conversation is indeed prophetic: instead of Misra's people killing Askar without asking who he is, confident in their own knowledge of community and identity, Askar's people kill Misra. Or is it Askar himself who kills Misra, as she anticipates and "prophesies" here? The police who come to question him at the end of the novel seem to think so, and though no reader of Farah's novels can have any confidence in the procedures of the Somali police, nothing in the narrative invites us to view their taking him for questioning and their apparent arrest of him for murder as a frame-up of the kind found in *Variations*.

In my reading of *Maps*, not a lot hangs on whether Askar actually killed Misra or not. The crucial point is that he might well have killed her, that as Misra herself understood, killing her is a logical outgrowth of the politics to which he has committed himself. In order to make "the dream" of nationalism "tangible," in order to carve nation-states out of the tangled web of intermingled identities which make up the world in which we live, the Misras of the world must be killed because they don't fit. They blur the distinct lines of Askar's dream-world, and in order to make these artificial distinctions real, Misra must die. The point here is not to demonize the Somalis who kill Misra, which is one reason why the identity of her killers is left unclear. After all, Askar's going with Misra to "her people" is presumably a real possibility in the context of the novel, and it is easy enough to imagine Askar's death happening just as Misra prophesies. Both sides are committed to values which ultimately and inexorably lead to genocide and the slaughter of the innocent.

Nuruddin Farah is obviously opposed to such values, but these are difficult values to oppose in anything like a straightforward manner. If one is criticizing a view in which the world is divided into black and white, how does one oppose that view vigorously without constructing it as an other to be eradicated and therefore returning to the either/or vision one opposes? This is Farah's dilemma in *Maps*, and one way of defining what he attempts to do in *Gifts* and *Secrets* is to try to construct narratives about this confused, not either/or world and to watch characters try to negotiate the complexities which result.

But having told a story in which I present Farah as a novelist to be a complicator of other people's narratives, I need to complicate my own narrative a little. My comparison of *Maps* to *Variations on the Theme of an African Dictatorship* has to this point been a narrative of development, in which *Maps* is intellectually more sophisticated than the earlier work and therefore an improvement on it. I do take *Maps* to be Farah's single most successful novel, but the many passages in all of his novels—especially *Gifts*—which reflect ironically on the language the West uses to present itself as developed, Africa as undeveloped and in need of gifts from the West, gifts which always come with complex strings and conditions attached, should make us pause before committing to any singular narrative of development here. In a manner something like Yeats's gyre, the second trilogy does not simply move beyond the concerns of the first. It also loops back to incorporate them, and there is a series of thematic and structural echoes between the two trilogies.

Let me try to sketch some of these echoes which relate to the themes of family and identity central to the new trilogy. *Variations* has an intricate pattern of variation in terms of gender and generational concerns. *Sweet and Sour Milk* is centered on the relation of sons and fathers, *Sardines* on daughters and mothers, *Close Sesame* again on sons and fathers or perhaps fathers and sons. In each novel, it is easy to assign one gender and one generation the primary role, and the primary relationships are across generations but not across genders. The third novel is the hardest to fit into this schema, because the brother-sister and father-daughter relations are almost as important as the father-son relation in *Close Sesame*. This pattern is echoed but varied elegantly in the new trilogy, though in each case the central relation is across genders and not necessarily generations. Hence, the two first novels in each trilogy—*Sweet and Sour Milk* and *Maps*—have a young man as their protagonist who is engaged in inter-generational conflict, and both end with the families falling apart: the central figure in *Sweet and Sour Milk,* Loyaan, tries to find out the truth about his brother Soyaan's mysterious death. As he comes to understand that the General's regime was involved and that his father Keynaan is urging him to accept the regime's bribes and remain silent, he revolts against the patriarchal structure represented by his father and the General alike. The second novels of the two trilogies—*Sardines* and *Gifts*—are dominated by female protagonists, Medina and Duniya, are about relations which are not grounded in conflict (though they may involve it), and move toward a harmony which is never fully achieved. What drives Medina's actions in *Sardines* is her desire to keep her daughter Ubax from undergoing female circumcision at the hands of her mother-in-law: this leads her to move away from her husband, who is a minister in the government. The male protagonists of the first novels choose a concern for the nation over their own families, and the conflict which results is destructive for both. The female protagonists of the second novels are concerned with their families precisely as a reflection of their concern about the nation, and they manage the conflict much more successfully at least as far as their immediate family is concerned. Finally, both of the third novels—*Close Sesame* and *Secrets*—complicate this dyadic relation in a similar direction, since very old characters—Deeriye and Nonno—come to dominate each work, though there is also an important and complex relation between a man and a woman of a younger generation in each. This parallel is not exact: the complex brother-sister relation of *Close Sesame* between Deeriye's children Mursal and Zeinab is replaced in *Secrets* by a very odd relationship between the protagonist Kalaman and his former lover and childhood sweetheart Sholoongo, who returns from the United States expressly in order to have a child with him, a demand which he does not satisfy. But each novel ends with the death of the father figure, a death which, though also not solving the national dilemma, is redemptive and integrative at the familial level.

However, there is a stark difference between all the families in the first and second trilogies which is worth exploring for a moment. The first trilogy always involves real, legitimate families and focuses on the relations between parents and children. Those relations are complex and often dysfunctional: Farah sees the tyranny represented by the General as little more than a reflection of the tyranny found in most Somali families, and this means that he welcomes the revolt of the sons and daughters in *Sweet and Sour Milk* and *Sardines* and welcomes even more the fact that Deeriye's children do not need to revolt against him. In contrast, the novels in the second trilogy are about relations which might best be called quasi-familial, since they have the character of familial relations though they turn out mostly not to be. Hence, *Maps* turns on a son-mother relation, except that Misra turns out not to be Askar's mother. At the center of *Gifts* is a foundling child who appears mysteriously out of nowhere: though treated as family, she clearly is not family. The "foster parents," Duniya and Bosaaso, are also not related, though they fall in love in the course of the novel and we suppose at the close that they will marry. Finding out the facts about the mysterious quasi-familial relations is an important theme in all these books: we ultimately learn who the parents of the foundling are in *Gifts* and also why the foundling was unacknowledged, whereas the central action of *Secrets* turns on Kalaman's painful discovery that Nonno is not in fact his biological grandfather, that he was instead born as a result of a gang rape. Since *nonno is* Italian for "grandfather," the question is whether Nonno is indeed Kalaman's *nonno.*

Most of Farah's novels can be presented generically as elegant variations on the genre of the detective story, but the space between his fiction and the genre of the detective story is established by the fact that the discovery of the hidden secret is never as important in his novels as what the characters do with—how they react to—the secrets they discover. The contrast I have established between the first trilogy, mostly about legitimate families, and the second, mostly about illegitimate ones, is not a contrast in ethical terms; it is a central part of Farah's point that he wants us to question the value we assign to terms like *legitimacy* or *natural.* The familial structure created across *Gifts* among people who are not related (at least not yet) is presented as much less dysfunctional than the biological families which are represented in the first trilogy. Although the foundling dies, Duniya and Bosaaso at least took responsibility for it and took care of it. The central resolution of *Secrets* is that the relation between Kalaman and his grandfather is essentially unaffected by the revelation that they are not in fact related. To put this another way, they are in fact related, related by emotional bonds, by the life they have lived together, even if they are not blood relations. The authenticity of that relation is unaffected by the absence of a genetic basis to the relation. Thus Kalaman continues to call Nonno Nonno because Nonno is his *nonno.*

This returns us to the large themes of *Maps* I sketched above, themes which persist throughout the second trilogy. One of the central problems with Somali society is the strong us-them difference instantiated in the clan structure of Somali society and which sustains the Somali nationalism on display in *Maps.* Central to any form of nationalism is a sense of the entire nation as an extended family: hence, foreigners and strangers are not kin, not family. The harm done by this view, for Farah, is not just that in this view we must construct the other as the enemy; it is that we must also construct our own relations as somehow ourselves in a way which may not be the case. Farah is happy to celebrate the relation we call brotherhood, but he is not so sure that it is always or even often found among brothers. The complex, fractured, inauthentic families of the new trilogy are there because they represent what life is really like today, not the world of Askar's dream in which identities are discrete and worn on our skin like clothes, but rather a complex landscape in which the very relations we take as natural—mother, grandfather— may be no such thing.

For me, the most moving relations in Farah's fiction are those which involve the construction of a genuine connection across complex and tortuous distances. Hence, the devout Muslim Deeriye has a Jewish American daughter-in-law, Natasha, who speaks no Somali (and he speaks no English). They meet each other halfway therefore in Italian, and the very strong human connection which emerges between them in *Close Sesame* is all the stronger because it has had to be constructed across this enormous gap. Duniya and Bosaaso are attracted to each other from the start of *Gifts,* but it is their relation as foster parents of the foundling which builds the durable relation which we feel has been established by the end of *Gifts.* The relation of Kalaman to his *nonno* is in an important sense strengthened, not weakened, by the revelation that Nonno is not his actual grandfather. The connection of this to the larger themes could not be more direct: we cannot build a stable society on group notions of identity, for those notions depend upon there being an other who is not us, and our relation to that other is necessarily antagonistic. We need to be able to find a way to relate to those who are not our relations.

It goes without saying that any actual realization of this ideal in the world of Farah's novels is fleeting and transient. If *Variations* is set during the struggle against the General, the new trilogy is set against the backdrop of the slow disintegration of the Somali state in the last years of Siyad Barre's rule and the chaos which has followed. During *Maps* the General's power is essentially intact, though the failure of the attempt to reclaim the Ogaden marked the beginning of a process of erosion of support for his rule. In *Gifts* the General is still in power, though his power is increasingly weakened by the economic difficulties, shortages of fuel and food, and outright famine facing Somalia. In *Secrets* the central state has crumbled after Siyad Barre's fall from power in 1991, and the militias control the roads outside Mogadiscio to the extent that travel just a few miles outside the city involves taking one's life literally in one's hands.

Somalia thus is a good image for us of the other whom we need to find a way to relate to. But we would not have learned anything from Farah's fiction if we were to ascribe all this to anything narrowly Somali, to a mysterious property which belongs to "them," not to us.

63

The figure from the outside who comes to Somalia is a common figure in Farah's novels, and it is easy to see these figures as versions of us, the reader from the outside who comes to Farah's world knowing little about Somalia but the complex prejudices we have. Farah's call is always to move toward an affirmation of human solidarity across the differences which may separate us, and that includes the readers of as well as the characters in his novels.

Farah himself is a writer in the tradition of cosmopolitan modernism, a writer who seeks to "fly by" the nets of nationalism and ethnic particularism which has done so much damage to his own people. Yet in that tradition, he should be identified with writers such as Joyce, who retained a primary commitment as an artist to depicting a particular culture and place—his culture and place—not because it is uniquely valuable but, on the contrary, because of its typicality. The problems of Somalia are the problems of California, if in different registers of intensity, if only because they are the problems of all of us. Perhaps it is Farah's good luck as a writer (even if this is obviously not a matter of good luck in other respects), and it is certainly our good luck as readers, that he was born in a country like Somalia which has experienced all the travails of the commitment to a vision of the nation as a singular identity which led either Askar or someone with his beliefs to kill his foster mother Misra. Farah's call is Misra's call: that we have a more spacious sense of who and what we are which will allow us to accept others and not kill them to make our "people's dream a tangible reality." I think it is impossible to read Farah's fiction without responding to that call: to read his fiction is to have one's world become a more capacious place. That is a lot for a writer to accomplish.

NOTES

1. Nuruddin Farah, *Variations on the Theme of an African Dictatorship*, a trilogy consisting of *Sweet and Sour Milk* (London: Allison &

Busby, 1979); *Sardines* (London: Allison & Busby, 1981); *Close Sesame* (London: Allison & Busby, 1983).

2. Nuruddin Farah, *Maps* (New York: Pantheon, 1986); *Gifts* (London: Serif, 1993); *Secrets* (New York: Arcade, 1998).

3. Feroza Jussawalla and Reed Way Dasenbrock, "Nuruddin Farah," in *Interviews with Writers of the Post-Colonial World* (Jackson: University Press of Mississippi. 1992), p.53.

4. *Maps*, p.42.

5. *Maps*, pp.94-95.

NURUDDIN FARAH:
Tribalism, Orality, and Postcolonial Ultimate Reality and Meaning in Contemporary Somalia

John C. Hawley

*"Everybody had turned the foundling into what they
thought they wanted, or lacked."*
—NURUDDIN FARAH, *Gifts*

1. Introduction

F̲ew would contest the observation of Matthew Horsman and Andrew Marshall that "fragmentation within existing nation-states—along ethnic, linguistic and religious lines—is occurring in eastern Europe, in Africa and in the states of the former Soviet Union"; that even in the "traditional nation-states," as the authors describe them, "tribalism is growing. Scots in the United Kingdom, Catalans and the Basques in Spain, and Lombards in Italy are increasingly vigorous in their demands for an even greater measure of self-

67

administration." Some would perhaps wish to qualify the reasons that Horsman and Marshall offer to explain this phenomenon but, again, most would agree that those who participate in this resurgence of tribal consciousness "seek a level of comfort in their communities to withstand the complexity and atomization that modern capitalism has wrought on their lives and to free themselves from domination by 'alien' elites."[1] But if this search for "comfort"—which one might interpret as a search for meaning—is a regressive and relatively recent event in some countries, in many parts of the world where nation-states have been arbitrarily carved out of a map by colonizing powers, such tribalism continues less as a vehicle for personal liberation and more as the very mechanism for domination by native elites. This is especially true in a country like Somalia, where factional battles resist national coalescence. The question citizens of such an inchoate country must ask themselves, in terms of their personal *and* national search for meaning, is how to find a voice, how to find an audience, how to begin a dialogue from which a consensus may emerge. Must each citizen remain a foundling, seeking an individual and national identity that has not been imposed by others?

While granting that it would be simplistic to propose that all 'postcolonial' peoples are seeking the same ultimate reality, it will be the purpose of this paper to suggest that in Nuruddin Farah of Somalia, roadblocks to the search for ultimate meaning dominate his fiction in a way typical of many third-world novelists. As Barbara Harlow points out, for writers such as Amilcar Cabral (the leader of the Guinea-Bissau liberation movement and a major theoretician of African resistance and liberation struggles) and Ghassan Kanafani (author of *Literature of Resistance in Occupied Palestine 1948-1966*), the resistance movement and the armed struggle for national liberation were to accomplish the political and economic liberation of the people from the thrall of imperialism.[2] But they were also expected to bring about, in that process, a revolutionary transformation of existing social structures. Whether in liberating women from traditional tasks, organizing democratic processes or decision-making and counsel, building schools or training cadres of peasants and workers, the "armed liberation struggle," as Cabral says, "is not only a product of culture, but a *determinant of culture.*"[3]

This suggests that belief in a particular ultimate reality (whether sacred or, in Marxist-inspired revolutions, profane—or, perhaps, so deferred as to become at least ethereal) that might be construed as a product of culture inspires in many of these politically-committed writers a revolt against the more rarified aesthetic concerns of western novelists in favor of a decision to reshape society and, in the process, to unearth the foundation of that culture's ultimate meaning. I will argue that this project defines Nuruddin Farah's corpus, most obviously in his trilogy jointly entitled *Variations on the Theme of an African Dictatorship*. At the heart of his interrogation of Somali culture is his examination of the tectonic friction between self-definition and tribal loyalty, between nation-building and diurnal obligations. He is especially noteworthy because of his interest in his country's transition from an oral to a written culture. The place of the word, and principally the revealed word of Allah, in such an age of change, directs the reader to the central questions of meaning that preoccupy both the author and his characters. Who can speak in such countries, and to what effect?

Nuruddin Farah was born in Baidoa in 1945, in what was then Italian Somaliland. The British and Italian territories were united in 1960 to form Somalia. Farah grew up, therefore, understanding Italian (he lived for some time in Italy) and English, the language in which he writes his novels (he has recently lived in Nigeria and now resides in Cape Town, South Africa). He worked for the Department of Education and then went to India and attended the Punjab University in Chandigarh to study literature and philosophy. While there he wrote plays and his first novel, *From a Crooked Rib* (published in 1970), which was one of the earliest African novels written by a male that clearly portrayed the inequities that women endured in Somalia and, by implication, throughout most of Africa. His interest in women's rights continued, as seen especially in *Sardines*, the second novel of his political trilogy. But his focus was to broaden a bit when he returned to Somalia in 1969, for this was the year that Major-General Siyad Barre staged a bloodless coup and, with Soviet assistance, imposed a system of "scientific socialism" on the country.

Farah quickly grew to hate this regime, with its near deification of Siyad Barre; it produced, as he describes it in *Sweet and Sour Milk*,

> a nation regimented, militarised. A nation disciplined and forced to obey the iron-hand directing thc orchestra of moans and groans...The politics of mystification kept everybody at bay. People were kept in their separate compartments of ignorance about what happened to other people and what became of other things.[4]

The regime became symbolic in Farah's mind for all such rulers throughout Africa—men who played one faction against another to maintain personal power, and who encouraged narrow tribal interests in opposition to the broader national concerns. When Farah wrote the novel in Somali, the views he embodied sufficiently alarmed the new government that the serialization of a novel similar to *A Naked Needle*, and containing the germ for *Maps*, was suppressed. He next wrote *A Naked Needle*, a novel with autobiographical overtones about a disaffected teacher. Before it was published in 1976 he had moved to Britain to study theater. Upon the publication of the novel he was warned that if he were to return to Somalia he would be imprisoned for thirty years.

It became clear to Farah that a generational crisis faced his homeland: those who were his parents' age who had stronger faith in traditional Islam were being pushed aside; those of his own generation, who were now assuming important positions in society, found themselves disaffected from the religion of their parents; those of his children's generation were the least rooted of all, and found themselves metaphorically set adrift in an increasingly secular society—almost like spiritual orphans.

2. The Three Political Novels of Nuruddin Farah

It was at this point that he turned his attention more pointedly upon the Siyad Barre regime, producing three novels (*Sweet and Sour Milk*, *Sardines*, and *Close Sesame*) whose characters become enmeshed in "the General's" political machinery. The General is the unifying focus of the three books and it is clear he would like to be the ground of ultimate meaning for the people whose lives he dominates. Running throughout the first book of the series, *Sweet and Sour Milk*, is the sacrilegious phrase "Labour is honour and there is no General but our General" (*SSM*, p.97)—Farah's none-too-subtle suggestion that military might has sought to take the place of the power of Allah. Throughout Farah's writing there is a cynical suspicion of political action, since in a tribal context it is so quickly corrupted.

The trilogy traces the fates of eleven members of a resistance movement who have vowed to do whatever they can to overthrow the General's regime: Ahmed-Wellie (he apparently betrays the group), Jibriil (dies in an assassination attempt), Koschin (imprisoned and reduced by torture to an automaton), Mahad (imprisoned), Medina (silenced and portrayed as a scandalous woman), Mukhtaar (killed), Mursal (killed in an unsuccessful suicide bombing), Samater (co-opted by being made a minister in the General's government), Siciliano (imprisoned), Soyaan (apparently poisoned by Soviet agents) and his twin brother Loyaan, who attempts to take his place in the movement (exiled to Belgrade as an ambassador). Although their plotting proves to be ineffective in overthrowing the General, their resistance to his presentation of himself as the center of meaning for Somalis offers readers something of a negative theology: though they do not assert an alternative 'god', they at least can say what their god is not.

The novels center around the personal struggle that faces each member of the group, and show how their decisions affect members of their families. The books give no sense that these decisions have any effect on the larger society, or any significant effect on the

71

General himself, who maintains control as easily under the Soviets in the first two novels as he does under the Americans in the third. Similarly condemned by Farah is the General's version of socialism and of democracy, since both are manipulated to serve the ends of totalitarianism. The General never personally appears in the novels—his is an absence around which all the characters must define themselves. Again, a kind of negative theology seems to play into this theme of absence, since Allah's enduring presence in the lives of Farah's powerless characters seems to indict the form of power that a secular regime embraces. The activities of the revolutionary Movement never fully materialize in the narrative. These remain shady happenings as if taking place in an alternative universe that somehow influences the real world that Farah describes. We hear about it all secondhand, off the cuff, muffled by sobs, interrupted, misinterpreted. The reader, like the characters themselves, is victimized by that offstage world of history and finds in the narratological world of Farah's creation whatever meaning may be possible. In other words, Farah's characters learn (and teach) the lesson that imagination, while ineffective against the political powers that control one's environment, is powerful in providing a shape for one's vision of self. As will be seen, religion in such a context offers much the same paradoxical hope as do other forms of imagination.

Emphasizing Farah's implied suggestion that 'movements' and tribal loyalties neither significantly ameliorate the conditions in which we must function nor, perhaps ironically, protect us from the necessity of individual choice, the novelist devotes the bulk of the first and third novel in the series to characters who do not belong to the Movement itself and who do not draw their power from the machinations around them.

Sweet and Sour Milk begins with the death of Soyaan, one of the revolutionaries, who dies in the arms of his twin brother. Loyaan then seeks to discern the cause of his brother's death, the ideological purposes to which the General is putting that death, and the consequent responsibilities that he has to counter the official rewriting of his brother's 'meaning' in the eyes of the common people. Whereas Soyaan went to his death defying the General, his dead body has been confiscated by the state and he has been posthumously honoured as a national hero who respected the regime. The novel focuses on Loyaan's struggle to understand the cause of his brother's death, and the meaning of his life. Farah's purpose in the novel seems to be to show the conscientization of an individual: Loyaan ultimately decides to take his brother's place in the struggle. The fact that the choice is rendered 'meaningless' by the General's decision to exile Loyaan as an ambassador to Belgrade does not significantly diminish the importance of the process whereby Loyaan moved into the struggle itself. The book, therefore, has the existentialist overtones informing Camus' *Myth of Sisyphus*: once the character has become enlightened, the burden of choice becomes heavier, inescapable, self-defining. There is no one to lift it from the character's shoulders. But with the enlightenment comes the transformation of the absurd into the tragic.

The third book in the series, *Close Sesame*, emerges principally through the consciousness of Deeriye, an elderly and devout Muslim whose son, Mursal, is one of the members of the Movement. In an interview Farah noted that "I think that *Close Sesame* is probably the one novel that will outlive all my other novels...It is difficult to explain why it is that I am more attached to [it] than to the others."5 Deeriye was once a 'player' in the political game, having defied the Italians during their occupation. But his defiance was akin to conscientious objection, a Gandhian non-violent resistance and refusal to cooperate with the imposing power. As chieftain he bore full responsibility for this decision, and he was imprisoned for twelve years. At the same time, his decision resulted in the Italians slaughtering the tribe's cattle and causing starvation among his family—while he ate well in jail. Again, as with Loyaan's exile, the power of the institution seems to have been to render the personal choice meaningless or destructive of innocents (and innocence).

The middle book in the series, *Sardines*, orchestrates more members of the Movement itself, focusing principally on Medina, one of the few politically-active women, and on her husband, Samater. The story allows Farah to show a woman revolutionary behaving something like the women of Aristophanes' *Lysistrata*: she separates from her husband until he lives up to his responsibilities as a man, resigns from his cushy and corrupting position as a member of the regime, and silences his reactionary mother. Her decision does, therefore, have a desired effect and weakens the General's power in one very small area. But this is a minuscule grain of sand compared to what the General has done to her: she is a very well-educated woman and had been one of the few involved in publishing in the country; her punishment for spreading incendiary ideas has been a type of silencing— she is forbidden to publish anything other than children's literature.

3. Traditional Religion as Portrayed in Farah's Novels

The role of Islam in this world of institutionalized frustration is significant and Farah's approach is respectful. Nuruddin Farah's own understanding of ultimate reality and meaning does not necessarily squarely coincide with that of conservative Islam. He does note that "Islam is most peculiarly more tolerant of Christianity than Christianity is of Islam...I would accuse Christians of being intolerant when it comes to other religions and of accusing Muslims of being fundamentalists," but he admits, as well, that "there are many varieties of Islam too, and there is more enmity between Muslims than there is between Christians."[6] Of those in the trilogy who call themselves Muslims there seem to be three categories: the cynical politicians, the self-enslaved fanatics, and the devout. There are those characters who use the trappings of religion for political ends, and they are roundly condemned; the General, of course, heads this list. In fact, in *Sweet and Sour Milk* Loyaan eventually discerns that his brother was killed because he answered honestly when the General asked if his rule was supported by the Koran. There are those characters who use

74

their religion to absolve themselves from involvement in the world around them, or who use their interpretation of its precepts to discipline the more creative and more daring among their family members. The most conspicuous member of this group is Idil, Samater's mother in *Sardines*. She attempts to enforce the discipline that has been imposed on her daughter-in-law, Medina, and plays to the hilt the stereotype of a vindictive mother-in-law. But the characters in the final category (the devout) abound, and one plays the foil to Idil: Fatima, Medina's mother, is actually far more religiously observant than Idil, more conservative in her daily life, and completely genuine in her attempt to live the teachings of her religion without condemning those around her. Of similar simplicity and religious honesty is Ebla, the central character in *From a Crooked Rib*, who travels from the countryside to Mogadiscio and meets with a good deal of sorrow. In *Sardines* she attempts to transfer all her love, which is grounded in her religious sense, to her troubled and worldly daughter, Sagal. But Farah's most striking portrayal of the results of a long life of sincere devotion to Allah and to the teachings of Muhammed is the central character of *Close Sesame*, Deeriye. Sixty-nine years of age, asthmatic and nearsighted, his faith remains unshaken.

> He bent double, murmuring a series of sanative phrases, breathed with lungs of gratitude and meant for the ears of his Creator...The beads again. A litany of Koranic verses. As he counted and re-counted the ninety-nine names of Allah, as he multiplied and subtracted the number of times he had said them, he realized that the world outside had begun to wake up...And then he prayed: 'O Allah who art just, give us true peace, bless us with the inner tranquillity that Thou art, make us apprehend the enemy within us, deliver us, help us, O Allah, descend from the greater heights of selfishness, help us reach and be content with what we have or who we are: weak and helpless

without thy guidance...Help us, O Allah, help us find peace in ourselves, in our friends, in our families and in our neighbours.' He held out his hands, rubbed them together, brought them closer to his face and spat a salivaless emission of breath and (with the prayer beads still in the grip of the index and middle fingers) rinsed his face in his dry but blessed open palms. Then he recited a mumbled Faatixa. With all this done, his features cast in worshipful mould, silent, reverent, he got up, caught the prayer rug by the corner and hung it on the nail on the wall above his bed.[7]

In the course of this novel Deeriye's son, the last of the revolutionaries, is killed in his attempt to assassinate the General. Apparently unshaken in his faith by this loss, Deeriye nonetheless seems to take on the younger generation's philosophy of violence—where necessary. He borrows a military uniform and a handgun, goes to see the General, and is himself killed when he attempts to withdraw the gun from his pocket: he has, instead, pulled out his prayer beads. Even in death he willy-nilly embodies the Gandhian principles that had ruled his life. His out-thrust symbol of Islamic devotion, Farah seems to suggest, is what will ultimately overthrow the General. At any rate, in the closing pages of the novel the populace recognizes his greatness and his spiritual strength—a power that means more than the brute force that controls the profane world around them. If the General's approach seems to hold them variously in his sway, ultimately even the General and his minions must answer to one more powerful than they. In the meantime, whether devout or cynical, the people of Somalia live under the reign of a tyrant.

Such a repressive regime, coupled to the wider world's profane philosophy, quickly exhausts the idealism of its citizens. The response of the younger generation to religion is embodied in the exchange between Zeinab, Deeriye's daughter, and her father:

"Excuse me," said Deeriye, "I'll see you later."

> "The muezzin calls," said Zeinab, "and you cannot *not* answer."
>
> "Earnest praying is a vocation, my father used to say," Deeriye said.
>
> "And is that what *my father* says?" she said.
>
> He did not rise to her challenge. He said, "I will see you later." (*CS*, pp.186-87).

He goes off to pray; she does not.

4. Portrayal of Politics in Farah's Trilogy

Throughout the trilogy Farah portrays the younger (that is, thirty-something) generation as action-minded, well-educated, generally well-travelled and cosmopolitan, but sadly lacking in a moral center or clear sense of what might be called ultimate reality and meaning. They have become politicized at the expense of their moral grounding. Deeriye and those of his children's generation come to much the same end, but Deeriye does so with the sense that, in the larger scheme, his life has been meaningful. Zeinab and her generation do not share that assurance. Farah is interested in charting the effects of modernity and neocolonialism on the members of his own generation (Zeinab's generation)—those who have been faced with an increasingly secularized world, a national oppressive government, and few roadmaps that would suggest a direction in which to take oneself and, by extension, one's 'emerging' nation. Though the details of the Movement that plays itself out in the background of this trilogy are sketchy, the reader will recognize in the various deaths and career collapses of its members a bravery that should have produced more impressive results: these, after all, are some of the best-educated and highest-placed members of the younger generation. Instead, the only hope for mobilization of a larger percentage of the population comes (and only paradoxically and somewhere off in the future) through Deeriye's almost ludicrous assassination (or sui-cide?) attempt. He, of course, is a member of the older generation whose time, one would have thought, had passed.

The trilogy targets those aspects of the historical Somalian *modus vivendi* that perpetuate patriarchal dominance. "The reason why I have always fought against authoritarianism," Farah writes,

> even when it comes from Somalian traditional society, is that if we accept authoritarian rule within our own societies, then we must also per force accept authoritarian rule coming from outside. Democracy suggests equality, and there must be equality, we mustn't say we (men) would rule women ruthlessly, unkindly, undemocratically but we would not want the Italians to come and colonize us. We shouldn't colonize other peoples. There is a hierarchy of injustice, and the weaker the person the more likely for that weaker person to do more harm to those persons who are weaker than he. For example, in societies where there is political terrorism, the weakest animal is the one who suffers most. In Somalia, for example, we usually chase children who have always been hit. If you have a small child who is about eight and who comes home and his parents hit him, and he goes out and another person who is more powerful hits him, and they go about doing nothing because they can't come home for fear of being hit...well, they are more likely to be tempted to chase a dog. This is the spiral of violence, a product of this hierarchy of injustice.[8]

Farah thus returns again and again to his despair over the Balkanising effects of tribal patriotism within a new nation like Somalia. Farah's trilogy has overtones of a Kafkaesque subterranean web of interconnecting, inscrutable happenings, wheels within wheels, that move without apparent causality or purpose. The members of Farah's generation, many of whom would naturally be the strongest leaders of their society, eventually fill the role of beaten children so eloquently described by the author: they are beaten by the evacuation of meaning from their most idealistic actions. The reader ultimately shares the debilitating confusion and malaise of the characters who begin with determination, and who end as demoralized isolates cut off from whatever trans-tribal hopes might enlist their energies in a national Movement. If one is not a member of the General's tribe, there is little possibility of 'networking' in an effective way to change society. On the other hand, if one is a member of the General's tribe the suasive charms of wallowing in one's potential dominance of others, of playing along with one's own family preeminence, are practically irresistible.

5. Valorizing the Word

Coupled to this tradition of tribal loyalty is Farah's ambivalence toward his country's oral traditions, which record the highest aspirations of its people but which also serve as the most effective agent for social control. Somalia has a long and vibrant history of oral literature, and its poetry fills the pages of the trilogy. Deeriye, especially, quotes from Sayyid Mohamed Abdulle Hassan, a legendary warrior poet, and Sultan Wiil Waal, ruler of Jigjigga. This tendency to 'live' the poetry of an earlier age, however, and to find sustenance and a meaningful thread of continuity in memorized verses seems, much like the tenets of Islam, to belong to Deeriye's passing generation and not so obviously to that of the members of the Movement. The Somali language had no accepted script and was, therefore, only oral until the early 1970s. In an interesting parallel to the observation that the fascists at least kept the trains running on time, the imposition of a script came very shortly after the imposition of Siyad Barre's regime. The movement from a fluid, personal, performance-based culture that may be suggested by orature, to a regimented, standardized, and anonymous culture that may be suggested by written 'literature' almost inevitably suggests a devolution rather than the liberating modernization that most westerners would immediately champion. However, Farah has, on a number of occasions, publicly indicated his view that the transition from oral to written expression in Somalia is a movement towards greater freedom, power, and reach for the verbal artist. Secondly, Somali oral poetry diverges in many respects from an understanding of African orature in the West gleaned largely from West African genres and practices; in contrast to these it features highly "regimented" and "standardized" conventions and performances that intentionally avoid the "fluid" and the "personal."

It is good to recall that the Koran was transmitted to the illiterate Mohammed without the aid of the written word. Nonetheless, a romanticized version of oral culture raised to its highest literary form, (and regardless of its obvious value in the lives of characters like Deeriye), overlooks the negative aspects of word-of-mouth communication in a tribal and/or tyrannical culture. Farah expends a great deal of energy in demonstrating the consequences of the horrible power of the spoken word to distort, obfuscate, disempower.

In his excellent analysis of this aspect of the trilogy, Derek Wright notes that

> reality in the oral society is unwritten, unwritable and, ultimately, unknowable...The indeterminacy of oral modes of interpretation make it difficult to distinguish between the true and the imaginary, between what does and does not exist...The political-criminal plot launched against Soyaan [in Sweet and Sour Milk] by an oral-based dictatorship and hunted down by Loyaan is, in the last analysis, unwritable and never materializes. Accordingly, the narrative plot eventually runs out unresolvedly in loose ends or, rather, unstitches itself deconstructively in the penultimate chapter and unrav-

els in a welter of conflicting oral testimony.[9]

"What I like to do, in telling a story," Farah writes,

> is to study the numerous facets of a tale and to allow
> very many different competing views to be
> heard...coexisting with the contradictions...I don't
> imagine that there is any single voice, so this is why
> my novels are multi-voiced.[10]

But, like life itself, his books written in this polyphony generally enact the confusion that their characters endure at the hands of a regime that manipulates the truth by mis-speaking, lying, telling half-truths, using a variety of speakers to broadcast conflicting interpretations of events that did or did not happen. And, as Barbara Turfan points out, "the feeling of an omnipresent uncertainty and tension is deftly evoked also in conversations, conversations which leave out more than they include but form, with the speaker's unspoken thoughts, a continuous stream to which the reader, but not the other participants, has access."[11] The result among the people is frustration, suspicion of each other, and paralysis. The misuse of speech, and the consequences of this manipulation, begin early: in *Close Sesame* a little boy is sent with a message that has a dubious source. Can it be believed? "The little boy's voice grew faint the moment he realized all these eyes were focused on him: for eyes which could hear frightened him: eyes which could register the movement of lips; eyes which could betray; sell information they deciphered. A young boy of eight carrying an important message: a history to be relived through...politics again" (*CS*, p.105).

By manipulating the powerful forces of social control inherent in an oral culture the General's regime undermines another of the strengths of the people. But this is not as it could be. As M.M.G. Mugo, Kavetsa Adagala and others have shown, true orature traditionally works as a reminder of the demands for human rights—

81

demands that would challenge any totalitarian system. Adagala notes that there are two types of orature in Africa, each reflecting the era and political system from which it arises: the first is feudal-oriented, in which there exists not only division of labour. but also division of society into classes. In these narratives the focus is on the struggle between these social classes. The second form of orature is communal-oriented, and in these "the social relationships depicted show the communal nature of society: people work together to overcome the difficulties in life and to fulfil their material needs."[12] In this latter form, the group, the family and the community feature prominently. Mugo points out that in these stories the narrator

> would view reality as constituting layers upon layers of interrelated co-existence. There is the individual, the corporate personality and the collective group. There is the family unit, the extended family, the clan and the community. There is the inner 'world' of the personality—the sound, the heart, the intellect, the imagination, etc. There is also the outer 'world' of being—the physical human appearance. Then there is the outside world—the environment, the natural world and the physical features that define it. The utmost circle of the outer world defines the world 'up there'—the sun, the moon, the stars, the sky and the rest of the elements.[13]

Considering the remarkable lack of harmony in the lives of most of Farah's characters, and their ultimate isolation from one another, it is significant to note that, in Mugo's view of traditional communal-oriented orature, "all the layers of the 'human onion structure' must harmonize or the world will step out of measured rhythm and cause chaos. An individual can only fully *be* if he or she is a part of the collective group."[14]

Such traditions are easily corrupted by a regime interested only in preservation of its own tribe in opposition to all others in the nation, since, in the world of orature, one becomes one's brother's keeper. The emphasis on collectivity and interdependence can be transformed into spying. But, at its best, orature is, in Mugo's words, "antithetical to individualism, egocentricity, isolationism, alienation, cutthroat competition and so on."[15] The artist assumes a special interactive role in society, giving voice to community concerns and also reminding the community of their dreams and responsibilities. Again, Mugo:

> Over and above the responsibility of exposing, satirizing and denouncing anti-social behaviour and the abuse of human rights, he or she was also expected to inspire those struggling against injustice to change the oppressive conditions facing them. He or she was expected to point out alternatives and options that would help the oppressed to eradicate an oppressive system and create a more humane world in which they could reach a full realization of themselves as whole, dignified human beings.[16]

If the tales were sometimes sexist, pro-patriarchal, and warlike,[17] they were also used to castigate society and bring it to its senses. It is against this cultural background that Farah valorizes such characters as Khaliif in *Close Sesame*. Lest there be any misunderstanding of Farah's true target—*all* misuse of the word whether spoken or written—the novels demonstrate that in a totalitarian state print can be similarly manipulated—rendered, in fact, a more enduring form of 'gossip' that constructs a totalitarian hermeneutic. In *Sweet and Sour Milk*, even though Soyaan has been a member of the Movement that opposed the regime, and even though it appears that he has been killed by the General's agents (or by the Soviets who support the General at this time), following his death he is declared a national hero—an artifact like the type moved about the page by a printer telling the 'history' of his country:

"Soyaan is from this day onwards state property and will be treated as such. They've come for and have taken his file. I worked on the file last night. Soyaan: a property of the state."

"Property of the state?"

"Yes. He is the property of the General."

"How do you mean?"

"They are rewriting your family's history, Soyaan's and the whole lot. Like the Russians rewrote Lenin's, Stalin's or that of any of the heroes their system created to survive subversion from within or without. They will need your cooperation, I am sure."

"That they won't get."

"I wouldn't be so certain" (*SSM*, pp.106-107).

Consequently, if the written word can be as deceitful as the spoken, Farah must find new avenues for 'truth' to break through in his pressurized society. This he finds in the ongoing tradition of the *revealed* words of the religious prophet—seen to be living, effective, and motivating in the lives of Deeriye and several of the other characters and in the 'crazed' words of a political 'prophet', who is similarly motivated by religion .

Running throughout *Close Sesame*, and acting much like the crazed and blinded confidantes in *King Lear*, is Khaliif, a former highly-placed civil servant who one night simply becomes a madman. Such a member of the totalitarian regime can say the forbidden because he is not taken seriously by the powerful. He is nonetheless recognized by Deeriye and principal characters in the novel as a reliable source of truth—even if that truth remains the inscrutable aphorisms of a Delphic oracle:

Now, sitting in the sun's brightness, Deeriye started: he could hear Khaliif's magical voice, complemented by some welcoming remarks, like a chorus, from a small crowd that had already gathered to listen. Deeriye craned forward. Khaliif did not suggest a broken man on the fringes of society; nor an alienated man whose mind buzzed with mysterious messages so far undeciphered; nor a man invalidated by or overburdened with guilt. No: his demeanour forestalled everyone's fear, prediction or worry: he sold to everybody the very thing no one was prepared to buy, and bought from everybody the very thing no one was ready to sell. His discourse was clear, grammatical and logical: "There are wicked houses in which live wicked men and wicked women. Truth must be owned up. We are God's children; the wicked of whom I speak are Satan's offspring. And night plots conspiracies daylight never reveals." And he held his hands together in a namastee, clowned a bit, entertained the younger members of the audience by doing a somersault, a karate ghost-dance, and then returned to his peaceful corner and fell quiet. Applause. He curtsied; grinning, grateful and graceful (CS, pp.16-17).

Khaliif's untrumpeted appearance is always remarkable, providing a focal point for the creation of a possible Somali society that remains free to hear the truth about itself from a sincere Islamic point of view. Surrounded by children as well as by thoughtful adults, Khaliif's undisputed personal marginalization allows his message to cut through the devious plots by a government intent on dissipating the disturbing idealism of the younger generation. It is the content rather than the form that is of importance, as Fiona Sparrow suggests: "His authority as prophet cannot be attributed to a return to oral traditions after fruitless years spent relying on written forms."[18] The power comes from a word that is neither written nor spoken but revealed.

Khaliif remains on the margin, however. Farah does not hold out easy optimism; he constantly counters hope with a heavy dose of

realism. He begins the concluding section of *Sardines* with this ominous quotation from Franz Kafka: "The crow maintains that a single
crow could destroy the heavens. Doubtless that is so, but it proves
nothing against the heavens, for the heavens signify simply: the
impossibility of crows."[19] Perhaps in a totalitarian regime, one that is
in transition from a far simpler age to one of multicultural confusion
and challenge, the most that an artist can offer is inscrutability, a
holding in abeyance of finality. Ever-suspended in the air, perhaps
one's characters and oneself must simply try to negotiate a personal
integrity that respects the traditions in which one was raised. In that
context, Farah concludes his trilogy with questions, simple questions of a mother with simple hopes in the face of a violent world:

> Would his body be given to her for burial? she won-
> dered to herself, as she cringed, for she now heard
> Natasha and Samawade crying to each other in anoth-
> er room. Would Mursal's corpse be handed over too so
> she could have them buried side by side in the same
> tomb—so they could continue uninterruped the dia-
> logue they had begun? At least, she thought, looking
> up and seeing Natasha and Samawade in the doorway,
> sobbing in chorus, at least neither died an anonymous
> death—and that was heroic (*CS*, p.237).

6. Conclusion

Thus, in his trilogy, Farah shows the crippling effect of totalitarianism and the devastating impact of secularization on his own cosmopolitan 'second' generation of citizens of the new state. His characters, even when they somehow gain access to the reins of power,
have little sense of common purpose and, therefore, little occasion to
display a commitment to any ultimate reality or meaning. It is little
wonder that a mother would find solace in the fantasy that her

child's *death*, at least, was not anonymous: increasingly, the child's *life* had been emptied of defining characteristics. What Farah's fictionalized older generation might lament as the passing of tribal affiliations that had provided, however narrowly, a sense of identity and purpose, the author's own generation might simply recognize as, on the one hand, the gratefully- welcomed but long-delayed collapse of the tribal structure and, on the other hand, its replacement by a sense of drift away from traditional moorings: the meaningless freedom to enter into the larger modern world of massive international business conglomerates, intolerance of the powerless, and avoidance of eccentric self-definition.

In the works that followed *Variations on the Theme of an African Dictatorship*, at any rate, Farah focuses his attention less obsessively on 'the General' and the imposition of this man's tribal defensiveness on the entire nation, and instead makes a foundling child the center of his attention. The child becomes symbolic at once of the new nation in search of a parent who will be neither a colonizing foster father nor a neocolonial patriarch, and symbolic as well of Farah's own generation of deracinated Somalis. *Maps* (1986) and *Gifts* (1993) move in these new directions, and they seem to have brought to a close, at least for a while, Farah's work in the novel form. He is reportedly at work now on a journalistic account of Somalis living abroad, having apparently concluded that the Somali that he has been describing all these years while in exile himself has been increasingly a world of his imagination—increasingly the projection of his inner world of turmoil over the implications of the life forced upon his generation of writers from postcolonial countries.[20]

Maps is Farah's most complex novel, in which an orphan named Askar from the disputed Ogaden region ultimately betrays his adopted mother, Misra, who is Ethiopian. It is, therefore, literally a novel dealing with 'border' identities, where one's nationality changes from one war to the next. The novel demonstrates this increasing mongrelization of national identity; as Askar notes, speaking to himself,

You doubt, at times, if you exist outside your own thoughts, outside your own head, Misra's or your own. It appears as though you were a creature given birth to by notions formulated in heads, a creature brought into being by ideas...you wonder if your existence is readily differentiable from creatures of fiction whom habit has taught one to talk of as if they were one's closest friends.[21]

As Derek Wright observes,

In the book's parabolic scheme Askar, representing the Ogaden, is born to two patriotic martyrs who give their lives for the cause of its liberation from Ethiopian liberation: his father dies on the day of his birth and his mother soon afterwards. He is thus the posthumous mythic offspring of Somali nationalist aspiration and the motherland of the Republic.[22]

But this identity must shift as the world 're-maps' him. The question that seems to haunt the novel is one which exiled writers like Farah must frequently ponder: whose geometry plots one's identity? Whose values outline one's perimeter? In its multiple layers of complexity the book ridicules the patriarchy that is everywhere attacked by Farah's novels. There is, in Wright's view,

a habitual erosion of the public into the personal, and of topographical into physiological space, which allows Askar to view the political destiny and military fortunes of the nation, analogically, through his adoptive mother's biological rhythms.[23]

How this is achieved is ingenious, resulting in "the first African novel of the body."[24] But it is important to note that the body in question is Misra's. Typical of Farah, the woman is portrayed as victimized by the males—and betrayed by her adopted son for his own misguided ethnic dreams. In fact, Askar assumes the reigns of heuristic control, becoming a mapmaker. In this role he asserts an oppressive ethnicity and suppresses his own hybridized identity in favor of an imposed national uniformity. No longer truly identifiable with his natural parents and their traditions, Askar escapes the discomfort of a complex existential situation by embracing a new hegemony. Like several of the plotters in Farah's earlier trilogy, this member of the younger generation sacrifices his integrity along with his ambiguity.

The novel opens with a telling quotation from Socrates: "Living begins when you start doubting everything that came before you," followed immediately by one from Charles Dickens: "No children for me. Give me grown-ups." One suspects that the latter is tongue-in-cheek; the former, completely sincere. In Dickens, after all, adults prey on children, and in Farah one sees a similar pattern: his adults seem frequently enough to be those who cannot stand the unsettling demands of Socrates' injunction. The challenge is presented to Askar late in the book by his uncle: "He said, 'Tell me, Askar. Do you find truth in the maps you draw?...Do you carve out of your soul the invented truth of the maps you draw? Or does the daily truth match, for you, the reality you draw and the maps others draw?...The question is, does truth change?'" (*M*, pp.216-17). To illustrate the implications of his rhetorical question the uncle points to a map of Somalia and concludes, "There is truth in maps. The Ogaden, as Somali, is truth. To the Ethiopian map-maker, the Ogaden, as Somali, is untruth" (*M*, p.218). As Derek Wright concludes from this passage, "the stable identity presupposed by the idealistic vision of the map-maker [is] non-existent."[25] But few are able to live with the openness demanded by a resistance to such 'maps'.

Gifts is a cautionary tale that appears to be a meditation on the demands placed by First World countries when they offer 'gifts' of financial aid to Third World countries but ends as an indictment of those who implicitly reject the gifts of Allah by acting on their fears and their petty bickering rather than on their ideals. At the center of the story is another apparent orphan, around whom all the characters project a meaning. Who is he, and from where does he come? Should he be welcomed or shunned? And to whom is he 'offered' as gift; who has the right to claim him? Almost as if the bickering of the adults convinces Allah to take back the gift he had offered, the foundling child dies halfway through the novel. In this first of his books to be published in Africa for an African audience, this 'truncation' of the plot stylistically has the same effect on his readers as it does on the characters themselves: as in Dickens's *Dombey and Son*, with the death of young Paul, we are offered a figure who appears to be the center of meaning in the novel, and then, after we begin to invest our imaginations in a projection of what that meaning might, in fact, be, the center does not hold. Things fall apart. We are left without a central focus, and our sense that we *understand* is suddenly confused.

The sense of closure that Western rationality so desires is, in fact, represented as premature, falsely static in the human context. Duniya, the child's temporary guardian, knows this at story's end—which, emphatically, does not end. "As the others engaged in polite talk," Farah writes,

> Duniya thought to herself that little is revealed to oneself directly. Revelations are received from out of a mist of doubts, in caves, in the dark, out of a child's mouth, or via the wise utterances of an elderly or mad person. She decided that her own epiphanic instant had occurred at a moment, on a morning, when a story chose to tell itself to her, through her, a story whose clarity was contained in the creative utterance, *Let there be a man,* and there was a story.[26]

The notion that truth—the truth of one's identity, the truths of history—cannot remain fixed, is an idea that runs through Farah's novels as the converse of the notion that the fascistic imposition of one tribe over another is unnatural, untrue. Deeriye, in *Close Sesame*, had pondered the role of the individual in what one might call the narrative of history. "Time was the travel," he imagines,

> the journey each undertook so that *another* arrived, because each would eventually reach his or her destination having become *another*...Time was also the abyss with the open door...Time was history: and history was a shy little thing hiding in the folds of its robe a giant: i.e. a little boy...burdened with a message heavier than his years...(*CS*, pp. 94-95).

But if that message is to be anything more than a profane political plan to supplant one unjust ruler with another, if it is to transform its hearers by revealing a *sacred* truth that somehow steps outside time, there seems little appreciation of such a possibility in the world of Farah's generation. On the other hand, Farah seems to offer Deeriye as an alternative to the General. This character maintains his patriarchal role without becoming a dictator in his household. As Maggi Phillips notes,

> though one part of his life is devoted to Allah, he is also a benign and monogamous patriarch who, after his dear wife's death and toward the end of his own days, is still genuinely interested and concerned in family and social matters. Moreoever, Deeriye's family brings different points of view together into a unit that advocates equality between generations, sexes and different ethnic roots: there is the religious Deeriye, the legal Mursal, the scientific Zeinab. the celestial Nadiifa, the Jewish daughter-in-law Natasha, and Samawade, the young and innocent translator. On a metaphorical level, Deeriye's storytelling places the family cluster

within the traditional continuum that carries oral wisdom through generations, while Nadiifa's spiritual leadership provides a channel for sacred wisdom to illuminate the family's secular state.[27]

Deeriye has enough trust in Allah that he can allow his family to enter the abyss, knowing that time is but one more creation. Those who cannot share this sacred covenant have less peaceful lives. Many readers will conclude that Nuruddin Farah, and many other exiled intellectuals like him, write because they are still seeking an ultimate meaning to explain this *bricolage* that is their hybridized reality.

NOTES

1. Matthew Horsman and Andrew Marshall, *After the Nation-State: Citizens, Tribalism and the New World Order* (London: Harper Collins, 1994), p.185.
2. Barbara Harlow, *Resistance Literature* (New York and London: Methuen, 1987), pp.11-12.
3. Amilcar Cabral, *Return to the Source: Selected Speeches of Amilcar Cabral* (New York: African Information Service, 1973), p.55.
4. Nuruddin Farah, *Sweet and Sour Milk* (St. Paul: Greywolf, 1992) [Allison and Busby, 1979; Heinemann, 1980], pp.190, 198-99. Subsequent references appear in the text after the abbreviation *SSM*.
5. Armando Pajalich, "Nuruddin Farah Interviewed by Armando Pajalich," *Kunapipi* 15, 1 (1993), 69. Other interviews and essays by Farah that were consulted for this essay are: Maya Jaggi, "A Combining of Gifts: An Interview," *Third World Quarterly* 11, 3 (1989), 171-87; Nuruddin Farah, "Why I Write," *Third World Quarterly* 10, 4 (1988), 1591-99; and Nuruddin Farah, "Childhood of My Schizophrenia," *The Times Literary Supplement*, 23-29 November 1990, 1264

6. Pajalich, 65.

7. Nuruddin Farah, *Close Sesame* (St. Paul: Greywolf, 1992) [London: Allison and Busby, 1983]. pp.4-5. Subsequent references appear in the text after the abbreviation *CS*.

8. Pajalich, 63-64.

9. Derek Wright, "Unwritable Realities: The Orality of Power in Nuruddin Farah's *Sweet and Sour Milk*," *Journal of Commonwealth Literature* 24, 1 (1989), 188, 190; reprinted in revised form as "Orality and Power in Nuruddin Farah's *Sweet and Sour Milk*" in the present volume.

10. Pajalich, 63-64.

11. Barbara Turfan, "Opposing Dictatorship: a Comment on Nuruddin Farah's *Variations on the Theme of an African Dictatorship*," *Journal of Commonwealth Literature* 24, 1 (1989), 174; reprinted in the present volume.

12. Kavetsa Adagala and Wanjiku Kabira Mukabi, *Kenya Oral Narratives: A Selection* (Nairobi: Heinemann Kenya, 1985), pp.xii, xiii.

13. M.M.G.Mugo, *African Orature and Human Rights: Human and Peoples' Rights*, Monograph Series No 13 (Roma, Lesotho: Institute of Southern African Studies, National University of Lesotho, 1991), pp.12-13.

14. ibid., p.13.

15. ibid., p.14.

16. ibid., p.22.

17. ibid., p.38.

18. Fiona Sparrow, "Telling the Story Yet Again: Oral Traditions in Nuruddin Farah's Fiction," *Journal of Commonwealth Literature* 24, 1 (1989), 170.

19. Nuruddin Farah, *Sardines* (St. Paul: Greywolf, 1992) [London: Allison and Busby, 1981; Heinemann, 1982], p.202.

20. Pajalich, 71.

21. Nuruddin Farah, *Maps* (New York: Pantheon, 1986; London: Pan, 1986), p.3. Subsequent references appear in the text after the

abbreviation *M*.

22. Derek Wright, *The Novels of Nuruddin Farah* (Bayreuth: Bayreuth African Studies, 1994). p.110.

23. ibid., p.108.

24. ibid., p.118.

25. ibid., p.120.

26. Nuruddin Farah, *Gifts* (London: Serif, 1993), pp.240-41.

27. Maggi Phillips, "The View from a Mosque of Words: Nuruddin Farah's *Close Sesame* and The Holy Qur'an," in *The Marabout and the Muse: New Approaches to Islam in African Literature*, ed. Kenneth Harrow (London: James Currey; Portsmouth, N.H.: Heinemann, 1996), p.194.

MAPPING FARAH'S FICTION:
The Postmodern Landscapes
Derek Wright

A common feature of postmodernist fiction has been the para-doxical, "heterotopian" space in which are superimposed, by a kind of literary double-exposure, disparate and incompatible orders—the factual and the fantastic, the "real" and imaginary, this and other worlds—and which has come to be known by the name of "the zone."[1] These spaces overlap, and overstep, conventional national and geographic as well as moral and ontological boundaries: into them may be projected any approximation to or misrepresentation of "truth" in the encyclopediac sense, any interpolation or misattribution, so that "reality", in its zonal version, is anti-verisimilar in character, multiple in perspective and indeterminate in form. Here it is possible for things simultaneously to be and not be true and for a person to be both one thing and another. A space is "zoned" in the sense of being occupied by rival or even mutually exclusive and incommensurable presences—be it a place by incursive powers, an object by a number of language-signifiers, or a character by different personalities—with the result that it may appear to be broken down into warring constituents or to be itself a component of some larger whole. "In such a state," writes Foucault, the originator of the concept of *heterotopia*, "things are 'laid', 'placed', 'arranged' in sites so very different from one another that it is impossible to find a place of residence for them, to define a *common locus* beneath them all."[2] It has been implied that the heterotopian zone in the colonial and postcolonial contexts begins, in its inherent multiplicity, either to correspond or at least to have certain points of contact with historical reality:

> Objectively, Latin America is a mozaic of dissimilar and, on the face of it, incompatible cultures, languages, world-views,landscapes, ecological zones. Its condition is, we might even say, intrinsically postmodernist. Even a "straight" realistic representation of the continent would have to take this multiplicity into account; and from such a representation to a postmodernist one is only a few short steps.[3]

Much of this is, of course, also true of Africa, whose countries are even more nakedly the results of competitive historical zoning, their irrational, often nonsensical frontiers freaks of colonial whimsy, their identities accidents of naming, their ethnic and geographical spaces subordinated to the free play of colonial signifiers. Such nations, whose boundaries consist of at least one arbitrarily drawn straight line for every natural contour provided by a river or mountain range, are artificial intellectual constructs which have never had any natural homogeneity except in the minds of colonial Governor-Generals and District Officers. Their postcolonial histories—catastrophic in the case of Nigeria, whose diverse peoples have proved equally unable to live together or apart—and the doomed attempts to salvage ethnic nations like "Biafra" from the colonial carve-up have been, to a large extent, the legacies of imperial political cartography which have taken little account of ethnic and linguistic variations.

Arguably, the colonial concoction which issues in the postcolonial nation-state is everywhere an unreal construct insofar as it is a mere fiction of political geography—an imperial invention or imaginative projection which is more often than not, in Salman Rushdie's description of Q/Pakistan in *Shame*, "insufficiently imagined...a failure of the dreaming mind."[4] Exploiting the potential parallels between the political remaking and the fictional rewriting of history in the postcolonial era, Rushdie's own treatment of India and Pakistan in *Midnight's Children* and *Shame* suggests how readily nations which are themselves, in some sense, fictions lend themselves to the most arbitrary and indeterminate (and the most flamboyantly experimental) of fictional forms. The more unlikely and unimaginable the postcolonial history, the more improbable and wildly imagined is the novelist's reinvention and its narrative modes and devices (one such device is the mythical collective-narrator to whom the whole of his nation's postcolonial history happens or is revealed, thus identifying his autobiography with the history of the nation and making his consciousness the repository of the communal or racial memory: Rushdie's Saleem, Vassanji's Salim in *The Gunny Sack*, Farah's Askar in *Maps*, Awoonor's Amamu in *This Earth, My Brother*).

Africa, more than most, has been peculiarly prone to the literary as to the political rezoning process, though its "intrinsically postmodernist" qualities have understandably been exploited in colonial and expatriate writing about Africa rather than in African writing itself. Notoriously, Africa has occupied in the European imagination a conceptual rather than a geographical space. It has been less an actual place than a protean literary zone which in Western fiction has been mined for its endless possibilities, serving as a screen for the projection of imperial fantasies of adventure and exploration (Rider Haggard's romances and their contemporary counterparts); as a void which, confused with its blank space on the imperial map, is made simultaneously to absorb the intruder's own imported nightmares and to provide him with an alibi for colonial occupation

(Conrad's *Heart of Darkness*); and, more recently, as a playground for lexical and ontological improvisation (Walter Abish's *Alphabetical Africa*) or, with parodic deliberateness, as fodder for European fantasy-lore (Angela Carter's *The Infernal Desire Machines of Dr Hoffman*). Some of these writers, it has been noted, have been troubled by the ease with which Africa has been reinvented by the non-African author and by a resulting imperialism of the imagination which reenacts at a different level the political rezoning of the continent.[5] Naturally, African authors themselves also have a stake in such concerns, particularly when, like the novelist Nuruddin Farah, they have skirmished with postmodernism in their own work. During its colonial and postcolonial history Farah's native Somalia—a strange mixture of nomadic herdsman and cosmopolitan urban intellectuals which a decade of clan warfare and famine has virtually wiped from the map—has seen its political and cultural space expropriated, in turn, by British, Italian, Ethiopian, Russian, American and United Nations forces, often with local reinforcement from the indigenous despotic regime.

It would be perverse to claim Farah as a thoroughgoing postmodernist or to try to limit him to any one school of writing, since his writing is as richly diverse in its origins as his personal background and education, his wide travel and work experience (in a score of countries over four continents), and his prodigious linguistic resources (Somali, Arabic, Amharic, English and Italian). Farah is one of Africa's most multicultural and multilingual writers and his highly eclectic body of fiction draws freely upon many cultural and religious sources and upon readings in many of the world's literatures. It is a living testament to the process of cultural hybridization which is a standard feature of the postcolonial world and its essence, as some recent commentators have observed, is to be found in an open-ended intellectual debate that is not resolvable into the stark binarisms of the pro- and anti-verisimilar, or postmodernist experimentalism and psychological realism, or any other alternative "isms."[6] I propose in this article, however, to limit myself to some of the quasi-postmodernist tendencies at play in Farah's work, bearing in mind that many of these are resemblances to rather than replications of the genuine article, and to focus on the points where postmodernism and postcolonialism appear to converge, paying special attention to the literary and cultural rezoning habit which has become a distinctive mark of the Western postmodernist imagination.

In particular, Farah's sombre, nightmarish trilogy of novels, *Variations on the Theme of an African Dictatorship*, reveals many of the standard features of the postmodernist fiction: for example, the collapsing of ontological boundaries by multiple, superimposed orders of reality; the conspicuous and ingenious play of analogic motif and parallelism; the "transworld" identities of characters who reappear in novel after novel (and, as with the respectively adolescent and mature Eblas of *From a Crooked Rib* and *Sardines*, do not always correspond with their intertextual signifiers and maintain a realistic illusion of their continuing lives outside the texts); and the favoring of fragmented, composite characters—spaces inhabited by multiple presences—over unitary personalities. As Ian Adam has observed, Farah patterns his people compulsively into pairs, paralleling rival parents and children, domestic and political patriarchs, victims and avengers, teachers and pupils, in ways that put the Western reader in mind of alternative mirror-worlds or parallel universes.[7] The latter tendency is particularly marked in *Sweet and Sour Milk* (the first novel of the trilogy) where confusions of identity amid a malaise of political misinformation cause Loyaan, during his investigation of his brother's death, to fear that he may not be an autonomous being but is perhaps really part of a composite fabrication put together from the literature of twins, a Siamese-soul called Soyaan-Loyaan, with interchangeable parts. In *Sardines*, the second novel of the sequence, Farah provides not a collection of individuals but a syncretic portrait of Somali womanhood in which all the women, packed into the same suffocating social sardine tin, become aspects of one another, their characters interpenetrative and complementary. Farah has said that "everyone contains different things—the woman in the child, the man in the woman and so on," that in his novels "an intellectual and psychological debate is going on between two selves—the woman's self in the man, the man's self in the woman."[8] Thus, in *Sardines*, Westernization brings out the latent feminine in Samater and the masculine in Medina.

In *Maps*, however, even these conventional categories are dissolved and the bounds of the realistic frame burst both by collapsing ontological divisions and by interchanging sexual roles. "Every image floats vaguely in a sea of doubt," runs the epigraph from Conrad, and on the dreamscapes of this novel everything is of transitional and indeterminate identity, melting from one form into another. Even in the twilight zone of *Close Sesame*, the third volume of the *Dictatorship* trilogy, the reality/metaphor axis turns on a fine but firm line (between, for example, the mysterious Khaliif's literal madness and symbolic sanity), whereas in *Maps* sexual, national and ontological boundaries are straddled —by the hero Askar, a child of the disputed territory of the Ogaden—in such a way as to dissolve the distinctions between the things they divide. Thus there is in this multilayered fiction a puzzling indeterminacy as regards where metaphor ends and literal reality starts; where mindscape passes into landscape, the personal into the public body, physiological into topographical space. In *Maps* the reductive elements in Askar's behavior which are privileged by conventional psychological-realist readings (for example, his obsessed idea that his dead Somali mother still lives inside him) are countered by more expansive, postmodernist tendencies. Askar aspires to be, at once, male and female, "half-man, half-child", ethnocentric Somali and culturally hybrid Ogadenese. He also fancies himself to be both a real child and the epic miracle-child of his adoptive mother's oral tales who was present at his own birth and born out of his mother's death (one who has "met death when not quite a being"). He claims to hold "simultaneously multiple citizenships of different kingdoms: that of the living and the dead; not to mention that of being an infant and an adult at the same time."[9] Like his prototypes, Grass's Oskar (=Askar) and Rushdie's Saleem, he is a liminal creature, an occupant of the between-worlds space of the zone. Like them, he behaves as a composite construct assembled from diverse sources and finally, as he struggles on the last page of the novel to free himself of blame for his adoptive mother's death, fragmenting back into his constituent parts: defendant, plaintiff, juror, witness, judge, and audience. The dreamscape of the novel is the improbable space where alone these incongruous elements can coexist.

In these novels Farah also shares concerns expressed by more conventional African authors who owe little or nothing to postmodernist writing. Like them, he is troubled by the imperial powers' zonal expropriation of Africa's political, ethnic and cultural space in both the colonial and independence periods; and, moreover, by the continuation and reinforcement of these territorializing habits by postcolonial African regimes. But it is in his treatment of this very process, and of these regimes' tyrannical imposition of arbitrary, quasifictional identities upon their nations, that Farah's work comes closest to postmodernist fiction.

Farah is perhaps at his most openly "postmodern" in the early *jeu d'esprit, A Naked Needle*. The most self-consciously "zoned" of his fictions, the book both is and is not about the progress of the Somalian revolution between 1969 and 1972, its "truth to reality" problematized at the outset by the disclaimer's enigmatic warning that there are "no real characters where none is intended" and "no true incident where none is mentioned" (what are "real" characters and "true" incidents?). Farah's Mogadiscio, as presented by his erratic and mercurial guide Koschin, is a jumble of languages and cultures, ethnic quarters and ghettos, and of migrating embassy officials, foreign experts and Italianized intellectuals with English girlfriends, American wives and Russian mistresses in tow. Even in its "straight" realistic representation, it is a patchwork product of the colonial imagination and a post-colonial variant of those zoned postwar European cities that feature in American postmodern fiction (Pynchon, Hawkes, Vonnegut), in which the locales traversed are so diverse and disparate that they seem to belong (and often do) to different worlds. As if to compound the very arbitrariness of the colonial "fiction", Koschin undertakes the further reimagining of the city and its postcolonial African context by the tried postmodernist technique of displacing and deranging customary historical and geographical associations. Written at a slight angle to historical reality, Koschin's narrative mischievously piles misquotation upon misinformation and mixes invented anecdotes with recorded ones, so that the facts are given to us more than a little askew. Bakhtu-Rida secondary school in Khartoum where Koschin claims to have been schooled is not a secondary school and is not in Khartoum,[10] while the real Fanon's death was from leukemia, perhaps less romantic than the cigar-toting guerrilla's death from lung cancer which is substituted for it here. Both Fanon and Nietzsche are misquoted in order to advance stock colonial paradigms of white mistresses and black love-slaves and, though the cameo of Mahed and his graceless Russian mistress is the only episode in the novel that upholds this model, each of the book's mixed marriages and relationships is routinely passed through the postmodernist fiction's deconstructive strainer and sifted for comic-strip stereotypes (the Dark Lady, the Colonial Mistress), with the effect that representations are given problematic priority over their referents. Koschin, moreover, leaves unclear both the exact status of the exotic, novelettish revolutions which he fantasizes into his visiting English girlfriend's past and their relation to the contemporary Somali revolution which is raging around them. The two revolutions come to coexist in an impossible space which exists nowhere except in the projected fictional universe of the written text. What kind of narrative needle is Farah/Koschin using to stitch together the different orders of reality zoned in his novel?

Koschin expresses the wish not to be the needle of the novel's title and epigraph, the needle that "clothes others whilst it remains naked" which Flaubertian and Joycean artists, denuding themselves of material for their art and remaining "naturally leafless, naked during all seasons and at all times, while on other trees flowers are conceived and blossom."[11] Of course, even if we allow for the novel's verbal pyrotechnics (the virtuoso alliteration, graphic onomatopoeia and outlandish homonymic punning), Farah's committed stance is as far removed as is imaginable from Joyce's neutralized aestheticism. But the book does bear many of the hallmarks of the postmodernist metafiction, notably its self-preoccupied textuality and linguistic self-absorption (the incestuous literary allusions and interior word games), and its narrative reflexiveness. Nancy is described at the beginning as "an epilogue that spoils the strong point of a novel" (*NN*, p.2), the book contains at least one reference to its own publisher and the series in which it appeared, and Koschin confesses to have written a thesis on Joyce (this habit of incorporating a character's written work into the author's is repeated with Margaritta's thesis on African National Security Services in *Sweet and Sour Milk*, Medina's critique of the revolution in *Sardines*, and Askar's court defence on the last page of *Maps*, which refers us back to the novel we have just read). Also conspicuous are the metafiction's playful, parodic manipulation of stock literary figures and the accompanying narrative needle that *un*stitches and pulls things from together. The Fanonian stereotypes exist in contradistinction with what substantial human reality is constructed in the illusionist mode and,insofar as they fail to develop the book's cross-racial sexual relationships as valid vehicles for social and political comment (on Russian and American neo-colonialism), they are *de*constructed by them. During the geographical and historical tour of Mogadiscio in the last two movements, in which the sexual centre of interest is virtually dissolved, the private relationships become unstitched from the political commentary, and the flat "literary" representations—the types and archetypes—come away from the more "realistic" ones. The psychological interest has been taken out of the mythological arena and rezoned.

In Angela Carter's *The Passion of New Eve* the heroine, who travels across a futuristic America of similarly arbitrary, warring zones, recalls having "lived in systems which operated within a self-perpetuating reality, a series of enormous solipsisms, a tribute to the existential freedom of the land of free enterprise."[12] Into this epistemological wilderness the denizens import their own significances, all believing themselves to be in possession of the "true" reality. Medina and Sagal, in Farah's *Sardines*, engage in much the same sort of mental activity in the quite different political environment of totalitarian oppression, though the postmodernist indexings to "objective" reality are here more political than cultural and psychological, and the peculiar affirmation of spirit essentially private and dualistic rather than public and collective. In *Sardines* we are aware, as with Loyaan's re-assembling of Soyaan's life in the previous book, of minds self-consciously engaged in the quasi-fictional reconstruction of reality after the event. It is another of Farah's novels of discourse and debate (with Medina as a more serious, female Koschin), written at an intellectual distance from and on a theoretic slant to events. Sagal, whose element as the national swimming champion is water, is conceived by Medina as "wearing a watery grin, squinting slightly" at an imperceptive angle to reality and is much given to "inventing futures for herself,"[13] while in the psychology of her mentor fluidity and fixation paradoxically mingle. On the one hand, it is Medina's habit to fictionalize her own past and reconstruct a multiplicity of possible motives for her actions, none of which is apparently to be preferred above the others, and she is abetted in this by the plurality of oral versions of her doings (notably, her abandonment of Samater) which are rumoured into circulation hot on the heels of the event.

Delighting in her existential doubts, Medina appropriates others' versions of her own actions (Sagal's, Nasser's) as is convenient (*S*, pp.63, 82). The flexibility, however, is born of fixation. Medina is the bookish intellect caged by political repression, struggling to construct its own human reality to rival the political unreality outside but, in the process, driven paranoiacally in upon itself to the point where it confuses the personal with the political and starts to mistake its own fictional reconstructions for fact. According to Ebla, "Medina was offered the pen with which she wrote herself off" (*S*, p.41). Placed under a banning order and virtual house arrest, Medina writes herself out of the public, political world and into a private, fictional world, where she has but a single disciple, her protege Sagal, and a captive audience of one, her eight-year-old daughter Ubax. From the boundaried isolation of a room in her brother Nasser's house—"In Medina's mind the world was reduced to a room" (*S*, p.24)—Medina proceeds privately to restructure the world in the light of a few narrow, self-righteous ideological principles:

> She reconstructed the story from the beginning. She worked it into a set of pyramids which served as foundations for one another. Out of this, she erected a construction of great solidity and strength. She then built mansions on top of it all, mansions as large as her imagination and with lots of chambers that led off corridors in which she lost herself...She roamed about in the architecture of her thoughts. (*S*, p.2)

If the house is Medina's life—"a life defined like the boundaries of a property" (*S*, p.6)—and the room her mind, in which her thoughts walk up and down unhindered, its spaces are the blank pages on which will be constructed her book criticizing the revolution (*this* book, in effect, since her consciousness occupies the largest space in it), and the furniture signifies whatever inconveniences distract the writer from her obsession: "one's mind bumped into things, was distracted by the material things around" (*S*, p.17). It is all, in reality, a giant solipsism, a monstrous projection of the subjective will which claims immoderately to have shaken the foundations of the national house of Somalia, overrun by Soviet "white ants"—"the ground below her shook with seismic determination"—and rendered her "a full and active participant in the history of her country" (*S*, p.250). The room is, finally, a reductive metaphor for the intransigent idealist's and self-absorbed novelist *manque*'s selfish rearrangement of others' lives, as if they were merely the furniture of her own brain, and of her own life in a way that is heedless of the effects upon others who come into contact with it: "She has created a habitat in which she alone can function...She put the chair in the wrong place in the dark. When Samater awoke he stumbled on it and broke his neck" (*S*, p.243).

The challenge to the regime issued by Medina's desertion of house and husband amounts to little more than a self-indulgent ideological gesture that takes little account of the circumstances at hand (does she expect Samater to wink at the wiping out of his clansmen by refusing the ministerial appointment?) and finally leaves the enemy (Idil and the General) in charge of the spoils (Samater and Somalia). Sagal, who learns well from Medina's doctrinaire vision of the whole of reality as political and all the nation's ills as explicable in terms of the dictator's personality, even deceives herself into interpreting her seduction of an ill-treated West Indian visitor as a political act—the child she bears him will "prick the nation's conscience with guilt" (*S*, p.116). But what is doubly disturbing about this fantasy-ridden politics is that it shares the totalitarian state's own frightening capacity for making a merely verbal, nominal sense of reality prevail over the actual, for promoting principle irrelevantly over particulars, ideology over instance (significantly Medina, in the first chapter, is described as being as unbending as her patriarchal father). Medina's ability, illustrated in the room-imagery, to proliferate metonymic motifs regardless of occasion is evidenced, ominously, in the political rape of Amina, who is regarded by her assailants merely as a metonymic attribute of her father, so that the attribute becomes the thing it stands for: "We're doing this not to you," they tell her, "but your father" (*S*, p.119). It is also present in the wilful official fiction perpetrated by the state that a sixteen-year-old American-born daughter of Somali expatriates on her first trip, as a tourist, to the land of her ancestors is really a Somali citizen on whose person they have licence to perform a brutal circumcision.

In *Sardines* the solipsisms are realistically framed, the paranoia politically placed. Medina and her pupil compulsively ideologize everything because they are victims of a confusion of the personal and the political which has become a standard feature of existence in a country where it is no longer possible not only to challenge the dictator's power but also to disentangle private matters from his stranglehold on public life: hence the equations "Idil *in* the General, the personal *in* the political" (*S*, p.245). Moreover, the uncertainties are mainly of the epistemological kind, the results of ideological fixations, alternative rumored versions of the same event, and speculative reconstructions of motives. In *Sweet and Sour Milk*, however, it is the individual's ontological hold on the world that is rendered insecure; the questions raised are ones of existence rather than identity, not of knowing but being; what is now uncertain is not who but what and *if* people are. In this novel we are back squarely in the postmodern literary terrain.

In *Sweet and Sour Milk* the General's dictatorship is built around a security corps of illiterate spies and informers working entirely in the oral medium (thus there are no arrest warrants, death certificates, or lists of detainees), and the fate in store for literate protest against unalphabeted tyranny is sounded proleptically in the novel's Prologue during the retrospective beach scene between Soyaan and his mistress Margaritta: "The solidity of his body in the water's transparency flowed into ripples of fantasy...She wrote his name on the sand. The sea washed away her writing. They silently watched the water recede. He wished he could read her message in the water receding."[14] Here, in the dissolving of solid, stable realities into fantasy, the washing away of words, the pattern for the book is set and the implications for written texts, including this one, in a mode of reality built on oral discourse—what happens to language when nothing is happening, in the sense of being written, in it—are darkly hinted at. After a while, as I have demonstrated at length elsewhere,[15] the public oral code of discourse privileged by the regime begins to infiltrate Farah's own written text. The latter takes on, insidiously, the oral narrative's reconstructive and reinventive capacities, its talent for improvising alternative versions in the retelling of tales; its subsequently unstable order of meaning, susceptible to variation, omission, and shifts of emphasis; its vagaries of characterization;

and, most dangerously in the present political context, the fluid indeterminacy and interpretative openness that follow inevitably from a
form of discourse which is audience-oriented rather than performer-
centered. "Let everybody interpret things as they wished," Loyaan
laments, in despair at the systematic misinterpretation of the facts of
his brother's life by their policeman-father and the police-state that
he serves (*SSM*, p.138). In this novel lives, like plots coming and going
in an epic narrative, are reimaginable and, in theory, infinitely interpretable. In *Sardines* the oralist Idil, who is the General's matriarchal
representative on the domestic front, is fully at home in this many-
versioned reality:

> And by the time you were ready to ask her a question,
> you would discover that she had already moved
> on...she had changed residence and had nomaded
> away, impermanent...

> Idil's ball of thread rolled away...She began to thread-
> draw in her mind a past with patterns different from
> the one she had the intention of re-narrating....Idil
> counted the number of holes she had to jump in order
> to form a pattern. (S, pp.7, 78)

In the tangled webs of both the General's and Idil's oral texts the
lacunae—the interpretative spaces and absences around the
words—are as important as the words themselves: the anti-matter
generated by the text is equal to its matter. The oral mode is, in a
very postmodernist way, an uncentered or off-centered mode of discourse, subject to the law of the excluded middle, and there is in
Sweet and Sour Milk a prevailing motif of uncentredness which index-
es its protagonist's psychological and philosophical dilemmas and
Africa's crises of national identity to the vagaries of the oral convention. Here ontological traumas become part of a broader national and
continental malaise.

In Margaritta's polemical monologue and in Loyaan's reflected responses Somalia, serving as a microcosm of modern Africa, is itself envisaged as a centerless and featureless void into which anything can be put and of which anything can be made. It is a space inhabited by so many inauthentic foreign and indigenous presences but without any inner core of identity: after the British and Italian colonizers come "KGBs and CIA espionage networks" to take up residence alongside "wizardry and witchcraft and hair-burning rites of sorcery" and the "make-believe" lives of western-educated elites who turn Africa into "a textbook reproduction of European values and western thinking" (*SSM*, pp.124, 148). The history of the ancient European world as presented through the twins' Italian education is a mass of solid documentation: "history as chiselled out of the harshness of rocks, come the Greeks themselves, the Sicilians, the Normans, the Arabs" (*SSM*, p.168). Meanwhile, "they were told *they* had no history" (*SSM*, p.131). Its past envisaged as an oral blank, Somalia has no history or, alternatively, has too much history and in too many variant versions for any of it to be certain. Its preliterate, precolonial history is conceived as an endlessly reinvented narrative, improvised over a factual vacuum and on which each successive regime plays its own variations before an obliging mass-audience. Its more recent, postcolonial history is reconstituted at the whim of dictators, frequently in terms of the flat, cartoon-like fictions that inform Keynaan's traditional pre-heliocentric view of the universe—"the flat universe of Father's calculable dimensions" (*SSM*, p.106)—but even these are imitative of foreign propagandist practices: Loyaan refers us to the Hungarian Uprising and Prague Spring, and to the "official" government version's polarization of the population into heinous reactionary rebels and heroic "revolutionary" armies (*SSM*, pp.103, 106).

Somalia's political uncenteredness is matched by the decentered lives of its intellectuals. Margaritta, limiting the relevance of her past affair with the Minister in the matter of Soyaan's death, marginalizes her influence—"I am not central to all that has taken place" (*SSM*, p.228)—while Beydan has a recurring dream in which she is not only not the center-point but is not even there, and at his funeral "Soyaan [was] the centre of this festivity although, just like Beydan in her dream, he too wasn't there" (*SSM*, p.231). Because there is no route by which his writings might pass into the oral discourse privileged by the regime, Soyaan's fate will be to be remembered not by their complex truths but by the oral slogans that refashion him into a myth. These lives are not centered upon themselves but are satellites of other forces, rotating in an interpretative void, and their meanings are not traceable to any single stable order of reality but float in a multiplicity of versions. The manufacturer of this many-versioned malaise and the ringmaster of its peculiar epistemological circus is, of course, the General. Somalia's Islamic militarism is centred on key political and religious signs in a written code, but the General's substitution of his own personality for the constitution ("I *am* the constitution") and his bowdlerization of the Koran into a collection of slogans and hackneyed praise-songs ("There is no General like our General") has had the effect of decentering Somalia's political reality, placing phrases like "radical governments" and "revolutionary socialism" in parentheses and inverted commas that hold them at a remove from the real thing.

Farah has said in his essay "Why I Write" that "Somalia was a badly written play" and "Siyad Barre was its author....he was also the play's main actor, its centre and theme; as an actor-producer, he played all the available roles."[16] The more precise analogy that suggests itself in the novel is of the General as a species of debased oral performer; a malevolent, diabolically inventive kind of oral historian, ringing endless surprises and variations on the theme of silencing dissidents, fabricating imagined alternatives for the lives of his trampled victims and, with the help of men like Keynaan, breathing life into lies that travesty their real ones. An astute and wily performer, he serves up for his nation's oral epics, sung by his "griots in green", new "heroes and legendary figures about whom one tells stories to children and future generations" (*SSM*, p.183). The General's ideal

110

audience, however, is not the active, contributing participants of the oral tradition but passive assenters who can rearrange themselves into any shape that is required: brainwashed buffoons mouthing official dogma; political stooges like Keynaan, men with no core of identity who will stoop to any baseness to ingratiate themselves with power; and beggars, who are compliantly impressionable and manipulable in all things. "Here was an audience willing to hear anything," says Loyaan of the latter. Appropriately, those who are most attuned to the General's protean oral reality are themselves adept shape-changers who, in one symbolic scene, actually transform themselves before Loyaan's eyes in response to the visitations of power: "The beggars no longer resembled the remnants of a plane-crash. No, they were the passengers of a third-class train, stirring forward, jerking, shaking, speaking...Power had chosen to visit them. The Minister to the Presidency and his entourage of cars and security men had arrived" (*SSM*, p.229). Loyaan notes that beggars, unlike Beydan, Soyaan and Margaritta, "are the centre of their dreams," but it is a hollow center, a void where identity should be, a blank ready to be moulded into any form.

Sweet and Sour Milk, Ian Adam argues at the end of his penetrating article "The Murder of Soyaan Keynaan," uses the forms of the detective novel, and the mystery-suspense and political thriller, only to depart from them, and it does so, I think, because its ontology is essentially more complex and sophisticated than theirs. Adam is reluctant to reduce the novel's rejection of final answers to the hermeneutic scepticism of the *nouveau roman* and thus to "post-modernize" Farah's text in any hardline way, arguing that the novel's comparative lack of closure is more ethical than epistemological in origin: Farah, he contends, "clearly sets the notion of collective activity, of collaboration and consensus" against the detective novel's relatively egocentric and authoritarian notion of a single leader and rescuer (a General-figure) who "ties up all the loose ends."[17] It is certainly true that, even though the clandestine organization has been decimated at the end of this novel and lies dormant in the next one, the ideal of collective resistance to one-man rule is kept alive as a positive force throughout the trilogy. It is also true, of course, that the figure of authority in Farah's novel could hardly fill the detective's role of tying up loose ends since he himself is the creator of them. Here the patriarchal messiah-figure is himself the mystifier-criminal element in the plot, the fabricator of an obscurantist order of reality, and there exists no other authoritative hermeneutic agent to counter his fabrications and provide a definitive version of events. Thus it is to be wondered (and Adam partly concedes so much) if Farah really intends us to be much closer at the end of the book than at the beginning to a true account of the events surrounding Soyaan's death. It is surely significant that Soyaan's fatal injection, like Mulki's torture, is perceived through a frenzied hallucinatory haze—he raves of "pale, ghostly beings which jabbed [him] with needles" (*SSM*, p.17)—so that unreality is deliberately conferred upon it, making it impossible to distinguish the true and the imagined. There is finally no way that we can separate the "real" from the theatricalized Mulki, the actual secretary from an incompetent actress who is wheeled onto the set at ministerial cue in the interrogation scene's "badly written farce" (*SSM*, p.199); and, given the elusiveness of the Prologue as a touchstone for objective reality, there are ultimately no means by which we can know the "real" Soyaan from the propagandist myth into which he is transformed. In what senses other than their outward representations can these persons be said to have existed since the facts of their lives are but figments of the General's personal scenario? Is Farah not undermining the whole idea that a knowable and verifiable personal reality is still discernible behind a coercive system of mystificatory political representations?

Even if the novel's vaporous, polymorphous political reality is not in excess of the requirements of the detective and political thriller genres, the highly poetic meteorological matter in which it is reflected surely is. Cloud formations, the night's phantasmagoric skyscapes, and the sun, which "poured its blazing vapouriness upon everything" (*SSM*, p.146), constantly assume different shapes—

camels, trees, garments, pillars, skulls—to the imagination playing its variations upon them. Like the regime's political enormities, they keep the beholder guessing, keeping always one step ahead of Loyaan's imagination which walks "the untrod landscape of the unknowable" (*SSM*, p.59). But when night falls "in a veil of darkness," Loyaan finally discovers, in one of the novel's crucial reflexive scenes, that there is really nothing behind this political reality, which is compared to a shoddily built, badly painted stage set: "Empty at my touch like a soap-bubble, everything reducible to nought, nothing. Inexistent at my remembering, like a dream" (*SSM*, p.143). Somali reality under the dictator constitutes not so much a slippery and confusing multiplicity of signs as a signless void, providing no forms in which coherent meanings can be expressed:

> The night unrolled like a cotton thread, unfolding inch by inch; the night wove words of thready thoughts; the night stitched for him a blanket of comfort and warmth...Every movement he heard had a meaning, and if it didn't he gave it one. The security men were following him and making sure he stayed indoors, in one version...Then, right before Loyaan's and the world's eyes, all suddenly began to disintegrate like a worn-out piece of cloth a thick set of fingers has pulled asunder. (SSM, pp.205-06, 210-11)

The sun's sudden dismantling of the "fabric of schemata", the text written upon the night by Loyaan's imagination, signals the deconstructive implosion of Farah's own text. What looks like an unfolding of meaning turns out to be an unravelling of the entire fabric in which meaning should reside: the novel's ontological barriers are themselves breached and the proliferation of "versions" precludes the literary representation of reality as the discovery of indivisible truths. The oralized political plot to assassinate and apotheosize Soyaan, apparently commandeered by the General, is finally unavailable to the narrative plot of the novel and its details and motives fail to materialize. Behind the mystificatory malaise of political misinformation, no verifiable reality is discernible.

Reality is no more verifiable or determinable in the final volume of the *Dictatorship* trilogy, *Close Sesame*, though for very different reasons. "It is the prerogative of God alone to be sure of anything," says its ailing veteran protagonist Deeriye. "I am only a human. And therefore I am in doubt."[18] Its menacing title notwithstanding, *Close Sesame* is not about closure, except in the limiting political sense of democratic freedoms being closed off by tyranny; it is, in fact, one of the most elusively open-ended and unresolved of Farah's fictions. Deeriye's is a "life resplendent with contradictions" (*CS*, p.159) and his narrative is an elliptical one in which the vagaries of perception are largely the result of his physically frail, asthmatic condition. Deeriye drifts in and out of consciousnesss, nodding off to sleep or falling into fits of absent-minded abstraction in conversations and political meetings, so that he is often unable to distinguish what he has heard from his daydreams and from the visions that precede his asthmatic seizures. He is at a distance from the world around him and only fitfully observant of it, his intermittent perceptions filtered through rumors and intuitions as much as through reports and observations. Deeriye's life has, as he explains, been "landmarked by absences" during lengthy spells of imprisonment by both the colonial and independence regimes. The exhausted asthmatic is mentally absent from his present life as the imprisoned political martyr was physically absent from his past one. But his asthma is part of a pervasive image-complex in which absence and presence are, complementarily, aspects and conditions of one another in a continuum, insofar as absence implies presence, an absence in one place being a presence in another, a departure here an arrival somewhere else, an act of omission one of commission at another level. Paradoxically, the imprisonment which absented Deeriye from his private life in the past has earned him a very public, if figmentary, contemporary presence as figurehead, household name and living legend. His life, he says,

114

"was a life developed, like a negative, in the darkroom of isolation" (*CS*, p.31). Though absent from the family photograph, he sees his life as figuratively developed in the darkness of the prison cell into the print-image of the national hero and historical celebrity. It was also during his period in prison that there developed an occult, extra-sensory communion with his wife Nadiifa, and since her death she has visited him, posthumously, in *her* absence, as he once visited her, psychically, during *his*. Subsequently, Deeriye's mental absences from his present material existence during his asthmatic blackouts tend, problematically, to signify power in another, spiritual realm.

Indeed, the protagonist, and the action, of *Close Sesame* are not entirely of this world. Deeriye lives, and much of the novel takes place, in a twilit half-world between sleep and waking, the time between dark and dawn when his dead wife comes visiting. The narrative is situated, problematically, in a transitional zone between different orders of reality, where phenomena are simultaneously present and absent, dark in one order and light in another. In the few seconds before his seizures, Deeriye "crosses over into a world whose logic is unknown to any living soul," and finds himself "living with different realities" and duelling value systems—with "two selves, two souls" as Nadiifa tells him—until he is "not sure of anything any more" (*CS*, pp.116, 143, 198). The reader, like Deeriye, is never quite sure whether his visions and visitations are the result or the cause of his illness; whether the asthmatic attacks induce or are a side effect of a higher spiritual experience which leaves him physically incapacitated; and whether the apparition of his wife is conjured from his imagination or breathed into existence by his religious devotions. "You have asthma, your lung is your soul," Nadiifa tells him at her last visit (*CS*, p.198). In fact, lungs and soul, breath and spirit, are bracketed throughout the novel, as if a compound entity, and the constant coupling of pneumonic and pneumatological motifs results in an unusually physical eschatology, in which the catarrh-clogged nasal and bronchial passages do service for the soul's numinous passageway to the spirit realm. Once this image-complex is exploded into the fabric of Farah's many-layered text, however, it acquires a curiously polyvalent, multidirectional quality. On the one hand, there appears to be a direct correlation in the novel between Deeriye's faltering religious faith and his lung ailment, between failing respirational powers and a dwindling expenditure of spiritual energy. On the other hand, by an inverse proportion, Deeriye's shortage of breath, his failure of exhalative power in the physical world, also connotes a corresponding enhanced inhalation of spiritual power—of God's breath—in his visionary realm, an intake of divine energy that leaves him physically breathless. Expansion issues from constriction (like illuminated prints from darkrooms); spiritual strength emanates from shrunken lungs.

The novel's secular-religious contradictions are crystallised in the episode of Deeriye's death in an abortive attempt on the life of the General, an event which is left deliberately indeterminate and is not closely investigated for motive. There is in this episode no unequivocal opting either for this life or an afterlife, only the familiar antinomous tropology of arrival and departure, negative presence and positive absence, that has attended Deeriye throughout the book. The revolver's failure to go off in the failed assassination is prefaced by a series of thwarted or muffled explosions, of bangs that end as whimpers, and the inward, asthmatic explosion in Deeriye's chest also fails to happen, as is evidenced by the two unused inhalers found on his corpse. Appropriately, the whole episode of Deeriye's death is, politically and narratively, a non-event. It is, in effect, a speculative, other-worldly action which occurs in the realm of absence, death being the supreme absence, and for this reason it is neither witnessed nor narrated but exists only in reported and rumored versions.

Farah's symbolism in this episode imparts a crucial ambiguity to the moment of martyrdom. Though committed to non-violent opposition, Deeriye embraces his son's retaliatory code in order to avenge his murder by the regime, but there also appears to be present a death-wish yearning to rejoin his beloved wife, who in her final visi-

116

tation is envisaged as an *houri* beckoning him to the paradisal gardens. "A hero must not die an anonymous death," Deeriye tells himself, "he must die, like the Sayyid, in the full knowledge of his actions, bearing the consequences" (*CS*, p.35). But while the Sayyid died secure in his accomplishments, leaving his brand of nationalism on Somali life, Deeriye fails to invest his death in the Sayyidist cause to which he has devoted his life. This death is not his warrior-hero's demise on active service but the relatively futile sacrifice of the suicidal martyr—he fumbles his weapon and is mown down by machine guns. At least one of the versions of the failed assassination partly bears out this reading. In this version, Deeriye pulls his revolver and rosary together out of the same pocket and entangles the revolver in the prayer-beads, which entwine themselves around the muzzle of the gun in droll parody of the rosary and Sura attached to the tip of the Islamic warrior's lance (Deeriye's Sura is in his pocket). In this case the rosary intervenes, divinely, not to steel the heart against the infidel but to prevent Deeriye from committing an act of cold-blooded murder that would violate the basic tenets of his religious beliefs and cause him to forfeit his place in paradise. The rosary thus ensures that he dies both a martyr and a man of peace. Meanwhile, at the level of practical action and political realism, the sacred object does not energize or empower the weapon but impedes it. Deeriye assaults the General's tyrannical regime with a devotional fervour which simultaneously inspires and inhibits action; which is a source of strength and solace during his long sleep of imprisonment but has no empirical power in the waking world and issues in no effective action at the material level. In pragmatic terms, Deeriye is a would-be political activist distracted and disabled by his religion, as the Sayyid was a religious leader diverted by politics. The ostensible aim of his deed appears to be, at once, sacrificial martyrdom and the overthrow of the government (with the implication that one will be achieved through the other), but the conclusion seems finally to opt, escapist-fashion, for bliss in the next world rather than redress in this one: "Nadiifa: the reward his martyrdom would gain him in the form of her companionship" (*CS*, p.205).

There is, however, another version of Deeriye's death. In this alternative scenario the would-be assassin mixes up his pockets and draws his prayer beads from the pocket where he had previously put his gun; thus, he pulls out his rosary not as well as but *instead of* his weapon. What is uncertain here is whether this is an alternative reading of the event or is essentially a thread of the same thought, with the same failure to issue in effective action. The symbolism may be read as offering an optional, anti-escapist reading, signifying that rosary and gun, faith and political violence, belong in separate pockets. Farah writes: "He walked straight, neither looking back nor to the sides, his right hand clutching the beads while his left held on to the bulge which was the revolver" (*CS*, p.205). Faith and violence adhere to different orders of experience and have no place together; the realization of one cannot advance the cause of the other, and Deeriye can maintain his moral uprightness and firmness of purpose only if they are kept apart. It is significant that, in this alternative (though not definitive) version of the event, Deeriye pulls out his rosary *in the place of* the weapon. While in one version, the rosary impedes the weapon, in the other version it has *become* the weapon. The prayer beads replace the gun, which plays no part in the event. In one version Deeriye fails to shoot the General in any sense; in the alternative version he shoots the tyrant down—not with gun-fire but with the holy purifying fire of Islam, the idealistic religious ardour of the zealot.

The reader is thus left in some uncertainty as to whether the final effect of the double-ending is to produce a fertile polyvalency of meaning or an impenetrable aporia in which the rival religious and political options cancel each other out. In his juggling of alternatives, Farah refuses to opt unambiguously for either spiritual or material options, never losing sight of the sacrificial logic by which Deeriye acquires more power over the General as a political martyr and religious symbol, as well as a guiding posthumous influence from the afterlife, than as an assassin. In the final postmodern-style double exposure, Deeriye's death—his final meeting with Allah, the Divine

General—is envisaged by turns as both an access and a loss of power, an empirical and an eschatological victory. Deeriye's "two souls, two selves" are as imponderably in evidence in his death as in his life, and, appropriately, the episode is informed by the dominant tropology's customary, closure-resisting antinomies: presence and absence, arrival and departure, negation and power.

This instability of meaning to which readers of the *Dictatorship* trilogy have grown accustomed is felt most acutely, however, in Farah's next book, his sixth and most radical novel. *Maps* is the story of Askar, an orphaned Somali child of the disputed Ogaden, and his shifting relationship with his adoptive mother Misra, an Oromo woman from the Ethiopian highlands who at the climax of the novel is doubtfully accused of betraying the Somali army to the forces of her homeland during Ethiopia's reconquest of the Ogaden and is murdered by a partisan group of which Askar is a member. In the book's allegoric scheme Askar, representing the Ogaden, is born to two patriotic martyrs who give their lives for the cause of its liberation from Ethiopian occupation: his father dies on the day of his birth and his mother soon afterward. He is thus, selfconsciously, the posthumous mythic offspring of Somali nationalist aspiration and the mother-Republic, and he signifies what is salvaged by his country from the colonial carve-up of the Horn of Africa (his mother's unread journal, predating Somali orthography, is written in Italian). In *Maps* the postcolonial nation is not so much parented as foster- parented: the privileged form of signification for the relations between a nation and its members—not surprisingly in Farah's fiction, where domestic and political patriarchies are mutually reinforcing—is to be found in the roles of surrogate parents and children. Nationality categories are best read through the positions which the novel's various guardians assume towards their charges, and the destabilization of these categories is, conversely, registered through a series of pseudoincestuous role-reversals which subvert these positions. The postcolonial territory of Askar's birth is, like Askar himself, without natural parentage (neither is it self-creating, as Askar fancies himself to be, though it has the opportunity to take charge of its own destiny). Such territories are, as Rushdie observed in *Shame*, the imaginative constructs of colonial and postcolonial cartographers (in this case, British, Italian, Ethiopian, and Somali). They are conceived not biologically but intellectually: Askar, who is the human analogue of the Somali Ogaden, describes himself as "a creature given birth to by notions formulated in heads" (*M*, p.3). Such creatures are adopted beings with adopted identities defined by adoptive parents, and Farah sustains the analogies between the child's ties with the family and the individual's more artificial ties with the nation only by replacing Askar's real parents with a range of surrogates and guardians. These are his foster-mother Misra who, albeit in a purely nominal way, represents the Ethiopian occupier; the childless Mogadiscio intellectuals Hilaal and Salaado who represent the modern Somali Republic, seeking to complete itself by the addition of the motherless male child of the Ogaden; the Koranic schoolteacher Aw-Adan, who represents the unifying power of Islam; and the Ogadenese Somali, Uncle Qorrax. At the end of the book each of Askar/Ogaden's five guardians have had parts of themselves chopped away—by, respectively, mastectomy, vasectomy, hysterectomy, amputation, and exaction of blood—and these truncations seem to signify, allegorically, the dismemberment of the Ogaden and the further fragmentation of the territories of Greater Somalia.

Askar is himself a principal agent in the artificial imposition of identity which is a part of this allegorizing process, most particularly through his use of maps. Farah has said of the colonial maps of Africa that "we should redraw [them] according to our economic and psychological and social needs, and not accept the nonsensical frontiers carved out of our regions."[19] And yet it is no accident that Askar has a nostalgic hankering for the time, during World War Two, when all of the Somali territories except for Djibouti were under a single, colonial administration: his own politico-linguistic map of Greater Somalia is, in reality, as much a fiction of cultural geography as the colonial maps were figments of political geography. History, Hilaal reminds us, is made by those who have access to sign-systems (*M*, p.168) and is imposed upon those who have not, and the coercive cartographic enclosures enforced by the newly-literate Somalis override socio-political (and, increasingly, cultural) divisions as the old Western imperial ones overrode ethnic and linguistic barriers; their ethnocentric organization of political space is, arguably, as distortive of reality as the Mercator projection's Eurocentric organization of geographical space. The members of the Western Somali Liberation Front, to which Askar belongs, regard their people as united by language, divided by maps, and the independent nation-state of the Somali Republic imagines that its cultural-linguistic "specificity" gives it a unique claim on those territories where Somali, in one fashion or another, is still spoken. The chief objection to this new cartographic hegemony, after noting the shakiness of its political propositions, is that it claims to unite people who, both linguistically and in other respects, are becoming more and more diverse—who have in fact become irredeemably mongrelized— while it artificially sets apart other groups of people who, in reality, are much more closely bonded. In the former category are the Somalis scattered through Kenya and Tanzania who, when they are not speaking Swahili, use a bastardized, ungrammatical form of Somali similar to that spoken by the Ogadenese Somalis, and whose subscription to Somali cultural values is as adulterated and compromised by the dominant host-cultures as is that of the Ogadenese marginal groups, the Oromo and Qotto, by the Somali one (all the indicators suggest that the linguistic homogeneity and cultural exclusiveness of Greater Somalia, if they ever existed, are rapidly disintegrating). Conversely, in the second category there is Misra, a non-ethnic Somali speaker who, though fully acculturated, is automatically mistrusted and is denied a place on her ward's identity papers, while honorary citizenship is granted to another non-ethnic Somali, the sullen Qotto schoolteacher Aw-Adan, for no other reason than that his Arabic input into Somali culture is, politically, more acceptable than Misra's Amharic one.

What is a Somali and what does it mean to be one? The question opens up a Pandora's box of political, ethnic and moral quandaries. Is it to speak or to read the language, or to be born in the homeland or in one of its territories? (in fact, few of the novel's Somali speakers are Somalis by birth: most are Qotto, Oromo, Boran, or Adenese). Is it to be a patriot in the cause of the Ogaden?—in which case what right has Qorrax, who openly collaborates with the Ethiopian conquerors, to his Somali identity? Who, if anyone, is fit to be awarded parental authorship or political guardianship of the disputed Ogaden territory to which Somalia lays claim? Certainly, the criteria for nationhood postulated by Askar, Hilaal and the WSLF patriots are, like the Somali map of the Ogaden which ignores its multilingual character and fifty per cent Amharic-speaking population, increasingly erratic and capricious, leaving little ground for belief in anything that could be described as a "pure," "authentic" or "natural" Somali identity. In one way or another, each of the characters mapped by the narrative stands, like the girl in Askar's dream, "in a borrowed skin" and the Somali map, in its peculiarly monolithic contours and fine disregard of multiculturalism, provides an inexact, inadequate model of reality. Maps, like the wars fought over them to redraw national terrains, distort and destroy (they are attended by funereal images throughout the book). The "notional truths" expressed by the Somali maps correspond to the political actuality of the Horn of Africa as little as Askar's moral conception of Misra coincides with the real woman (Misra, significantly, has no understanding of maps). But Askar's consciousness is *our* map in the novel, his the conceptual space which annexes and determines the signified reality. Consequently, in this protagonal consciousness Misra, like the political map of the territory of which she is the figurative custodian, is a suitably floating signifier, zoned into many stereotyped figures and rival fantasy embodiments: on one side, mother-martyr and victimized nation; on the other, wicked stepmother, betrayer and national enemy. A nominal sense of reality so prevails over the actual, the signifier over its referent, that Askar even thinks of her at one point as "a creature of his own invention" (*M*, p.107); and it is difficult to say exactly what does constitute her reality, or if a coherent reality has been provided for her to resist Askar's ontological inversion, since she seems to live (like the Ogaden) solely through the guardians and wards who control her existence in one way or another.

Not only does Askar not know, and not only is he unable to reveal, what Misra is: more bewilderingly, he does not know what it is that he has done to her. The text of *Maps* is surrounded by epigraphs about the necessity and inevitability of doubt, but Farah is not concerned in this novel with epistemological questions about the ultimate meaning of the deeds performed by the guilty party and with the gradual revelation of his hidden traumas (as, for example, a late modernist-realist like Graham Swift is in *Waterland*). Rather, he is breaching ontological defences by posing the problems of *what* it is that the narrator has done and is now concealing from himself, or, indeed, *whether* he has done anything (which things are not clear to the reader or to the character), and how, if at all, these things can be made known. There are two dream sequences in *Maps* (pp.211, 214-15) which could be interpreted to mean that Askar was at least an accomplice in Misra's murder and dismemberment, but it is difficult to say exactly what is happening in either of these passages and at what level their images of cannibalistic violence and bloodshed are meant to be read.

If Askar has little success in finding an authorizing parent-nation to authentically "engender" his homeland territory, he is even less successful in his use of Misra to "gender" the nation along falsely heroic, patriotic lines. Askar refers the reader to a Somali poet's fable of national identity in which Somalia, portrayed as a beautiful woman, freely accepts the advances of five suitors. These represent the original five territories of Greater Somalia, and three of the children she conceives by each of them miscarry: namely, the three provinces (one of them the Ogaden) which were not absorbed into the Somali republic at independence. The figure in the novel whose personal history approximates closest to the archetype in the fable is, ironically, the non-Somali Misra, who is also pursued by five men, some of them from the disputed homeland territories; only in Misra's case, she is the object of their largely unwanted sexual attentions. These are the Amhara abductor of her childhood; the wealthy Muslim who adopts her and then forces her to become his wife; the Qotto teacher Aw-Adan who exploits her sexually and finally betrays her; Askar's brutal Ogadenese uncle Qorrax; and the Ethiopian captain with whom she forms a liaison in the Ogaden war. In Misra's story the miscarriages become the abortions forced upon her by Qorrax and Aw-Adan. In each relationship Misra is an enslaved victim of patriarchal tyranny rather than a free agent: the point of Farah's self-subverting use of the fable is that no woman in the Horn of Africa, whether Somali, Oromo or Ethiopian, can serve in a signifying system which genders national freedom in such spurious idealized terms. It is, moreover, significant that, although the political tenor of the fable's metaphor connotes an expansive, unifying generosity, it is eclipsed by its sexual vehicle which, more in line with prevailing Somali male psychology, presents the woman as promiscuous and treacherous. The Somali poets, Misra reminds Askar, obsessively stereotype woman as a betrayer: in the words of Askar's school-mates, "if she isn't your mother, your sister or your wife, a woman is a whore" (*M*, p.98). The nation is disingenuously gendered as an imaginary woman, for whom lives must be laid down, by patriots like Askar who in fact despise the real women in their daily lives. Once again, Askar's fictionalizing of the nation has missed the mark, falling wide of what little "objective reality" is constituted by the narrative.

Askar, the girl in his dream tells him, is "almost always satisfied with the surface of things...a mirror in which your features...may be reflected" (*M*, p.130). For him Misra is an image of the Ogaden insofar as both are mirrors in which the beholder sees his own desires reflected. Maps, like mirrors, reflect the dispositions of their makers. "There is truth in maps," Hilaal concedes but, aware of the dangers of pursuing chauvinistic myths of ethnic nations, adds the rider: "The question is, does truth change?...The Ogaden, as Somali, is truth. To the Ethiopian map-maker, the Ogaden, as Somali, is untruth"

(*M*, pp.217-18). Meanwhile, like the "real" Misra (whose name means "the foundation of the earth"), the neutral ground of the disputed strip of land does not discriminate between its diverse occupying nationalities and the rival maps that overlay it like the layers of a palimpsest. Whatever the true nature of the external reality which they contour, the "truth" of maps is, finally, a highly subjective, ethnocentric kind of truth, and the stable identity presupposed by the idealistic vision of the map-maker non-existent.

Farah's sceptical line of inquiry in *Maps* is extended, in his most recent novel *Secrets* (1998), from national to clan identity and takes into account the damage that clan fanaticism, even more than nationalism and ethnic patriotism, has done to his country. In the last days of the Barre regime and under the shadow of impending inter-ethnic warfare that will make clan lineage a matter of life and death in Mogadishu, Kalaman, the foremost of the novel's five narrators, seeks to settle doubts about his paternal ancestry. Like Askar, he discovers that origins, whether of individuals or nations, are an obscure, imponderable business and may finally be irrelevant. Kalaman, it transpires, was the issue not of Yaqut, his supposed father, but of the revenge-gang-rape of his mother for refusing to comply with a forged marriage. Thus he finds, at the end of his search, only a host of untraceable progenitors, of clans nameless and unnumbered, and he subsequently learns of people many of the things that Askar learns of countries: firstly, that they have many parents; secondly, that the kinship groups into which they are formed have no congenital authenticity or, as the grandfather Nonno puts it, "primordial blood identity"[20] but are man-made, opportunistic political inventions camouflaging powermania and greed (Nonno prefers to have the more openly political designation "British" on his passport); and thirdly, that (as Askar learns too late and to his cost) the emotional bonds of parents and children who freely choose each other are finally more flexible and liberating than identities constructed along bloodlines. It is not that love is necessarily stronger than blood and semen (and Farah rubs the reader's nose in both in this most sexually explicit of his novels) but that it is more reliable and certain, and healthier and more valuable insofar as it is more productive of freedom. As Kalaman puts it: "In place of sperm, I thought it was the river of [Yaqut's] humanity which flowed into my blood, everlasting in my memory...How I loved him, the certainty that was Yaqut!" (*Secrets*, p.254).

In *Secrets* there is a decisive rejection of a system that gives priority to paternal blood lineage over and above all other allegiances, even to the extent of ratifying fraudulent marriages with oaths by false male witnesses (the bride *in absentia*) and depriving a child of unknown paternity of both clan and individual identity. Farah loads the dice against male genetics by making the father-centred family of Kalaman's childhood-love Sholoongo the site of every imaginable form of paternal unnaturalness and inhumanity, including bestiality (with heifers and donkeys), incest, the rape of a sister-in-law and aborting of her child, and the exposure of a girlchild (Sholoongo) at birth, to be raised in the wilderness by lions. "Curse the blood that binds!" is Kalaman's apt comment (*Secrets*, p.201). Indeed, the escalating havoc of Sholoongo's family begins in time to eat into the country's civil chaos, with which her destructive antics so uncannily coincide that Kalaman comes to see her as a key agent in both family ruination and national apocalypse. His grandfather, however— though he sees his country "fragmenting into family fiefdoms," becoming an extension of the clan as the clan is of the family— remains wary of the generalizing, allegorizing habit of mind that is given to glib analogies of the family, through the clan, with the nation: "I doubt that local scandals have earth-shattering proportions to them...I can't bear the thought of generalizing. I am a person. A clan is a mob...I am reasonable. Clans are not" (*Secrets*, p.190, 114, 297). As in *Maps*, the signifying system is a postmodernly unreliable one which operates with a too-suspicious neatness. Though aware that both individuals and families must bear the blame for their failure to resist Barre's clan dictatorship, Nonno, like Hilaal in the earlier novel, regards the relations of personal and national responsibility, and the extent to which one may be represented by or distinguished from the other, as ultimately imponderable. Indeed, far from mirroring the national collapse, his own family is, ironically, salvaged from it by his son Yaqut and Damac's refusal to marry.

For Nonno, as for Hilaal in *Maps* (and for *Secrets'* professional shape- shifter Sholoongo), "truth changes," confusing identities and blurring borders—including, in the new novel, the boundaries between natural and supernatural, animal and human, animate and inanimate. In this extraordinary novel—in which human mothers grow supplementary breasts, crows help to restart cars, and an elephant, emulating clan fanaticism at its most vindictive, treks across international boundaries to kill the hunter who massacred its kin—power is located at the point where different orders of being intersect and interdepend. To experience this power, here and elsewhere in Farah's work, is to be, in Nonno's words, a "citizen of the crossroads where several worlds meet" (*Secrets*, p.236).

NOTES

1. Brian McHale, *Postmodernist Fiction* (London & New York: Methuen, 1987), pp.43-45.

2. Michel Foucault, *The Order of Things: An Archaeology of the Human Sciences* (New York: Pantheon, 1979), p.xviii.

3. McHale, p.52.

4. Salman Rushdie, *Shame* (London: Picador, 1984), p.87.

5. McHale, p.54.

6. See Charles Sugnet, "Nuruddin Farah's *Maps*: Deterritorialization and "The Postmodern," *World Literature Today* 72, 4 (1998), 745-

46; and Patricia Alden and Louis Tremaine, *Nuruddin Farah* (New York: Twayne, 1999), pp.159-60.

7. Ian Adam, "Nuruddin Farah and James Joyce: Some Issues of Intertextuality," *World Literature Written in English* 24, 1 (1984), 40-42; and "The Murder of Soyaan Keynaan," *World Literature Written in English* 26, 2 (1986), 205-07.

8. Robert Moss, "Mapping the Psyche" (Interview with Nuruddin Farah), *West Africa* 1 September 1986, 1827-28.

9. Nuruddin Farah, *Maps* (London: Picador, 1986), p.11. Further references are given in parentheses after the abbreviation *M*.

10. D.R.Ewen, "Nuruddin Farah," in *The Writing of East and Central Africa*, ed. G.D.Killam (London: Heinemann, 1984), p.199.

11. Nuruddin Farah, *A Naked Needle* (London: Heinemann, 1976), p.70. Further references are given in parentheses after the abbreviation *NN*.

12. Angela Carter, *The Passion of New Eve* (London: Gollancz, 1977), p.167.

13. Nuruddin Farah, *Sardines* (London: Heinemann, 1982), p.128. Further references are given in parentheses after the abbreviation *S*.

14. Nuruddin Farah, *Sweet and Sour Milk* (London: Heinemann, 1980), pp.124, 128. Further references are given in parentheses after the abbreviation *SSM*.

15. See Derek Wright, "Zero Zones: Nuruddin Farah's Fiction," *ARIEL* 21, 2 (1990), 21-42; and, in the present volume, "Orality and Power in Nuruddin Farah's *Sweet and Sour Milk*."

16. Nuruddin Farah, "Why I Write," *Third World Quarterly* 10, 4 (1988), 1597.

17. Adam, "The Murder of Soyaan Keynaan," 210.

18. Nuruddin Farah, *Close Sesame* (London: Allison & Busby, 1983), p.202. Further references are given in parentheses after the abbreviation *CS*.

19. Patricia Morris, "Wretched Life" (Interview with Nuruddin Farah), *Africa Events*, September 1986, 54.

20. Nuruddin Farah, *Secrets* (New York: Arcade, 1998), p.193. Further references are given in parentheses after *Secrets*.

The Novels of Nuruddin Farah

Florence Stratton

Despite a steady stream of novels and his evident ability as a writer, the work of Somali novelist Nuruddin Farah has not attracted wide critical attention until relatively recently. The purpose of this discussion is to provide an overview of Farah's early novels[1] and to highlight some of the relationships among them. As an analysis of Somali institutions is at the heart of the novels, an attempt to elucidate Farah's assessment of them is central to the discussion. A certain amount of attention is paid to Farah's craftsmanship, but because of space limitations it is less than is merited.

Farah focuses his novels on Somalia's political and social structures. Politically, he looks at Somalia's government by a Supreme Revolutionary Council headed by Major General Muhammad Siyad Barre, who came to power in a coup in 1969. On the social plain, he centres on the composition of the traditional Somali family and its organization, in particular the position of women and the relationship between elders and children within the family structure. In simple terms, Farah's ideals are probity in public life and egalitarianism in all relationships. As he finds the composition of the traditional family a corrupting influence in the political domain and the organi-

131

zation of both the family and the government very authoritarian, he attacks the two institutions. The central characters in all of the novels are rebels, activists, radicals, iconoclasts struggling against the established order.

All of the novels except *From a Crooked Rib* are set during the rule of the Barre regime and are explicitly political novels. In them Farah exposes what he sees as the increasingly repressive nature of the General's government and the growing disenchantment of Somalia's intelligentsia with it. The novels are set at successive intervals during the period starting in 1974 with *A Naked Needle*. Through Koschin, the central character of this novel, Farah makes clear that at the time of the coup a change in the political system was sorely needed.

> Before the Revolution...there were over sixty political parties in this Country of Curiosity, and the majority of them came into being with the approach of general elections and became defunct, out of function, with loss or gain of seats in the dissolved National Assembly. Each major tribe had a party to its name, each major party had a major tribe to support her. To finance her, to vote for her, and parties would be offered a democracy-progress-coated name. Some minor but influential tribes had several. And there were the parties under the American umbrella of democracy and there were those under the inspiration, the love-for-liberation movements of progressive Russian communism, not to forget of course the one under chummy Chinese Maoism. The religious partisans had one or two to their name: the Geilani or Saleh Brotherhoods. (p.99)

One of the aims stressed by Barre's Revolutionary Council was the elimination of the clanship system. The government also proclaimed its dedication to the principles of scientific socialism. Koschin, who is a Marxist, is a supporter of the new government, and his stance is representative of that taken by the educated elite during the first few years after the coup. However, by 1974 when the novel is set, Koschin is presented as being one of the few who has remained loyal to the Revolution. The majority, represented by Koschin's friend, Mohamed, has become disillusioned. Koschin, however, is by no means entirely uncritical of the government. He worries, for example, that the General is allowing himself to be deified, and he complains of incompetency and bureaucracy. His uneasiness over some of the developments is also indicated by his membership in an independent political organization made up of Somali intellectuals, although the group has at this point, we gather, a non-subversive function of offering the government constructive criticism. Rather, Koschin believes that for the sake of national development the people must be patient. He is impressed by what the government has undertaken so far, in particular the establishment of a script for Somali and the nationwide literacy campaign. He believes that "a revolution...is a pill that tastes bitter, the benefits of which are felt only when one has gone through the preliminary pain and pestilence" (p.4). "Loyalty to the Revolution," he feels, "is a necessity" if the government is to achieve its goals, the "unification of the different sectors of [the] society" being for him paramount among them (p.16).

A year later in *Sweet and Sour Milk* and still later, in the time of *Sardines,* the government has become in the eyes of Samater, one of the main characters in *Sardines,* "a facsimile of the fascist left anywhere" on which is superimposed "the tribal motif" (p.71). Somalis now live in abject terror of the midnight knock on the door, the prelude to imprisonment without trial and to torture. Rather than pursuing "the unification of the different sectors of [the] society," the government now operates according to the dictates of "inter-tribal, inter-clannish allegiances" (*Sardines*, p.53). It is itself, according to Medina, another of the main characters of *Sardines,* "an incestuous circle which draws its members from the General's clan and those related to this tribal oligarchy through marriage" (p.87). In the one-year interval between the settings of *A Naked Needle* and *Sweet and Sour Milk,* the independent political organization to which Koschin belonged has become a subversive, anti-government organization whose aim is to arouse the masses from the lethargy induced by government rhetoric and to awaken them to the true state of the nation by clandestine dissemination of information on the tyrannical and corrupt practices of the government. By the time of *Sardines,* the organization is moribund. About half of its members have been either killed or imprisoned, while others are in exile and two have betrayed the cause. Even Medina, who, as she is neither in prison nor in exile, is in essence the sole survivor of the group, has been rendered ineffective by the government, which has placed her under a banning order. However, her response to the group's failure to initiate change indicates that Farah is at least cautiously optimistic about the future. She says to her husband, Samater: "We've tried. Koschin. Soyaan. You. And me. Now it's the others' chance to try" (p.241). "The others" appears to refer to the next generation of educated Somalis represented in the text by Sagal, Medina's young friend and disciple. The subversive activities of this group are much more daring than those of their predecessors. They paint anti-government slogans on the walls of the city at night, purposefully courting arrest in order to become "makers of a people's history of resistance" (p.128). Should these fail, then there is still the next generation represented by the children, Medina and Samater's daughter, Ubax, and Sagal's unborn child. Farah seems to have a particular faith in this latter group because of the way he envisages its members will be socialized, a topic which will be returned to later.

At the same time as these novels provide an historical perspective on the shifting attitude of Somalia's intelligentsia to the government of the General, they also reveal that Farah, at least since he started writing *A Naked Needle,* has maintained a hostile attitude towards the regime. This becomes evident, however, only with the recognition that Farah's novels, rather than being separate works, form a series. Not only are all of the novels concerned with the same issues, but many of the characters from each of the novels reappear in the others and, after the first book, all of the main characters belong to the same clandestine organization. This point, which is one of the most interesting of Farah's work, has, in fact, been overlooked by one critic, Kirsten Holst Petersen, who as a result has been unable to distinguish Farah's perspective on events from that of his characters. Writing just prior to the publication of *Sardines,* Petersen reaches the conclusion that "Nuruddin Farah's two books which deal with the revolution, A *Naked Needle* and *Sweet and Sour Milk,* reflect a degree of uncertainty which, however, crystallizes into an opposition to the regime in the manuscript of *Sardines.*"[2] The uncertainty about the regime that is reflected in *A Naked Needle* and *Sweet and Sour Milk,* is not Farah's, but that of his characters. Farah in both cases clearly indicates his own opposition to the regime through his revelation in the succeeding work of the fate of the main characters. For example, at the end of *A Naked Needle,* Koschin, who has resigned from his teaching post because he believes that the behaviour of his principal, a government appointee, is "incompatible with...the aims of the Revolution" (p.18), is safe in bed with Nancy, his English fiancèe. However, at the beginning of *Sweet and Sour Milk* he has been imprisoned and is being tortured. Koschin, not Farah, is, in the words of the novel's epigraph, "the needle that stitches the clothes of people and remains naked itself."

Textual evidence does not indicate at precisely what point in his career Farah discovered the possibility of creating a series of novels rather than individual works. He had certainly mapped out a plan by the time he was writing *A Naked Needle,* for Ebla, the central character of *From a Crooked Rib,* makes a brief appearance in this novel as a shopkeeper with a daughter (p.86), as do Margaritta, one of the major characters in *Sweet and Sour Milk* (p. 90) and Samater of *Sardines,* whom Koschin describes as "the son of a tribal member of a tribal constabulary whose mother bakes maize-cakes on contract for an eating-house" (p.95). In addition, the membership of the political organization to which Koschin belongs becomes the structuring

135

device of the series from this point on. Soyaan, Ibrahim Musse, Ahmed-Wellie, Medina, Samater, and Nasser of the later novels all belong to the same group as Koschin and their fate and the fate of the organization itself is the focal point of the novels. By the end of *Sardines,* Farah has made us aware of the identity of seven out of the ten original members of the group.

Possibly Farah conceived the plan for the series at the time he was writing his first novel. *From a Crooked Rib* certainly belongs to the series. As noted above, its heroine, Ebla, makes a brief appearance in *A Naked Needle,* in addition to which she plays a major role in *Sardines.* But *From a Crooked Rib* is in many ways so different from the other novels that its integration into the series might have been an afterthought. It is linked with the others only through Ebla and through Farah's continuing concern with the suppression of women, which is its theme. Set just prior to Independence, it has no place in the overall design of the following novels and unlike them it contains virtually no explicit allusions to political matters. Furthermore, it was written by a young man who seemingly was in haste to make his appearance on the literary scene. Farah states on the last page of *From a Crooked Rib* that he wrote the novel in less than a month, and this is only too evident. Stylistically and technically, *From a Crooked Rib is* a most unsatisfactory piece of work. It does not prepare the reader for the elegant prose, intricate structures, or displays of technical virtuosity of the later novels. It is marred by infelicities of language, occasional incoherence in its story line, and the inclusion of all sorts of irrelevant and uninteresting details, the last being particularly irritating as Farah, in what appears to be an attempt at naturalism, often points to details such as dandruff (p.4) or a dirty navel (p.160) which, because they are unsavory, lodge themselves in the reader's imagination and putrify there. Given what seems to have been Farah's state of mind at the time, he would very likely have lacked the patience to map out a series.

In addition to allowing Farah to distinguish his own voice from that of the central consciousness of each novel, the novels' serial relationship also produces a number of other effects. With the exception of Ebla, who plays a major role in two of the novels, the other characters who make several appearances have very minor roles in all of the novels but one. When the minor role precedes the major one, which is often the case, no special significance can be attached to a character's first appearance until the series is re-read. When the reader thus encounters someone in one of the earlier novels whom he now knows quite intimately, he experiences a pleasant shock of recognition and the satisfying illusion of participating in a familiar world. In addition, in certain instances of this situation the reader finds that he is required to view a character's behaviour from two different perspectives. This is the case with Samater's brief appearance in *Sweet and Sour Milk:*

> From the distance, Loyaan couldn't make out the others of whom the Minister's entourage was composed...Could that possibly be Samater, the man with whom the Minister was talking now—Samater, Medina's husband...Samater, once a member of the clandestine movement which Soyaan and Ibrahim had started? If it was Samater, could Ahmed-Wellie be far? Give him another five minutes and perhaps he, too, would come.
> "That bastard!" from Ladan.
> Loyaan turned round and with touching sincerity said: "Can't you think of other appellatives, for God's sake? 'That bastard, that bastard, that bastard.' Think of a designation pregnant with generic contempt and universal hate. Traitor. Inhumane. Something like that." (p.230)

As the point of view of much of *Sweet and Sour Milk is* Loyaan's, even on a second reading, the reader is inclined to share Loyaan's complete disgust at Samater's alignment with the government. At the same time, *Sardines* has made the reader aware of the reasons behind Samater's defection from the group. He is not an evil man, covetous of money or power. He is simply overwhelmed by the pressures of conflicting loyalties, a common enough human frailty. The effect created is not unlike what Ngugi achieves by withholding information in *A Grain of Wheat*. The reader is reminded of the hidden complexities underlying much of human behaviour and is warned against making hasty judgements.

However, Farah achieves his main effect in the instances where the minor role follows the major one. In each case a note of doom is sounded as the names of the characters become a litany of the results of the government's repressive measures. The following is from *Sardines:*

> "So Soyaan is dead? And nobody knows what has become of Loyaan? Someone saw him briefly in Rome in the back seat of an embassy car. He looked ill, this person said, and his cheeks were puffed up. The others are in prison; so is Siciliano; Koschin is broken and foams at the mouth, you say, unable to hold his saliva." (pp.22-23)

By delaying imparting information on the fate of his main characters, Farah shocks the reader into an acute awareness of the brutal nature of the General's regime. His handling of Koschin is particularly effective. The news of Koschin's imprisonment announced at the beginning of *Sweet and Sour Milk* gives the reader a severe jolt. The focus of attention at the end of *A Naked Needle* has been on Koschin's relationship with Nancy, and whatever doubts may have been raised about the compatibility of these two, on the last few pages of the novel they seem to be groping their way towards an understanding. The reader does not expect to learn anything more about Koschin because until his imprisonment is declared in *Sweet and Sour Milk* there has been no real indication that the novels constitute a series. The reader thus finds himself wistfully hoping in *Sweet and Sour Milk* that this is not the same Koschin. Farah continues the shock treatment by intermittently referring to Koschin's deteriorating condition.

Several years later when *Sardines* is set, he has been "reduced to a vegetative state" (p.241). The reader eventually acquires the uneasy feeling that Farah has used Koschin, the first of his political heroes, to establish a pattern. Loyaan is already ill. Will Nasser and Dulman, who are arrested at the end of *Sardines,* also be "reduced to a vegetative state"? And what about Medina and Samater? Will they retain their liberty? Thus by withholding information on the fate of his characters from one novel to the next, Farah also creates for his readers a sense of the uncertainty that he sees as dominating the lives of his people under the General's regime.

As stated at the beginning of this discussion, Farah is concerned not only with political tyranny, but also with social tyranny, in particular with the oppression of children and women within the structure of the traditional Somali family. In both *Sweet and Sour Milk* and *Sardines,* Farah focuses on the traditional family as a social unit ruled, as he describes it, with brutal authority by the matriarch or patriarch of the clan. He portrays three of these figures in some detail—in *Sweet and Sour Milk,* Loyaan and Soyaan's father Keynaan, and in *Sardines,* Medina and Nasser's grandfather Gad Thabit and Samater's mother Idil. The effect of these despotic figures on the victims of their power is quite terrifying, as the following passage from *Sweet and Sour Milk* indicates:

> [Loyaan] was a child again; the moon was mild, and he and Soyaan had quarrelled over a ball. Keynaan's crooked smile; his towering height. The fist of power; the power of the patriarch; eyes hard as knuckles. Keynaan had picked up the ball and, without much ado, without any uprush of rage or anger, punctured it and tore it in two. "I will kill him one day," Soyaan had said. (p.36)

Idil's methods are more subtle. She dominates Samater by playing on his filial feelings:

It was an hour later. The sun searched the width and breadth of the sky for a cloud behind which to hide. Idil had made herself comfortable like a queen in her residence.

"Who is this woman?" Samater asked.

"She is your cousin. Your uncle's daughter."

"And where is Rijo, Medina's and my maid?"

"Don't mention that woman's name."

"Did you fire the maid, Mother?"

"Yes."

"By whose authority? Who do you think you are?"

"I am your mother."

He was irritated. He was angry. He was so enraged he was afraid he would do something unbecoming of a son. He walked up and down like a wounded tiger. His eyes were red: he was livid.

"I want this woman out of here. Immediately," he said.

"No. She will not leave. She has every right to be here where I am. She is your cousin, she is your blood."

"I want her out of here, I said."

"You will have to force me to do that physically and I am sure you won't. After all, I am your mother and I want her to be where I am."

"I give you half an hour. I'm going to shave. When I come out, I want her gone. If she isn't, I shall throw her out myself. And if you say so much as a word about it, I shall throw you out too."

A cautious silence; then:

"No respect for your mother?" (p.74)

A lifetime of his mother's emotional harassment has weakened Samater's moral fibre and Farah uses him to illustrate the deleterious effects of the authoritarian family.

These two repressive institutions, the authoritarian family and the authoritarian state, do not, for Farah, exist independently of one another. The structure of the family, he suggests, has conditioned the people to tyranny, so that, despite the fact that traditional Somali political institutions are egalitarian, the people are easily induced to accept despotism. In addition, as indicated above, Farah sees the authoritarian family as an institution which enervates a society by producing individuals whose moral courage has been sapped by a lifetime of intimidation. Much of this surfaces in a conversation between Medina and her mother in *Sardines*:

> "I remember something my grandfather used to say, [said Medina.] 'A woman, like any other inferior being, must be kept guessing, she mustn't be given reason to believe she is certain of anything.'"
>
> "That's right. Children must be kept guessing. They must never see you in your weakest moment. A child is an inferior being when it comes to that. As for the half-raised hand about which the child isn't sure..."
>
> "But that's precisely the same concept as the General's. The masses must be kept guessing. The masses are inferior, they cannot in any case understand how a government functions, they cannot appreciate this or that. No one is sure what will happen; no one is certain who will come knocking on your door; no one must be in a position to know in advance what will take place. It's the same thing..."(p.140)

The two institutions are also mutually supportive, each using the resources of the other to crush opposition to its authority. In *Sweet and Sour Milk* Farah makes explicit the government's reliance on the family by employing as an epigraph Wilhelm Reich's statement that "in the figure of the father the authoritarian state has its representative in every family, so that the family becomes its most important instrument of power" (p.97). He also dramatizes it through Keynaan, who is used by the government to dissipate the effect of the subversive activities of his son Soyaan. In *Sardines* he shows how the family is able to bring political pressure to bear on any of its members who attempt to break with tradition. When Samater, whose mother has been plotting to break up his marriage, finally drives her from his home, she informs her clansmen, who respond as follows:

> One of them predicted he would lose his job. Another threatened to have him fired. A third spoke of how Stalin, when the most powerful man in the world, was forced by the politics of the day to visit his aged mother in Georgia...Another recurring image was how the clan was united against him, how the clan would ask the General to unseat him. (pp.175-76) Samater ignores these threats, and he is detained by the authorities and beaten.

The conclusion that Farah reaches as a result of his analysis is that social conditions in Somalia virtually preclude the development of an effective opposition to the government. The traditional family structure in a modern political state severely retards, if it does not completely prevent, the evolution of political institutions which, rather than serving the self-seeking interests of the authorities, serves the needs of the people. Social reform, Farah believes, is a prerequisite to political reform. Without it, as Sagal says in *Sardines,* even if the General's government is overthrown, it will merely be a matter of one "dictatorship [being] toppled by another military dictatorship, and so on and so forth" (p.32). This is why children like Ubax are so important to Farah's vision of a new society. The process of socialization that they have expe-

142

rienced within the family has been very different from
that of their predecessors. Family relationships have
been egalitarian, not authoritarian. The needs of the
children have not been "taken less seriously than an
adult's" (*Sardines,* p.14).

Because these children have not been subjected to the traditional child-rearing principle of "the half-raised hand" they should have
fewer complexes and be more able than those like Samater to stand
firm against tyranny.

In addition to analyzing the relationship between these two institutions Farah also uses the traditional family to serve as an image of
the state, as a microcosm of the macrocosm. By doing so he is able
to convey a very vivid and immediate impression of the nature of the
General's regime, while at the same time avoiding to a fair degree the
practical problems of dealing directly with recent historical events.
In both *Sweet and Sour Milk* and *Sardines,* Farah makes his intention
quite explicit through his characters' meditations on the organiza-
tional parallels between family and state. The following forms part of
one of Medina's reflections in *Sardines:*

> Medina said that one reason why she opposed the
> present dictatorship was that it reminded her of her
> unhappy childhood, that the General reminded her of
> her grandfather who was a monstrosity and an unchal-
> lengeable patriarch who decreed what was to be done,
> when and by whom. (p.16)

If, on one level, Gad Thabit, Keynaan and Idil represent the
General, what, then, is to be made of Medina's defeat of Idil near the
end of *Sardines?* It does seem to suggest that Farah is hopeful.

Farah treats the suppression of women in much the same way. In
an interview he made the following comment about the women in his
novels: "Like all good Somali poets I used women as a symbol for

Somalia. Because, when the women are free, then and only then can we talk about a free Somalia."[3] Two of Farah's novels, *From a Crooked Rib* and *Sardines,* can be classed as feminist novels and in *Sweet and Sour Milk,* also, the oppression of women is a major concern. In the late 1960s when Farah was writing his first novel, the position of women in African society was not the popular literary theme it later became. At the time only a few authors such as Farah and Flora Nwapa were writing about a situation which has since attracted the attention of many others including Mongo Beti, Buchi Emecheta, Bessie Head, Ngugi wa Thiong'o and Sembene Ousmane.

Although, as noted earlier, *From a Crooked Rib* suffers from serious technical flaws, it is not without merit. Even today when so many other novelists have also dealt with feminist issues, there is something refreshing about Farah's treatment of them in this novel. This arises mainly out of his farcical presentation of the misadventures of Ebla and his portrayal of her character. Ebla is a lively individual and a unique and original thinker. When her grandfather offers her in marriage to an old man in exchange for some camels, Ebla runs away to the city where she takes refuge with her cousin, who first treats her like a slave and then gives her hand to a man with tuberculosis to whom he owes money. Still determined to control her own fate, Ebla elopes with Awill, a young, educated man who carries her off to Mogadiscio, marries her, and then leaves her for several months when his work takes him to Italy. When a photograph of Awill and an Italian woman accidentally falls into Ebla's hands, she takes a second husband in order to spite the first. With Awill's return impending, she regrets what she now considers a precipitous act and engineers a divorce from her second husband. Then she discovers that she is pregnant with a child whose father she cannot with any certainty identify. The story ends with Awill's return and leaves Ebla debating whether or not she should confess to him.

A plot summary does not do justice to the boisterous, farcical element in the novel, nor does it bring out the grim irony inherent in Ebla's situation. Her sex precludes her from determining her own fate. In the absence of independent economic means, a woman is chattel. Ebla slowly gropes her way towards an understanding of this. When she is for the second time sold, she assesses her position and then rails against it:

> From experience she knew that girls were materials, just like objects, or items on a shelf of a shop. They were sold and bought as shepherds sold their goats at market-places, or shop-owners sold the goods to their customers. To a shop-keeper what was the difference between a girl and his goods? Nothing, absolutely nothing.
>
> What agony, what a revolting situation! Naturally women are born in nine months (unless the case is abnormal) just like men. What makes women so inferior to men? Why is it a must that a girl should refund a token amount to her parents in the form of a dowry, while the boy needs the amount or more to get a woman? Why is it only the sons in the family who are counted? For sure this world is a man's—it is his dominion. It is his and is going to be his as long as women are oppressed, as long as women are sold and bought like camels, as long as this remains the system of life. Nature is against women. (p.84)

But in the face of tradition, Ebla is powerless. What she eventually concludes is that the best she can do is develop a strategy that will at least serve her own interests too:

> "With her hands she felt down her body, naked under the sheet; she scratched her sex, then chuckled. 'This is my treasure, my only treasure, my bank, my money, my existence'" (p.160).

Farah's point is that the structure of the Somali family makes prostitutes of all Somali women. The only variable in the situation lies in whether a pimp in the form of a male relation or the woman herself arranges and benefits from the economic transaction. Ebla decides that, rather than being sold by others, she will now merchandise herself. She accepts that she is an object to be bought and sold but she will at least determine the buyer and pocket the profit.

Ebla's pragmatism pays off. When she reappears twenty-one years later in *Sardines,* she is the owner of a prosperous business which she has built up out of property she inherited from the man she married after divorcing Awill. Wealth being the prerequisite for freedom, Ebla is now able to ignore traditional constraints. She is also able to give Sagal, her daughter, "the happy childhood which she herself had not had" (p.33).

Not only, as was stated earlier in this discussion, does *From a Crooked Rib* contain virtually no explicit allusions to political matters, but it appears to have only a social level of meaning until it is considered in the context of the later novels. This context, however, suggests to the reader the possibility of ascribing to Ebla's experiences a quasi-allegorical level of meaning. As the novel is set on the eve of Somalia's Independence, Ebla's status in the society as a material object to be bought and sold with no reference to herself seems to mirror the fate of Africa during the colonial era; and the economic dependency that circumscribes her emancipation is a reflection of the realities of the post-Independence era.

In both *Sweet and Sour Milk* and *Sardines,* Farah makes overt connections between sexual and political oppression. For example, in *Sardines* Medina says, "I'm fighting for the survival of the woman in me...while demolishing 'families' like Idil's and regimes like the General's" (p.246). In *Sweet and Sour Milk* the feminist issue is polygamy. Keynaan takes Beydan as a second wife, makes her pregnant, and then maltreats her. Her constant refrain is "I keep wondering if I will survive this" (p.154 for example). She does not. When she gives birth to the baby she dies.

Although Sardines is in many ways a remarkable novel, one of its most outstanding features is the extent to which Farah has made it a woman's novel. Not only do all of the ideas and actions originate with women—even the children are female—but Farah has given the novel a feminine ambience by suffusing it with female images: "[Ebla and Sagal] would link arms after such an argument and go further into the night which opened up like the teased lips of a vagina" (p.35); "Ebla's smile was light like the water of childbirth, her teeth white like diluted milk" (p.25). The feminist issue in the novel is female circumcision which in Somalia involves infibulation. Farah sees this practice as being at the heart of the suppression of women: "Circumcision reduces the woman to property. A man likes to know that the shirt he's wearing has not been worn by someone else. It is the same with his woman."[4] The operation itself he finds abhorrent, a reaction he conveys very powerfully in the novel by presenting several detailed descriptions of what it entails from the point of view of a woman who has been circumcised, Medina:

> "If they mutilate you at eight or nine, they open you up with a rusty knife the night they marry you off; then [when you give birth to a baby] you are cut open and re-stitched. Life for a circumcised woman is a series of deflowering pains, delivery pains and re-stitching pains." (p.59)

Medina fights desperately to save Ubax from this pain and humiliation and as far as *Sardines* is concerned she is successful. But the social force behind circumcision, the pressure exerted by the traditional family, is extremely powerful, and the experience of the teenage girl born in America of Somali parents who was forcibly circumcised while visiting Somalia hangs ominously over the novel.

Its authoritarian structure is not the only aspect of the traditional family that Farah condemns. He also finds its group loyalties a menace to the proper running of the state: the extended family, according to Farah, precludes probity in public life. Farah conveys his attitude again and again in the novels through the reactions of his protagonists to situations that are common within an extended family framework. Koschin's refusal to give an old man who comes to him a contribution to be used in aid of a kinsman is one example (A *Naked Needle*, p.13). Samater's response to the presence in his house of a cousin is another:

> He was thinking: *I must de-tribalize this house.* He remembered something similar to this which took place not here but at his sister Xaddia's a year before. His mother had filled Xaddia's place with tribeswomen and tribesmen of hers. It was during the worst period of the famine and all the malnourished clansmen and clanswomen who managed to run away from the camps specially erected for them went and were given shelter there as though Xaddia's was a rehabilitation centre. (*Sardines*, p.73)

In the context of African literature, Farah's position on this issue is clearly an extreme one. Many other African writers who, like Farah, are looking for integrity in the public sphere, defend the extended family, arguing that the two are not mutually exclusive, that nepotism and corruption can be rooted out of public life without destroying the traditional social fabric of a nation. At least part of the reason that Farah takes such a hard line may lie in the uniqueness of the Somali situation. The social groupings in Somalia are of a different kind from those in other parts of Africa. All Somalis belong to the same ethnic group, that is they share the same language and culture. Their group loyalties are not to an ethnic group but to kin and clan. Some analysts of the situation, including Farah, feel that this network of family and clan membership permeates Somali life more completely than do ethnic ties in other African nations. In *Sweet and Sour Milk* Farah tries to convey an impression of just how pervasive their influence is through Loyaan's thoughts as he considers how to ask directions to Margaritta's:

> Maybe he should ask the shop-keepers in the area if
> they knew Margaritta or her mother, Loyaan thought.
> Describe? A tall, beautiful woman, with large breasts,
> half-Italian, half-Somali, and with a child; and a villa,
> her own. Can't you do any better, Loyaan? challenged
> the voice in him. Ask. They know no better, anyway.
> Unless you play the game by its rules: identify the per-
> son by tribe. And the computer in their heads would
> be set into motion. If they didn't know the person you
> wished to contact, the villagers would give you the
> address of another clansman or clanswoman who
> would become your honeyguide, buzzing ahead of you
> until you are shown the honeysuckle you're looking
> for. (p.112)

I.M. Lewis, an historian, has the following to say on Somali sec-
tionalism at the time of Independence:

> The divisive influence of Somali "tribalism" was felt as
> more, rather than less frustrating by the fact of its per-
> sistence within an already achieved cultural unity.
> Nationalist leaders saw only too clearly how clan dif-
> ferences and jealousies had in the past facilitated the
> partition of their people by foreign powers. Now these
> same factors, with little diminished vitality, impeded
> not only the full realization of the Pan-Somali goal, but
> also seemed to imperil the stability of the Republic
> itself. Here Somali fears may seem exaggerated; for
> sectional interests and differences of one kind or
> another exist in all countries. Yet it has to be borne in
> mind that what is specific to the Somali case is the
> strength of these particularistic divisions, their uni-

versal appeal, their pervasiveness, and their organization along a single principle of grouping. And, despite
the efforts of some nationalists to deny their existence, there could be no doubt of their continuing
importance in the political life of the new state.[5]

Nonetheless, many will no doubt disagree with Farah. The
extended family may have been romanticized by some writers, but
the communal life it affords and its values of hospitality, generosity
and assistance are very attractive when set against the personal dislocation and bureaucratic institutions of other systems. Farah completely ignores these positive values and thus lays himself open to
the charge of scorning his roots. As well, in societies in which the
nuclear family is the basic unit, non-familial social networks such as
class and institutional ties function to the same end as extended family bonds. Farah's position cannot, however, simply be dismissed. In
addition to the uniqueness of the Somali situation, the combination
of the extended family and public integrity is certainly a difficult one
to achieve.

Thus the main thrust of Farah's novels is an exposition of the
social and political realities in Siyad Barre's Somalia. However, he
also clearly believes that part of the critic's responsibility is to propose alternative structures to the ones he condemns. This is particularly evident in *Sardines,* in which on several occasions he presents
the challenge to his protagonists. Idil, for example, accuses Medina
and Samater of being merely destructive in their criticism:

> "Your generation hasn't produced the genius who
> could work out and develop an alternative cultural
> philosophy acceptable to all the members of your rank
> and file; no genius to propose something with which
> you could replace what you've rejected." (p.78)

As noted earlier in the discussion, Farah believes that social reform is a prerequisite to political reform. At the core of his vision of a new society is the replacement of the clanship system by the nuclear family. Farah clarifies this vision in *Sardines* by focusing on two nuclear family units, the one comprising Medina, Samater and Ubax and the other Ebla and Sagal. As the discussion of the importance of children like Ubax to the process of change in the society indicated, these family units differ from the traditional family not only in composition but also in structure. Relationships are democratic, not authoritarian. The degree of harmony Farah envisages as attainable is revealed in a very beautiful and almost unforgettable passage describing the relationship between Ebla and Sagal, portions of which Farah repeats again and again to emphasize the creative nature of this kind of parent-child relationship:

> They would go together through the entrance of the night's starry doors like two feathered doves, proud in their plumage—two vessels of purity. Like egret, like cattle! They would keep pace with each other and together move in the direction of the nodal knot within the circle which their presence created: an image as fascinating as the whirlpool of a herdsman's dust. The slight wind of the night's sleazy feeling, Ebla's silky touch, Sagal's voice a sort of whisper, coming in waves of words out of which one could build a castle of meanings. Ebla, once provoked, would say: "A myth is butterfly-fragile. Brush the silky dust off it and you kill it. So is motherhood. Sure, she and I disagree on a hundred and one things. Of course, we do. Each of us speaks for a generation, each of us is like a clock keeping its own time. What one gains, the other loses. What my daughter does not have, I have. But we are two persons with two different backgrounds and two separate minds. Although the hands of clocks might not point at the same second, there is no doubt the difference is minor,

particularly when both are functioning well." (p.35)

These new relationships between people individually different but equal, like the traditional family pattern they here supersede, not only illustrate the kind of social order preferred by Farah, but also serve, if not as an image of, at least as a clue to his political ideal. The label which best seems to describe Farah's political views is "democratic socialism." Possibly Farah was at one time attracted to Marxism. In any case, several of his protagonists have been Marxists at some point in their lives. Koschin is one at the time *A Naked Needle* is set and Samater, Medina and Nasser were members of the Communist party during their student days. They soon become disillusioned, and whether Somalia is seen as a true or pseudo-Marxist state seems irrelevant to Farah's view of scientific socialism. On the level of practice, he points to the development of an impenetrable bureaucracy and a self-serving dictatorship. On the level of theory, he finds Marxist doctrine narrow and rigidly Eurocentric. This is the essence of Medina's thoughts in *Sardines:*

> She was a "guest" in the Marxist ideology which she couldn't twist as she pleased for she needed the Soviet or the Chinese or the Yugoslav stamp to give it credibility, she needed the approval of the European intellectual left; in that ideology, at any rate, there wasn't enough space in which she could spread her mat and her exhausted bones. (p.207)

For Farah, Marxist categories are incompatible with certain Somali social realities. The theory does not take into account the centrality of the clan system to all aspects of Somali life. The struggle, as Farah sees it, is not between classes or even clans. Rather it is between the forces for and against the clan system, between the traditionalists, whose basic concern is the maintenance of clan power, and the progressive, advocating change for the betterment of the

152

individual. The main issue for Farah is not the economic oppression
of a class, but the total oppression of women and children by the clan
and of the Somali people by the government. What he wants is freedom from the tyranny of the clan and its political ally.

The agent of change for transforming society for Farah is education. He sees it as the only means of liberating the individual from a
world of narrow constraints. His belief in its efficacy is perhaps best
conveyed in Soyaan's explanation in *Sweet and Sour Milk* of the differences between himself and his father:

> "Not so much generational as they are qualitive—the
> differences between us twins and our father. My father
> grew up with the idea that the universe is flat; we, that
> it is round. We believe we have a perspective of an
> inclusive nature— more global; our views are 'round-
> er'. We believe that his are exclusive, that they are flat
> (and therefore uninteresting) as the universe his insu-
> larity ties him to...My father sees himself as a miniature
> creature in a flat world dominated by a God-figure high
> and huge as any mountain anyone has seen." (p.85)

The members of Somalia's educated elite have all received their
higher education in Europe or America. Farah asks that they adapt the
knowledge and skills they have acquired to suit home conditions. Their
most immediate task, which Farah dramatizes through the activities of
the clandestine organization, is to expose to the masses the real nature
of the nation's political and social institutions and to reveal to them
other possibilities.

Farah does not, however, underestimate the difficulties in effect-
ing the social and political transformations he is looking for. In addition to acknowledging the entrenchment of the establishment, he
points to the capacity of ordinary human failings to frustrate the
potential for change. Education is no absolute panacea. Both
Samater and Ahmed-Wellie betray the cause of freedom. Authority, in

practical terms, is never equally shared and each individual has the propensity to misuse whatever power is invested in him. Medina is accused several times of "trying to shape [her] child in [her] own image" (*Sardines,* p.14), and even Ebla occasionally lapses into the martyred-mother role: "You can't say I haven't tried. All my life I've done all I could to make your life the happiest, all my life, Sagal" (*Sardines,* p.34). Nonetheless, Farah's view of history is a progressive one. He has faith in the ability of individuals to develop the capacity for self-regulation, and although he does not seem to anticipate an immediate change in conditions in Somalia in these early novels, he does envisage a time in the future when a collective effort will bring into being a nation which truly nurtures its people.

NOTES

1. The novels by Farah discussed here are: *From a Crooked Rib* (London: Heinemann, 1970); *A Naked Needle* (London: Heinemann, 1976); *Sweet and Sour Milk* (1979; London: Heinemann, 1980) and *Sardines* (London: Allison and Busby, 1981). Further references are incorporated in parentheses in the text.
2. Kirsten Holst Petersen, "The Personal and the Political: The Case of Nuruddin Farah," *ARIEL,* 12, 3 (1981), 95; reprinted in the present volume.
3. Julie Kitchener, "Author in Search of an Identity" (interview with Nuruddin Farah," *New African,* December 1981, p. 61.
4. "Author in Search of an Identity," p.61.
5. I.M. Lewis, *A Modern History of Somalia: A Nation and State in the Horn* (London: Longman, 1980), p.167.

This paper was written with the support of the Dame Lillian Penson Travel Grants Awarding Committee and the University of Sierra Leone.

NOMADS AND FEMINISTS:
The Novels of Nuruddin Farah

G. H. Moore

Nuruddin Farah has always been a difficult figure to absorb into the emerging categories of African literary discourse. To begin with, he is a Somali, and Somalis are not really expected to write in English, although the poet William Syad had already broken precedent by producing a book of verses, *Khomin,* some years earlier. Indeed, the emergence of a written literature in Somalia is a recent event in any case, since there was no orthography for the language before the early seventies. Until that time, Arabic was the language of the literati, and its uses were homiletic rather than literary. What Somalia did possess was a particularly rich oral literature, most remarkable for its poetry.

The rarity of the Anglophone Somali writer as a species has placed Farah in a situation where his work cannot be seen in a national context, although the unpublished novel he wrote in Somali might have provided that basis for comparison, had its serialization not been stopped by the authorities. Again, Farah writes of a society in which nomadic values seem to be strongly enshrined as central to the national self-image, unlike neighboring Kenya or Ethiopia, where they are the values of a marginal minority, however beloved of the photographer and the tourist brochures. Lastly, and most significantly, Farah intruded a marked sympathy and sensitivity towards womanhood into African Literature, which has generally remained as male-dominated in its orientation as the societies producing it. Such eccentricity can be tolerated in a woman writer but is scarcely looked for in the work of an author who is not only a man but a Moslem too.

Farah's first novel, *From a Crooked Rib* (1970), will do as well as any other to localize these observations. Not only is its central character a girl in flight from her society, but she is one who has been entirely formed by a nomadic pastoral community. Ebla, however, seems to carry her nomadism into sexual matters, where it is scarcely expected of her, and thereby hangs the slight plot of the tale. She changes men with the insouciance of the innocent rather than with that of the libertine, but with no more moral anguish than the latter. Fleeing from bartered marriages with two men she does not accept, she ends up married to two others, simultaneously, who have no knowledge of each other's existence.

Farah tells the story of her sexual pilgrimage in a narrative style that is already unorthodox. The wide-eyed ingenuousness of the heroine is conveyed not only in her own thoughts and utterances, which predominate in the text, but in the naivete which pervades the narrative voice itself: "The lives of these people depended upon that of their herds. The lives of herds depended upon the plentiness [sic] or the scarcity of green grass. But would one be justified in saying that their existence depended upon green pasture—directly or indirectly? Yes: life depended upon green pastures."[1] The tone here is reminiscent of an oral tale, where the teller will often pause to examine rhetorically the truth of what he has just said, before going on to confirm or modify it. This is the literary tradition in which Farah was reared, in which his mother was a well-known oral poet. Although touched from an early age by a multilingual and literary education, Farah still sometimes reverts to this ancient tradition when he writes; not only in his choice of material, but in his very way of presenting it.

Farah's narrative style may be compared with that in which he renders Ebla's own vaguely rebellious inexperience and lust for life. She is a girl who lives entirely in the present and who, having fled from the restraints of tribal life and the confining love of her grandfather, is without any guide to conduct except the usually self-interested advice of others: "Ebla thought over the question many a time, and finally she made up her mind. 'Asha doesn't have to tell me what to do and what not to do. I am twenty, or almost twenty. It is me who marries or is divorced, so she doesn't have to put her nose into my private business. I will tell her to keep out of it. In future I am responsible for whatever I do. Tomorrow, I will tell her. Tomorrow. In future I will be myself and belong to myself, and my actions will belong to me. And I will, in turn, belong to them'" (*FCR*, p.142).

All this is, of course, pure self-delusion. Adrift in the city, without means or family of her own, Ebla is a pawn in the hands of those around her. In the circumstances she is remarkably lucky to have been taken up by the personable young man Awill. But she convinces herself that he has "abandoned" her, merely because he has been sent to Italy by his government, and "divorced" her because she glimpses a photograph of him embracing a white girl over there. She conveniently forgets that he has sent her money through a friend. But her confusion is as much Awill's fault as her own. Typical of this society, he makes no attempt to explain things to her or discuss them with her. The promise of mutual "explanations" with which the book closes is perhaps unlikely to be fulfilled.

"Should I tell you everything, Awill?" Ebla asked
after a long silence.
"Maybe tomorrow when you have thoroughly decid-

ed," he said...

"Tomorrow," said Awill, moving towards her with desire.

"Tomorrow. We will tell each other everything tomorrow. You'll tell me everything, and I shall tell you everything."

Ebla smelt his maleness. She touched his forehead and, as usual, he was hot with desire . . .

"Yes. Tomorrow," Ebla murmured and welcomed his hot and warm world into her cool and calm kingdom." (FCR, p.179)

Farah's own inexperience as a novelist shows in that last, would-be balanced sentence, where "hot" and "warm" conflict with rather than complement each other. *From a Crooked Rib* was completed in India in 1968, when the author was twenty-three. The same period saw his marriage and the birth of his son Koschin. The four years of study at Chandigarh are not directly reflected in his work, but it must be supposed that they helped to determine his choice of English as the language of his first novel.

The path which led Farah to become an Anglophone writer in a society still dominated by Somali oral tradition was a complex one. At the time of his birth in 1945 his native Ogaden, like the whole of Somalia, Eritrea and Ethiopia, was under British military administration. Hence Somalia's claim to the Ogaden and Eritrea's to independence, both the causes of bitter wars since, were temporarily suspended. Everyone held his breath for the European departure which, beginning in Ethiopia, culminated in the independence of a unified Somalia in 1960. At the British withdrawal from Ethiopia, the Ogaden was transferred to the Ethiopian Empire. Amharic was then imposed on the area, as the official language of the Empire. Arabic was acquired through the Koranic School and Italian through the educational system in most of Somalia. Last came English, but this last was the only possible preparation for higher studies in India.

The language and culture which are transliterated in that first novel are, however, Somali, Islamic, and nomadic. The reader is made to feel as strange and ill-at-ease in Mogadiscio as Ebla herself. By contrast, Koschin, the protagonist of his second novel *A Naked Needle* (1976), is a sophisticated, urbanized young teacher, a "been-to" who has studied in England and acquired an English mistress there. Nancy, this last, has firmly taken up Koschin's youthful offer of marriage if neither of them finds a partner within two years of his departure from England. When the novel opens, her arrival is imminent and throws Koschin into a welter of confused emotions every time he hears a plane arriving.

Farah's formal experiments here are far more radical than in the rather simple chronicle of his first novel. There, Ebla's muddled reflections alternated with passages of colloquial, mundane dialogue, as limited in its references as the speakers were in their experience. By contrast, the long monologue through which Koschin conducts the newly-arrived Nancy on a walking tour of Mogadiscio exhibits a wide and often rather showy ingenuity. But through it we gain as sharp a picture as African literature has yet given us of a desperately poor society, boasting only one real city with a few thousand meters of tarred roads before the sand begins; full of prostitutes, suddenly enriched bureaucrats and competing, often bullying foreign aid missions:

> But Nancy, the Russians, with all their political piracy have agreed to construct a dam, Fanoole Dam ...Russians know how to sing their own praises, as Dawn has said. Whereas the Chinese, Nancy, are a very honest people. That dam...
> -Is it half as big as that of Egypt?
> -Aswan?
> -Is that what it is called?
> -Yes
> -Is it?

-Not even a quarter. And they haven't even started a plan. They take their sweet time just like the Americans, the Russians do.

-What friends, the Russians!

-And this is the Chinese Embassy in Mogadiscio, red-starred flag and all; and a little farther up is the Korean Embassy. Neighbours even in the grave, eh, Nancy!

-Romeo and Juliet died separately for the same cause.

-Cause, you said?

-Love is a cause.

-Let us march on, servants of the Lord that we both are, although with different beliefs and different hues, and may He be pleased with him that he sent to preach to all mankind.

-Amen!

-Business streets, Nancy, seldom annoy me. In fact, I am fascinated by them, with everybody girded up as if in a hurry, intent on fighting against the current of time.'[2]

This is generally effective, though one wonders who or what "Dawn" is supposed to be. The relaxed, humorous, observant and noncommittal tone is equally typical of Koschin whether speaking or thinking. It is what keeps him at a distance from Nancy and from all others with a claim upon him. It is what prevents him from giving sincere advice to Barre, a friend who has contracted a disastrous marriage to an American woman, and which prevents him from any real intimacy with Mohamed and Barbara, a much more successfully mixed couple who are frankly and deeply in love. It permits him also his barbarous rudeness to an old man who comes to make tribal claims upon his pocket. Finally, perhaps, it protects him from a full and serious exposure to Somalia itself. The gradual penetration of his defences by Nancy's patient tenderness may be exactly what he needs. The novel ends upon that possibility.

In *From a Crooked Rib*, Farah had already begun to intersperse dialogue with monologue in a manner ultimately derived from Joyce. We are required to jump constantly between what Ebla says and what she thinks but does not dare to articulate. In A *Naked Needle*, monologue becomes really the dominant mode through which we get to know Koschin. It would not be true to say of the above passage that the first and last paragraphs, framing the direct exchanges between Nancy and Koschin, are sharply differentiated from them. They differ in being cast as monologue rather than dialogue, but Farah has already begun to move away here from any hard distinction between what is thought and what is spoken. The opening chapters of the novel, for instance, abound in monologues addressed to Nancy before she had even arrived in Somalia. Koschin is addressing the idea of Nancy, whom he has not seen for two years. They mingle dread with hope, for Nancy's imminent arrival will certainly force him to alter his drifting existence, for better or for worse: "He replaces the book under the pillow, he heaves heavily under the white sheet that now covers him up to his waist.—An epilogue that spoils the strong point of a novel, that is what you are to me, Nancy. However, I do hope that I am wrong in my judgement: that you have changed since we last met" *(NN*, p.2).

This deliberate blurring of the familiar distinctions between the modes of fictional discourse is carried further in the later novels. Passages of dialogue are sometimes so poetic and elaborate in their imagery that they strike the reader as more like thought or authorial description than actual speech.

A *Naked Needle* was written during 1972, when the Somali Revolution of October 1969 was still fresh in its impetus, although its cost to civil liberties was also growingly apparent. In the following exchange, Farah does not manifestly take sides between Mohamed's humanism and Koschin's revolutionary zeal. The latter's attitude towards the Revolution is one of fairly open-minded respect. He does not deny its excesses, but prefers to dwell upon its necessity and its achievements:

> Koschin sits forward.
> -Somalia very badly needed a revolution.
> -Was Somalia in need of terror and horror from dawn to dusk?
> -A revolution, any revolution anywhere at any time, thrives on loyalty. Loyalty is the first code of a revolution's law...To intellectualize about a revolution is certainly trifle-sweet, but to plunge into the depths of its bitterness, only a few can stand. Che Guevara and Fanon, you once said, were your men . . .
> -But they were great!
> -What context? What place? Where? For Somalia?
> -The world.
> -First here. Then elsewhere!
> -Do you believe in all that?
> -Yes. (NN, p.149)

Even Mohamed here displays none of the deep anger which we find later among the embattled heroes and heroines of *Sweet and Sour Milk* or *Sardines*. He registers the terror, but his own life within the novel does not convey the impression that it is all-pervading, penetrating every thought and every action. The leader is still "The Old Man" rather than the General. Farah's approach to the truth about his society has been circumspect because, like Koschin, he recognized the Revolution as a stage in its development from the old tribal politics of 1960-69. A national movement and ideology seemed to be the only way forward, but that ideology has not been made any clearer by the abrupt switch away from Russian and International Communist influence, back to the former American sponsorship, which followed the Ogaden war of 1976. At the time of writing *Sweet and Sour Milk* (1979), however, Farah was unaware of that imminent reversal. Russian influence is not only strong but dominant, extending to penetration of the whole machinery of security, interrogation and incarceration. *Sweet and Sour Milk* is relentless and terrifying in its presentation of tyranny. This is no longer the tragicomedy of revolutionary rhetoric in the midst of obstinate underdevelopment. Rhetoric here is only the least of afflictions to a people who live in the constant presence of fear. What is a boring speech or two, compared with the dawn disappearance of friends headed for detention or execution? The political illusions which present Fascism in the guise of dedicated revolutionary struggle are something more deadly than failure; they suggest that there was never even the promise or prospect of success. Relentless power manipulation, backed by Soviet example and "technical assistance," is what this novel exhibits in daily action and intimate detail. As if to underline the change of mood since 1972, the Koschin of *A Naked Needle* is now in detention and believed by his friends to be in serious danger.

The detail is intimate because here the apparatus of terror is literally "in the family." Keynaan, the father, is a retired security officer, soon to be reemployed by a grateful government. His two sons, by his senior wife, are the twin heroes of a mythic quest, in which Loyaan restlessly searches for the key to his brother Soyaan's sudden and mysterious death.

Because of the novelist's fluid approach to time, the lost Soyaan is as much present to our imagination as the questions of Loyaan, although his death is described in the opening chapter. Moving step-by-step with the survivor, we too piece together the scanty evidence until we are convinced—though without conclusive proof—that Soyaan was eliminated by a government plot, with the aid of an obliging Russian doctor. Handily, the devout Muslim family refuses a postmortem as sacrilegious, so the cause of death remains unknown. The government shows its guilt, if anywhere, by its calculated appropriation of the dead Soyaan, who was a secret but active dissident, as a "Hero of the Revolution." His father eagerly collaborates in the process, and the unpoliticized family cannot really understand Loyaan's indignation and disgust at this betrayal of his brother's memory. After all, the possession of a dead hero should at least bring them some measure of protection, or even patronage. Loyaan's persistence in his quest earns him, however, not patronage, but enforced departure as a supernumerary diplomat in the Moscow embassy. The facade of the regime remains intact and the epic journey in search of truth breaks off inconclusively, lacking any cyclical fulfillment. In the world of "the General" and his advisers, there can be no ritual renewal, because there is no perception of their own decay.

And yet the book does close on a hesitant note of renewal, something a little more definite than a question mark. We are not certain whether Loyaan will after all acquiesce in his "deportation" even though the alternative might be an indefinite imprisonment in which he will ask himself a hundred times a day what good his gesture has done, for himself or his society. In the moments preceding the arrival of his escort to the airfield, his stepmother gives birth to a boy who is duly named Soyaan. Father and son even discover a possibility of communicating with each other. All three of these developments converge with the knock on the door which ends the book. But a synopsis of *Sweet and Sour Milk* can give little idea what it's *about*. As much as anything, it is about the art of narration. Farah's control of time, tense and space keeps us continually moving between obsessive recollections of the boys' childhood; Soyaan's last days of life, with their involvement of his political collaborators, his mistress, and his child; and Loyaan's own discoveries as he moves about the city and gradually discerns the lineaments of his half-known brother's personality and significance. This inclusiveness is not achieved by means of rigid flashbacks, but by the seamless weaving together of impressions, memories, premonitions, and desires. Here the dying Soyaan contemplates telling his brother about their father's impending marriage to a third wife:

> No. He chose not to tell even Loyaan about the young woman whom Keynaan proposed to marry. That would only make matters worse. Soyaan: a man

of intrigue, rhetoric, polemic and politics. Loyaan: a man of melodramatic scenes, mundanities and lost tempers. Loyaan would insist, for instance, on removing all inverted commas from phrases like "revolution in Africa," "socialism in Africa," "radical governments," whereas Soyaan was fond of dressing them with these and other punctuational accessories; he was fond of opening a parenthesis he had no intention of closing. Years ago as a matter of fact it was Soyaan who had suggested that Loyaan should avoid politics as should a patient unprescribed drugs; "You stay where you are, in that region of Baidoa, you do your job well and you are the most revolutionary of revolutionaries"—inverted commas removed! Hiccup. Soyaan lay quiet under the sheet like a tucked-in child. Hiccup . . .

"And how is Father?"

"He was hic here a while ago."

"How is he?"

A powerless patriarch, the grandest of them hic all.

"We are on the worst of hic terms."[3]

Here we move in a few lines from the immediacy of Soyaan's decision of silence to his (or the author's) ironic reflections on the differences of temperament between the twins which have shaped their recent careers (Soyaan as a high government functionary, Loyaan as a provincial medical officer). Soyaan's silence returns to our attention at the end of the paragraph and is made louder by his brother's sudden question and his evasive reply. Irony returns to patch over his reticence, which protects his identity right up until the ensuing moment when he "hiccups his last," clutching the hand of the brother he hardly knows, and perhaps thereby drawing him after, filling Loyaan's mouth with questions he had scarcely dared to ask before.

The quest motif means that the consciousnesses of the two

brothers dominate the action. Having diverged in adult life, they gradually converge again as Loyaan discovers more and more details of Soyaan's public life and of his private convictions, which are profoundly against the whole trend of the Revolution. A scrap of paper found under the pillow of his deathbed reads in part: "The withered hope of a dream leafy as autumn. Our throats have pained, the latest encomium is too long to give an encore to. Listen to the knock on your neighbour's door at dawn. Hearken: the army boots have crunched grains of sand on the pavement by your window. Listen to them hasten. Listen to the revving of the engine. They've taken another. When will your turn come?" (*SSM*, p. 39). The path of Loyaan's quest, however, is illuminated mainly by the women who have loved his brother. Their sister Ladan has had to content herself mainly with a domestic role, but has radiated upon him a deep and piercing tenderness. Understanding both brothers and needing what both represent, she takes refuge in imagery to express it: "To Ladan, Soyaan was the braille of her otherwise unguided vision. Loyaan was the brother who enabled her to sow her moons and bright days with nightly stars" (*SSM*, p.17). More actively involved with Soyaan's projects and concerns is his emancipated mistress Margaritta, a divorced Italian-Somali journalist who has borne him a son. Margaritta is protected to some extent by her wealth and her Italian citizenship, but it is rumored that she is also, or was, protected by the Minister to the Presidency. This Russian-trained politician seems more and more likely to have been involved in Soyaan's murder (by a lethal injection), and is certainly involved in the plot to "steal his soul" by proclaiming him a posthumous Hero of the Revolution whose last words were "Labour is Honour." Hampered by his own hot temper and indiscretion, ill-suited to assume his brother's mantle, Loyaan is well aware that he is walking through a minefield in quest of Soyaan's ghost. When a man cannot trust his own father, whom is he to trust?

The dialogue in *Sweet and Sour Milk* (images of the two brothers, perhaps?) is generally tauter than that of A *Naked Needle,* with its ironic digressions and more relaxed tempo. Words here are used to

166

locate the other person in a kind of moral darkness where few are what they seem. Occasionally Farah's search for the poetic phrase to decorate the speech of his characters goes a bit off the rails, however. His aim, though, is to articulate the images which glow in the minds of his character, but which may not rise into speech in everyday reality.

Just as Koschin was used to provide a frail link between the action of the last two books, so Medina provides a bridge into the next one. She has been mentioned by Margaritta as a sophisticated journalist, but the reader has not encountered her. In *Sardines* she occupies the center of our attention. This Balzacian device of slightly overlapping casts of characters helps to give Farah's work an air of comprehensiveness in its treatment of the Somali scene over the past two decades. A reflection of Medina's about whom to put into the rooms of her imaginary house brings the reader up to date on what has happened to the principal cast of *Sweet and Sour Milk:* "She crossed out the names of Soyaan (dead), Loyaan (forced into exile), Koschin (in prison), Siciliano (in prison), Dr. Ahmed-Wellie (traitor)..."[4] So we learn that Loyaan did after all accept to be silenced and neutralized in Moscow, that his suspicions of Ahmed-Wellie were well-founded, that two members of Farah's earlier casts are in prison. But there, with the labels attached in that early paragraph, we leave them. Our concern in *Sardines* will be principally with Medina and her search for "a room of one's own. A country of one's own. A century in which one was *not* a guest (*S*, p.3).

The trouble with this search, as the reader perceives it, is that everyone and everything around Medina becomes the casualty of it. By abandoning her husband Samater for ill-defined reasons, she deprives her daughter Ubax of a father whom she desparately needs to counterbalance her mother's voracious attention. By fleeing from her own house and moving to her brother's, she leaves Samater to the mercy of his implacable mother Idil. Medina indeed *has* a country, Somalia, but has become alienated from it both by upbringing (mainly overseas) and temperament. The latter is summed up by an aside of the author: "She was, in a manner, like her father Barkhadle. She was as confident as a patriarch in the rightness of her decisions" (*S*, p.5). Such decisiveness would be all very well if her decisions did not so often strike the reader as ill-considered and poorly-motivated. In a rare flash of self-knowledge, Medina wonders at one point whether her search for "a life defined like the boundaries of a property" may make her "harsher towards herself, unfair to Samater, obsessive about Ubax" (*S*, p.6). All these doubts are well founded. Samater loves her deeply and her desertion causes him to deteriorate rapidly. His acceptance of a ministerial post earns Medina's outright condemnation, but no account is taken of the real difficulties of the choice. Leaving aside the steady pressure of friends and clansmen to accept a promotion which will benefit them also, there is the more complex question of allegiance. Above a certain level of education, an individual is likely to find that refusal to serve the regime amounts to a refusal to participate in the nation's development in any capacity. Active opposition will certainly not be tolerated and can only end in death or imprisonment. The alternative of exile too often leads to a situation where one is contributing to the development of other countries rather than one's own. There remains the choice of covert opposition, of doing good by stealth and avoiding open confrontations with authority. This was Soyaan's choice, and nothing in the book indicates to us that the well-intentioned Samater was incapable of making it. Medina's own action in accepting editorship of the national daily and immediately using it as an instrument of challenge seems flamboyant rather than useful. She cannot seriously have expected the regime to let its one national organ be used in this way. Unless she was more intent on self-glorification than on positive activity, she would have done better to reject the post.

Later, we learn that by accepting it she was to some extent playing out a scenario written for her by the General. Two weeks after sacking her and placing her under a banning order, he offered Samater the Ministry. But it was understood that his refusal of it would entail imprisonment and perhaps death for some of his tribesmen. These realities are clearer to the uneducated Ebla, heroine of Farah's first novel who now reappears as a middle-aged mother, than they are to the sophisticated but self-absorbed Medina.

As for Medina's obsession with Ubax, the following exchange conveys it as well as any:

> "You want me to be just like you, remember titles of all the books I see, remember every story anybody tells me, remember who said what to whom...Leave me alone. I'm only eight years old" . . .
>
> "Of course I want you to be like me. But I want you to grow up healthy and independent. I want you to do what you please."
>
> "Why don't you let me go and play with Abucar, Omar and Sofia?"
>
> "When you come home, your language suffers from lack of originality. You keep repeating yourself, saying the same thing. I want you to speak like an enlightened child."
>
> "Why don't you let me go to school like the other children, then?"
>
> "Because schools teach you nothing but songs of sycophancy and the praise names of the General. And because I can teach you better than they..." (S, pp.12-13).

Thus Ubax is harnessed to the chariot of Medina's search for independence. Denied a father, playmates, toys, or normal schooling, she is in effect denied a childhood, in exchange for an enforced precocity and a devouring possessiveness.

The fact that Medina occupies center stage for so much of the book's action creates, therefore, certain problems. The reader is likely to be exasperated quite as often as sympathetic. Her self-righteousness seems to make her incapable of seeing the reality which others, lacking her privileged and alienated upbringing, are forced to inhabit.

Hence her example, if intended as a bravely feminist search for liberation, is unlikely to be of much use to them. Leadership there has to
come from those who are deeply in and of the society, rather than from
those who wilfully seek "a life defined like the boundaries of a property," something quite beyond the possibilities of most Somalis.

To take one example, Medina's flight from her mènage with
Samater and Idil is seen by her as a noble act of self-liberation. But it
can equally be seen as a flight from the challenge of the situation. Nor
can the old lady be expected to throw her traditional education aside
and embrace a secular way of life she has been brought up to consider sacrilegious. What is called for, then, from the younger, better-
educated and supposedly more flexible woman is tact, understanding, and sympathy. Idil does, after all, love Samater in her own peculiar way. Perhaps the core issue of the fight, the refusal to have Ubax
circumcised, could have been won by such an approach. Medina
prefers to give up both the fight and Samater, leaving Idil in full possession of the field. Her own mental imagery accepts this:

> "The General's power and I are like two lizards
> engaged in a varanian dance of death"—the emphasis
> on power and not on the General, power as a system,
> power as a function. Was Idil part and parcel of that
> power? The sky would fall in on anyone who upset a
> pillar of society—in this case Idil. So Medina would go
> about with care; they were like monitor lizards in com-
> bat, each dancing the tango of its strategy, chest to
> chest, face to face...She would rather be like the mata-
> dor who gives way when the bull charges at him blind
> as red blood. (*S*, p.52)

To the relationship of Medina and Ubax is counterposed that of
Ebla and her daughter Sagal. Circumstance rather than choice has
forced intimacy upon these two. Ebla has borne only one living child
and, long divorced from Awil, has been widowed of her second hus-

band. A deep physical love and sympathy binds Ebla to Sagal, but she is careful to avoid the sort of mental and emotional tyranny which Medina often displays. And Sagal has taken the intellectually dominating Medina as her mentor; the prompter of her reading, her ideas, her generous but confused ideals. She does not recognize that Medina is in some way using her as a teenage proxy, just as Ubax is her proxy in the younger generation. In her anxiety to protect these two from the sort of traditional subjection she suffered as a child, Medina has fallen into the role of a new-style matriarch.

Sagal believes herself to be all head and her mother Ebla all heart. But Ebla's radiant common sense has a much juster picture of Sagal's nature: "Her ambition knew no limits, her daydreams knew no end, her goals were unreachable. She was never realistic, never walked with her feet on the ground, never woke to reality when she had dreamed" (*S*, p.40). Farah's other full-length portraits of women in this novel include the raped girl Amina who, in defiance of her society, has rejected her rapist but kept her child. There is Samater's sister Xaddia, whose job as an air hostess enables her to act as courier for friends and whose use of the pill has caused a bitter quarrel with her mother Idil. There is the rather dubious Black American girl Atta, whose conspicuous seduction of Samater leads to his disgrace and her deportation. There is Sandra, the Italian communist who has known Medina and Samater at university, who waltzes into Mogadiscio as a privileged visitor whose approval is valuable to the threadbare regime, and whose air of condescension towards her friends is especially responsible for Medina's sense of being a guest in her own continent and her own century. Of all these, it is Xaddia who surprises Medina with a few home truths about herself:

> "I cannot take it any more," Xaddia said.
> "What? What is it that you can't take any more?"
> "The charade. Your politics. The fact that you will not accept defeat. You are a gambler who having won thinks that another win is in the offing. You are a habit-

ual gambler."

"You don't understand anything," Medina said.

"No, my dear Mina, and I am not a Sagal or one of those you give a book to read when something goes wrong," shouted Xaddia...

When Medina didn't say anything Xaddia continued:

"You pawn and pawn until there is nothing or nobody left to put up to auction. Yesterday it was Samater, today Nasser [Medina's brother] and Dulman; tomorrow—who knows?—Maybe it's my turn; the day after tomorrow, Sagal. When will you stop being obstinate and start seeing reason? Will you never concede or accept defeat?" (S, pp.245-46)

Medina comes badly out of this exchange. Yet beneath Medina's arrogant defiance may linger a recognition that she has for too long confused the personal and the political; that the price to others is somehow always higher than to herself. That this is not a specifically feminist insight on Farah's part is shown by comparison with the rather similar manipulative role of Yussuf in his unpublished play *Yussuf and His Brothers,* produced at the University of Jos in 1982. The constant manipulation of others, in whatever cause, is a form of domination which perpetuates the power relations that both Medina and Yussuf claim to oppose. The last pages of *Sardines* gleam with a faint recognition of this in Medina's mind as she and Ubax are reunited with Samater at last.

But if the feminism of *Sardines* can be, and doubtless will be misconstrued, the book remains a powerful and ranging account of embattled Somali womanhood. In that sense, it is a nice complement to Farah's first work in which, on an obscure impulse of revolt, Ebla crept out of the nomadic encampment all those years before. Ironically, the illiterate Ebla has proved to be a more effective feminist than the sophisticated Medina. She demands less from her society, yet she has succeeded in winning from it a space in which to live her own life. As a mother too, she displays a clearer understanding of the respect owed to others' personal freedom. In her, nomad and feminist have achieved a curious fusion.

NOTES

1. Nuruddin Farah, *From a Crooked Rib* (London: Heinemann, 1970), p.7. Subsequent references to this edition appear in the text after the abbreviation *FCR*.

2. Nuruddin Farah, *A Naked Needle* (London: Heinemann, 1976), p.105. Subsequent references to this edition appear in the text after the abbreviation *NN*.

3. Nuruddin Farah, *Sweet and Sour Milk* (London: Allison and Busby, 1979) pp.19-20. Subsequent references to this edition appear after the abbreviation *SSM*.

4. Nuruddin Farah, *Sardines* (London: Allison and Busby, 1981), p.8. Subsequent references to this edition appear in the text after the abbreviation *S*.

AUTOCRACY AND THE LIMITS OF IDENTITY:
A Reading of the Novels of Nuruddin Farah

Felix Mnthali

Authoritarianism in the family as well as autocracy in the state, against a background of an intense and passionate search for and assertion of identity by individuals and by groups, form the alternating and often interlocking angles of vision towards which the fiction of Nuruddin Farah moved in the trilogy, *Variations on the Theme of an African Dictatorship.*[1] The clusters of linguistic resources mustered by Farah in all of his novels point in two directions which continually criss-cross along an enormous historical and spatial canvas. Elsewhere in a study of the symbolism and imagery of change in African literature a similar use of recurrent clusters of linguistic resources was termed "semiotic constants."[2]

In Farah's novels, especially those of the trilogy—*Sweet and Sour Milk* (1979), *Sardines* (1981) and *Close Sesame* (1983)—the unnamed General casts a shadow over everyone and everything in Somalia. He

175

is presented to us complete with his ninety-nine names and his slogans including one which tells us that "there is no general but our General."[3] He is a product of the peculiar circumstances surrounding the history of Somalia. In his manipulation and oppression of the people of Somalia, however, he belongs to a type which has become all too familiar on the African continent. Nothing, and certainly no one, seems able to dislodge him from the strangle-hold which he exercises on his country. It should surprise no one that he is able with impunity to blaspheme the discourse of Islam. His faith-like ideologies which he discards at will are only marriages of convenience. What really matters to him is a kinship system which dates back to nomadic times. His policies, such as they are, are built around a Machiavellian manipulation of the clan structure of Somalia. It has been observed that in "real" life General Siad Barre pays his greatest attention to three clans. These are: firstly, the *Marehan*, his own clan; secondly, the *Ogaden*, his mother's clan; and thirdly, the *Dulbahante*, his son-in- law's clan.[4] It is important to distinguish the novelist's General from that of historians and social scientists as failure to do so has often resulted in reviewers and critics insisting on reading or wanting to write books which they feel Farah should have written. Farah's General is the sum-total of the motifs, images, symbols, episodes, and even epigraphs employed in his novels.

In *Sweet and Sour Milk*, for example, Keynaan exercises his prerogative as a father and as a patriarch to cause pain to his sons. When they are young he vividly implants in their tender minds the image of absolute cruelty: "Loyaan was with Soyaan, and the twins were fighting over a ball. Towering above was this massive figure, their father, who snatched the ball from them and cut it in two."[5] That such a cruelty is defended on cultural grounds enables Farah to neatly equate Keynaan with the General and to show how the General, like a typical authoritarian father, is dispensing cruelty, intrigue, and secrecy as well as the rewards and punishment characteristic of a regime which thrives on sycophancy and the manipulation of ethnic divisions in society. Keynaan appropriates to himself the power of life and death over his wife and over his children in the same way that the General appropriates to himself the power of life and death over the people of Somalia. We are then able to see why Farah's General exercises such a strangle-hold over his country. Above all, we are able to seriously ponder over the real source of the "staying power" of some of Africa's more notorious dictators. Their authoritarianism is accorded a base in social arrangements which have long become a burden to contemporary Africa but which continue to exercise a great influence on the majority of Africa's populations. When the General decides to undermine Soyaan's standing among the members of his band of intellectuals who have resolved to "tackle" the regime, he uses Soyaan's own father to have the dead Soyaan posthumously made out to be a supporter of the regime's policies. Soyaan is falsely said to have uttered with his dying breath one of those very slogans he has been detesting all his life: "Labour is honour and there is no general but our General".6 The basis of the General's success here is to be found in the attitude of Soyaan's father, Keynaan, towards his sons. He feels and maintains that he can do with them whatever he wants, including handing over the story of Soyaan's life to the General's functionaries who "doctor" it according to their own image. His reasons for such a sacrilege are as old as patriarchy and the nomads' wells in the desert:

> I am the father. It is my prerogative to give life and death as I find fit. I've chosen to breathe life into Soyaan. And remember one thing, Loyaan: if I decide this minute to cut you in two, I can. The law of this land invests in men of my age the power. I am the Grand Patriarch.7

In "real" life the "Grand Patriarch" of Somalia cut people in halves as if their lives did not mean very much. Between October 1969, when he took power, and the middle of 1980, Siad Barre had already executed sixty-one people and imprisoned without trial many others.[8] Many more executions and detentions followed. In *Sweet and Sour Milk* Farah mentions only one execution, that of the ten sheikhs who are accused of using religion "for the purpose of breaking up the unity of the Somali people or weakening or damaging the authority of the Somali state."[9] The seemingly muted voice which such a selection carries has its own quiet strength. It is not until the third part of the trilogy, in *Close Sesame*, that Farah takes us back to the murderous sanctions through which the General keeps the people of Somalia in perpetual fear of his secret police. In *Close Sesame* one of the people accused of a failed plot to assassinate the General happens to be a member of the clan which is in alliance with the General's own clan. This man is neither detained nor charged with any crime. The General simply orders the man's clan to "look into the matter" and the clan prevails on the man's father to kill his own son to appease the General. The logic behind this kind of cruelty is similar to the one used by Keynaan in *Sweet and Sour Milk* to desecrate his son's memory. A father's unquestionable right to deal with his son as he sees fit derives from his having been "the man who planted and watered the tree in question. If a farm is yours, what you do with your trees is primarily your business and no one else's."[10] It is in *Close Sesame* that the General's manipulation of the clan structure of Somali society comes into its own. The remote and shadowy figure of the General is in everything and in everyone's life and yet the immediate impression is that of clans fighting among themselves while the real culprit continues to remain detached from it all. He resuscitates clan animosities by seeming to give power to the clans while closely monitoring their discussions and making sure that his secret police plants the right amount of fear in everyone's mind.

The power of Nuruddin Farah's fiction lies less in any of its plots than in the author's ability to compress time to a few days and space to a remarkably limited geographical area at the same time that he covers events which encompass the lives of several generations and the landscape of the whole of Somalia. In Farah's fiction very little seems to happen and yet we are shown a great deal of what constitutes the lives of ordinary people. *Sweet and Sour Milk* is the most accomplished example of Farah's handling of compression. We do not begin the story at the beginning but somewhere near the end which is itself a beginning. Most of our time will be spent not with the central character who suddenly "hiccups his last" after a food poisoning in which the hands of the General and his KGB advisers hover in the background, but with his twin brother who in arranging his brother's funeral comes face to face with the kind of intrigue, bureaucracy, and persecution from which his work as a provincial dental officer has until now shielded him. What we end up following with keen interest is the education of the dead man's twin brother into the intricate web of life and death in a police state. The twin brothers have similar sounding names: Soyaan and Loyaan. Indeed one of the mourners at Soyaan's funeral continually speaks of the deceased as Loyaan even after being corrected by Loyaan himself and by the other mourners. The national daily speaks of Loyaan when it means Soyaan and ends up canonising the wrong "martyr". What Farah is doing here is to make the individual identity of the victims of autocracy less important to the reader than their representational or symbolic significance. Soyaan becomes everyman, though by his education, training and position as an economist in the office of the President he belongs to his country's intelligentsia. Farah is consequently showing us that even this group is powerless before the General. Loyaan's father tells us that the General has nothing to fear from Somalia's intellectuals:

> "The General fears no threat which might come from you and your lot. You have no common ideology for which you fight. You have no organised protest. Skirts. Air tickets to Europe. Posh cars. These are what you are after. Security provides them and you are no threat. The General fears tribal chieftains or men of his age."[11]

We have already seen how even those men of his own age can be made to do what the General wants them to do. *Sweet and Sour Milk* gives us not only an intellectual who represents the other intellectuals in his country but also manages to show us in what way these intellectuals are now "captives"in their own country.[12] We also see how one family has become the symbol of all the divided families in Somalia where children see one thing and their parents see something else. Soyaan's funeral enables us to see all classes of society and to gather both from what they say and what they can only say in whispers the atmosphere of silence and fear which the General's regime has inculcated in everyone. As the funeral arrangements slowly unfold and the procession unwinds its way to the cemetery we learn about the Byzantine ways of Somali bureaucracy which bear an uncanny resemblance to other bureaucracies all over Africa. Farah's portrayal of autocracy shows how closely African dictatorships resemble one another. The scene at Soyaan's funeral could have taken place anywhere in Africa today. The obligations towards beggars and towards the poor are similar to those we see in Sembene Ousmane's Senegal. The treatment of beggars during the visits of foreign heads of state is also familiar. In some countries the police go so far as to lock up people with criminal records even though at the time of the visit such people have not actually committed any crime.

From the day Soyaan dies after coming home complaining of a stomach disorder to the day his brother Loyaan is forced into the splendid exile of a minor diplomatic posting takes only a week. Yet it is within the space of that week that we are able to learn a great deal not only about the twin brothers and their family, but also and especially about their unhappy country. It is everyday life we see in Farah's novels. What is new and refreshing is how in presenting everyday life Farah manages to take us on a journey of exploration through the intricate tangles of life in the Mogadiscio which the General's repression and ethnocentrism have created. We see how ordinary people have learned to distinguish fact from the regime's fiction. We see the social life of all classes of society, especially that of the country's middle-class intelligentsia. Above all, we see how the regime closely watches the movements of this intelligentsia and how it succeeeds in neutralising whatever thoughts of resistance such an intelligentsia might be capable of organising. Soyaan comes across as a lonely figure and it is easy to see how an unscrupulous regime would find it advantageous to co-opt him posthumously and destroy his standing among his friends. He has been fighting lonely battles with the General, trying to humanize what is essentially an inhumane way of running a country. During one such confrontation the General is irritated by Soyaan's insistence on constitutionalism and by his protest at the execution of the ten sheiks who had been accused of using religion to undermine the unity of the people of Somalia. We find the General resorting to the kind of argument dictators have used throughout history: "...have I ever introduced myself to you, young man? I *am* the constitution. Now you know who I am, and I want you out of here before I set those dogs of mine on you and you are torn to pieces. Out."[13] Fighting lonely battles is as frustrating and as futile as attempting to change autocracy from within. The problem with the "captive intelligentsia" of Farah's Somalia, as with their equally captive brothers and sisters in other parts of Africa, is that they have been either politically marginalised by being isolated from the rest of society or co-opted into their countries' ruling and exploitative elites.[14] In such a situation any meaningful attempt at influencing change is bound to lead to the sort of bizarre preoccupation with secret memoranda and "kamikaze "attempts at assassinating the General which form the bulk of the "detective" layers of both *Sweet and Sour Milk* and *Close Sesame*. The ennui of a life in which revolution and discussions on change are confined to the closed doors of the houses of a close-knit band of intellectuals can be seen in the demandingly slow pace at which *Sardines* moves. Little happens here—precious little that we do not already know from earlier novels about the repression and ethnocentricity which characterize the General's rule. What Farah achieves in *Sardines*, although the novel is part of the trilogy concerning dictatorship, is a dramatization of the kind of narcissistic "much ado about nothing" which now takes up most of the time of Somalia's frustrated intellectuals, especially that of women such as Medina and her disciple and protege Sagal who appear to be steeped in mere frivolities.

We need to take a closer look at Farah's intellectuals. They are determined to do something about their country's repression but what they actually plan does not measure up to the magnitude of the repression going on in Somalia. That is why a close examination of Soyaan's famous memoranda may throw some light on the failure of Soyaan's group to bring about any meaningful change. Initially there seems to be only one memorandum which has now become the bone of contention between Soyaan's twin-brother Loyaan and the regime represented by the Minister to the Presidency. We later see that there are, in fact, several memoranda including one on which Soyaan had been collaborating with one of the General's Vice-Presidents. Taken together these memoranda accurately describe the level of repression going on in Somalia. They are also fairly detailed on the kind of culture of fear and silence which the regime has created.

> "Clowns, Cowards, and (tribal) upstarts: these are who I work with. The top civil service in this country is composed of them. Men and women with no sense of dignity, nor integrity; men and women whose pride has been broken by the General's Security; men and women who have succumbed and accepted to be humiliated. Are you married? Do you have children? How many? Five? A wife and a mistress? Plus the tribal hangers-on who have just arrived and whom you support? Listen to the knock on your neighbour's door at dawn. Hearken: the army boots have crunched grains of sand on the road leading away from your house. Listen to them hasten. When will your turn come? Yesterday was your colleague's turn. You saw his wife wrapped in tears, you saw how she averted her eyes. Does she know where they have taken her

husband? She goes from one police station to another. The police know who she is, and what she is seeking, but no one will tell her anything...Hearken: the army boots have crunched grains of sand on the pavement by your window. They've taken another. When will your turn come?"[15]

It is in the area of what needs to be done that the memoranda reflect weaknesses which are common to the thinking of intellectuals all over Africa. Those who become aware of the problems around them rarely come around to broadening their support among the peasants and the "people of the city" in their countries. There is in Soyaan's memoranda no mention of any recruitment drive beyond the circle of those intellectuals who know one another well. There is no analysis of the country's economic, social and political needs beyond the regime's repressive practices and the inordinate influence of the Soviets and their KGB. Admittedly, when the power of the secret police is as extensive as it is in Farah's Somalia, proper organization and a thorough analysis of a country's deep-seated malaise become extremely difficult. What Soyaan's memoranda tell us about his group's programme of action as well as about its membership does not give us reason to expect any momentous change. His friend and close collaborator Ibrahim "Il Siciliano" tells Loyaan that the clandestine group of intellectuals and professionals who have taken an oath "to serve not the interests of any superpower but this nation's" would collect, disseminate and eventually publish information about the regime's atrocities:

"We can foretell that the written word, more powerful than the gun, will frighten them. In the chaos ensuing from that, and just as they start their purge, we will announce our clandestinity and publish a leaflet of our intention, and you will see that more people will adhere to it. Then we will baptise it as a movement, we

183

will give it a name."[16]

No sooner are these words said than the speaker is taken into detention and Loyaan is forced into exile. The regime is not only ruthless but efficient in its ruthlessness. By the end of *Close Sesame*, which is also the end of Farah's trilogy devoted to the ways of the Siad Barre dictatorship, Soyaan's group has neither embarked on a recruitment drive nor expanded its membership beyond the confines of its own class, that of the petit bourgeois intellectuals. That makes the group an easy target for the regime's secret police and it comes as no surprise that by the end of the trilogy the group has been decimated through detentions, exile, co-optation, and murder. Meanwhile the regime is saturating the nation with its propaganda and its slogans. Its Green Guards are busy turning their head of state into a god against whom all assassination attempts will prove futile. Against such an objective situation the kind of resistance chosen by Soyaan's group assumes the puny stature of the helpless little creatures pitted against implacable forces dramatized in the epigraphs to the chapters of *Sweet and Sour Milk*. Nowhere is the futility of attempting to assassinate the General made more poignant than in the final chapter of *Close Sesame*. In this chapter a nationalist hero who has distinguished himself in the struggle against colonialism and who has also suffered at the hands of Somalia's post-colonial rulers is drawn into his son's anti-government plot after his son is killed in yet another unsuccessful assassination attempt on the General. The old hero, Deeriye, comes close to shooting the General. He succeeds in infiltrating the presidential guards and is standing at attention as the President is awarding medals to heroes of the land. Deeriye also fails to assassinate the General and his failure brings home to Farah's readers one of those quirks of irony which come perilously close to lending ambiguity to the author's point of view. Deeriye pulls out, "by mistake, prayer-beads instead of a revolver to shoot the General..."[17] In a different version of this tragic episode we are told that "the prayer-beads like a boa-constrictor, entwined themselves around the muzzle of the revolver—and Deeriye could not disentangle it in time."[18] As the old hero slumps to his death his body is nearly cut in half by the machine-gun fire of the presidential guards.

It would not be correct to see in the old hero's manner of departure both from the trilogy and from the political scene any questioning by Farah of the old man's combination of righteous indignation against political chicanery with religious devotion. After all, one of Deeriye's greatest charms is his attachment to both his religion and his nationalist principles. Indeed one of the articles found on the old man's person is "a pamphlet on the underground activities of the ANC."[19] What Farah is most clearly emphasising here is the fact that Soyaan's group has been out-maneuvered at every turn in its struggle against the regime by forces which were not carefully taken into account when the group formed. The regime's use of the tactics of "divide and rule" through both co-optation and ethnic rivalries is such a force. Its ability to "mobilize" the population against any particular group of people is another. Its ability to manufacture slogans and any hotch-potch of "ideologies" to disguise its reliance on and exploitation of the country's clan structure is yet another. The list is endless and Farah appears to acknowledge his intellectuals' shortcomings by allowing them to explain their own position. An examination of the thinking of one of them will shed light on some of the causes of the group's failure. The physician Ahmed-Wellie maintains the following position:

> "Against the ethics of political violence, the weak have
> no means of survival other than to collaborate, up to a
> point, with the powerful. It is while collaborating that
> strategies can be studied...I consider it symbolic: that
> I wash the blood they shed; that I bandage the sores
> they open; that I nurse the wounds they inflict upon
> the innocent..."[20]

This seems to be the kind of position most likely to play into the hands of any repressive regime. By choosing to ameliorate the wounds of repression Ahmed-Wellie is conceding to the regime the initiative for change. From such a position to one of collaboration is only a step away. Although in *Sweet and Sour Milk* we last see Ahmed-Wellie being taken into detention there has been so much ambivalence about him that Loyaan concludes he is an informer, a conclusion which, like Soyaan's national honour, sows confusion among the members of his group. What we see in Farah's Somalia is fascism gone wild. To confront such a fascism Soyaan's group needs a much better organization and greater dedication than we are allowed to see.

It is no doubt from a realisation of the Herculean task confronting all those who seek change that the edge of gloom intrudes on Farah's fiction. The allegorical thrust of the epigraphs which precede every chapter in *Sweet and Sour Milk* is that a wall of insecurity surrounds everyone and everything, especially around those little things and little people who have no way of defending themselves, let alone confronting unaided the immovable forces around them. Among the most vulnerable members of society featured in these epigraphs are women and children. In the epigraph to the novel's prologue we see deception which prepares us for the policy of exploitation through "divide and rule" contained in the epigraph to Chapter One. Dried twigs and grass fly helter-skelter around a lonely tree in the epigraph to Chapter Two and in their own way prefigure the fate of the week-old baby who is dumped into a garbage-bin in the epigraph to Chapter Three. In the epigraph to Chapter Four we come to a kind of "homo homini lupus" popularized by the "social contract" school of political philosophers. A victorious cat walks away licking its whiskers as it leaves behind it the dead rat for which it was fighting as well as its rival whom it has viciously killed. It now flaunts a majesty born out of cruelty and ruthlessness. With the epigraph to Chapter Five we come to a child who is a victim of his own curiosity. He is gazing helplessly at a toy which he has dismantled but can no longer put together because he has lost the toy's crucial part. In the epigraph to Chapter Six a lonely child is swallowing dangerous pills while the adults in the room are consummating what turns out to be a disappointing sexual union ending in the woman's shrieking cry of "I didn't come, I didn't. It is unfair." With the epigraph to Chapter Seven we return to yet another baby facing imminent danger, that of drowning. This danger is as frightening as the famine which stalks the child in the epigraph to Chapter Eight who must depend on a stranger's milkless breasts. In the epigraph to Chapter Nine more danger stalks the tiny and the helpless. The only visible guardian of a child who is crunching and munching naked radio wires is a bed-ridden hundred-year old woman. In the epigraph to Chapter Ten we see a fetus which may turn out to be either a child or a miscarriage. In the epigraph to Chapter Eleven we see one ant trying to rescue another. Both are in the end swept away by a roaring river. We begin Chapter Twelve with the picture of a child about to move from a gecko to a scorpion; of similar metaphorical import is the epigraph to Chapter Thirteen, where a butterfly which has lost a wing and a feeler is to be smashed by the boy with a tennis racket. The crowning epigraph is the one to Chapter Fourteen where a crow on a minaret sits pretty as the stones thrown by the attendant to the mosque keep falling on the thrower. We have in all a picture of those without power or authority being abandoned to the mercy of those who have.

It would be unfair to Farah to ignore these epigraphs because, whether they come into the novel consciously or unconsciously, they form part of the author's total vision. Whether they are taken singly with the chapters which they precede or together with the novel as a whole, they deserve attention. At one level they are part of the funeral oration which might have been made for Soyaan. At another level they are a critique of power in Somalia and at yet a slightly different level they are a measure of the task confronting Soyaan's group. It would not be correct to read their meaning in the manner of Gloucester in Shakespeare's *King Lear:*

"As flies to wanton boys, are we to the gods;
They kill us for their sport."[21]

187

Farah is less concerned with fate, fortune, divinity and things of that nature than he is with the authoritarian state now prevailing in his country. One of the epigraphs to Part Two of *Sweet and Sour Milk* is a quotation from Wilhelm Reich: "In the figure of the father the authoritarian state has its representative in every family, so that the family becomes its most important instrument of power." Although the intellectuals who decide to take up the cudgels against the General's regime do not make any meaningful dent into that regime's entrenchment in the national life of Somalia we remain aware of an intense and passionate search for and assertion of identity in all of Farah's characters. The sphere of identity is the sphere of freedom and in denying freedom to the people of Somalia the regime is limiting the extent to which the people can assert their identity. The sphere of identity is also that of personality and Farah devotes a great deal of space and time to the denouement or unfolding of his characters' personalities through dreams, premonitions, fantasies, regrets, hopes and fears.

In Farah's novels individuals and groups search for and assert their identity. Children are fascinated by their childhood and try to find out in what way it makes them different from adults and above all why such a difference should be the cause of the "raw deal" given to them by adults. Women are concerned about the discrimination meted out to them on the grounds of their sex. They do not wait for anyone to acknowledge their rights. They assert these rights. It is in the process of acting out this search and assertion of identity that Farah compresses both time and space, making us see how "in the choir of the nation's sad song...a million waves broke on the sandy shores of the nation's discontent."[22] In *Close Sesame* our attention is focused on Deeriye whose heroism goes back to colonial days but who in his last days is haunted by the fact that in spite of his achievements in the national interest he has been absent from his family on all the important occasions on which his presence might have meant a great deal to his children. His identity as a father is now in question. It is, in fact, partly to assert that identity that he finds himself drawn

188

into his son's plot to assassinate the General. The details of Deeriye's youth and manhood are a way of showing us the extent to which both the objective reality around him and the subjective inner world created by his background have led him to the kind of decisions which he now makes, including the decision to assassinate the General. Deeriye is a man surrounded by both history as contained in the deeds of men and history as the sum-total of our aspirations, our dreams, our fantasies, our frustrations, and our fears. In this sense he prefigures Askar, the central character of *Maps*, who is surrounded by dreams, premonitions, and the kind of fears which suggest an unending search for identity. Deeriye's visions invariably come to pass. He is able to tell his family about events which only someone who had been present when the events occurred would know—and yet he had been in detention for the best part of his life. The most lingering vision in his life is that of his dead wife Nadiifa who becomes the guardian of his principles and the symbol of his aspirations for his country. She is the anchor of his identity: "What is Nadiifa but honour, good memory, and faith in life, trust in love and friendship?"[23]

We see here the source of the strength which has enabled Deeriye to survive eight years in colonial prisons and four in post-independence jails. Askar, the central character of *Maps*, does not possess this kind of strength. What he does have is a thorough and passionate desire for identity as manifested in all his boyish longings as in his extraordinary premonitions and fears. Askar's dreams and fantasies are the kind of material out of which reputations in the study of psychology are made and yet his maternal uncle who is doing research in psychology burns all his notes when Askar tells him that he once menstruated. All the uncle can say at this point is that "wars are rivers that burn...rivers whose waters, rough as crags, distort reality..."[24]

The most perceptive reviewer of the novel *Maps* is Hussein A. Bulhan who recognises the scars of oppression and war which produce personalities like that of Askar.[25] In the authoritarianism of Askar's paternal uncle Qorrax we are reminded of Keynaan who in

Sweet and Sour Milk claims the right to inflict pain on his children. Bulhan sees in *Maps* "the unexplored contours of oppression in the Horn of Africa."[26] We come face to face with those indelible scars which in the end leave us with an Askar who remains an unfulfilled dream, a "soldier" whose emotional and spiritual paralysis render him ineligible for the great mission of liberation for which both his name and the extraordinary circumstances of his birth have prepared us. Askar does not complete his quest for identity and the most haunting question he leaves with us is: "Who is Askar?"[27] This question has been with us from the very beginning of the novel, right through its intricate and groundbreaking narrative design. Askar repeatedly asks himself, "Who am I?" His dreams and his daydreams, his fears, his fantasies as well as his premonitions continually conspire to ask him the same question. His fascination with menstruation is part of that questioning and not, as one critic maintains, "an example of how Nuruddin fetishizes women."[28] Nuruddin Farah does not "fetishize" women. He creates situations in which they assert their identity with all the consequences which such an assertion brings from a male-dominated world. Ebla in *From A Crooked Rib* is a case in point. Medina in *Sardines* is another. The Hilaal household in *Maps* is organized along complete equality between husband and wife and a mutual caring which enables Hilaal to choose a vasectomy to prevent the suffering which comes to his wife with pregnancies which invariably end in miscarriages. The fate of Misra does not imply that Farah has now deviated from his usual understanding of women in society. Misra's situation has to be understood in relation to Askar's quest for identity. She is the mother Askar never had, a symbol of tangible human love with which Askar is being called upon to identify himself as opposed to the abstract notion of a greater Somalia which at any rate he fails to honour. Hilaal, his maternal uncle, acts as the understanding father Askar never had, a foil to the cruel and authoritarian paternal uncle Qoraax and to the other men in Misra's life such as Aw-Adan and the father-husband before Aw-Adan. As in *Sweet and Sour Milk*, we are here covering a vast expanse of space stretching all the way from Ethiopia and the Ogaden to Mogadiscio. The time-scale is just as vast. It takes in the childhood of both Misra and Askar and includes the war in the Ogaden which is won and lost to Somalia with all the attendant problems of displaced persons of whom Misra is one and towards whom Askar is a passive spectator.

Hilarie Kelly finds Farah's virtuosity in *Maps* tainted with "stylistic peccadilloes" which are to her "not just a question of form, but more seriously of content."[29] The example given for such an observation is a conversation in which Hilaal and Askar refer to gurus like Freud, Jung, Otto Rank, Toni Morrison and Adler. This criticism becomes more disturbing when the critic regards people like Hilaal and Askar as distinct from "ordinary Somalis" and asserts, "In all of Nuruddin's books, his main characters are never in any sense ordinary Somalis."[30] However debatable we may wish to make the concept of an ordinary Somali, we must grant that those who can discuss Freud or Toni Morrison still qualify to be ordinary, especially if, as in the case of Askar's uncle Hilaal, they happen to teach psychology and are looking after a precocious adolescent who is also a voracious reader. We Africans should be excused the exasperation we often feel at not being considered "ordinary" unless we are poor and live in the rural areas, a classification which has its roots in colonial anthropology. In literary criticism the corollary to this classification is the demand that writers eschew "virtuosity" in favor of a certain bucolic simplicity, a practice which Ayi Kwei Armah has lampooned in the novel *Fragments*. In *Maps* Farah has reached a new height in the development of technique. Askar's search for identity is dramatized in his dreams, his fantasies, and his premonitions. Above all, it is dramatised in the structure of the narrative which flows along four streams marked by three voices and a string of dreams with all their Freudian implications.

At the end of *Maps* we are told that we have come to the beginning of the story of Misra/Misrat/Masarat and that Askar tells it first to the police, and then to lawyers:

And time grew on Askar's face, as he told the story yet
again, time grew like a tree, with more branches and
far more falling leaves than the tree which is on the
face of the moon. In the process, he became the
defendant. He was at one and the same time, the plaintiff and the juror. Finally allowing for his different personae to act as judge, as audience and as witness,
Askar told it to himself.[31]

We have here Farah's own explanation of his narrative design.
The voices we hear are those of Askar but an Askar wearing different
masks and in his own youthful and sometimes confused way going
over his life and judging it, sometimes severely, sometimes leniently,
but never with sentimentality or self-pity. He recognizes the suffering
inflicted on Misra both by those who wrongly accuse her of betraying Somali combatants and by his own cold withdrawal from her. The
variations on the name of Misra are important since they stand for
the concept of both "motherhood" and "motherland" which exercises Askar's mind and leads his uncle into making the distinction
between an essential and a generic nationhood. Misra is a symbol of
both motherhood and nationhood. In distancing himself from her,
Askar is creating a distance between himself and all the deep human
and humane values which both nationhood and motherhood stand
for. In the end the question seems to be not whether Askar is right or
wrong in identifying himself with the one or the other, but whether
the identification measures up to the expectations we have of him
from all the linguistic resources that have gone into his creation. It
does. A precocious child is, after all, only a child and no amount of
promise will remove the possibilty of his ending up as a disappointment. He has indeed been given an epic stature from the opening of
the novel and it is this stature which is linked to his association and
fascination with maps and with the sea. Misra explains to Aw-Adan:
"Perhaps his stars have conferred upon him the fortune of holding
simultaneously multiple citizenships of different kingdoms: that of

the living and that of the dead; not to mention that of being an infant and an adult at the same time."[32] Askar has also been afflicted with dreams presaging failure and disappointment, insecurity and help-lessness. That path of the narrative is powerful enough to remove any doubts about Askar's "ordinariness." He is, to paraphrase Nietzsche, "human, all too human." That is why when he adopts the mask of a second-person narrator he also continually criticizes him-self, as if he is not at all sure that he is telling the whole truth. He accepts his fallibility which is a foil to any delusions of grandeur. The first-person and third-person narratives are checked and cross-checked by this second-person voice and vice-versa. Dreams and premonitions enlarge the novel's universe of discourse. The world of Askar is as fascinating as a Dickensian novel of growing up and yet it also remains an adult world of the "here and now" where values are revalued and traditions overturned by the hand of war, of repression, and of geopolitical calculations. In *Maps*, as in *Sweet and Sour Milk*, Farah ascends to a new level of artistic power. This power derives from clusters of linguistic resources centred on certain recognizable motifs. Reference has already been made to the omnipresence of the General and his paraphernalia of repression in Somalia. The authori-tarianism prevailing in the traditional Somali family has also been looked at and an attempt has been made at linking the authoritarian-ism of the family with the autocracy in the state. The search for and assertion of identity stand as foils to the repression prevailing in Somalia. Men, women, and children in Farah's novels search for and sometimes successfully assert their identity. This is particularly true of women and in that respect Farah enjoys the distinction of placing the women of his novels in a position where they not only talk about their identity but are seen to assert it. The same cannot be said of other male African writers who took much longer to wake up to the reality of women's rights. Medina in *Sardines*, Soyaan's sister in *Sweet and Sour Milk*, Ebla in *From A Crooked Rib*, Deeriye's daughter in *Close Sesame*, and Salaado in *Maps* are all women who are no longer tied to the whims and/or egos of men. They act and are seen to act in their own right. We have also looked at Farah's intellectuals and examined their weakness in the light of the enormous responsiblity facing them and have sadly concluded that they have not shown themselves to be equal to their task either in terms of organization or in terms of expanding their recruitment beyond their own class of the petit bourgeois intellectuals, a weakness which they share in good measure with other intellectuals all over Africa. A writer who has given us this amount of "food for thought" deserves to be read more seriously than Farah has been for much of his writing career.

NOTES

1. Nuruddin Farah, *Variations on the Theme of an African Dictatorship,* consisting of *Sweet and Sour Milk* (London: Allison and Busby, 1979); Sardines (London: Allison & Busby, 1981); and *Close Sesame* (London: Allison and Busby, 1983). All references will be to these editions.

2. Felix Mnthali, "Semiotic Constants and Perceptions of Change: A Study of the Symbolism of Change in African Literature," *Africa Development* 11, 4, 133-173.

3. *Sweet and Sour Milk,* p.99.

4. Mohamoud Hassan, "The Status of Human Rights in Somalia," *Horn of Africa* 3, 2 (1980), 3-11.

5. *Sweet and Sour Milk,* p.53.

6. Ibid., p.99.

7. Ibid., p.95.

8. Hassan, 5.

9. *Sweet and Sour Milk,* p.93.

10. *Close Sesame,* pp. 117-118.

11. *Sweet and Sour Milk,* p.93.

12. Hussein Abdillahi Bulhan, "The Captive Intelligentsia of Somalia," *Horn of Africa* 3, 2 (1980), 25-37.

13. *Sweet and Sour Milk,* pp.226-27.

14. Felix Mnthali, "Change and the Intelligentsia in African Literature: A Study in Marginality," a paper read at the First Symposium of the Special Committee on Africa, Nairobi, March 1985.

15. *Sweet and Sour Milk,* pp.38-39.

16. Ibid., p. 139.

17. *Close Sesame,* p.207.

18. Ibid., p.207.

19. Ibid., p.207.

20. *Sweet and Sour Milk,* pp.159-160.

21. Shakespeare, *King Lear* IV.i. ll.38-39.

22. *Sweet and Sour Milk,* p.56.

23. *Close Sesame,* p.26.

24. Nuruddin Farah, *Maps* (New York: Pantheon Books, 1986), pp. 151-53.

25. Hussein A.Bulhan, review in *Africa Events* (July 1987), 78-79.

26. Ibid., 79.

27. *Maps,* p.245.

28. Hilarie Kelly, "A Somali Tragedy of Political and Sexual Confusion: A Critical Analysis of Nuruddin Farah's *Maps,*" *Ufahamu* 16, 2 (1988), 21-37.

29. Ibid., 27.

30. Ibid., 28.

31. *Maps,* p.246.

32. Ibid., p.11.

THE SOCIOPOLITICAL EVOLUTION OF A SOMALI WRITER

Peter J. Schraeder

A lthough traditional Somali society engendered a rich oral literature,[1] and in the colonial period certain authors adopted other
European languages and the Western novel form,[2] the modern
writer Nuruddin Farah is unique as the first Somali author to publish
novels in English.[3] Although his works have been favorably reviewed
for the most part, overviews of Farah's novels have tended to discuss
only his earlier work or have centered on a particular theme in discussing only a limited number of his works.[4] This article focuses
Farah's evolution as a socially and politically engaged author, emphasizing the political content of his works. It proposed that Farah's evolution as a novelist is not unique but rather is indicative of a process
potentially applicable to other African writers. As socially engaged writers perceive political authority as becoming increasingly authoritarian
in nature and unresponsive to popular needs, their novels will become
increasingly politically engaged and anti-government in nature. Farah's
novels are analyzed according to three evolutionary phases: initial concern for social issues, increased political awareness, and acute political

engagement with perceived political and social injustices.

Farah's first novel, *From a Crooked Rib* (1970), typifies the first phase of his evolution as a socially engaged novelist. Although published in 1970, the novel was written in 1968 while Farah was a student of literature and philosophy at the University of Chandigarh, India, before the 1969 Somali revolution that gave power to the military and Siyad Barre. The novel presents less a political than a sociological study of the subordinate role of Somali women and the effects of urbanization during the 1950s, indicative of Farah's commitment to social issues.

The central character of the novel is Ebla, a woman pastoralist from the Ogaden who desires emancipation from her subordinate role in Somali society. Ebla first runs away from her clan to the city of Belet Wene because she refuses to accept her "arranged" marriage with Giumaleh, "an old man of forty-eight fit to be her father" (p.9). Once established at the house of her cousin Gheddi, however, Ebla learns that, to pay off some debts, he had secretly offered her hand in marriage to a "broker" friend. Ebla thus flees a second time by eloping to Mogadishu with a civil servant named Awill, only to become infuriated when she learns that, on a government-sponsored trip in Italy, he cheated on her. Ebla reasserts herself and gains revenge by secretly marrying Tiffo, a wealthy man of the city with whom she trades sexual favors for money. Ebla has learned to manipulate men through a brand of prostitution in which she realizes that her body is "my treasure, my only treasure, my bank, my money, my existence" (p.160). Eventually Ebla discards Tiffo and confronts Awill upon his return to Mogadishu. Rather than bringing each other's infidelity into the open, however, the pair leave resolution of this issue for "tomorrow" (p.179).

The subordinate nature of women in Somali society is clearly the dominant image of the book. This is emphasized continually in Farah's authorial commentary, as when he asserts: "From experience [Ebla] knew that girls were materials, just like objects, or items on the shelf of a shop. They were sold and bought as shepherds sold their goats at market-places, or shop-owners sold their goods to cus-tomers. To a shop-keeper what was the difference between a girl and his goods? Nothing, absolutely nothing" (p.84). Farah is particularly opposed to the continuing traditional Somali practice of circumci-sion and infibulation of young girls.[5] This intense concern for women's rights is best expressed by Kirsten Holst Petersen: "He would seem to be the first feminist writer to come out of Africa in the sense that he describes and analyzes women as victims of male sub-jugation."[6] Farah, in a 1983 interview, underscored the consequence of not treating women as equal partners: "We have to be aware of the opportunities that we lose by not using women to their full, for their contribution to the general welfare of humankind."[7]

The second dominant image of *From a Crooked Rib* is the problem of urbanization and the rural-urban dichotomy. Ebla, who sees flee-ing to the city as her salvation, loses the security of her clan and is forced into various forms of prostitution to support herself. Kenneth Little puts the newly urbanized woman's plight in perspective: "By entering into a modern type of marriage or by migrating, [women] have exchanged family and other traditional forms of security for the prospect of personal liberty. However, as a result of the deal, they are more dependent upon their own resources."[8] Ebla epitomizes the problems faced by the newly urbanized individual who wishes to escape certain aspects of traditional Somali culture (for example, arranged marriages), while retaining other aspects of traditional life, such as the affection felt for beasts of burden. Ebla asserts: "People here in Mogadiscio and in the towns don't have the slightest idea how to take care of beasts, how to milk them, how to love them, how to sacrifice their own lives to make the beasts happy and fat and healthy. They know how to eat meat and drink milk, but that is all they know. How ignorant and proud they are! A white man's language is no knowledge" (p.178).

Farah's second novel, *A Naked Needle* (1976), was written in Mogadishu in 1972, enabling him to have digested the preliminary successes, failures, and effects of the 1969 military revolution. The book represents the second phase in Farah's evolution. He remains socially engaged, and portrays an increased political awareness, typified by a general questioning of the revolution's "successes." Farah's description of continued political corruption and tribalistic practices at the highest levels of government, despite official statements to the contrary, put him in conflict with the ruling regime (this and all his subsequent novels were banned in Somalia). Whereas *From a Crooked Rib* stresses Ebla's individualist struggle against traditionalism within Somalia, *A Naked Needle* emphasizes "national identity and national unity" within an "expansive and internationally oriented world."9

The main character of the novel is Koschin, a teacher and fervent revolutionary committed to the advancement of socialism and the welfare of the masses. Espousing an idealist faith in the goals and aims of the 1969 revolution, Koschin is appalled by the tribalist and immoral tendencies of his college Principal, ultimately choosing to resign his position rather than compromise his revolutionary standards. In addition, Koschin is nervously awaiting the arrival of Nancy, a woman he had met in London and had agreed to marry if within two years neither had found someone else. Koschin wonders how Nancy, a white non-Muslim who has never been to his country, will fit into Somali society. The rekindling of their relationship is set against those of Koschin's Somali friends and acquaintances who have married foreign white women.

These relationships with foreign white women seem to symbolize Somalia's external relationships with foreign powers. Barre's relationship with his "American" wife is fraught with problems and viewed with disdain by Koschin. Similarly, Warsan's "Soviet" wife irritates Koschin with her overbearing manner, despite the existence of a "political alliance between Russia and Somalia" (p.167). Mohamed and his "British" wife, although enjoying a successful relationship, disgust Koschin with their reactionary statements concerning the revolution. Koschin thinks only British-born Barbara, with her lower class origins and socialist sympathies (her former fiancè and her father were both revolutionaries), understands the true principles of the Somali revolution. Shunning the reactionary nature of the United States and the overbearing, doctrinaire nature of the Soviet Union, Farah, through the character of Barbara, seems to extol an independent path of socialist development reminiscent of some traditional British socialists of the 1930s and 1940s.

Rather than denouncing the 1969 revolution as a failure, *A Naked Needle* represents the increasing political engagement of Farah as he probes several questionable aspects. As already stated, Koschin is disturbed by the tribalistic practices of his superior and the revelation that the top echelons of the government are hesitant "to take any steps to bring this ill-practice and what it entails to an end" (p.17). Koschin states unequivocally: "I do not owe any loyalty to any tribe...I owe loyalty to the nation, the government in power" (p.14). In fact, a general dialogue between Koschin and his friend Mohamed is perhaps indicative of Farah's attempt to sort out the necessity of the revolution. Koschin states that "Somalia very badly needed a revolution," and Mohamed replies: "Was Somalia in need of terror and horror from dawn to dusk?" (p.149). The reader is reminded by Koschin that "a revolution, y'know, is a pill that tastes bitter, the benefits of which are felt only when one has gone through the preliminary pain and pestilence" (p.4). "If this one doesn't remain loyal to the basic truths of a Somali-African humanity, then it must be denied the rights to dominate the minds of the honest ones" (p.149). One therefore receives the impression that although there are negative aspects of the revolution, a "wait-and-see" attitude is appropriate in order to judge whether it will degenerate or remain true to its goals. For example, one result of the revolution viewed favorably by Farah is the introduction in 1972 of a written Somali script. Koschin proclaims: "Why, Somali is a written language! Bless the Revolution" (p.134).

But this compromise position of qualified optimism could not last; the rather hopeful "wait-and-see" attitude of *A Naked Needle* is firmly rejected in the subsequent trilogy *Variations on the Theme of an African Dictatorship*. This trilogy represents the third phase in Farah's evolution; he comes out adamantly opposed to the Barre regime, writing his novels from self-imposed exile in England and Italy. The trilogy goes beyond the mere social engagement of *From a Crooked Rib* and the subdued political themes of *A Naked Needle*, portraying instead an intense awareness of perceived social and political injustices.

The pivotal factors in this stage of Farah's development were events occurring within Somalia between the writing of *A Naked Needle* in 1972 and the publication in 1979 of the first volume of the anti-government trilogy. Opponents of the Barre regime claim that, from 1974 onward, various instruments of the Somali government, such as the National Security Service (NSS), the National Security Court (NSC), the Somali Revolutionary Council (SRC), and the *Gulwadhayal* (Victory Pioneers) "were increasingly being perfected and their full weight brought to bear on what the regime had classified as 'anti-socialist,' 'anti-revolutionary,' and naturally anti-Siyad."[10] Opponents cited numerous examples of political excess by the government: April 1974, the imprisonment of thirteen teachers on the charges of organizing and taking part in strikes; January 1975, the execution of ten Muslim leaders on the charge of "exploiting religion to create national disunity and subverting state authority"; October 1978, following Somalia's defeat in the Ogaden war, the public execution of seventeen army officers for attempting a coup; late 1978, the execution of five students on the charge of anti-government demonstration.[11] The Somali regime in mid-1978 was said to be "exposed for what it really was: a repressive, frightened and desperate government unable to take chances with anyone, however apolitical."[12]

The first part of the trilogy, *Sweet and Sour Milk* (1979), won the 1980 English-Speaking Union Literary Award. The novel is representative of Farah's third phase, in which he virulently attacks the tribalistic and authoritarian practices of the Barre regime, its links with the Soviet Union, the traditional patriarch of Somali society, and the elites who have sold themselves to the government. Conversely, Farah now portrays those who write and distribute anti-government pamphlets as the heroes and future salvation of Somalia.

The novel begins with the mysterious death of Soyaan, an economic adviser answerable only to the General and a leading member of a clandestine opposition movement composed of Somali intellectuals and professionals. Soyaan's twin brother, Loyaan, is gradually drawn into a personal investigation of the circumstances surrounding his brother's death, eventually learning that his brother was "silenced" by the regime because he secretly wrote and distributed anti-government pamphlets. In order to discredit the movement and keep Soyaan's true actions from reaching the general populace, the government proclaims him a "hero of the revolution" whose last words were "Labour is honour and there is no General but our General." Loyaan's efforts to keep the government from making a mockery of his deceased brother's true political beliefs eventually bring him into direct opposition with the regime. The novel ends with Loyaan facing either exile overseas or imprisonment if he refuses to leave.

Sweet and Sour Milk reveals how a burgeoning opposition within the educated upper class of Somalia prepared and distributed clandestine material which violated national security statutes. Farah's opinion of the ruling elite is summarized in a secret memo penned by Soyaan: "Clowns. Cowards. And (tribal) upstarts: these are who I work with. The top civil service in this country is composed of them. Men and women whose pride has been broken by the General's security; men and women who have succumbed and accepted to be humiliated" (p.38). Special ridicule is reserved for the national leader. In Soyaan's words: "Listen to these ludicrous eulogies of the General...The father of the nation. The carrier of wisdom. The provider of comforts. A demi-god. I see him as a Grand Warden of a Gulag" (p.15). Even more disturbing to Farah is the degree of control and influence that the Soviets maintained over the Barre regime. This is portrayed in the novel by Loyaan's anger when told that an accomplice of Soyaan was arrested for anti-Soviet activities. Loyaan proclaims: "But we are not in the Soviet Union. We are in the Somali Democratic Republic, a sovereign African state. Not in the Soviet Union. We are *not*" (p.198).

The role of the patriarch in traditional Somali society, as well as traditional authority in general, is attacked in the character of Keynaan, the father of Soyaan and Loyaan. Keynaan epitomizes the patriarch who rules his family with an iron hand and has become a willing instrument of the clannish policies of the Barre regime. Furthermore, Keynaan is portrayed as oblivious to the valuable role of women in Somali society. He asserts: "Women are for sleeping with, for giving birth to and bringing up children; they are not good for any other thing" (p.84). The father summarizes his position in Somalia in a conversation with his son. "And remember one thing, Loyaan: if I decide this minute to cut you in two, I can. The law of the land invests in men my age the power. I am the Grand Patriarch" (p.95).

Sardines (1981), the second part of the trilogy, is an intensification of the political engagement characteristic of his third phase. Reiterating many themes from *Sweet and Sour Milk*, the novel breaks new ground by exploring the role of Somali women in opposing the ruling regime. Farah blends his understanding of women's issues with the polemics of politics to create a powerful novel.

The story revolves around Medina, an avowed feminist and sole female member of the clandestine anti-government movement composed of members of Somalia's educated upper class. Medina has been banned from publishing and fears that Ubax, her daughter, will be "forced" to undergo the traditional circumcision and infibulation performed on nearly all young women in Somalia. Medina also guides the intellectual development of her friend's daughter, Sagal, who is a nationally recognized swimming star. Sagal is a potential representative for the "Africa-Comecon Meet" in Budapest, and dreams of "painting the dawn" with anti-government slogans. Furthermore, Medina's husband, Samater, has been blackmailed by the government to accept a cabinet position—from which he ultimately resigns, only to be jailed.

Like *Sweet and Sour Milk*, *Sardines* portrays the growing political opposition and activities of the educated elite. In the latter novel, however, the primary elements of opposition studied are women and female students, representative of Farah's concern for this segment of the Somali population. Medina, for example, typifies the educated, cosmopolitan woman who wishes a better life for her daughter. Medina is concerned about the intellectual freedom of Ubax and is disgusted with the traditional customs which call for the subordination and circumcision of women: "I want to spare my daughter these and many other pains. She will not be circumcised. Over my dead body" (p.59).

Individuals comprising a second group of opposition within the novel are female students, indicative of Farah's impression of growing student unrest in Somalia. Sagal, who has always dreamed of "painting the dawn" with anti-government slogans, is extremely jealous when her two closest competitors are arrested for committing this act. The girls had painted the slogan: "Down with the one-man, one-tribe dictatorship! Down with the General's regime" (p.125).

Despite the rise of opposition groups within Somali society, Farah warns through Samater that most of the intelligentsia are corrupt and self-serving: "We the intellectuals are the betrayers; we the so-called intellectuals are the entrance the foreign powers use so as to dominate, designate, name and label; we the intellectuals are the ones who tell our people lies" (p.72).

Finally, Farah emphasizes the extreme pressure put upon individuals of the ruling hierarchy by members of their clan to amass wealth and manipulate the patronage system to their benefit. Samater's mother, Idil, epitomizes this aspect of Somali clan politics: "And what are you a minister for? How many more months will you hold this important position, occupy the throne of power? Why don't you use it? Why don't you get richer while you can, amass the wealth that is yours by right? Or have you taken to heart what the General says about socialism?" (p.65)

Close Sesame (1983) is the final novel of Farah's trilogy and is the most politically engaged work of his third phase. Rather than discuss mere protests or the distribution of secret memoranda, the novel seemingly calls for the leader's assassination and seeks to rationalize such a call.

Once again, one can hypothesize that the primary impetus for Farah's increased political engagement stems from his perception of events taking place in Somalia. Opposition groups have described the period between 1981 and 1983 (during which *Close Sesame* was written) as one in which "mass discontent with the regime intensified to such an extent that it has become a national phenomenon."[13] Furthermore, these groups assert that numerous anti-government demonstrations, ambushes of military convoys, and bomb explosions in Mogadishu "provide good examples of the nation-wide manifestation of discontent with the regime."[14]

The plot of *Close Sesame* revolves around Deeriye, a nationalistic Muslim pan-Somalist and pan-Africanist who has been a "Sayyidist" all his life. Unfortunately, Deeriye has paid for his beliefs by spending eight years in colonial prisons and four in post-independence jails. A respected man within Somali society in the 1980s, Deeriye is confronted with a personal dilemma when he learns that his son Mursal, with three accomplices, is plotting the assassination of the General. Originally stating that he would never make use "of violent means to overthrow a tyrannical regime" (p.13), Deeriye changes his political opinions as the regime seeks, for self-serving tribalistic purposes, to isolate him from his clan and discredit his public image. Upon learning that his son has been killed, presumably by the regime, Deeriye is finally driven to an assassination attempt on the life of the General, "not to avenge his son but to vindicate justice" (p.180). He dies in this unsuccessful attempt.

Close Sesame is an especially powerful novel because the call for the overthrow of the ruling regime comes not only from upper class intellectuals but also from Deeriye—an extremely nationalistic Somali, a hero of the revolution revered by his peers. Drawing parallels with the colonial past, the plot shows how the regime's attempt to isolate and intimidate Deeriye replicates what the Italian colonialists had done to him in 1934. Just as the Italian authorities had wanted Deeriye to hand over a suspected assassin and dissociate himself from the individual's actions, so the present government is portrayed as attempting the same thing. "The only difference, *if there is a difference*, is that in 1934 the enemy and the famine-creating power was colonial and foreign; and now it is neo-colonial and local" (p.147). In essence, Farah is condemning the Barre government for committing the same or worse crimes against the Somali people as did the colonial powers. Farah accuses the regime of presently attempting to defuse legitimate and ideologically-based nationalist movements by isolating a certain act as tribally based, thereby "denying it a national base by showing its tribal support" (p.79). Furthermore, the regime's ability to control the flow of information keeps "the populace underinformed so you can rule them...imprison them with shackles of uninformedness and they are easy to govern" (p.68).

All of Farah's novels embody certain themes: the subordinate role of women in Somali society and a need for their emancipation, the disastrous effects of clan competition and struggle, the role of the traditional authoritarian patriarch, and the pivotal role of the educated intelligentsia in acting as both a force of opposition to and a maintainer of the ruling regime. What differs among the novels is the amount of emphasis placed upon the various common themes. The social concerns of Farah's earlier works, although represented in his later novels, have given way to explicit political issues in his evolution.

More important, we can derive through an examination of Farah's evolution a general model potentially applicable to other socially and politically engaged African writers. At the beginning of this article, it was suggested that as a socially engaged writer perceives political authority becomingly increasingly authoritarian and unresponsive to popular needs, his or her novels will become more politically engaged and anti-government. The evolution of the political content of Farah's novels supports this hypothesis. Indicative of a primary phase in which the socially engaged author examines the society's cultural defects is *From a Crooked Rib*, primarily concerned with the subordination of women within Somali society. With the advent of a revolution (or peaceful transfer of power which entails a radical political departure) and the installation of a new regime, the socially engaged author will enter a second phase, questioning the various social and political aspects of the revolution in general and the new ruling regime in particular. This phase is represented by *A Naked Needle*, following the 1969 Somali revolution. A third evolution occurs when the author perceives the revolution or the new government as not remaining true to its original objectives. As the regime is perceived as incrementally resorting to coercive and authoritarian practices in the face of growing domestic dissent, the socially engaged author writes increasingly about anti-government political involvement. This development is represented by Farah's *Dictatorship* trilogy. Unfortunately, the writer who does become politically engaged and takes a negative stance against the ruling hierarchy, as Farah did in Somalia, is often banned and forced to write in exile.[15]

Somali officials generally have declared that Farah's novels are unrepresentative of Somalia's true conditions. A common claim is that Farah has been out of the country so long that he is unable to interpret events as only an insider can. Furthermore, Farah is described as an intellectual who would rather highlight the negative aspects of the revolution than recognize the "advances" that have been made since 1969 (for example, the institution of a written Somali script).

Farah undoubtedly does not present an "exact" image of Somali society and politics. For example, in *From a Crooked Rib*, Ebla responds to a query made by nomads as she is fleeing her clan that she is going to the city to get injections and buy some clothes. The nomads enquire, "For your wedding?" and Ebla responds, "Yes" (p.20). In Somali society in the 1950s such a question would not be asked because the marriage outfit could not be bought by the woman; it was ordered well in advance and paid for by the man. Likewise in the political realm, certain of Farah's images may be exaggerated or unrepresentative of actual occurrences. The writer, however, need not be expected to deliver mere documentary realism. Rather, it is by capturing the concept and the image, such as the subordinate status of women and the increasingly authoritarian nature of the Barre government, that the author presents his case to the public, which can then judge it upon its own merits. The author is not a recorder of events but an interpreter acting upon his perceptions of them. While the Barre government may have stated that it banned Farah's novels because they misinterpreted Somali society, Barre's opponents might note that they were banned because they represented Somali society all *too well.*

Deviating from the political, one of the most interesting aspects of Farah's novels is that they often represent a continuous story; characters live on from novel to novel, and those whose fates are not resolved at the end of one volume may be resolved in the next. For example, the reader does not know at the end of *Sweet and Sour Milk* whether Loyaan will accept exile overseas in terms of a government post or whether he will continue to fight for the vindication of his twin brother's name and risk a lengthy jail term. The story ends thus: "It was seven in the evening. There was a knock on the outside door" (p.237). In *Sardines*, however, the reader learns that Loyaan has been jailed by the government, intimating that he refused to accept exile. In similar fashion, Ebla, who remains unsure of her destiny at the end of the first novel, shows up in *Sardines* as the mother of Sagal. She had left Awill, remarried, and then divorced. The reader familiar with Farah's previous works will gain a better understanding of the secondary characters in the latest novel.

Farah's ongoing exploration of the social and political evolution of Somalia continues to generate much discussion; whereas critics may dismiss his novels as unrepresentative of Somali society, supporters will argue that they are completely on target. In any case, Farah's novels remain an important aspect of Somali studies, serving as a unique means for transmitting one man's interpretation of Somali politics and society. Indeed, espousing his perceptions of the

state of the field, Farah characterized African writers (and undoubtedly himself) as managing to "touch the raw nerve of the reader."
Alluding to what drives his critical fiction, Farah stated: "There is
something virgin about writing in Africa. There are certain aspects of
the writing which are like social documentation, writing about things
which have never before been written about."[16]

NOTES

1. For two excellent overviews of Somali oral poetry, see
   B.W.Andrzejewski and I.M.Lewis, *Somali Oral Poetry: An
   Introduction* (London: Oxford University Press, 1964); and Said
   S.Samater, *Oral Poetry and Somali Nationalism: The Case of Sayyid
   Mohammed Abdille Hassan* (Cambridge: Cambridge University
   Press, 1982).

2. For a general overview of this topic, see David F.Beer, "Somali
   Literature in European Languages," *Horn of Africa* 2 (October-
   December 1979), 27-35.

3. The editions of Nuruddin Farah's novels employed in this article
   are as follows: *From a Crooked Rib* (London: Heinemann, 1970); *A
   Naked Needle* (London: Heinemann, 1976); *Sweet and Sour Milk*
   (London: Heinemann, 1980); *Sardines* (London: Heinemann,
   1982); and *Close Sesame* (London: Allison & Busby, 1983).

4. Discussions of Farah's first two novels include: Judith Cochrane,
   "The Theme of Sacrifice in the Novels of Nuruddin Farah," *World
   Literature Written in English* 18 (1979), 69-77; and Shuaib Ahmed
   Kidwai, "The Two Novels of Nuruddin Farah," in *Somalia and the
   World*, Vol.1, ed. Hussein M.Adam (Mogadishu: State Printing
   Press, 1980), pp.191-201. Two reviews centering on the political
   content of Farah's work and each covering three novels are:
   Kirsten Holst Petersen, "The Personal and the Political: The Case

of Nuruddin Farah," *ARIEL* 12, 3 (1981), 93-101 (reprinted in the present volume); and Juliet I. Okonkwo, "Literature and Politics in Somalia: The Case of Nuruddin Farah," *Africa Today* 32, 3 (1985). Two other excellent reviews, covering respectively three and four novels, are: Ian Adam, "Nuruddin Farah and James Joyce: Some Issues in Intertextuality," *World Literature Written in English* 24, 1 (1984), 34- 43; and Florence Stratton, "The Novels of Nuruddin Farah," *World Literature Written in English* 25, 1 (1985), 16-30 (reprinted in the present volume).

5. For a review of this topic, see Raqiya Hahi Dualeh Abdalla, *Sisters in Affliction: Circumcision and Infibulation of Women in Africa* (London: Zed Press, 1982).

6. Petersen, 98.

7. "Close Sesame: The End of a Trilogy" (Interview), *Africa Now* 32 (December 1983), 82. Okonkwo is another critic who has put Farah's beliefs into proper perspective: "Farah's championing of the cause of women is part of his crusade against tyranny and victimization not just of women, but of all who are denied their legitimate rights—social and political, private and public." See Juliet I.Okonkwo, "Nuruddin Farah and the Changing Roles of Women," *World Literature Today* 58, 2 (1984), 215-21.

8. Kenneth Little, *West African Urbanization* (Cambridge: Cambridge University Press, 1965), p.122.

9. Cochrane, 73.

10. Mohamed Hassan, "Status of Human Rights in Somalia," *Horn of Africa* 3, 2 (1980), 4. For a pro-government interpretation of events taking place in Somalia, see "Concerned Somalis," *Horn of Africa* 6, 3 (1983), 46-48.

11. Ibid., 5.

12. Ibid., 5.

13. "Somalia on the Brink of Civil War," *Horn of Africa* 6, 1 (1983), 40.

14. Ibid., 40.

15. Anne Walmsley, "Nuruddin Farah and Somalia," *Index on Censorship* 10, 2 (1981), 17-19.

16. "Close Sesame: The End of a Trilogy," 82.

Note: The author extends special thanks to Patrick A.Scott, Mark W.DeLancey, Abdi Awaleh Jama, and Mohamed Haji Mukhtar for their constructive comments and criticisms.

PART THREE
Early Works

FARAH AND THE (RE)WRITING OF SOMALI HISTORIOGRAPHY: Narrative As a Politically Symbolic Act

Ali Jimale Ahmed

In the figure of the father the authoritarian state has its representative in every family, so that the family becomes its most important instrument of power.[1]
—WILHELM REICH

Nuruddin Farah's first two novels, *From a Crooked Rib* and *A Naked Needle,* shed light on acute and simmering contradictions in Somali society. These contradictions are captured in their inchoate forms and early manifestations, especially in *A Naked Needle.* By identifying contradictions before they have a chance to ferment, a writer attests to the truth in Adonis' assertion that "[literature] is not [only] a stage in the history of human consciousness but a constituent of this consciousness."[2] As a gendered text Farah's first novel, *From a Crooked Rib*, clearly reveals the inadequacy in

Jameson's arguments that "the oral tale of tribal society...[is] the irre-pressible voice and expression of the underclass of the great systems of domination..."[3] For Jameson, the assumption is that the oral tale depicts a single undifferentiated group with one world outlook, thus forgetting that the so-called tribal society is not itself a cohesive group. In other words, "the oral tale of tribal society" could on cer-tain occasions represent "the great systems of domination" for sec-tions of its own audience. The ability of the oral tale to hide the schism within tribal society through either self-effacement or through intricate maneuvering which direct our attention towards the great systems of domination in the center, does not mean that all is well in the periphery. The oral tale, in this case, becomes what Geertz calls "a tale a culture tells about itself."[4] So much that humans tell about themselves and their institutions fails to square off with reality. Farah's novel gauges the truth the culture tells about itself. *From a Crooked Rib* shows deliberately that the tale Somali culture tells about itself is not a holistic one that emerges from the agonies, hopes, and aspirations of all the members of the community. (That even Farah's tale sometimes cannot break out of the hegemonic hold of Somali culture is but one indication of the survival power of offi-cial orthodoxy.)

From a Crooked Rib is divided into four parts, each of which is introduced by an appropriate epigraph. Part One begins with the Somali proverb from which the novel gets its name, " God created woman from a crooked rib; and anyone who trieth to straighten it, breaketh it." The solemnity of the proverb is underlined by the words "trieth" and "breaketh," which add a scriptural aura. In the prologue an omniscient third person narrator tells us of a weak man whose only remaining weapon is the authority to curse. The gaunt figure is the grandfather of Ebla (the protagonist). He is squatting, " his but-tocks resting on his heels"—waiting expectantly to hear from his grandson. The image of the squatting frail man is important. In Somali culture, which is not over-dependent on chairs, *kadaloob (squatting)* conjures up many images, such as a sense of urgency and a seriousness of intention. A suitor, for example, squats outside the hut of his intended, and so does the man with the "evil eye" squat in front of the house he expects to destroy. It seems that to hurl harm at an enemy, one has to fulfill certain rituals commensurate with the intended efficacy of the curse; as in fighting a lion, the curser has to create a mental poise and crouch before taking aim at the beast. Ebla's grandfather squats so that he can give serious thought whether to curse her or not. When Ebla's sixteen year-old brother comes back to the old man to report her flight from home, the old man already expects the worst. That his wife had eloped with him years ago does not alleviate his fears nor does it assuage his resentment. Lost in his thoughts, his prayer beads fall apart. Again this conjures up well-known images in Somali society: *"sida tusbax go'ay taladaada Allaha ka yeelo"* [May Allah disperse your objectives as a strand of beads that has broken] is a powerful curse. The old man secretly utters his imprecation, "May the Lord disperse your plans, Ebla. May He make you the mother of many a bastard. May He give you hell on this earth as a reward."[5]

Ebla is an eighteen- or nineteen-year-old girl who, as her name in Somali suggests, is "graceful at six feet." She is running away from a marriage arranged by her grandfather with a much older man. It is for this reason that she has lost all respect for him. Her anger against her grandfather finds expression in her total disillusionment with the so-called egalitarian system of the nomad. She believes that each is for himself or herself, especially since no one accompanies anyone at the time of birth, and that when one's time comes, one dies alone. As a result of that, "One tried to solve one's problems alone" (p.7).

Ebla flees from the Ogaden, the place commonly referred to as *Ulasan* in the de facto border between Ethiopia and Somalia. She goes to Belet Wein in central Somalia and her connection to her homestead is symbolically severed as soon as she steps out of her hut. Her "My God, I am out" (p.9) is as literal as it is metaphorical. Outside of the kraal symbolizes individual freedom. The family enclosure symbolizes protection provided by the community.

Disenclosure, i.e., stepping out of the kraal, implies that protection must be sought for one's self. She joins a caravan on its way to Belet Wein, a town on the other side of the border, in Somalia proper.

Life in the town constitutes Part Two, which is introduced by a quotation from *Waiting for Godot*: "There's a man all over for you/ blaming on his boots/ the faults of his feet." The epigram is sugges- tive of the role of women in society. They are nothing more than boots for men—so important to protect their feet, yet when things go wrong, it is easy to blame the victim. She comes to visit and perhaps stay with Gheddi, a male cousin she has never seen, and becomes a servant maid for his family. Ebla is told to care for the pregnant wife as well as for their cows. A neighborly widow helps her become familiar with the town and becomes Ebla's best friend, acting as her conduit to the larger world.

Four days after her arrival in Belet Wein, Gheddi takes Ebla with him to a smuggling rendezvouz but the deal goes sour as the opera- tion is foiled by the authorities and he runs for his life. She goes to the house of the widow, who explains to her what has become of the contraband scheme. Her cousin is forced to sell one of his cows and Dirir, the broker, who helps him sell the cow, also comes up with some cash for Ebla's hand. Gheddi unreasonably blames Ebla for the aborted deal, reasoning that the loss he incurred forces him to recoup by marrying her to Dirir. Ebla's escape starts all over again and she ponders inequality among people, and about women being treated as "slaves," daughters less cherished than sons. Her verdict, transmitted to us by the narrator, is categorical: "For sure this world is a man's...nature is against women" (p.84).

Her castigation of the colonial government is as harsh as her crit- icism of patriarchy, envisaging it as nothing more than an extension of patriarchal supremacy. It is men who run the state machinery, she sees, and it is to them that women must go to demand justice. It becomes obvious why despotic governments easily become models for father-figures to emulate. Ebla's inner thoughts are again trans- mitted to us by the narrator. "Before she has opened her mouth, she is condemned to the grave. Aren't men the law?" (p.85). The narrator is a vehicle for her inner feelings, the quotation clearly alluding to infanticide practiced in pre-Islamic Arabia against daughters. In a patriarchal society, it is the woman's gender which, *a priori,* determines her role. In such times, she is better off if she can sell herself without a mediator. As Ebla argues, "Without a broker there is no bidder-and no auctioneer. All I need is the Sheikh's fee if Awill wants to marry me" (p.85).

Ebla's words suggest an inversion of the traditional method of contracting marriage in Somali society, as the groom is normally the one who pays the Sheikh's fee in that traditional method: institutionalized religion becomes a tool for men to oppress women. The sheikh is only a broker, but a broker profits by his trade. In this sense, the institution of marriage is nothing more than a commodity, bought and sold to the highest bidder, with all the attendant haggling over prices. By "selling" herself, as she does in the novel, Ebla knocks other auctioneers (her grandfather and later her cousin) out of business at least in this one transaction. The Sheikh and the grandfather play nearly interchangeable roles.

Ebla agrees to elope with Awill, a relation of the widow. When the widow comes back from town and is told of the elopement plans, she is happy that she had taught Ebla a few things about life. The widow's own life story is of an embittered woman whose relationships with men (and by extension with society) have soured. Farah never gives the name of the widow, suggesting the symbolic importance of her role to all women as a potential ally. She herself did not re-marry because, we are told, no one thought of her as desirable. A widow is seen by some as a sign of malediction, a curse. The death of a husband is, in certain places and on certain occasions, interpreted as a manifestation of a woman's sins.

Part Three opens with a quotation from Arthur Miller's *After the Fall*: "Why do I ever think/ of things falling apart/ were they ever whole?" The allusion is to Achebe's *Things Fall Apart*. Ebla is the same generation as Okonkwo's grandson, Obi, in *No Longer at Ease,* when

219

the falling apart of African traditions has already taken place. Farah's allusion to *Things Fall Apart* goes beyond what is suggested by Harold Bloom's thoughts on "the anxiety of influence," whereby a novice writer wants to emerge from the shadow of a father figure. The allusion to Achebe no doubt enhances Farah's position as a 23-year-old novice but, taking issue with Achebe's portrayal of the African past, Farah engages in "rhetorical self definition." As Henry Louis Gates, Jr., writes, "It is clear that black writers read and critique other black texts as an act of rhetorical self-definition. Our literary tradition exists because of these precisely chartable formal literary relationships, relationships of signifying.[6] But in Ebla's story Farah perhaps wanted to shed light on Achebe's blindness to the plight of Igbo women, and by extension the plight of all African women. Trying to redirect our attention to such blindness is at times more difficult than correcting an error. As Wlad Godzich writes, "Correcting errors sets the record straight, eliminates impediments to thought; reflecting upon blindness, on the other hand, forces thought into a reflective judgement about its own torturous and discontinuous path, the very blindness of which consists in the fact that it has no guide to warn against its vagaries."[7] Achebe's analysis in *Things Fall Apart is* focused more on the disintegration of an African society as a result of colonialism than on women's special plight. The oversight is more the result of an engendered emic approach than it is a deliberate error.

Awill takes Ebla to his rented room in Bondere, the biggest quarter in Mogadishu. Aunt Asha, so-called not out of any blood relationship but out of respect for an older person, is Awill's landlady. Asha calls for some Sheikhs to perform the marriage ceremony, after which Jama, one of Awill's work mates, delivers to him the news that he (Awill) has to go to Italy for a short government course and is expected to leave in a week's time. The author contrives this scene to show that Ebla is not important enough for Awill to delay or decline an opportunity to go study in Italy. Anticipating Jama's question, Awill preempts him by stating in Italian that he is not going to destroy his life for a woman.[8]

Awill's program in Italy is about the grooming of Somalis to run the Ministry of Education after independence (this story takes place sometime in February, 1960). The Ministry expects them to return a month before independence, i.e., before June (Somalia's southern section became independent on July 1, 1960). Awill tells Ebla on the seventh day of their marriage that he will be leaving in two days' time and she has to accept his departure for "It was part of a man's life to travel for the benefit of the family" (p.113).

The last part of the novel, Part Four, opens with a Sicilian proverb, "Don't tamper with Camarina."⁹ A week or so has passed when Jama delivers a letter for Ebla, inadvertently forgetting to take out photographs of Awill and a semi-nude Italian woman. Ebla is incensed by the photos and feels betrayed, whereupon Asha, who now takes the place of the widow, suggests that Ebla should likewise cultivate relationships with men. She tells her of a rich acquaintance who has visited her place several times, and who has shown some interest in Ebla. Asha is now playing the role of procurer for the rich man, Tiffo, and it is here that her function in the plot differs from that of the widow, who did not encourage an illicit act when she wanted her nephew to marry Ebla. Asha is the quintessential town dweller who, with no one to turn to for help, must rely on her wits. It is not impossible to imagine that she expects her share of the gravy and, even though she is not in charge of a *maison de societè,* she nonetheless expects a cut of whatever Ebla gains from the deal. They also talk about the implications of polyandry, which in essence is what they are planning—a secret marriage between Ebla and Tiffo. Ebla is pragmatic about the secret marriage.

After the women discuss the final details of their "new project" over tea, each goes to her room. Ebla dreams of the arrival of her brother from the interior and also of her grandfather's death—an important dream in that the grandfather had symbolically died before she went to sleep. The consummation of the new marriage will destroy the sway of patriarchy over women, the act of polyandry being the final stage of her challenge to the system. As far as Ebla is

221

concerned, her grandfather was the paramount patriarch whose presence and deed in the community stood for the transmission of gender-biased tradition to posterity. The death of her grandfather was always in her subconscious and, though the intended act of polyandry only closes that chapter of her life, the specter of the grandfather never really leaves her subconscious. Ebla is somewhat resigned to the fact that she will not get away with impunity: in her dream, she is trampled by camels fleeing a herder's stick, and the herder is always a male.

When Awill's return to Mogadishu nears, Ebla gets into an argument with Tiffo. She asks for his senior wife's name and when he refuses to tell her, she tells him of her other husband. Now, his wife's name must be traded for Awill's. Tiffo still does not believe her and when he insists that she is a liar, Ebla calmly answers, "Why should I [tell a lie]? You have another wife and I have another husband. We are even; you are a man and I am a woman, so we are equal. You need me and I need you. We are equal" (p.145). Ebla is adamant on this point, male and female being even. No one part of a pair can stand by itself: it is what it is because of the complementary nature of the other. Her argument is based on a Somali proverb (culled from a poem); *"Istaageerid bay laba gacmood, tamar ku yeeshaane/ Tiska waxa la qaada hadday, tiirisaa bidixe/ Hadday midigtu keli taagantahay, taxar ma goyseene."* ("It is supporting one another that two hands find strength,/ A thorny branch can only be carried, if the left hand is helping [the right one],/ The right hand raised alone could not cut even a morsel of gristle.")[10] When Asha confirms Ebla's story, Tiffo divorces her right there and then. Awill is expected on the morrow and she has pleasant dreams that night.

Ebla's happiness, however, is short-lived. As a novelistic character, she indeed represents a challenge to tradition and her ordeal is similar to Emma Bovary's, about which Edward Said argues: "In Emma Bovary's refusal to be the same kind of wife that her class and the French provinces require of her, the filiative bonds of society are challenged."[11] But, challenging the filiative bonds of society is not

222

enough to break from the hold of tradition. To transform tradition, Ebla, Emma and their ilk must remember the dual aspects of tradition, namely, structure and ideology.[12] By challenging the structures of tradition one is only able to call attention to the institutions. To effectively and dialectically supersede existing negative structures, one has to challenge tradition ideologically, for it is in ideology that a structure is nurtured, justified, and legitimized. It is here where Ebla shows a relative ambiguity common to individual consciousnesses which are ready to question certain aspects of tradition but are not sure of themselves as yet. Ebla, at times, doubts her moral strength. The ingredients that inform her suspicions emanate from warped and distorted superstructural tenets. She thinks that because women were created by God from the crooked rib of Adam, she is too crooked to be straightened. Ebla's belief that her situation may be preordained indicates that she has internalized her subservient role.

An important aspect of Farah's endeavor to bare the trappings of hegemonic hold is reaccentuated at the end of the novel when Awill, in an attempt to remind her of her inferior position, rhetorically asks Ebla, "You know how you were created?" The fighting spirit in her manages to subvert the original meaning of the rhetoric when she answers him, "From clay, like you." Awill then shifts the second person in his rhetorical question to a third person plural in his matter-of-fact rejoinder: "Let me tell you that they were created from the crooked rib of man" (p.179). This statement, which has a condescending tone, is also revealing in that it speaks about an absent group, a *they.* For the oppression to materialize, however, the initial "you" that became a "they" must metamorphose into an "it" that is uttered by the "oppressed" herself. The "it" is indicative of Ebla's self-denial, of having come to a cul-de-sac. Ebla completes the linguistic base of the triangle of oppression; "And if any one tries to straighten *it* he will have to break *it"* (p.179; emphasis added). Yet Ebla's statement, uttered as self-effacement of a sort, could ironically proclaim a latent, perhaps coded wish: To make women viable

223

members of the community, one will have to do away with the oppressive shell that impedes the full realization of their inherent value. It is in this sense that *From a Crooked Rib* anticipated the Family Law statute of 1972. This statute was meant to give women equal rights with men but, while the spirit of the statute was noble in its design, the same cannot be said of the intentions of some of its principal originators. Had the intentions of the Barre regime been other than political expediency, a greater emphasis would have been placed on tradition as ideology.

The beauty of the novel lies in its ability to capture the troubles a Somali woman had to go through in a world created and dominated by men. The patriarchal nature of that world is shown through Ebla's grandfather and the other men whose paths cross with hers. The creation of a fictional Ebla who could vote with her feet is not only found in Farah, but also in Somali lore regarding elopement. The case of Kaba'alaf in the second chapter is a case in point. Ebla's own grandmother is another one. Elopement is a way out for couples in love to escape parental injunctions. *From a Crooked Rib,* therefore, reveals an ambivalence in Somali culture: the possible escape of those in love to defy outside interference and the eventual potency of the curse of the parent.

It is a dilemma. The uneasiness of a plausible solution bespeaks a rife contradiction within the superstructure of the society. Even though Farah deftly handles the subject, the dilemma holds his art hostage and generates inconsistencies in the text. This hesitancy on the part of the author to wholly commit himself to the taming of patriarchy can also be taken as a symptom of his own ambivalence. The fictional period of *From a Crooked Rib* focuses on the pre-independence era. The novel comes to a close at the return of Awill from his trip to Italy, sometime in May, 1960. Awill and his friends have ostensibly returned to Somalia to lead the country to a new dawn. Women were not among the trainees, thus exposing the future form of a male-dominated government. The novel is the first of its kind in Somali literature to focus on gender biases and inequities. By focusing on the plight of Ebla, Farah was able to teach the Somali culture about its blind spots. With the coming to power of Barre, women played a dominant role in the democratization of Somali culture that took place early in his regime. This role was at its peak when Barre's project still represented the national popular will. In Farah's second novel Barre is firmly in power.

A Naked Needle deals with Somalia after the military takeover in October, 1969.[13] The title comes from an Arabic proverb: "The needle that stitches the clothes of people remains naked itself."[14] The profession of the major protagonist is not in a sartorial field, but in teaching. The title alludes to either one or both of the following: the utter disorganization and carelessness of the teacher-protagonist or the moral turpitude of his nemesis, the principal of the school.

The novel is divided into "movements" instead of chapters, and these movements go back and forth in more ways than one. Ideas in any movement become incomplete without their being associated with other ideas in preceding or succeeding movements. The novel displays a cinematic technique and is written in a stream-of- consciousness style. The plot, if there is something of that nature in *A Naked Needle*, is based on movement.

Nancy, the protagonist's British girlfriend, is coming from England; the protagonist Koschin is anxious with expectation. When Nancy finally arrives, he shows her around. They go to a party. People come and go all the time. It is three in the morning and they walk home. The characters are always on the move and, on a different level, Somalia is also on the move with the "revolution"—with all the connotations of the word. The nature of this novel is that it moves on many levels. But it is the need for these movements that catch our interest. It is possible to argue that constant motion affords little time for contemplation or brooding over ideas. It is only after the day's grazing that ruminating animals chew their cud. The absence of serenity encourages the protagonist to think over ideas in motion, actions in full swing. The surge of motion allows the protagonist to procrastinate as he pleases. In a nutshell, movements of the plot reflect the protagonist's own ambivalence and his groping in the dark for answers to difficult metaphysical and existential questions.

There are many personal and political events that Koschin is not emotionally prepared to either castigate or lend his blessings to. The arrival of Nancy, to whom years ago he had given his word to marry, disturbs him. He has his doubts about the viability of their would-be marriage. At times, his doubts are not confined to Nancy personally, but reflect his resentment towards her background and, by extension, towards her culture. His juxtaposition in his mind of his Muslim amulet against the rosary beads given to Nancy by her mother reveals the extent of his frustrations with her culture, while, in his over-sensitivity, he assumes that Nancy's culture calls his memories of his mother "leftovers from superstition."[15] In contrast to Senghor's ardent defense of his own "totem" in his poem of that title, Koschin grumbles and whines, "Because despite all that I have seen, read, learnt of yours I am still afraid of labels designed, pregnant with prejudices" (p.6).

On the political level, Koschin is torn between praising and lambasting the military government. For example, he momentarily decides to lend it his support: "The most outstanding government Somalia has ever had...in many fields, the stability of the state, a statedom, neutral not among the neutralized, effulgent Somalia has become radiant in the Eastern horn of prostituted Africa" (p.93). But 58 pages later, Koschin is not so sure after all if his earlier characterization of the government was that apt. For "Isn't it the same people doing the same jobs as before the revolution!" (p.151). So the movements seem to come in waves, which punctuate the inchoate ideas of the protagonists as well as, to use a Joycean phrase, the "uncreated conscience of the race."

The breaking down of the novel into movements instead of chapters does not have any significant impact on characterization. Koschin is as wavering at the end of the book as he was in the prologue. And if man is what Lacan calls "hommolette," breaking and forming under the heat of experience and pressure without losing his fundamental humanity, then Koschin cannot be argued to have

226

changed a bit;[16] he comes out at the end only to lend credence to Lawrence's "the old stable ego of the self."

Koschin is awakened by noises and voices which carry through the quietude of the wee hours of the morning. There are also the voices of his co-tenants, all eight of them, that is if one does not count the guests "on an away day from where they live." The building he shares with these nocturnal creatures is not only in shambles but is also cramped and rodent-infested. If, as Wellek argues in his *Theory of Literature,* it is true that "a man's house is an extension of himself," then Koschin's existence in such an environment could perhaps be viewed "as metonymic, or metaphoric, expressions of [his] character."[17] His living in this place is necessitated by "silly governmental interference, intervention if you like, with regard to rent" (p.3). Koschin's house is also symbolic of Somalia.

Metaphorically, the depiction and imagery of filth in this book symbolically reveals a corresponding impoverishment in the material and spiritual being of the society under scrutiny. In a passage reminiscent of Ayi Kwei Armah's description of the bus conductor and the tattered paper money in his hands in *The Beautyful Ones Are Not Born,*[18] Farah writes about Koschin:

> His hands in his pockets, there is only a tenner, a filthy, aged, Xaaji Faarax [named after a one-time finance Minister] note (A note that must have been clutched in the folds of many an elderly woman's sweaty hands, or warmed in the safety of the aged breast of a milk-woman). Only ten poverty pills, with Nancy coming! (p.19)

Awake at an early hour, Koschin engages in a conversation with Nancy through an interior monologue. His neurotic behavior comes to the fore when, scared by the sound of an aircraft, he goes into fits, weeping and foaming at the mouth. Koschin then thinks, "A snake that hisses as if in preparation of an attack? Nancy you are...a snake.

227

Or, aren't you?" (p.5). This quotation hints at the unreasonable fear that seizes Koschin every time Nancy's name is mentioned, or even when something reminds him of her. He even asks himself, "Why am I drunk with hatred when Nancy's name is mentioned?" (p.6). Koschin's bizarre internal state necessitates the fear. He associates Nancy with Death, especially when he pronounces her last name, Stonegrave, as "grave." The "tomb" image is important: she will seal him off from his people, he fears. The juxtaposition of Nancy, the country, and the Revolution signifies that they are potentially in conflict with one another. The symbolic entombment explicit in Koschin's use of the word "grave" is best grasped when read in the context of cultural domination and hegemony. Nancy, and by extension her European background, will entomb the Somali intellectual in a cocoon. This view of Nancy is similar to the depiction of Maria, the Italian wife of Muuse in Xuseen Kaddare's *Waasuge iyo Warsame*.[19] The two novels were perhaps written at about the same time. Farah's Koschin and Kaddare's Muuse are involved with Western women at a time when their country was drifting towards the Soviet bloc. In the early days of Barre's regime, Westerners were viewed with suspicion. By 1972, for example, the U.S. Peace Corps was expelled from the Somali Democratic Republic.

To Nancy, Koschin is the Devil, and she recites weird hymns from the tenth century during their sexual encounter. Koschin believes the hymns, which are followed by her display of the cross, "are the Crusade ones." "A Tau cross she holds in her hand when we make love. Ancient Tau cross her great-great-grandmother got from her grandfather. It has come through all ages of metal, and she clasps the cross in her hand" (p.76). Nancy's ambivalence, to put it mildly, is obvious in the text. Her display of the cross during her sexual enchange with Koschin could indicate that she is as anxious about her vulnerability after engaging in pre-marital sex as was Ebla in *From a Crooked Rib*. Farah is making a point here by having Koschin be self-absorbed in his own neurotic, bizarre fantasies, which he projects onto Nancy's behavior. Her brandishing of the cross reminds one of the many uses to which the cross is put, especially for exorcising ghosts and evil spirits which haunt the living. Through her brandishing of the cross, Farah is perhaps showing how Nancy feels sinful herself. Koschin is not unaware of the spectacle the couple makes when he asks: "What are we after, the so-called intelligentsia of this country, running like Paris after those foreign women...? Why are we unsatisfied with our own?" (p.42). The allusion to Troy is important. It was Paris' flirtation and elopement with Helen that caused the destruction of a whole city and its civilization. A similar catastrophe is to befall Somalia and Africa in general. The agents of this imminent danger are none other than the intelligentsia of the land.

Here, Koschin is not all alone. In "Movement Two," he is visited by a Somali friend, Barre, who is married to an American, Mildred. Barre met Mildred in Minnesota when he "was a participant in an AID course." But today Barre comes to consult with Koschin about the next step he must take, since Mildred has left him and was spotted in the bathroom of a missionary. Barre cannot expect a high level of fidelity from Mildred, since he had had sex with Barbara, the American wife of his Somali friend, Mohamed. There is a kind of soap-opera-like, incestuous circle here which Koschin does not condone. He reminds Barre how Barre engaged Mildred with the ruses men use to woo women. Echoing Soyinka's poem "...And the Other Immigrant," in which the first-person narrator of the poem has his dignity "sewn/ Into the lining of a three piece suit" he has rented, Koschin teases Barre by mimicking the scene in which Barre used his meager scholarship allowance to beg Mildred to marry him: "Why not now dear, why not now in this hired car, me in my borrowed suit and you in yours..." (p.35). Koschin's harsh words register his indignation with the way that men like Barre bring Mildred's kind to their respective countries, only to let the poor women fend for themselves once the bitter reality hits home. In Barre's case, his dreams of rearing children were shattered when the doctors told him he could not have any. His story is that of a broken man unable to collect the pieces and embark on another journey. But when Koschin answers,

"I am afraid I can't" to Barre's question of why he does not fight the corrupt principal of his school, it then dawns on Barre that impotence has different forms. His verdict, "The bear, for all its fur, feels absolutely cold, is that it?" (p.40) harkens back to the nakedness indicated in the title of the novel.

Koschin attempts to analyze the locus of their problem: Barre is troubled by Mildred while he, Koschin, is scared to death of Nancy's impending arrival. Like existentialist characters in contemporary fiction, Koschin and his peers "give birth to thoughts that generate further thoughts, which in turn breed a further progeny of thought *ad infinitum*."[20] Their casuistry culminates in a lack of action. Koschin's after-thoughts reflect his desperate need for answers. His frustrations are directed inward, causing him to see the world in himself. Losing track of his identity, he interprets his problems as a microcosm of the social world. Unable to grasp reality, he walks around like a zombie:

> I have been let loose on this city [Mogadiscio] by boredom-cum-fear, which to me is a personality tangible. Bored with life I am no doubt, but do I really know what life is—or even what fear is, or what boredom is if I deal with each separately?" (p.42)

Like an ostrich that hides its head in the sand in order to ignore a potential hazard, Koschin, as usual, runs away from reality, afforded an escape by seemingly random associations of ideas. A conversation reminds him of his last trip to Kismayo, where he went to find his dying step-father. Once in Kismayo, he met Meyran, a former prostitute, who "had left Mogadiscio, determined never to return, made a home in Kismayo, where she worked the Port as a clerk/typist" (pp.47-48). To prove that his compatriots are afflicted with indecision, Koschin succeeds in sleeping with Meyran, who had vowed earlier not to lapse into her old profession. Koschin stayed at the Enrico Hotel, "the only decent hotel there." The Italian owner admires Chairman Mao Tse Tung, which prompts Koschin to question him:

> "Come Mai ammiri questo uomo?" asked Koschin [How come you admire this man?]
> "Troppo en gamba e un grande politicante del secolo," replied the Italian [(because) he is very smart and one of the greatest politicians of the century] (p.46)

Once in his own room, Koschin hunts for his favorite novel of the year, *The Interpreters*. He browses it "trying to find passages on Sekoni."[21]

The journey motif here does not fit into the traditional mold, where traveling entails the acquisition of new, transformative experience. Consistent with its plot, the journey motif in this novel has an important use, i.e., that of a diversion to enable the protagonist to indulge in his quandary. Other than that, Koschin's journey to Kismayo does not demonstrate anything save his pedantic inclinations. We are not, for example, given an opportunity to see what is in the hotel owner's mind when he, a member of the Italian settler-bourgeois community in Somalia, admires, of all people, Mao Tse Tung.

Walking uphill towards the school, Koschin meets Mary, whose sophistications are seen in the different ways her name is pronounced. Merriam, Mary, or Maria belongs to a group of sixteen or so girls who are referred to with the sobriquet of "party-girls." She and Koschin first met at Barbara and Mohamed's party. After that Merriam never left Koschin alone. When she learnt that he had written a thesis on Joyce, she told him of her spiritual affinity with "great men of old." She also told him that *"Finnegan's Wake* is my night cap" (p.52). The allusion to Joyce and *Finnegan's Wake is* important in that it attempts to preempt the reader from associating the text with another Joycean text which calls for more than comparison. *A Naked Needle* resembles *Ulysses* in a number of ways.[22] The most obvious resemblance lies in the span of the 24-hour period during which each text delivers its message. Also, reminiscent of Joyce in *Ulysses,* Farah has his characters resort to vulgar street language on many occasions. For example, there is no love lost between Koschin and Faduma, the maid who cooks for him and three other men who live within fifty meters of each other, who pool in and share a meal . . ." (p.8). He becomes irritated by Faduma's answer to his statement that his clock has stopped:

> *"Mac Sokor* [serves you right], she says, sarcastic and bitter. I shall crawl into you one day, I swear, he says to himself, as he notices the way she is sitting, her legs one east, the other west" (p.6).

Koschin says good bye to Merriam and heads towards the school where he teaches. After a brief argument with the school principal he is taken to Barbara's house by a mutual friend, though he still does not understand why he is there. Despite their mutual dislike of each other, they conduct some kind of discussion on a variety of subjects. Then Mohamed, Barbara's husband, comes in with a bleeding neck. Barbara hands her daughter to Koschin, but her query "Where is Nancy?" is answered with a thud on the floor as Koschin drops the baby. Again, Nancy's name disorients Koschin. His reply, "I always called her Grave," reverberates in the text with an eerie feeling. The way he and Nancy met in the first place—at a pub in England at month's end—could perhaps shed light on the nature of his "Nancy-phobia." Koschin, like Barre and Soyinka's narrator in "Other Immigrant" had just collected [his] monthly fortune of a scholarship allowance and [his] purse in the hip-pocket was bursting with pound notes" (p.74). Nancy was at the pub to meet her boyfriend and "decide on the fate of their friendship." The boyfriend never showed up. Koschin, on the other hand, had just terminated an affair with another woman. There was also a second woman who claimed to be pregnant by him. When she called from a telephone booth in

Edinburgh, she, or rather "the instrument threatened, the instrument, mind you, for I can never distinguish voices of women, the instrument threatened . . ." (p.75). This quotation reminds one of Soyinka's "Telephone Conversation" in which the protagonist tries to rent a room over the phone.[23] The landlady cannot tell the color of the caller but when he tells her of his pigmentation, she abruptly terminates the conversation by telling him that there is no vacancy. Koschin's allusion to Soyinka's poem alters the racist rhetoric into a sexist one. The remark about distinguishing women's voices is consistent with his earlier remarks about Faduma, the maid, and Meyran, the ex-prostitute who moved to Kismayo.

Mohamed and Barbara serve lunch to Koschin and Nancy, after which they are given a room to themselves. Nancy wastes no time, asking immediately if Koschin loves her. True to his ambivalent character, Koschin responds with "I don't know." To mollify her tears and anger, he treats her to a walk around Mogadishu, but Koschin's action is not wholly for Nancy's benefit. Walking around Mogadishu, he treats the city both as a backdrop and as a political space both to attack Barre's regime and to rewrite Somali historiography. But, as Michel de Certeau shows, "Historiography (that is, 'history' and 'writing') bears within its own name the paradox—almost an oxymoron—of a relation established between two antinomic terms, between the real and discourse."[24] Koschin's historiography, however, is more a discourse intended to twist and manipulate than real history. Ironically, Koschin's discourse, especially when he engages in Somali clan politics, shows little substantive difference from Siyad Barre's. In other words, there is a wider narrative that informs both Siyad Barre's and Koschin's consciousness. Such clan-based narrative seeps through Farah's text. Reflective of opposing narratives which have been simmering and which later partially informed the Somali civil war, Farah writes: "Mogadiscio. Mogadixo. Maqaldisho. Muuqdisho. Its populace: gangsters with no gang, a town with no treasure, no history..." (p.21)

To understand the importance of this quotation in relation to the dialectics of the Somali clan system, one must decipher the last two spellings of Mogadishu, the Somali capital: "Maqaldisho" (that which taints fame), "Muuqdisho" (that which ruins the appearance). Koschin's way of spelling Mogadishu is perhaps necessitated by the counter-narrative that thrives in Somali orature. The counter-narrative concerns the disparaged city and its residents, who are synechdochically represented by what Farah, through Koschin, calls "a donkey water-man" (pp.19, 21, 22, 95, 96). People who are well-versed in Somali history and politics will understand that the respective clans of Koschin and the donkey water-man have fought for supremacy and control over state politics for the last fifty years. The presence of Nancy, who listens to Koschin's interpretations of events in Somali politics, is important: few outsiders had ever had a holistic view of the Somali problem. Much of what they learned really depended on which Somali version of the past the non-Somali was privileged to hear.

Koschin's incursions into Somali history take a surrealistic turn when he tells Nancy, "Mogadiscio, in the good old oldies, in the ancient of ancients, wrote an Englishman, I don't know how true it is, he wrote that Mogadiscio came under a donkey water-man's dynasty" (p.96). Farah is here referring to a historical fact, the Abgaal-Hawiye dynasty of the early fourteenth century. Koschin's "I don't know how true it is," is a subtle juxtaposition against the Abgaal claim that the city is theirs. As Seamus Deane explains, "These are not nugatory distinctions, for it is from them that so much of the latter history of strife and disagreement evolves. Priority is a claim to power."[25] In the Somali civil war, members of the Daarood clan family, to which Koschin evidently belonged, were expelled from Mogadishu after Siyad Barre's ouster from power. It cannot be ruled out that much of the strife that followed Barre's overthrow is also related, directly or indirectly, to claims of priority among the different Hawiye clans.

Farah's *A Naked Needle* has a prophetic depth, in that it fulfills Balzac's claim that "the novel is the private history of nations." It is in the last two movements of the book—Five and Six—that *A Naked Needle,* as the private history of a Somali nation, assumes a poignant position.

The last movement of the novel, Six, starts with Koschin and Nancy alighting from a taxi, for which Nancy pays the fare. They come to the party thrown by Barni and her husband Dulmar, who has been re-appointed as an ambassador. Many, if not most, of the Somali elite are at the party. The characters, "disjoined" as they are, are nevertheless connected "by acquaintanceship and history."[26] The party is comparable to an assembly of crooks that cuts across gender and ideological lines. There is Ambera, a teacher trained "somewhere south of the Dixon line at a second rate religious institution." There is also the more flashy character, Xaali, whose ostentatious personality includes flaunting her degrees from Padova University in Italy. Then there is Bulxan, a political scientist and a potential candidate for General Secretary of the Somali Socialist Party. The man has bandages all over his legs and feet. His confessions as to the nature of his "ailment" could send shudders down one's spinal cord: "My dozen pairs of socks, all of them, were dirty. I washed them this afternoon. They wouldn't dry in time and I so much wanted to come to the party. So!" (p.137). So much for honesty and integrity, if these were necessary qualities for the post. Bulxan's character also suggests foolishness and stupidity. Farah's point here is to make us laugh at him and wonder at a government for which he is a candidate for a high post. There is also Amxad (a bastard, as his name suggests, being a bastardized form of Ahmed), a graduate of Lumumba University in Moscow. Amxad is an atheist in a sea of believers. His heterodoxy is predicated on his attendance at the famous Russian school for Third World peoples. Amxad does not entertain any sense of decency: he is a man who borrowed some money to have an advertisement for himself as a newly-returned graduate of a foreign university published in the Corriere Della Somalia. The depictions of the last two characters have relevance beyond their fictional lives in the novel.

At the time *A Naked Needle* was written, Somalia was supposed to be on a socialist road to complete emancipation. The Supreme Revolutionary Council had created what it called the "Public Relations Office" of the Council. Later, that name metamorphosed to Xafiiska Siyaasadda Madaxtooyada GSK (Political Office of the SRC Presidency). Cadres were sent to East European countries for training. People who had never had an opportunity to read Marx began professing Marxist-Leninist ideology overnight. Before long, Hantiwadaagga Cilmiga Ku-dhisan (Scientific Socialism) became more than a fad among city dwellers, genuine intellectuals, and quacks of all shades. The political sifting process did not develop an apparatus which could separate the chaff from the seed. It was that first false (some would argue intentional) step which begat people like Bulxan and Amxad. The type these last characters represent has frustrated and at times foiled the aspirations of the few sound and genuine socialists in that desolate strip of land. In his characterization of charlatans like Bulxan, the potential candidate for the position of General Secretary of the Somali Socialist Party, Farah predicts two important and related events: first, Barre's Supreme Revolutionary Council will one day dissolve itself to form a Socialist Party; and second, quacks will swell the ranks of that party. Both predictions came to pass. Barre would have done himself a great service had he allowed the serialization of *Tolow waa talee, ma...*(the original Somali version of *A Naked Needle*). The story in Somali would have helped Barre and his lieutenants avoid many pitfalls that later led to their demise.

A Naked Needle marks a sharp break with tradition, both in terms of content and form, which cannot be separated because the kind of information the novelist imparts is closely linked to the mode of its dissemination. The novel utilizes a stream-of-consciousness technique to deal with contemporary Somali society, evaluating opposing political views within Koschin's consciousness. The absence of an evaluation which caters to and emanates from a consensus is not depreciative of the author's authentic interpretation of reality from a specific historico-political clan background. A case in point is the fourteenth stop in Movement Five, in which Koschin is a Cicerone to Nancy. They come to the statue of Xawo Tacco (Hawo Tako), near the National Theater. Koschin gives this explanation of the lady of the statue: "She was in the Jihaad against the Italian infidels and a Somali whose son is now a governor of a region, hit her. The arrow was poisoned, and she died of it" (p.104).

The Jihaad against colonialism is a theme that is largely absent in Somali fiction writing. The reason is that each sub-culture in Somalia developed its own version of the struggle for independence. It becomes obvious then that Koschin and the man alleged to have killed Xawo Tacco hail from two different clans.

In conclusion, the beauty of *A Naked Needle* lies in its parodic style. It caricatures Siyad Barre's inchoate and primordial ideas about what kind of community to constitute. Farah's reading of the early period of the Barre regime unmasks the revolutionary rhetoric of the time. Koschin, like Bloom in *Ulysses*, goes through life distorted by machinations and lies. Farah depicts decadent life in Mogadishu. Like Bloom, Koschin attempts to fight from within himself. Cantor writes, "The language of lies that Bloom must survive in is what is usually called propaganda. *Ulysses* is a compendium of this language: newspapers, hand bills, the advertising sandwich boardman, popular novels, magazines—all are forces, systems, languages that are outside the ego's control. And they are all forces that impinge on Bloom's consciousness."[27] Farah's text is also paradigmatic of this kind of propaganda. While it creates its own agenda through labyrinthine systems, not least of which is that effacing the agenda of its opponent, *A Naked Needle* does not extricate itself from what Ellul calls "political and integration propaganda meant to induce conformism."[28] The inability of Koschin to rid himself of all forms of Barre's effects on the psyche, reminds one of Julia Kristeva's indictment of "narrativity as the instrument by which society produced the self-oppressing compliant 'subject'..."[29] This is clear from the text's mode of explication and exegesis of rife contradictions emanating from subtle and suppressed forms of enunciations.

Koschin's selective forays into the Somali "liberationist anti-imperialist resistance,"[30] to borrow a phrase from Edward Said, reveal how historical elucidations in the form of fiction could be read as socially and politically symbolic acts.

NOTES

1. Quoted in Nuruddin Farah, *Sweet and Sour Milk* (Saint Paul: Graywolf Press, 1992), p.95.

2. Adonis, *An Introduction to Arab Poetics,* trans. Catherine Cobham (Austin: University of Texas Press, 1990), p.97.

3. Fredric Jameson, *The Political Unconscious* (Ithaca: Cornell University Press, 1981), p.105.

4. Clifford Geertz, *The Interpretation of Cultures* (New York: Basic Books), p.5.

5. Nuruddin Farah, *From a Crooked Rib* (London: Heinemann, 1970), p.6. All subsequent references to this book are given in parentheses in the text.

6. Henry Louis Gates, Jr., "The Blackness of Blackness: A Critique of the Sign and the Signifying Monkey," in *Black Literature and Literary Theory,* ed. Gates (New York: Methuen, 1984), p.290.

7. Wlad Godzich, "Afterword" to Samuel Weber, *Institution and Interpretation* (Minneapolis: University of Minnesota Press, 1987), p.155.

8. *From a Crooked Rib*, p.110 ["Ho mio moglie. Ma non voglio distruggiare la mia vita per una donna."]

9. Nuruddin Farah told me, when we met in East Lansing, Michigan, in 1989, that the Sicilian proverb comes from Robert Graves' *I, Claudius.*

10. B. W. Andrzejewski and I. M. Lewis, *Somali Poetry: An Introduction* (Oxford: Oxford University Press, 1964), p.57.

11. Edward Said, *The World, The Text and The Critic* (London: Faber, 1983), p.117.

12. Abdallah Laroui, *The Crisis of the Arab Intellectual,* trans. Diarmid Cammell (Berkeley: University of California Press, 1976), p.33.

13. Even though the novel was published in 1976, its manuscript form was finished by 1972—almost two years after the military takeover. And while it may be easy to become wise after the event, the same cannot be said of an author trying to capture the essence of an inchoate moment.

14. cf. The following Gurage proverb: "The needle does not cover its own hole, [instead] it covers that of others [of people]. [Refers to a person who tries to solve the problems of others instead of solving his own problems]," From Wolf Leslau, *Gurage Folklore: Ethiopian Folktales, Proverbs, Beliefs, and Riddles* (Wiesbaden: Franz Steiner Verlag GMBH, 1982), p.247.

15. Nuruddin Farah, *A Naked Needle* (London: Heinemann, 1976), p.6. Subsequent references to this book appear in the text in parentheses.

16. Quoted in Catherine Belsey, *Critical Practice* (London: Methuen, 1980), p.60.

17. Rene Wellek and Austin Warren, *Theory of Literature* (New York: Harcourt, Brace, 1949), p.229.

18. Ayi Kwei Armah, *The Beautyful Ones Are Not Yet Born* (London: Heinemann, 1969), p.3.

19. Xuseen Sheekh Axmad Kaddare, *Waasuge iyo Warsame* (Mogadishu: Akadeemiyada Cilmiga iyo Fanka, n.d.).

20. Charles I. Glicksberg, *The Literature of Commitment* (Cranbury, NJ: Associated University Press, 1976), p.14.

21. cf. Lennard J. Davis, *Resisting Novels* (New York: Methuen, 1987) p.148: "Novelists are forever slipping other novels into the pockets of their characters. In *Tom Jones,* Partridge carries his copy of *Robinson Crusoe,* Frankenstein's monster keeps his copy of *Werther...*"

22. cf. "[*Ulysses*]—a book, as he [Joyce] said himself, about 'the last great talkers—is itself a result of imperialism, which condemns Ireland to an older rhetorical past and to the survivals of oratory (in the absence of action), and which freezes Dublin into an underdeveloped village in which gossip and rumor still reign supreme." Fredric Jameson, "Modernism and Imperialism," in *Nationalism, Colonialism and Literature,* Intro. Seamus Deane, eds. Terry Eagleton, Fredric Jameson & Edward Said (Minneapolis: University of Minnesota Press, 1990), p.63.

23. Wole Soyinka, "Telephone Conversation," in *A Book of African Verse*, eds. John Reed and Clive Wake (London: Heinemann, 1964), p.20.

24. Michel de Certeau, *The Writing of History* (Minneapolis: University of Minnesota Press, 1988), p.xxvii.

25. Seamus Deane, "Introduction" to *Nationalism, Colonialism and Literature*, p.17.

26. Jameson, "Modernism and Imperialism," p.63.

27. Jay Cantor, *The Space Between: Literature and Politics* (Baltimore: John Hopkins University Press), p.38.

28. A.P. Foulkes, *Literature and Propaganda* (London and New York: Methuen, 1983), pp.10-11.

29. Quoted in Hayden White, "Figuring the Nature of the Times Deceased: Literary Theory and Historical Writing," in *The Future of Literary Theory,* ed. Ralph Cohen (New York: Routledge), p.37.

30. Edward Said, "Yeats in Decolonization," in Eagleton, Jameson, and Said, *Nationalism, Colonialism and Literature*, p.74.

THE PERSONAL AND THE POLITICAL:
The Case of Nuruddin Farah
Kirsten Holst Petersen

"The Somali are intelligent, sophisticated, subtle, inordinately proud and extremely individualistic."[1] This quotation from a reputable ethnographical survey sums up the Western folklore image of the Somalis as kings of the Africans, but too proud for their own good. In such responsible literature these generalizations are followed by references to the lack of hierarchy in traditional Somali social structure and by the exigences of nomadic life, whereas the popular imagination dwells upon a Karen Blixen inspired oriental mysticism and the romanticism of fierce desert warriors, disappearing into a sun-drenched never-never. Another reality is suggested when Koschin, the hero of Nuruddin Farah's *A Naked Needle*, quotes a colonial English saying that "Somalis are like Epsom salt, which spurts, foams and settles to the bottom in the time it takes to bat your eyelids" and he agrees: "we are a people that need constant changes in government, in leadership. We rise, we revolt against any power and eventually tend to accept it as our fate...In short, we are a people of God."[2] Although this statement, like others of Farah's authorship, is qualified and circumscribed and perhaps not really meant it is still true that in his novels the folklore Somali turns into a poverty-stricken city slum dweller or a Western educated African, hesitant and bewildered by his complex mixture of worlds. Thus another myth goes by the board, another area of Africa enters the mundane world of party politics and literacy campaigns. The contrast is all the more striking because of the characters' (and perhaps the author's) inability or unwillingness to commit themselves to a final point of view. One symptom of this state of mind is the fact that the novels are not concluded, but simply fade out mid-plot, leaving the reader as bewildered as the characters. Farah sifts the modern Somali experience through an exceedingly sensitive mind, and it is not surprising therefore that he eschews easy solutions and instead poses a set of questions. The questions he asks are to a very large extent the questions asked by the majority of modern African writers, and his authorship is very much part of the established African literary tradition in which the educated elite takes a "critical-and-yet" view of their societies.

Farah's early novels, *From a Crooked Rib* (1970), *A Naked Needle* (1976), and *Sweet and Sour Milk* (1979), deal with the role (or perhaps plight) of women in a Muslim society, the role of the educated elite, the corruption of the political elite and the repressive nature of the Somali revolution. Both by virtue of his educated background and his themes, Farah conforms to the established canon of African writing, and a useful angle from which to investigate his work would seem to be to try and discover if he has added any new insight to it. Looked at in that way he is least interesting when he discusses the tribalism and corruption of the military/political elite. His description of the alcohol, cars and fast women syndrome adds nothing to the already existing picture, except perhaps a well-chosen quote from Clemenceau to the effect that America "in only one generation" had "ceased being referred to as a barbaric nation and had qualified itself to be labelled decadent."[3] The quotation is used with reference to

Africa, but maintains the characteristic ambiguity found in all of the novels. A much more interesting point is the author's description of and developing attitude to the Somali Revolution and its leader.

The Somali revolution which took the form of a bloodless coup in 1969 was the result of growing despair over the increasingly obvious failure of the parliamentary model which Somalia had inherited from Italy when it gained formal independence in 1960. Despite obvious advantages of ethnic and linguistic unity the country fell apart into a large number of parties based on clan allegiances. In the 1968 election more than 70 parties contested fewer than 130 seats. Like countless other coups in Africa, the 1969 one was greeted with a sigh of relief, but unlike most of the other military take-overs which ended the post-colonial experiment in transferred democracy, this one did not content itself with trying to curb the worst of the political excesses. Instead it tried to steer an entirely different course and involve the hitherto ignored and fairly inaccessible nomadic masses of the Somali people. Trained in the Soviet Union Siad Barre and his colleagues developed their own brand of "scientific socialism." In doing this they had the co-operation of a small group of left wing intellectuals, and there can be no doubt about the idealism and also the promise of this new beginning. The spectacular achievement of the literacy campaign, following the long overdue agreement on a script for the Somali language in 1972, is a testimony to this idealism, as is the Supreme Military Council's concern for the rights of women. In 1975 the S.M.C decreed that women should have equal inheritance rights with men, something which caused much consternation in a Muslim society where such a decree amounts to a heresy. Thus, despite the regime's heavy leaning on Soviet aid and technical assistance, Western observers tended to take a benevolent view of the Somali revolution.[4] But the military regime also developed a repressive aspect, exhibiting the only too well-known features of sudden arrests, torture, disappearances, censorship, and in 1980 power to detain without trial for 90 days. Members of the corrupt political class seeped back into power, and corruption and a clan-based nepotism flourished. This combination of positive and negative aspects created a complex situation in which one's answer will have to be the result of a careful weighing up of means and ends. Farah's two books which deal with the revolution, *A Naked Needle* and *Sweet and Sour Milk*, reflect a degree of uncertainty which, however, crystallizes into an opposition to the regime in the later *Sardines* (1981).

The naked needle in the book of the same name is Koschin, a young Somali, living in Mogadiscio during the early days of the revolution. In the prelude, which is written in first person narrative, he states the two events which are causing him his present concern and which are the two interwoven themes of the book. They are the revolution "to which I am loyal" and the fact that an English girlfriend, Nancy, whom he has invited to Somalia "on the whim of a day" has just sent a telegram announcing her arrival. These two events on their different levels are forcing him to make decisions, a thing he has never been able to do. This state of affairs is not much improved in the course of the book. On the political level he assesses means and ends by way of an image: "A revolution, y'know, is a pill that tastes bitter, the benefits of which are felt only when one has gone through the preliminary pain and pestilence" (p.4). Loyalty to the revolution is considered necessary, and towards the end of the book a somewhat toothless and pompous stance is made. "Whoever will do any good for this country and for Africa, I shall back till I die. Go up to the pulpit, do something good and I shall certainly be on your side. If these fail to do that they owe us, I shall declare war against them, single-handed even though I am" (p.152). The author is, of course, hiding behind his character, and there is no precise indication of his attitude towards him. On the personal level Farah discusses the problems of a small group of Somali/white couples to which Koschin belongs. This is given a political dimension, not in relation to Somalis, although it is stated that white wives are a handicap, but in a wider perspective of sexual power-relations between races. However, here also there is a lack of a final point of view. The first half of the Somali man/American woman love story is very much in the vein of Armah's *Why Are We So Blest?*, but the second part blames the man for trapping the woman in an alien society by not telling her the truth beforehand. The moral, as pronounced by Koschin, is to make sure not to be trapped. "I prefer whoring to marrying, I, for one, feel free" (p.32). There is nothing wrong with that as a solution, but the whole incident is yet another example of an irritating tendency in the book to touch on vital topics only to drop them in an offhand manner. The style also suffers from this indecision. Sentences like "I...blinded to his wishes by a belief that may be killed no sooner than tomorrow" (p.134) leave one visionless.

Although some of these flaws are still present in *Sweet and Sour Milk* the higher degree of firmness in both character development and statements of opinion makes it a more rewarding book to read. The book centres on a pair of identical twins, Soyaan and Loyaan, and their different attitudes to the revolution. The tone of the book is much more sinister, and arrests, imprisonments, tortures, informers and generally an atmosphere of fear prevail. Soyaan dies mysteriously in the beginning of the book under circumstances which indicate that he has been poisoned by the regime. Trying to ascertain the truth, his brother traces Soyaan's movements using the few clues left to him—cryptic notes and coded messages found in his pocket. This is reminiscent of the detective story technique, but as well as finding out some facts about his brother, Loyaan also undergoes a reluctant and fumbling political development. The shadow aspect of the twin situation is stated explicitly: "One in two: Loyaan and Soyaan. 'My brothers in twins,' says their sister" (p.53). Soyaan is the political activist who has seen through the regime and is trying to subvert it by writing illegal pamphlets, whilst Loyaan seems naive and without any real interest in political matters. He is driven by a personal wish to vindicate his brother, but the insight he gains into the machinations of the regime eventually forces him to accept the vadility of his brother's vision and to try to incorporate it into himself. In a situation of stress he tells himself, "you must help encounter and then fuse the talents of Soyaan and Loyaan; in you must encounter the forces of life (Loyaan) and death (Soyaan)" (p.102). To a reader who is used to more heroic stances against oppression, like, for example, Armah's *Two Thousand Seasons*, Loyaan's political maturing may seem excessively slow and naive, but Farah shares with Ngugi a concern for the doubts and failings of ordinary people who find themselves in extraordinary situations with which they cannot quite cope. Unlike Ngugi's characters, however, Farah's do not reach a definite point of view as a result of their deliberations. At the end of the novel Loyaan, despite his new insight, is still unable to act and the reader is still not certain just how much insight he has gained. The two novels represent a small and somewhat timid beginning of a crucial awareness which, however, in the Somali context, was enough to keep Farah in exile.

A critical view of present political powers, whether black or white, is a theme which in modern African literature is often combined with a search for roots, an affirmation of the validity of traditional society and its potential as a source for a new beginning which should replace the society under attack. One could mention writers like Achebe, Soyinka, Kofi Awoonor, Armah, and Ngugi. In this respect Farah differs radically from the established canon. He finds no virtue in traditional Somali social organization: indeed his two pet hatreds seem to be the patriarch in the traditional Somali Muslim family and the concomitant subjection of women. The patriarch or head of an extended family group as represented by Loyaan's and Soyaan's father is a petty tyrant with unlimited power over the members of his family, and in the larger context of the society he is a cowardly police informer. In the novel Farah connects these two social levels through a quotation from Wilhelm Reich: "In the figure of the father the authoritarian state has its representative in every family, so that the family becomes its most important instrument of power" (p.98). This juxtaposition of negative aspects in traditional and modern society amounts to a heresy in African writing. It is closely connected with Farah's unique sensitivity towards the situation of women in traditional Somali society. Ironically, he would seem to be the first feminist writer to come out of Africa in the sense that he describes and analyzes women as victims of male subjugation. Both the Nigerian writer Flora Nwapa and the Ghanaian Ama Ata Aidoo have dealt with the lives of women, but not with the same emphasis on their social victimization. This is obviously connected with the fact that they are attempting a synthesis of traditional values and modern life. The detached view of Farah's book, which coincided with the ideology and anger of the Western feminist liberation movement, has only become possible in West Africa with a second generation of writers, some of whom have gained enough self confidence to question and reject aspects of their heritage. The Nigerian writer Buchi Emecheta's description of the subjugation of women in traditional Ibo society is a result of this development and an approximation to Farah's work. *From a Crooked Rib* will I think go down in the history of African literature as a pioneering work, valued for its courage and sensitivity.

Due to a mixture of Islamic law and the needs and hardships of nomadic life, the position of women in traditional Somali society would seem to be extremely low. A woman is the property of a patriarch. As such she has no individual rights, but she is protected as a member of her lineage group against outside abuses. Thus blood compensation in slaughtered camels is demanded if she is murdered, even though the amount is only half of the blood compensation demanded for a man. Marriages are arranged by the patriarch who also settles the bride price. Farah incorporates into *From a Crooked Rib* the ethnographical information which is necessary for an understanding of the dilemma of the main character. This information coincides with what one can learn from reading an ethnographical survey, but his use of it is strongly coloured by his attitude. The information that "the engagement and marriage are ratified by a series of presentations"[5] is expressed in the following way in the novel:

> From experience she knew that girls were materials, just like objects or items on the shelf of a shop. They were sold and

bought as shepherds sold their goats at market-places, or shop-owners sold the goods to their customers. To a shop-keeper what was the difference between a girl and his goods? Nothing, absolutely nothing.[6]

The main character in the novel, Ebla, a young nomad girl, is sold several times in the course of the story, and when she understands the connection between her human value and money she draws the logical conclusion. "She scratched her sex, then chuckled 'This is my treasure, my only treasure, my bank, my money, my existence'" (p.160). This realization is made probable by the story. In order to avoid a forced marriage to an old man, Ebla flees from her nomadic kinship group to the city. By doing this she becomes a woman who is not owned by anybody, and as such she has no legal protection. She joins the marginal group of widows, spinsters and divorced women whose only means of survival is prostitution or shades of it. Ebla marries a student who soon after leaves for Italy, and she is left to fend for herself. Marriage is the purpose of her life, but she has confused ideas about it, and the book is somewhat contradictory on this point. On the one hand she says "I love to be a wife. I don't care whose" (p.125), but on the other hand she also has Western ideas about individual choice and love: "I won't marry a broker. Unless I choose him, I cannot think of anything else to do" (p.80). These ideas do not easily fit into Somali society, and Ebla's choice (or choices, for she marries twice) are not based on a knowledge of the men chosen but rather forced by circumstances she cannot control. Marriage may be the purpose of her life, her only means of self-definition, but she is to find no satisfaction in it. "Enslavement was what existed between the married couples she had met. The woman was the slave" (pp. 83-84). Women in Somali society are not only slaves, they are also sexually abused. The Somali practise clitorization and infibulation, and the book stresses the physical pain attached to these customs. After the consummation of her marriage (which, incidentally, according to tradition is preceded by her husband beating her up),

Ebla wishes that she were either an old woman or a man so that the experience would not have to be repeated. None of her problems are solved in the course of the book, but the reader is left with a very clear vision of the narrow space within which a Somali woman can define herself, and the virtual impossibility of breaking down the walls of tradition and widening the space.

With no sympathy for traditional society and a critical attitude towards the Revolution, pushed by his own sympathy and sensitivity, but not pushed too far, and anchored to a modified Western bourgeois ideology, Farah battles valiantly, not for causes, but for individual freedom, for a slightly larger space round each person, to be filled as he or she chooses. It is a thankless task, and Farah stands guard over liberty in Somalia like the camel owner of an anonymous traditional Somali song:

> One of my she-camels falls on the road
> And I protect its meat,
> At night I cannot sleep,
> And in the daytime I can find no shade.[7]

NOTES

1. I.M.Lewis, *Peoples of the Horn of Africa* (London: International African Institute, 1955), p. 150.

2. Nuruddin Farah, *A Naked Needle* (London: Heinemann, 1976), p.21. All subsequent references will be to this edition and cited in the text.

3. Nuruddin Farah, *Sweet and Sour Milk* (London: Heinmann, 1979), p. 149. All subsequent references will be to this edition and cited in the text.

4. See for example Colin Legum and Bill Lee, *Conflict in the Horn of Africa* (New York, London: Africana Publishing Company, 1977); and Basil Davidson, "Notes on the Revolution in Somalia" in *The Socialist Register* (London: The Merlin Press, 1975), pp.198-223.

5. Lewis, p.135.

6. Nuruddin Farah, *From a Crooked Rib* (London: Heinemann, 1970), p.84. All subsequent references will be to this edition and cited in the text.

7. B.W. Andrzejewski and I.M. Lewis, *Somali Poetry: An Introduction* (London: O.U.P., 1964), p.142.

MISOGYNY MISCONSTRUED:
A Comment on *A Naked Needle*
Derek Wright

Nuruddin Farah has made known his preference that his second novel, *A Naked Needle* (1976), should remain out of print. This is not, it seems, the mature author's disowning of a youthful *jeu d'esprit*, written at the age of 27, or his harbouring of regrets about its mercurial young narrator's misguided enthusiasms for a post-revolution regime which would be targeted in his subsequent *Dictatorship* trilogy. Rather, Farah's discomfort with the novel has to do with his concern—understandable in an author who has done more than any male African writer to spotlight the plight of African women—that it might be misinterpreted as a misogynistic work. Farah has said in a recent interview: "I thought at the time that I was being satirical about misogynists, in addition to many other things, and people misunderstood the sarcasm and the satirical nature of the book and took it literally to heart. I didn't want to add one more misogynist to world literature. It's not an easy book to read if you're prone to not seeing beyond the surface."[1] In fact, one does not have to look very far beyond the surface of *A Naked Needle* to discover that

Farah accomplished, more or less, what he set out to do—to be "satir-ical about misogynists." The problem, however, is that what is being satirized in the novel is often difficult to place and pin down, partly because the erratic narrator is no more consistent and coherent in his misogyny than in anything else he says or does and partly because the author's angle on him wavers between intermittent identification and sustained dissociation, with the result that the narrator serves, by turns, as both a victim and a vehicle of Farah's satire.

The novel is set in Mogadiscio during the early days of the Somali Revolution, sometime between Siyad Barre's Soviet-backed military coup of October 1969 and December 1972, when the book was fin-ished. As it opens its narrator Koschin, a young Western-educated Somali intellectual, is thrown into a state of panic and confusion by the imminent arrival of his English girlfriend Nancy who has sudden-ly decided to take up his half-serious offer of marriage if neither of them were to find partners within two years of Koschin's leaving England. Koschin remembers that once, in England, he had beaten Nancy, which now causes him both remorse and embarrassment, particularly in the light of his recent progressive thinkings—"Women should be seen, not hurt"—and he is haunted by traumatic child-hood memories of his mother's beatings at the hands of his father. He is, contradictorily, both critical and defensive of the state's degrada-tion of Somali women but the defence is deliberately ironic and is made only before the American woman Barbara. Women are "serviles in the society," he tells her. "They like it that way, being Somalis," and then adds, to himself: "And they being what they are, superior Somalis, may scorn the speech you may use."[2] Koschin's misogyny is, in fact, highly selective, the hysterical diatribes that punctuate his rambling narrative being reserved exclusively for foreign wives. Though he is himself a party to the offence, and perhaps partly because of this, Koschin is preoccupied by the threat to national unity, to the social fabric and its cultural integrity, posed by the pres-ence of foreigners and infidels, particularly white women, in a devout Muslim society ("Do not hold on to your marriages with unbelieving women," runs one verse of the Koran[3]). Koschin's scorn, largely misdirected and unfounded, is unleashed upon both these women and the Somali males who seek "honorary" whiteness through their foreign sexual conquests, even though the Soviet Embassy, in true imperialist style, penalizes the Russian women who marry them. The point is driven home during the novel's last long "movement" at the Europeanized Mogadiscio Club in the cameo of Mahed, a new Soviet-trained power *arriviste*, for whom any white woman will do, and his graceless Russian mistress, whom Koschin dubs "a thing of laughter for a wife" (p.167).

In its treatment of interracial marriages and relationships Farah's novel makes considerable play, whether of a serious or satiric kind, with race-sex archetypes inherited from colonialism. This is done, however, in a generally playful and selfconsciously parodic manner. Indeed, each of the book's racially mixed relationships is passed as a matter of course through a deconstructive sieve of stock literary types and tropes, reduced by time and over-familiarity to comic-strip level (here, the Dark Lady, the Colonial Mistress, the White Destroyer), with the effect that the symbolic or representative signifier is given a provisional priority over its referent: "I don't like what you *represent*," Koschin tells Barbara (p.145). Ultimately, however, the archetypes and tropes from the world's literatures and philosophies which the narrator tosses casually around come to exist in contradistinction with whatever substantial human reality is realized in the novel and to be grotesquely unequal to "reality" as constructed in the "realistic" or illusionist mode. Koschin, for example, devises for Nancy an unashamedly novelettish past full of grandfathers and fiances martyred in the noble struggles of romantic Latin American insurrections, mixing historical anecdotes with imagined ones and revolutionary romances (Nancy's supposed ancestry) with "real" ones (her present). Subsequently, it is left unclear whether or not these exotic magazine-romance revolutions are to be seen as existing in the same world as, and being of the same status and order of experience as, the historical Somali revolution which she now finds herself in the midst of. Because the distinctions between thought and speech are blurred in Koschin's egocentric, freewheeling monologue, it is never certain whether his tirades are delivered in actuality or in imagination; whether they are addressed to the real Nancy or to an idea or memory of her. Thus it is not clear if the romance-material invested in Nancy is the stuff of stories previously narrated by her to him and now relayed, with additions, to the reader, or if it is all a wild concoction of Koschin's exuberant imagination and part of the satiric author's all-embracing literary fabulation.

Indeed, Koschin's playful, parodic manipulation of the types and tropes of race and sex in the context of mixed marriages and engagements—tropes that are by turns challenged and upheld—needs to be seen in terms of the book's problematic metafictional mode and with reference to narrative needles that may *un*stitch and pull things apart as well as sow things together. In this novel the human reality of the female interlocutor, ominously surnamed Stonegrave, has to fight its way through a dense narrative fog of stock literary figures and stereotypes, spread by her intended before she appears. Nancy, whom Koschin has inexplicably "always associated with death," becomes, in rapid succession, a shadow and ghost, "a human deformity, the white person,...a ghost of the living dead" (p.113), La Belle Dame sans Merci, the Dark Lady, the deathly white mistress given to the pathological clutching of crucifixes and the recitation of medieval hymns during love-making, and much more of the same kind. The writing in these passages has a precious, self-parodying and self-debunking literariness which seems deliberately to disarm belief and which culminates in Nancy's hysterically overstated introduction: "She offers him a love that has decayed inside her heart...Dressed in a black nylon two-piece dress, and a dark jumper, and dark shoes: and this, a pact with the darkness of death, my God!" (p.78). Once the Gothic trappings have been removed, what emerges from the caricature is the female sexual archetype of the colonial mistress, the white dominator and destroyer. But then, when he has to bring the real Nancy's gentle, patient nature to bear upon this cartoon-model that he has prepared for her, Koschin is unable to negotiate the gulf that he has opened up between trope and truth, and he embarks on an impossible attempt at a "contractual marriage...between the image he hated and the woman he cared for" in order to "crush out of existence an image of the dominator" (p.134).

This latter image rampages through most of Koschin's speculations about interracial sexual relations, particularly his fantastic projections from the Mildred-Barre marriage shortly before Nancy's arrival:

> Nietzsche said never wed a woman without her whip. Ask for the whip before the hand...Never buy a Nigger without a stick to beat him with.

> And this poor fellow from the land of the pagans, green in his hand-me-down suit, falls for an American dream of a woman, and licks the ground she walks on...And this pagan chooses to prostrate himself before the American dream of a woman, what boobs, what a figure, what a mouth to to kiss, he chooses to flatten himself on the tiled floor, he argues, because he needs her, and she chooses never to pick him up, never to offer him a helping hand...The man straight from the land of jungles, he continued sinking down more and more, never denying her the rights of a deity, until he had been reduced to a bare physique with no mind.

> What are we after, the so-called intelligentsia of this country, running like Paris after those foreign women, sluts of a kind, in their own countries, despised here in ours—what are we after? Is it what Fanon says we are after? Or something below that?...Why are we unsatisfied with our own? (pp.31, 33, 42)

Of course, Koschin protests too much, and the author's satiric irony resounds through his narrator's frantic hyperbole. His too glib espousal of the stereotype, whether genuine or ironic, is clearly meant to be taken as an index to his own immature, almost paranoid, anxiety over Nancy's visit and is sustained only by misquotation and misrepresentation. Nietzsche's famous quip about the whip is inverted— "never wed a woman without *her* whip"—to promote the stale sado- masochistic colonial paradigm of white female power-lust and black male prostration; and thence the Fanonian model, treated in *Black Skin, White Masks*, of the white mistress and the black love-slave who, in a white society, desires only to be loved as if white.[4] A few minutes later Koschin is ready to admit his blunder in his assessment of the Mildred-Barre marriage: the latter, as his own interrogation of Barre reveals, in fact reverses the Fanonian model. Here the white woman is not the victimizer but, lured by lies of wealth and tribal hospitality, is the duped, trapped victim for whom the husband impossibly seeks acceptance as an "honorary" Somali in a culturally alien society. The black man does not, in this case, want to be loved as "white" by the white woman in her white society; he wants *her* to be loved as a Somali in a Muslim one. Most of the unhappiness in this marriage is hers, and it is chiefly his doing. Stereotypically, Barre blames the nuclearization of the extended Somali family upon the foreign wife—"They make you cut off your ties with your brothers and sisters, they insinuate the idea from the moment they set their feet here that you must live your own life with them" (p.28)—but in fact the opposite is true. Barre beats his wife, exposes her to the rigid customs and codes of an alien clan culture, and, finally, by abandoning her to its suffocating intimacies and boredom, drives her to a suicide attempt. The misogyny here is entirely the character's; it is the narrator's only indirectly, by way of error and guilty confession; and it is the author's not at all.

Farah tentatively offers, as an alternative to the cultural collisions of the Mildred-Barre marriage, the more realistic compromise, albeit with built-in infidelities, achieved by the American Barbara and the

Western-oriented Mohamed, a Somali who has already "detribalized" himself. "I have adjusted totally, I should say, to the conditions that are prevalent here, conditions that may put off any woman from anywhere else in the world," Barbara claims, offering herself as the model of cultural compromise. The claim rings hollow, however, when she reveals that her knowledge of her husband's language extends only to "the basic Somali words for communication" and adds the qualifier, "But it is only him [Mohamed] that I must get used to, not a whole tribe, if you see what I mean" (pp.62, 64). Moreover, when Barre discloses to Koschin that Barbara turned to himself for sexual satisfaction within a month of the birth of her daughter and during Mohamed's brief absence, the American woman's abject failure to observe or to understand Islamic conventions becomes glaringly evident. Subsequently, it transpires that whatever happiness Mohamed and Barbara have found in their flexible relationship has been achieved by his shift towards Western behavior patterns rather than by any accommodation of Somali traditions and values on her part (we hear in the later novel *Sardines* that Barbara is living in Rome, revelling in her new freedom, and assume that the marriage has failed). Whatever the relative merits of these two relationships, it becomes clear in the first half of the novel, in any case, that race and colour are not the real issues at stake but religion and the devout Muslim code on women: thus Koschin foresees that Nancy's Western Catholicism, not her whiteness, will be the main source of Somali hostility.

In *A Naked Needle* Farah constantly complicates racial polarities with other factors and his use of Koschin to play off figure against fact, image against particular instance, effectively sets up misogynistic racial stereotypes only to dismantle and demolish them. It is not the author but the narrator who endeavors to turn European and American wives into merely figurative and representative characters and, even then, in a half-serious and partly self-mocking way which precludes any serious correspondences between black-white sexual relations and patterns of African powerlessness and Western domination. In these respects the novel is a world away from the politico-sexual polemics of, for example, a book like Ayi Kwei Armah's *Why Are We So Blest?* (1972), in which the white American woman is invested with a solemn rhetoric of "white devilry" and a succubus-like sexuality that sucks life from her black prey, so that she is imaged as an engine of destruction or a demonic contraption rather than a human being. The crucial distinction here is between stereotypes as a literary failing and stereotypes as social and political reality reproduced by the writer for satiric effect. The satiric levity of *A Naked Needle* is, finally, too deliberately self-evident and self-advertising for its "misogyny" to be misread in serious, unironic terms or, as the author puts it in the interview, to be taken "literally to heart." In Farah's novel the writer's fair-minded openness to experience and the narrator's self-satirizing histrionics combine to debunk all types and tropes, while Armah's book—a truly misogynistic work—is itself heavily implicated in stale, sensationalist myths of race and sex to which no counter-truths are opposed.

If anxiety about misogynistic misreadings do not quite justify Farah's virtual withdrawal of *A Naked Needle*, however, a possible alternative explanation—that the author is embarrassed by his narrator's long discredited pro-revolutionary sentiments—also creates some puzzles for the reader. Koschin's naive revolutionary idealism is a self-willed and self-consciously hollow phenomenon, maintained only by artificially suppressing his growing awareness of the Supreme Revolutionary Council's betrayal of the revolution's original ideals of economic independence, sexual equality and detribalization. These betrayals, and Somalia's subsequent drift towards tribal oligarchy and totalitarian dictatorship, complete with state surveillance and police terror, will preoccupy Farah in the novels of the *Dictatorship* trilogy, in which we hear that Koschin himself has been arrested and reduced to a vegetable in one of the state's mental asylums. Yet even in the earlier novel there is abundant evidence of the gathering forces of political repression: the bandaged feet of Bulxan just back from the police cells, his friend Mohamed's razor-cut after a political argument with his barber, and the menacing police car hovering over the last pages of the book. Koschin's blithe attempts to "turn a dead ear" to these developments meet with little success, for the grim warnings keep breaking through his euphoria, and the liberal humanist Mohamed, who exposes Koschin's disingenuous double-think and sounds the first alarms about the "terror and horror from dawn to dusk" being ushered in by KGB-trained revolutionaries, surely speaks for the author and reinforces the repudiative authorial irony. Moreover, Koschin himself—if he would but admit it—is already deeply suspicious of propagandist art, government indoctrination programs and the deification of Generals (even if he does naively attribute the latter to sycophantic underlings and an ignorant populace). Consequently, his admiration for the national leader's achievements is guarded and at times jeeringly ironic, for his alert critical eye falls also upon abuses that are becoming impossible to ignore: nepotistic government appointments, gross maladministration and venality; the neocolonial connivance with Catholic mission profiteering and the use of Italian workmen in preference to the Somali unemployed; the flocking of the intellectual elite to United Nations sinecures abroad while poorly trained teachers struggle with a dearth of school laboratories at home; and, above all, the strengthening and increasingly sinister Soviet presence.

All of these details add up to a novelistic vision that is in essence deeply critical of the Somali revolution, whatever the narrator's professed loyalties and sympathies, and surely the most decisive testimony in this respect must be the response of the Barre regime iself. Even if Farah did not think he had written an anti-revolutionary book, the regime certainly did, promising him thirty years of imprisonment if he dared to return to Somalia in 1976. The fact is that *A Naked Needle* was the book that first got Farah into major trouble with his government and its publication marks the beginning of his long exile. As such, the book is an oddity in African and world fiction. Usually, it is the fashion for controversial works of this kind to be turned into a *cause celebre* and thereafter to be never out of print: witness *Lady Chatterley's Lover, Lolita, The Satanic Verses. A Naked Needle*, meanwhile, remains a little-known, seldom-read work which has received only one reprinting (in 1980) and has been out of print ever since. Perhaps one day, when the author is satisfied that there exists a readership that is sufficiently deserving of and adequate to his satiric subtleties, and forgiving of his narrator's political incorrectness, he may change his mind about this neglected novel.

NOTES

1. Patricia Alden and Louis Tremaine, "How Can We Talk of Democracy?: An Interview with Nuruddin Farah," in the "Farah on Farah" section of this volume. p. 39.

2. Nuruddin Farah, *A Naked Needle* (London: Heinemann, 1976), p.68. All subsequent references are to this edition and are cited in parentheses in the text.

3. *The Koran* 60: 10; trans. N.J.Dawood, 1956 (Harmondsworth: Penguin, 1974), p.268.

4. Frantz Fanon, *Black Skin, White Masks*, trans. Charles Lam Markmann (New York: Grove, 1961), p.63.

PART FOUR
THE FIRST TRILOGY:
Variations on the Theme of an African Dictatorship

OPPOSING DICTATORSHIP:
A Comment on Nuruddin Farah's
Variations on the Theme of an
African Dictatorship
Barbara Turfan

Three novels comprise the trilogy retrospectively entitled *Variations on the Theme of an African Dictatorship—Sweet and Sour Milk, Sardines* and *Close Sesame*, and it is with these three only that I shall deal in this paper. The novels do form a whole in that together they trace the activities of selected members of a clandestine opposition group in present-day Somalia; more than this, Farah introduces the participants' various ideological platforms, their "world-views", as well as their perceptions of aspects of Somali and other societies. My intention, then, is first to examine the Somali regime as it is portrayed in the three novels together with the views of it held by members of the secret opposition group and the different tactics for its removal adopted by them; secondly, I shall consider some of the questions arising from Farah 's use of his subject-matter and the way in which he approaches it.

The ruling regime is continuous throughout the trilogy in the sense that the ruler, known as "the General", continues uninterruptedly in power. The irony is that the ideological basis of his rule changes from the Russian-backed " Socialism " of the first two books to the American-backed "democracy" of the third, yet nothing changes in the country other than the substitution of western for eastern aid and technicians. The iron hand of the General does not relax its grip over the ruled: suppression of information and oppression of individual opinion and action is the rule; arrest and imprisonment without charge, torture and even execution are so commonplace that few families or clans remain untouched and inviolate. It is the first two novels that convey directly and succinctly the methods of the government in its efforts to establish total control over its citizens. Soyaan and Ibrahim ("Il Siciliano"), two of the founder members of the opposition group, have prepared a subversive Memorandum which, but for Soyaan's mysterious and untimely death, they would have circulated clandestinely. The Memorandum is called "Dionysius's Ear" after the legend of the Syracusan tyrant who constructed a cave in the shape of an ear which echoed the secret whispers of his prisoners:

> Soyaan and I saw a similarity between this and the method the General has used so far. The Security Services in this country recruit their main corps from illiterates, men and women who belong to an oral tradition, and who neither read nor write but report daily, report what they hear as they hear it, word by word...They need no warrant to arrest anybody. Everything is done verbally...We've found that two thirds of the prisoners have no files, that over two thirds of them are serving indeterminate prison sentences...We say in our Memo that the General (with the assistance of the Soviets) has had an ear service of tyranny constructed.[1]

The universal use of spies and informers is bound to create an atmosphere of suspicion, fear and isolation—an atmosphere heightened by laws such as ban the assembly of more than five people except at an Orientation Centre (at which civil servants and their families must attend thrice-weekly programmes of orientation on pain of losing their jobs) or to chant the praises of the General. Tension and suspicion are almost tangible throughout the trilogy, even after the switch to a western alliance with its insistence on at least the forms of democracy if not the spirit. Indeed, *Close Sesame* dwells no less than do the preceding novels on the strangers who approach one in the street to open up a conversation and prove one's political allegiances—the security men nicknamed the "pederasts" by Medina because "they walk with the ease of a pederast scouring the streets they've always hunted in."[2] The feeling of an omnipresent uncertainty and tension is deftly evoked also in conversations, conversations which leave out more than they include but form, with the speaker's unspoken thoughts, a continuous stream to which the reader, but not the other participants, has access. The conversational style is, like Farah's narrative, further enhanced by symbols and metaphors which enrich the most banal of exchanges and lend a profundity and a dignity to the characters themselves.

Another characteristic of the regime of which Farah clearly tries to make the reader aware is that of its dependence upon foreign powers, be they from the eastern or the western bloc, both to support its continued existence against subversive activity and, more fundamentally, to provide the very ideological foundation on which it bases its validity. There is not necessarily an identity between real and "validating" ideology. For example, the General espouses socialism and receives aid in the form of huge prisons built by the East Germans and medical doctors sent by China and the Soviet Union; yet he relies upon traditional tribal loyalties and family ties in selecting his ministers and administrative officers, always alert to the threat of ideological ties developing between members of different tribal groups and creating a dangerous potential "national" awareness and "nationalist" opposition. Yet is this not a major contradiction in terms? How can a regime truly espousing an ideological cause seek to deny the development of an ideological awareness among its own populace? How can it seek instead to graft the official ideological superstructure onto an unprepared tribal, or clannish, infrastructure? But of course the General is depicted as not truly seeking to graft the ideology he ostensibly espouses onto a society being educated to understand and embrace it. For him, socialism is merely a means to an end and can be dropped when other, more useful means come to hand—as indeed occurs. As Nasser writes to his sister, Medina, while there can be no doubt that the Soviets used the General for their own purposes, " '...he used them too. He made them train his clansmen; he used them to build himself a system of security as tight as the KGB.'"3

As for tribal loyalty, this is a theme to which Farah returns time and time again. In *Sweet and Sour Milk*, Loyaan's father rounds on him for his misplaced "self- importance":

> "The General fears tribal chieftains or men of his own
> age. Not you, nor Soyaan, nor anyone of your genera-
> tion. You have no common ideology and no principles.
> You work for the interests of the countries in which
> you received your academic training. Some for
> Western Europe, some for Russia."4

Sardines turns on the appointment of Samater as Minister of Constructions, a post he is reluctant to take up since it is incompatible with his subversive inclinations as a member of the group, but which he feels obliged to accept, against the group's instructions, in the face of open threats against his tribe and his duty as a clan member to save them. It is, we find, for Samater's ambivalent behaviour—his reluctance to condemn his kinsmen in order to uphold a principle—that his wife, Medina, leaves him until he has faced his own conscience and made his own decisions. Again, the plot of the final novel, *Close Sesame*, revolves around the relationship between four young opponents of the regime who are drawn from different tribal backgrounds. The aim of the General after the first, abortive assassination attempt is to isolate Mahad's tribe and family (in that order) and to play down the likely involvement of Mukhtaar, a member of the General's own clan and "the water he cannot swallow" of Somali lore. As the opposition realize, should more than one tribe be seen to be involved, the plot would assume ideological implications and hence nationalist proportions not possible in a purely tribal incident. Deeriye, the father of one of the four, has proved himself a long-standing and staunch opponent of oppression at the hands of the Italian colonialists and the succeeding Somali dictatorship; his friendships have been formed across the clan barriers, against all advice, and it is perhaps to establish beyond all doubt the nationalist, non-tribal basis of the ineptly managed assassination attempts of the four youths as much as to avenge the death of his own son in one of those attempts that Deeriye himself dies in a futile but extremely public attempt on the life of the General. Clearly, Farah sees the clash between traditional tribal and modern national awareness as a major flaw in the development of a modern, independent nation-state:

> Must everything be interpreted according to the code of clan-, class- or group-interest, must everything be seen in this light?...This country hasn't a tradition of protest movements, trade unions or organised groups of any kind. There is no tradition such as there is in Egypt, Ethiopia or Sudan, of student movements which can help form or unform governments or shape public opinion.[5]

One of the " group-interests" seems to be that of religion, again presented as an inconsistency in present-day Somali political life. For the traditional religion of Somalia, Islam, provides a firm cultural foundation for the society at large, a foundation, like tribalism, which

269

is incompatible with a genuinely socialist superstructure. Yet the General has been able to distort his subjects' interpretation of Islam, bribing or coercing the sheikhs to support his rule and to lead their followers in singing his praises and comparing him, grotesquely, with the Prophet or even with Allah. In *Sweet and Sour Milk*, the dead Soyaan is posthumously turned into a "Hero of the Revolution" whose last words are given out as "Labour is Honour and there is no General but our General"[6] —a perversion of the most fundamental tenet of the Islamic faith. The sheikhs are in total confusion, those who support the General being rewarded with stipends and honours, those who refuse being imprisoned, tortured, even executed . The provision of an Islamic legitimacy for a dictatorial, Marxist-Leninist regime is something the General obviously finds of extreme impor-tance in securing at least the passivity and at best the full support of the populace. Much care is taken in the pursuit of this aim, to the extent of hiring the best and most famous popular singers; such is Dulman (*Sardines*)—the "Lady of the Revolution"—hired to sing praise-songs in his name both at home and on propaganda tours of Europe and the Middle East where she is reviled by the numerous Somalis in exile. But Farah's own attitude towards Islam is by no means hostile. Rather, it is the distortion of Islam by its practitioners and by those who seek to use it to their own advantage that provokes his criticism. His portrayal of strongly religious figures, such as the older women (particularly Medina and Nasser's mother, Fatima bint Thabit), may not always show them up in a particularly good light but nor does his portrayal of the bright young atheistic generation they have spawned. The chief character in *Close Sesame*—to my mind Farah's richest and most human novel—is the aged, asthmatic and devout Deeriye, a tribal elder who has spent his life in the strug-gle against oppression or actually in prison for his beliefs. He is most sympathetically drawn as a character and is shown as a man who has come to terms with himself, who knows who he is and where he stands, unlike so many of the confused and rootless adolescents and young people of Farah's novels (and whom, perhaps, Farah himself

270

represents?), and especially of *Sardines*.

Sardines stands rather alone in the trilogy in that while it is, like the others, very much about personal relationships, it is particularly female—and most of all mother/daughter—relationships that form the texture of the book. And it is among the younger women that the confusion and rootlessness seem most prominent. To me, the adolescent Sagal stands out as the epitome of this; Sagal, described by various of her friends and relations in terms of flowing water:

> Sagal is a river changing course, country, beds, master and lover. She is the river which floods the farms it has watered. Where will she go? To Budapest, then London? It's not the first time she's talked of that. No nothing will surely come of it: she will not paint the dawn walls with slogans against the General...[7]

Sagal is bright, alert, intelligent. Yet she is curiously transient in her attachments, with only a superficial interest in her enthusiasms; for example, she has on her wall stills of Marlon Brando in the film *Queimada* but is unable to explain to her questioning mother such basic points as who was the hero? What was the revolt he led? What other revolutions were taking place at that time in other places, especially Africa? Then it turns out that in Somalia only a very heavily censored version of the film was shown, and that for just one night—moreover, Sagal had not even seen it! "So why must you hold the banner of the revolutionary when you are not properly initiated...?" queries Ebla, her mother.[8] Besides *Queimada*, Sagal has the usual poster of Che Guevara, records of Stevie Wonder, pictures of Malcolm X and Martin Luther King; she bubbles with flippant, revolutionary remarks, her naivete and insincere enthusiasm as transparent as the pyjamas which so dismay her mother:

> "All the men worth falling in love with either live in exile or are in prison. Both categories are outside my

reach. That's why I want to go abroad: to join the ones
already in exile. "

"And if you can't?"

"I'll paint the morning leaves with slogans and go
to prison. Possibly I shall meet some of them there "9

Medina herself, the chief character of this book, is a more
interesting personality. The daughter of a Somali ambassador, she
has grown up in numerous European and African capitals, attended
an Italian university and published occasional papers, speaks four
European languages fluently as well as Arabic and writes two of them
well, and was, albeit for a very brief period, editor of Somalia's only
daily newspaper. She is cosmopolitan, relaxed in mixed company—
indeed is never debarred from any group or activity on account of
her sex, a characteristic shared by few women —and is one of the
leading members of the original clandestine group of ten. She is
deeply critical of the General and his regime which, as a declared
Marxist-Leninist, she pronounces Fascist and intolerable; she is evidently sincerely concerned with her country's problems. She is a
thinker, yet not profound enough to realize that it is a mistake to
underestimate and despise one's enemy and is thus responsible for
the split in the group between those like herself who consider the
General an evil buffoon of no historical significance and those who
believe the General to be following a definite policy and to be a foe
worthy of circumspect observation and careful planning. She shuns
convention wherever and whenever she finds the opportunity, bringing up her daughter, Ubax, in a way that scandalizes not only her
detested mother-in-law but also her own mother and even, at times,
her liberal minded, co-revolutionary brother, Nasser. Yet she wonders why she feels like a "guest" in her own country, her own home,
unable metaphorically to move the "furniture" without being invited
to do so. She seeks a place for herself and longs to fit. In the view of
the reviled Idil, her mother-in-law:

"I am the product of a tradition with a given coherence and solidity; you [she is speaking to her son, Samater], of confusion and indecision. I have Allah, his prophets and the Islamic saints as my illustrious guides. For you, nothing is sacred, nothing is taboo. You are as inconsistent as your beliefs and principles are incoherent."[10]

A remark such as this could be made of most of the youthful protagonists opposing the regime, in all three books. Indeed, we come across the same characters again and again as the novels unfold. All told, the youth portrayed in these pages are, to my mind, a reflection of a greater or lesser degree of the spoilt, rich, urban elite of western Europe and America with their fancy toys and gadgets, their expensive tastes, their passion for new and exotic experiences and their playing at revolution. Yes, playing; for while one by one the opposition group and their companions are eliminated from the struggle by imprisonment, exile or death—and they are certainly prepared to suffer and die for the cause—they none of them seem to have a clear idea of what they actually want to replace the hated General and his system with, nor do they have a clear idea of how to achieve their immediate objective of removing the General as a political force. It appears almost as if, for some of them at least, it is more important to strike a blow and win a heroic martyrdom than to achieve a positive gain for their peers, let alone for the "suffering masses". Loyaan, in *Sweet and Sour Milk*, is caught up by events on the mysterious death of his activist twin, Soyaan; he has no course mapped out in his mind except that of defending his brother's name against the encroachments of state propaganda which is claiming Soyaan for its own. Medina is a leader of the ten, but in her extremism misuses her one major opportunity to influence the state's propaganda as editor of Somalia's single newspaper, is sacked and refused permission to publish anything at all. She criticizes the General for ignoring her on the grounds that she is a woman and therefore insufficiently important. Yet other women are imprisoned and tortured, as we hear from

273

Dr.Ahmed-Wellie's graphic accounts in *Sweet and Sour Milk* as well as the case of Ibrahim's sister, Mulki, and as we see in *Sardines* with the arrest of Sagal's chief rivals in swimming, Cadar and Hindiya. In *Close Sesame*, Deeriye is caught up, in the twilight of his life, in the activities of his son and three others; Deeriye, a man who has always professed his belief in non-violent opposition, eventually comes round to sharing Mursal's faith in "lex talionis," or the right of the victim of state oppression to exact personal vengeance on the state itself in the form of the General, its leader. The four plotters in this final part of the trilogy are the most coherent in their ideological grounding; they have based their argument upon Qur'anic teaching (Mursal has a doctorate in the political relevance of the Qur'an in an Islamic state and engages his father as well as his colleagues in long debates) and have clearly laid their plans in a systematic way. But like previous attempts, it is all rather "other-worldly" and is bungled from start to finish. These idealistic youths are no match for the worldly realism of the General and his state machinery. Similarly naive were the opposition group's original plans to collect information for a common pool and disseminate the information to the populace at large:

> "We can foretell," we added, "that the written word, more powerful than the gun, will frighten them [the government]. In the chaos ensuing from that, and just as they start their purge, we will announce our clandestinity and publish a leaflet of our intention, and you will see that more people will adhere to it. Then we will baptize it as a movement, we will give it a name."[11]

I have tried so far to show how the regime is seen by the young subversive activists and what the background and views of the members of this group are. It appears that Farah's movement consists of a group of young intellectuals who belong to a small elite of educated, cosmopolitan and sophisticated Mogadiscans, sincere, idealistic and not very competent in practical terms. What then, may we ask, is Farah's intention in writing these novels? What does he wish to achieve? What point is he trying to drive home? Does he find action against state oppression pointless, in the sense that it cannot succeed? If he does believe there can be a solution to African oppression, does he offer any clues to this solution in his fiction?

I would aver that there are two principal themes present in *Variations on the Theme of an African Dictatorship*. The first is hinted at in the inclusion of "African" in the title of the trilogy. While, as we have seen his protagonists are sophisticated and cosmopolitan— apparently more versed in chic European modes of thinking than in their own society's—and many Europeans appear and have their say in the pages of these novels, Farah's fundamental concern does appear to be the position of Africa (and of Somalia in particular) in relation to colonial and neocolonial powers. Somalia, indeed, provides a good case-study for European interference in African development—first as an Italian colony, later a Soviet Russian satellite and still later an ally of "Western democracy." Farah seems to be pleading for a native settlement of native problems and a native development within a native-inspired framework. While he is critical of governmental reliance upon the economic aid and ideological format of foreign powers, there is surely also present an indictment of an opposition's reaching likewise for foreign ideologies as remedies to be applied wholesale in the fight against tyranny.

This is the core of the clash between Medina and her erstwhile friend and co-revolutionary in Italy, Sandra. Medina's antagonism dates from the occasion when Sandra told her not to include Italy in their discussions about imperialism and socialism since as a foreigner Medina cannot and will never be able to understand Italy. When Medina takes her to task, therefore, for discussing Africa without restraint, she is brusquely told:

> "I'm not talking about Africa. I'm talking about Marxist theory, the Marxist ideology which is basically European, both in its outlook and philosophical devel-

opment. Hegel, Marx, Engels, Lenin. They are all European."[12]

This I believe to be the crux of the matter. That it is in the minds of Farah's opposition group is clear from the oath of the intellectuals and professionals who created the clandestine movement "to serve not the interests of any superpower but this nation's,"[13] and also from Deeriye's response to his daughter's query whether he would not inevitably become a dictator if he were head of state:

> "I am not a black ape imitating the monkeys who trained me. For no man trained me. I did not learn what I know from a white man whose ways I hold sacred."[14]

Is not Farah—himself cosmopolitan, multilingual, rootless—then questioning the relevance of foreign ways and ideologies to African countries? There can be no doubt that the foreign supporters of a regime do so in their own interest and assist in the development of those aspects of the state that accrue to their own advantage; there are, indeed, numerous references to such a view in the novels, from Loyaan's irrelevant training in Italy as a dentist when Somali teeth have not yet suffered enough from the diet of "civilization" to require the services of dentists to the statistics of infant mortality and the unequal distribution of economic aid between vast state prisons, unimportant public buildings and monuments, and vital hospitals for the population at large.

But is there not also implicit in the novels the idea that changes arising out of the wholesale adoption of alternative foreign ideologies and economic systems will compound rather than solve the existing problems, and that therefore the idealistic revolutionaries are in their own way just as culpable as the regime they oppose for the ills of Somalia? As Idil argues:

"What is more, your generation hasn't produced the genius who could work out and develop an alternative cultural philosophy acceptable to all the members of your rank and file; no genius to propose something with which you could replace what you've rejected." [15]

Just as socialism is seen not to have been appropriate for Somalia, especially so in the distorted version foisted upon the nation, so do Deeriye and his daughter, Zeinab, discuss the more tempting bait of "western democracy" in order to expose it as a sham, a fraud and an instrument of repression, particularly when applied by those "western" powers of African states.

Hence, throughout his trilogy, Farah seems to me to be making the point that African countries, including Somalia, must solve their own problems, work out their own destinies, not rely on wholesale importations from the outside world of ideas and methods evolved for the specific needs of other societies. The outside world will neither act from disinterested motives in promoting the well-being of African states or citizens, nor are the ideologies themselves, as the products of European thought geared to European situations, relevant to Africa.

As for the second theme of the trilogy, I feel that Farah may be preoccupied with a related problem—that of the position of the intellectual in a modern African state. As I have attempted to show, most of the prominent characters in these novels, that is those of the younger generation who have been brought up and educated in the "modern" Somalia or abroad, do not appear to have a firm grounding in their own society. Moreover, the Somalia portrayed by Farah is an extremely limited one, that of a narrow circle of "privilegentzia" in Mogadiscio who all know one another, are well-to-do, sophisticated, widely travelled. It is interesting that despite the noble ideals they profess, our subversive figures rarely, if at all, mention the poor, the under-privileged or the harsh and worsening conditions of drought and warfare in the rural areas; and this in spite of the fact that they all have clan relations and therefore connections in different parts of the country. Indeed, when Deeriye refers to "the natural famine [which] claims lives daily and a nationalist war in the Ogaden,"[16] it comes as rather a shock to the reader who has been fed almost wholly on a diet of very personal and very abstract problems so far. There is, I must admit, more comment on the urban mal-development of Mogadiscio—the traffic problems, the violence and the beggars—but these are more closely related to the lives of the urban elite with their fast cars, vouchers to avoid queuing for essential stores and food, and all the other modern gadgets that make life easier for those who can afford them. The reader gets the impression that most of these elite neither know nor care about their fellow countrymen except in the most abstract way, but are far more absorbed in their selfish, cosmopolitan interests and pursuits. Sagal, for example, practices her swimming every day and hopes to represent her country internationally as a swimmer, and this in a land where drought is endemic—yet she never mentions it and we can only assume that it never crosses her mind. One is reminded of the criticism of Jane Austen, that the War is never mentioned in her novels even though she lost a brother in it; either she is not interested in that side of life or she writes simply to entertain. I don't think Farah is writing simply to entertain, but it is not clear in these novels whether he himself is not interested or whether it is is his characters that are so. This is an imbalance in Farah's work that is to a large extent redressed in his next novel, *Maps*,[17] which does focus upon the very topics of famine, drought, poverty and war along the Somali/Ethiopian border. Nevertheless, this weakness in *Variations on the Theme of an African Dictatorship* remains, I think, a very real one.

More questions, indeed, arise from speculation along the same lines. Is this evasion in *Variations* of important aspects of Somalia's existence as an independent state what Farah deliberately intends? Is such a morally ambiguous position avoidable for such an elite as he portrays? What, moreover, is the position of the intellectual in a modern African state? What of Farah's own position as a Somali intellectual living abroad and therefore even more cut off from his countrymen? For such an intellectual wishing to impart his own knowledge and communicate to his less-advantaged citizens his desire to help them and his country advance and prosper, what are the channels when he has no obvious links with them at any level? If one bases one's judgement on some of the popular heroes on the books and posters mentioned in these novels, Pablo Neruda, for example, or Che Guevara, the parallels seem ominous; the peasants whom Guevara came to liberate seemed not to appreciate his intentions but saw him as an interfering foreigner and he died unfulfilled, while the Chilean regime was able to corrupt Neruda's poetic idealism by appointing him ambassador to France—a technique also used by the Somali government in Farah's trilogy. Would a sophisticated "modern" Somali in the mould of Medina, Nasser, Sagal, Soyaan or Loyaan fare any better than a Guevara in the remoter parts of rural Somalia? And the question arising from this would of course be: to what extent can the intellectual and social elite seek to change and advance a society with which they have no real contact or identity? Such a question is clearly related to my previous discussion of whether a foreign ideology can or should be implanted in a developing state, for how can the country's intellectuals produce a homegrown remedy if they are steeped in the ways of societies not their own?

All these questions seem to me to be highly pertinent to Farah's novels of present-day Somalia. Perhaps it is partly for this reason that I find the last book of the trilogy, *Close Sesame*, the most satisfying. For unlike the earlier ones, which present the reader with a segment of the society quite out of context, *Close Sesame* has a historical dimension and a cultural context in which to weigh the principal figures. Indeed, the selection of the elderly Deeriye as the chief character is invaluable in this respect; he does not follow Farah's more usual pattern of brash and youthfully cosmospolitan protagonists. That Farah should portray a rather narrow section of society does not in itself merit criticism—witness Anthony Powell's *A Dance to the Music of Time*, for example, in British literature—but if he is trying to hint at something broader and more significant, as I think he is, then such an oblique angle of vision might be construed as a weakness.

To conclude, I find Farah's trilogy in many ways extremely convincing and powerfully written. He is, for example, an artist in the use of language which he makes almost tangible at times; he has a knack of offering slightly off-key metaphors and similes which strike one all the more vividly for this reason, and he can be very gentle and sensitive in his treatment of such minor characters as Beydaan and Dulman, who draw from the reader an instinctive compassion. Moreover, Farah's writing provokes much thought on topics wider than the subject matter might initially suggest. Yet, I feel some doubt as to the underlying aims of his work in *Variations on the Theme of an African Dictatorship*—I am not certain whether he intends to provoke some of the lines of thought I have picked up or whether these have been provoked unwittingly by Farah's falling into the very trap that I have suggested he may be pointing out for us to observe. And it is in this ambivalence, perhaps, that Farah's main weakness lies . He cannot be putting over his message sufficiently clearly if the reader remains uncertain as to what that message actually is.

NOTES

1. Nuruddin Farah, *Sweet and Sour Milk* (London: Allison and Busby, 1979), p.136.

2. Nuruddin Farah, *Sardines* (London: Heinemann, 1982), p.151.

3. ibid., p.22.

4. Farah, *Sweet and Sour Milk*, p.93.

5. ibid., p.139.

6. ibid., p.99.

7. Farah, *Sardines*, p.26.

8. ibid., p.29.

9. ibid., p.31.

10. ibid., pp.77-78.

11. Farah, *Sweet and Sour Milk*, p.139.

12. Farah, *Sardines*, p.204.

13. Farah, *Sweet and Sour Milk*, p.138.

14. Nuruddin Farah, *Close Sesame* (London: Allison and Busby, 1983), p.85.

15. Farah, *Sardines*, p.78.

16. Farah, *Close Sesame*, p.147.

17. Nuruddin Farah, *Maps* (London: Picador, 1986).

NURUDDIN FARAH'S VARIATIONS ON THE THEME OF AN AFRICAN DICTATORSHIP: Patriarchy,Gender, and Political Oppression in Somalia

Dubravka Juraga

One of the main projects of Nuruddin Farah's fiction is to expose the complicity between the traditional patriarchal Somali family and oppressive political conditions in his native Somalia. For Farah, the Somali regime of the 1970s and 1980s was in many ways an extension of the Somali patriarchal family. But many aspects of Farah's critique are relevant outside of Somalia as well, and his work resonates with that of a number of modern cultural critics who have seen the patriarchal family as a central tool of political oppression in a variety of social situations. Paraphrasing Aristotle, Michel Foucault explains that the structure of the ancient Greek family is inherently asymmetric because "to govern a wife is to exercise a 'political' authority in which relations are permanently unequal."[1] That model of unequal relationships within the ancient family is, for Foucault, an illustration of the wider political context of a Greek polis where all social relationships were seen as the "relationship between a superior and a subordinate, an individual who dominates and one who is dominated, one who commands and one who complies, one who vanquishes and one who is vanquished."[2] According to Foucault, the Greeks regarded the family as a site where a free Greek male citizen had to prove his ability to rule in order to participate in governing the Greek state. Thus in Greek thought there existed a "continuity and homogeneity between the government of a state and that of a household."[3]

Foucault suggests that strategies for governing the state in ancient Greece paralleled strategies for governing the family—the primary ones being hierarchy and domination. Those are main characteristics not only of the ancient Greek family, but also of any other types of family based upon patriarchal principles. Indeed, Foucault's primary object of inquiry (even when he speaks of the ancient Greeks) is the patriarchal family of nineteenth- and twentieth-century bourgeois Europe, which he sees as the locus where various social alliances of power converge to create obedient subjects compliant with the current power distribution in the society. Thus, for Foucault, the patriarchal family in general serves as a powerful participant in larger alliances of power. Foucault here radically departs from Freud, for whom the family is a potential site of resistance to social power because of its insularity and exclusivity: "The more closely the members of a family are attached to one another, the more often do they tend to cut themselves off from others, and the more difficult it is for them to enter into the wider circle of life."[4]

The sociologist Jacques Donzelot follows Foucault in describing the nineteenth- century French patriarchal family as "a relay, an obligatory or voluntary support for social imperatives." Instead of Freud's characterization of the family in opposition to the government, for Donzelot, as for Foucault, the traditional patriarchal family was actually conscripted by the bourgeois system to function as "a

284

government through the family."5 For Farah, similar strategies were applied in the rather different social context of twentieth-century Somalia, where the fundamental premise of the patriarchal family as the basic unit of Somali society parallels the same premise in European bourgeois society. As in Europe, the Somali society of the twentieth century is based upon a patriarchal hierarchy. And, as in European society, power alliances in Somalia use the traditional family as an instrument for the maintenance of the status quo.

Farah's primary concern is with Somali society during the regime of Mohammad Siad Barre, who came to power in a 1969 coup deposing the previous pro-Western regime that had failed to establish a satisfactory postcolonial government in Somalia. After the coup, the Soviet-educated Barre banned all political parties or opposition to his regime and declared his intention to create a socialist society based upon the traditional Islamic religion. That was supposedly possible because of Islam's emphasis on justice and equality among people, but in reality, the socialist-religious mixture of the new and the old actually enabled Barre to manipulate both new and old technologies of power, rejecting or invoking tradition as it suited his purposes. Barre declared that his main goals were the eradication of tribalism and the rapid economic development of Somalia. However, many observers soon noticed that anti-tribalism was only a rhetorical strategy used by Barre to destroy his opponents. Actually, he favored his, his wife's, and his son-in-law's clans while persecuting members of other clans. Barre also powerfully endorsed the traditional patriarchal family, which he regarded as a useful tool for the manipulation of his Somali subjects. As time progressed Barre's oppressive rule relied more and more on traditional strategies of clan and family domination in order to destroy opposition by all available means.6

The relationship between political power and the family in the Somali society of the 1970s is meticulously examined in Farah's trilogy *Variations on the Theme of an African Dictatorship*, which consists of the novels *Sweet and Sour Milk*, *Sardines*, and *Close Sesame*. Like his other novels, the trilogy is firmly embedded in the social and political reality of Somalia in that period. In particular, Farah suggests a quite direct relationship between the traditional patriarchal Somali family and the authoritarian regime in Somalia under the rule of Mohammad Siad Barre. Because Farah sees that close connection between the family and the state as crucial to the adverse social conditions in Barre's Somalia, he is, in the words of Derek Wright, "unrelenting in his pinpointing of patriarchal bigotry and brutality as the sources of current political authoritarianism and police-state terrorism."[7] Farah suggests that any attempt critically to evaluate the present and its potential transformation ought to start with the critical evaluation of traditional Somali institutions, in particular the family.

Traditional Somali society was divided into six large clan-families that consisted of different associated clans. These clans in turn contained different sections, lineages, and affiliations. Within the clan, all Somali males enjoyed equal rights and respect from all the other members of the clan. Western historians and sociologists like I.M.Lewis and David D.Laitin have often described Somali society as very egalitarian because "a hierarchical pattern of authority is foreign to pastoral Somali society which in its customary processes of decision-making is democratic almost to the point of anarchy."[8] Interestingly, while praising this "egalitarian" society, those Western scholars fail to point out that the equality of status in clan affairs extends only to men and that women are utterly deprived of the right to participate in clan politics. Like the ancient Greek democracy, the Somali democracy applies only to men, regarding women only as men's property.

Unlike those Western scholars, Farah, from the beginning of his literary career, has been aware and critical of the oppression to which women are subjected. His first novel, *From a Crooked Rib*, is largely a critique of the traditional treatment of Somali women as the property of men. Ebla, the book's protagonist, is a young woman who runs away from two marriages, one that her grandfather arranges for her (and for which he receives a handsome bride-price) and another one that her cousin in Mogadiscio later arranges as a compensation to a man to whom he owed a large sum of money. Ebla is well aware of her subaltern position in these marriages:

> There is no friendship between a husband and a wife; the husband is a man and the wife is a woman, and naturally [sic] they are not equal in status. Friends should be equal before they can become friends. If you despise or look down upon somebody, he cannot be your friend, neither can you be his friend.[9]

Further, Ebla is aware that she has been marketed to each of her husbands very much like a piece of personal property:

> From her experience she knew that the girls were materials, just like objects, or items on the shelf of a shop. They were sold and bought as shepherds sold their goats at market-places, or shop-owners sold the goods to their customers. To a shop-keeper what was the difference between a girl and his goods? Nothing, absolutely nothing.[10]

Farah thus indicates that the problem of the traditional patriarchal family and its inflexibility is inextricably connected with the problem of rigid gender roles in Somali society. As long as people are not allowed to choose roles and lifestyles that suit them best, or freely to create their identities, the society as a whole will suffer. Farah emphasizes that any fundamental change in Somali society must therefore start in the family and clan structure, and in particular in the treatment of women. He suggests that it is not possible to have a society free of political tyranny if half of the population will suffer under the oppressive conditions that patriarchy has assigned to women.

In *From a Crooked Rib* Farah focuses his attention exclusively on

the position of women in the Somali society. In his later work, especially in the *Dictatorship* trilogy, Farah broadens his critique, directly
associating gender and patriarchal oppression with general political
oppression in Somalia. Farah explores the ways the patriarchal clan
structure of the traditional Somali society is reflected in the larger
political reality of Barre's Soviet-backed regime. The dystopian
Somalia of Farah's novels is ruled by the almighty father figure of the
"General," based quite transparently on Barre. In that terror-ridden
society the boundaries between the state and the family are blurred:
traditional family values are modern shibboleths of the General's rule
of oppression, terror, and tyranny. Farah raises his voice against
what he sees as a dangerous practice of excessive idealization of and
reliance upon the traditions of the past in order to establish a new,
postcolonial cultural identity. His work thus parallels the criticism of
many other postcolonial writers and intellectuals (like Soyinka and
Ngugi) of the appropriation and manipulation of traditional culture
and the past. Such writers agree with Frantz Fanon that the past
should be used "with the intention of opening the future, as an invitation to action and a basis for hope."[11] Indeed, Fanon strongly
warned against excessive use of the past in the creation of new post-
colonial cultural identities. In his view, no viable cultural identity can
be created completely out of the past, because culture in general is

> opposed to custom, for custom is always the deterio-
> ration of culture. The desire to attach oneself to tradi-
> tion or bring abandoned traditions to life again does
> not only mean going against the current of history but
> also opposing one's own people.[12]

Similarly, for Farah, the practice of excessive reliance on the traditions of the past amounts to no more than a disingenuous manipulation of the past in the interest of the oppressive present. As Derek
Wright points out, Farah does not see traditional values as an effective counter to the tyranny and corruption of postcolonial Somalia:

> On the contrary, he sees the traditional forms as being
> implicated in the new terror. For him, the General rep-
> resents something authentic. He answers some funda-
> mental need in Somali life. Despotism by a tribal oli-
> garchy is but the family's patriarchal authoritarianism
> writ large.[13]

Farah painstakingly compares the power relationships within the traditional family and those established between the state and its subjects. Although he acknowledges that some negative aspects of the Somali family are due to their heritage of Italian and British impe-rialism, he continuously denounces the Somali patriarchal tradition for its role in the perpetuation of despotism. Farah suggests that the authoritarian structure of the Somali family makes Somali society inherently susceptible to political oppression. In that he parallels Foucault, who points out that in bourgeois Europe the family organi-zation is used to support other "maneuvers" of the larger alliances of power in the society.[14] In a sense, the family acts as a "back-up" to other strategies of power by enacting the power hierarchy already existing in the society. Therefore, to make substantial changes in Somali politics, Farah suggests that fundamental changes must be made in the clan-oriented patriarchal structure of Somali society.

Many critics have pointed out the importance of Farah's percep-tion of the traditional Somali family as one of the fundamental sources of authoritarianism in Somalia. Dasenbrock sees Farah's intense preoccupation with the Somali family as a necessary and log-ical extension of his interest in the Somali political structure because "the politics of the nation are the politics of the family, and an author-itarian state depends upon a nation of authoritarian families."[15] The patriarchal family, with its omnipotent ruler, is the instrument that generates subjects accustomed to subjugation who will unquestion-ingly accept the power of the state. Therefore, it is of crucial impor-tance for an authoritarian regime to stimulate authoritarian relation-ships within the family. Wright points out that "the embodiment of

289

political and paternal tyranny in the same person makes for the efficient stamping out of subversion, simultaneously, at both public and private, state and familial levels."[16] Authoritarian upbringing does not train one to think critically, creatively, or independently, but to obey the authority of the father (or mother) and unquestioningly to follow orders. It is much easier for the state to manipulate such subjects and to turn them into obedient, if fear-ridden and impoverished, subjects who can only perpetuate the oppressive relationships they were conditioned to live in.

Farah, of course, is not alone among postcolonial writers in his concern with the resemblance and complicity between familial and state authoritarianism. In *The Laughing Cry* Henri Lopes depicts an unnamed African country suffering under the military regime of a despotic ruler, significantly nicknamed "Daddy," who claims that his authority is that of the head of a family. Just as "in a sound family, there was no place for a child who wanted to command in place of his father," there is no place for opposition to the ruler in the country: "Because, after all, the country was one big family."[17] V. S. Naipaul also insists that the extended family often functions as a microcosm of the authoritarian state—witness his depiction of the suffocating Tulsi clan in *A House for Mr. Biswas.* Echoing Freud's account of strong leaders whose regimes can provide (some of) their subjects with a sense of security, Naipaul describes the Indian patriarchal family and clan structure as a reflection of state authoritarianism. The clan that "gave protection and identity, and saved people from the void, was itself a little state, and it could be a hard place, full of politics, full of hatreds and changing alliances and moral denunciation."[18]

The cruelty of family life is one of the major motifs of Farah's trilogy. The patriarchal Somali family is merciless in imposing its rule on its members, to whom it denies any separate individual identity. The first part of the trilogy, *Sweet and Sour Milk,* depicts the attempts of a young professional (the apolitical dentist Loyaan) to investigate the sudden and mysterious death of his twin brother Soyaan, who had been an important political figure in the Somali government and a member of a secret organization whose aim was to overthrow the General's regime. Loyaan is unable to find out what really caused his brother's death. Besides struggling with the secrecy that envelopes Soyaan's life, Loyaan unsuccessfully struggles with their father, Keynaan, an ex-policeman and torturer, whom the regime has now conscripted to help create the posthumous myth of Soyaan as a loyal worshiper of the General and his regime. That creation of the social-ist "saint" Soyaan is yet another example of the General's skillful use of the tradition, in this instance of Sufi Islam that creates Muslim saints by appropriating dead ancestors into their pantheon. By grant-ing Soyaan the status of "hero of the revolution," the General suc-cessfully diffuses the danger that might arise from the underground resistance to his regime and its potential appropriation of Soyaan as its own hero. The General's strategy succeeds because he conscripts Soyaan's father, the traditional patriarch and an active supporter of the regime, who would side with it against his sons and the rest of the family if need be. By the end of the novel, the regime and the father are still firmly in power; they succeed in their fictionalization of Soyaan's biography, which symbolically indicates the extent to which their power is absolute. Soyaan's subversive organization completely fails; its members destroyed one by one.

Authoritarian relationships as portrayed in Keynaan's family sat-isfy what Freud sees as the basic human need for protection, which arises during early childhood when infants feel extremely helpless and in need of security. On the one hand, the father provides that security, whereas on the other he simultaneously establishes his domination over the children. Keynaan is a father who brutally impos-es his authority on his children, exemplifying well Freud's discussion of the function of the father as the primary agent for introducing the concept of authority to the child. Keynaan assumes the role of an all-powerful Grand Patriarch who "rules, with the iron hand of male-dom-inated tradition, over his covey of children and wives."[19] Paralleling Freud's suggestion that a strong leader provides a similar kind of security to the members of a society, Farah indicates that the iron hand of a patriarch closely resembles that of a dictator like Stalin or Hitler, or in the Somali case, Barre. Keynaan's family relationships in *Sweet and Sour Milk* are the mirror image of political relationships in the larger society. He rules his family with the firm hand of a dictator; the General rules Somalia with the iron fist of a patriarchal father. The father Keynaan parallels the image of himself that the General wants to convey to the Somalis. He presents himself as the great patriarchal (authoritarian) Father of the Nation. The parallel is not lost on the Somalis. While listening to the songs played on the radio in honor of the General, Soyaan remarks: "Listen to these ludicrous eulogies...The father of the nation. The carrier of wisdom. The provider of comforts. A demi-god. I see him as a Grand Warden of a Gulag" (*SSM*, p.10).

The ineffectuality of Soyaan's fight with the General is foreshadowed in an event from his childhood that establishes the relationship between Keynaan and his sons. Loyaan recalls this traumatic childhood experience, which began with a fight he had with his brother over a red ball. Echoing Freud's notion of the fear of castration as a major source of the submission of the young boy to the authority of the father, Keynaan ends the fight by mercilessly cutting the ball in two and threatening to cut the twins up as well. Both Soyaan and Loyaan dream of revenge for this tyrannical act, but these dreams never lead to action. Farah suggests that as long as it is possible for such relationships to exist within the family, the society will produce Generals who rule in the name of the father and people who define their identities from the prescribed obedience to such father figures.

The second part of the trilogy, *Sardines,* provides a singular picture of the claustrophobic atmosphere that characterizes relationships in the Somali family and the strategies the Barre regime uses to replicate this atmosphere within the Somali society. Farah critically examines the mechanisms of social control that the regime has appropriated from the traditional Somali culture, from Western European bourgeois culture, and from the Soviet masters with their Stalinist techniques of power. He suggests that all these mechanisms operate in complicity with the regime and therefore render the Somali society incapable of creating a successful opposition to the General.

Sardines focuses on Medina and her husband Samater, European-educated intellectuals trying to adjust to the Somali context. Medina is a journalist who challenges the regime and therefore loses her job. Being a woman and thus not very relevant, she is spared harsher punishment. However, she refuses to accept the subservient position of women in the Somali society and gathers a group of female friends whom she wants to help escape the feminine predicament of submission. She places great emphasis on education and literature as ways of understanding the world. Thus, she and her friends read Fanon, Achebe, Flann O'Brien, Yeats, Tagore, Camus, Sartre, Virginia Woolf, Beckett, and many other writers. One of their secret projects is also opposition to the regime, which they see as the purveyor of traditional social relations based on the oppression of women. The narrator explains Medina's position:

> One of the reason why she opposed the present dictatorship was that it reminded her of her unhappy childhood, that the General reminded her of her grandfather who was a monstrosity and an unchallengeable patriarch who decreed what was to be done, when and by whom.[20]

Medina's grandfather was a difficult tyrant who constantly abused his power. However, his power and tyranny were not confined to his family. He was also one of the slave-owners with whom the Italian government had the most difficulty in persuading to free his slaves. Farah here again draws a parallel between the General's rule and the patriarchy he emulates. Just as the "monstrosity" of a grandfather owned and freely disposed of the lives of his family and slaves, the General freely disposes of his subjects that he "owns."

When Samater is blackmailed into accepting a position in the General's government to save his fellow clansmen from torture, prison, and death, Medina strongly objects and condemns his act as cowardly. She eventually leaves their home because she can no longer endure the tyranny of her authoritarian mother-in-law, Idil, who lives with her son's family. Samater then rebels against his mother and orders her to leave his home, which she has destroyed. However, the government, which relies for its power on the perpetuation of traditional family structures, immediately reacts against Samater for both his disrespectful behavior toward his mother and his inability to control his wife. His career is destroyed; he immediately loses his position in the government and is even imprisoned. The government's support of the traditional patriarchy is unequivocal.

Farah is primarily concerned with the traditional Muslim family within the supposedly socialist Somalia. However, his analysis has implications for patriarchal family structures in general. For example, his view of the function of the family as a tool of official oppression closely parallels Foucault's description of the bourgeois family of Victorian England as a focal point for power relations in a society. Farah's suggested link between the patriarchal family and the authoritarian state also recalls Foucault's argument in *The Use of Pleasure* that the ancient Greeks saw the function of the father as head of his household as directly analogous to the role of the ruler of a city-state. For the Greeks, according to Foucault, there is a "continuity and homogeneity between the government of a state and that of a household."[21] The husband's first responsibility, like that of the political leader, is to exercise self-control, or *enkrateia*. His next responsibility is to see that those under his governance exercise a similar restraint:

> The husband's self-restraint pertains to an art of governing—governing in general, governing oneself, and governing a wife who must be kept under control and respected at the same time, since in relation to her husband she is the obedient mistress of the household.[22]

In *Close Sesame,* the third part of the trilogy, Farah provides yet another example of the extent of parental power in Somalia. Here the young man Mukhtaar is literally driven insane by his domineering father. After many clashes between the two, Mukhtaar and his father finally come to blows in which (it is rumored) Mukhtaar is killed by his father. Mursal, Mukhtaar's friend, comments on the reasons for Mukhtaar's disintegration:

> A father can beat his son to madness in full public view and the son is expected not to raise a hand but to receive the beating in total silence...As for public justice being confused with private justice, what would happen if Mukhtaar were to receive a fatal blow on the head and die? Nothing. Nothing would happen to avenge Mukhtaar's life and his father would not be submitted to questioning: after all, it is the prerogative of a parent what to do with the life and property of an offspring.[23]

On the other hand, in *Close Sesame* Farah attempts to examine alternative, potentially positive aspects of patriarchy by portraying a traditional patriarchal family that is not based on oppression and domination. Mutual respect and love for each other are the foundation of the relationships among the members of this family. Deeriye, the patriarch of the family, is an old and respected anti-colonial fighter who enjoys his old age living with his son, Mursal, and Mursal's family. However, Farah's use of Deeriye as a positive figure appeals not to the mainstream tradition of patriarchal Somali culture but to the more marginal tradition of anti-colonial resistance, especially as represented by the Dervishes. Deeriye was born in 1912 at the peak of the Dervish war against the British colonialists, and Deeriye sees the timing of his birth as symbolic for the later course of his life as a fighter against colonial oppression. Deeriye tremendously admires Sayeed Mohamed Abdulle Hassan, the famed and fierce anti-colonial fighter and the leader of the Dervishes in their struggle against the British in the first two decades of the twentieth century. However, despite their avowed devotion to the values of the traditional Somali society, the Dervishes employed methods of anti-colonial struggle that were radically untraditional:

> They even fought using guns—the weapons of the infidel. While they claimed they were defending that which was most traditional in Somali life, their actions severed them from their clans and threw them together in a pan-Somali movement that was quite untraditional. Only in this way were they able to transcend the limits of the old order and point the way to a new and revolutionary one.[24]

Within the context of this revolutionary past Deeriye and his family attempt to model their identities. For example, in his intense preoccupation with the importance of friendship as opposed to the allegiance to one's clan and family, Deeriye draws his inspiration from the Dervishes' pan-Somali solidarity.

Similarly, even though the Dervishes led their struggle in the name of a return to Islamic purity, their attitude toward women was highly unorthodox. Although the Dervishes followed the basic instructions that Islam prescribed for women, they allowed their women a much more prominent role than in the traditional Muslim household. They rode horses and fought against the British next to their male companions. Likewise, Deeriye accepts his daughter's independent life-style that radically differs from the conventional norm for a Somali woman. She is a medical doctor with a successful professional career. Even though she is a widow whose husband died fighting for the Somali cause during the 1977-78 Ethiopian-Somali war, Deeriye does not insist that she remarry—the standard course for a Somali widow. Deeriye's son Mursal also leads an unorthodox life. He is married to an American Jewish woman whom the family has warmly accepted into its circle.

Unfortunately, this idealized family situation inevitably comes into conflict with totalitarian conditions in the Somalia of the General's regime. Mursal and some of his friends, including Mukhtaar, are involved in a conspiracy to assassinate the General. Deeriye does not want to get involved in this political battle. He believes he has contributed enough to the political life of Somalia by fighting Italians before the liberation and spending long years in Italian (and later in the General's) prisons. He sees Mursal's struggle strictly as the business of Mursal's generation. However, too late he realizes that it is impossible to stay neutral in such a politically charged environment and that he has to take a stand. When all the conspirators have been arrested and executed, Deeriye himself attempts an assassination, only to be gunned down by the General's guards. Farah suggests that the deep division between the generation of Deeriye and that of Mursal needs to be overcome before a successful challenge to the regime can be mounted. Even though Deeriye and Mursal mutually respect each other, they cannot communicate or jointly create a resistance that would bring down the General and establish a meaningful and democratic society.

The destruction of the "disloyal" family is complete. They have been punished for their betrayal of the social order and the state, and their punishment can be interpreted as a warning to other potentially deviant patriarchs. But Deeriye's family is more an aberration than a common practice. In most families the dominion of husband and father goes unchallenged by any member of the family. Just as the dictator's domination encompasses all subjects, patriarchal domination is aimed at all members of a patriarchal family, women and children. The traditional patriarchal family is firmly backed by the state and the consequences of a refusal to submit are often drastic, as Farah shows in the trilogy.

This story of Deeriye's failure to protect his society from political, cultural, and social oppression can be read as an allegory of the failure of postcolonial Somali society successfully to establish a new identity that would be based on energies derived from both traditional and contemporary sources. Deeriye is simultaneously a symbol of the anti-colonial struggle and of postcolonial impotence. Thus, although Farah offers some positive alternatives and venues for a patriarchal society, and even though in *Close Sesame* he gestures toward the idea that patriarchy can be a possible source of love and mutual respect as well as strength and power, he concludes that traditional social and political sources are tragically insufficient within the contemporary Somali context. Consequently, for Farah, the traditional institutions have failed to produce a healthy social environment in Somalia. Potentially positive traditional energies, like those in Deeriye's family, are ultimately inadequate and even pernicious within the larger oppressive structure—both Mursal and Deeriye die in their attempts to counter the regime's tyranny.

Although the regime's tyranny is aimed at all members of the Somali society, it is focused primarily on Somali men, whom the government holds responsible for governing their wives and children. It is the duty of the husband and father to exert authority and rule his family. Other writers have also noted this emphasis on the domination of women in patriarchal societies. In *Possessing the Secret of Joy*, the African American writer Alice Walker tells the story of an African man who is thrown out of his community because "he lost control of his wife, [which was] a very evil thing to do in that society because it threatened the fabric of the web of life."[25] As in Foucault's ancient Greece, men are here defined as owners and rulers of women; it is a man's duty to dominate his wife—and the rest of the household, including children, servants, and slaves. Walker suggests that this identity of the man as the master is one of the major patriarchal assumptions that must be rejected if a just society is to be established.

Farah agrees with Walker's condemnation of patriarchy and also notes that in Somalia, the traditional patriarchal family and in particular the traditional institution of marriage are two main strategies of oppression. For that reason, Farah especially concentrates his critical attention on the traditional institution of marriage. In *From a Crooked Rib* Farah demonstrates his awareness of the fact that traditional marriage is a form of subjugation. Ebla, the young protagonist, muses about the predicament of women in Somali society: "Enslavement was what existed between the married couples she had met. The woman was a slave. And she was willing to be what she had been reduced to, she was not raising a finger to stop it."[26] Indeed, within marital and familial relationships much of the violence endemic to Somali society occurs. Moreover, such domestic violence is an accepted and condoned practice. In *Sweet and Sour Milk,* Qumman, Keynaan's first wife, and her children are in the position of abused and dominated victims:

> Whenever some superior officer humiliated him, he came and was aggressive to the twins and his wife. He would flog them, he would beat them—big, and powerful that he was, the Grand Patriarch whose authority drenched his powerless victims with the blood of his lashes. (*SSM*, p.84)

Qumman dreams of the day when her sons will grow up and she will be free to leave. However, by the time they are grown up and gone she has come to terms with her position and stays with Keynaan even though her humiliations escalate. Qumman is especially humiliated when Keynaan contracts a second marriage to Beydan, the young widow of a man whom Keynaan had tortured to death in the course of his work as a police interrogator. Indeed, Keynaan is ordered by the government to marry the widow as compensation for the death of her husband.[27] Keynaan's "punishment," of course, is curiously double: he now has to support another woman, but his reward for his zealous service to the regime is the sexual services of a young and pretty second wife, who has no choice but to accept the marriage. The very private affair of the marriage thus becomes a political weapon, a punishment or a reward for the service done to the state.

Marriage as a strategy of political manipulation is not, however, the invention of Barre's regime but yet another strategy of the traditional Somali culture that he has appropriated for his "socialist" rule. As I.M.Lewis points out, marriage was one of the frequent strategies of the great national hero Sayyid Muhammad for establishing political alliances with different tribes.[28] Farah suggests that the traditional inability of the Somalis to dissociate private and political aspects of their lives is one of the most important facts of life under the regime of Barre. Private life is just another domain of public politics for the regime. And just as the political life of Somalia is marred by torture, imprisonment, and always imminent physical annihilation, the private life of the Somalis, both women and men, is characterized by abuse, physical and psychological violence, and terror. For Farah, the sexual violence that thoroughly permeates the lives of Somali women is one of the most important manifestations of violence in Somalia. Not only are women regarded as powerless and insignificant, but they are considered to be legitimate instruments of political manipulation. As in the case of Keynaan's marriage to the widow of the tortured man, sexual politics are part of the larger political strategies of power.

In his discussion of the manipulation of sexual energies in the interest of political power in modern society, Foucault suggests that modern (bourgeois) society seeks not to repress sexuality as proposed by Freud but instead to encourage sexual energies so that they can be administered as a technique of domination: "Pleasure and power do not cancel or turn back against one another; they seek out, overlap, and reinforce one another."[29] In opposition to the Freudian "repressive hypothesis," Foucault regards sexuality as a potential tool of oppression, noting that "we must not think that by saying yes to sex, one says no to power; on the contrary, one tracks along the course laid out by the general deployment of sexuality."[30] A similar politicization of the sexual is central to the fiction of Farah. In *Sardines,* Farah again underlines that sexual power and political power are closely aligned and that the sexual is another strategy of the political system. In a situation in which no other venue for the expression of political dissent exists, everything and everybody becomes a pawn in the game of politics.

In particular, Farah in this novel explores rape as a weapon of political power. Amina, the daughter of a powerful politician close to the General, is raped by three men from a clan that has been continuously terrorized by the General. They have nothing against her personally, they tell her. Her rape is their revenge against her father, the agent of the hated regime. After the rape one of the rapists "comforts" her: "We're doing this not to you but your father" *(S,* p.126). When Amina's father, following the same pattern, remarks that her rape is a political act, Amina angrily retorts *"But which rape isn't?"* *(S,* p.127). Fearing that the rape might set an example of a new tactic for political opposition to the regime, the government allows two of the rapists to escape abroad, thus avoiding trials and the ensuing publicity. Meanwhile, in an echo of Keynaan's forced marriage to Beydan, the General and his regime (with the complicity of Amina's father) unsuccessfully pressure Amina to marry the third rapist, which would be a traditional "punishment" for a rapist in Somalia. Amina is outraged by such political machinations and by the total indifference of the General and her father to her plight. She insists that *all* three men be brought to trial and she wants "every Somali to see the political significance [of the rape]. I want everybody to know that every rape is political, that the powerful rape the weak" *(S,* p.129). In the Somali situation, the weak are not only women, Farah implies, but all others who are symbolically raped by the General's regime.

Rape, of course, has frequently been used as a metaphor not only for the subjugated position of women in patriarchy, but for the subjugated position of the colonized as well. Sara Suleri notes that "the geography of rape as a dominant trope for the act of imperialism" has been recurrent in literary and theoretical discourse (in particular about India) so often that it is no longer "critically liberating."[31] Nevertheless, the metaphor of rape calls attention to the significance of sexuality and gender and their relationship to the politics of power, in the context of colonialism and of postcolonialism. In postcolonial countries the powerful also rape the weak; the difference is that in the colonial time the powerful were British, French, Italian, and others, whereas in a postcolonial situation the powerful are of the same nationality as the weak. As Fanon has emphasized, the postcolonial situation often differs from the colonial only in the fact that the oppressors have black skin instead of white.

Therefore it is not surprising that Farah extends the metaphor of rape into the postcolonial context. Gender oppression is common to both colonial and postcolonial situations, and Farah emphasizes that general oppression as a form of social intercourse will be endemic in a society that condones gender oppression as a way of constructing social reality. The position of the postcolonial subject is similar to the position of women in patriarchy. Like the prisoners in Foucault's panopticon, the identity of the postcolonial subjects is also formed by force imposed from above through the violent gaze of the authority, just as the identity of women is circumscribed by the violent gaze of the opposite sex. The subjugated are perceived as *objects* of domination, to be studied and then inscribed within the worldview of those in power, men, colonizers, or both. As Catharine MacKinnon puts it, "Men *create* the world from their own point of view, which then *becomes* the truth to be described...*Power to create the world from one's point of view is power in its male form.*"[32]

A patriarchal society exercises that power through various strategies of sexual politics. Rape and marriage are only two techniques designed to establish women as second-class citizens. Medina fights simultaneously against the matriarchal domination of Samater's mother Idil (whom she perceives as a symbol of the larger political oppression in the society) and the General, whom she regards as a staunch supporter of patriarchy.[33] One of the main reasons for the conflict between Idil and Medina is Idil's insistence that Ubax, her granddaughter and Medina's daughter, undergo the traditional ritual of female circumcision, to which Medina violently objects.[34] As Awa Thiam points out, the purpose of such circumcision is "to guarantee the total possession of [men's] wives' bodies."[35] It is an act of humiliation intended to emphasize woman's status as male property in a patriarchal society. Therefore, circumcision is often regarded as the

302

ultimate symbol of women's subjugation.

Farah suggests that, like rape, circumcision is a powerful political weapon that the General's regime in Somalia unscrupulously uses. Medina tells her brother Nasser a story of a Somali couple, now American citizens, who return to Somalia with the sixteen-year-old daughter whom they have brought up as an American. When the family arrives in Soviet-dominated Somalia their passports are appropriated by the police, and the regime announces its refusal to acknowledge their American citizenship. They are arrested for some undefined anti-government activities, tortured, and then released to the custody of their clan members. But their ultimate humiliation will be administered not by the regime but by their own extended family: the women of the clan secretly kidnap and circumcise the American daughter as a preparation for her marriage to a clan member. Here again the oppressive family operates in complicity with the regime: "All this...was done in cahoots with the Generalissimo. The tribal chieftain knew about it" (*S*, p.98). Like Amina, who is raped in order to "punish" her father for his political activities, and like Beydan, forcibly married to the torturer of her late husband, the young American girl is mutilated as a means to "punish" her father for his political opposition and the criticism of the Somali regime that he published while in the United States. In all those cases women are treated simply as objects for political manipulation by the oppressive regime.

For Farah, women often function as allegorical representations of modern Somalia because in both cases the violence perpetuated on them impedes the successful establishment of cultural or individual identity. Circumcision, rape, terror, and other forms of physical and psychological abuse are the hallmarks of woman's condition and are at the same time emblematic of Barre's political regime. Therefore, Farah suggests that to create a viable Somali society that would be suitable for all of its members, a significant change in the society's attitudes toward women is necessary. Farah's fiction represents an extended attempt to bring about those attitudinal changes.

NOTES

1. Michel Foucault, *The Use of Pleasure,* trans. Robert Hurley (New York: Vintage-Random, 1986), p.216. Foucault's work, although situating itself in opposition to the European philosophical tradition, nevertheless clearly remains embedded within a European discursive context. However, thinkers like V.Y Mudimbe (while remaining aware of the potential dangers of drawing upon European theoretical models) have recently employed Foucault's work as a resource in the exploration of African social and philosophical issues: see V.Y.Mudimbe, *The Invention of Africa: Gnosis, Philosophy and the Order of Knowledge* (Bloomington: Indiana University Press, 1988). As Manthea Diawara notes, for Mudimbe "Foucault's archaeological approach to discourse is doubly enabling: first, for thinking against the grain within the Western canon, and second, for proposing alternative discursive formations outside the West": see Manthea Diawara, "Reading Africa Through Foucault: V.Y.Mudimbe's Reaffirmantion of the Subject." *October* 55, 3 (1990), 80.

2. Foucault, *The Use of Pleasure*, p.215.

3. ibid., p.171.

4. Sigmund Freud, *Civilization and Its Discontents*, trans. James Strachey (New York: Norton, 1961), p.56.

5. Jacques Donzelot, *The Policing of Families,* trans. Robert Hurley. (New York: Pantheon, 1979), p.92.

6. Barre's regime had a notorious record of human rights abuses: ordering genocidal massacres of people and their livestock, poisoning wells crucial for a clan's survival, mass torture, detention and execution without trial, and many other atrocities.

7. Derek Wright, "Parents and Power in Nuruddin Farah's Dictatorship Trilogy," *Kunapipi* 11, 2 (1989), 96.

8. I.M.Lewis, *A Modern History of Somaliland: From Nation to State* (Boulder, Colorado: Westview Press, 1988), p.10.

9. Nuruddin Farah, *From a Crooked Rib* (London: Heinemann, 1970), p.156.

10. ibid., p.84.

11. Frantz Fanon, *The Wretched of the Earth*, trans. Constance Farrington (New York: Grove, 1968), p.232.

12. ibid., p.224.

13. Derek Wright, "Somali Powerscapes: Mapping Farah's Fiction," *Research in African Literatures* 21, 2 (1990), 26.

14. Michel Foucault, *The History of Sexuality: An Introduction.* 1978; trans. Robert Hurley (New York: Vintage-Random, 1990), p.100.

15. Reed Way Dasenbrock, "Creating a Past: Achebe, Naipaul, Soyinka, Farah," *Salmagundi* 68-69 (Fall-Winter 1985-86), 327.

16. Wright, "Parents and Power," 96.

17. Henry Lopes, *The Laughing Cry: An African Cock and Bull Story*, trans. Gerald Moore (New York: Readers International, 1987), p.75.

18. V.S.Naipaul, *India: A Million Mutinies Now* (London: Penguin, 1990), p.178.

19. Nuruddin Farah, *Sweet and Sour Milk* (Saint Paul, Minnesota: Graywolf, 1992), p.50. Further references are given in parentheses in the text after the abbreviation *SSM*.

20. Nuruddin Farah, *Sardines* (Saint Paul, Minnesota: Graywolf, 1992), p.17. Further references are given in parentheses in the text after the abbreviation *S*.

21. Foucault, *The Use of Pleasure*, p.171.

22. ibid., p.165.

23. Nuruddin Farah, *Close Sesame* (Saint Paul, Minnesota: Graywolf, 1992), p.121.

24. Lee V.Casanelli, *The Shaping of Somali Society: Reconstructing the History of a Pastoral People, 1600-1900* (Philadelphia: University of Pennsylvania Press, 1982), pp.252-53.

25. Alice Walker, *Possessing the Secret of Joy* (New York: Harcourt, 1992), p.137.

26. Farah, *From a Crooked Rib*, pp.83-84.

27. According to the Koran, a man can have as many as four wives simultaneously. As Keynaan is married only to Qumman, he is eligible for marriage.

28. Lewis, p.71.

29. Foucault, *The History of Sexuality*, p.48.

30. ibid., p.157.

31. Sara Suleri, *The Rhetoric of English India* (Chicago: University of Chicago Press, 1992), p.17.

32. Catharine A.MacKinnon, "Feminism, Marxism, Method, and the State: An Agenda for Theory." *Signs* 7 (1982), 537.

33. As Farah makes clear, in the absence of a surviving father Somali mothers are traditionally granted considerable authority over their sons and daughters-in-law.

34. Two forms of *female circumcision,* also known as female genital mutilation, are performed on girls age 4-12. Infibulation is the removal of the clitoris and labia minora. Excision is a more drastic procedure that includes the removal of external labia as well. Usually, the operation is performed by any suitable sharp object (a sharp stone, a piece of glass or metal), with no anesthesia. After the removal, the wound is stitched together with long thorns or thread leaving only a minuscule opening for urine and menstrual blood. The opening is enlarged on the wedding night, often by knife. Afterwards, every sexual act is a constant source of pain and resembles more a rape than "lovemaking." The operation incapacitates the woman for the rest of her life causing numerous physical and psychological problems.

35. Awa Thiam, *Speak Out, Black Sisters: Feminism and Oppression in Black Africa* (London: Pluto Press, 1986), p.76.

ALLEGORIZING TERROR:
A Comparative Study of Novels by Farah and Soyinka

Armando Pajalich

In Farah's *A Naked Needle* (1976), there is a revealing intertextual link with Soyinka's first novel *The Interpreters* (1965): "...he woke up, took a shower after re-activating the water pipe, back to his room, and for no reason he knew, he hunted for *The Interpreters*, his favourite novel of the year, read a few passages on Sekoni. His hand stammered as he underlined some lines."[1] One cannot help thinking that the statement Koschin makes (that *The Interpreters* was his "novel of the year") was a vehicle for Farah's own taste: Koschin's badly-digested readings and 60's culture[2] had a great deal in common with Farah's own careful studies and interests and with his admiration for Soyinka's writings. As he has admitted, through Koschin, Farah also tried to acknowledge, and free himself from, his early apprenticeship to literature.

Farah's protagonists, however, are far from expressing full authorial opinions. Koschin—a "satirist satirized"[3]—had the complex task

of voicing the author's own disgust about the way politics and society were moving and, at the same time, of becoming himself one of the
very targets of that criticism.

Apostasy & Anomy

Soyinka's two novels—*The Interpreters* and *Season of Anomy*
(1973)—expressed two significant moments, or "seasons", in post-
colonial African society: that "of apostasy" and that "of anomy." It is
quite possible to interpret Farah's first important novel and his later
Trilogy along much the same lines: through Koschin (and his
entourage), *A Naked Needle* fully expressed the climate identifiable as
apostasy. Koschin is indeed an "interpreter" and, very much like
Soyinka's early novel's protagonists, he is an apostate. He represents
the intelligentsia whose misreading of the catastrophic days of Somali
history ended in their total failure to contribute to the newly-achieved
Independence. In Farah's *Trilogy*, the attempts at revolt and the overall climate of fear and struggle experienced by families and State point
to an anomy which fails to explode as civil war but which nevertheless permeates the whole country through many of its families
(Loyaan and Soyaan's, Samater and Medina's, the Four Messengers'—
to name only the central ones in the three novels). Of course, it would
have been utterly unrealistic for Farah, whose fictions are grounded
in history, to depict a civil war in pre-1991 Somalia.[4]

To my mind, it might also be interesting to compare the two
chronologies: Soyinka (born in 1934) was 26 when Nigeria became
independent (1960). Farah (born in 1945) was 24 when Siyad Barre's
Socialist Revolution took place (1969). Soyinka published *The
Interpreters* five years after Nigeria's Independence, Farah published
A Naked Needle four years after the Somali Revolution. *Season of
Anomy* came out 13 years after Independence, Farah's *Trilogy* respectively 10, 12 and 14 years after Barre's coup. The two patterns of
hope, disillusion, total disappointment and chaos are quite similar,

though distanced by approximately a full decade.

Both Farah (as well as his protagonists!)[5] and Soyinka had read and admired Fanon's works. Fanon had emphasized how the role of the new middle class and that of the intellectuals were essential to new independent countries. According to Fanon, the intellectual had to mobilize the peasantry and, by educating them, had to "interpret" the values of democracy and to avoid or limit the corruption of the newly formed (or forming, informing and disinforming) urban bourgeoisie. For the urban middle classes, privileges were such an attraction and a possible trap that their intellectuals could also be easily seduced by them. Farah's notion of a "priviligentsia" was a variation on Fanon's ideas: his own contribution was to create that brilliant verbal pun, embodying it in fictional terms. Soyinka's apostates, with their night clubs and bohemian lifestyle, and the members of the Cartel, with their super-glamorous and parodistic mansions and parties, have offered other fictional embodiments of Fanon's theories. Fanon's two other main roads to democracy were signposted as the struggle for women's rights and the formation of workers' cooperatives.[6] Farah—the "feminist"—has insisted on women's role in society.[7] Soyinka—the "ideologue"—has insisted on communality of property, work and profits.[8]

The second stage in our two novelists' progress, that of anomy, reveals two very different stances, which may be attributed also (but not only) to their respective historical realities. The first and foremost difference was that Soyinka was able to turn Fanon's scheme into a fictional fresco since Nigeria (and West Africa) did have a peasant class, which could be mobilized by such a skilful intellectual-cum-artist like Ofeyi. Farah, instead, had to confront a country where the "peasantry" was constituted by a scattered population of extremely poor starving men and women still rooted in a nomadic culture. In Farah's Somalia there could be no Aiyèró with its Pa Ahime. Instead, the country had the pacifist and mystic ethics of one of the faces of Islam to possibly rely on (as seen in *Close Sesame*).

If Fanon's ideas involved a project for the future (and not merely a description of society as it was), Soyinka's *Season of Anomy* followed suit by embracing Socialist "utopian" tenets. Despite the fictional tragedy occupying most of the novel (and evoking also the tragic massacres which occurred in Nigeria during its Civil War), the message is not invalidated, and Ofeyi will continue to incite the masses of peasants in order to overturn tyranny. Ofeyi *is* the ideal Fanonian intellectual-cum-artist who puts his creativity at the service of the peasantry, not only to educate them, but also, with an important extension to Fanon's ideas, to be educated *by* them. His message is that land and labor, the "capital" of the nation, must be owned and managed by the people—*that* was the Aiyèró ideal that Ofeyi wanted to spread throughout the country. His art (lyrical, theatrical, filmic) had to be instrumental to that message. Ofeyi was a mouthpiece for Soyinka (also a poet, dramatist, and film director). Nothing of the kind is found in Farah's *Trilogy* (published in 1979, 1981 and 1983). His intellectuals (Loyaan and Soyaan, Medina and Samater, Deeriye and Mursal, etc.) operate within Mogadiscio. These protagonists never leave the urban space, and their attempts to overturn the regime remain a middle-class struggle. In Farah's novels, the anomy occurs inside that class, and not within society at large.[9] This might in part explain the limitations and failures of his protagonists: their culture is an urban one and is, after all, the culture of an èlite which has been educated abroad.[10] (As we shall see, Deeriye is an exception to this.) In fact, Farah's heroes and heroines do nothing to mobilize the masses of non-urban citizens.[11]

An intellectual's aspirations do not necessarily coincide with those of State politicians, based in the capital and major cities, and territorialized inside their tribes (as in Nigeria), clans (in Somalia), and patriarchal families (in both countries). The projects of the intellectual and those of the State machinery may find themselves positioned on grounds not only different from but also opposed to one another. The role of the post-colonial intellectual may thus become a subversive, revolutionary one. When an individual or a group of people *act* against the State machinery (of military power and national propaganda), the regime labels this counter-action as terrorism. In corrupt and tyrannical newly-independent countries where *State* terrorism rules, the intellectual seems to have two possible strategies: either nihilistic apostasy or revolution through terrorism. Hence the central theme in the two novelists (that of terrorism) and our possibility of comparing their elaborations on it. To these two strategies, a third one will be added later.

Tyrants & Terrorists

In order to understand their fictional uses of terrorism, one first has to consider the historical moment when these novels were written, since both authors meant to describe a local reality in order to construct allegories which had some relevance for Africa as a whole. This is evident by the subtitle of the *Trilogy* ("on the Theme of an *African* Dictatorship") and by the absence of specific allusions to Nigeria in *Season of Anomy* (which takes place somewhere in *Western* Africa). What is meaningful for Africa is, obviously, of extreme relevance for the world, since the recent history of Africa has shown it to be not only a battlefield for local power struggles but also for the larger interests of neo-imperialism.

Soyinka's *The Interpreters* was written during the events that precipitated the Civil War (1967-1970) which was to destroy earlier hopes of a peaceful national unity, and *Season of Anomy* when political chaos was ravaging Nigeria. On the African continent, the most extreme tyranny was South Africa's apartheid regime, against which, in 1961, the African National Congress responded by forming the Umkhonto we Sizwe (or MK) "terrorist" group. It would take three decades for the armed struggle, also led by intellectuals and writers, to put an end to *State* terrorism—and this probably only when foreign powers found it expedient to include Southern Africa in the global market. On a world scale, the Vietnam War (1962 or 1965-1975)— the most important bellic event of those decades—was still raging.[12]

There are at least three major considerations about the Vietnam War which are relevant to this discussion: Firstly, the US and their allies *apparently* started it to support a local leader (who refused to accept the United Nations' partition of Vietnam) but *in reality* their objective was to strengthen American (and Japanese) imperialism in that part of the world; secondly, the war was fought by Americans who never received a proper mandate by the American people, following axioms of the "intelligence community" (and particularly Henry Kissinger) that "American interests" could be promoted thanks to the workings of agencies (read: CIA and USIS) which did not necessarily have to answer to Congress; and, thirdly, the war was won by local guerrilla forces consisting mainly of peasants.[13]

These three points foreground a pattern which constituted the post-colonial tragedy for many countries all over the world as well as a "Fanonian" solution. If a corrupt local leader is supported by an all-powerful foreign (theoretically "democratic") country (like, first, the USSR and East Germany and, later, the US and Italy in Somalia, and like US "vested interests" in Nigeria), how can local opposition be organized and succeed? The intellectuals may find two kinds of support: that of mass resistance (as in Vietnam) or that of a resistance inside the èlite embracing terrorism (as in South Africa, and as—in fictional terms—in the Somalia of Farah's *Trilogy*). However, the two possibilities can (fictionally, at least) coexist: thanks to the Dentist's contribution, in *Season of Anomy*, Ofeyi, the artist-cum-intellectual, turns out to be the mediator between the peasants and the terrorist.

The subject of terrorism is a frightening one. Nobody likes to admit that this—the ultimate political resource?—might be a necessary reply to State terrorism which is what occurs when the workings of a State rely on "agencies" deprived of any control exercised by the representatives of the people and engineered by local tyrants and foreign support. The issue, though painful, cannot be ignored. It is to the credit of our two novelists that they had the daring to face it full on. If we look at Farah's rebels in *Sweet and Sour Milk* and *Sardines*, their "public actions" may be easily summed up. What Soyaan did remains

314

quite vague. Probably, he only wrote some Memoranda (which will be found by Deeriye, in *Close Sesame*, but not taken into consideration!) and organized a small group of rebels which broke apart, as one may infer, because of internal disagreements during their political discussions.[14] It appears that at the end of the novel Loyaan accepts exile. What Medina did was to denounce the Grand Patriarch in her articles. As a result she was sacked, and stayed in that small group of rebels started by Soyaan. They acted mainly through words, like all "pure" intellectuals. But their "private actions"—inside their families—were much more relevant. In this regard, what happens in *Close Sesame* deserves more careful analysis.

In Farah's masterpiece, resistance to the Generalissimo also takes the form of an armed struggle: the novel opens with a debate between father and son about the viability of terrorism, and—as we shall see—also *closes* on that issue. The author delegates most comments on terrorism to his wise protagonist who, in turn, leaves the reader uncertain about his final option. Of course, the meaning of a novel does not rest only on the actions of its characters themselves, but on their roles as masks within a structured carnival inside the overall work of art and its unity. Through that work of art, they operate at the same time *inside* history and *beyond* history, offering a comment on contemporary life but establishing its relevance for future generations as well.

The apparent "open ending" of *Close Sesame*[15] will continue to arouse disagreements among readers on how the option of terrorism is dealt with in that novel. In order to interpret what happens in the "Epilogue", one may recall what Deleuze and Guattari had to say about the issue of terrorism and its struggle against the State machinery.[16] Their own stance seems to be that terrorism stops being revolutionary and creative ("deterritorializing", "a mutating flux of quanta") when it becomes organized and structured as a rival force to the State machinery. At that point it so resembles the State machinery that, instead of deterritorializing tyranny, it territorializes itself into an alternative closed space, "an overcodified or overcodifying line", and into a possible new authoritarian rule.[17] Deeriye's wisdom cannot accept that reterritorializing possibility: he is the potential terrorist[18] afraid of becoming a new tyrant. He says his "NO in thunder" and stops before crossing the border into murder and imitating the tyranny of the State machinery. The ending of the novel is less open than it appears to be. Deeriye says his "NO" to both State terrorism and counter-state terrorism. He chooses his prayer-beads. He saves his soul, perhaps. However, he does not save his country. For him, one's soul is more important than one's country. He is convinced that politics and revolution must be in accord with the ethics of Islam. Deeriye's revolutionary message is *not* in the final pages of the book; it lies in the way he has created a new modern and hybrid form of home and of father-son and man-woman relationships. Revolution must start inside the home and the family. That is his (and Farah's) message: Deeryie, the messenger, an ethical exemplum, has made it possible. While the Four Messengers embody "the message of the Lord; the message of the revolution; the message of a future happier than the present we live in; the message of brotherhood and true peace",[19] Deeriye seems to embody the message that nothing justifies murder, not even the need to bring about social justice. Real revolution has to take place in homes and individuals: this is the third strategy intellectuals may pursue.

If we look closer at the writings of the two French philosophers, we will have a clearer view of which fears the potential terrorist may experience. The "rebel" runs four risks: Fear (of losing), Clarity (of having a "mission" to fulfil, thus becoming a sort of dogmatic justice-maker), Power (which alienates and territorializes desire), and the great Disgust (a desire and passion for mere destruction and abolition, with the consequent longing to kill and die).[20]

When desire accepts destruction and abolition, it is no longer "mutating" and may even "kill itself." In *Close Sesame*, the center of tyrannical power (which "overcodifies", the "primitive" territories of nomadic culture, and those of patriarchy, of orality and of clans) is opposed by the "molecular quanta" of the open family, inter-clan and

316

inter-cultural siblinghood, writing, feminism and rebellious sons: while these latter accept the risk of turning their rebellions into fear and destructiveness (the great Disgust), Deeryie, rather than accepting destructiveness and the possibility of "killing" his own rebellion, opts for martyrdom to *his* cause, not to his son's. His strategy (revolution inside the home) remains valid—much as Ofeyi's does—well *after* the end of the novel. His God is Allah, not Ogun.

Deleuze and Guattari's philosophy remained only apparently open, in the same way that Farah's novel remains only apparently open in its form and allegorical stance. For them, one's existential drama comes before historical tragedy. Terrorism is accepted as a deterritorializing force (consisting probably of *intellectual* struggle and scheming) but not as an *armed* organized group action. Similarly, in *Close Sesame*, the option, rather than being left open, is *closed*. The members of the terrorist cell are blown up when Deeriye rings at their *closed* door. In some of his later essays, Farah has rather coherently stated that in the face of State terrorism and tyranny the intellectual's only option is existential and/or physical exile.[21]

In spite of its seemingly "open" ending concerning the physical conditions of Iriyise, *Season of Anomy*'s allegorical pattern is an outright and marble-like stigmatization of contemporary totalitarianism. Soyinka's art was meant to "deflate the bogey": the great anathema pronounced by Soyinka against the Cartel was pronounced also against its foreign allies who very thinly disguised the petrol multinationals, the "seven sisters" who were destroying peasant life in Nigeria. The destruction of the communal life of the peasantry meant more than a change in the economy and a drastic impoverishment of the population, since it involved also the annihilation of its ethics, and of its very capacity to *resist* foreign imperialism. Terrorism (as embodied by the Dentist) may survive but, if deprived of the support of the masses of peasants and of the creative urge of the artist, it would be as pointless as the actions of the Four Messengers in *Close Sesame*.

What Soyinka was attacking was the principle of globalization itself, according to which some areas of the world are compelled by multinationals and world-finance to specialize in only one phase of the chain of production, and not in the entire (small or large scale) production necessary for human survival. This limitation means dependence on the global system and its manipulators: it results in neo-imperialism. After all, nothing much has changed since the days of "old" imperialism, which was also based on the exploitation of raw materials and cheap labor from the colonies; the amount and quality are slightly different: instead of sugar, coffee or cocoa, etc, we now have strategic raw materials like uranium (to make plutonium with), oil, and diamonds, for export, or materials essential to industries in that portion of the global market, and instead of compulsive emigration (read: slavery and indentured labor), neo-imperial subjects now *beg* to be allowed to enter rich countries, or children and women work in slave-like conditions in that local area of production. This is what has happened in South America, the West Indies, the Indian subcontinent, South-East Asia, and many parts of Africa. The aim of this historical phenomenon is more and more wealth for the centers where globalization is masterminded, and more and more extreme poverty for the areas depending on them for their survival. The huge world-scale implications of this globalization have recently caused the indignation and protest of leaders of "poor countries" and especially that of Fidel Castro:

> The images we see of mothers and children in whole regions of Africa under the lash of drought and other catastrophes remind us of the concentration camps of Nazi Germany...We lack a Nuremberg to judge the economic order imposed upon us, where every three years more men, women and children die of hunger and preventable diseases than died in the Second World War...If money is capital for the rich, labor is the capital of the poor countries. They should be allowed to migrate to the rich countries to compete for the jobs there just as the powerful corporations of the rich

must be allowed to compete with their tiny counterparts in the poor countries."[22]

Soyinka was aware of the risks of globalization, and he has continued to stigmatize it in his essays.[23]

By comparison, Farah seems not to address his allegories to the
macro-systems of world economy.[24] He remained (and remains) more
interested in the micro-politics of family and gender relations and in
socio-cultural issues (equality, siblinghood, orature, the power of the
pen), and also in experiments with the novel form (which have made
him popular also with postmodernist criticism). His concern is certainly of enormous relevance, since no macro-system has (so far)
been able to construct itself without the support of a molecular mirroring of its tenets and principles in the family, clan, tribe, or other
institutions. And no democracy can be achieved without locating
gender relations at the forefront of the ethical and economic debate.

However fictional Farah's characters and stories (or fables) may
be, they remain grounded in contemporary events and, therefore,
subsume some basic pseudo-realistic elements. This is not true of
Season of Anomy, which lowers all boundaries between fiction, poetry, drama, and oral mythological tales. In *Season of Anomy* there are
no pseudo-realistic characters, and not even postmodernist variations on characterization. Ofeyi is a hybrid reincarnation of Orpheus
and of Ogun: he is the embodiment of a voyage into the chthonic
world and, as such, a message, more than a messenger. Farah's characters are messengers whose messages remain vague and partial, if
not entirely mysterious.

Farah has constantly insisted on his being "democratic" in his
own relationship with his characters and their ideas.[25] If one limits
oneself to their positivity or negativity, his insistence appears only
partly true (since, after all, Farah allows them to voice their own
goodness or wickedness), but it is definitely true if one analyzes the
structures of his fiction and his avoidance of the transparency and,
yes, dogmatism, of the message which Soyinka has constantly

319

embodied in his works. From this point of view, it seems that Farah's democracy needs a multiplicity, a dialectic or a polyphony of voices. On the other hand, Soyinka is not a "Bakhtinian" writer. For him, collective history is more important than individual and existential needs. If necessary in order to achieve real democracy, man must be ready for an armed struggle, prison, death. A soul —like his favourite god, Ogun—may be saved through murderous wars.

The Message & the Messengers

This comparison does not intend to suggest that one or the other of these two great novelists has more relevance for Africa and for the world. Its purpose instead is to emphasize how two writers who were writing a decade apart—and definitely affected, in their aesthetics, also by the spaces of their indigenous cultures—opted for two different kinds of novel-writing. The Message or the Messengers? How did this choice affect their narrative strategies?

I opened this essay suggesting that Farah was a great admirer of Soyinka's works. Obviously, this also means that the two writers are not exactly contemporaries, and therefore must be seen in a chronological sequence, representing two different moments in post-colonial African fiction. In spite of his personal tragedies and those of his country, Soyinka's novels were written during a phase of hope, political commitment, utopianism. Once he abandoned fiction, Soyinka continued to expose African dictatorships in some of his greatest plays, notably *Kongi's Harvest* (1967), *Opera Wonyosi* (1981) and *A Play of Giants* (1984), which, farcically, had Jean-Bedel Bokassa (the dictator of the Central African Republic, 1966-1979) and Idi Amin Dada (the dictator of Uganda, 1971-1979) as their main targets.[26]

Farah's early works represented the phase of disillusion, physical or existential exile, dreams. In our own days, Africa (and the poor countries in general) seems to have abandoned utopia and to have found dreams less and less possible. Farah's later works—*Maps*

(1986), *Gifts* (1992), *Secrets* (1998)—indicate the possibility of a reconstruction of identities (however split and fragmented): they deal more (though not only) with individual and private issues than with collective history, so much so that Farah's aesthetics have come closer to post-modernism. Farah has continued to insist that, to change society, first individuals and their micro-organizations must change.[27]

The novels we have focussed upon, written only a few decades ago, speak of an Africa which is no longer, an Africa hoping for the end of colonialism. Since then, imperialism has struck once again, and most African countries are bogged down with tyrannical regimes and civil wars and/or devastating and increasing poverty.

Our reading leads us to yet another drastic difference in their narrative strategies regarding the use of allegory. Post-colonial fiction has accustomed us to split allegories—decentered, asymmetrical, even chaotic ones. Farah's fables belong to this kind of allusive and non-declarative allegory which relies on polyphony and messengers. Soyinka's fictions, by comparison, are closer to classical allegories. Their patterns are as clear as narrative structures can be. In spite of their multiple levels and echoes from different civilizations and epochs, both *The Interpreters* and *Season of Anomy* foreground a central message to which all characters contribute in a centripetal mode. They stare at the reader like a prophecy, a Truth delivered without any ambiguity. This might even account for some ostracism (in the academic and publishing fields) of Soyinka's works. Farah's fictions are pluralistic in their allegorical strategies: they deal with centrifugal messengers, maps, gifts, and secrets (as recent titles suggest), overlapping and interacting; they imitate thrillers without introducing all-knowing detectives; they compare and contrast ideologies, religions, cultures, "truths", without opting for one or the other, but foregrounding their ways of producing desire and economy. They offer examples of multi-centered allegories and of the ontology of the "multi-verse." The corollary is also true: if Soyinka's molar allegorical strategy is centripetal, his balancing molecular strategy must be centrifugal—with a continuous branching off into

321

details, digressions, allusions, epochs, styles, modes of narration. Conversely, if Farah's molar allegorical strategy is centrifugal, his balancing molecular strategy must be centripetal—with the use of a filtering central consciousness, an obsessive iteration of similar episodes, parallel characters, analogous micro-narratives, doublings, statements (also through quotations, folk stories, articles, dreams).

Still, one cannot avoid concluding that all these differences between our two authors are relevant only when readers understand what both of them share: their struggles against tyranny and despots—inside and outside their countries—place their novels in a friendly dialogue. One has privileged the Message of the Revolution against tyranny, capitalism and imperialism, while the other has insisted on the need for revolutionary individuals (messengers) who can help build a new form of democratic African society. However different, Soyinka and Farah belong to a small group of contemporary African novelists whose target is our awareness of the dangers of totalitarianism, projecting Africa onto the screen of our minds as a historical but also "imaginative" territory where forces (messages and messengers) collide and fight for hegemony and dominance or for coexistence and equality. Their messages and messengers, from this point of view, can even be seen as complementary.

Ngugi's statement that neo-imperialism exploits African writers (much as it does African raw materials) so as to enrich its own literary traditions in European languages[28] finds its best counter-statements in Soyinka's and Farah's novels. If they enrich world literatures, they do so by subverting static and reactionary ideologies and by warning against Empires *of the lands and of the minds*. Whatever their language (their "tool of convenience"), they express the views of the exploited peoples and classes and not of the oppressing and privileged centers of power. As for terrorism—is it the most extreme political resource or a willful act of elitist and narcissistic destruction and self-destruction? The rub remains: thanks to the work of such novelists as Farah and Soyinka, it exists also as a "literary" issue in this age of recent Cold Wars (were they cold?) and of new empires (are they new?).

NOTES

1. Nuruddin Farah, *A Naked Needle* (London: Heinemann, 1976), p.46. The novel, finished in 1972, is set in 1970 or 1971, soon after the 1969 Somali Revolution. By "novel of the year" Koschin obviously referred to its relevance *for him* in Somalia and not to its year of publication. Koschin's favorite character seems to be Sekoni (see pp.46 and 146), the engineer whose power plant is never allowed to work and who is first confined to a mental hospital and finally dies in a car crash; Sekoni, with his idealism, religious zeal and artistic bent is definitely one of the most appealing among the "interpreters"; Koschin also refers to Noah (p.50).

2. Apart from references to classics (Plato and Nietzsche) and modernists (Joyce, Faulkner, Eliot, Pound), Koschin mentions Moravia, Cary, Okigbo, Sartre, Tutuola, Albee, but also Malcom X, Martin Luther King, Miriam Makeba, James Brown, The Beatles, Dylan Dog...

3. It might be interesting to compare this novel not only with Soyinka's *The Interpreters* and Joyce's *Portrait*, but also with Kingsley Amis's *Lucky Jim* (where the "angry young" protagonist is also a teacher who leaves his job out of his disgust for society) and Wyndham Lewis's *Tarr*, probably the greatest example of modernist satire introducing the protagonist as a "satirist satirized" and revelling in abrasive images derived from technology and machinery which Farah also employed in this novel. In 1994, in response to my question whether he had read *Tarr* before writing *A Naked Needle*, Farah replied with a "probably"...For the strategy of the satirist satirized, see: Robert C. Elliott, *The Power of Satire* (Princeton: Princeton University Press, 1960) and, for its application to Lewis, see: Fredric Jameson, *Fables of Aggression: Wyndham Lewis, the Modernist as Fascist* (Berkeley: University of California Press, 1979), or my *Wyndham Lewis: l'apprendistato e il vortice* (Brescia: Paideia, 1982).

4. It seems that Farah had been working on a novel about a civil war when the fall of Siyad Barre (January 1991) made the war such a reality that the novelist had to desist; see his "Savaging the Soul of a Nation," *In These Times*, 28 December 1992, 14-17.

5. Koschin quotes Fanon on p.114. Many of his ideas seem a parody of Fanon's.

6. See Frantz Fanon, *Les Damnès de la Terre* (1961), translated into English in 1965 as *The Wretched of the Earth* (Harmondsworth: Penguin, 1967). Fanon believed that former colonies were turning from areas of production of raw materials into markets of consumers. So far, his prediction has proved only partly true, unless we consider as consumer goods the surplus that the rich countries dump on them.

7. Especially, of course, in *From a Crooked Rib*, *Sardines* and *Gifts*, but also throughout his work.

8. See the section "Seminal" devoted to Aiyèró in *Season of Anomy*.

9. The obvious exception is *From a Crooked Rib*: Ebla, a peasant, goes through her own urbanization in a plot which is typical of many African novels (so much so as to create an important genre in South Africa, the "Jim comes to Jo'burg" fiction). If Ebla allegorizes Somalia's 1960 Independence, she also embodies the transition from a nomadic to an urban culture.

10. Koschin studied in England. Loyaan, Soyaan, and Margaritta studied in Italy. Medina, Samater, and Nasser "studied in Milan around 1968."

11. At the end of the Nineties, another African novelist, Ngugi, has continued to insist on this role of the post-colonial intellectual

and writer: nothing can be accomplished if he/she does not address the masses of peasants. All attempts to reform society and attain democracy are in vain if he/she engages only the urban middle classes—and for Ngugi this adds meaning to his obsession about the need to use African languages instead of European ones. According to him, the fact that most African writers have been using "European" languages (if the word "European" still makes any sense: is English still a European language?) have led to the fact that "The peasant and the worker in Africa have been denied participation in discourses about their own economic, political and cultural survival". See: Ngugi wa Thiong'o, *Penpoints, Gunpoints, and Dreams: Towards a Critical Theory of the Arts and the State in Africa* (Oxford and New York: Oxford University Press, 1998), p.92.

12. To mention only two other examples of local tyrannies supported by foreign agencies in those decades: the Greek Colonels' dictatorship (1967-1975) and Pinochet's Chile (1973-1990) both supported by the US. As to the other side of the "Cold" War for world supremacy—which has caused more havoc and casualties than the first two world wars put together—there is the fact that Hungary was invaded by the USSR in 1967, Czechoslovakia in 1968, and that the USSR supported some of the bloodiest tyrannies in Africa: ideologies had often very little to do with the scramble for global markets.

13. My interpretation is based on Noam Chomsky, *For Reasons of State* (New York: Pantheon, 1973), published in the same year as *Season of Anomy*. Chomsky's conclusion was that even if the Vietnam War was going to be lost by the US, they had managed to succeed in their main goal, which was to absorb Vietnam and Southern Eastern Asia into the global market (into the American and Japanese "sphere of influence"). This was made possible by the building of airports, roads and other modern infrastructures nec-

essary for the war but also for joining in the global economy, and by the arrival of masses of desperate peasants to towns to work as cheap labor in factories. Of extreme relevance are also Chomsky's elaborations on the role of the scientific intelligentsia in rich countries: it might be useful to compare and contrast them with Fanon's ideas about the role of the intelligentsia in the poor ones.

14. The group includes also Medina, Samater, and Sagal (who would reappear in the following novel, *Sardines*); Koschin (from the previous novel); and other minor characters.

15. It would be erroneous to consider "openness" as a characteristic only of modernist and postmodernist Western fiction. According to Adonis (a pseudonym for Ali Ahmed Said), in *An Introduction to Arab Poetics* (London: Saqi Books, 1990), Koranic exegesis underlined how the "beautiful text" is "the one which the spirit can approach in all manner of ways, or in modern critical terminology, the open text, the text with multiple meanings" (p.39); "True poetic beauty was to be found in ambiguous difficult texts which permitted a variety of interpretations and offered a multiplicity of meanings" (p.52).

16. The two philosophers have suggested how a totalitarian State and revolutionary terrorism have more in common than one might think: "un Etat devient totalitaire quand, au lieu d'effectuer dans ses propres limites la machine mondiale de surcodage, il s'identifie à elle en crèant les conditions d'une "autarchie", en faisant une reterritorialisation par 'vas clos', dans l'artifice du vide (ce qui n'est jamais une opèration idèologique, mais èconomique et politique).

D'autre part, à l'autre pôle, il y a une machine abstraite de mutation, qui opère par dècodage et dèterritorialisation. C'est elle qui trace le lignes de fuite: elle pilote les flux à quanta, assure la crèation-connexion des flux, èmet de nouveaux quanta. Elle est elle-même en ètat de fuite, et dresse des machines de guerre dans ses lignes.

Mais aussi, entre les deux pôles, il y a tout un domain de nègo-ciation, de traduction, de transduction proprement molèculaire, oû tantôt les lignes molaire sont dèjà travaillèes par des fissures et des fêlures, tantôt les lignes de fuite, dèjà attirèes vers des trous noirs, les connexions de flux, dèjà remplacèes par des conjonc-tions limitatives, les èmissions de quanta, converties en points-centres." Gilles Deleuze & Fèlix Guattari, *Mille Plateaux: Capitalisme et Schizophrènie* (Paris: Les Editions de Minuit, 1980), p.273.

17. This is what happens in the film version of Soyinka's *Kongi's Harvest*: "The tyrannicide fails in the play. It succeeds, however, in the film by the same title—in which Soyinka acts the part of Kongi—although the conclusion is even more pessimistic. In the last sequence the leader of the opposition is seen taking on the dictator's role." Josef Gugler, "African Literary Comment on Dictators: Wole Soyinka's Plays and Nuruddin Farah's Novels," *The Journal of Modern African Studies* 26, 1 (1988), 175.

18. Both Deeriye's "doubles"—his dead wife and the mad prophet—incite him to rebel and kill the tyrant. See *Close Sesame* (London: Allison & Busby, 1983), pp.21, 198.

19. Ibid., p.137.

20. There are: "quatre dangers, d'abord la Peur, puis la Clartè, et puis le Pouvoir, et enfin le grand Dègoût, l'envie de faire mourir et de mourir, Passion d'abolition-." As to the great Disgust: "le qua-trième danger: que la ligne de fuite franchisse le mur, qu'elle sorte des trous noirs, mais que, au lieu de se connecter avec d'autres lignes et d'augmenter ses valences à chaque fois, *elle se tourne en destruction, abolition pure et simple, passion d'abolition...*c'est prè-cisèment quand la machine de guerre n'as plus pour objet que la

guerre, quand elle substitue ainsi la destruction à la mutation, qu'elle libère la charge la plus catastrophique...on doit dire, de la guerre elle-même, qu'elle est seulement l'abominable rèsidu de la machine de guerre, soit lorsque celle-ci c'est fait approprier par l'appareil d'Etat, soit, pire encore, lorsqu'elle s'est construite un appareil d'Etat qui ne vaut plus que pour la destruction. Alors la machine de guerre ne trace plus des lignes de fuites mutantes, mais une pure et froide ligne d'abolition." Deleuze & Guattari, *Mille Plateaux*, pp.277, 279-281.

21. See "Do Fences Have Sides?" in *The Commonwealth in Canada*, Proceedings of the Second Triennal Conference of CACLALS, vol. 2, ed. Uma Parameswaran (Calcutta: Writers Workshop, 1983), pp.174-182.

22. From Fidel Castro's speech delivered at the three-day Summit of Poor Countries Leaders held in Cuba in April 2000, quoted in John Rice, "Castro Viciously Attacks Capitalism," *Associated Press*, 13 April 2000.

23. See Wole Soyinka, *The Open Sore of a Continent: A Personal Narrative of the Nigerian Crisis* (Oxford: Oxford University Press, 1996), where he denounced the ethnic cleansing done by the Nigerian despot Abacha, at the expense of the Ogoni, whose land is a strategic oil-producing area, and where he mentioned Ken Saro-Wiwa's protest to the United Nations Minorities Council, which would later lead to the popular writer's execution by hanging; and Wole Soyinka, *The Burden of Memory, the Muse of Forgiveness* (Cambridge, MA: The W.E.B. Du Bois Institute Series, 1998), where he exposed recent African tyrannies, raising doubts about the viability of The Truth and Reconciliation kind of solution in South Africa.

24. *Gifts* is only a partial exception to this.

25. See my interview, "Nuruddin Farah Interviewed by Armando Pajalich," *Kunapipi*, 15, 1 (1993), 61-71.

26. See Gugler, "African Literary Comment on Dictators," 171-77.

27. Many critics have emphasized Farah's focus on the family issue and the relationship between patriarchy and tyranny. For example, see: Derek Wright, *The Novels of Nuruddin Farah* (Bayreuth: Bayreuth African Studies Series, 1994) pp.46-52; or, for a reading of Farah's entire oeuvre on those lines, my "Padri tiranni e ribellioni di figli e di figlie nei romanzi di Nuruddin Farah", in *Filiazioni e affiliazioni (nel testo periferico africano)* (Venezia: Supernova, 1995), pp.255-349.

28. Ngugi wa Thiong'o, *Penpoints, Gunpoints, and Dreams*, pp.126-27.

THE MURDER OF SOYAAN KEYNAAN

Ian Adam

No reader of Nuruddin Farah's *Sweet and Sour Milk* can be long engaged with the work before sensing its generic affinity with the detective story, or, more precisely, with that variant of the detective story, the thriller, in which the detective himself is imperilled by the scheming of the murderer. While a strict identification with the genre would not do justice to a work as thematically and formally rich as this novel, an examination of points of structural contact and departure might be illuminating to both. The simplest point of contact is immediate and obvious. At or near the beginning of a detective novel someone dies and murder is either suspected or directly established. The opening section of *Sweet and Sour Milk is* titled "Prologue": in it we trace, through the concerns of his family and the fluctuations of his own consciousness, the last hours of a young man, Soyaan Keynaan, economic advisor to the president of the post-1969 revolutionary Somali Republic. Normally healthy, he lies ill at home: medical attention by a friend, Dr. Ahmed-Wellie, modern drugs prescribed for him, traditional remedies offered by his mother, do not help; he mutters incoherently and utters obscenities in his sleep, talks in lucid moments with family members, including his twin brother, hiccups, his hiccups become spasms, and he dies grasping his brother's hand. Poison is suspected, but by whom administered and by what means?

The mood of detective fiction is interrogative, and the questions—which may be asked by all—are definitely framed in the consciousness of a detective investigator, who ponders the circumstances of the death and begins a reconstruction of the events leading up to it, basing his re-creation of the past on such clues as he can discover. In *Sweet and Sour Milk* this role is undertaken by an unlikely candidate, the twin brother, Loyaan, a dentist turned health officer in the plague-stricken region of the inland town of Baidoa, who has always stayed clear of the highly engaged political life of his brother and whose knowledge of its labyrinthine complexities is relatively naive. Loyaan immediately puts to one side the accusation of their mother Qumman that his brother has been poisoned by her husband's second wife, Beydan, with whom he dined the night before, and instead ponders fragments of evidence that turn up and disturbing events that transpire shortly after the death. In Soyaan's diary he finds the baffling entries "M to the power of 2. I/M comrade in project."[1] The Minister to the Presidency attends Soyaan's funeral, alludes briefly to "a certain woman" to Loyaan, challenges his account of his brother's last words, and asks if he knows of a "Memorandum" Soyaan was working on. In Soyaan's pillowcase his mother finds a paper which, being illiterate, she cannot read, and which she turns over to Loyaan: it is a diatribe against upstart leaders and political terrorism in the state, of an authorship which remains obscure. The twin's sister, Ladan, finds in the pockets of a pair of Soyaan's trousers copies of two government statutes prescribing the death penalty for dissemination of matter deemed anti-revolutionary and for the use of religious office for anti-government political ends. These too are given to Loyaan.

The emphasis in the detective novel is hermeneutic, as the investigator fits fragmentary clues into patterns, patterns which sometimes become established as final but more frequently disintegrate or assume minor importance in the light of subsequent discoveries. From greater to lesser provisionality the patterns move in the course of the narrative towards a final coherent and correspondent truth. The "certain woman" mentioned by the minister is rather quickly identified through the woman herself, Margaritta, a half-Italian, half-Somali Christian student of law who calls at the family home with a child a few months old, Marco, fathered by Soyaan, her lover. "Margaritta. Marco. *Marco mio. Margaritta mia.* M to the power of 2" (p.71). The discovery of the "certain woman" leads to the decoding of a diary entry, but it is in the nature of the hermeneutic activity of the genre that such evidence may always be further decoded in the interest of a higher pattern: later "M to the power of 2" is seen to allude as well to the government's close involvement with the Soviet state, to the capitals "Mogadiscio /Moscow" (p.127).

Everything points to political motivation behind the death. Soyaan's secretary, Mulki, is taken for interrogation, and she is reported to be tortured to reveal the contents of the memorandum, which she apparently typed. Margaritta tells Loyaan that there are two memoranda, one in her possession, the other with a friend of Soyaan, Ibrahim Musse Ilmog, "Il Siciliano," a civil servant also, and brother of Mulki. From Ibrahim Loyaan learns that the memoranda were written in connection with the activities of two small clandestine nationalist political groups allied in opposition to the regime, that one, titled "Dionysius's Ear," was an exposè of the network of informers used by the government, and the other an assessment of the cost to the nation of the imprisonment of intellectuals and professionals replaced by Cubans and Russians. "I/M and comrade-in-project: Ibrahim and Margaritta: comrade in my project?" (p.126) he speculates. He is also shown, on the back of a photograph of Marco, portions of a poem about pursuit, flight and murder (John Wain's "The Murderer") transcribed by Soyaan, with the "theys" designating the pursuers underlined, and a date of three months earlier inscribed, along with the symbol "M." The date matches that of the regime's legislation: the copies of the two statutes prescribing the death penalty clearly apply to such papers as the memoranda and the specific activities of the sheikhs. The poem was portentous for Soyaan and now is for Loyaan: as he further pursues the cause of his brother's death he becomes himself embroiled in a counter-action against him.

The detective story, suggests Michel Butor, "must...have two murders; the murderer is the victim of the second, which is committed by the detective, his weapon an 'explosion of truth.'"[2] Such an explosion is carried out by Loyaan in the following sequence, without, however, fatal result. In a visit to the family home shortly after Soyaan's death Beydan had mentioned to Loyaan that a man had accompanied his brother to dinner at her place; visiting her after his talk with Ibrahim to learn more about the dinner he finds that the man is the same minister who had spoken to him at the funeral, that he is a frequent visitor there with the twins' father, Keynaan, and that he too ate the meal prepared, emerging unharmed. Soyaan looked tired and was abnormally thirsty; drank beer while the minister had a soft drink; spoke of his thirst ("I am thirsty like the sand of the sea" [p.153]) and of the need to see a doctor; took pills. Ahmed-Wellie calls on Loyaan at Beydan's unexpectedly, not to say inexplicably, and as he drives him home gives the news that Ibrahim Siciliano has been arrested for interrogation and that Mulki has broken under torture. Outside his home Loyaan finds Margaritta waiting in her car; the memorandum she was to show him that day has been taken from her bank locker, which has been forced open. Loyaan has questions for the minister when he meets him for an appointment the next day, and the thrust of a bold and dangerous interrogation is the charge of Soyaan's murder through injections given after the meal by a Russian doctor in a Military Hospital where he was taken for treatment. The deductive processes leading to this charge are unstated, but clearly a link has been made between the disclosure of the minister's presence at the meal, Soyaan's casual mention before his death of a visit to a doctor at the Hospital, and Ahmed-Wellie's discovery, related to Soyaan on the drive home, of a Russian doctor used by the Security for clandestine work. (Soyaan also raved in his sleep in the final restless hours of "pale ghostly beings which jabbed [him] with needles" [p.17], though Loyaan was not present at the time, and there is no record of any report to him.)

If there are two murderers in the detective story there are also two detectives, the second carrying out the charge laid on him by the first, the victim, to seek out and bring to justice the perpetrator of violent crime. Further, the victim often has some intimation of danger to himself, and has begun to seek its source, frequently hiring the detective as his "second self" in the task. One notes frequently a strong identification between the two, often extending beyond that of role to occupation or personality, as in Dashiell Hammett's *The Maltese Falcon,* where the victim is the detective's partner. Few identifications could be closer than that of *Sweet and Sour Milk,* where the victim is his twin brother! Further, Soyaan until his death has been a detective of sorts, an investigator of a horrifying series of offences against human freedoms, rights and physical well-being. His history, reconstructed in the fragments of writing and personal recollections brought out in the course of the narrative, makes him still a powerful presence even though physically absent, and indeed it is through such presence that Loyaan is guided in his new role. He progresses from deep fraternal affection and physical identity almost comically underlined at points (a newspaper praises the dead Loyaan and similarly captions Soyaan's photograph; a friend of the parents from the boys' childhood praises to Loyaan his dead brother "Loyaan"), to a spiritual affinity that touches on the uncanny. Their sister Ladan, who speaks of "One in two: Loyaan and Soyaan. My brothers in twins" (p.53), has long recognized the latent Soyaan in Loyaan, but the murderer's act makes the latent manifest. He is offered Soyaan's place in one of the clandestine organizations, has a dream in which he sleeps, erotically though not overtly sexually, with Margaritta, and in his close friendship with her takes his brother's place as her companion. Most strikingly, on his first visit to Margaritta he has an extraordinary sense of *déjà vu*:

> Quiet the night. Soft the breeze. The moths moved in frenzy. The *mayooko* buzzed in their ears. They sat in silence. Loyaan felt he had been through this before. He sensed he had known all this. Something in him told him that he had sat in the same place, that he had used the same rocking-chair, that he had drunk from the same glass. But had he ever known Margaritta? (p.114)

At the novel's end, his investigations thwarted, Loyaan's apparent destiny is to fulfil the official government plans for Soyaan's future as he departs to take up the position of Somalia's councillor in Belgrade.

In most detective fiction the normal official agencies of public order are shown to be at best less competent and at worst corrupt in relation to the detective, whether he be a private operator or Scotland Yard representative: he represents a new order both in understanding and explaining more than they and in implicitly or explicitly establishing the need for their reform or removal. The official agency of public order is usually the police force, and it, or others who perform its functions, is certainly evident in Sweet and Sour Milk, running very much on the corrupt end of the scale of inadequacy. Its representatives act in compliance with the wishes of the murderer or murderers, and Loyaan's relation with them is as troubled and danger-ridden as his brother's. At odds with them and all enforcers of the regime's tyranny, he is shadowed throughout by a sinister one-armed man, and is himself arrested for interrogation shortly after his visit to the minister. Further, far from investigating the circumstances of Soyaan's death the police collaborate with official attempts at his spiritual murder through an Orwellian rewriting of history proclaiming him a dedicated son of the revolution who died with praises of the General on his lips.

Only brief hours before Soyaan's death Loyaan reads a passage his brother has underlined in Machiavelli's *The Prince,* part of which reads: "There is nothing more difficult to take in hand, more perilous to conduct, or more uncertain in its success than to take the lead in the introduction of a new order of things. Because the innovator has for enemies all those who have done well under the old conditions, and lukewarm defenders in those who may do well under the new" (p.21). In the action described of displacing established authority at considerable personal risk for the sake of a "new order," we can see the ghost of a pattern which underlies the detective story: the Oedipal. *Oedipus Rex is* the first detective story, its hero, as Michel Butor suggests, not only solving a riddle, "but also...[killing] the man to whom he owes his title . . ."[3] Oedipus's father is literally and biologically such, but every detective owes his existence as detective to the murderer who provides him with the crime to solve. The Oedipal pattern in all detective fiction is seen displayed in the investigator's relation to the police, whose role as protector of the public weal he usurps, but it is sometimes even more strikingly evident, with the detective challenging the authority of a figure associated with the paternal role and taking as his own a woman linked with him. Frank Kermode, for example, has demonstrated such an action in E.C. Bentley's classic *Trent's Last Case,* in which the murdered man, an American millionaire named Manderson, is ultimately discovered to be a suicide who has elaborately contrived his death to throw suspicion for it onto his English secretary, Marlowe, whom he believes, with obsessive jealousy, to be having an affair with his much younger wife. As it turns out their relation has been entirely innocent, but the detective, Trent, like Marlowe young enough to be Manderson's son, falls in love with and marries the widow.[4] In *Sweet and Sour Milk* three analogous patriarchal figures are closely linked literally and symbolically: the General, the President of the Republic, the Minister to the Presidency, and the twins' father, Keynaan. All three work for the common end of perpetuating the regime, and all three have a hand in the soiling of public memory of Soyaan through the refashioning of his history. Though they are anal-

337

ogous in function, emphasis on aspects of their role varies: the president representing supreme political authority, the minister sexual rivalry, and Keynaan literal paternal tyranny.

Behind the revision of Soyaan's life story lies the power of the General, who takes (or rather thinks he takes) complete possession of his spirit. As Xassan, a civil servant responsible for the files of his fellows, tells Loyaan as he informs him that his brother's file has been removed for rewriting: "He is the property of the General" (p.108). It is of course the General who is the prime mover of the corruption and terror denounced in the fragment found in Soyaan's pillowcase ("Listen to the knock on your neighbours' door at dawn" [p.391]), and dramatized throughout, with special vividness in Dr. Ahmed-Wellie's accounts of his blindfolded transport to treat tortured prisoners. He rules through tribal patronage, bribery, surveillance, brute force, fear and collusion with the Soviet Union and its police arm, the KGB. Loyaan deals with him only through his agents, never directly, but towards the novel's end Margaritta recounts Soyaan's confrontation with him over the execution of the ten sheikhs:

> And the General had looked at him, he told me, looked at Soyaan with disdain. "Is it unconstitutional to shoot these sheikhs because they oppose my directives, the laws which I've passed, the decrees which I've signed?" had challenged the General. "Yes, it is unconstitutional to pass laws, sign decrees, run a martial-law government and then sentence these sheikhs to death. It is against the teaching of the Koran on which they base their arguments. It is unconstitutional," Soyaan concluded. "Well, in that case, have I ever introduced myself to you, young man? I *am* the constitution. Now you know who I am, and I want you out of here before I set those dogs of mine on you and you are torn to pieces. Out." (pp.226-27)

Such centralization of state authority in one person leaves little option for others to become anything but instruments or opponents of public policy, and its execution through terror inevitably leads to intrigue and counter-intrigue. In such activity the state is the captive feminine, her being subject to abuse beyond the darkest imagining, and the goal of the investigator is to set her free for a new and creative partnership.

The basic pattern is duplicated at an explicitly sexual level in the relations of Soyaan and Loyaan to the minister, Loyaan's prime suspect as the immediate hand in his brother's death. He is, as Beydan has told Loyaan, in close and mysterious association with the twins' father; as Minister to the Presidency he has a similar relation with the prime political patriarch. It is he who first issues at the funeral the challenge to Loyaan's account of his brother's last words. He is also the unnamed presence in a chilling scene recalled by Soyaan in the prologue, where he and Margaritta (also unnamed, but in retrospect obviously her) swim in the sea at an isolated beach, believing "they had the beach to themselves" (p.12). This phrase would seem to allude to a child who appears shortly afterwards, but it is ambiguous: Soyaan wonders "if there were other persons, adults, in the area" (p. 13); there is "another" in Margaritta's life, "[a] man important enough to be recognised in public at every gathering in Mogadiscio (p.12), who accounts for their need to meet in private; and near the scene's end, ominously, Margaritta "thought she saw a vulture perched on the precipice at the far end of the shore" (p.14). Soyaan at this point has been the minister's sexual rival for nearly a year and a half and Margaritta has already borne his child; by the time of his death she has left the minister altogether. Circumstances encourage the suggestion of at least some sexual motivation behind his death. Loyaan replaces Soyaan in the relation with Margaritta in all respects but the sexual (but we should note the erotic content of his dream of her on p.206); he is companion, confidant and friend; he has, as we have seen, an uncanny sense of having lived through his relation with her before; despite Soyaan's physical death the Oedipal displacement of the minister continues.

In an epigraph to part two of the novel the author deliberately underlines the parallel between the patriarchs of state and family with a quotation from Wilhelm Reich: "In the figure of the father the authoritarian state has its representative in every family, so that the family becomes its most important instrument of power" (p.97). In his public office Keynaan represents that striking arm of the state discussed above: he is a policeman, and furthermore, in a clear displacement of Soyaan's death, one implicated in the murder through torture of a political prisoner.[5] It is his newspaper interview which gives the first "official" account of his son's last words and begins the process of falsification of his history. Farah devotes chapter six of the novel to an exploration of the relation of patriarch to family through an extended conversation between Loyaan and Keynaan. While the chapter is a fair-minded one, showing Keynaan's affection for his son and concern with what he considers his folly about his brother, and allowing Keynaan to defend his life, conduct and values, it leaves no doubt about his readiness to exercise brutal power as he chooses. His attitude to women (always a touchstone for enlightenment in Farah) parallels that of the General to his subjects: it is tyrannous, dismissive of their capacities and proprietorial of their role. "They can serve the purposes Allah created them for originally, and no more" (p.84), he declares to Loyaan, who disagrees. Soyaan is recalled speaking of his outlook generally:

> When once addressing himself to these differences, Soyaan said: "Not so much generational as they are qualitative—the differences between us twins and our father. My father grew up with the idea that the universe is flat; we, that it is round. We believe we have a perspective of an inclusive nature—more global; our views are 'rounder.' We believe that his are exclusive, that they are flat (and therefore uninteresting) as the universe his insularity ties him to." (p.85)

In its reference to the contrast between "flat" and "round" views the passage alludes, as do many others more or less directly, to a childhood incident in which the twins are at a seaside beach at the town of Merca and find a large round object, a ball or globe representing the world, which their father severs as false and abominable. The violent act haunts their memories: here, waiting to meet Ibrahim, Loyaan's:

> The sea foamed, it frothed, it flirted with the sun which teased it. The sea roared. It made Loyaan rehearse a line just half-recalled. And in the distance, way down waveful of events: the twins. There were ships flying foreign flags, big and small boats carrying bananas and other merchandise, ships which had dropped anchor. And out of the blue clearness of the waters emerges Keynaan, the tyrant: in his right hand, he grips a club at its butt-end; in his left, the rubber ball which he has torn in two, the rubber ball upon which the twins had together drawn a complete and an illustrated mini-atlas. A world with no frontiers. A world of their own fantasies. (p. 131)

The act represents at once his cosmology and despotism, as well as foreshadowing the physical severance of the twins, the "one in two." The repeated note of division is echoed in Keynaan's last words in the chapter, a defence of the official glorification of Soyaan:

> I am the father. It is my prerogative to give life and death as I find fit. I've chosen to breathe life into Soyaan. And remember one thing, Loyaan: if I decide this minute to cut you in two, I can. The law of this land invests in men of my age the power. I am the Grand Patriarch." (p.95)

341

I am the father. I am the Grand Patriarch. I *am* the Constitution.
I *am*.

In the classical detective story the patricidal journey through the
maze of clues and false clues, patterns and discarded patterns, raising and violation of readerly expectations, ends with the illuminating
order of truth: the labyrinth is mapped, signs direct you away from
the wrong turn and blocked exit; deceitfulness is unmasked and mystery unveiled: from multiple possibilities, polygraphy of meaning,
emerges meaning single and definitive. From what has been said so
far it seems clear that *Sweet and Sour Milk* departs radically from the
classic genre in this pattern of closure. New puzzles arise to replace
the old, and many of these are not satisfactorily resolved by the time
the novel comes to an end—if "end" is the term for such openness.
Loyaan suspects Dr. Ahmed-Wellie to be an informer, and then has to
deal with the apparent contradiction of his subsequent arrest; a
woman claiming to be Mulki appears before him while he is detained
and tells him she was never tortured; he is told just before the
novel's close that Ibrahim and Mulki will see him off on his flight to
Belgrade, a fact incompatible with their imprisonment; Margaritta
tells him that her former relation with the minister had nothing to do
with Soyaan's death, but we have no way of knowing whether she is
right or wrong. Furthermore, it is still not clear who killed Soyaan and
by what means. Was it through the beer at dinner which only he
drank? The pills he took? A poison ingested *before* the dinner which
accounted for his feeling unwell, his thirst? The injection—if there
really was one—by the Russian doctor, if indeed he treated Soyaan?
The detective, far from pursuing his investigation to a conclusion,
has it aborted through his enforced "appointment" to Belgrade, and
is shown in the last line of the novel hearing a knock on the door from
the escort that is to take him to the airport, though whether or not
he will in fact be taken there is an ominously open question.

It would be tempting to reduce the novel's rejection of final
answers, its refusal to tie up all the loose ends, to the hermeneutic

scepticism of a *nouveau roman,* but at the most I think only affinities can be argued here. For one thing, the *degree* of scepticism we find in a Robbe-Grillet is absent. If we are not given a definitive version of past events we are somewhat closer to a true account than at the novel's beginning. It seems highly likely, for example, that Soyaan was the victim of a murder that was largely politically motivated, whose goals were to rid the state of a perceived subversive, terrorize those associated with his activities, and provide the regime with a revolutionary martyr, and it is certain that those goals were achieved. For another, one senses the relative lack of closure to derive less from epistemological scepticism than from an ethical principle which looks with mistrust at the egocentric tyrannies of the General's or Keynaan's "I am." The notion of a single superb deductive intelligence implied in the figure of the traditional detective, a Sherlock Holmes or Hercule Poirot with all the answers, comes rather too close to the belief in one leader, one rescuer, that the novel opposes. Against such authoritarianism it clearly sets the notion of collective activity, of collaboration and consensus: Soyaan dies, but Loyaan continues his work, and the members of the clandestine groups are in the background putting together pieces of a puzzle having to do with more than Soyaan's death. Just before Loyaan's departure Beydan dies giving birth to a boy, who is given the name Soyaan: new generations will bury the old, the Soyaans the Keynaans, the process of enlightenment will continue. The establishment of a new order will not give any one person the responsibility for final solutions, and indeed will preclude such absoluteness in favour of the endless provisionality of group agreement.

NOTES

1. Nuruddin Farah, *Sweet and Sour Milk* (London: Allison and Busby, 1979), p.27. Further references are incorporated in the text. The pagination of the 1979 edition is identical with that of the more accessible Heinemann paperback (1980).

2. Paraphrased in Frank Kermode, "Novel and Narrative," in *The Theory of the Novel: New Essays,* ed. John Halperin (London: Oxford University Press, 1974), p.166.

3. Kermode, p.166.

4. Kermode, pp.161-63.

5. Beydan, his second wife, was the wife of that prisoner, a fact which gives Qumman's suspicions of her as poisoner some plausible ground in motives of retaliation. Personal animus, however, remains self-evidently the determining force behind the accusation, and finally discredits it. The marriage of Keynaan to Beydan of course only reinforces the Oedipal parallels.

ORALITY AND POWER IN NURUDDIN FARAH'S *SWEET AND SOUR MILK*

Derek Wright

Nuruddin Farah grew up in a genuinely oral world which communicated in a virtually unwritten language, his imagination nourished by the legendary oral poets of his Ogaden childhood (Somali acquired no orthographic script until 1972). His novels, in his own words, chart the passage of a "society coming out of the oral tradition into a written form."[1] He has insisted, however, that "you cannot divorce the oral and the literary from one another,"[2] and in his fiction the two modes have an interpenetrative existence. Ebla, in his first novel (*From a Crooked Rib*, 1970), and Askar, in *Maps* (1986), live, idiomatically and stylistically, as oral beings on the pages to which they are transcribed, their questing intelligences and intuitions fed by remembered anecdotes, parables and folk-wisdoms imbibed with the oral cultures of their childhoods. Even the mercurial Koschin of *A Naked Needle* (1976), for all his literary allusiveness and his pride in the revolutionary government's scripting of the Somali language, is at heart a garrulously oral creature, given to torrents of talk and intoxicated, as is evidenced in his pun-power and virtuoso alliteration, with the sheer sound of words. Though he has come a long way from it, Koschin comes originally from the same eloquent, bookless culture of Somali tradition.

Nevertheless, these continuities notwithstanding, Farah's fiction has been slower than some of his contemporaries—notably Ngugi and Armah—to recognize the positive strengths and reconstructive potential of oral cultural values and modes of expression and, unlike them, he has not conceived these values and forms in an unequivocally polemical way: for example, as unsullied alternatives and possible modes of counter-discourse to the evils of post-colonial politics. In his trilogy of novels, *Variations on the Theme of an African Dictatorship* (1979-1983), Farah seeks neither to rehabilitate traditional forms, like the later Armah, nor to discredit and repudiate them, like Ouologuem, but rather to show how indigenous traditions, both oral and domestic, have themselves been implicated in the new political tribulations and terrors of the independent state. On the domestic front, the totalitarian tribal oligarchy imposed on post-revolution Somalia by General Siyad Barre's Soviet-backed regime is revealed to be but the old patriarchal (and matriarchal) despotism writ large. Thus, in *Sweet and Sour Milk* (1979), the police informer and "grand patriarch" Keynaan connives at the death and defamation of his dissident son, the government minister Soyaan, to stamp out subversion at both state and familial levels; and in *Sardines* (1981) the tyrannical Idil, when evicted by her son Samater (also a government minister), is able to invoke the wrath of the state to bring about his political degradation.

As regards the oral tradition, Farah had already provided, through the medium of Ebla in *From A Crooked Rib*, a glimpse of an oral culture in something closer to a pristine healthy state prior to its perversion by the General. Meanwhile, at the other end of the spectrum he presents in the barely literate, eloquent figure of Dulman in *Sardines* a revolutionary image of an ancient oral Somalia, a guest in a century of high-technology which it now turns to its own account by

346

fighting despotism with its own weapons. "Our tradition is oral," says Dulman. "One can communicate with the hearts of Somalis only through their hearing faculties."[3] The former "Lady of the Revolution" whose songs were exploited as revolutionary propaganda, Dulman has now joined the struggle against the regime by smuggling underground tapes of subversive poems, recorded straight from the poet's mouth, then learned and worked into unscripted theatrical pieces for outside performance. Significantly, the girls arrested for painting anti-government slogans sign themselves 'Dulman,' with the implication that the voices of protest have combined, the power of the spoken word added to that of the written one. In *Sardines* the cassette becomes the oral tradition's answer to the debased oral techniques that help to keep the General in power. In the third novel of the trilogy (*Close Sesame*, 1983), the protagonist Deeriye is a living reminder of a radical Somali oral tradition that fostered the talents of the warrior-poet the Sayyid and the Sultan Wiil Waal, who fought colonial and clan enemies with the power of the spoken word as well as with conventional weapons. The historical original of Deeriye's beloved legendary Sayyid inspired both devotion and terror in his people, however, and his revolution was nationalistic rather than social, whilst Wiil Waal was an absolute, albeit a benevolent, dictator; and Deeriye, who was given the works of Mussolini to read when a prisoner of Italian colonialism, is alert to the political uses and misuses of both the spoken and the written word.

Farah has described the Somalis as a people "moving straight from the oral tradition in the African sense to the oral tradition in the technological sense (television and radio) without going through that middle stage of the written word."[4] This process acquires sinister implications, and the oral tradition darker dimensions, in *Sweet and Sour Milk*, where the oral culture is effectively allied with the reactionary forces of tribal authoritarianism and obscurantism, thus polarizing oral despotism and written revolution, unalphabeted tyranny and textual subversion. It is Koschin, in the earlier *A Naked Needle*, who raises the first alarms about the dangers of excessive reliance on the oral code's modes of communication, sounding an ominous warning note for the forthcoming trilogy. "There is no government-fixed price, neither do you get a receipt," Koschin remarks ominously. "All is done orally, we are an oral society, and one has to trust. . ."5 In the sombre trilogy of novels that follows, the Somali populace is short- changed by a military dictatorship that lives in terror of the written word and whose repressive surveillance techniques thrive on oral exchanges and are steeped in the existing oral traditions of a still largely illiterate society. The General knows as well as Dulman that Somali hearts are won through their ears and though, in the Dulman episode, Farah gives a nod of acknowledgment to the outspoken oral poets who also fell victim to the Barre regime, it is his sole concession to the oral mode's radical possibilities in a trilogy that generally opposes a progressive sophisticated literacy to a primitive reactionary orality. In the next novel, *Sardines*, literature is in effect compulsorily oralized by banning orders. Medina is forbidden by the regime to publish her translations of world classics and so serves them up oral-fresh—"hot like maize cakes from the oven"—as a domestic diet of bedtime stories for her young daughter Ubax. For Medina communications with the world outside the house where she is virtually under arrest are possible only on an oral basis, and that world is governed by gossip, libellous rumor and speculation, which foster and sustain the atmosphere of suspicion and uncertainty, of being "kept guessing", required by the dictator: a Somali poet notes that the ear, the organ of both the oral culture and the General's police system, is shaped like a question mark. Medina's clanswomen "live in the innards of a whale which hardly went ashore," insulated by the oral code's watery unreality of rumor and hearsay. She has scarcely made her decisive departure from home and husband when a generous supply of oral versions of the event are already in circulation and on their way back to her, presenting her with four possible reasons for her action: Idil's threat to have Ubax circumcised, the compromising of her anti-government position by Samater's ministerial appointment, Samater's rumoured infidelity with the maid, and the creation of a need for herself through absence. The result is that the agent herself is no longer sure of her motives and neither she nor her author ever confirm that any one of these alternatives is to be preferred above the others. Whatever private certainty and personal individual reality exists is thus dissolved into public indeterminacy, and the oral convention, in its reconstruction of multiple possibilities, poses not merely an invasion of privacy and a moral usurpation but an ontological threat.

In the Somalia of *Sweet and Sour Milk*[6] power is still largely oral-based. According to the system of "Dionysius's Ear", the oral network uncovered in Soyaan's Memorandum, a barely literate General recruits his security corps of spies and informers from illiterates working entirely in the oral medium and reporting verbally everything they hear. As Ibrahim explains to Loyaan, the domestic and oral traditions are very close here, for the "ears" planted by the security system "sprout in every homestead"; in the absence of trade unions or organized protest groups, informers are easily recruited from the family unit by threats to its members. Under the "ear-service" of tyranny, little or nothing is written down: there are no death certificates, birth registers, lists of detainees or arrest warrants (phoned instructions suffice), and no written reports and particulars. In any case, the few files which exist can, like Soyaan's, be immediately confiscated for purposes of rewording "history." Where rumor rules, nothing is ever confirmed: as Medina notes in the next novel, it is in the General's interest for the populace to be "kept guessing", and it is rumor rather than information which is published. "No information was released until a rumour had been published, and nothing was made official until the General's informants had reported back the mood, the feeling of the general public" (p.196). There is an embargo on books and written information. Texts like Soyaan's Memorandum and his "Clowns" piece (which apparently had a real underground circulation in a Somali translation)[7] are automatically subversive and are ruthlessly hunted down, with dire results for those found in possession. The written word certifies reality by providing an evidential record of people and events which insists that things happened. Thus it poses to an oralized power-system the greatest threat: "The written word, more powerful than the gun, will frighten them," predicts Ibrahim optimistically and Loyaan trusts that a written public statement will refute the lies fabricated about his brother by his father. Soyaan, who kept his official memos short because of the semi-illiteracy of the ruling oligarchy, seems from the scraps of his writing to have shared this forlorn belief in the authority of the written word, in a desperate bid to resist the real power bases in Somali society.

The floating oral reality, in which truth is as indeterminate as the jail sentences imposed by the regime, mirrors the malaise that has become the new political status quo of Somalia. In the oral-dominated culture faith must be pinned to the few signs that exist since there is nothing else with which to fix the flux, or even prove the existence, of human experience. Signs, for those challenging obscurantist power, are crucial for an objective notation of reality: they mark limits, define and identify, measure and record. Thus, it is no surprise that all those who oppose the dictatorship in the book are Westernized, university-educated literates and that there is an absolute polarization of speech and text, of a reactionary oralism and a reformist literacy. All of Farah's rebels, up to this point, are revolutionaries of the written word: we hear nothing of the outspoken oral poets who also fell victim to Siyad Barre's regime.[8] It is not until the Dulman episodes of *Sardines* that Farah demonstrates an awareness of the oral mode's revolutionary possibilities.

Sweet and Sour Milk, as one critic has observed, probes its own language, which both *tells* and *is* the story.[9] It reveals what happens to written language in a culture built on oral discourse and, most particularly, how it is suppressed, undermined and driven into secret codes such as Soyaan's "I/M" and the ambiguous "M to the power of 2" (Margaritta and Marco, Mogadiscio and Moscow?); the John Wain poem and the "Clowns" fable; and enigmatic signs like the one scratched in the sand by Margaritta at Soyaan's funeral. But beyond these language concerns, the novel raises deeper existential and ontological doubts about the nature of reality in an oral culture. In the "unmapped city" of Mogadiscio the established oral codes take a number of forms from the badly to the barely scripted, the ill-written (in the sense of being inauthentic) to the entirely unwritten. In the first category come the hackneyed praise-songs of the General sung by the "griots in green" at the meaningless purification ceremony, the Koranic slogans bowdlerised and parroted by cartoon-like military stooges at Loyaan's interrogation, and the "badly written farce" staged for Loyaan by the Minister to the Presidency to persuade him that "Mulki", a character of uncertain existence, is really safe and well and will come out to farewell him at the airport. Soyaan comments ironically in his Memorandum on the banal idiomatic oralization of history itself: Mussolini is remembered not by the achievements and atrocities recorded in the history books but by the trite oral quip about making trains run on time that has passed into the folk-memory. As there is no route by which writing can pass into speech in the regime's repressive, text-exclusive oral culture, it will be Soyaan's fate to be remembered not by the complex truths of his writings but by the oral lies and cliches used by the regime to refashion him into a revolutionary hero.

Alternatively, reality in the oral society is unwritten, unwritable and, ultimately, unknowable (Loyaan's thoughts walk "the untrod landscape of the unknowable"). The indeterminacy of oral modes of interpretation makes it difficult to distinguish between the true and the imaginary, between what does and does not exist. In what sense, for example, can Soyaan be said to have existed except as a mythical property of the government, a revolutionary artifact like the parks, streets and towering buildings named after him? Loyaan is repeatedly mistaken for his twin and feels *deja-vu* affinities with him, hearing Soyaan's voice speaking posthumously inside his head, tempering his impetuosity with its secrecy and discretion, until he begins to wonder, like his mother Qumman, if he and his brother are not really the same person: "Could one search for Soyaan in Loyaan? Might one find the dead in the living?" (p.55). This fogging of narrative fact and dissolution of time-sequences is then furthered by the hypnotic and hallucinatory aspects of Farah's style in this novel, particularly in the epigraphic poetic passages which have the elusiveness of parabolic oral texts requiring the audience's complementary interpretation. *Sweet and Sour Milk* is full of multilayered, microcosmic oral "texts" of this kind, notably the symbolic vignettes of weather and skyscape which open the chapters, and the recurring epigraphic refrain of rival poisons fed to an infant who is denied his mother's milk (variously construable as the "sour" and "sweet" sides of the Somali tempera- ment, represented by Loyaan and Soyaan or by Keynaan and his wives; as the mixed bag of colonial education which opposes a glob- al view to Keynaan's flat conception of the universe but also teaches that Africa had no pre-colonial history; or as the successive poisons of colonial and the General's regimes).

Indeterminacy is also the informing principle of the vagaries of characterization in oral societies. Mulki, for example, is an entirely "oral" character for whom there is neither documentary evidence in photographic or written records within the contexts of realism nor narrative confirmation from the author. She suffers—and exists—on hearsay alone, and on doubtful hearsay at that: Keynaan and Ahmed- Wellie (government spies), Ibrahim (whom Loyaan does not yet trust), Margaritta (ex-wife of the Minister), and the tribally antago- nistic receptionist at the government office where Loyaan goes in futile pursuit of Soyaan's death certificate (possibly a spy recruited from the tribe most hostile to the General to arouse least suspicion). The ministerial files disclaim all knowledge of Mulki's existence and it is not even completely clear that the unnamed typist and Ibrahim's sister are one and the same person: the name is supplied by Loyaan himself, who has previously never heard either of Ibrahim or his sis- ter, and its source is one of the text's many lacunae. Though Ahmed- Wellie insists that the blindfolded torture-victim he was taken to tend was not "Mulki," Loyaan does not believe his claim to know her and the suspicious doctor is later called away to deal with "a mad case of euthanasia administered to a woman." Is this Mulki? In the interrogation scene staged for Loyaan by the Minister to the Presidency, "Mulki" is apparently represented by an unconvincing actress who is cued by the Minister to protest that she has been neither detained nor maltreated and promises to be there at the airport to wave him off to the foreign diplomatic post which the embarrassed regime has hastily created for him. If Mulki really does exist, clearly this is not she; but, depending upon oral testimony alone, we have no way of knowing whether there really is such a person or, if there is, whether she has indeed been arrested for typing Soyaan's Memorandum and has broken under torture. In any case, political detainees whose arrest and sentences are nowhere on record become, in Farah's favorite word, "inexistent." Moreover, Mulki's torture, like Soyaan's lethal injection by Russian doctors, is presented in the form of a delirium in the protagonal consciousness, blurring the border between the real and unreal, so that we can no more distinguish the "real" from the merely "represented" Mulki than we can the "real" Soyaan from the government stage-property which he is posthumously turned into.

All of this naturally problematizes the epistemological status of Farah's own text, particularly in a context where written texts are both threatening and threatened. The novel's narrative plot of Loyaan's quest for the truth of his brother's death is finally unable to unravel the details and motives of the political plot to murder and then mythologize Soyaan. Thus, Loyaan in the labyrinth of the Somali Security system: "Every movement he heard had a meaning, and if it didn't he gave it one. The Security men were following him and making sure he stayed indoors, in one version" (p.206). Somali oral reality under the dictator has become the equivalent of an obscure hermetic text to be "read," a darkly opaque hieroglyph layered with possible versions of reality. The butcher's riddling oral text of the tribal goat, tortured for its own enlightenment before being ritually slaughtered, stands perhaps as a sinister paradigm for the regime's uninterpretable—or infinitely interpretable—political imbecility insofar as it resists intelligibility in any single set of terms other than those

of personal powermania. But Farah's own narrative develops, mimet-
ically, into a correspondingly obscure text for the reader as the
uncertainty of the questing protagonist becomes the reader's own.
The text's defensiveness and evasiveness before the reader's interrogation of it for possible clues imitates and re-enacts Loyaan's suspicions of "friends" whom, for one reason or another, he is afraid to
tell everything he knows: Ahmed-Wellie, a seeming spy despite his
later arrest; Margaritta, compromised to an unknown extent by her
former marriage to the Minister; Ibrahim, an unknown quantity; even
his sister Ladaan, for whom knowledge may mean danger. Thus the
atmosphere of confusion and mistrust spread by the General is recreated by the narrative's own refusal to clarify and its subsequent
retreat into secret codes like Soyaan's. In a more insidious way, the
narrative consciousness, given the paranoid context of persecuted
print, behaves as if it were itself being plotted against and interrogated by an implied reader, looking over the writer's shoulder like
some hermeneutic thought-police—D.R.Ewen has commented
astutely that "one feels relieved to have got out of the book safe-
ly"[10]—and this feature is instanced in the text's plethora of echoing
questions and inquisitorial exhortations: "Address yourself to the
question!" Most of the questions, however, appear to be without
answers, and the outcome is that the expected definitive closure of
the political thriller and detective novel—forms which, as Ian Adam
has noticed, the narrative simulates[11]—is finally dissolved in a polygraphy of possible meanings. The political-criminal plot launched
against Soyaan by an oral-based dictatorship and hunted down by
Loyaan is, in the last analysis, unwritable and never materializes.
Accordingly, the narrative plot eventually runs out unresolvedly in
loose ends or, rather, unstitches itself deconstructively in the penultimate chapter and unravels in a welter of conflicting oral testimony:
"Then, right before Loyaan's and the world's eyes, all suddenly began
to disintegrate like a worn-out piece of cloth a thick set of fingers has
pulled asunder" (pp.211-12). We are told in the final chapter that only
Ladan, who has hidden Soyaan's writings in a place known to herself

alone, will be able to resume control of Loyaan's narrative quest and restitch the true text of Soyaan's life: "Ladan is that Solomonic thread which connects all, which stitches the holes its needle has made. Follow the hints of that thread, follow it with patience" (p.225). Yet Ladan, puzzlingly, is one of the few characters who fails to reappear or even get mentioned in the trilogy.

There are in the novel two more positive poles of resistance to the frightening indeterminacy of the Somali political reality. One of these is the lush poetic lyricism which endows weather, light, sunrise and the descent of night with a physical and at times earthily feminine sensual dimension. The recurring images of wombs, fertilizing sperm, foetuses and eggs are not merely symbolic of the aborted hopes of the 1969 Revolution or of the faith in the future which is pinned to Somalia's women, but appear also to represent the private physical and sexual reality to which the state has no claim of ownership, that tender pragmatism of the flesh which becomes the only touchstone, the only tangible thing individuals have to hold onto to prove they exist, in the enveloping public malaise (though Loyaan's feeling for Margaritta is more erotic than sexual). The other point of resistance to oral chaos is an aesthetic one: namely, Farah's own defiantly ordered textual patterns which impose clear definition and design even upon a mad and meaningless world. Striking among these, particularly in the light of the close physical intimacy of Somali family life, are the analogic devices and parallelisms through which Farah, in the dream-sequences of surreal poetic passages, couples brothers and sisters, pairs off parents and children, and marks whole family groups and modes of parenthood (a feature that will become more pronounced in *Sardines*). Equally striking are the grand microcosmic metaphors which draw together in a single swoop a number of the book's key thematic threads. Thus the recurring childhood memory of Keynaan tyrannically bursting the atlas-covered, egg-like ball played with by the twins gathers many motifs at once: the rival cosmologies of fathers and sons and their respective codes of unthinking despotism and free inquiry, narrow bigotry and global vision; the full 'roundness' of human complexity, gained from knowledge and experience, as against the 'flatness' of propagandist lies and the cartoon-caricature that Keynaan has let himself become; the creative potency of the fertile brain and the anti-creative brute force of the "Grand Patriarch", for whom the 'round' world is "an egg that awaits your breaking it" and who chooses to "breathe life" not into his dead son but into a lie that travesties his life.

These are the things that stay in the mind as the narrative dissolves at the end of *Sweet and Sour Milk* and Beydan, as in her dream, dies delivering a child to be called Soyaan. Whether or not the new birth represents a hope for the future and for the recovery of the truth about his dead namesake is left uncertain: "Twenty years later, for all one knew, a Soyaan who survived Beydan's death in childbirth might walk a street named after a brother Soyaan knighted by a false revolution, made a hero in order to hide in the virtuosity of the generosity of politics" (p.218). What is delivered, at least, at the end is the book itself: the written record of courage and integrity which posed a significant threat to oral-based power in totalitarian Somalia.

NOTES

1. Mary Langille, "Coming out of Oral Tradition to Write about Dictatorship" (interview with Farah), *The Varsity* (University of Toronto), 26 November 1987, 7.

2. Robert Moss, "Mapping the Psyche" (interview with Farah), *West Africa* 1 September 1986, 1827-28.

3. Nuruddin Farah, *Sardines* (London: Heinemann, 1982), p.170.

4. Langille, 7.

5. Nuruddin Farah, *A Naked Needle* (London: Heinemann, 1976), p.111.

6. Nuruddin Farah, *Sweet and Sour Milk* (London: Heinemann Educational Books, 1980). All page references are to this edition and are given in parentheses in the text of the essay.

7. Anne Walmsley, "Nuruddin Farah and Somalia," *Index on Censorship* 10, 2 (1981), 18.

8. Ibid., 19.

9. D.R. Ewen, "Nuruddin Farah" in *The Writing of East and Central Africa*, ed. G.D.Killam (London: Heinemann Educational Books, 1984), p.205.

10. Ibid., p.202.

11. Ian Adam, "The Murder of Soyaan Keynaan," *World Literature Written in English* 26, 2 (1986), 203-11; reprinted in the present volume.

NEW WOMEN AND OLD MYTHS IN ACHEBE'S *ANTHILLS OF THE SAVANNAH* AND FARAH'S *SARDINES*

Patricia Alden

One of the triumphs of Beatrice's creation [is that] the things that fell apart under the impact of Europe in Mr.Achebe's first novel...come together in this woman. She is a true world-historical figure in Georg Lukács's sense, and it is Mr.Achebe's victory that she is also one of the most extraordinary, attractive and moving women characters in any contemporary novel.
                                        —Nadine Gordimer[1]

Medina's consciousness, exasperatingly, occupies the largest space in this portrait of embattled Somali womanhood. [In Sardines] Farah has warned us...of her egotistical possessiveness towards her daughter and the self-absorbed ideological purity of all her actions....Medina's challenges to the regime are merely flamboyant and self-indulgent ideological gestures...The problem is that so much of the narrative is presented from the perspective of this intransigent idealism and coloured by Medina's priggish self-righteousness that these...come to have a ring of doctrinal finality and authorial approval.
—Derek Wright[2]

Guided by the above remarks, a reader interested in successful fictional representations of women would with confidence select Achebe's work in preference to Farah's. But she would be wrong. Indeed, the above assessments of the characters themselves and, implicitly, of the writers' skill in controlling narrative need to be reversed. Achebe's stature as a distinguished novelist is beyond question, and much of *Anthills of the Savannah* is a compelling account of political turmoil in an African nation. However, Achebe's portrait of Beatrice Okoh betrays a significant failure of imagination—a failure to take seriously, as part of contemporary political struggle, the feminist challenge to patriarchal authority, and a corresponding failure to create convincing, interesting women characters. Offered as an example of a new African woman, Beatrice is effectively removed from the brawl of politics to assume traditional roles as her Dantean namesake, as the water goddess Idemili, and as Mother Africa. The novel achieves its closure in an uncritically examined connection between the fertility of woman and the rebirth of a nation.

It is rather in the work of a younger writer, Nuruddin Farah, and in particular in his novel *Sardines*, that we find a genuinely "world-historical" character in the Lukácsian sense, a "typical" figure in

whose temperament and experience are registered critical contradictions of her time.³ Positioning Medina within several different
groups of female relatives and friends allows Farah to capture the
diversity in women's experiences and to examine through multiple
perspectives the several ways in which their domestic, private lives
are imbricated in the political order. Such representation suggests
how profound the cultural transformation must be in order to free
everyone from invisible, because accepted, bonds of oppression.
Rather than aligning his female characters with traditional mythic
figures, Farah shows women interrogating their experience by
reworking old myths to new purposes. They see their sexuality, a
focus at once of male oppression and female power, not in connection with the fertility goddess Idemili but with Prometheus and
through him with agency and with the creative as well as the destructive potential of fire.

Chinua Achebe's *Anthills of the Savannah* (1987) and Nuruddin
Farah's *Sardines* (1981) probe the causes for the emergence of dictatorship in post-colonial Africa and overtly connect feminism to the
larger political struggle at the state level. Their female protagonists
are ideologically situated in similar ways. Beatrice Okoh and Medina
belong to an urban elite; they have been well-educated abroad, hold
advanced degrees, and are professional women with access to government circles, Medina as a journalist and Beatrice as Senior
Assistant Secretary in the Ministry of Finance. Among the privileged
of their nation, both feel a responsibility to resist the growing atmosphere of repression. Both women define themselves as feminists who
understand that the liberation of women from patriarchy is a necessary part of the social transformation required to bring about a more
equitable order. Their intellectual commitment to feminism is sustained in part by their western education and in part by traumatic
experiences as children within patriarchal societies. For both characters this has entailed overt disparagement as a daughter and an
atmosphere of family violence; for Medina, it has entailed infibulation. Distanced from the majority of women in their countries,

Beatrice and Medina each has as a close friend a "woman of the people" in Elewa and Ebla; these friendships allow their ideological commitments to be contrasted with more pragmatic, grounded, less theoretical perspectives. Medina, however, is located within an extensive network of female relationships, and this allows the reader to see her in multiple contexts and from multiple perspectives. By contrast, Beatrice, though she holds a responsible position in the government, is largely restricted to the role of girl friend (her author names her as "girl" in contrast to the "men" who are her contemporaries). While husbands, brothers, presidents and politicians do figure in *Sardines*, Farah allows women to fill the foreground; Achebe's few women appear just over the shoulder of the men on whom he focuses. Farah's larger canvas allows him to represent a wide range of women's experiences and so to register contradictory ways in which their oppression mirrors and sustains dictatorship and sometimes leads them to challenge it. In Achebe's more spare world the two women characters become freighted with symbolic significance in order to enrich their presence in the text, and the weight of this symbolic meaning seems to fix and limit them in prescribed roles: woman of the people, goddess and prophetess.

Although, as I shall argue, Beatrice is diminished in *Anthills* in a variety of ways, it is appropriate to compare her with Medina for she is clearly intended to have major standing in the novel, serving with Chris Oriko and Ikem Osodi as one of the narrators of the novel. Her autobiography is at the center of the novel, her past given equal treatment with the men's, and she, like Chris and Ikem, is rushing to write down the novel we have before us.[4] Thus she lays claim with Chris and Ikem to the important role of storyteller, the one whose voice is heard after the battle (*AS*, p.113). However, the men are disposed to equate their personal history with "the story of this country" (*AS*, p.60) while Beatrice anxiously questions herself ("Who am I that I should inflict my story on the world?" (*AS* p.80). Beatrice offers an ironic reflection on male egoism, but her own, compulsory self-diminishment is not commented upon. Still more troubling is the fact that her version of her history is essentially the same as that told by the men; at times they are said to know more about her than she herself! That male and female narratives would be the same is itself startling—a failure of the imagination mentioned above—and the more discouraging in a novel which makes it so clear that there are distinct class versions of history, indeed distinct, class-marked languages in which the different versions are told. While the novel urges us to attend to such class divisions and potential resolutions, gender differences do not receive comparably serious attention.

Beatrice, like her Dantean namesake, serves as a guide and teacher of the men who are the real actors in this story. She urges Chris to mend his friendship with Ikem and alerts him to the coming danger from Sam, the President. She educates Ikem, poet and dissident editor of *The National Gazette*, to see the need for including women in new roles in his utopian political order. However, the way in which this education is narrated reveals much about what happens to female agency in the novel. Beatrice is recalling their university days in London, in terms that verge on caricature of a committed feminist:

> I was determined from the very beginning to put my career first and, if need be, last. That every women wants a man to complete her is a piece of male chauvinist bullshit I had completely rejected before I knew there was anything like Women's Lib. You often hear our people say: But that's something you picked up in England. Absolute rubbish! There was enough male chauvinism in my father's house to last me seven reincarnations! (AS, pp.80-81)

[Her strident tone here is belied in a later scene when she tells Chris that she is, after all, a traditional "girl" who wants a certain kind of "man" to be sexually possessive of her (*AS*, p.103).] But back in their university days, Beatrice recalls, she and Ikem "argued a lot about what I have called the chink in his armoury of brilliant and original ideas. I tell him he has no clear role for women in his political thinking; and he doesn't seem to be able to understand it" (*AS*, p.83). Eventually he does. Several years after they had returned to Kangan, Ikem appeared on Beatrice's doorstep in the midst of a driving rain—"it was literally like barging into a pillar of rain," he says (*AS*, p.85)—to tell her he has come on a "'mission...to thank you for...the gift of insight...into the world of women'" (*AS*, p.88). In vocabulary as politically correct as Beatrice's in her London days, Ikem claims to have learned the folly of putting women on a pedestal, of being too respectful, of saying "Mother is supreme" and yet allowing women's participation in daily affairs only as a last resort. Women, Ikem says, will have to tell men what "the new role for Woman will be" (*AS*, p.90), characteristically hypostatizing myriad women as "Woman" even as he speaks of their empowerment. Equally characteristically for this unreconstructed imagination, having said that women must speak for themselves, Ikem goes on to do all the talking, and this in a chapter that is supposed to be Beatrice's narrative. Beatrice the teacher has in fact become the auditor, while Ikem controls the conversation. In the next chapter Beatrice is explicitly identified with Idemili, the goddess who manifests herself "in the resplendent Pillar of Water" (*AS*, p.93), and it is clear that we are invited to read back and see in that "pillar of rain" into which Ikem barged, a Beatrice who is merely the fertile environment which sustains male agency. Beatrice is essentially passive in her role as goddess/teacher, and in the following chapter (which develops her connection with the goddess) we are told that she is like "the village priestess" who is ridden by her divinity (that is, the power possesses her, rather than she possessing the power) and that, furthermore, Ikem "knew [this] better than Beatrice herself" (*AS*, p.96).

In Ikem's long speech, which begins with his new insight that women are "the biggest single group of oppressed people in the world," he moves to the issue that most fully engages Achebe's attention in this novel: how to achieve political reform in desperately economically divided, underdeveloped societies. This material is couched in language that ignores gender: "Man will surprise by his capacity for nobility as well as for villainy. No system can change that. It is built into the core of man's free spirit...Experience and intelligence warn us that man's progress in freedom will be piecemeal, slow and undramatic" (*AS*, p.90). At one point in his very substantial speech, the reader infers that Beatrice has got a word in edgewise as Ikem appears to respond to a comment. "Bloody reformist?...Reform may be a dirty word but then it begins to look more and more like the most promising route to success in the real world...We can only hope to rearrange some details in the periphery of the human personality. Any disturbance of its core is an irresponsible invitation to disaster" (*AS*, p.91). If Beatrice has a more revolutionary vision of social change, she has been silenced—by the character and by the author. Perhaps the prospect of sharing the podium with women ("*You* have to tell us") has prompted this affirmation of "reform" rather than fundamental "rearrangement" of the "core" of the "human personality." The door is open at this point for Beatrice to respond to or criticize Ikem, but she is silenced by his passionate kiss which leaves her "trembling violently...struggling for air" (*AS*, p.92). The storm is over, the goddess Idemili has manifested herself and given Ikem his insight, and then moved on.

Beatrice's major act in the novel occurs when she is invited to the President's for a private dinner; she and Chris assume she is being asked to advise Sam on the dangerously widening rift betweem him and his two oldest friends. But the plot stalls at this point, and the dinner party becomes trivialized as an arena for sexual combat around a different issue. Miffed that she has been invited merely to provide "the woman's angle" for a visiting white American journalist, Beatrice first snubs, then attacks Miss Cranford for her position on foreign debt. She sees this "Desdemona" seducing the President and goes to work to woo him back to his proper place among fellow black Africans.

> I did it shamelessly. I cheapened myself. God! I did it to your
> glory like the dancer in a Hindu temple. Like Esther, oh yes
> like Esther for my long-suffering people.
> And was I glad the king was slowly but surely responding!
> Was I glad! The big snake, the royal python of a gigantic erec-
> tion began to stir in the shrubbery of my shrine as we danced
> closer and closer...soothing our ancient bruises...Fully
> aroused he clung desperately to me. (*AS*, p.74)

She then takes President Sam aside to explain that she's merely
making a political point about racial solidarity. Perhaps not surprisingly, he shows her the door. Beatrice's feminist loyalties and racial
loyalties are interestingly at odds in this scene, but this contradiction
is not developed, nor elsewhere alluded to; the occasion provides no
more than a farcical peek at Sam's gigantic erection and Beatrice's
bumps and grinds.

The next chapter opens with a lyrical tribute to Idemili and ends
with a scene of love-making between Chris and Beatrice, which we
are clearly supposed to take "straight" as she, the goddess, leads him
into the depths of her "heaving groves" to "her own peculiar rites
over which she held absolute power" (*AS*, p.104). Brought to the
point of sexual ecstasy, Beatrice prophesies the climax of the novel,
the coming political resistance and consequent repression: "I see
trouble building up for us. It will get to Ikem first. No joking, Chris. He
will be the precursor to make straight the way. But after him it will be
you. We are all in it..." (*AS*, p.105). Cassandra-like, Beatrice can foresee—but she cannot act.

In the coda to the novel, the symbolism of the goddess is
mobilised to persuade us further about women's power. With their
male lovers dead, Beatrice and Elewa are the nucleus of the new, egalitarian, inclusive community, whose future is promised in the figure
of the daughter Elewa bears after Ikem's death. However, this new
holy family of women preempts investigation of ideological differences which exist between Elewa and Beatrice, differences of class

which have been at the heart of the novel. Beatrice takes the lead, appropriating a traditionally male role in the naming ritual, giving the daughter a male name, "Amaechina: *May-the-path-never-close*." The future she inaugurates appears open to new possibilities, new combinations of male and female roles, new empowerment of ordinary people like Elewa. But Beatrice is upstaged (as previously in the scene with Ikem) by the arrival of the anarchic figure of Elewa's uncle, drunk and late for the naming, initially threatening in his peremptoriness, demanding to know who has presumed to name the child. When he is told of the non-traditional ceremony, his "explosion into laughter took everybody by surprise and then dragged them all into his bombshell of gaiety" (*AS*, p.209). The uncle presides over the breaking of the kola nut, offering a rousing toast/speech which has the effect of fixing our attention on a male speaker who powerfully articulates the vision that has most deeply informed the novel of a humane, inclusive social order in which "all of us" participate. And "all of us" is certainly intended to include the women—women as child- bearers and fertility figures, women as goddesses or Dantean guides to men. But not women as speakers, women as autonomous seekers after their own ends, women who have serious ideological differences to work out, women whose claims to authority must be, *should be*, disruptive. The very sense of unity and resolution here at the end of the novel testify to the fact that Achebe, like Ikem, has shrunk from imaging those "disturbances at the core" which would occur if women were to become equal participants in making the history of Kangan.

It is precisely in their role as historical actors that we can distinguish the women of Farah's fiction from those of Achebe's. Farah's Medina is at the center of a novel that is at the center of a trilogy about political oppression in Somalia, a work to which Farah has given the collective title *Variations on a Theme of an African Dictatorship*. His representation of women's experience is more meaningful than Achebe's not merely because he affords it more space (extended coverage does not guarantee depth, though it is perhaps a necessary condition) but because Farah explores a vital connection between patriarchal and other forms of oppression. In the first volume of the trilogy, *Sweet and Sour Milk*, Farah captures this theme in a quotation from Wilhelm Reich: "In the figure of the father the authoritarian state has its representative in every family, so that the family becomes its most important instrument of power."[5] This quotation is paraphrased by Mursal in *Close Sesame*[6] and by Sagal in *Sardines*.[7] The insight is developed throughout the trilogy in conflicts between parents and children, in the rhetoric of the General and the rhetoric of the resistance group, in the claustrophobic atmosphere of oppression on the streets and in the homes of the characters. All three novels, but *Sardines* most comprehensively, incorporate the view that patriarchy is a key "variation" of African dictatorship and indeed the fundamental ground upon which it flourishes.

Sardines is about political dissidents (the Group of Ten) who oppose an increasingly terrifying military dictatorship. It is also about political struggle within domestic spaces and within women's bodies, a struggle that affects the lives of all the women in the novel. At the opening, Medina has left her husband Samater, taking their eight-year-old daughter Ubax with her. Husband and wife, members of the governing elite, have joined the clandestine Group of Ten and must now consider how most effectively to influence the political destiny of Somalia. In the recent past, Medina has been fired, after a four-day stint as editor of the national newspaper, for challenging the General's censorship. Samater, however, has reluctantly accepted a post in the General's cabinet. Medina deplores his refusal to cut his ties to power and influence; she sees him as someone who has learned too well in the bosom of the family to "bow his head" to authoritarian power. Moreover, Samater's mother Idil is threatening to have Ubax circumcised, a practice which Medina knows herself, through her own flesh, is a hideous form of control of women, whether exercised by patriarch or matriarch. She has little confidence that Samater will resist his mother's plans for Ubax any more than the General's tyranny. Thus she leaves, silently challenging him to resist the dictator at home and in the palace.

Medina's situation is only one variation on the theme of patriarchal control of women's lives. Her mother Fatima, in Yemeni purdah, reigns pathetically over children and de facto slaves. Her mother-in-law Idil was compelled to exchange her body for a bread concession to keep herself and two children from starvation. Her young friend Amina was raped by political dissidents as an indirect way of punishing her father's complicity with the General; Amina then resists her father and the General, who are eager to hide this evidence of dissent, by insisting on bearing the child of the rape. A girl of sixteen whose family had emigrated to America and then returned for a holiday in Somalia is forcibly circumcised in order to teach her parents a lesson in patriotism. Other stories remind us that even when male power is not direct and brutal, women live in bodies which are highly controlled by patriarchal requirements for virginity and fertility. Medina's protègè Sagal, moiling in adolescent confusion, compromises her vaunted autonomy when she finds herself pregnant from a one-night stand. Xaddia is divorced when her husband discovers she uses birth control, Sandra is permanently harmed by her abortion, and Dulman despairs because of her infertility.

These stories represent myriad ways in which women are trapped in the sardine tin of patriarchal culture. Their responses range from Fatima's passive acceptance to Idil's insistence on her own limited authority to tyrannize others, mirroring the General's, to Ebla's and Dulman's mix of complicity and private refusal, to Medina's determined resistance. Further, by placing Medina within this network of relationships, giving her many roles as mother, daughter, sister, wife, friend, mentor and dissident, Farah allows us to compare her experience with that of other women and to view her from their several perspectives. While her fundamental political understanding is authorially underwritten (her position is articulated in the Wilhelm Reich quotation, used throughout the trilogy), how Medina chooses to live, in light of that understanding, is open to criticism and interpretation.

This uncertainty about how we should judge Medina troubles critic Derek Wright, whose words I quoted at the beginning of this essay. Irritated by her "compulsive [feminist] ideologizing," he finds Medina "egotistically possessive" towards her daughter, given to "flamboyant and self-indulgent" political gestures, and "priggish[ly] self-righteous" (Wright, 101, 99).

> The freedom which Medina forces prematurely upon Ubax is at times almost as oppressive as the obedience Idil has forced upon Samater, her emotional and intellectual tyranny over her daughter as stifling as its physical counterpart...Medina terrorizes her young daughter with knowledge, as does Idil with the circumcisional knife. (Wright, 101)

Wright's negative assessment of Medina misses the power and appeal, the sheer interestingness of her character. Thus he is puzzled when Medina's closing claim to be "a full and active participant in the history of her country" (*S*, p.263) has the ring of "authorial approval" (Wright, 99). For him her "status" has been uncomfortably "problematized" by the indeterminacy in the way she is presented. I hope both to rescue Medina from the hostile assessment of this influential critic and to suggest how carefully Farah has structured the novel to provide the multiple, discordant perspectives on his central character which Wright finds a liability. Through these Farah succeeds where Achebe falls short, providing critical perspectives on salient contradictions and refusing to foreclose prematurely the conflict they engender.[8]

In the opening sentences of the novel, Medina is given to us as a storyteller and architect: "She reconstructed the story from the beginning, [built] mansions large as her imagination," rooms for herself and her friends, "a room in which one was *not* a guest . . ." (*S*, pp.3-4). Leaving home has prompted her to imagine a new space that will include women and children because "*He is not all of us!*" (*S*, p.3). The reference is to a favorite folk tale from Achebe's *Things Fall Apart*, in which the tortoise claims all the food at a celestial dinner by telling his hosts that his name is "All of us." In translating the story for Ubax, Medina in effect constructs a feminist revision; her new title, "He," draws attention to the false universal of the masculine pronoun.

This capacity to dream of other possibilities, to make her private crisis with Samater a metaphor for restructuring society, the breadth of learning suggested in her references to Woolf and Achebe, the confident appropriation of those sources to her own needs, the recognition of the power in narrating one's own story—all of this gives Medina authority in the opening lines of the novel. She is in many ways a heroic figure: the only woman in the Group of Ten, she has put at risk her privileged life and her career to keep faith with her political commitments. She is further represented, in this opening chapter, as a passionately involved mother. Bent over her sleeping child, Medina recalls a birth made agonizingly painful because of her infibulation. She opposes the present dictatorship because it reminds her "of her unhappy childhood...the General reminded her of her grandfather who was a monstrosity and an unchallengeable patriarch...`I want Ubax to be free of all that...to live her life like a dream. I want her to decide when to wake up, how to interpret her dreams...'" (*S*, p.17). Medina is determined that Ubax and other girls will be spared the knife of tradition and allowed to direct their own lives, interpret their own dreams. Despite the intimacy between mother and daughter, Medina understands that her ultimate role is to sponsor her child's autonomy. Ubax challenges, argues with her mother, scolds her for smoking and for not bringing toys with them from the old house. She tells her mother, "`One day, I will have outgrown you, become independent. Then I will leave you.' `I look forward to that,'" responds Medina (*S*, p.17). She tells her daughter: "`You are the sunflower of my life...You are the bird which leans against the air from which it seeks support; like the bird, you are the one who upsets and breaks the very air whose support you seek" (*S*, p.15). Deeply attached, Medina is alert to the mysterious nature of their relationship in which she who supports is also she who must be resisted.

Other characters suggest that Medina may be an overly posses-sive mother, a new version of the tyrants whom she opposes. She remembers that her father Barkhadle once said: "You must leave breathing-space in the architecture of your love...You mustn't indoc-trinate, mustn't brainwash her. Otherwise you become another *dic-tator*, trying to shape your child in your own image" (*S*, p.16). When Idil, determined to contain Ubax in a traditional world, harangues Samater with her criticisms of Medina's mothering, he "bows his head" to her matriarchal authority and turns on Medina asking "whether or not she realized that she was flooding the girl with her love and understanding, breaking the small girl's dam with her affec-tion" (*S*, p.17). Sagal, the perennially inconsistent teenager, wavers on her view of mothers, finding at one point that Medina is "a great improvement on Idil" (*S*, p.43) and later asking: "Mother-as-martyr or mother-as-the-all-knower. In the final analysis, what is the difference between yourself, Idil and Ebla?" (*S*, p.55).

These perspectives by no means automatically confirm Wright's view of Medina's "egotistical possessiveness of her daughter." All who view Medina have their own interests at stake. The text requires us to consider numerous interactions between mother and daughter, Medina's meditations on mothering, and these external perspectives; it does not do the work of synthesis for us. Judgments about good mothering obviously are grounded in judgments about the larger social context. Those who desire to adapt children to the world and those who prepare them to challenge it will certainly differ. Beyond this, good mothering involves the paradoxical effort to foster intima-cy and autonomy, a balancing act which changes moment to moment and is hardly ever judged the same by two onlookers—or indeed by the participants themselves.

This issue of mothering is connected to our assessment of Medina's political gesture of leaving home. In both the domestic and public arenas, she claims that she acts to liberate others but is criti-cized for her egotistical desire to control. As we have seen, Barkhadle suggests that Medina could become a "dictator"; her brother Nasser wonders whether she is not practising on Samater a policy not unlike the General's: "*starve and rule...*had it all started with a small notion, with her saying that she wanted to change the position of a chair...the bed and other furniture...did she want to be the centre of everything?" (*S*, p.109). Does Medina's effort to build a room of her own mean that "she has created a habitat in which she alone can function...No room for either Samater or Ubax...She put the chair in the wrong place in the dark. When Samater awoke, he stumbled on it and broke his neck" (*S*, p.255). Nasser's speculations become Xaddia's (and Wright's) certainties: namely, that Medina is to blame for forcing Samater to oppose his mother and the General. Samater's sister Xaddia puts this accusation directly to Medina: "'Tell me, then. What was the point of the charade in which Samater lost face and his job, my mother her son and dignity, Nasser and Dulman their freedom? What point have you made?'" (*S*, p.259). Xaddia's words support Wright's estimation of Medina's flamboyant, self-indulgent political gestures that hurt others and leave her unscathed. But Xaddia's are the anguished questions of a family member, close to someone in danger. It is appropriate that she should put the questions, and that we should have to weigh seriously the value of Medina's and others' resistance. Zeinab asks virtually the same questions of Mursal in *Close Sesame*, shortly before he sacrifices himself in a futile attempt to assassinate the General (*CS*, pp.127- 28). There are, of course, responses to such questions. Medina thinks to herself: "*If only Xaddia could understand that I'm fighting for the survival of the woman in me, in her—while demolishing `families' like Idil's and regimes like the General's*" (italics in original, *S*, p.259). Characterizing such language as Medina's "compulsive ideologizing," Wright ignores the painful dilemmas which emerge in the women's argument: familial versus civic responsibilities, the intertwined threads of egoism and honor. Accepting another of Xaddia's accusations, Wright mistakenly blames Medina for the arrests of Dulman and Nasser, who are clearly presented in the text as independently engaged in a separate resistance action. They, like Sagal's friends and perhaps even like Samater, are imprisoned in a general crackdown, which has nothing to do with Medina's departure (except insofar as all are responding to the paranoid tyranny of the General). Wright's negative assessment of Medina's political acts depends partly on an assumption contradicted in the text.

Farah's trilogy focuses repeatedly on acts of resistance which are, in the short run, apparently futile. Some sacrifices, as Deeriye reflects in *Close Sesame*, serve only "to keep the flames going, keep the live coals under a bed of ashes" so that the next generation will "find the fire buried under the ground" (*CS*, p.218). His view of Mursal's sacrifice exists in tension with Zeinab's plea that Mursal think first of his family, just as the several views of Medina's act (even the several understandings of what motivated her act) exist in tension and are not finally resolved. Farah's novels reflect the human condition: there are no positions outside of history from which we can judge with certainty the acts of others. There are only interested perspectives, on resistance as on mothering.

In offering a more positive perspective than Wright's on Medina, I do not want to present her as unquestionably heroic. Allusions and symbolic associations throughout the novel require us to see Medina in contradictory ways. Her name connects her to the "the city of righteousness," central in Islam, but also to "Mina: the place where pillars are stoned, a symbol of Satan" (*S*, p.154). She is associated throughout the novel with fire and with the figure of Prometheus, the demi-god whose gift of fire to humankind inaugurated a new order but also entailed his own extended torment. At the time of Medina's birth, a wing of her home was set on fire, perhaps by her dreadful grandfather, bent upon killing an unwanted female child. This circumstance connects her to another child who is burned to death, an event narrated in a chapter which offers the fullest treatment of the Promethean associations and extends their meaning from Medina to other women in the novel. I explicate this material in some detail as an example of Farah's complex treatment of myth.

In Chapter 6, Sagal and Amina are celebrating the birth of the sun and the new year with a bonfire. Concerned that she may be pregnant, Sagal is torn between fascination with the new life that may be within her and thoughts about her own dubiously heroic future: will she be swimming champion? Will she "write on the walls of dawn" as a resister? Are these roles emphasizing her autonomy now foreclosed by her pregnancy? Sagal tells Amina about a fire that destroyed their neighbor's one-year-old, a child already near death from malnutrition and disease. Her mother had been abandoned by the father, who had gone to work as chauffeur for a Party official and given his ration card to his new mistress. Unable to buy her child milk, much less medicine, rumor has it that the mother may have purposely locked the child in the house while she stood in a queue for her rations, leaving it to die. To the girls the child represents "a young fire extinguished—the old not yet!" (*S*, p.117). The old dispensation allows the misery of the urban poor, the slow death of children by starvation or their horrifying destruction in fire, the possible madness of a woman abandoned by all the male power structures of her world—a dispensation represented by Medina's grandfather who tried to destroy her in a fire (*S*, p.121). The girls conclude that "A Promethean intervention is in order!" (*S*, p.122).

But who has the power to create and nurture "a young fire," to bring about a new order in which women and children are no longer locked in the horrifying sardine tins of homes which are domestic prisons? And who is willing to risk the dangerous potential of fire? Fire and fertility, power and destruction are figuratively connected in this narrative, and connected to women. Amina recalls that in a Hindu myth "the two lips of the vulva of a woman [were] that slot in which two sticks were rubbed together and that friction made the first fire. That's why Hindu women burn themselves at the funeral pyre" (*S*, p.125). Where other women have only suffered, Medina and Amina and Sagal consider the possibility that they could be Promethean figures, challenging the patriarchs and harnessing the fire that was woman's to begin with to create a new world. This cre-

375

ative potential is implied in their fertility which, like fire, can be either affirming or destroying. Amina's story testifies to a woman's ability to assume control, even over the violent rape which caused her to be pregnant, and defy her rapists, her father, and the General, by insisting on bearing her child and raising it in a community of women which includes Medina and Sagal. Pondering all this Sagal thinks that she too may be able to take charge of her own unplanned pregnancy and begin to "*narrate*" (*S*, p.123) her own, until now indecisive, life. Their night-watch concluded, Amina and Sagal turn from their dying fire to "the sun [which] had begun to crown herself with a halo of brightness: she surrounded herself with a congregation of clouds...Sagal emptied a bucket of water on the fire, kill it lest it claim another young life" (*S*, p.124). In the presence of this female sun,[9] the two girls assume the power to control the bonfire they have made and to control choices about their fertility; figuratively they assume the responsibility to extinguish the old dispensation and to bring the new into being.

This scene can be compared to the coda in Achebe's novel, discussed earlier, in which the birth of a child signifies a potentially different future for the nation, a future over which women, at least nominally, preside. As we saw, Achebe firmly, and almost exclusively, associates women with Idemili, the fertility goddess, and with the power to bring forth life. In Farah's novel mythic associations are interrogated in complex ways in the text. This passage, like his work as a whole, is riddled with indeterminacy. Sagal is not sure she is pregnant; though the neighbor's child was certainly killed, it is only rumor that the mother locked her inside intentionally; it is only rumor that Medina's grandfather set his fire. Amina tells an inaccurate version of the Hindu myth, but Sagal chooses not to correct her. At the opening Sagal intends to tell Amina about her possible pregnancy, but she doesn't. The language in which she imagines her pregnancy and childbirth is suffused with a romanticism worthy of Stephen Dedalus ("the wild fields of a future emerged from behind the greener courts of others. . . this future of futures" *S*, p.123) so that

376

we cannot be sure that she has matured beyond the adolescent confusion that has thus far characterized her. The community of supportive women, which she here idealizes, is internally divided, Medina and Amina in particular at odds. Sagal may, in fact, have carelessly lost her best opportunity for her own development as an autonomous individual. Is her "future of futures" to be just another "close sesame"? The potency associated with the sun, with fire and with the allusions to Prometheus is thus seriously qualified in the context of the novel, and the connections between women and myth are both surprising (a female Prometheus) and indeterminate. Moreover, the women themselves choose to contemplate their futures through these associations and allusions, but the author offers no assurances beyond the understanding that all futures are to be made by humans imagining their lives, their choices, and their agency. In Farah's work women are not just midwives to history but actors in their own drama, narrators of their own lives, interpreters of their own dreams. Like Prometheus, they will figure as victims and rebels; they too will destroy and create. They will not escape the paradoxes of development nor easily resolve the contradictions deeply embedded within Somali society. Farah offers not a symbol of hope for the future ("Amaechina: May-the-path-never-close") but a representation of the complexity of the present—a complexity which, however else we read it, nevertheless authorizes Medina's claim to be "a full and active participant [inevitably a flawed participant] in the history of her country" (*S*, p.263). That is what makes her, to borrow from Gordimer, "a true world-historical figure in Georg Lukacs's sense...one of the most extraordinary, attractive and moving women characters in any contemporary novel."

NOTES

1. Nadine Gordimer, "A Tyranny of Clowns," *New York Times Book Review*, 21 February 1998.

2. Derek Wright, "Parents and Power in Nuruddin Farah's *Dictatorship Trilogy*," *Kunapipi* 11, 2 (1989), 94-106. Hereafter cited in the text as "Wright."

3. Georg Lukács, *Studies in European Realism* (New York: Grosset & Dunlap, 1964).

4. Chinua Achebe, *Anthills of the Savannah* (New York: Doubleday, 1988), p.75. All references are to this edition of the novel, hereafter abbreviated in the text as *AS*.

5. Nuruddin Farah, *Sweet and Sour Milk* (St Paul: Graywolf Press, 1992), p.95.

6. Nuruddin Farah, *Close Sesame* (St Paul: Graywolf Press, 1992), p.104.

7. Nuruddin Farah, *Sardines* (St Paul: Graywolf Press, 1992), pp.66-67. All references are to this edition of the novel, hereafter abbreviated in the text as *S*.

8. Wright is not alone in objecting to the open-endedness and indeterminacy which characterize all of Farah's work. Matters of plot are left uncertain (Was Soyaan poisoned? Is Sagal pregnant?), motives are continually re-examined (Why did Medina really leave Samater? Why is Mursal pursuing his kamikaze mission? Why does Deeriye follow him?), and the ultimate value of the Group of Ten's resistance remains in question. Barbara Turfan wonders whether Farah is sufficiently cognizant of his characters' defects; if he is, why is he not more overtly judgmental of their inadequacies? Indeed, why not give us characters more adequate to the challenges they face? ("Opposing Dictatorship: A Comment on Nuruddin Farah's *Variations on the Theme of an African Dictatorship*," *Journal of Commonwealth Literature* 24, 1 (1989), 173-

84; reprinted in the present volume). Part of my argument here is that Farah's refusal to give us characters who have resolved contradictions and his determination to present the contemporary situation in all its indeterminacy contribute to his strength as a writer. Much criticism of Farah's work reflects an anti-modernist preference in readers of African literature, where modernism and indeterminacy are equated with an insufficiently committed position on the part of the writer. Achebe's Ikem, facing a version of this argument, says, "Writers don't give prescriptions...They give headaches!" (*AS*, p.148). Farah has not shrunk from treating seriously the feminist challenge to patriarchy, nor has he resolved all issues by giving us an unproblematic representative.

His presentation of Medina is in some ways similar to Virginia Woolf's of Clarissa Dalloway, both novelists refusing to resolve highly contradictory evaluations of their protagonists. However, there is this critical distinction in their works. The positive evaluation of Clarissa requires us to assent to a transcendental realm, outside time, wherein she communes with Septimus, her social opposite but spiritual companion. Only her capacity for a mysterious empathy with others saves Clarissa from being merely a society hostess. With Medina the positive and negative perspectives are located within history: the unresolved questions involve evaluating the efficacy of her actions in history, and this efficacy cannot yet be established. Thus the indeterminacy of Farah's novel keeps us engaged with historical process while Woolf's tempts us to escape it. It is important to see that the literary technique of modernism, critiqued by Lukács as a decadent form of bourgeois evasion, can in fact work to quite different purposes in the African context.

9. In the Somali language the sun is feminine.

TO A ROOM OF THEIR OWN:
Structure and Shadow in Nuruddin Farah's *Sardines*

Maggi Phillips

Words written about the celebrated storyteller Nuruddin Farah have begun to indicate this writer's fascination with both the prismatic potential and the insufficiency of the stuff itself—language. *Sardines* marked my first encounter with Farah's cache of diaphanous images which, a decade later, still radiate shadows that, as this author reminds us, cast further than the originating forms. One specific shadow glides into the network of women within the novel, the purdah-imprisoned Fatima bint Thabit, who characteristically steals into her daughter's presence, "light like the night's sudden tropical darkness...quiet as a shadow...a shadow which doesn't get wet and is not consumed by fire."[1] In another stratum, however, this novel, unbounded by the femininity of its protagonists, collaborates with shadows. When Farah alludes to the Somali proverb that compares women to shadows adjusting their shapes to the external circumstances in "The Women of Kismayo," he indicates something of his own storytelling craft. Doubtless, the traditional grain of the proverb is a warning of female 'fickleness' but in the eye of the expert shape-shifter himself shadows represent the amorphous wisdom of women's grasp of community, extending laterally towards mediation, compromise, harmony, towards all things unfixed.

> Women are aware of the importance of the multiplicity of connections the warring communities have, seeing themselves now as mothers to children of one family, now as daughters of another, and on remarriage, as mothers to offspring from yet another lineage. The men remain true to their father's ancestral identity, the women do not.[2]

Like Salman Rushdie's mediator of *Haroun and the Sea of Stories*, Mudra, the personified liminal figure between light and dark, speech and silence, Farah's women (and men vulnerable to femininity) move across boundaries to construct in the flow of time. At least, given Farah's adherence to the variance innate in any idea, *some* women do behave with such positive mobility, *some* of the time.

Farah's tales, intricate calligraphies of doubt, alternatives and tolerance, deliberate upon but offer no definitive picture of how to contest political oppression. Instead, Farah's tracings spin off and create other doubts, alternatives and tolerances, other shadows in which light transpires and occasionally blinds. *Sardines*, the womb-like centre between *Sweet and Sour Milk* and *Close Sesame* in the trilogy *Variations on the Theme of an African Dictatorship*, is a mere movement in the ongoing orchestration of resistance. Like a symphonic movement, *Sardines* is permeated with motifs which re- emerge in different configurations throughout his *oeuvre*: identity, family, clan, nation, shadows, construction, resistance, collision and coherence of orality and script, are all transposed within the myriad ways in which language and storytelling make manifest the Somali culture. Although Farah takes care to point out the imaginative constructiveness of his version of Somalia, his tales illustrate James Clifford's observation that "we should attempt to think of cultures not as organically unified or traditionally continuous but rather as negotiated, present processes."[3] I hope to suggest in this discussion some of the strategies by which Farah incorporates the specific fluidity of Somali culture and, through the centrifugal momentum of interpenetrating ideas, of culture *per se* in a novel that is ostensibly about a single and singular woman, Medina.

Beneath the explicit aim of examining how women could attempt to subvert the oppressive dictatorship of the General, Farah's well-known cypher for the notorious autocratic head of state, Siyad Barre, is an architectonic design interrogating the act of storytelling itself. As D. R. Ewen noted in one of the early commentaries on Farah's writing, "the author probes the language as he uses it, so that often the language does not tell the story but *is* the story."[4] This characteristic of Farah's work has been analyzed by a coterie of critics over time and surfaces clearly in recent contributions like those to *World Literature Today*'s commemorative issue. Central to these analyses is Farah's particular poetic craft informed by the historical conditions of Somalia itself. From pre-Islamic traces, through the waves of colonization of Islam and the European powers to nationhood, orality both binds within itself and vies with written scripts. *Waaq*, the iconic crow deity known as the "Speechless One," haunts contemporary systems of noise and inscription through telephones and tape-recordings, newspaper propaganda and subversive writings on walls. Each historical layer embeds meanings and/or interconnections with other signs and notions. A single word theoretically carries entrails of other words, other images and other stories: molecular motions are transposed onto linguistic and epistemological fields. Farah's storytelling unfurls in a tension between the conventions of a long lineage of distinguished pastoralist poets of his homeland and the threat of nihilism inherent in Jacques Derrida's proposal of an infinite *deferral* of meaning. His narrative art is as rich as Qur'anic exegesis and as subtle as shifting desert sands. It is through this probing of linguistic permutations that Farah replicates the foundational design of the "inordinately varied cosmos" of each and every manifestation of culture.[5] The ideas, symbols and metaphors that surface from the probe contour the unique Somali-ness of Farah's investigation of identity.

When asked about his motives for writing, Farah invariably points to a need to articulate Somalia's socio-political dilemmas. This campaign is unashamedly announced in the title of the first trilogy and is borne out in the committed moral stance Farah adopts in each novel, essay and interview. However, activists who choose the pen over the sword, especially one riven to fiction, do so for reasons that appear inevitable and, at once, obscure. With a mother who was an oral poetess in a culture prone to value such aptitude even in women, and a father who translated in the fertile linguistic environment that was Somalia during the colonial tug-of-war of possession and dispossession, the son was bound to be involved in language one way or another. In "Childhood of My Schizophrenia," Farah points to the further complication of his convergence with language.

> We spoke Somali at home, but we read or wrote in other languages: Arabic (the sacred tongue of the Koran); Amharic, that of the colonial master, the better to know what he thinks; English, a tongue that might one day afford us entry into a wider world. We moved from one language universe to another with the disquiet of a tenant on a temporary lease. We were conscious of the complicated state of affairs, conscious of the fact that we were being brought up not as replicas of our parents but as a strange new species.[6]

The 'new species' according to this telling is bound to the written word. But what makes the child-to-be-a-man the peculiar storyteller he became? Nonno, the charismatic grandfather in *Secrets* and a fitting shamanic counterpart to *Close Sesame*'s devout Muslim Deeriye, offers a clue to his author's impulsion towards storytelling when he observes that the "living listen to stories, which they tell to others in the hope of weaving strands of their personalities into the mysteries of the tale."[7] Identity and mystery, as so often in Farah's work, coalesce but Nonno's words also suggest that human life itself is an embodied idea constructed of strands of signs only intelligible when filtered through the skeins of a story. Farah has alluded to the conceptual significance of images, symbols and metaphors in his worldview and writing. "The writer speaks of hell and heaven in a language of images, symbols and metaphors. In other words, the images, the symbols and the metaphors are his guide: they communicate the incommunicable. The writer is himself an image, symbol, a metaphor—no more."[8] Even more directly—if Farah in fact can be direct—is his brief description of characterization to an audience at a bookshop launch of *Secrets*: "We're all not people so much as just ideas. We are stories, ideas, bits of other people too. This is what I am interested in."[9] Little is revealed here about the complexity of such statements: one needs to enter his fictions, like *Sardines*, to find the communal scheme of cultural maintenance and change in overlays of individual stories. A single psyche's anomalous pattern of ideas illuminates the cornerstones of cultural identity just as the accumulated system is the blueprint for the formation of the individual. Both ends of the spectrum belong to the same interpenetrating instability.

A principal word in *Sardines* is 'construction,' making the novel an illuminating text for examining the architecture of Farah's art. Medina, at once a pragmatic journalist, translator and idealistic advocate of feminist aspirations, is introduced in a daydream in which there is a metaphorical interpenetration of language and architecture.

> She reconstructed the story from the beginning. She worked it into a set of pyramids which served as foundations for one another. Out of this, she erected a construction of great solidity and strength. She then built mansions on top of it all, mansions as large as her imagination and with lots of chambers that led off cor-

385

ridors in which she lost herself but which led her finally, when she chose to follow, to a secret back door in
another wing of the building (p.2).

The bricks and mortar of Medina's imaginative castle are ideas bridg-
ing the ancient African world (pyramids) with the future through
words constructed to puzzle and, at the same time, to foretell the
narrative movement from one house to another until the central protagonist chooses a back door leading to an alternative space. The
short passage signals Medina's pivotal position in the narrative and,
through Farah's investigation into the subterranean leakage of language, also plots her uncompromising individuality. Except for the
lapse indicated by "she lost herself," Medina is portrayed as self-consciously in control of the construction of *her* imagination, *her* story
and *her* sphere of influence. She is a matriarch, though one with a
peculiar slant, who views herself as a counterpart to the unseen but
metaphorically ever-present patriarch, the General. "The General's
power and I are like two lizards engaged in a varanian dance of death;
we are two duellists dancing a tarantella in which they challenge
their own destiny" (p.45). Hints of the tussle between the two figures,
whose equality extends only to a certain similarity in their will to
power, occur on the opening page. While roaming in "the architecture of her thoughts," Medina encounters an agonistic sign, "Stop
and give heed: *He is not all of us*" (p.2). In the first appearance of ital-
icised words, an extra-linguistic device in Farah's repertoire to signal
attention, an enigma hovers. Who is '*He*'? Could it be the generalised
male, Allah or one of the two pivotal characters yet to be introduced,
Samatar, her husband or the General? Alternatively and quite probably, in view of the internal molecular-like structure of words
described above, '*He*' could embrace every one of those assorted
masculine ideas simultaneously activating one another.

This disruptive sign seeps through unanswered questions to
Medina's wish for a 'room of one's own,' which introduces a literary
allusion and raises the stakes in the language/gender game. The allu-

sion evokes Woolfian overtones and draws another set of ideas into the peculiar floor-plan of the Medina cluster. Medina's education in Italy and travels in Europe (together with foreign characters such as Sandra, Atta and Wentworth George) enable Farah to extend the narrative's diachronic linguistic resonances along a synchronic axis of contemporary cross-cultural (and multi-linguistic) thought. Feminism, the primary discourse tapped through the allusion, is one that runs counter to traditional Somali assumptions about the place of women in society and situates Medina in tension with her mother's acquiescence to male authority. Medina's feminist agenda also clashes with the views of her mother-in-law Idil, an antagonism brought to an incisive head over the matter of female circumcision. Here Farah shares Medina's moral indignation over the savagery of a practice that Idil threatens to inflict upon Ubax. In contrast to other issues raised in the novel, infibulation and rape are the two subjects about which the writer admits no equivocations. At the same time, there are other aspects of the Medina-Idil clash which are not so cut and dried. If Medina's feminism aims for gender equality, she often expounds her views with an egotistical authority that differs little from Idil's autocratic manipulation of the household. The behavioral similarities in two women whose ideas are diametrically opposed raises doubts about the assumed gender inequities of Somali culture. Variables in power relationships, Farah suggests, are more complex than those portrayed in simplified programs pitching feminism against patriarchy.

Another pivotal element of construction within the design of Farah's introductory pages is the description of Samatar, Medina's husband, as seen from the restricted viewpoint of their young daughter, Ubax. Strange deviations to family patterns have brought an end to mother and daughter storytelling sessions and the only reason Ubax can find for the change is a picture in the newspaper announcing Samatar's appointment as Minister for Construction. For the reader, on the other hand, the announcement and subsequent move of Medina and Ubax to another house signal an ostensible collision of imagination and pragmatism within the construction complex. If not for Ubax's observation of the adults' behavior as a domestic irregularity, it would seem as if Farah aligns metaphors of construction and gender along the stereotypical spatial grid of domestic and public spaces; the woman in the home and the man overseeing building in the political arena. Those readers familiar with Farah's deconstruction of categorisation will be prepared for the cross-weave of contradictory forces that follows.

As the novel proceeds, Medina, already marked as politically conscious and in *control* of her thoughts, may be physically confined to a domestic space and yet, psychologically, she is the driving force and decision-maker within the family. Contrary to gender norms in Somali society, Medina owns and practically runs the family home. Moreover, her imaginative sensibilities are often channelled into a reified, even imperious sense of principles that at times causes her feminism to be strident and unbending. In this configuration of identity she is a matriarch, a modernised counterpart to Idil, the nomadic strong-woman who is "as powerful as providence itself" (p.5). The two women create a doubled mirror image of the General's autocratic manipulations of state power. Medina corrupts normally sound principles of gender equity by her inflexibility, whereas Idil compromises and connives to ensure that her family and clan maintain their political influence. Medina, with an intellect that aspires to roam freely across many rooms, is ironically confined to a solitary cell. As her mother, Fatima bint Thabit, observes: "You are a prisoner of your principles and your secret dreams, Medina; I am a prisoner of tradition, that I won't deny. One is always a prisoner of one thing or another: a prisoner of acquired habits or a prisoner of the hope that chains one" (p.144).

In contrast, Samatar, the engineer, allows himself to be forced into a politically untenable position (another image of imprisonment) as Minister of Construction in the frail hope that this role may enable him to deflect some of the more sinister and inhumane aspects of the regime and thus to benefit the population in general. Closer in many respects to the feminine *shadows* that Farah conceives as arbitrators of unyielding male ideologies, Samatar is viewed by his mother Idil as a weakling who is not man enough to control the whims of his domineering wife. In the mutable terrain of Farah's characterisation, however, weakness is but another name for gentleness. The perspectival shift is indicated almost microscopically by the textual focus on Samatar's offer of a "bridge of a hand" to save an ant in the wash basin while his mind is consumed by the life-threatening situations he may face in terms of the regime and of filial ethics. Further deviations in the gender fabric are encountered in Samatar's relationship with Fatima bint Thabit, who describes him as a sensitive man with an artistic nature. On the other hand, Samatar ultimately makes the toughest decision of any character in the novel when he throws his mother out of the house.

Farah imbues the two metaphorical edifices of construction, Medina and Samatar, with internal contradictions that are further enhanced by structuring a curious distance between them. Apart from speculation generated by rumours outside the relationship, there is nothing in the surface writing that counters the impression of an implied intimacy and exchange between the couple. Curiously then, and excepting the final glimpse of the nuclear family departing together, interaction between the two remains textually hidden. Major scenes revolving around Medina or Samatar, together with the circulating suppositions about their estranged relationship, provide a smokescreen over actuality. Medina's evasion of thoughts about her husband when the narrative voice permeates her consciousness only exacerbates the restricted vision. Physically, Medina and Samatar are never portrayed together, whether from the point of view of the omniscient narrator or any other of the participating characters who have a narrative voice. *Sardines*, like the trilogy in total, rehearses the narrative experiments with shifting perspectives that reaches radical proportions in *Maps* and its ordered puzzle of alternative speaking positions. In the earlier novels, narrative points of view appear as fluid responses to what can be known or expressed

and only when one is puzzling over questions of why one relationship appears transparent while another is obscured do deep-struc-
tural designs emerge. Why, for instance, is the central relationship
between Medina and Samatar veiled when the omniscient narrator
reveals so much about the other significant (and aberrant) family,
that of Ebla and Sagal? The linguistic architect plumbs many tensions
and dynamics in the plan of Mogadiscio's domestic territory.

In Farah's examination of families, the unconventional single-par-
ent group and quintessential example of a mother and daughter relationship, Ebla and Sagal, act as the novel's emotional centre and
counterpart to the intellectual force of Medina's matriarchy. Whereas
politicised frictions sever communication between Medina and
Samatar, the two women constantly strive to overcome dissonances
arising from their generational differences. Fundamentally, the distinction between the two family situations lies in Ebla's willingness,
as a mother, to compromise even over the bitterest quarrels with her
daughter. The maternal empathy is underscored by Farah's decision
to comment on the aftermath of such disagreements, noting that "the
two would link arms...and go further into the night which opened up
like the teased lips of a vagina. The masked opaqueness of the hour
would open like a tunnel of softness to welcome its own breed"
(p.35). Unvoiced shadows hover over the image, extending tenuous-
ly to another pivotal topic of debate, compromise. Ebla's voice gives
further weight to the external narrator's licence: "Each of us speaks
for a generation, each of us is like a clock keeping its own time. What
one gains, the other loses...Although the hands of the clock might not
point at the same second, there is no doubt the difference is minor,
particularly when both are functioning well" (p.35).

In contrast, Medina is forthright about her principled approach
to motherhood, encouraging Ubax's right to defy parental dictates
except, and this point has been well noted by Jacqueline Bardolph,
when Medina's idealism is challenged. Quarantined from the street
dirt and smutty language of other children of her age, Ubax retorts to
Medina's insistence on uniqueness (following the dictates of free

speech encouraged by her mother) with "But I want you to be like other mothers" and not smoke (p.150). Farah implies that, as sound as Medina's stance on modernised ideas may be, her unbending attitude and Ubax's unfamiliarity with children's games could have adverse repercussions as regards social integration later in life. As Bardolph notes: "There is some irony in [the metaphorical flower of Ubax's name] as Ubax has not any existence outside her mother's project for her and is paradoxically denied her own language, as Medina often excludes her by speaking Italian."[10] Issues of multi-lingualism constantly resurface in Farah's work, fluctuating between negative and positive poles. In this instance, Ubax's exclusion echoes the rhetoric employed by the General to confound the populace as well as the exclusion practised on the foreign wife in *Close Sesame* until rectified by the observant Deeriye who perceives a disjunction between language and feeling. Given this context, Medina's principles further alienate her from the love that she desires to give. Gifts, like threats, have many and varied points of reference.

Moreover, Sagal, as Medina's favored disciple in feminist stratagems, aspires to but lacks the resolve for astute and committed political action. Instead of the planned graffiti denouncing the General, Sagal, the potential swimming champion, is true to her watery element and becomes sidetracked by currents of emotional turbulence. Throughout the novel, she is preoccupied with thoughts of repercussions from a one-night sexual liaison with the foreign journalist Wentworth George, an act to which she had succumbed out of sympathy following his mistreatment by the regime. In reflection, she justifies her submission as a positive subversion of the General's influence while, at the same time, admitting that the encounter will be seen as a serious political misjudgment in Medina's eyes. In other words, she is a failed pupil and an inconsistent human being faced with an incisive problem, pregnancy. In the characterization of Ebla and Sagal, Farah poses questions about moral values that are equally uplifting and disturbing. Is Ebla's ability to compromise a sign of weakness or a potent means of dealing with human vagaries? Is

Sagal's inconsistency a failure to live up to the intellectual rigor of resistance or a demonstration of an empathy and vulnerability that needs to be acknowledged in human affairs? How can resistances to clear cases of political injustice like the General's be effected by such ineffectual and inconsistent means? Farah turns conclusions over to the reader although his focus on Ebla and Sagal indicates that resisting the regime may be fought in other than the General's own terms.

Ebla's maternal empathy and Sagal's indeterminacy, etched within the clear passages of their communicative relationship, bridge back and forth with the issue of the obscured marital rift. Another tangential corridor of ideas opened by Farah's strategy of silence between the two rooms of Medina's and Samatar's thoughts relates directly to the General's rule by secrecy. The domestic fabrications mirror the large-scale obfuscatory tactics of the General's propaganda machine and in so doing implicate the average citizen in the political language games. More interestingly, though, Medina's evasions and rubber stamping of any external conjecture about why she left the house—and Samatar as a consequence—suggests to readers who have privileged insight into her thoughts that she herself cannot explain her actions. Medina's internal reaction to Sagal's explanation of the rift as the result of Idil's wish to have Ubax circumcised is typical: "Why not appropriate Sagal's version and make it work? Everyone would believe it" (p.63). In contrast, speculations from other characters all assume that Medina is adopting a critical stance. Controlled intentions figure in every explanation about the separation, whether they be Medina's direct attack on the General's schemes, her protection of Ubax against Idil's threats of infibulation, or her revenge for Samatar's weakness before his mother's orders for a new and compliant wife. It is the *projection* of her principles, rather than the principles *per se*, that implicates Medina in the General's imposition of tribal and totalitarian rule.

In overview, the strategy of maintaining the two metaphorical structures at a distance provides Farah with a narrative device to explore the variations in his own resistance to stereotypes which, at another remove, is synonymous with resistance to dictatorships. Ideologies of dictatorship and of militant resistance to that dictator-ship admit no hint of vulnerability; like forts, the ideational armoury is built to withstand and/or deny structural errors. Commenting on her body language at the final gathering in Nasser's house, the narra-tor pointedly notes that Medina seemed to say: "Insert another bullet, have the General in person come within shooting range of me and we'll see who falls" (p.237). In this moment, her external projections fuse with conditioned readings of her character within which all hints of vulnerability have been erased. However, the reader, exposed to her inner indecisiveness over separation from Samatar, perceives a behavioral fault-line that admits other possibilities. Subversion, per-haps, involves not a matching of strength as Medina's projected char-acterization suggests. Instead, what may be required is some kind of denial of the structure of assumptions on which the ideology rests. Although tempered by inconclusiveness, the novel's ending indicates that Medina relinquishes the center stage of her political opposition in favor of the two most important people in her life.

> *The journey to the acceptance of roles is final*, she thought. Samatar. Ubax. And Medina. There wasn't time to tie up the loose ends of the story, though there was a need to tell one another what had happened, a human need to touch the nerve...It wouldn't be diffi-cult to explain to Samatar when the others had gone, wouldn't be difficult to put their house in some order...The three walked away, refusing to play host to the guests who waited to be entertained with explana-tions, explications and examples. Medina, Samatar and Ubax behaved as though they needed one another's company—and no more (p.250).

Farah intimates, time and time again, that the smallest, almost ineffectual challenges are often paradoxical means to unhinge or at least make dents in the strongholds of inhumane power. As I have argued elsewhere, the clutched prayer-beads in Deeriye's failed attempt to assassinate the General in *Close Sesame* signal martyrdom and the recruitment of God's invincible powers for the resistance.[11] Thus the death of one small and disease-ridden old man can make a difference. Ultimately, there are no manuals nor formulae articulating the 'right way' to demolish structures of injustice. Shadows and small acts exposing human vulnerability may be the answer.

Indeed, the notion of small movements is encoded in the metaphoric fabric of the novel's title. Itala Vivan notes Farah's play on the Somali children's hide-and-seek game of *dhundhunmashaw* (sardines)[12] which extends the usual Western interpretation of the confined situation of womanhood. At the same time, sardines are small fish that have the potential to be lively agents of change. When Medina turns to her family, her motivation seems to arise from an expression of personal love beyond the bounds of political intent. Ironically the 'back door' option, announced in the opening paragraph, may lead to a small yet alternative means of resistance, although Medina's familiar tactic of following up the disappearances of the singer Dulman and her brother Nasser is noted in the omniscient narrator's final entry into her thoughts. Nonetheless, Medina's choice signals a compromise with her principles and, more importantly, a small victory in the face of the General's project to wrench them apart. Three people depart to create a new story out of the loose ends left by others, a story that they need to tell each other "in the hope of weaving strands of their personalities into the mysteries of the tale."[13] At a fundamental level, the family aspires to construct a home designed by their shared sense of identity, a room of *their* own.

This discussion has only begun to touch upon the materials and structuring strategies in Farah's verbal architecture. Extensions to the foundational ideas, such as the dynamic tensions between men and women, mothers and daughters (and sons), orality and script, feminism and patriarchy, inflexibility and compromise, state edifices and domestic dwellings, are found in the important clusters erected around other protagonists. The celebrated performer Dulman, the "Mother of the Revolution" and its symbolic victim, represents the extreme maternal position because her infertility bars her from the realization of her most sought-after goal, a child. She also opens debates on the power of the oral culture when it is jolted into modernity by audio technology and, on another linguistic level, the semantics of 'performance' through an anguished acknowledgment of the corrupted system of Somali gift-giving. Medina's brother Nasser likewise plays into the polysemic design in his membership of the inner circle of resistance and his compassionate liaison with Dulman, his fathering of a deaf-mute child, and his championing of the maimed and injured. Together with Samater, Nasser is the feminine principle that is close to Medina's unbending feminism. Additionally, there is the brutal rape of Amina that desecrates womanhood in the name of politics, an inexcusable act that has other ramifications in the young woman's decision to bear the child and compromise with her father's guilt in the affair. As Medina's reaction to Amina's decision demonstrates, principles can be destructive when they are unbending before complex human experiences. The foreigners, in their varying degrees of abuse, Eurocentric narrowness and pathos, become the mortar in the issue of habitation and shape the vital motif of 'hosts and guests,' resonant with colonialism. Through such clusters of variable ideas, Farah draws up a sceptical, critical layout of the indeterminacy and contradictions of cultural identity. In the very foundations of textual construction, the architectonic metaphor falters. Ultimately external forces, whether architects or dictators, cannot design culture. Culture organically becomes.

In a poet's activism, the city of ideas also becomes something other. The bricks and mortar of Farah's scheme would not be complete if his ideational drawings failed to admit emissions of that phenomenon called beauty. Farah's words construct a logic of variables and, at the same time, they permeate another, arabesque dimension, an aesthetic and semiotic network that is recognizably Islamic in origin. When Seyyed Hossein Nasr points out the significance of light as a symbolic resonance in Islamic cultures, he could equally be referring to Farah. "Arabic and Persian literature, and even everyday language, are replete with expressions which identify light with joy of the soul and correct functioning of the intellect...Moreover, this light is ultimately the same as the Word."[14] Furthermore, he notes that the structuring of Islamic architecture "relates outward forms to inner meaning and architectural utility to spiritual significance."[15] While *Sardines*'s spiritual significance is low-keyed and may be better encapsulated by *moral* significance, the work's outward form (women's resistance to dictatorship) relates to the ideas, symbols and metaphors embedded in linguistic systems drawn from the synchro-diachronic axes of Somali culture. The architectonic nature of the text, focused as it is on domestic environments, gives rise to a moral questioning of the potential dictator in each of us and suggests that human beings seek freedom through small steps to that place where construction melds with shadow, a *feminine* shadow. By a similar argument, storytelling is the fusion of a rigorous structure of ideas and a de-*light* in language itself, analogous in the broad scheme to the great mosques where architectural form combines with artistic embellishment to enhance the light-filled sanctity of their interiors. Ultimately, Farah's optimistic faith in the human spirit shines through in the poetic tonalities of his novel: "A galaxy of charred stars in flight. A deposit of the day's tears in smoke, tears of ash sprinkled on the year just ended. The year's blessing was expressed in burning ashes light as dead leaves, which flew and floated here and there and in the air like dust, and fell like dusk" (p.110). In the passing of one year into the next, and against the thrust of dictatorship, beauty is a slender yet enduring dream.

Multivocality and shifting perspectives, webs of history and individual contradictions, are ores poured into the founding ideas of people and their stories. *Sardines* drafts but a small portion of the architect's plan to span the profiles of Somali identity through the lens of doubt. It is a shadowy, insubstantial plan: the book traces an identity already past, though the present is still redolent with it. Thus

396

Farah can claim of his writing as does Wentworth George of his photography: "I instil stillness in movements" (p.226). In the stillness of structure and light, a future dawns. Medina, Samater and Ubax move on to construct their small home in a continuing story of symbols, metaphors and ideas.

NOTES

1. Nuruddin Farah, *Sardines* (London: Heinemann, 1982), p.135. Further references are given in parentheses in the text.

2. Nuruddin Farah, "The Women of Kismayo," *The Times Literary Supplement*, 15 November 1996, 44.

3. James Clifford, *The Predicament of Culture: Twentieth Century Ethnography, Literature and Art* (Cambridge: Harvard University Press, 1988), p.273.

4. D.R.Ewen, "Nuruddin Farah," in *The Writing of East and Central Africa*, ed. G.D.Killam (London: Heinemann, 1984), p.205.

5. Nuruddin Farah, "Why I Write," *Third World Quarterly* 10, 4 (1988), 1591.

6. Farah, "Childhood of My Schizophrenia," *The Times Literary Supplement* 23-29 November 1990, 1264.

7. Nuruddin Farah, *Secrets* (New York: Arcade, 1998), p.244.

8. Nuruddin Farah, "The Life and Death of Words," *South* (April 1984), 54.

9. Megan Rooney, "Neustadt Winner Brings *Secrets* to Brown Bookstore," *The Brown Daily Herald*, 13 November 1998.

10. Jacqueline Bardolph, "Women and Metaphors in Nuruddin Farah's *Sweet and Sour Milk* and *Sardines*," in *Proceedings of the Second International Congress of Somali Studies*, University of Hamburg, 1983, ed. Thomas Labahn (Hamburg: Helmut Buske Verlag, 1984), p.437.

11. Maggi Phillips, "The View from a Mosque of Words: Nuruddin Farah's *Close Sesame* and *The Holy Qur'an*," in *The Marabout and the Muse: New Approaches to Islam in African Literature*, ed. Kenneth Harrow (Portsmouth, N.H.: Heinemann, 1996), pp.191-204.

12. Itala Vivan, "Nuruddin Farah's Beautiful Mat and its Italian Plot," *World Literature Today* 72, 4 (1998), 790.

13. Farah, *Secrets*, p.244.

14. Seyyed Hossein Nasr, *Islamic Art and Spirituality* (Albany: State University of New York Press, 1987), p.51.

15. ibid., p.49.

TIME AND HISTORY IN NURUDDIN FARAH'S *CLOSE SESAME*

Jacqueline Bardolph

C*lose Sesame* is the third book in the trilogy *Variation on the Theme of an African Dictatorship*. The connecting theme in the novels is arbitrary power, that of the President, the police state or the patriarchal family, as seen by some of the oppressed, young intellectuals or women. In the third book, the approach is paradoxically centred on an old man, a traditional and pious character, and from this unexpected angle, the debate on the legitimacy of rebellion against an unjust ruler will take a new dimension. Through him, time and history will be the main subjects of *Close Sesame*, as well as giving shape and texture to a complex narrative technique.

Close Sesame being part of a trilogy, this in itself gives a temporal dimension to the experience of reading, as we meet again characters who have matured or changed from *Sweet and Sour Milk, Sardines*, and even *From a Crooked Rib*. The other novels, set in the contemporary world and in a recognizable political system, revolved around fictitious events. This time, fictitious elements are secondary to the urgent choices to be made in a context anchored in reality with dates and known facts. By examining how fiction and historical facts are organized and balanced in the book, we can see how the scope and craft of Farah as a novelist are evolving and also how the text can function as fiction and comment on Somalia's history, past and present, for its various readers.

The structure is organized around two different visions of time. On one hand, the narrative covers a few days in the life of Deeriye, an old man, ailing with asthma. Most of the action takes place within the house of his son Mursal, and is very static: talks with family and friends who try to understand the current turn of events as, first, Mursal's friends, and then Mursal himself meet tragic ends. Deeriye ventures out a few times, to see friends in the Novecento Bar (nineteenth-century bar), to a meeting of the clan's elders, and for a final visit to the President after his son's death, the outcome of which is not made clear: it has all happened "off stage"...The reports say that, as the old man was shot by the guards, he held his prayer beads and a gun, entangled in his hand: did he or did he not intend to kill the unjust ruler? We are not told.

A tense few days, then, with very little action from the main character, who seems to be a passive and powerless witness to external events. But as a counterpoint to this static core of the plot, the reader is made to explore the history of Somalia from the remote, quasi legendary past of King Wiil-Waal to the time of the Dervish movement in 1912, from the Italian Fascist occupation to the present day, with references both to the history of the African continent at large, and to the early days of Islam, and the Caliphate.[1] This massive use of real facts could easily unbalance any novel. We shall see how these known data are interwoven in the reflections and dreams of the imaginary characters, how the apparently timeless waiting inside the household is examined and given meaning by the vast panorama of facts, myths and memories through which the protagonists try to understand the present and decide on a course for future action.

To give coherence to various perceptions of time, the novel relies first on the central character, Deeriye. The whole narrative is focused

on his point of view. From the first lines, we are immersed in his subjective vision of things, which in itself is an experience of displacement for the reader. This kind, pious Muslim patriarch, as seen from
the inside, is very new to fiction in English. So, modestly, we share his
experience of physical time: time as dictated by the rhythm of the
body, with the difficult breathing, the naps and dreams that punctuate the day of an old man. But this man is no slave to natural time and
his day is ordered and regulated by prayer:

> He clocked his heart-beat. He timed the breathing-in
> and the breathing-out of his lungs: all normal. He con-
> cluded what had preceded with the saying thrice of
> the Islamic transcendental unity. He thanked God for
> the inner peace obtained with the *modus vivendi* of his
> own condition. (p.167)

The narrative is given pauses by such prayers, the words of
praise, the privileged moments when he establishes contact with his
God in the serenity of his faith. So the cycle of each day from dawn to
sunset, as described from chapter to chapter, takes into account both
the natural law of ageing and the religious ordering of each moment.
This frame is important, because there will be the same search for
ordering and meaning on a wider time scale, the scale of centuries.
For this old man, if there is a meaning in the rhythm of daily ablutions
and prayers, there must be a meaning to a larger scale of time.

The first chapter also establishes another scale by which to measure time, that of a lifetime as seen by an old man at the close of his
days: "Will he survive another day, another month, another year?" say
his friends. (p.23) He is tolerant of daughter Zeinab, who is a doctor,
as she counts his pills, but his way of counting is different: he wonders if a man's lifetime can be measured by the number of daily
prayers he has said. His daughter's efforts at curing him meet with
this comment: "Not a day, not a single second will either be added to
or substracted from the precise hour prescribed by Allah - whatever

401

you or I do. How often must I tell you this?" (p.54). This vision of human life, from a religious and philosophical distance, is not shared by all the characters, especially the young ones, and it is not necessarily the vision of the book as a whole, but it serves as a frame of reference from which the tensions and agitations of his modern children who "never have the time" can be seen. The acute consciousness Deeriye has of being at the sunset of his days gives both urgency and serenity to his final attempt at understanding and acting.

The long life of the protagonist also gives unity to the novel through the various moments of meditation when he looks back to his past. It is not so much the fact that he has lived through important years in the history of Somalia that makes him such a privileged witness: it is that his "twelve to fourteen years' imprisonment" in the days of Italian Somalia, then, in the days when Somalia was a UN Mandate Territory, and again "a couple of years ago," have made him paradoxically a privileged observer, through the clarity of vision given by his displacement, just as when Medina in *Sardines* moved house to find herself:

> Twelve years in rooms dark as a photographer's, twelve years framed as one's picture of oneself or one's dearest, there for him or her to see, speak about,point at the developed print, point out the hiatus, mentioning why he was not there when the family portrait was taken. (p.32)

Thus he keeps establishing parallels between the present and past events. The news on the radio makes "his mind travel back to 1934; and to the Italian colonial officer who had brought him 'peace' and in the end created 'famine': did peace from a superpower always mean that they would sweep clean your natural resources and make you live on the dry sticks of famine and total economic and political dependence?" (p. 115). Prison and solitude have given him the habit of this permanent confrontation of past and present: "I have to reinvent my tenses" (p.192). His memories colour everything and make him compare the present days to the stagnant time of his detention: "we are quarantined with the cordons of fear around us."

The memories of the old man open possibilities for comparison within the narrative. They also underline the theme of the importance of action: is one passively carried by the flux of history, or are there choices to be made which could alter its course? Deeriye was first thrown in jail for opposing the Italians, not in violent fighting, but by his refusal to betray and to give them the name they wanted. Can this action, praised as heroic by the new generation, provide him with a reference for future decisions? For him the incentive to act or resist does not stem from abstract political theories, but from strong moral issues, from a personal code of honour and faithfulness to what one has been. Will his past heroic deed be a guide? A choice once made seems to live with you for ever, and even lives through one's descendants. This theme is reinforced in the book by the repeated pattern of fathers and sons: are the sons of traitors to be rejected as traitors, are the sons of heroes heroic, is the young Yassin born outside wedlock an evil child because of that? The concept of free choice, of the momentous historical decision to be made, seems at times to be contradicted in the fiction by the more ancient notion of the curse determining men's lives from one generation to another.

Thus Deeriye is the memory of the novel, comparing independent Somalia and colonial days, always aware of the long history of his nation as he is driven through the streets of Mogadiscio, a town which is to him like an open history book. His life is also used in an allegorical manner. In the same way as Ebla's journey to Mogadiscio and freedom in *From a Crooked Rib* can be seen as an evocation of the various stages of Somalia's independence, Deeriye's life is deliberately conceived in symbolic terms:

> He was born in 1912. He would add for the benefit of those who did not know or might have forgotten it that it was in 1912 that the first African party of resistance

was formed, a party, *magac lagama miskiin maahee*, known as the African National Congress; it was also in the year 1912 that the Dervish movement of the Sayyid in Somalia defeated the British imperialists; and Corfield died in this war and the Sayyid composed Deeriye's favourite poem. (p.15)

Deeriye, under such auspicious beginnings, is clearly meant to be remote from the mere politics of clan or tribe: he stands for national-ism and Pan-Africanism through the date of birth the novelist has thus chosen and underlined. His life history can also be read as the fate of the nation, as he was jailed by the Italians, released by the British in 1943, and jailed again by the Italians. This invites the reader possibly to see a similar allegorical meaning in his recent term of detention in independent Somalia, his present sickness and waiting; the implica-tion is that the whole country is still somehow in detention.[2]

We have seen how this inside focus on Deeriye's consciousness and the presentation of his life's experience helps to weave present and past events.[3] But history in this novel is not only alive in an old man's reminiscences. It is dramatized as it would be in a play, by the creation of suspense and by the relationship Deeriye establishes with his son's generation and with his grandson Samawade. Each of these elements of the plot throws a different light on the central con-cern—the meaning of history—while adding human dimensions to characters with whom the reader can identify, with their lives full of tensions, dreams, and also affection.

Space and time are restricted to a few days in a house: suspense builds up as Mursal and his friends seem involved in mysterious doings and as one after the other, characters are reported missing, with no clear indication as to their fate. This dramatic waiting helps to underline another dimension of history: the meaninglessness and confusion of history in the making for the direct participants. Texts, legends, collective knowledge make sense of the past century, and by contrast the hours lived now seem totally formless. Again and again

the opposition is created in the narrative between the neat organisa-
tion of cause and effect and the easy moral judgements one can for-
mulate as far as the past is concerned, and, on the other hand, the
uncertainty of present experience. It is impossible to establish links
between events and, what is more, it is impossible to be certain of
the events themselves. Characters are shown trying to decode the
news bulletin and to deduce information from what is said, not said,
or implied. Witnesses are not reliable or speak with innuendoes and
hints which are not easy to decipher. There are several versions of
the same incident, none of which is attested or refuted within the
text. As in *Sweet and Sour Milk*, the official account of an event can
replace in people's minds their actual experience of it. Rumours are
spread, intentionally or not. For instance, the actions and death of
Mursal can only be inferred from his silence and reticence, then from
an incomplete news bulletin and intermittent ringing of the phone,
silence and a song on the radio. The papers do not tell the whole
story; neither can radio news, national or foreign, be considered as
entirely reliable. The actions which are "off-stage," Rooble's disappearance, for instance, or Mukhtaar's killing by his own father, are
pieced together by the protagonists who are never certain that their
guessing is correct, still less that they can construe an overall meaning considering the circumstances. Up to the last page, as in *Sweet
and Sour Milk*, there are contradictory reports on Mukhtaar's and
Deeriye's deaths. The reader, like the characters, is left to grope and
infer, left to the responsibility of the plot he thus traces and of the
conclusions he comes to. The certainty of history books and national heroic myths is not for the present.

If much of present history is pieced together with difficulty by the
characters and reader alike, the comments on past history are given
explicitly, mainly in the long debate Deeriye has with the generation
of his children, and chiefly with his son Mursal. In *Sardines*, the novel
was organized around many such intellectual debates. Here the confrontation of ideological systems is concentrated more effectively in
the arguments exchanged by father and son. Such moments, in

varous parts of the novel, help to take stock of Deeriye's gradual evolution . For here, unlike Keynaan and his sons in *Sweet and Sour Milk,* both of them are engaged in an earnest dialogue, trying to find common terms of reference: Deeriye's detention seems to have made him more receptive to others and to change than other members of his generation. When he meditates he has at his disposal quotes provided by Mursal (p.94), and part of his political analysis stems from contemporary ideas:

> ...history was as much about the movement of tribal peoples with no technological know-how as it was about the conquest of territories, of "protections", of "pacificatory" methods and of created famines whether in Vietnam or in the Ogaden. (p.86)

From the first pages, it is clear that their debate will revolve around the legitimacy of violent action, with examples taken from the history of the Caliphate to modern egalitarian ideologies. For Deeriye, an action must be in agreement with the fundamental tenets of Islam if it is to be justified and to represent the culture and nation it sets out to protect. The debate about the right to violence and the justification of *lex talionis* is saved from being too abstract by the constant interplay between historical references and fictional events. The parallels made between known events like the killing of the first Caliphs, passages from the Koran like the Sourah of Yassin, and the fictitious episodes where the little boy Yassin throws a stone at Deeriye connect reality and fiction in a way that gives verisimilitude to the novel and helps to make it a comment on the present situation—a present that, at the moment, for the characters and readers alike, is in the 1980s.

Through these exchanges, Deeriye appears as a man who in spite of his age still lives for the future of his nation, whereas the elders of his clan seem to him stuck with outdated values and modes of reasoning:

> They hadn't the sensitivity to understand the subtlety
> of this statement: that confinement to prison opened
> to Deeriye a vista of a wider larger world: detention
> compelled him to think of the history and contradic-
> tions which the neocolonial person lives in; detention
> forced him to see himself not only as a spokesman of
> a clan, but made it obvious to him that he was a mem-
> ber of the world's oppressed...You found the likes of
> them all over Africa, the Middle East and Asia. (p.93)

The bland talk of the other old men sends him to sleep; their automatic consensus precludes any stimulating debate and, hence, any creation of new solutions.

If the relationship between Deeriye and his son helps to establish two diverging ideological starting points, which in their attempted convergence provide an intellectual frame to the issues in the novel, the bond between Deeriye and his grandson is of a very different nature. In *Sardines*, mother and daughter, brother and sister were shown in a relaxed immediate contact, nearly animal in its warmth and instinctive quality. Here the warmth of the old man, and to a great extent, the warm tone of the novel, is established mainly through Deeriye's caring relationship with his family and old friends: the daughter, the Jewish daughter-in-law, the brother-in-law, and Rooble, the old friend from another clan. But the daily contact with Samawade also helps to introduce another vision of history: at the end of his day, the old patriarch feels he has to transmit the culture of his people to the very young.[4] This is why he narrates traditional tales and fragments of history . This oral storytelling is as much an expression of his love, in the warm closeness of their daily contact, as of his concern for Samawade's future life. In that way the novel can integrate two full length texts about King Wiil-Waal (pp.50-52, 123-26). The insertion of these long quotations from oral tradition, about "the king of the Somalis a thousand or so years ago", gives authority to the general debate on kingship and wisdom or madness. They function within the plot as indirect moral lessons to the young boy, in the same way as the long tale about the blind man, also in italics (pp.174-76). But they also fit in the general pattern of the book by extending the time-span of Somali identity and showing at least ten centuries of national pride. By using such large extracts, in the way other African writers like Ngugi or Achebe have done within their novels, Farah lets the collective memory speak and inserts his written work in the continuity of a long genealogy of oral texts. History does not start with the nineteenth-century struggles for power nor with written scholarly works; it is kept active and works for the present every time an old man speaks to his grandson. What is interesting here also is that this age-old practice is given modern relevance by the discussion that extends it: young Samawade can compare Somali history with his growing knowledge of the world at large, as he learns about Ataturk for instance.

If history is present for Deeriye in explicit debates with Mursal and in the tales told to his grandson, it is repeatedly referred to through another device, the cassettes the old man listens to. Cassettes here are symbolic, belonging both to the oral modes of transmitting and feeling, but also to modern technology. The earphones isolate the old man from the everyday bustle around him and connect him, in an immediate manner, to the Egyptian who reads his favourite Sourah or to the rhythm and beauty of the poem he is most fond of, "The Death of Corfield" by Sayyid Muhammad 'Habdille Hassan, called the "Mad Mullah" by the British.[5] Cassettes are not too dissimilar to the voices he hears in his dreams, especially that of his dead wife, but they are also material objects: he nearly throws them like stones at Khaalif, the madman—can one lapidate with revered texts? Deeriye has read widely in prison, and the mention of the biographies he remembers echoes again the whole issue of leadership: the lives of the Sudanese Mahdi, Shaka Zulu, Ataturk, Garibaldi or Napoleon. Yet somehow, paradoxically, books are dismissed as sources within the novel, maybe because they were once given to him by his jailers: books like the writings of the Duce or *The Collected*

Wisdom of the General are clearly issued by a similar power.

Cassettes can also be listened to collectively, and listening to them is an action that involves one physically and emotionally as when Deeriye listens again and again to "The Death of Corfield" in the company of his son. The emotion is evoked within the novel for the Somali reader by the extract of eleven lines, untranslated. All readers are reminded by the untranslated extract of the way this poem acts as a fundamental intertext for the whole of *Close Sesame*, by the way it is referred to page after page, each time giving meaning to present day events. The heroic deeds of the Sayyid, his nationalist courage, and the beauty of the text itself act as touchstones to all that occurs in past or present history. It is striking, after *Sweet and Sour Milk* and *Sardines* with their many references to foreign ideologies or intellectual comments—Wilhelm Reich, Ho Chi Minh, Bertolt Brecht—to find that the third book of the trilogy is thus entirely centred on this seminal national text, as if any relevant understanding had to be looked for essentially in Somali values.

As a touchstone, this poem gives rise to a whole series of parallels between past and present events. The most important is established by the old man who listens alternatively to the Holy Book and the poem, historical Islam and Somali nationalism being to him the two solid stones on which to found the judgement of current events. The story of the "Mad Mullah" and the Sourah of Yassin help him to ponder on the general theme of madness: does history consider as mad the heroes who succeed? Or again, if the Sayyid had no known tomb, that of the Sudanese Mahdi was desecrated by the British. The Sayyid is compared in talks with children to Ataturk, "a good man for Turkey, definitely the Kurd's greatest foe indubitably, but a defiant Muslim" (p.145) or to Cabdunnaasir, or to Shaka Zulu, "a great warrior nationalist, another Sayidd." Through this device, the history of the Somali people is placed firmly alongside the history of Islamic countries and of the whole African continent. Non-African references, important in the previous books, would seem irrelevant here.

The life of the Sayyid provides parallels to and comments on daily events within the present of the plot, for instance when traitors are mentioned:

> After a brief pause, he spoke and touched on aspects
> of betrayal and spoke of known historical precedents
> already documented such as the constabulary Haalo
> who, having sold his gun to the Sayyid for four camels
> reported to his British masters that the Sayyid had
> "stolen his rifle." (p.80)

When Deeriye is invited to meet the "clan's peace makers", he interprets the summons thus: "Do you remember the historical trial of the elders and clan leaders the Sayyid was invited to in 1897?...I am on trial by a tribal council for my ideological stand vis-a-vis state power" (p.134). Other parallels are drawn when the whole issue of madness is raised by Khaalif, the mad man, and his rantings in the streets: is he inspired in his raving accusations like the "Mad Mullah" was? The acts of Mursal and his friends Mahad and Mukhtaar are also weighed according to this criterion: is Mahad's action "a premeditated act of madness" like the "courageous charge of the guns of the Somali nationalist dervishes?" (p.76). Yet, the Sayyid's British-termed "madness" was not the lunacy of a man alone. Mukhtaar's act, if it was mad, is not in the Sayyid's tradition: "Which means that Mukhtaar had crossed the frontier Khaalif had crossed before him, a frontier Deeriye hadn't gone beyond, or the Sayyid or Wiil-Waal, for that matter" (p.109).

This last example is typical, in the way it blends history and fictional characters, adding verisimilitude and a sense of urgency to the debate. Again it shows the exploratory nature of the whole text: from the same premises, young men feel justified to resort to violence, sane or mad, whereas Deeriye to the last finds his strength in connecting the Sayyid with resistance, but a resistance which is not necessarily a shedding of blood. In the same way as his stand against Italians was marked by a refusal to betray a name, the great men he quotes include different approaches to nationalist integrity, and it is significant that the last one on the wide-ranging list should be Gandhi, next to the Sayyid: "all great men—Shaka Zulu, Ataturk, Nkrumah, Cabral, Garibaldi, Lenin, Cabdunnaasir, Gandhi, the Sayyid—have one thing in common: the shaping force of their lives has been resistance" (p.147).

As we have seen, if the history of Somalia is essential to the novel, it is presented in a very complex manner, lit from many different angles. We may examine briefly what function is fulfilled by this blending of national figures and fictitious characters, of truth and verisimilitude.

The most obvious effect is to make the history of the Somali people better known to the English-reading public, in Africa and elsewhere, who had read Farah's previous novels. After the original assertion of the dignity and richness of their culture African or North African writers have in similar ways written novels referring to precolonial history—the Ghanaian Armah, the Moroccan Driss Chraibi, for instance. The present, even in fiction, can only be understood if one takes into account years and centuries gone by, contrary to the view imposed by all conquering powers who called Africa, after Pliny, "a continent without history." Not only are the facts mentioned but also the way in which history is perceived by the people and, to an extent, fashions their lives. As we have seen, mention is made not only of the scholarly reporting of facts, as in the erudite books mentioned in the postface, but also in the well-known texts that belong to oral culture: tales, epic narrative, verse by famous poets. History is thus shown to be not just the prerogative of specialists, confined within the pages of serious books, but as the fruit of a collective effort at memorizing, commenting, choosing what is to be remembered and what is to be forgotten in genealogies, past conflicts and heroic deeds.

The history of the Somali people is here placed fully on the literary map: the references surely mean more to those already acquainted with the tradition, yet they are clear enough for readers of any origin who can grasp the plot and the issues at stake, without having the feeling that they are being taught by the "novelist as teacher." The book makes a point of dealing with Somali issues with references to Somali values and history, yet some comparisons are established with the world at large: the persecutions of the Jews or the founding of the ANC are mentioned; Deeriye has memories of a trip to New York. A nationalist stance does not preclude an attempt at understanding current events in a worldwide context.

Close Sesame is not, however, a " historical novel" in the way there are "ethnological novels" in Africa. History is questioned for the answers it may give for the present. Underlining all the book, as with the other works of the trilogy, is the certainty that there is a meaning in human lives which has to be deciphered. History here is not an absurd sequence of chance occurrences, nor a determined concentration of cause and effect which would render moral decisions irrelevant. The novel underlines the idea that there is a latent pattern to history by pointing repeatedly at coincidences, parallels, echoes, facts that through decades seem to refer to one another. One may feel at times that the writer, playing the part of the Omnipotent Creator, accumulates too many coincidences. The year 1912 seems already symbolic with the birth of Sayyidism and pan-Africanism; he chooses it as the birth-date of his hero. In this way an allegorical mode is established, as with the birth of the *Midnight's Children* on the night of independence. But the many echoes and similarities between past and present events (pp.61,63,146) express something which Farah also has in common with Rushdie: the Indian writer explains that among his people there is a "lust for meaning," a "lust for allegory." When he looks for recurrences in real events, or twists the known facts a little, mixes them with imaginary incidents, he is not apologetic for this authorial freedom: "everything has shape, if you look for it. There is no escape from form."

Farah also wants the reader to start looking for pattern in the fiction which is both image and representation of the real historical world: there is meaning for those who try hard to make sense of fragmented experience, especially by interpreting cycles and situations which are repeated across the years. In a way, in this search for meaning, past and present are coexistent. The quest for knowledge or even revelation of the old man is like that of the blind man with his stick in the last tale, who tries to understand both the world made by the creator and the mound of earth made by the minute *aboor* insect. The novel itself is such a groping quest, as described also in *Sardines*:

> The earth's surface is read like a book in braille: the stick sees a small hole in the ground; the hole obstructs the slick's movement upwards or downwards, as irritating as the grit in Medina's rice, which her tongue busily sorts from the grains, Medina whose eyed tongue, flat against the floor or the wall of her mouth, sees, tastes, takes its time as it travels up and down the blind molars. The stick of the blind man sees...(p. 150)

At times the narrator paradoxically marvels at coincidences which are of his own making, as when he ponders on the very apt meanings of the names of Mursal's friends, but this trick is not too conspicuous, and reminds one of the determining role played, after all, by the names chosen at birth by one's parents. If the writer seems to mimic in his fiction the power of the Creator, allotting names and destinies to the creatures of his brain, he is also in the text, humbly, the blind man of the fable, or possibly even the lonely madman, or the isolated detainee who names the world to attempt understanding and just to keep sane: "The very old and the very small: they keep sane by constantly naming the objects and things they come into contact with lest they lose touch with the reality they know" (p.116). The protagonist, at times, seems to stand for the writer himself, "displaced" for many years when he states:

> "Did I ever tell you why I conjure up interlocutors, why I have visions, why it is that I invent histories, why I try

to create symbolic links between unrelated historical events, why it is that I speak to your mother in my sleep...did I ever bother to explain myself?"..."To speak of that about which others are silent and to remain sane at the same time is a very difficult task." (p.200)

Close Sesame can thus be said to dramatize a cognitive quest, an old man' s attempt at reading the world. Yet this quest is not a gratuitous, dispassionate, philosophical exercise. On the contrary, the book imparts the feeling of the urgency of this understanding. Page after page, people have to make dramatic choices; they suffer, they love: "We are not only ourselves, we are others too, those whom we love, those who have influenced our lives, who have made us what we are" (p.202). They are goaded by this sense of their interdependence. Their collective future is at stake in each decision made, and that is why an understanding of history is so essential to read the present. The tension is made all the more acute as the past seems so easy to analyse, so clearcut in the certitudes given by epic or heroic tales, so conveniently labelled in retrospect (p. 117), whereas the present is confused, painful. The issues are not clear, and yet one has to act: "Is there no avoiding that one should belong in one camp or another? Is there no avoiding belonging on the inside or outside of this camp?" (p. 167).

One of the merits of the novel is to make one feel how a reference to history, far from being an imaginary escape into the more tolerable past, is part of the life and blood of men confronted daily with difficult and urgent choices. History, in such a novel steeped in emotion, is made flesh, and its understanding is shown to be a task in which all members of society are involved—elders, but also young men, women, children even.

The feeling of urgency in other situations has led novelists to a more and more militant tone. When Ngugi wa Thiong'o describes the history of Kenya in *Petals of Blood*, to an extent he preaches from the pulpit at his Kenyan readers; there is only one way to interpret the events he narrates, and, possibly, one type of action expected. Here a space is created for the reader to analyse and decide by the function the central character plays in the novel: Deeriye is a positive centre, yet he is not the only holder of truth in the book, no mere "spokesman" for the writer. The focus on his inner life helps us to sympathize and identify with him to an extent, but what we can infer from the facts and issues, as seen by other characters or evoked by the narrative voice, adds other dimensions, and leaves us free to reconstruct our own judgement on history. Some values which are essential to Islamic faith and Somali culture, as exemplified in the Koran and in traditional poetry, are stressed many times. But these fundamental criteria—faith, honour, love of family and friends—do not provide easy answers. Deeriye is a complex character. In all the serenity of his faith, he is tortured:

> "Is it the prerogative of God alone to be sure of anything?" "No doubt, no doubt," she said, unwilling to get carried away again.
> "I am only a human. And therefore I am in doubt," he said. (p.202)

He is anguished by the feeling of what he still cannot see clearly, even in history:

> "My life is landmarked by absences I cannot account for: naps, daydreams; and just before the seizures, there are the few seconds during which I cross into a world whose logic is unknown to any living soul. How else can I describe the hole in my memory tonight?" (p.116)

The uncertainty about the cause and meaning of his death at the end does not let us know if his prayer has been answered:

> Help us cope with our weaknesses, show Yourself to

us every now and then, forgive us if, when feverish, we conjure up nebulous visions: when these cause us some disquiet, when these cause disturbances in our minds and lead us astray, help us, O God. The ways of the soul are mysterious and so are Yours. Make us wiser, make us understand, O God, the contradictions in which we find ourselves. (p.165)

In its treatment of history, *Close Sesame* is committed, but not didactic. The novel gives us too much a sense of the complexity of human interaction for that. Farah, in thirteen-year exile at the time of writing, addresses his people, clearly stressing the need for reflection and action. Yet the book, with its direct historical references, far from being a pamphlet, is more a meditation on time and history. The subject is Somalia, but the scope of the book can be extended to the whole of postcolonial Africa. It can be read also, more generally, as a dramatization of human consciousness of the past and of time fleeing. The subject is very ambitious, but in presenting a protagonist who was a national hero and is a mystic, the book presents us both with a sense of eternity as felt in repeated moments of prayers, and of the sequences of human conflicts and achievements. Some of the best passages, blending the awareness of the minutiae of daily life with the feeling that there is an overall meaning to human endeavour, as with the *aboor* "constructing an ant-hill with her own saliva after nightfall," are passages of poetry, close to the poetical vision and rhythm of the great oral intertexts:

Time was also the abyss with the open door; it was human for it had hands: one for seconds to give the minute and another for minutes to tell the hour, fingers praying deferentially to the God who created the hands that are in motion, like a clock's, losing; gaining time; eyes of quartz in the darkness of a room; ears of ticking time, adding a second only to take the same

416

from the life of those who have experienced it, who have lived through it. Time was also the rest of sleep, a cat-nap, the night-cap, the uncounted heads of cattle chewing the cud in peace and quiet, the prayerless screams, the absent father-husband and the loved wife...Time was history: and history consisted of these illuminated prints—not truths...(p.86)

NOTES

1. On the history of Somalia, see I. M. Lewis, *A Modern History of Somalia*, 1965 (London: Longman, 1980).

2. On the use of modern allegory in new literatures in English, see: Stephen Slemon, "Revisioning Allegory: Wilson Harris's *Carnival*," *Kunapipi* 8, 2 (1986), 445-55.

3. One may compare this narrative technique with that of *The Stone Angel* by Margaret Laurence, the Canadian writer who played a role in Farah's life and writing in connection with her stay in Somalia.

4. The name in Somali means "conciliator, he that opens the road to peace."

5. Sayyid Muhammad 'Abdille Hassan was at the head of the twenty years Dervish struggle against the British, Ethiopian and Italian colonizers. A political, military leader, he was also a theologian and poet and left a body of oral poetry which is still well-known and recited today in Somalia. For the poem "The Death of Richard Corfield," a "savagely brilliant poem" (Lewis) celebrating a victory over the British, see the full text and translation, along with other poems in B.W.Andrzejewski and I. M. Lewis, *Somali Poetry* (Oxford: Clarendon Press, 1964).

Page references to Nuruddin Farah's *Close Sesame* are to the Allison & Busby edition (London, 1983).

MYSTERY AND MADNESS IN
CLOSE SESAME
Claudio Gorlier

C *lose Sesame*[1] is the third volume in a trilogy which began with *Sweet and Sour Milk* (1979) and was followed by *Sardines* (1981). It is probably Nuruddin Farah's most complex and highly structured work, one that obliges the reader to employ more than one hermeneutical framework if s/he wishes to avoid being led into an erroneous, simplistic reading that the deployment of a single interpretative strategy would inevitably produce. We may embark on our critical journey with this preliminary remark, even though a master code is offered by the general title of the trilogy: *Variation on the Theme of an African Dictatorship.*

This establishes a primary interpretative structure that must be employed in decoding the novel, one which involves the domains of politics and history. Farah, the Somali, tackles a phenomenon which is anything but rare in the postcolonial African landscape, namely the emergence of a tyrannical regime which usurps authority, brutally stamps out all dissent, and maintains power through the use of ruthless repression. To name a few other significant examples in the literary field: the Kenyan writer Ngugi wa Thiong'o, and, in particular, *Petals of Blood; Anthills of the Savannah* by the Nigerian writer Chinua Achebe; *The Voice,* by Achebe's compatriot Gabriel Okara; and *This Earth, My Brother*...by the Ghanaian Kofi Awonoor. The emphasis placed on the adjective African which qualifies the word dictatorship is by no means accidental. This emerges with great force from chapter eight of *Close Sesame*, which contains one of the novel's sustained ideological debates. In conversational exchange of views with his father, Deeriye's son argues that the only difference between Italian domination and the present dictatorship—if there is one—is that the former is a foreign, colonial power while the latter is a local, neo-colonial power. The old man strenuously corrects the younger one, claiming that when one is dealing with an external, colonial power, one is able to establish the identity of the enemy with great precision, whereas when the enemy is internal, as is the case with a national dictatorship, then he is like a slippery eel which cannot be pinned down, like a malignant tumour which attacks suddenly and unexpectedly, from unknown quarters, spreading like wildfire.

The three books of the trilogy are set during the first stage of Siyad Barre's dictatorship—"the General" in the novels—when the political referent at an international level was the then Soviet Union and the so-called countries of "Real Socialism." These countries provided Barre with economic and military support, as well as with advisors who were present in the country. One of the central characters of *Sardines,* Medina, professes radical principles, and judges the Barre regime to be essentially Fascist, which is not surprising since the President had received his training from the Italian colonialist troops. On the other hand, Medina denounces the Western matrix of Marxist-Leninist ideology as being foreign to the country, adopting a stance which is very close to that of another African writer, the Ghanaian Ayi Kwei Armah, who, in an essay of fundamental importance, "Masks and Marx," not only denies that Marxism may be applied to Africa, but even accuses it of being a racist doctrine, given its Western roots. Later, when Ethiopia under Menghistu entered the

420

Soviet sphere of influence, Barre nonchalantly reversed his political position and moved under the Western and "democratic" sphere of influence without making even the slightest changes to the iron structures of his regime.

Close Sesame follows on from the first two novels. The ninth chapter reintroduces, by reference, some of the earlier characters: Koschin, Soyaan and Loyaan, Samater and Medina, and Ibrahim (called Il Siciliano—the Sicilian—in the text). One distinguishing feature of the novel, however, is that the temporal dimension is dilated, so that it delves deeper into the past. The events recounted in *Sweet and Sour Milk* and in *Sardines* are centered on the present and the past is introduced as part of historical memory. Meanwhile, in *Close Sesame*, the past takes on flesh and blood, in the form of the novel's protagonist, the patriarch Deeriye, born in 1912, imprisoned by the Italians, and later discriminated against by the British because of his Somali nationalist views. History and memory coincide in this character. This enables the writer, who has no first hand experience of Fascist colonialism because he was born in 1945, to establish a perspective. Indeed, this perspective is generational, for the book recounts the doings of Deeriye's children and grandchildren, as well as his own. As if this were not enough, it is Deeriye, with his decisive presence, his words, his behavior, and his own tragic destiny, who determines the different levels of reading in a book which is both mysterious ("mystery," "mysterious," "inexplicable" are key words in *Close Sesame*) and whose crucial moments are deliberately impossible to decipher. The profound and intriguing originality of this novel, its unique dimension, lies in the extraordinary interdependence that exists between action and speculation, imagination and the debate of ideas, and between phenomena and mystery, reason and madness. If, as has been correctly noted by more than one scholar, African literature is characterised by this dimension of interface, that is, by the "encounter" of two cultures—hegemonic or subaltern, or at least multiple—which both meet and come into conflict, then *Close Sesame* offers incontrovertible evidence of the point no less than

421

does Frederic Jameson's theory concerning socio-symbolism and the permanent, fixed relationship between private history and public event, which, in contrast, are often inexorably divided in the contemporary Western novel.

This gives rise to a whole series of paradoxes. Deeriye is not only a man of the past generation; he is also the representative of tradition, even though he is anything but averse to change, and is hostile to the persisting and deeply rooted tribal divisions in his country. From childhood he learned to venerate the charismatic figure of the Sayyid, the legendary Mohammed Abdullah Hassan, a national hero, a symbol of independence, and a poet, who died ten years after Deeriye's birth. We know he was devoted to the Sayyid, whom he took as a model both because he was a proud supporter of Somali independence, hunted in vain by the British for years, and because of the importance his hero attributed to the creation, to the world. Here another aspect of the interface emerges, that is to say the essential function of orality, the relationship between the oral and written modes, which constitutes one of the basic structures of the novel. According to his biographers, the Sayyid, the legendary hero, had recourse to the word as a weapon, using it to hearten his companions and to strike fear into the hearts of his enemies. Thus, at the very beginning of *Close Sesame*, the discussion of the *lex talionis* and, subsequently, of the legitimacy of the use of violence may be traced back to the Sayyid and to Deeriye's religious background, centered on the study and reverence of the Koran. He believes in the word as truth, as logos and not simply as communication, while he rejects violence and rebellion. The Italians arrested him not because he had taken part in the armed resistance, but because he had refused to betray friends who belonged to the movement; the importance of the point is underscored by the fact that the resistance did have traitors among its number, such as the detestable and detested Haji Homer.

It is no coincidence that Deeriye's other important model also belongs to the oral tradition, and is enshrined in the roll of national legends in the figure of an absolute monarch. But in contrast to the

General's, his is a wise and well-balanced personality. The figure is that of Wiil Waal, who lived around the sixteenth century and who gave life to a whole series of popular tales, two of which are recounted by Deeriye to his grandson Samawade. In these tales, too, the literary component—which is firmly entrenched in the oral tradition—and the political, or rather institutional, component are intertwined, leading us back, as does Farah's apt title, to the novel's supreme referent and primeval, inexhaustible fountainhead, *The Arabian Nights.* It should be noted, from the outset of the novel, to what extent historical-legendary memory, in the shape of the Caliph's memories, unrolls the carpet of a continuous stream of ideas, in evocative conversation, employing the Chinese boxes technique which is characteristic of *The Arabian Nights.* Zeinab's daughter, to underline the point, is called Sheherazade. Such a structure substantiates the pressing flurry, the "flash of vision, as though in a pocket of memories" in the Epilogue, which culminates in an emblematic phrase—"The mad discourse of the sane" (p.204).

The discussion about the Caliph leads into another crucial question: Is the Somali dictatorship invested with legitimacy by the Islamic religion? Does it have roots in Somali thought? The question obviously fills Deeriye with anxiety and distress: here lies the origins of his worry and his fear, a condition which is exasperated by his rejection of violence and his doubts about clandestine organisations whose aim is the violent overthrow of the regime itself. Nevertheless, we should remember that Farah had already drawn attention, in *Sardines,* to the lack of a tradition of popular protest movements, of organised trade unions in Somalia, in contrast to Egypt, Ethiopia and Sudan.

In the main, the generational conflict revolves around these themes. Of course, Deeriye's son, Mursal, never renounces his Islamic matrix, and his Ph.D. dissertation is on the relationship between the Koran and the political structure of the state; the rebels base their actions on the Koran. But the old patriarch has no desire and no intention of following the young rebels along the road of armed violence; in addition, his is the wisdom of popular culture, of tradition, which is largely oral, while his two children are part of an intellectual elite which is now the product of a university education: his daughter has a degree in medicine, and Mursal has gone one better, inasmuch as he now teaches at university. It thus happens that Deeriye feels the need to redefine the perspective of time in his relationship with his children, even to the point of re-thinking the tense system of the language; his temporal universe risks being deconstructed as much as other fundamental and irreplaceable aspects of life, such as social reality, public relations, and family relationships.

At this point in *Close Sesame* madness acquires a very special relevance. The reader is induced to reflect, from a Western viewpoint, on the question of folly, and of the mental asylum as a prison; on the basis of socio-psychoanalytic theories from Szasz to Foucault; on madness as an Orwellian classification of dissent; or, retracing steps back to antecedents, on Poe's work or George Eliot's *Middlemarch,* where the intruder in the community, the person who does not conform to society's norms, is branded as mad. This parallel is legitimated by the grotesquely ironic episode in which the General has the director of a mental asylum interned as a madman in his own institution because the latter is guilty of declaring a "political" internee to be of sound mind. But such behaviour—recent evidence of which has been gathered, for example, in Kenya—is in actual fact only one aspect of reality in these countries. In this specific case, the General employs imported methods, for elsewhere Farah informs us that the mental clinics in Somalia employ "experts" from eastern Germany. There are echoes of these trends in some episodes of *This Earth, My Brother...,*and even more markedly in *The Voice,* where the protagonist clashes with the power of the Elders as a result of his quest after truth, and is first branded as mad and then put to death.

The emblems and manifestations of madness in *Close Sesame* are open to diverse reading strategies. One master reading is the specular interchange between mystery and reality, the latter often being hidden and unfathomable. Khaliif is, or should be, mad, since he walks the streets at night with his face painted half white and half

424

black, a "wonderful" mystery since no one really knows whether this respectable ex-government official, who has perhaps already received psychiatric treatment after disturbances which developed mysteriously, is mad or not. Whether he be sane or insane, Khaliif takes on internal value as an instance of mediated oral narration. Mogadishu is populated by madmen whose condition is an expression of fear, perhaps, and of insecurity, or of mysterious revelations; madness borders on magic, for the expressions of madness, both in word and in song, may also be expressions of magic. In its perturbing concreteness, Muhktaar's madness is emblematic of a lack of harmony, of the fragmentation caused by the regime, the consequences of which may be visited upon the population and live on in individuals in a strange symbiosis until their tragic physical death. This is the case with Mahad. Zeinab speaks of collective madness, but Mursal describes Khaliif's case as one of individual insanity. Indeed, after Deeriye makes his confession concerning the strange "absences" which he suffers from, Mursal goes to the root of the problem, in pinpointing madness as stemming from disjointed values and confused behavior. Escape from madness is obtained though naming objects. Nevertheless, this strategy also requires the maintenance of a solid relationship between the word, thought and factual reality. This is a characteristic of the young people in the novel, and becomes particularly significant when compared to the absences of Deeriye, who is losing his grip on reality or the ability to comprehend reality. The British defined the Sayyid as being mad; if Mahad had realised his plans, he would have been a hero, not a madman. The rift between generations could hardly be more marked, in the sense that, at bottom, Deeriye considers madness as organised revolt, the attempt to overthrow the regime through the use of violence—collective madness, of which his son is an active part.

The close relationship between mystery and madness reaches a climax in the final pages of the novel, after Mursal's disappearance and the knowledge that he has been killed by the General's police. Here the two components become one and are channelled through

Deeriye's mind, his memory, his dreams about his wife and his neighbor's illegitimate son Yassin who perversely throws stones at him. There is here a symmetry and specularity which send the reader back to the third chapter, with its discussion of the symbolic and religious significance of the stone, of Satan or *rajiim* whom stones are thrown at, and of madmen—that is, saints—who are stoned by boys who have not yet reached maturity.

Nobody would throw stones at a dog in New York, or at a sheep dog in Somalia. They would at a mongrel whom they were afraid of, and which would fight for its life. But the Wailing Wall, the Kaaba, are stones. And Khaliif, who asks the provocative question about who is mad and who isn't, is, to tell the truth, the saint. His discourse may be taken as being suffused with the holiness of the Sufi Islamic mystique. Thus, after Mursal's disappearance, his father's mind brims over with questions, sudden illuminations, associations, unravelled mysteries, and all this is permeated by the extreme irony that everybody carries the divine message, but no-one is aware of the fact. But at that moment revelation is at hand: while everyone is waiting for the General, Khaliif appears in full uniform, solemn and stiff. What is the truth? Is Khaliif the general, whom a delegation of madmen move off to meet?

Mystery thus finds its ultimate seal. In *Sweet and Sour Milk* and in *Sardines,* the disappearance of the regime's opponents had already been a mystery. The same is true for Mursal. Deeriye's final gesture is ironically mysterious, incomprehensible, and thus open to different readings. Does he really intend to kill the General and do the beads of his rosary prevent him from doing so? Does he simply wish to bear witness through the sign of a talisman, that he is repudiating violence once more? Does he wish to carry out a sacrificial act, a gesture? We will never know, nor, if we think about the matter carefully, does it really matter whether we do. The ironic paradox comes to a close, as had happened with Soyaan in *Sweet and Sour Milk,* with an extreme form of mystification, when the victim of the despot was honored as a national hero. Deeriye is left wearing the medal, but

426

Zeinab provides an accurate portrayal of her father's heroism. Over and beyond the mystery, his heroism derives from his faith and precipitates at least one death that is not anonymous (another component of heroism). But all the heroes have been defeated, Sesame closes, and it is left to the narrative voice to recount the story and keep hope alive, provided that—and here another unanswered question is set—it is capable of transcending individual destiny, generation after generation. In this sense, *Close Sesame* is neither wholly a political novel nor wholly a historical novel.

Another aspect of the interface has yet to be considered. One of the book's novelties, when it is placed beside Farah's preceding works, is the presence of an Other, an outsider who is extraneous to the Somali context. Mursal has, in fact, married an American Jewess, Natasha. Her presence enforces a confrontation with a different culture, a different standpoint, and gives substance to as well as substantiating one of Farah's persistent practices in his work—interlanguage. In normal circumstances, Farah's English is modulated by ingenious verbal inventions, intertextual play, illuminating metaphors and semantic games. But he often has recourse to Italian, without ever furnishing a translation; and he implants it into the English texture of his discourse. In the case of Natasha, interlanguage duplicates the operation of the interface: in order to communicate, neither father nor daughter-in-law speak a language which is their own. This language thus represents a meeting ground, and Italian is the language that serves this function. Deeriye's learning of the language during incarceration, as a prisoner of the colonialists, deepens his paradoxical dimension. Italian, the language of communication in Somalia where the national language affirmed its existence late, surfaces every so often in Farah's novels, no less than the mediated presence of Italy or of the relationship which still exists between the two countries, so much so that many of his characters go to Italy to carry out their studies. In *Sardines,* the 1968 student revolution in Milan is observed through Somali eyes. The presumptuous arrogance and peremptory judgements of Sandra when she visits her friends in Somalia express what on the surface appears to be a revolutionary stance but which is actually a version of colonialism that has changed only its outer dress, not its substance.

The Somali intellectual must face his problems by himself, and must try to solve them, paying a price which, in his case, is exorbitantly, if not desperately, high. But Farah's narrative line constantly underlines this presupposition from his very first books, *From a Crooked Rib* and *A Naked Needle,* whether he is attempting to break the back of a ruthlessly authoritarian regime or describing, with unusual subtlety, the effort of woman to free herself from centuries of serfdom. Here, one might fruitfully add, Farah demonstrates exceptional skill in creating female characters. As has been noted by other scholars, *Close Sesame* seems to be directed not only at the generation gap, but also at young people themselves. Deeriye's privileged interlocutor is beyond a shadow of doubt his grandson, and the old man's message is entrusted ideally to him, because he is so young, so different, and yet, despite this, an idealist. We are not just ourselves, warns Deeriye: we are everyone else too. Only God is certain of everything and everybody. The prerogative, the bitter though conscious privilege of those mortals, those heroes who inhabit Farah's novels, is to be sought in the continuous, experienced and suffered practice of doubt.

Translated from the Italian by John Douthwaite.

NOTES

1. Nuruddin Farah, *Close Sesame* (London: Allison & Busby, 1983). Page references are to this edition.

PART FIVE
THE SECOND TRILOGY: Maps; Gifts; Secrets

SELF AND IDENTITY IN THE *BLOOD IN THE SUN* TRILOGY

Guillaume Cingal

In the Epilogue to his most recent book, *Yesterday, Tomorrow*, a non-fiction that stands generically in between essay and *témoignage* literature, Nuruddin Farah insists upon self-centredness as an obstacle to individual progress. He goes as far as contending that most Somalis are prevented from taking a turn for the better in exile not only because of their status as refugees or asylum-seekers (which is described as alienating throughout the book) but also because of what he calls "blamocracy," i.e. their natural tendency to blame others for everything that happens to them:

> Being blamocrats par excellence, Somalis do not place themselves, as individuals, in the geography of the collective collapse, but outside of it. It is as if they did not inhabit the territory in which the disaster occurred, many ascribing the collapse to Siyad's dictatorship, or more recently to the warlords and their politics. The collapse in and of itself, some of them explain, was a

consequence of an inherent failure of the nature of the post-colonial state, to which the idea of democracy was anathema. But the generality of them attribute the failure to the workings of a clan structure. In short, the self is not to blame.[1]

He also insists on the fact that collective (clannish) identity is a convenient means of keeping the self pure and untainted:

> The generic references to their clan identities serving as mere markers, many of the self-identifiers are intent on subsuming their individual identities in the larger unit, thereby not sharing in the censure. Implicit in the idea is that the self is not to blame, but that civil society is![2]

In that respect, the self serves as a form of hidden identity, one that is not claimed or advocated, in order to remain irreproachable. This is a form of escapism, as the Somalis here described are intent on avoiding their fair share of the blame: in other words, they refuse to act as responsible adults. Hence, to question one's own self is the best solution if one does not want to become a blamocrat. It may well be a privileged method to define one's own identity without depending too much on collective definitions, which are seen here as restrictive or even irrelevant.

Nuruddin Farah's second trilogy, *Blood in the Sun*, tackles the twin notions of self and identity in a very elaborate way, as each of the three novels pays attention to different aspects of the conflict that divides individual identities and collective definitions of identity. In *Maps*, for instance, Askar rejects his foster-mother's "cosmos" in order to identify with abstractions. The process of identification is seen as a direct consequence of Askar's circumcision, which reinforces the idea that the fusion (not to say the confusion) of the self with a larger unit, namely the nation, has to do with rejecting the mother-figure and the female cosmos to which Askar belonged. As such, assuming an identity which is no longer individual is synonymous with rejecting previous self-definitions:

> In a month or so, especially now that his manhood was ringed with a healed circle, the orgies of self-questioning, which were his wont, gave way to a state in which he identified himself with the community at large. And he partook of the ecstasy of madness that struck the town of Kallafo, an ecstasy that expressed itself in a total self-abandon never known, never experienced in the history of the Somalis of the area. The war was on...Who knows, he thought, he could become, at such a tender age, the movement's flag-bearer; who knows, the Ethiopians might forcefully conscript him if the Somalis lost the war; who knows!
>
> What mattered, he told himself, was that now he was at last a man, that he was totally detached from his mother-figure Misra, and weaned. In the process of looking for a substitute, he had found another— Somalia, his mother country.[3]

Two contradictory features stand out in this passage: Askar's identification with the nation and with Somalia's war against Ethiopia in the Ogaden results in a tendency to "total self-abandon"; and yet, this identification "with the community at large" coincides with Askar's indulging in wild dreams about his future, thus pointing at self-assertion of the strongest kind. "Self-abandon" is a mere pretence. Indeed, the rest of the chapter shows clearly that what is at stake in this process of identification is Askar's own definition of individual identity. Askar is more than ever imbued with his own plight. His desire to become "the movement's flag-bearer" makes it obvious that his biography is what matters most. Replacing Misra by Somalia is a self-centred abstraction, not one that *actually* results in "self-abandon." In fact, circumcision has helped Askar build a new set of references, including the belief that he is "at last a man." In that respect, identification with notions originally alien to individual iden- tity reinforces individual identity by making it more abstract. The word "ecstasy" points to the fact that Askar does not indulge in a questioning of the self any more. He thinks he has finally managed to stand (ec-statically) outside his own self, which is perhaps the most hazardous fiction there can be. By imagining that he is no longer con- cerned with self-questioning, Askar becomes even more dangerously self-serving.

Self-questioning has been replaced by one-way answers that are as subjective as the questioning proper used to be, though they seem to be objective. When Askar decides to re-draw the map of Somalia on his own skin, he is utterly convinced that he has reached "self- abandon," but he is unable to disregard the self as a means of expres- sion. When all is said and done, his body is the only reference he can adjust to:

> He was adrift (and so was the Somali nation every-
> where) on a tide of total abandon. At least, he kept
> thinking to himself, staring at the map on the wall,
> there would be changes in the cartographer's view of
> the Horn of Africa. And so, with his felt-pen, using his
> own body, he re-drew the map of the Somali-speaking
> territories, copied it curve by curve, depression by
> depression. Which reminded him of his father's nick-
> name: Xamari. At last, he would be reunited with the
> city of Xamar from whence came his father's nick-
> name. (*M*, p. 97)

As any narcissistic person will do, Askar mistakes his own body for an objective reference, thus indulging in his own image while think- ing he faces reality and the world-at-large. He even goes as far as using his body as a means of representation. It is obvious that he has replaced Misra not by Somalia but by himself, thus having no other perspective but himself. It is fairly ironical that he should refer to his father with the sole mention of a nickname, i.e. a surface-signifier that points at a fully symbolical identity. His father is a pure geographical abstraction and has no body of his own; he is not so much a biological father as the abstract figure-head of the Somali capital.

Collective definitions of identity are rejected by less neurotic, more mature characters, such as Nonno:

> "I can't bear the thought of generalizing. I am a person, a clan is a mob. Talk to me, sell things to me, I am reasonable. Clans are not." I wish many of the fighters visiting havoc on people's lives had been born with the luck to hear him. "If we had many like him, there would be no civil strife," Talaado said earlier that day.[4]

As both Kalaman's and his wife-to-be Talaado's comments show, Nonno's viewpoint is in sharp contrast with Askar's phantasmic identification with the father's name, i.e. with lineage. If probing deeper into intratextuality is deemed necessary, Askar's own progress from Misra's cosmos to his problematic self-definition as a Somali 'warrior' can be said to be reflected in Nonno's analysis as regards one tragic and yet possible outcome for his grandson's identity quest:

> "As an animal with a high sense of taboo, will you be upset if you learn that you are somebody else's child, not Yaqut's? Will doubts shatter your certainties? What will become of your relationships with us, your kith and kin all your life? Will you kill me or your father if it turns out that your family is at war with ours, in the current struggle for political power?" (*S*, p. 203)

What Kalaman actually faces at the end of the novel is the choice between identifying with an abstract (though founded on biology) allegiance to lineage, on the one hand, and sticking together with the family "life" imposed upon him on the other. As is clear later in the novel, his choice runs counter to Askar's and he does not take part in the collective bloodshed.

In Askar's case, the trend towards abstraction has its origins in the very nature of self-questioning. The fact is that he does not so much question his origins as try to justify his situation at the age of eighteen, hence the completely retrospective structure of the novel: Askar does not go "backward and forward in time" (*M*, 138), as he pretends to do; instead, he prefers to indulge in recollections of the past. Time structures are clearly different in *Gifts* and *Secrets*. In *Secrets*, thirty-three year-old Kalaman only investigates his origins in order to settle accounts and to move onwards to what seems, at the end of the novel, a promising existence. As the discussion with his mother at the end of chapter 11 indicates, Kalaman takes both the past and the future into account, thus defining his own identity in dynamic terms:

> "You remember how often you pestered us with your gimme-a-sibling plea," she said. "Well, it wasn't for lack of trying, it wasn't."
>
> Now we hugged. Now we kissed. "I have a triad of unshaken loyalties," she said, "you and Yaqut and Nonno, and I imagine my faith in these three allegiances would be all the more solidified if we sealed it with a sacred trust—the fact that Yaqut and I have never married, and aren't planning to. The sacred trust of a family secret."
>
> In the silence that came after this, a disjointed body of ideas entered my mind. I felt cold to the bone, then was warm as the blood circulating in my veins of my self-doubt. I surprised even myself as I said: "I suppose

> it is high time I married Talaado and gave you a grand-
> child, and made Yaqut *another* Nonno!" (*S*, p. 265)

Kalaman clearly moves on from his childish plea, in which he wanted to be given a brother or sister, to the mature decision of giving his parents a grandchild. He also makes up for his parents' sterility as a couple. Whether Yaqut, who is not Kalaman's biological father, was unable to have children, or whether Damac became sterile as a result of the gang rape, the move is at the same time retrospective and prospective: Kalaman decides both to have a child and to confirm Yaqut as his father. He conceives his identity both in terms of what he can achieve (as a father) but also in terms of whom he depends on (as a son and grandson). The italicization of "another" shows that the double bind, the simultaneously prospective and retrospective invention of identity, is everywhere, linking not only Yaqut and the child to come as grandfather and grandchild, but also Kalaman himself and *his* Nonno. In that respect, the term "Nonno" refers to *actual* rather than biological grandfathers.

In chapter 5, Nonno's narrative insists on the fact that Kalaman has to face this double bind, which proves problematic:

> He was confronted with no easy matters, and was having to reexamine his beginnings. You cannot help entertaining your past as you entertain an unwelcome guest, when you cannot think of a pleasant association with which to celebrate the present. You cannot help wanting to construct the solidity of a future with the female companion of your choice, when the world, in the form of a haunting past, is collapsing around your ears. (*S*, p. 111)

Unlike Askar, who cannot escape the sterile "reexamining" of the past and is thus confined in a monolithic representation of identity, Kalaman will manage to move forward. In an even less dramatic way,

Duniya faces her past only when she is about to have dinner with Bosaaso and tries to imagine what kind of women he might like:

> Somali men are said to be turned on by the mound of flesh round a woman's navel. But what kind of women did Bosaaso like? Did he prefer them slim, young-bodied, with not an extra ounce anywhere? For a woman of her age and background, Duniya knew her body was still in good shape. Surely, she thought, it wasn't a body to turn up one's nose at. It had served her faithfully all these years, giving of itself all it possibly could, and it had known only two men, one of them sixty-odd years old. In the two years she had been Zubair's wife, they could not have made love more than thrice a month...
>
> Her second husband Taariq wanted it nightly...
>
> By leaps of logic she found herself considering the women Bosaaso had known, who might have left indelible influences on him."[5]

In Duniya's mind, identity is a result of past physical experiences, love affairs and sexual intercourse being here foregrounded. Duniya's self-narration focuses on the past in order to determine what "indelible influences" it might have had on present circumstances. Her phantasmic projection into Bosaaso's tastes and personal experiences is synonymous with her desire to interpret what may happen according to what did happen. Self-questioning is here presented in a casual way, in complete contrast with Askar's "indulg[ing] in metaphysical evasions" (*M*, p. 245). Besides, whereas Askar is more or less unable to act in a positive way, introspection enables Duniya to take decisions:

> Duniya's feeling of weightlessness returned directly [when] she was alone, so that she had to lean against the outside door once she opened it. She remained

438

> where she was until her chest rose with her breathing,
> her heart beating faster in anticipation of self-hatred, a
> notion which nauseated her. Or was it love? Whichever
> it was, she wished to have nothing to do with it. Surely
> to be affected by such a nebulous sensation of sickness
> is no love, or is it? Her self-questioning inspired
> courage in her *and she was able to walk through the*
> *entrance*, her gait uncertain, her whole body numbed
> by worry. (*G*, p. 133, emphasis added)

Though she remains in a critical situation, she does not remain on
the threshold. Her highly symbolical state of spatial in-betweenness
only lasts for a few moments, before she manages to pull herself
together. Self-questioning is considered as a necessary but also a necessarily temporary phase. The self is positive only as far as it provides
a transition. The problem with Askar is that his self-questioning
extends to the novel as a whole and engulfs it, thus shadowing and
obliterating everything else. This is what Hilarie Kelly calls Askar's
"agonizing quest for an appropriate identity,"[6] further arguing that
Askar's self-centredness is an obstacle both to a coherent definition of
identity and to a transparent reading of the author's motives:

> Several times during the reading of *Maps*, I found
> myself wanting to throttle the whining, narcissistic
> Askar and shout "Stop dithering and get on with it!
> You're not the most important person in the world."
> I'm not at all convinced this was the reader response
> Nuruddin intended.[7]

Therefore, the shift from passive self-indulgence to active self-
narration is already a step towards a positive, creative definition of
one's own identity. Kalaman's emblematic move from the desire to
"be given" a sibling to his intention of "giving" can be compared with
the very structure of the previous novel: as a matter of fact, the first

439

part of *Gifts* is called "A Story is Born," and the last is called "Duniya Gives," thus showing that Duniya discovers new perspectives through self-narration. Self-absorption on the threshold between yesterday and tomorrow is only momentary and opens onto actual gifts that still imply the self as such: "And suddenly, she knew what she was going to do. 'Tomorrow evening,' she said, 'Duniya will spend the night at Bosaaso's to make of her body a gift to him. Tomorrow evening'" (*G*, p.198).

Identity is thus found through a confrontation in time and space (i.e. through the process of story-telling, of writing, or of addressing one's own experiences) with others. Duniya's classical interpretation of personal pronouns shows not only that identity is inherited from the past, but also that it is a transformative process that depends on the individual's constructive relationship with the community:

> Duniya took note of the flourish of pronouns, some inclusive, some exclusive; pronouns dividing the world into separable segments, which they labelled as such. Apparently, the two of them were *we*, the rest of the world were *they*. Together, when alone with each other, they in turn fragmented themselves into their respective I's. That is to say, they were like two images reflecting a oneness of souls, more like twin ideas united in their pursuit to be separable and linked at the same time. Is this the definition of love? (*G*, p. 148)

Identity becomes possible only when the self is no longer regarded as the sole reference. Askar's tampering with personal pronouns shows that there is no real dividing line that separates him from the others: "He was, at one and the same time, the plaintiff and the juror. Finally, allowing his different personae to act as judge, as audience and as witness, Askar told it to himself" (*M*, p. 246). Askar's self-narration is all-inclusive, which means that what stands *outside* the self is immediately *integrated* into Askar's self-centred investigation, oth-

440

erness being constantly (and perversely) transformed into a mode of the self. As though unable to admit that someone else gave birth to him, he indulges in the well-known Protean fantasy of self-creation:[8] "It feels like yesterday, the day I was born; and it feels as if I were there, as though I were my own midwife" (*M*, p. 24). As a young male unable to cope with sexual difference, he convinces himself that he can menstruate: "I have a strange feeling that there is another in me, one older than I—a woman" (*M*, p. 151).

Self-narration is of the utmost importance, providing that the narrator does not indulge in introspection to the point of forgetting his own existential agenda. As Patricia Alden and Louis Tremaine have well shown, Kalaman "seek[s] out others for information" and "cannot control, as Askar does, the other voices in his story."[9] As a consequence, "the struggle is not only for individual identity and autonomy, but for identity in relationship to others."[10] In fact, if Kalaman cannot control the whole story, it ought to be considered as a positive trend rather than as a drawback: for a character who is aware of his own failures, the dynamic interplay with other, divergent figures is necessary.

Both *Maps* and *Gifts* end with the main protagonist's decision to "tell the story yet again" but Duniya chooses to have an audience, unlike Askar, whose centripetal narrative evades the questions of the real policemen to "tell it to himself" (*M*, p. 246). Whereas the stories built up by Duniya and Kalaman depend on the presence of other characters both as audience and as external viewpoints, Askar's story is completely self-referential. Duniya's point of view at the end of *Gifts* is at the same time self-centred and opened to others:

> Then Duniya smelt Bosaaso's odour, because he had come round to where she was sitting, and they were kissing while the others toasted them again and again. The world was an audience, ready to be given Duniya's story from the beginning. (*G*, p. 242)

Duniya's desire to address *others* and to face a multiplicity of view-points combines self- narration (which is what Askar practises in the paradoxical form of the polyphonic soliloquy) and story-telling proper (which implies the presence of a real audience). As a matter of fact, her story is deprived of meaning if it has no audience:

> She said she wanted to talk, explain all that had happened, including the reason why she hadn't told him all that she suspected she knew about the foundling's identity. It was up to him to trust her or not.
>
> She started the story from the beginning, omitting nothing, arguing that the foundling had become and would remain for her a symbol uniting the two of them. Would their affection survive such self-questioning?
>
> Nature had supplied Bosaaso with an accommodating spirit. He listened attentively, did not speak nor move any part of his body for a long time. Then his nose twitched involuntarily, as if overcome by a musky sexual odour or something as vital, as immediate. 'Will you marry me, Duniya?' he said. (*G*, p. 179)

Self-narration implies a double speech-orientation, as the story is addressed both to the speaking subject and to the listening audience. It also requires a response on the part of the audience, as is the case with Bosaaso's marriage proposal. Though it may seem irrelevant at first, his reply is in keeping with Duniya's final query concerning "their affection." As was the case with Kalaman's decision to marry Talaado, marriage is a symbolical act which prevents relationships between characters from becoming too abstract: Bosaaso does not comment on the foundling's possible status as "a symbol uniting the two of them", to quote Duniya's words, but he moves on to give a more literal meaning to the verb "unite." "Seeking out others" is seen as the open-sesame that enables characters to emancipate sterile definitions of the self and to grow aware of what identity ought to be:

a construct that has its roots in the individual person but cannot subsume differences in a self-centred unit. Dialogue and mutual trust are necessary foundations of a coherent self-questioning identity.

For Kalaman, who cannot, unlike Askar, get on with the dream of biological filiation, there is a strong need to find (or to invent, in the etymological sense) "a *different* foundation for his *identity*,"[11] to quote an almost oxymoronic statement by Alden and Tremaine that points to the coexistence of complementary, not to say contradictory, realities within *one* definition of identity.

As such, self-narration consists in duplicating reality so as not to disregard the possible contradictions within oneself. Self-narration is necessary to go beyond monolithic or escapist definitions of identity. Duniya's self is not monolithic but binary, thus reinforcing the idea that Farah's approach to identity in this trilogy rejects reductive definitions of identity as "sameness" to enhance its polyphonic aspects.[12]

As a result, identity is more a hybrid construct than a homogeneous notion. To give a figurative example, the invention of identity can be compared to Duniya's decision to wear her hair uncovered in chapter 13:

> Wearing her hair uncovered brought along with it a change of dress style, in a sense a change of personality. Bosaaso liked it a great deal, her children approved of it too, but were they the only ones who mattered? Obviously not. For some of her colleagues at work had commented on it adversely. She herself had often described a woman's bare head as being narcissistic, and requiring the use of mirrors and similar modern gadgets. After lunch, for instance, Duniya gave herself a few moments alone in the bathroom, absorbed in an act of self-regard, her attention totally engrossed in the three white hairs that wouldn't curl no matter what she did, three flimsy white thread-like filaments

with a slender body, unhealthy and pale...She might never have taken notice of these emaciated hairs if she had been wearing her hair hidden in the prudence of an Islamic tradition which instructs women to cover their hair with scarves of modesty. (*G*, pp. 148-9)

Duniya's decision here is the right compromise between tradition and modernity, between self-denial and self-centredness. As she wears her hair uncovered, Duniya is neither confined in a self-denying pattern inherited from Islamic patriarchy nor proving narcissistic, as she actually does it to please others, viz. Bosaaso and her children. It also implies that she plays close relatives and friends off against professional acquaintances.

In a recent article, Kelly Oliver argued that abjection, i.e. the self-centred rejection of what is different, is a necessary phase but that it ought not to become the main reference in the construction of identity:

If abjection of the mother or maternal body is described as a normal or natural part of child development, then one consequence is that without some antidote to this abjection, all of our images of mothers and maternal bodies are at some level abject because we all necessarily rejected our own mothers in order to become individuals. On the level of social identification, if group identity is formed by rejecting what is different, then war, hatred, and oppression are inevitable and unavoidable parts of social development.

If overcoming oppression or living together as persons is possible, we must reject normative notions of abjection. We can endorse theories of abjection as *descriptions* of the dynamics of oppression and exclusion without accepting that abjection is necessary to self-identity.[13]

The *Blood in the Sun* trilogy suggests that self-narration may be the antidote that enables the individual to emancipate her or his own self, thus "celebrating differences," to quote the title of Farah's Neustadt lecture.[14] What Oliver has to say about abjection leading to war is illustrated in the trilogy, as Askar's attitude finally leads to justifying the war in the Ogaden at all costs and rejecting the mother-figure. In *Secrets*, the collapse of the Somali nation is mirrored in a contrastive way by Kalaman's decision *not* to identify with abstract constructs. Yet, *Secrets* also stresses the reversal of the conventional shift from mother-figure to father-figure (as it is expressed in *Maps* for instance), by having Kalaman first reject Yaqut as he still believes he is his true father, and then accept him though there is no biological link between them. Kalaman's childish statement *"fathers matter not, mothers matter a lot!"* (*S*, p. 66) is finally turned into *"Mothers matter a lot! Yaqut matters too!"* (*S*, p. 262). The use of the name "Yaqut," which serves here as a specific signifier as opposed to the generic term "fathers," shows that Kalaman rejects abstraction and abjection to celebrate his "foster-father"'s difference.

Unlike Bosaaso's former girlfriend Zawadi, who fully identifies with the Black Americans' collective struggle for freedom in the United States and points out that she is "too old to unlearn all [she has] learned" (*G*, p. 144), Askar, Duniya and Kalaman decide to question what they had taken for granted and to unravel the multiple threads of their life experiences. In that respect, identity can be considered as the ultimate goal to be reached after a phase of self-questioning and self-narration, though it is not a static construct and it constantly needs to be redefined all over again. At the end of the day (or, most certainly, as an overall reading of the trilogy shows), identity is a dynamic construct; though it has its roots in the self, it needs to take otherness into account. It is a complex construct, insofar as it moves away from identity as 'sameness' without advocating selflessness. The only instance of a positive selfless character is Yaqut, who is said to have helped Kalaman's mother Damac overcome her suicidal crisis by resorting to a fully unselfish strategy:

At some point my mother said, "Yaqut was a godsend to a woman in my state of feverish need. I might have conjured him up if he hadn't existed. But he was there, a healer of wounds, a mender of my shattered self-reflections, a bringer together of all my fragmented selves. He used to tape my fragmented parts together nightly, daily, never failing in his determination to make me whole again. I was a candle beam, he the light within its penumbra. I was the twilight, he a virtuoso of vintage godliness. I doubt that either of us would have survived if it hadn't been for his selflessness. (*S*, pp. 263-4)

The move towards the invention of identity is the result of a dialogical and dialectical structure that involves accepting others without having one's own self dissolve in the process. It is both an "ethical" (to quote one of Alden and Tremaine's key-words[15]) and a fictional endeavor, one in which self-narration plays a central role. As has been seen, the *Blood in the Sun* trilogy uses characters and fictional situations as dialectical modes, setting Askar's nationalistic predicament up against Kalaman's or Nonno's celebration of "difference", to take but one example. As a result, intratextuality is one of the essential keys to the trilogy, as the move from one situation to another, from one case of self-narration to another, exemplifies Farah's fictional strategy, one that functions as a pluralistic rather than as a monologic discourse.

NOTES

1. Nuruddin Farah, *Yesterday, Tomorrow: Voices from the Somali Diaspora* (London: Cassel, 2000), p.188.

2. ibid.

3. Nuruddin Farah, *Maps* (New York: Pantheon Books, 1986), p.96. Further references to this novel use the abbreviation *M* with the page number following.

4. Nuruddin Farah, *Secrets* (New York, Arcade, 1998), p.297. Further references to this novel use the abbreviation *S*, with the page number following.

5. Nuruddin Farah, *Gifts* (London: Serif, 1992), pp.102-3. Further references to this novel use the abbreviation *G*, with the page number following.

6. Hilarie Kelly, 'A Somali Tragedy of Political and Sexual Confusion: A Critical Analysis of Nuruddin Farah's *Maps,'* *Ufahamu* 16, 2 (1988), 22.

7. ibid., 28.

8. See Elisabeth Bizouard, *Le cinquième fantasme. Auto-engendrement et impulsion créatrice* (Paris: Presses Universitaires de France, 1995).

9. Patricia Alden and Louis Tremaine, 'Reinventing Family in the Second Trilogy of Nuruddin Farah', *World Literature Today* 72, 4 (1998), 763.

10. ibid., 759.

11. ibid., 763. Emphasis added.

12. On the debate between *idem*-identity ('mêmeté' or sameness) and *ipse*-identity (ipseity), see Paul Ricœur's *Soi-même comme un autre* (Paris: Le Seuil, 1990). Fictional characters make it possible to define identity as a process of self-reinvention (or even self-

regeneration) according to patterns that are originally foreign to the self proper. The very notion of self implies that there is some difference between the self and the thinking subject. In Farah's trilogy, self-narration serves as a transition from strictly tautological 'sameness' towards 'ipseity', which implies referring to the self as if it were at the same time intimate and foreign.

13. Kelly Oliver, 'Identity, Difference, and Abjection,' in *Theorizing Multiculturalism*, ed. Cynthia Willett (Malden, MA: Blackwell, 1998), p.175.

14. Nuruddin Farah, 'Celebrating Differences: The 1998 Neustadt Lecture,' *World Literature Today* 72, 4 (1998), 709-712.

15. Patricia Alden and Louis Tremaine, *Nuruddin Farah* (New York: Twayne, 1999).

THE POLITICS AND POETICS OF NATIONAL FORMATION:
Recent African Writing and Maps
Simon Gikandi

The Politics of Post-colonial Narratives

A useful starting point in my consideration of the politics and poetics of recent African writing is provided by Abiola Irele, the eminent Nigerian critic, who observes, at the beginning of a recent survey of contemporary thought in French- speaking Africa, that "there is beginning to be a redefinition of what we may call the 'African problematic,' and this redefinition appears to be related to the changed realities of the contemporary African situation in the post-colonial era."[1] Three key terms in Irele's assertion will frame my discussion and will help us to understand the function and nature of recent African writing, especially its continued concern with, and appeal to, notions of national identity and relations of power and knowledge in the post-colonial state: the African situation as a problematic with inherent theoretical problems, the redefinition of the

African terrain, and the assumption that the African space is indeed defined by changed political and social realities.

First of all, African writers and intellectuals are increasingly beginning to realize that Africa is not simply an entity whose nature and history can be taken for granted; rather, the African space is being re-configured as a theoretical problematic in the sense the term has been defined by Althusser and Foucault among others.[2] As a problematic, Africa is not considered to be a historical reality, a linguistic entity, or even a philosophical concept which exists in isolation from other systems of discourse; rather, there is an impulse to analyze the African terrain as part of a discursive formation which functions "in the theoretical or ideological framework in which it is used."[3] Instead of assuming that there is a unified African world view, African writers are beginning to pay closer attention to the discursive systems, both native and foreign, through which, to quote V.Y. Mudimbe, "African worlds have been established as realities for knowledge."[4] Such discursive systems, as Mudimbe argues in *The Invention of Africa*, are often the foundations of an African order of knowledge, and "today Africans themselves read, challenge, rewrite these discourses as a way of explicating and defining their culture, history, and being."[5]

The second important term in Irele's proposition is the strategy of redefinition inferred in any re-reading of African literature: African writers are increasingly obsessed with questions of redefining the African context and the transformation it has been undergoing since independence. If previous paradigms and literary ideologies, such as Negritude and the African personality, and the narratives they generated, were predicated on the assumption that African cultures and selves were natural and holistic entities which colonialism had repressed and which it was the duty of the African writer, in the period of decolonization, to recover (if only the right linguistic and narrative tools could be developed), there is now an urgent need to question the ideological foundations on which the narratives of decolonization were constructed. In the colonial period, narration,

450

and related acts of cultural production, were predicated on a simple ethical assumption: it was the duty of the African writer to recover the African political unconscious, a fundamental history which colonialism had repressed.[6] Indeed, in the nationalist period, it was taken for granted that the liberation of the nation was an important precondition for the generation of an 'authentic' African narrative. Clearly, nation, national consciousness, and narration would walk hand in hand in African literature.

Nothing illustrates this premise better than Frantz Fanon's influential theorizing on the relationship between the nation, national consciousness and cultural production in *The Wretched of the Earth*. For Fanon, the legitimacy of the nation was nothing less than the enabling condition for a new post-colonial culture; as a result, it was imperative that strategies of narration—in the narratives of the nation—be geared toward asserting this legitimacy, in the process restoring the form and content which the colonizer had emptied from the natives' mentality. Because the colonial ideological machinery was driven by what Fanon saw as a perverted logic, one bent on distorting, disfiguring and destroying the oppressed people and their history, the narrative of liberation derived its authority from its capacity to realize the "truths of the nation."[7] The African problematic was hence defined by its Manichean relationship to the very colonial culture it sought to negate.

In the first decade of independence, however, the colonizer/colonized paradigm became more complex, forcing African writers to reassess their commitment to the "truths of the nation," leading to the rise of the so-called literature of disillusionment. The forms and ideologies of works such as Ngugi wa Thiong'o's *A Grain of Wheat*, Chinua Achebe's *A Man of the People*, Wole Soyinka's *The Interpreters,* and Ayi Kwei Armah's *The Beautyful Ones Are Not Yet Born* seemed to have been over-determined by their author's disillusionment with the ideals of the nation evoked in earlier African texts. In the texts of the 1960s, narrative strategies are propelled by the belief that African countries had entered a neo-colonial phase, one in which colonial structures and institutions continued their gigantic hold on the new states wearing the ideological masks of blackness and modernity. But as Neil Lazarus has persuasively argued, this notion of independence as a fraud was based on an ideological misunderstanding, not so much of the terms of liberation and its narrative claims, but of the possibilities of an epistemological revolution inherent in the de-colonization gesture; the literature of 'disillusionment'

> remained possessed of the illusion that the era of inde-pendence marked a revolutionary conjuncture in African societies. It was this illusion that motivated the intellectual obsession with loss and failure and betray-al in these works of the 1960s. As such the prevalent way of thinking about post-colonialism, as it was artic-ulated during that decade, can be said to have been predicated upon a preliminary overestimation of the emancipatory potential of independence.[8]

Furthermore, the literature of 'disillusionment,' like the narratives of decolonization before, still suffered from the values and images generated by colonial discourse, even as it sought to evoke a world beyond colonial structures. To paraphrase Foucault's famous discus-sion of the relationship between madness and leprosy, colonialism had disappeared but its structures remained; thus the substitution of the theme of colonialism for that of neo-colonialism "does not mark a break, but rather a torsion within the same anxiety."[9] In this context, the third term in Irele's assertion—"the changed realities of the con-temporary African situation"—points to new conditions of possibility, signals ways in which recent African writing has attempted to break away from the colonial paradigm and its anxieties. For in trying to redefine the African context, and the forms which it takes in narrative and discourse, it is no longer enough to cast African culture as one long struggle with colonialism, a struggle which continues into the post-colonial period; in spite of the dominance of colonial structures and the colonial episteme in many African countries, there is a need to recognize, at least on the cultural level, that the "paradigmatic oppositions" engendered by colonialism are no longer enough to account for the contemporary African situation.[10]

My thesis here is that a new African literature is emerging in which notions of betrayal and the failure of nationalism are seen as inadequate strategies for representing and explaining a post-colonial situation which is proving to be much more confusing than earlier theories of neocolonialism entail. Writers who still seem to believe that the post-colonial situation is simply the continuation of colonialism under the guise of independence, or that the narratives of decolonization can be projected into the post-colonial world, seem to be entrapped in an ideological and narrative cul-de-sac. Ngugi's novel *Matigari* is exemplary in this regard; it is both a symptom of the problems which arise when the narrative of decolonization is evoked in a transformed post-colonial era and a commentary on the problematics of a belated national narrative.[11] The novel sustains a rhetoric which privileges the colonial paradigm and its anxieties, but it also uniquely ironizes the ideological assumption that national independence is a mask for new forms of colonialism. Thus, Matigari, the subject of the novel, is bewildered by the post-colonial scene precisely because his mode of knowledge is still imprisoned in the romance of the nation and of national independence, both notions triggered by the colonial epistemology.

If we accept the basic assumption that the desire for national independence is generated by colonial independence, then this desire and the forms it takes are still functions of the colonial episteme. What Ngugi does not allow for—hence his conception of Matigari as a heroic and allegorical character—is that the paradigms that define the nation, and hence the discourse on liberation, have changed while the hero was in the forest. Matigari, like the African writer in the nationalist period, conceived the nation as the highest stage of African consciousness; the national interest (embodied in the novel by the hero's house) was a divine right to be fought for and protected. In the post-colonial situation, however, the divinity of the nation has collapsed; the nation is not the manifestation of a common interest but a repressor of desires; class alliances are sometimes confused for, or rationalized by, ethnic configurations. In the circumstances, Matigari's search for his house is notable for the innocence that underlies it as well as its historical belatedness.[12] Matigari seems to search for truth in a world which he is not even equipped to understand; his mode of knowledge is structured in a Christian allegorical structure which pits goodness against evil, but the resulting insights are also forms of blindness. In other words, what Matigari does not understand is more important than what he purports to know. And there are many things which Matigari does not comprehend: there is intractable warfare between members of the ruling class which goes beyond the patriot/betrayer dichotomy; women now constitute a new and important centre of identity and are not simply whoring figures who offer their bodies to help the hero in the task of liberation. In short, Matigari is a prisoner of the emancipatory narrative he promotes.

Of course, the allegory of the nation is confounded by the fact that the national interest, which seemed so clear during the struggle for independence, has become paradoxical. Our new global situation demands narratives which face up to the task of representing the ambivalences of the post-colonial situation, a situation that is more ironic than we are often willing to admit: international capital continues to oppress many peoples in the so-called 'third world', but from the perspective of the governing classes in those countries, this is development; the oppressed continue to suffer under economic doctrines which are expressed through Orwellian doublespeak—'structural adjustment,' for example—but what they continue to aspire for, even as they suffer, are the values and images of the West, the juices from the source of suffering itself. For Africans, as Achebe has aptly noted, this topsy-turvy world presents new narrative challenges: We are in a period so different from anything else that has happened that everything that is presented to us has to be looked at twice.[13] The relationship between the imaginary space and its historical condition has to be re-evaluated.

Before independence, African writers committed their narratives to the articulation of the nation as what Benedict Anderson would call "the imagined community."[14] Even when they recognized that the nation in Africa was an invented community, these writers believed that their works would harmonize national ideals and values; by realizing the realities of the nation, to borrow Fanon's term, the writer would find "the seething pot out of which the learning of the future emerged."[15] After independence, however, the interests of the nation became more confused. For example, by the early 1970s Achebe would see the gesture of writing as an engagement with the seething pot of the nation even when his function as an ideologue of the Biafran cause might be construed as a commitment to the breakup of the Nigerian nation. Moreover, the novelist saw his narratives as forms of articulating the African revolution "that aims toward true independence, that moves toward the creation of modern states in place of the new colonial enclaves we have today, a revolution that is informed with African ideologies."[16] At the same time, however, Achebe would acknowledge that a consensus no longer existed on the meaning of the nation: "Having fought with the nationalist movement and been on the side of the politicians, I realized after independence that they and I were now on different sides, because they were not doing what we had agreed they should do. So I had to become a critic."[17]

Of course, what has changed in the last thirty years is not merely the relationship between the writer, the politician, and the people they both claim to serve; the terms of nation-building and the construction of identities have also changed, perhaps they have become more inscrutable; but the post-colonial situation is also a context that offers great possibilities for narratives concerned with national formation. The basic question which recent African writing has had to deal with, but one which we have yet to theorize adequately, is the problematic of power and the state. For if you look at almost any literary text published recently in Africa, the character of power and how it is exercised seems paramount. In Achebe's *Anthills of the Savannah* and Soyinka's *Play of Giants* the primary drama takes place in a field defined by relations of power; Matigari's allegorical quest in Ngugi's novel is certainly confined to a field delimited by relations of production, but the resulting struggle is one which pits an individual against the materiality of the state and its instruments of power and coercion. And as Nicos Poulantzas notes in his discussion of the State and ideologies of power, "Although the relations of production delimit the given field of the State, it has a role of its own in the formation of these same relations."[18]

In Ngugi's text, we cannot fail to see the ways in which Matigari's primeval ideology (expressed through Gikuyu legends and Christian allegories) is pitted against ideologies elaborated and reproduced through state apparatus and the discourses of organization which the state articulates to reproduce its power. Matigari's visionary world is built around notions of natural justice and truth; in contrast, the utterances of the Minister of Truth and Justice ("I am the soul of the government. I am the soul of the nation. I am the light in the dark of the tunnel" [p.102]) elaborate a political tactic which has become a technique of knowledge. Ngugi's text raises another question: who represents the interests of the nation, who speaks its truths? The text, of course, provides a rather simplistic answer: it insists that Matigari is the voice of the nation, he is the crystallization of the collective desires of the oppressed. This answer is, however, achieved only at the expense of repressing the reality that evokes it in the first place: Matigari may have right and justice on his side, but the interests of the nation and the national community, in all their contradictions and perversions, are ideologically manifested by the state in its master narratives.

Matigari's words may resonate with the truth, but the ideological machinery of the state determines the realities of the nation. To quote Poulantzas, again, "Ideology does not consist merely in a system of ideas or representations: it also involves a series of *material practices,* embracing the customs and life-style of the agents and set-ting like cement in the totality of social (including political and eco-nomic) practices."[19] The nation, too, is an ideological practice which is only available to us in its representations and contradictions. The paradox of national formation in postcolonial Africa, as I hope to show in my reading of Nuruddin Farah's *Maps,* is that the nation is the source of identities and, paradoxically, the entity that represses their formation.

Maps: **Nation, Body, and Text**

Now, the motive for narration in *Maps,* as in many other post-colonial texts, is the contemporary African writer's consciousness of his or her alienation and exile, an awareness that the nation does not naturally proffer identities, nor lead to the fulfilment of the desire to belong to a real or mythical community, but often comes between post-colonial subjects and their quest for a communal ideal, a *natio,* a space of belonging. But exile, by distancing the subject from the idealized space of the nation, also generates the desire for a com-pensatory national narrative—one in which the individual's longing for a unified image of the self is cast within the country's epic quest for its soul. In Farah's novel, however, Askar's quest for selfhood, which parallels Somalia's dream of unification during the Ogaden war of 1977, does not generate a linear narrative in which temporal pro-gression takes us from a situation of alienation and dispossession (in the past) to a sense of fulfilment and identity (in the present). At the end of the novel, which is also its inaugural moment of narration, Askar is no closer to discovering the meaning of his life—and of Somalia—than he was as a child seeking the signifiers of the nation in geography books. Indeed, the various strategies he adopts to evoke his Somali identity—for example his attachment to real and imaginary maps of his nation and even his desire to fight for the lib-eration of the Ogaden—have only complicated notions of national identity in the text.[20]

When Askar is arrested at the end of the novel, apparently to be questioned about his relationship with Misra, the Ethiopian woman who brought him up, it is no longer clear whether there is any natural difference between a Somali and Ethiopian, although this assumed difference is the source of the conflict between the two countries; a narrative which sets out to interrogate the two entities (Ethiopia and Somalia) will end up collapsing inherited notions of cultural and natural differences. *Maps* is, of course, the story which Askar tells the secret police ostensibly to assert his Somaliness; nevertheless, the narrative, by "going backwards and forwards in time" (p.138), and by shifting narrative voice between the first, second and third person, problematizes previous notions of selfhood and national identity. In effect, what makes narration possible in this novel is not the quest for identity (since this condemns the narrative to a circle or maze), but the narrator's reflections on, and positivization, of his alienation, a gesture which allows him to recognize that Somalia is defined, not by a unified signifier, but by its "split personality" (p.120). Like other post-colonial narratives of national formation, narration is not predicated on any positive affirmation of the nation as an imagined community, but what Jean Franco, in another context, calls "a sceptical reconstruction of past errors"; the novel makes "visible that absence of any signified that could correspond to the nation."[21]

Of course, Farah's narrative ideology has always been predicated on the adoption of alienation (itself a sign of absence and error) as a positive force rather than a problem to be erased or overcome. Despite Somalia's historical claims to a unified and integrating culture, Farah underscores the extent to which to be a Somali, especially under colonialism, was to be alienated from the idealized symbols of the nation. In a revealing reflection on his background in "Why I Write," Farah asserts that the text-books used for the Somali-speaking peoples of the Horn of Africa "were meant for *other people*...Not only did we feel alienated from the texts we read, but the universe which these portrayed had nothing familiar to offer to a Somali child like myself, in a Somali-speaking Ogaden."[22] Such forms of alienation are now, of course, familiar descriptions of the colonial situation; however, Farah saw them as conditions which made writing possible because "to live in the world of which I was part, I had to make it my own" (WW, 1592). Writing became a way of claiming the authority of invention; and narration a strategy of self-inscription: "the Quran could not be mine because it was God's and no human could own it, but at least I could make a small claim in other areas, recreating the cosmos as I knew it in the hope that I would see the world and my friends in it, the way one sees a mirror's reflection in another mirror" (WW, 1592). To write is to claim a text of one's own; textuality is an instrument of territorial repossession; because the other confers on us an identity that alienates us from ourselves, narrative is crucial to the discovery of our selfhood. The text is the mirror in which the Somali subject will see itself reflected.

But the relationship between narratives and mirrors is a problematic one in *Maps*. At the end of the novel, the secret police will pose a simple question to Askar: "What is your name?" (p.246). Simple as it is, though, this question can only be answered by tracing the history of the self against the background of the Somali mythology of nationhood, retracing the errors of the nation in the post-colonial period, thus exposing what Franco calls "the disappearance of the nation, its failure to provide systems of meaning and belief."[23] For what defines the Somaliness of Somalia—language, culture, or biology? As a boy, Askar is troubled by many questions, but none is as dominant as the nature of his identity on both the biological and cultural level: do mirrors reflect "the true identity of things and persons?" (p.43); and are "bodies tattooed with their identities" such that no nationality is interchangeable with another? (p.42). Because Askar is obsessed with such questions, questions that point to the absence of a stable system of meanings in the Somali cultural body, his frustration is heightened by the realization that answers to issues of identity must be self-engendered: "He was saddest that there was no one else to whom he could put questions about his own identity; there was no one to answer his nagging, 'Who am I?' or 'Where am I?'..." (p.44).

Narration creates a text which becomes the mirror in which the character hopes to identify himself. But there is no guarantee that the image in the mirror is authentic, for mirrors have immense powers of distortion. In his narrative mirror, Askar assumes one image only to see it wrenched out of his control and disfigured in the process. At one stage in the novel he looks at his "newer self" and sees it as a dot in the distance, a dot "which assumed features you could identify, becoming now a man, now a woman—or even an animal, your perceptions of the new self altering with the distance or nearness of the spot of consciousness" (p.61). Narration is adopted as one way by which the narrator can capture an image of the self and represent its uniqueness in language. In this instance, however, the act of identifying the self through writing leads to self-alienation; the mirror vanishes in front of Askar to be replaced by a wall on which "appeared shadows and the shadows were speaking with one another, some laughing, some listening and some holding hands or touching one another" (p.61). So, the self is alienated through the agencies it sought to represent itself. If narration was initially posited as the solution to Askar's crisis of identity—the resolution of his initial doubts on whether he exists outside his own thoughts and ideas—it seems to have compounded the problem because he still remains "a question to himself" even after narration is over.

There is even a prior, more elementary problem—the narrating self has no authority of representation because the narrator has no means of collectivizing the desires of the Somali nation. The ideal allegory of self—which is evident in the African epics which Askar tries to emulate—assumes a fundamental relationship between self and nation. For Askar, however, the relationship to his "people's past history and present experience" (p.3) is marked by misfortune and displacement just as his desire to reinvent himself is retarded by his confused origins. In both an individual and collective sense, Askar cannot derive his authority from any genealogy: "What survived my real mother was 'memory,' not I. People were, in a general sense,

460

kinder and more generous to me, because my parents had died and I was an orphan" (p.25). Without a mother to connect him to a genealogical tradition, Askar appears to many people "as though I had made myself" (p.23). His state of orphanage does not become the source of a melancholy that might allow the subject to identify with a nation, but it is an important licence to invent.[24]

However, it is Askar's sense of the incompleteness that haunts the Somali nation that allows his narrative to continue in spite of the crisis of consciousness that often grips him. Consider his reflections on his impeding circumcision: the moment when the individual is supposed to enter the *communitas* is here represented as one of confusion about selfhood and language. When Misra mentions the day of his circumcision, we are told, Askar is filled with fear that chokes his speech. When he recovers his composure, he observes that

> "I was back where I had begun—I was motherless, I was fatherless, I was an orphan and had to give birth to myself. Yes, I was an orphan and had to give birth to myself. Yes, *I* was to re-create myself in a worldly image, I thought to myself, now that the Word had deserted me, now that I couldn't depend on its keeping me company." (p.86)

In effect, Askar cannot substitute language for the absent mother figure: "The Word, I said to myself, was not a womb; the Word, I convinced myself, wouldn't receive me as might a mother, a woman, a Misra" (pp.86-87).

The conflict between the Word and the mother would also appear to be one between texts and bodies. After all, a major cause of tension in the novel, especially in regard to the source and nature of Somalia's identity, is whether 'Somalia' is a text, i.e. a map on the wall, or a body, a mother figure. When the Somali ruling class talks about the realities of Somalia and discourse about the Somali character, they take pains to emphasize the natural, or rather biological, nature of the nation. Because such notions of identity only lead to mystification or justify repression, Farah thinks that we can only penetrate the veil of nationhood which the Barre regime has wrapped around itself by foregrounding the textuality of Somalia: "Somalia was a badly written play...Siad Barre was its author" (WW, 1597). Moreover, Farah's anxiety about his position as a writer, especially at the beginning of his career, arose from the fear that his art could not measure to Barre's text and hence could not offer an effective counter-discourse: "You can imagine how Siad- Barre-as-subject oppressed and obsessed me. I was in awe of it, afraid that I was not up to it, that I would mess it all up for future writers dealing with the same material even if from a detached historical angle" (WW, 1597).

How does a writer counter an idea which has become nationalized and naturalized in public discourse? Other African nations may at least accede to their arbitrary invention in the halls of European imperialism, but not Somalia which, says Farah, "is a country peopled by a race of men and women who are decidedly united in their unmitigated arrogance and pride in being unique, the only country in Africa that qualifies to be called a nation" (WW, 1597). The "promiscuity of the Somali-idea," concludes Farah, is an instrument which the Somali ruling class or regime uses to repress other discourses on the Somali character; in the words of a Somali diplomat, "you cannot invent a nation as unique as ours. That's the truth that matters" (WW, 1598). Obviously, Farah will not subscribe to this 'truth'; as a result, his narrative strategies are often geared toward the deconstruction of the naturalized Somali idea. Many of the ambivalences toward the idea of nationhood which we see in *Maps* arise from the fact that Farah must simultaneously counter the dominant idea of Somalia as a natural entity, but at the same time propose alternative ways of constituting national formation, since, as he told Maya Jaggi in interview, the writer is "the depository of the nation's memory."[25]

In any case, the idea that the nation can be signified by its maps comes up for closer scrutiny in Farah's novel. The Somali nation lacks the authority of a state, since its people are spread across different countries, hence the ironic suggestion that the Somali people "have a case in wanting to form a state of their own nation" (p.149). One could of course argue, as many Somali nationalists have argued, that Somalia needs to redraw its maps to reinvent its nationhood. But such an act of reinvention would also threaten the mythology that gives the Somali idea its doctrinal hold—that the Somali are a homogeneous people; that they are "homogeneous culturally speaking and speak the same language wherever they may be found" (p.166). Does this mean that an Ethiopian who adopts the Somali culture and language can also be considered Somali? This is the problem posed by Misra in the novel: although she will not be accepted as a Somali, by all the indices used to determine a Somali, Misra is surely one. But since she will always be denied this identity because of her Ethiopian origins, Misra is the figure Farah uses to deconstruct the hegemonic doctrine of Somali national purity.

Furthermore, Misra allows Askar to recognize that given identities have an adverse effect, too, especially when they deform the self (p. 42), and that national identity is a strategy which goes beyond the cultural text and territorial claims. Indeed, an important strategy of national formation in *Maps* is the use of the human body as a third site of identity formation, a site beyond Askar's individual fantasies about Somalia as signified by maps and official doctrines of the Somali nation as a natural entity. In examining the relationship between Askar and Misra, in 'bodily' terms, the narrative questions the 'wall' that is supposed to separate Ethiopians from Somalis. This wall, it seems, has been elected at the expense of human bodies which the state finds it easy to dispense with to realize its ideals. To ally himself with "the notion of a nationhood," Askar is momentarily forced to detach himself from "his mother-figure, Misra" (p.96); his desire now is to become "a fully grown man, a man ready for a conscription into the liberation army, ready to die and kill for his mother country, ready to avenge his father" (p.105). The ideal of manhood, which underlies nationhood is, nevertheless, perverse—its logic demands that Askar should even be ready to kill the woman who has been his mother because she is of Ethiopian origin. It is also the source of acute anxiety, an anxiety that forces Askar's body to recoil from the doctrines of manhood as he begins to 'menstruate,' an act which dissolves the binary opposition between men and women (p.105). If men can menstruate, then the biological division between the sexes is called into question; and if such 'natural' divisions can be collapsed, then the fixedness of the Ethiopian/ Somali chasm cannot derive its legitimacy from the laws of nature.

In the end, Askar's body seems to reject notions of nation formation as defined by the state for three reasons: the ideals embedded in such notions can only be achieved at the expense of human bodies whose collective desires the state claims to represent; he cannot countenance his separation from the woman whom he has called mother just because she was born in another country; and because he realizes that the Somalia which Siad Barre has scripted is an ideological practice which the regime uses to justify its authoritarian grip and stifling of the Somali people. When Askar makes Misra, the Ethiopian woman, the heroine of his narrative—"Misra was the heroine of your tale now and you played only a minor supporting role" (p.141)—he begins to acknowledge that the official idea of the homogeneous and unique Somali nation is quite arbitrary if not false. Like other recent writing from Africa, *Maps* is a narrative whose goal is to critique, rather than simply valorize, the notions of African identity inherited from a colonial past and sanctioned by independence. In the process, the modern state becomes "a kind of illusionist which needs the past only as a lament and whose miracle is the economic miracle of dependency."[26]

ACKNOWLEDGMENT

I thank Juandamarie Brown for providing research assistance for this article.

NOTES

1. Abiola Irele, "Contemporary Thought in French Speaking Africa," in *Africa and the West: The Legacies of Empire*, eds. Isaac James Mowoe & Richard Bjornson (Westport: Greenwood Press, 1986), p.122.

2. Louis Althusser and Etienne Balibar, *Reading Capital,* trans. Ben Brewster (London: NLB/Verso, 1979), pp.25-28; Michel Foucault, *Madness and Civilization: A History of Insanity in the Age of Reason,* trans. Richard French (New York: Vintage, 1988), pp.3-37.

3. Ben Brewster, Glossary to *Reading Capital, p.* 316.

4. V.Y. Mudimbe, *The Invention of Africa: Gnosis, Philosophy, and the Order of Knowledge* (Bloomington: Indiana University Press, 1988), p.xi.

5. *The Invention of Africa*, p. xi.

6. Frederic Jameson, *The Political Unconscious: Narrative as a Socially Symbolic Act* (Ithaca, NY: Cornell University Press, 1981), pp.20-21.

7. Frantz Fanon, *The Wretched of the Earth,* trans. Constance Farrington (New York: Grove Press, 1968), p.225.

8. Neil Lazarus, *Resistance in Postcolonial African Fiction* (New Haven: Yale University Press, 1990), p.23.

9. *Madness and Civilization,* p.16.

10. *The Invention of Africa*, p.4.

11. Ngugi wa Thiong'o, *Matigari,* trans. Wangui wa Goro (Oxford: Heinemann, 1989). Further page references to this text are made in parenthesis after the quotation.

12. This point is made by Peter Nazareth in "Faking Fiction Beyond the Text," *Third World Quarterly* 11, 3 (1989), 204.

13. Bill Moyers, "Chinua Achebe: Nigerian Novelist," in *A World of Ideas*, ed. Betty Sue Flowers (New York: Doubleday, 1989), p.343.

14. Benedict Anderson, *Imagined Communities: Reflections on the Origin and Spread of Nationalism* (London: Verso, 1983), pp.14-15.

15. *The Wretched of the Earth, p.* 225.

16. "Interview with Chinua Achebe," in *Palaver: Interviews with Five African Writers in Texas*, eds. Bernth Lindfors et al. (Austin: African and Afro-American Research Institute, 1972), p.6.

17. "Interview with Chinua Achebe," p.8.

18. Nicos Poulantzas, *State, Power, Socialism,* trans. Patrick Camiller (London: NLB, 1978), p.25.

19. *State, Power, Socialism,* p.28.

20. Nuruddin Farah, *Maps* (New York: Pantheon Books, 1986). Further page references to this text are made in parenthesis after the quotation. Important studies of Farah's novels include, D.R. Ewen, "Nuruddin Farah," in *The Writing of East and Central Africa*, ed. G.D. Killam (London: Heinemann, 1984), pp.192-210; G.H. Moore, "Nomads and Feminists: The Novels of Nuruddin Farah," *International Fiction Review* 11, 1 (1984), 3-12 (reprinted in the present volume); Juliet Okonkwo, "Literature and Politics in Somalia:

The Case of Nuruddin Farah," *Africa Today* 32, 3 (1985), 57-65.

21. Jean Franco, "The Nation as Imagined Community," in *The New Historicism*, ed. H. Aram Veeser (New York: Routledge, 1989), p. 205.

22. Nuruddin Farah, "Why I Write," *Third World Quarterly* 10, 4 (1988), 1591. This article is henceforth referred to as 'WW' in the text.

23. "The Nation as Imagined Community," p.208.

24. The notion that melancholy is one of the ways subjects express identification with a nation was recently proposed by Homi Bhabha at a conference on "Nationalisms and Sexualities" held at Harvard University, 16-18 June 1989.

25. Maya Jaggi, "A Combining of Gifts: An Interview with Nuruddin Farah," *Third World Quarterly* 11, 3 (1989) 187.

26. "The Nation as Imagined Community," p.206.

RECALLING THE OTHER THIRD WORLD:
Nuruddin Farah's *Maps*

Francesca Kazan

*Your story, because it is not a translation of reality, interests me.
I take it as it is, artificial and painful.*
—TAHAR BEN JELLOUN

*...a remembered event is infinite, because it is only a key to every-
thing that happened before it and after it.*
—WALTER BENJAMIN

To say that cartography expresses ideology is hardly news, but perhaps nowhere are the crucial repercussions of this truth more evident now than in Africa.[1] As far as the visual image of this continent is concerned, after the period of *mappaemundi* (fifth to fifteenth century), the first relatively available representations emerged in the sixteenth century, the most popular of which was a map printed from a woodcut in 1540, Munster's *Cosmographia*. It lacks geographical detail, but is adorned with an elephant, a cyclops, and so forth. The sixteenth century saw a rise in accuracy though, as we might expect, by the nineteenth century the primary interest, according to R.V.Tooley, now lay in the "historical recording of the spread or penetration of a European element in the interior, the gradual discovery and naming of physical features, the towns and trading posts established."[2] It is worth remembering even now that the map of Africa we see most commonly today is not the Peters' projection, but that based on Mercator's sixteenth-century globe: the map where Europe's 9.7 sq.million kilometres appears larger than South America's 17.8 million, where the former Soviet Union's 22.4 million appears considerably larger than Africa's 30 million, and so forth. In fact, European colonialism in Africa is over 2,000 years old, beginning on a large scale with Carthage's defeat by Rome, and developing to its fullest expression during the 1880s, with "the scramble for Africa." The Berlin Conference of 1884-85 began a process which was to culminate after World War I with the partition of an entire continent: Africa was, in effect, (re)mapped.[3]

So it is in the context of these facts that we can turn to a post-colonial Anglophone African text entitled, quite simply, *Maps*. This work by the Somali novelist Nuruddin Farah investigates the fissures rent in national and personal identity in the disintegration that follows such topographical "reorganization"; not only the disintegration resulting from European colonialism (in this case British, French and Italian), but also the disintegration resulting from wars over the Ogaden territories—territories which were ceded to neighboring Ethiopia after World War II by the Allied Powers.[4]

To re-map is to re-border, and certainly borders are at the heart of *Maps*. This text demonstrates the drive and desire for, as well as the inefficacy of, borders—whether linguistic, temporal, corporeal, or psychic. Through multiple shifts in narrative voice, the "you," "he" and "I" of the single narrator renounce pronominal definition to weave us back and forth in a shifting temporal perspective from his mysterious birth to his writing present. In the process the boy's sense of gender dissolves (he even experiences a form of menstruation) in what I can only describe as a kind of psychic-somatic union with his surrogate mother, where he projects himself as her "third leg" or "third breast."

But Farah's itinerary is also clearly political, and these personal borders spill over, fuse with the larger issue of national borderlands.[5] He traces a route which traverses both the realm of personal identity characterized by diffused boundaries and liminal psychic zones, and the realm of politics where the Somali nation is in search of its state. Almost exactly midpoint in the text, Askar, the young Somali protagonist of *Maps,* asks his surrogate mother, "Misra, where precisely is Somalia?"[6] His poignant question pinpoints a problem which resonates throughout this work: can one define the borders of one's self (even provisionally) if one cannot define the borders of one's nation?[7]

Askar's parallel search for national as well as personal identity could in theory lead him towards nationalistic insularity. But, given the broadly exploratory and boundary-breaking nature of his inner self, I want to instead read his political quest as a demonstration of Frantz Fanon's expansive belief that "National consciousness, which is not nationalism, is the only thing that will give us an international dimension...It is at the heart of national consciousness that international consciousness grows and grows. And this two-fold emerging is ultimately the source of all culture." This meshing of the national with the international consciousness creates a larger entity. In addition, "If a man is known by his acts," writes Fanon, "then we will say that the most urgent thing today for the intellectual is to build up his nation."[8] So the intellectual concentrates on the "inside" space of the nation in order to move beyond, "outside" to the globe.

This raises an interesting problem for many of those post-colonial writers who are already firmly positioned within the international community, who are, in fact, exiled from their nation. They are *already writing from outside.* This politico-global expansiveness finds an aesthetic parallel in *Maps,* not only thematically with the breakdown of traditional gender assignation, but with the textual experimentation of narratival voice and the ambiguity of resolution.

In many ways, then, Nuruddin Farah is an exemplary figure in African letters. He has been actively publishing for thirty years, most of them in enforced exile from his native Somalia.[9] His own thoughts on exile are clearly stated when he refers to himself as a writer who, "in essence, has accepted the duality of his role: that of belonging to a particular country occupying a marked latitude on the globe, and of being a denizen of the world which he calls his home...I am home everywhere; and everywhere is home."[10]

This "worldliness," if I can call it that, marks a new breed of post-colonial writer. And I am using this somewhat differently to Edward Said, for whom the term signifies a "circumstantial reality," that reality where texts are "always enmeshed in circumstance, time, place, and society—in short, they are in the world, and hence worldly."[11] But it is "worldliness" in the sense that in re-positioning, re-situating themselves throughout the world these writers in some way call attention to, even theorize, their "displacement" and hybridity, and make productive use of the inevitable tension that results. Tim Brennan characterizes them as "spokespersons for a kind of perennial immigration, valorised by a rhetoric of wandering, and rife with allusions to the all-seeing eye of the nomadic sensibility."[12] But not only do these writers write outside their culture; they usually write outside their mother tongue—the advantages and drawbacks of which are increasingly debated. They operate, then, within a kind of double outsiderness. Farah's position as novelist takes this one step further, because Somalia's highly privileged oral literature is poetry, not prose, and it was only in 1972 that an official orthography for the Somali language was introduced. This latter fact, of course, raises a question regarding the virtues of writing in the indigenous language. Farah's first novel was published in 1970, two years *before* the official script for Somali was even introduced—prior to this time there was Cusmaaniya, an underground Somali script. It is another complexity to add to the debate on writing in the mother tongue.[13]

Finally, though, to be a Somali outside Somalia, writing prose rather than poetry; and in English rather than Somali, is to be triply outside. (Perhaps, even, three worlds removed.) Small wonder, then, that borders are the issue.[14]

1. Mapping the Mother/Land, or, the Other Third World

The narrator of *Maps,* Askar, is a child of the Ogaden: he is born in a border territory claimed by both Somalia and Ethiopia. This involution of origins is further exacerbated by the fact that, although born of Somali parents, his adoptive mother is Ethiopian. His natural mother having apparently died in childbirth, he is found unwashed and unattended with bloody finger stains round his neck. From these dubious beginnings Askar, an almost magically intuitive and preternaturally memoried child, negotiates his path through the fraught terrain of gender and nationality. *Maps* is in part a tale of divided loyalties, of a young man's struggle to define identity in relation to these opposing forces.

Chapter Five of *Maps* opens with something like a reverie on the protagonist's relation to Misra, his adoptive mother:

> There was nothing like sharing the robe the woman carrying you was wrapped in, nothing as warm, with the bodies, yours and hers, touching, oozing and sweating together—I naked and she not—and the rubbing together of the bodies producing itchy irritations, scratchy rashes and crotchy eruptions of skin. Then the quiet of the night would crawl in like an insect up one's back—ticklish and laughter-producing. The darkness of dusk would take over one's imagined sense of being: this time, like an insect bite so scratchy that you cannot think of anything else. And so, for years, I contemplated the world from the safe throne carved out of Misra's back, sleeping when I pleased,

473

swinging from her back as a fruit the thorn which is its twin, making water when I had to and getting scolded for it; for years I viewed the world from a height slightly above that of a pigmy's head.

I seem to have remained a mere extension of Misra's body for years—you saw me when you set your eyes on her. I was part of the shadow she cast—in a sense, I was her extended self. I was, you might even say, the space surrounding the geography of her body. (p.75)

I will return to the corporeal world so intimately evoked here, but first want to examine what may be considered something of a corporeal lack. Towards the end of the passage Askar describes himself both as a "mere extension...part of the shadow she cast" and as "the space surrounding the geography of her body." He is incorporated into her, while he simultaneously surrounds her. Her body defines the border where he begins, while he is simply space. But the "extended self" formed by his shadow also extends her boundaries, enlarges her, as it were. And space, in the abstract, is boundless and knows no limits. This is a system of complete, yet paradoxical, reciprocity, a system that cannot be fixed.

Askar's description of his relation to Misra is paradigmatic in *Maps* because it suggests the question that preoccupies the narrator throughout his narrative: where does the self begin, *the other* end? Farah's initial answer for Askar seems to lie in blurring both gendered and corporeal boundaries; these distinctions blur not just in androgynous empathy, not just in a pull towards a system of nurturance which depends on psychic merger (though it is both these things), but also in an intellectual striving to answer the question that resonates more generally throughout the text: what then, is *the other*? "Uncle Hilaal helped you home in on *the other*," Askar reflects to himself (p.149). (This phrase is always emphasized in *Maps*.) For postcolonial writers, engaged in re-negotiating their own subject positions, these are key questions.

The first thing to note is that in *Maps the other* is not the racial *Other* we have come to recognize in our recent readings of texts; at least, not a racial *Other* in the sense that black and white are inevitably *other* to each. There are no whites in this textual world, and while Western intellectual thought does influence some characters (in particular, Askar's uncle and aunt) "whiteness" and "blackness" are not given play in the actual narrative, which is set firmly in the Horn of Africa. So in a generalized sense *the other* is what the self is not, and here quite specifically it is female to Askar's male. But we are immediately diverted from such a conclusion because time and time again Askar empathizes with, is totally absorbed by, is initiated into, the world of women. He is finely attuned to Misra's menstrual cycle; it is something he envies her (p.98), and one morning there is even blood on his groin. Misra tells him with complete seriousness, "You've begun to menstruate...The question is: will you have the monthly curse as we women do or will yours be as rare as the male fowl's egg?" (p.105).[15]

So for Askar, the *other* is not simply female to his male, because the feminine and masculine co-exist: "I have a strange feeling that there is *another* in me, one older than I—a woman. I have the conscious feeling of being spoken through, if you know what I mean. I feel as if I have allowed a woman older than I to live inside of me, and I speak not my words, my ideas, but hers. And during the time I'm spoken through, as it were, I am she—not I" (p.151). The *other,* then, seems not to be opposed to the self here, but resides within as the complementary gender, not depending on binary opposition. It is not a stable entity, but a more complex mutable force which rejects the oppositional, hierarchized *other* typical of Western thinking.[16]

But if *the other* resides within the self, can self and identity ever be defined? Or is one somehow always marginal? The answer to the first question may be no—at least in the sense that identity can never be absolutely defined; instead it shifts continually, thus implementing a procedure of renewal. And furthermore, it is only the possibility of *the other* that makes the identity of *the self* a possibility. The answer to the second question concerning the endlessness of marginality may be affirmative, with the clear recognition that marginality has benefits: living at the border, living at the edge allows one the advantage of incorporating diverse qualities, allows one possibilities which the center cannot allocate.

These boundary issues inevitably return us to Misra, but here I want to consider her not just as female to Askar's male, but more specifically in her maternal role. In the lengthy description cited earlier her body is configured through geography; she is, it is obvious enough, the mother/land. However, this is complicated, and marred, by the fact that she literally represents Ethiopia, the enemy in the Ogaden border wars, and not Somalia. Eventually this adoptive mother will be renounced—in a violent and unsettling way. Years pass in physical separation, and Askar is briefly reunited with her just before she is washed ashore with her heart ripped out, dismembered in what is probably a ritualistic political murder. In fact, this renunciation is openly addressed early in the text when the narrator tells Misra in his uncannily direct manner, "To live, I will have to kill you" (p.57).[17] So Askar's earlier corporeal lack—when he perceives himself as virtually bodiless in his merger with Misra in the shadowy symbiosis that blurs the distinction between self and *other*— becomes instead Misra's corporeal lack. But this is not simply imagined or empathized, because Misra actually loses life. Her corporeal "lack" is final and complete.

This takes us back to the seductive intensity of the corporeal world evoked early in Askar's recollections, the world of the mother/land. This is a world where bodies blend in intimacy, where Misra whispers "endearments the like of which I am not likely to hear ever again" (p.23), and where in pronominal distancing mode Askar relates that "she smelled of your urine precisely in the same way you smelled of her sweat: upon your body were printed impressions of her fingerprints, the previous night's moisture: yours and hers" (p.9). While it is clear that Askar's memories of Misra are driven by nostalgia and longing as he attempts to recreate the past, they are nonetheless an unusually dense summoning of the mother-child dyad. This world collapses borders, and prolongs psychic bonding long after the sequestered space of infancy. Misra creates a secure mother/land, and yet is also perceived by him to be "the cosmos"—an entirely larger entity; certainly one that moves beyond the idea of the nation.[18]

So where is Askar sited? In the mother/land, or in the world beyond? There is a curious moment in *Maps* when Askar's uncle, Hilaal, asks, "Askar, where is *the third? Where's the other?*" (p.138). Askar, precocious though he is, cannot answer; the question is left hanging. This juxtaposition of third and other infiltrates the text in suggestive ways, and I want to read it as explicitly connecting the body with politics. Towards the end of *Maps,* after Misra has disappeared from the hospital and he is awaiting news of her whereabouts, Askar reflects that "she was my universe, she was the one who determined the circumference of my cosmos, her body was an extension of mine, my body her third leg as we slept and snored away time, my head her third breast..." (p.232).

As before, the system is reciprocal, her body extending his even as his enlarges hers. This time the intimate relation is evoked not only through the abstraction of space and shadow of symbiosis as self and *other* merge, but also through the accretion of body parts, a leg and a breast.[19] The body extends to include a *third,* and in so doing creates an alternative corporeal space—perhaps, even, an alternative "third world." Askar is sited both in the mother/land and in the world beyond.

This strategic revision of body space within the text enables us to reconsider national identity (Somali and Ethiopian converge) and to readdress that problematic term coined by a Frenchman, "the Third World," a term which Aijaz Ahmad argues (in many ways very convincingly) is a "polemical one, with no theoretical status whatsoever."[20] For while Askar's projection of himself as the "third leg" or "third breast" could possibly be read as a kind of grotesque representation, a distorted view of the filial, it can be read more productively as creating a site where "third" does not signify "less" in a vertical counting system, but rather counts for "more" in a system of empowerment, a site where consciousness is nourished, to summon Fanon once more, both nationally and internationally; a site, then, which denotes a potentiality in the term "Third World" and which enables Askar to be at home both in the body of the m/other, and in the body of politics.[21]

So why, we may ask, is this m/other (actually, both m/others) so violently eradicated? Misra is first hospitalized for a mastectomy, there she is abducted and her heart is literally torn from her body, when she is washed ashore; Askar's unnamed birth mother disappears after his birth, indeed, practically *at* his birth because in Askar's preternatural memory he tells himself, "you *were* an adult...you believed you were *present* at your birth" (p.13)—in a symbolic sense he delivers himself, and in a magical way is fully self-conscious from then on. The questioning of this violent eradication cannot be simply answered. Certainly it would be trite to imply that the maternal presence must be destroyed in order for the boy to achieve an independence. The point is, Askar does not achieve an independence—the text revolves round his entangled relation to Misra. Relating events does not necessarily result in a catharsis. Clearly there is a violence at work in the text, but one that goes well beyond Oedipal conflicts, and involves, among other things, a violence directed at the self.[22]

And among these other things is the "violence" that involves language. Askar must leave the "third world" of the nurturing body in order to enter the larger "third world" of politics, the world of social reality. Initiation into this world involves the acquisition of the Word, and even more importantly in Muslim culture, initiation into the language of Allah entails a separation from the world of women. The highly reflective narrator of *Maps,* just prior to his graphically described circumcision, muses, "The Word, I said to myself, was not a womb" (p.86). So one must leave nurture in order to enter language. Askar provides a rationale when he reminds himself, "Misra belonged to my 'non-literate' past—by which I mean that she belonged to a past in which I spoke, but did not write or read, in Somali" (p.164).[23]

To enter literacy is a proclamation of a new kind of power, one that differs from the immense power of the oral tradition to which he belongs, and Askar, whose name means "bearer of arms," has no doubt of the power of writing: ". . . every letter became a sword—by pronouncing it, I sharpened it; by drawing it, I gave it a life of its own; all I had to do was to say 'Cut' and it would cut the enemy's head" (p.168).[24] The text spans the eighteen or so years of his life's experience. It begins with him recreating his origins and attempting to "conjure the past" (p.3); it ends with him naming himself to the police. He repeats the story until "time grew on [his] face, as he told the story yet again, time grew like a tree..." until finally, "allowing for his different personae to act as judge, as audience and as witness, Askar told it to himself" (p.246). He leaves orality and enters literacy; he leaves the mother/land and enters the larger world. But the procedure of endless telling and re-telling from a variety of perspectives draws on Somalia's oral tradition, thus yoking it to the literacy he now so eagerly embraces.

The story he tells is the story of maps and borders, of political affiliation and national identity. The story that connects all these stories, however, is that of Misra. Perhaps a clue to the need for her violent eradication lies in the epigraph from Tahar ben Jelloun's *The Sand Child,* itself a tale of mis-sited gender and the retrieval of origins: "Your story, because it is not a translation of reality, interests me. I take it as it is, artificial and painful."[25]

It does not attempt to represent reality, therefore it is interesting. It is artificial; it is pained. Clearly, the tale of a boy who menstruates and remembers his own birth is not a "translation of reality"—in other words it does not follow literary conventions of realism. (Neither, for that matter, does it fall into the category of "magical realism.") But the connection of that which is artificial and painful is also of interest. It is artificial in the sense that it is artful, in that it creates an artifact from pain. Askar must painfully eradicate Misra in order to situate her and himself, in order to tell *her* story as well as his own, in order to attempt the story of *the other,* in order to determine if there is, or can be, separation.[26]

II. The Archives of Memory, or, "Do the Dead Dream?"

At the beginning of *The Art of Memory* Frances Yates repeats a story from Cicero where the poet Simonides escapes death when the roof of a banqueting hall falls in.[27] The corpses are so mangled that the relatives cannot distinguish them, but Simonides, said to be the inventor of the classical art of memory, remembers the seating arrangement and so is able to make an identification. Simonides, we might say, spoke for the dead. I repeat this story because it quite wonderfully demonstrates how memory and language cooperate to invoke that which is past, and thus compensate for its loss.

And it is memory's transmutative drive which impels *Maps.* Misra is the ghost who passes through, who is invoked through the vicissitudes of Askar's memory as he attempts to retrieve and situate her: "So, he asked, who was Misra? A woman, or more than just a woman? Did she exist as I remember her? Or have I rolled her into a great many other persons, spun from the thread leading back to my own beginnings, incorporating with those taking one back to other beginnings, other lives?" (p.243).

Shortly after reflecting on this question of Misra's past identity— "So, he asked, who was Misra?"—Askar returns to the present and asks, "Who is Askar?" (p.245). These two questions must be posed together in order for any answer to be attempted. At this point we learn that Misra's funeral has taken place. If questions of *the other* have preoccupied, even obsessed, Askar all along, then now he is faced with the ultimate *other*—in the form of death.

The text is drawing to its close: the point at which he recites the story of betrayal and political intrigue, both to the police court and to his various reflecting selves. And it is at this point that I want to draw attention to Misra's story, the story of her own self, the story that revolves not round Askar, but occurs before he is born, and then after he leaves the Ogaden to live with his uncle and aunt in Somalia. Both stories are in some sense elided, are almost parenthetical to the elegiac enterprise of *Maps*.

Misra's childhood beginnings are briefly recounted to Askar in Part One of the tripartite structure of *Maps* (another example, perhaps, of Farah's operating within three worlds). Part One opens with a tantalizing epigraph from Dickens: "No children for me. Give me grown-ups." We are duly warned.

From the security of their bed and "cuddled up in each other's embrace...she spoke to you of a raid, so far undocumented in history books" (p.68). But this is no bedtime story, because Misra is the offspring of a *damoz* union between an Oromo woman and a married Amhara nobleman—a temporary union which comes about as the result of the man's legal wives failing to produce sons. Misra's gender, of course, provides no solution, so she and her mother are abandoned. Misra is kidnapped, and eventually is taken in by a wealthy man who brings her up as his daughter, but "with an eye to taking her as his wife when she grew up." She is forced into complying, but "In the end, the conflicting loyalties alienated her, primarily from her self. And she murdered him during an excessive orgy of copulation" (p.69). Finally, she tells Askar of two miscarriages, and of carrying a dead child within her, only to be replaced by the "living miracle" of his own self, whom she finds abandoned. (The telling of this history takes about a page of the overall narrative.)

The second part of Misra's story, that which occurs after Askar leaves, is the story of possible political treachery, and whether true or not, it apparently leads to her brutal murder. She is accused of betraying a Somali freedom fighters' camp in which 603 men lost their lives; part of the impetus for the community's accusation comes from her living with a young Ethiopian soldier—that, and her own status as foreigner, makes her suspect. But this story and the first are linked further. It transpires that the young Ethiopian soldier is, in fact, her half brother. The Amhara nobleman finally found success in another *damoz* union, which bore a son.

So murder, betrayal and incest combine in two tales. This triad is difficult to situate within *Maps,* partly because of the melodrama of coincidence, partly because of the descriptive elements—murder after an "orgy of copulation" admittedly does not sit easy. It seems over-written. But it is difficult to situate mostly, I think, because the hasty rendition interrupts the primary narrative, the narrative of Askar, in a way that jars. And perhaps this is the point.

I said earlier that both stories are somehow elided, are almost parenthetical to the elegiac enterpise of *Maps.* The subject of the elegy is the lost object. Or, is it really the surviving subject?[28] Because if this is so, the story of *the other* is perhaps incidental to the story of the self, particularly when that self is young and striving to find its own identity—a fact that is made even more complex because Askar is clearly uncertain where self and *other* divide. So that which seems overwritten (both in terms of style and event) is also, paradoxically, underwritten, minimized.

A reading of *Maps* inevitably produces more questions than answers: questions of origin and memory, identity and violence. While we are left in doubt about many issues (something Farah would approve of, given his opening epigraph from Socrates: "Living begins when you start doubting everything that came before you"), I want to suggest that in *Maps* something like a post-colonial interrogation is initiated, a practice akin to what Edward Said has called, in the specific context of the exile, the aim for that writer's "scrupulous subjectivity!" He refers, I think, to the need for exiled writers to cultivate a subjective and rigorous questioning in response to the present, to "regard experiences *as if* they were about to disappear."[29] But this "scrupulous subjectivity" is pushed further in *Maps:* the post-colonial interrogation further extends this "subjectivity" to include an emphatic retrieval and re-negotiation of the actual *subject*, a subject who refuses objectification and allocated *othering,* and instead scrupulously seeks the *other* within the self. In a recent article Farah writes: "Colonial childhood such as mine is discontinuous: the child grows up neither as a replica of his parents, nor of the colonial ruler...It was with this in mind that I began writing—in the hope of enabling the Somali child at least to characterize his otherness—and to point at himself as the unnamed, the divided *other*, a schizophrenic child living in the age of colonial contradiction."[30]

This agenda is given further emphasis with Farah's displacement of a pronominal hierarchy; the "three worlds" of his divided self emerge as the "you," "he" and "I" of the narrator allow for the differing perspectives to engage. This interrogation relies on memory's archives even as it acknowledges possible inaccuracies: "I'll admit," says Askar, "that many things are confused in my memory. My head, I feel sometimes, will explode with the intensity of the anecdotes I remember—events which in all likelihood didn't take place, not, at any rate, as I remember them" (p.40). By creating a protagonist who constantly engages self with self in an endless retelling, Farah reminds us again that while Askar readily embraces literacy he is also the product of an oral culture which values the gifts of speech and memory above all, even when, as in this case, the educated young narrator acknowledges his own weakness, caught as he is at a transitional point in the culture.[31]

The postcolonial writer is "the divided *other*," writes Farah; it is not surprising that such division brings violence to the heart of this narrative of identity: the violence that allows the narrator to say, "What mattered, he told himself, was that now he was at last a man, that he was totally detached from his mother-figure Misra, and weaned. In the process of looking for a substitute, he had found another—Somalia, his mother country" (p.96). It is the violence that compels Farah to eradicate that which his narrator most depends on—Misra, who loses first her breast, then her heart.

Finally though, for all Askar's ambivalence towards his adoptive mother, for all his efforts to site himself in his motherland, we must remember that the project of *Maps* is to recall Misra, to recall *the other* Third World they inhabited so intimately—to recall both in the sense of remembering, and in the sense of renaming. Just prior to his hearing of her death Misra appears to Askar in a dream and says, "All that one hopes to remain of one is a memory dwelling in someone's head. In whose will I reside?" (p.237). It is a poignant statement, the foreshadowing of a demise; it asks to linger.[32] This takes me to my opening epigraph where Walter Benjamin states that "a remembered event is infinite, because it is only a key to everything that happened before it and after it."[33] This configuration of memory and boundlessness comes from Benjamin's essay on Proust, where he lovingly acknowledges the haunting power of remembrance—Proust is also hoping to reconstruct his origins, his private version of the mother/land, but is exiled only within corked walls. I turn to Benjamin because his words acknowledge the liminal space which memory inhabits; its power is infinite, without boundary, because even as it provides the *key* to experience (and Benjamin says in the first half of the sentence that "an experienced event is finite"), it cannot be contained: it is poised forever at a temporal threshold connecting past and future, moving freely from one to the other. Once again, boundaries are blurred.

The second part of this section's title is "Do the dead dream?" These words occur just after Misra appears to Askar in the dream which expresses "all that one hopes to remain of one is a memory dwelling in someone's head" (pp.237-38). Of course, "dwelling" here is used in its verb form, but we can transpose it for a moment into a noun so that we have a memory house, a home for recollection, an archival repository. And just a page further in Benjamin's homage to Proust he describes how "from the honeycombs of memory he built a house for the swarm of his thoughts."[34] The power of this statement lies, I think, in its evocation of the sweetness of the enterprise, an enterprise which culminates in what we can think of as a poetics of loss, but which may answer the question, "Do the dead dream?" The answer is yes: they dream to be spoken for.

484

NOTES

1. A shorter version of this article was read at the MLA's African Literature Division panel on Farah at San Francisco in 1991. I am grateful to the University of Alabama for a Summer Research Grant which enabled me to complete this piece. Richard Helgerson's important essay demonstrates how ideology is expressed through cartographic images. See Richard Helgerson, "The Land Speaks: Cartography, Chorography, and Subversion in Renaissance England," in *Representing the English Renaissance*, ed. Stephen Greenblatt (California: University of California Press, 1988). For an examination of how atlases facilitated the growth of capitalism see Chandra Mukerji, *From Graven Images: Patterns of Modern Materialism* (New York: Columbia University Press, 1983), pp.79-130.

2. R.V.Tooley, *Maps and Map-Makers* (New York: Crown Publishers, 1978), p.99.

3. G.N. Uziogwe tells us that there is some argument as to the nature of the boundaries. Around 30% were drawn as straight lines, cutting across ethnic and linguistic boundaries, but the remaining borders followed national boundaries: see G.N. Uziogwe, "European Partition and Conquest of Africa: An Overview." *UNESCO General History of Africa VII: Africa Under Colonial Domination 1880-1935,* ed. A.Adu Boahen. (California: University of California Press, 1985), pp.43-44. For graphic representations of Africa's history from 175 million years ago to 1978 see Colin McEvedy, *The Penguin Atlas of African History* (Harmondsworth: Penguin, 1980).

4. Such issues of place and displacement are frequently central to postcolonial writing. And I use the term "postcolonial" in the way defined by Slemon and Tiffin, as "writing that is grounded in the cultural realities of those societies whose subjectivity has been

constituted at least in part by the subordinating power of European colonialism": Stephen Slemon and and Helen Tiffin, eds. *After Europe: Critical Theory and Post-Colonial Writing* (Sydney: Dangaroo Press, 1989), p.ix.

5. Somali society is essentially homogenous, and in contrast to the vast majority of independent African states Somalis are essentially a one-nationality state. The particular tragedy is that of its esti- mated population of 6 million, only 3.5 million lived in the Somali Republic; the rest were dispersed in Djibouti, Kenya and Ethiopia— a situation magnified by the mass dispersal of refugees in the clan wars of the 1990s. Yet all Somalis "speak the same language, respond to the same poetry, derive their wisdom (and their expe- rience) from the camel economy, and worship the same God": David Laitin and Said S. Samatar, *Somalia: Nation in Search of a State* (London: Gower, 1987), p.xvi. See also I.M.Lewis, *A Modern History of Somalia: Nation and State in the Horn of Africa* (London: Longman, 1965).

6. Nuruddin Farah, *Maps* (New York: Pantheon, 1986), p.111. Further references are given in parentheses in the text of the essay.

7. A good deal has been written of late about the concept of the nation. For a collection on this subject, see Homi K.Bhabha, ed. *Nation and Narration* (New York: Routledge, 1980). Rhonda Cobham also connects the boundaries of nation and self, but her emphasis is on the destabilization of gender in the text which, she argues, challenges us to "resist the reflexive urge to pin down a single version of the African reality as 'true'" as well as uncriti- cally accept the notion of "essence that underlies much of the dis- course around nationalism and sexualities In modern African fic- tion": Rhonda Cobham, "Boundaries of the Nation: Boundaries of the Self: African Nationalist Fictions and Nuruddin Farah's *Maps.*" *Research in African Literatures* 22, 2 (1991), 96.

8. Frantz Fanon, *The Wretched of the Earth*, trans. Constance Farrington (Harmondsworth: Penguin, 1967), p.199.

9. Farah's first novel, *From a Crooked Rib*, appeared in 1970, followed by *A Naked Needle* in 1976. The trilogy *Variations on the Theme of an African Dictatorship*, consisting of *Sweet and Sour Milk, Sardines* and *Close Sesame*, was published between 1979 and 1983. *Maps* was the first part of a second trilogy, followed by *Gifts* (1992) and *Secrets* (1998).

10. Nuruddin Farah, "The World as a Writer's Home," *African Commentary* (January- February 1990), 58.

11. Edward Said, *The World, the Text, and the Critic* (Cambridge: Harvard University Press, 1983), pp.34-35.

12. Tim Brennan, "Cosmopolitans and Celebrities," *Race and Class* 31 (1989), 2.

13. For a polemic against the use of the colonial tongue, see Ngugi, *Decolonizing the Mind: The Politics of Language in African Literature* (London: James Currey, 1986). See also, for an argument supporting Afrocentrism: Chinweizu, Onwucheekwa Jemie, and Ibechukwu Madubuike. *Towards the Decolonization of African Literature* (Washington: Howard University Press, 1983). Soyinka and Achebe are examples of those on the other side, arguing for a syncretism. For a brief introduction to Somali literature, see Albert S. Gerard, *African Language Literatures: An Introduction to the Literary History of Sub-Saharan Africa* (Washington: Three Continents Press, 1981). For the crucial links between politics and poetry, see Said S.Samater, *Oral Poetry and Somali Nationalism: The Case of Sayyid Mahammad 'Abdille Hasan* (Cambridge: Cambridge University Press, 1982). The first literary publication in the Somali language appeared in 1981. Translated as *Ignorance*

is the Enemy of Love, by Faarax M.J.Cawl, the novel is approximately half poetry and half prose.

14. Of course, the whole question of this "outsiderness" and borders is exactly what is being addressed when established American critical journals put together issues on African literature or when *PMLA* calls for articles on "Colonialism and the Postcolonial Condition." There is currently a recognition that what happens at the borders and margins is that which is potentially most interesting. Some of those "outside" are therefore invited "inside" the academy. Farah's is an interesting case: he has not been a prominent "Third World cosmopolitan celebrity" (to use Brennan's somewhat unfortunate phrase that jars, I think, in an otherwise fine essay); his readership has been largely in Europe, and it would be productive to identify the criteria that allow one "third world" writer greater "access" over another. Ahmad points out that the useful inquiry would be to see "how the principle of selective incorporation works in relation to texts produced outside the metropolitan countries": see Aijaz Ahmad, "Jameson's Rhetoric of Otherness and the 'National Allegory'." *Social Text* 17 (1987), 17.

15. In addition to menstruating, Askar witnesses and describes in graphic detail an abortion. Hilarie Kelly misses the point, I think, when she sees what she calls Askar's "fixation on menstruation" as an example of how Farah "fetishizes women...Menstruation is a metaphor of destructive femininity, frustrated womanhood, and Misra's warped, sacrificial devotion to Askar rather than to a husband or a child of her own": see Hilarie Kelly, "A Somali Tragedy of Political and Sexual Confusion: A Critical Analysis of Nuruddin Farah's *Maps.*" *Ufahamu* 16, 2 (1988), 31. Derek Wright, however, argues that in creating such an emphasis on the corporeal, "Farah has written the first African novel of the body": see Derek Wright, "Somali Powerscapes: Mapping Farah's Fiction," *Research in African Literatures* 21, 2 (1990), 33.

16. Farah is not, I think, in any danger of becoming what Sara Suleri has called an "otherness machine." Rather, he uses the term in order to undo its restricted meaning, to expand its potential, to reappropriate it for his own purposes. Sara Suleri, *Meatless Days* (Chicago: University of Chicago Press, 1989).

17. This is not a literal intention, but one that Askar explains elsewhere: "only in [her] death could she and I be related, only then would I somehow feel as though we were a mother and her son. And then, and only then, would I find myself, alone and existing and real—yes, an individual with needs of his own—no longer an extension of a maternal hand whose touch quietened the childish cry in one" (p.37). And while Askar's statement is more premonition than threat, there is a constant slippage between the real and unreal in *Maps*, what Derek Wright calls a "deliberately puzzling indeterminacy...as regards where metaphor ends and literal reality starts": see Derek Wright, "Zero Zones: Nuruddin Farah's Fiction." *ARIEL* 21, 2 (1990), 28.

18. There are several references of this kind throughout *Maps*, from the example of Misra being "the cosmos," to their being so engrossed in each other that "they didn't need to acknowledge the existence of the outside world" (p.192). Clearly there are also erotic overtones to the relation: Askar is jealous of Aw-Adan (Misra's lover), and his descriptions of Misra linger at times on her body, and in a very moving moment he confesses (within a dream), "I was utterly in love with her" (p.214). While an erotically sensual longing is certainly present, and may indeed be more explicit because Misra is his "adoptive" rather than his birth mother, it is not, I think, the primary focus of his bond.

19. There are other specific references to this: "Misra who eventually tucked me into the oozy warmth between her breasts...so much so I became a third breast...and I would find myself between her

opened legs this time, as though I was a third leg" (p.24); "...and you were in her cuddle, you were her third leg or her third breast" (p.141). Cobham argues that Askar becomes "Misra's penis or third leg," reading this "either as Askar's masculinization (or empowerment) of Misra, or his erasure of her as he incorporates her entire feminine identity into himself": Cobham, "Boundaries of the Nation," 90.

20. Ahmad's essay (see note 14) is a response to Jameson's essay, which argues for a "theory of the cognitive aesthetics of third-world literature": see Frederic Jameson, "Third-World Literature in the Era of Multinational Capitalism," *Social Text* 15 (1986), 65-88. For another response see Ketu H.Katrak, "Decolonizing Culture: Toward a Theory for Postcolonial Women's Texts," *Modern Fiction Studies* 35 (1989), 157-179.

21. Fernandez Retamar is also concerned about this term: "If there is one thing that troubles me now about the term 'Third World,' it is the degradation that it perhaps involuntarily presupposes. There is just one world in which the oppressors and the oppressed struggle, one world in which, rather sooner than later, the oppressed will be victorious": see Roberto Fernandez Retamar, "Caliban Revisited," in *Caliban and Other Essays,* trans. Edward Baker (Minneapolis: University of Minnesota Press, 1989), p.55.

22. Kelly sees Farah's portrayal of Misra as disappointing, because his ambiguous treatment "implies that women's victimization is inevitable, and that women may even bring this on themselves by their own inherent "flaws"; she suggests it is a "classic case of unresolved Oedipal conflict [where] the boy child wants to sepa-rate himself from the mother, but he cannot accept her separa-tion from him" and where eventually he "compromises the female 'in' him...for male privilege and emotional remoteness, just as he compromises the warrior in him for the safety of abstractions and

an academic life": Kelly, "A Somali Tragedy....," 31-33.

23. It is clear enough, I think, that a Lacanian reading of *Maps* could prove fruitful. Along with the issues of self and other, there are several critical references to mirrors and mirroring, and Askar's acquisition of the Word initiates him into the "symbolic order"— after his circumcision. One could also speculate if Askar emerges from the "mirror stage."

24. And in fact this connection of the power of language to that of the sword is more than metaphoric, because it was actually enacted in Somalia's quite recent history. Poetry's force is so formidable that it enabled one of the nation's most acclaimed warriors, Sayyid Mahammad 'Abdille Hasan (known to his enemies as "The Mad Mullah"), to use it for political purposes and effectively defy the Ethiopian, Italian and British "infidels" in the holy war he led against them between 1900 and 1920. Samater has a fine analysis of the power of the Sayyid's poetry and oratory in political resistance in Somalia. He writes that his power was such that he "was thought to 'inflict wounds' on his enemies, and indeed those who were attacked by his literary barbs often responded as if they had received physical wounds": Samater, *Oral Poetry and Somali Nationalism,* p.1.

25. Tahar ben Jelloun, *The Sand Child,* trans. Alan Sheridan (New York: Harcourt, 1987), p.135. Jelloun's book is the story of a man with seven daughters who desperately wants a son; when the eighth daughter is born he announces the birth of a son and raises the child as male.

26. African writers have long criticized Western readers for their tendency to universalize, to ascribe their own values to other cultures. Perhaps the real problematic issue, then, lies with the critical enterprise itself, with (Western?) critics' disinclination to

accept ambiguous characters who disappoint them, ideologically speaking. The argument that the double death of the m/others is unwarranted carries with it the implication that African writers should assume the unreasonable burden of creating characters who are without contradiction in order to serve a specific political agenda, one that fulfils "first world" critical expectations of what might be considered ideologically "acceptable." A useful broad overview of the early critical reception of African literature is provided in Rand Bishop, *African Literature, African Critics: The Forming of Critical Standards 1947-1966* (New York: Greenwood Press, 1988).

27. Frances A. Yates, *The Art of Memory* (Chicago: University of Chicago Press, 1966), p.2.

28. I am indebted here to Peter Sacks, *The English Elegy: Studies in the Genre from Spenser to Yeats* (Baltimore: Johns Hopkins University Press, 1985).

29. Edward Said, "The Mind of Winter: Reflections on Life in Exile," *Harper's* (September 1984), 54-55.

30. Nuruddin Farah, "Childhood of My Schizophrenia," *Times Literary Supplement* (November 23-29, 1990), 1264.

31. In fact Somali respect for memory and oration is so strong that the pastoralist ridicules the urbanized for dependence on writing. Samater cites a traditional storyteller on the subject: "When such people are called upon to give a public speech, they resort to their written symbols. Without these they can hardly open their mouths. To register our contempt for such a person, we say: 'He who looks at a paper never becomes a memorizer'": Samater, *Oral Poetry and Somali Nationalism*, p.33.

32. Misra is just one representative of the dead in this text, and while she is clearly the most significant to Askar, there are many "unburied corpses" (p.122) whose stories remain untold. Misra's invocation through *Maps* simply suggests Farah's larger agenda of giving Somalia a voice and a homeland, a place where the living (and the dead) can be heard. It also, importantly, demonstrates that the novel, while not Somalia's traditional nor privileged literary form, performs the act of memorizing so crucial to that culture.

33. Walter Benjamin, "The Image of Proust," in *Illuminations,* trans. Harry Zohn (New York: Schocken Books, 1969), p.202.

34. Ibid., p.203.

"THIS IS A PEN": WRITING IN *MAPS*

Rosemary Colmer

The map as a paradigm of colonial discourse is subverted and revisualised continuously throughout Farah's *Maps*,[1] but the map is only one manifestation of literacy; other aspects also are explored. Somali essentialist nationalism is posited on the identification of Somalis as a uni-lingual cline, yet the central tenet, unity of language, is not preserved (as in Arabic or Chinese) by a tradition of script. In a fiction which allows free play of improbable possibilities, Farah invents situations in which relations of language, blood and nationhood are subject to unlikely but fascinating complexities which serve to interrogate the psychological interface between orality and literacy, thereby indicting literacy as an agent of cultural colonialism far more potent than geographical dominance.

The novels of the second trilogy present a critique of essentialist nationalism by problematising the central constructs on which its dogma rests. By placing his fictional— even fantastic—creatures in hypothetical situations, Farah demonstrates the necessity of a reformulation and revision of nationalist rhetorics. Farah's first five novels explore the nature of choice and the repercussions of past decisions on the individual. His sixth novel, *Maps*, again places the central character in an uncomfortable dilemma, one which is metaphoric of the ontological anxieties of the nation. Askar, a Somali refugee from the Ogaden, finds himself at a personal crossroads. The narrative is not, however, focused on the choice he makes but on the reasons why he finds himself unable to commit himself to either option.

Askar faces the problem of having to choose between two futures for his adult life. He can become a university student and middle-class intellectual or he can enlist as a soldier in the Western Somalia Liberation Front, but the two vocations are seen as mutually exclusive. At the end of the novel, the choice is still not made, and the application forms for both future lives remain blank, waiting for him to take up his pen and inscribe his own fate, because Askar has not yet established the answer to the vital question, "Who *is* Askar?" (p.245), towards which the novel moves. It is not possible for him to make a decision between the two alternatives while the identity of the person who must decide is indeterminate. Askar must settle who he is if he is to decide who he will be. The source of his confusion lies both in his relations with his foster-mother, Misra, and in his inability to emerge from the world of written texts in which he lives. Literacy, which confers power on its colonial possessors, leaves Askar uncertain of his own identity and powerless to choose between the opposing rhetorics offered to him.

Though his name suggests *a warrior*, the character he reveals for us is full of dreamy introspection, and haunted by ambiguous visions. Dreams legitimately present a state of slippage between body and self, the metamorphic flux which is Askar's habitual psychological condition. The fluidity of selfhood and otherness in dreams mirrors the indeterminacy of Askar's own concepts of self and, correspondingly, the inconstancy of his ideas of the Somali nation of which he is a reflection. In dreams he can escape the categories and classifications imposed on him by language; he can return to the raw emotions and unified understanding of his pre-literate infancy.

The narrative takes the form of Askar's account of himself as told to "*You* who sit in judgement over me" (p.41). Implicitly, "*You*" is the reader; explicitly, on the last page, the narrative is re-viewed as a confession: "*You*" is reassigned as referring to the officers of the law, and the story is multiply repeated. In the tale as he tells it, Askar's birth occurs in mysterious circumstances which lead his uncle Hilaal to liken him to the magically-born heroes of African epic, Sunjata and Mwendo. Farah's installing of Askar as culturally representative while simultaneously establishing him as socially marginalised is achieved by having his mythic status raised and questioned in a single inset document of encouragement and reproof. This is a letter from his uncle who solemnly considers the evidence that he is "an 'epic' child of the modern times" (p.21), but ironically concludes that the right signs and portents were not, after all, present. While Askar's father died the day before he was born and his mother shortly after his birth, the gestation period was normal, and no eclipse accompanied his arrival in the world; indeed, the solar eclipse in the novel signals Misra's death, not Askar's birth. Although Hilaal's avuncular wisdom may dismiss grandiose suggestions of Askar's epic status, this passage in his letter provides a hint to the reader which is sufficient to open up a reading of the novel that makes Askar's orphan status, fostering, journey, and choices emblematic of the Somali nation. Farah's richly allusive style enables the parallels between Askar and the nation to remain fluid, shifting and elusive, but nonetheless inviting.

The interrogation of colonial history in the novel indicts the local geographical colonizer, Ethiopia, but it also points to aspects of colonial power that are not driven by a territorial imperative. The cultural colonization of literacy allied with religion is accented in the scenes in which Askar, a Somali boy, first acquires literacy by learning in a foreign language and an imported script. The metaphor of mapping is the dominant one in the novel and it is invoked to describe several social and psychological processes: the mapping of the body and the process by which Askar comes to consciousness of himself and enters the "territory of pain" which is manhood; the mapping of boundaries between the human and the non-human; the mapping of the land, emotionally and geographically; the mapping of the people, colonially, linguistically, and politically; and the process of physically inscribing maps, on the body or with the pen. Mapping, nevertheless, is seen as only one form of inscription. Script, in this novel, is foreign to the oral Somali culture; script is experienced in association with Arabic and Islam, or with other foreign languages and cultural imports.

As teller of his own story, a teller who never suggests that his tale takes written form, Askar situates himself within an oral context. His account of his early life is importantly focussed on the immediate physicality of his apprehension of his surroundings and the oral medium of his earliest verbal knowledge of his environment. Orphaned at birth, Askar appears at first "as though I had made myself, as though I was my own creation" (p.23), but he comes to see his foster-mother as the universe he inhabits: "she *was* the cosmos" (p.9). He is her time; she is his space (p.11). As a child, Askar is inseparable from her. They are smeared with one another's body fluids, so close that Askar's body seems a part of hers:

> And let me not forget Misra—how could I? Misra who eventually tucked me into the oozy warmth between her breasts (she was a very large woman and I, a tiny little thing) so much so I became a third breast; Misra who, on account of my bronchial squeamishness, engulfed me in the same wrapping as her breasts—a wrapping as cosily couched as a brassiere; Misra who, as the night progressed towards daylight, would shed me the way a tree sheds ripe fruit and who would roll over on her back and away from the wrapping which had covered us both, and I would find myself some-where between her opened legs this time, as though I was a third leg. (p.24)

Askar is nourished by Misra, mentally as well as physically. He is taught the lore of his own people by Misra, who is a foreign woman (p.127). Through her experience he also apprehends the physical realities of the power structures which govern gender relations among his people and, guided by the grandmotherly neighbor, Karin, he understands the woman's intimate sensory world of powerlessness and pain, that is shown particularly in Misra's abortion. Despite Askar's belief that he has once menstruated, however, he rejects any identification of himself with women; he is very clear that he would rather believe that he is sick than that he has in any way become a woman. On a physical level, therefore, he identifies himself as male; as he grows up he learns to classify himself as masculine in his society.

The focus on Askar's earliest years enables Farah to propose a number of questions through the fiction, many of them relevant to the Somali nationalist claim that the common tie among Somalis is language. What *is* the Somali language? Is it the same when mispronounced by a child as when mispronounced by the Oromo woman who teaches him to speak? If written script is a twentieth-century imposition on a language with a rich oral tradition, what is the status of literacy in Somali (particularly before the normalizing pressure created by the adoption of an agreed authoritative orthography), and what is the validity of an educational system which relies on texts, or introduced systems of law or morality, which are couched in another language and proceed from another culture? Askar's passage from childhood involves his grasping the textual and symbolic, which provide a set of rules for human life, like the rules for sexual behavior marked out in red and green on the calendar that is designed to save Misra from another unwanted pregnancy. Farah does not suggest that Misra is illiterate—in fact she has taught Askar the alphabet—but she has to be socially coerced into making use of the calendar's textual message, and giving it control over her sexuality, whereas Askar's acquisition of masculine-owned Koranic literacy is the first stage of his intellectually-based separation from Misra's physical mothering: "I would sleep with the *loox*-slate between my legs...to keep her from coming anywhere near me" (p.86).

Askar is separated three times from Misra in the novel: once by time, as the transition from infancy to childhood is marked by writing lessons and circumcision; once by geographical distance; and once by ideological distance when he believes that she has betrayed six hundred Somali fighters. All three separations are represented as a passage across territorial boundaries. All three are traumatic; the first and third figure largely in Askar's narrative of himself, since they are deeply formative experiences, while the second more clearly takes its place as part of the political allegory in the novel. Each moves Askar further from the physically whole, intellectually unfragmented world of his Ogaden childhood.

Askar's first encounter with school and with the written word is heavily allegorised in the text: "Like a bewildered African nation posing questions to its inefficient leadership, I kept asking, 'Where are we going? Where are you taking me to?'" (p.80). Askar's introduction to writing is to Arabic, in Arabic script: "the brutal force of the written tradition imposed upon the thinking of one belonging to a non-written tradition" (p.84). His first lessons are accompanied by malice and violence. His mouth "a pool of blood" (p.82)—a phenomenon later associated with news of his journey to Mogadiscio and with his vengeful feelings towards Misra—Askar is inducted into the harsh world of the Koranic school kept by Aw-Adan, and soon his mouth is instead filled with the holy Word, replacing the blood-taste of hatred and even Misra's "profane name" as he chews, drinks and sleeps with the Word (p.86). Askar is passing from a world of touch and physical bonding into a new realm of the written and the symbolic. Letters, the Word, maps, and social boundaries are part of this new world. Almost immediately, circumcision takes Askar into a "territory of pain" leading to a "land of loneliness" (p.85), an experience which also forces him to "give birth to myself" (p.86). The ritual of circumcision and the "geographic dictates of pain" (p.90) which it involves mark his physical separation from the maternal cosmos of Misra, just as his first day of school had marked his intellectual separation from her to begin the creation of his new independent relation with the world. The gifts Askar requests after his circumcision are pen and paper, so that he can continue his devotion to the written text; he is also offered maps and pictures, other textual representations of the new, literate world. Literacy enrols Askar in a new set of alliances: "He, as prominent as the map he read to the illiterates surrounding him, spoke knowledgeably, enthusiastically about the liberation war which his people were waging against Misra's people" (p.97). Askar's "prominence" here underlines the way in which literacy has raised him to a higher, newly-defined status: prominent above non-literates and antagonistic to non-Somalis. Literacy elevates him socially and alienates him from linguistically defined categories of others.

So, too, does the process of understanding the classification of sexuality. As part of his male socialisation in his society, he learns the rules of sexual power which allow the man to exploit the woman but not to exploit those lower or higher in the sexual hierarchy than women. Boys and women can be beaten but only women are proper objects of sexual exploitation: "After all, she was a woman and she could be beaten or taken at will" (p.85). The border between higher and lower is clearly mapped and comprehensible to the young boy, who has before him the transgressive example of the Adenese who rapes hens and boys. The demarcation is invoked again later in the novel, when Misra's story of how her rapists claim to be her rescuers (from pack-rape by a gang of baboons) equates their vengeance with the actions of beasts, even as their false explanation purports to link her with the animals (p.186).

During the time when he lives in the Ogaden, Askar's accession to the status of literacy blends with his physical apprehension of the world. The Word is inscribed on the real. Askar's body is scarred with the letter-shaped marks of Aw-Adan's cane; he writes Koranic verses on his own body and draws maps on his skin; green days on the calendar smell differently from red days. Although he is literate, the sensory and the textual are not yet split. The rift occurs when he leaves Kallafo.

Askar's second separation from Misra is the geographic one created by his travelling from Kallafo in the Ogaden, home of his birth-mother, to Mogadiscio, whence his father and thus Askar derive part of their surname: Xamari. This journey from the world of his mother and foster-mother to his father's homeland is also, in the fluid set of referents Farah manipulates in the novel, the symbolic reunion of a child of the Ogaden with his Somali motherland, and the labelling of a human child with documented national identity. Askar's narrative is quite explicit about the replacement of Misra as mother figure with Somalia (p.96); yet the Ogaden, too, continues to be represented as a metaphoric motherland which the child will one day help liberate (p.158). Nor is "motherland" the only authentic concept of mother-hood, and the metaphor of fostering is further complicated by Farah's continued insinuation that a legalistic construction of nation-hood which fails to find a space in its definitions for socially and cul-turally nurturant relationships such as Misra's with Askar, while priv-ileging the status of violent instigators of cultural dominance, such as Aw-Adan, is faulty. Concepts of nationhood are overtly interrogated in the Mogadiscio passages of the novel, where Askar is offered opposing rhetorics of national duty.

Farah consistently highlights the disjunction between the real world and the text that culture and national aspiration attempt to inscribe on it. Not only are our allegorical readings of Somalia and the Ogaden indeterminate, but the geographical limits of the regions are ambiguous. Askar's passage from his past to his future crosses an imaginary but symbolically potent line between Ethiopia and Somalia, a line which has already lost its reality, as the border of the reclaimed territory has shifted during the fighting. Within Farah's fic-tion, this serves as a warning, about the separation between the real and the representational, that Askar would do well to heed as he enters the next phase of his life under the protective supervision of a couple who occupy a fully literate domain. Hilaal, a university lec-turer, and Salaado, a teacher, are explicitly linked with literacy and text, and their influence on Askar is primarily intellectual. His new foster-parents are overtly non-maternal and even, physically, non-reproductive: Salaado has had her ovaries removed (or just one ovary—the account varies) and Hilaal has had a vasectomy[2]. Askar's first meeting with Hilaal is in a room from which daylight is excluded and in which Hilaal's head blocks most of the light even from the lamp; here "Hilaal created another world, out of which he refused to surface" (p.137). Askar's room in their home bears on its walls a map, a calendar, and a mirror. No longer is his sense of space and time to be a part of his unified Misra-cosmos; instead his self-image is to take its framed place next to the cartographic and chronographic representations of space and time (p.145). It is under the patronage of Hilaal and Salaado that Askar acquires the *carta d'identitá*, the identity document which says in writing that he is a Somali national, but on which there is no room for Misra's name, because such documents deal with categories and classifications of the literate world, and take no account of the human relations of touch and nurturance. Although Askar plunges with enthusiasm into the sophisticated environment of his uncle and aunt, where floor tiles are "Italian and therefore attractive" (p.136) and "middle-aged men and middle-aged women behaved as though they were in their early twenties" (p.159), Farah is less enthusiastic. The language signals that these things, although delightful, are not necessarily admirable.

It is clear, particularly from Hilaal's persuasive writing in his letter, that although Hilaal and Salaado pay lip service to the idea of Askar's return to the Ogaden as a member of the Western Somalia Liberation Front, they try to influence him to remain in Mogadiscio as a student. Hilaal's letter, written to Askar when he is fourteen and struggling with his conscience, suggests that he has a duty to his nation to finish his education, "since you'll prove to be excellent material as a researcher, as a writer of articles and as one who can impart enlightened opinion about the cause" (p.20). The advice is valid, but it is hedged about with ego-deflating comments. Further, the fact that the letter, placed very early in the novel without much context, turns out to come from a man who shuts out the daylight makes the reader reassess it once we know more about its author. Askar is being pressed to stay in the world of letters, far removed from the real war.

His tutor, Cusmaan, applies a counter-pressure, marked in the text as subversive because it is explicitly banned by the boy's guardians. In the intervals between reading *Playboy*-type magazines, he harangues the eight year old boy about his duty to liberate his homeland by military action. When Askar is older, Cusmaan gives him a manual on car repair, full of technical signs and jargon. Ostensibly this is so that he can repair and use cars liberated from the enemy, but the gift of the incomprehensible manual is an emblem of Cusmaan's ability to preach theory without any connection with practice. Both *Playboy* and the repair manual are substitutes for the real thing. Thus, although both Hilaal and Cusmaan try to influence Askar, in opposite directions, both are limited by their reliance on the written word. They are abstracted from reality. Under their tutelage, Askar too is increasingly estranged, by his growing passion for inscribed systems of classification and codification, from the real world. The ironic inflections of Farah's language show his character's learned dependence on the authoritative (and often foreign) text, for instance when his interest in the reality of what makes a Somali a Somali takes him from the practical discovery that fluency in the Somali language is the criterion, to academic research: "I began to study with appropriate seriousness the linguistic map of the continent as updated by researchers at the AIA, London" (p.166).

There is a radical dichotomy between reality and its abstract representations. The "illustrated detail" (p.158) with which the theory and psychology of war is explained to Askar gives him an excellent grasp of the way in which war in Africa has become an incongruous testing site or playing field for the Western powers, but the discourse itself alienates Askar from the human realities of war and death: "The universe altered perspective, it shrunk into a tiny chessboard" (p.158). Hilaal's rhetoric becomes seductive in its own right: "I felt calm listening to the rise and fall of his beautiful rendering of his own ideas" (p.166), but the ideas are too abstract to survive Askar's attempt to apply them to any concrete example. Being able to read the text does not enable Askar to deal with the things he has read about. Possession of a manual on car repair does not help him when Hilaal floods the carburettor. Nevertheless, Farah uses the opposed rhetorics of Hilaal and Cusmaan to argue that both mastery over the real and command of the text can give rise to political power. Hilaal's philosophical discourses are full of examples of ways in which the pen, the book, the Word, and the map have been instruments of religious and political domination. Askar has already discovered that the first words in his English language textbook are, *This is a pen. This is a book.* Hilaal points out to him the ways in which the imposition of literacy on a non-literate people is part of the colonial process. The literate, in Hilaal's view, will prevail over the non-literate. For Askar, these observations ring so true that "every letter became a sword" (p.168). Askar cannot even go to the beach without reading a message in the waves about how colonisers exploit their ability to read text as much as their ability to control objects:

> The sea is a map: it tells those who are literate in its language where they are, it reveals, to those who are able to uncover secrets, where the treasures are. Haven't all the *daters* employed it, as they employed their intelligence and their map-reading facilities, their writing capabilities—haven't they crossed it to conquer, to subjugate, to colonize? (p.159)

The novel has already led the reader to a broader understanding of the dominance of literacy and literate modes of codified thought than this narrow appreciation of the role of literacy in the colonial territorial enterprises. The last part of the novel opens broader issues still, such as whether truth is accessible in language and whether, if orality is the state of childhood, it belongs with other intimate knowledges of the touch, the heart and the body, so that literacy, which marks a stage in (literal or metaphorical) separation from the nurturing "mother" also marks an estrangement from truth. Askar's floundering attempts to understand the uses of literacy and to disentangle the critique of literate dominance from the rhetoric of the critical discourse are interrupted by his third separation from Misra, this time an ideological one, for it appears (truly or falsely) that his foster-mother is a traitor to his motherland. One of the early categorizations of women Askar had been introduced to was the idea that all women except your mother, wife and sister are whores. For as long as Misra was conceptually classified as a mother, her position in Askar's filial affections was secure. She might have murdered her first husband and had several lovers, but she was still his foster-mother, and therefore blameless. Events require that the adult Askar reconsider Misra's position when her old friend Karin brings the news that Misra has betrayed a camp of liberation fighters to her Ethiopian lover (who may also, improbably but significantly, be her half-brother). A traitor to the motherland cannot also, in this code, be a "mother." Askar's attempts to come to terms with the reversal of his concepts complicate the difficulty he is already having in resolving the opposition between Cusmaan's theoretical advocacy of warfare and Hilaal's alluring rhetoric of educated liberalism. Cusmaan and Hilaal at least present conflicting logics, conflicting literate codifications of action, but Misra's appeal is from Askar's pre-literate past and it is sensory, emotional, and oral. Assuming a new identity with the slipperiness of one of Askar's dream-figures, Misra arrives in Mogadiscio to plead her innocence before a disbelieving Askar and his more impartial relatives. Her geographic and ideological displacement, and the mastectomy which symbolically renders her less of a nurturer, reverse the old relations between them: he becomes, we are told, her cosmos. Askar's inability to deal with the situation highlights the failure of either of his new rhetorics to cope with a non-rational, pre-literate human relationship. The re-categorizing of Misra as traitor makes her also a murderess, a whore, a witch, and Askar's psychological and almost physical revulsion from this version of her is radically and traumatically at odds with his residual memories of her vital, maternal role in his life. He has difficulty touching Misra, and he cannot give credence to her spoken word, so

506

it is impossible for him to reestablish the old bond of trust, or Misra's status as blameless mother. Two other responses lie open to him, corresponding to the opposing ideologies of his teachers, Hilaal and Cusmaan: he can make logical and unbiased inquiries, as Hilaal urges, or he can take violent action on behalf of the WSLF and avenge the deaths of the 600 fighters.

Hilaal's legalistic arguments proceed from his usual rational stance; he remarks, for instance, that in Islam adultery is a "complicated science" (p.225), and this comment underlines the way in which the laws of the Peoples of the Book regulate human behavior and codify human sin. Askar's sense of horror and repugnance at Misra's putative guilt makes a disinterested inquiry into the facts impossible; besides, he has only her spoken word to judge from. There are no documented facts on which a judicial decision could be made. The masculine rhetoric of war and bloodshed has more appeal for Askar, but he cannot get beyond symbolic, inscribed representations of action. He can draw a picture of a knife, but not use one. From early childhood, Askar had spoken of the possibility that he would kill Misra, as he had killed his birth-mother; now he veers between tender protectiveness and murderous disgust. She asks him if he will avenge her murder; he asks himself if he should avenge her betrayal of the fighters. His problem is that logic will not tell him whether Misra is guilty or not, and as a literate man in a logical world, Askar no longer trusts anything which is not logical. Neither the testimony of the spoken word nor the testimony of the heart is enough for him. Psychologically his refusal to trust her word tears the heart out of her and throws her to the sharks, but probably—the novel is reticent on this point—he plays no actual role in her real death. Misra's death eclipses the sun and turns the sea to a vast bloody womb, and Askar is left, once again, like an egg in a dead hen, a creature with potential born from a defunct possibility. In narrating his life as part of the inquiry into her death, he draws life from her corpse; he is reborn from her death in the act of narrating to the police and to the judicial court of his own conscience.

The novel ends not with action but with the initiation of the self-reflexive process of narrating. Farah's project is not to present a program but to open up an area of inquiry. *Maps* invites the reader to see Askar's crisis of identity as more than the plight of an individual caught between conflicting interests and incapacitated by inchoate passions. His is the predicament of a post-colonial nation, inescapably reconstituted by the multiple influences of its past and its present.

NOTES

1. Nuruddin Farah, *Maps* (New York: Pantheon, 1986). Page references are given in parentheses in the essay.

2. For a fuller treatment of fostering, mutilation and miscarriage as allegories of nationhood, see: Derek Wright, "Nations as Fictions: Postmodernism in the Novels of Nuruddin Farah," *Critique* 38, 3 (1997), 193-204; reprinted in revised and expanded form as "Mapping Farah's Fiction: The Postmodern Landscapes" in the preesent volume.

MAPS AND MIRRORS

Gerald Moore

Maps and mirrors reflect and clash against each other throughout Farah's sixth novel, in a pattern of imagery that makes this the most richly integrated of all his works. The "you" who is addressed in the book's opening word is not only the hero's younger self, greeted across time and space (from Mogadishu to Kallafo: from the late 1970s to the early 60s); he is the tool employed tirelessly to explore the problem of his identity; individual, familial, ethnic, and national. By addressing himself in the second person, the seventeen-year-old author establishes much more than sheer distance from his younger self; he establishes a profound strangeness. Who is Askar?: "It appears as though you were a creature given birth to by notions...a creature brought into being by ideas, as though you were not a child born with the fortune or misfortune of its stars, a child bearing a name, breathing just like anybody else."[1] These, then, are the mysteries that baffle the adolescent Askar and which "you" must illuminate. They surround the when, the where, and the how of his arrival. For the babe Askar was found, masked with blood, beside the body of his mother, who had crawled into a dark hiding-place to bear him. Did she, as he sometimes

509

believes, die before his arrival? Was the living body born from the dead? Or did she suckle him just once before expiring?

Askar is orphaned in a quite drastic sense. His Mogadishu-born father has died fighting to liberate the Ogaden from Ethiopian rule. His Ogaden-born Somali mother has died in childbirth. And, to deepen the anomalies surrounding his birth, his finder and foster-mother is an Oromo from the Ethiopian highlands who has been kidnapped and carried to the Ogaden in infancy. The map that he begins to learn from her lisping Somali is one whose truth depends upon who draws it and for whom. Is Kallafo in Western Somalia or in Ethiopia? Did his uncle, Qorrax, rape his widowed and helpless mother? Whose son is he? And, for that matter, has not Misra, his foster-mother, been more than a natural mother to him? Their beings have overlapped to such an extent that they virtually inhabit each other. The infant Askar has no existence apart from Misra, whilst she finds her body borrowed almost nightly by either Qorrax or the Koranic teacher Aw-Adan. If her body is a map, it is one ruled over by many, eventually mutilated and flung into the ocean without identity. If it is a mirror, what or whom does it reflect? Can a body so abused be recognized as that which was once virtually shared and inhabited by the child Askar? These are some of the questions that the young man, by roving to and fro in time and space, by roving between the "you" of then and the "I" of now, vainly strives to answer. One can only imagine the delight Mikhail Bakhtin would have found in such a text. For the dialogue here is not only between phases of the same being, but between that being and his female "half" or aspect. So intense is the latter that young Askar even imagines he has menstruated in sympathy with it, just as Misra did on first encountering his new-born "stare." And Askar's affiliation with the female "curse" is the more touching because it is precisely during her periods that Misra becomes irritable and violent towards him. Thus Misra's alleged treachery during his absence from Kallafo is something he simply cannot deal with; it touches him far too intimately. And the dialogic structure of the book extends to include alternative origins and alternative destinies; the elitist destiny offered by his mother's relatives in Mogadishu or a plunge back into the centuries-old conflict for the Ogaden. Enigma wraps both his beginning and his possible destination. Farah likes open endings, and the reader does not know which path Askar will choose.

Farah has long been interested in doubles and in overlapping or coinciding personalities. In *Sweet and Sour Milk* (1979), Loyaan's search for the truth about his dead twin Soyaan, who expired under his eyes, provides the structure of the book. And the reader is surprised to learn how little Loyaan really knew about his identical twin's movements, motives, and relationships. Even Soyaan's elegant mistress and baby son come out of the blue, so far as Loyaan is concerned. At the end he is still not able to say clearly what or who killed Soyaan, and his search is certainly not helped by his "sour," combative personality, so different from that of his twin. Their traces have seemed to diverge as well as converge during his pilgrimage through a corrupt and oppressive society, from which he has hitherto held his distance, working far away in Baidoa. But the irony of the ending is perfect; he is apparently doomed to take over the exile destined for his brother. The earlier media muddle over their respective names and photos, his own photo having been printed in an obituary of Soyaan, is simply a foretaste of that conclusion. Loyaan has almost become Soyaan, through tracing him so obsessively through his movements and acquaintances. Yet the search also brings out, ironically, the distance between the two. As Loyaan encounters the same people and situations that surrounded his brother during his last days, his irascibility strikes a false note. Soyaan, the reader senses, was not like that. But the pattern of final convergence works itself out inexorably nonetheless. The struggle over Soyaan's soul, which the regime is determined to appropriate, will perhaps only be resolved in the next generation, through his son. But, in the meantime, Loyaan is probably obliged to step into his shoes. The regime has succeeded in claiming not only Soyaan's soul, but his twin as well.

Askar's long absence from Kallafo and from Misra might be compared with Loyaan's absence from Mogadishu during his brother's prominent career. The activities during those ten years of a woman who was once almost his twin self are surrounded with ambiguities. Even her name and village of origin are shrouded in mystery. And this mystery will not "rub off" from the young hero, impatient for emancipation from that extreme dependence. Misra had once put it in these words: "You are a blind man and I am your stick, and it is I who lead you into the centre of human activities" (p.15). What she means is that both have an ambiguous status in Uncle Qorrax's compound. He, though a nephew, is also an orphan, born in apparent shame and obscurity, and thus not entirely welcome to Qorrax's own wives and children. She, though welcome to take the care of him off their hands, is a stranger, a woman with no husband or living child of her own. Though she has climbed from the status of servant to that of wife, her subsequent divorce and the death of her child have left her back where she started. Thus she elaborates her image to explain to Askar their situation: "You, the blind man, and I, the stick. And together we pierce the sore—that's their conscience" (p.15).

Askar's first childish instincts of rebellion against his extreme dependence upon his protector sometimes strike a sinister note. After threatening to kill her, so that she will become a corpse like his mother, he reflects upon his meaning:

> Of course I wasn't going to "kill" her because I hated her, far from it...What I meant was, that only in death could she and I be united...only then would I somehow feel as if we were a mother and her son. And then, and only then, would I find myself, alone and existing and real—yes, an individual with needs of his own. (p.37)

She must die so that he may live. Perhaps this is why Askar yields so easily to belief in Misra's rumored treachery: it is another way of "killing" her in his soul. When reproached for this infidelity by his uncle Hilaal, he is unable to justify it, but he remains inflexible.

512

It is Hilaal, the Mogadishu professor, who explains to him the partial truth offered by the maps which have come to obsess him. Mercator, he points out, had drawn a projection of the Earth which exaggerated the size of the northern regions of the world at the expense of the equatorial ones, producing a Greenland almost as large as Africa. And this at the very time, the mid-sixteenth century, when those northern regions were busy taking over the tropical areas, starting with the Americas. Hilaal's sometimes pedantic homilies serve to inform the reader, as well as the provincial young Askar, about the significance of contemporary events in the Horn of Africa. He points out Somalia's uniqueness in Africa, as a nation based on a single language, culture and religion, as opposed to an imperial construct like Ethiopia. Yet imperialism has left the Somalis divided between three states, their unity as a people denied by the maps which separate them. Askar's first interest in maps had been sparked by the Ogaden war against Ethiopia, which had brought home to him his anomalous situation: a Somali orphan living in Ethiopian-dominated territory and linked in extraordinary intimacy with an Ethiopian woman. How to map that? And mirrors could be equally treacherous as guides to identity:

> Then the mirror vanished from right in front of you and the wall which had been there replaced it. And there on the wall appeared shadows and the shadows were speaking with one another, some laughing, some listening and some holding hands or touching one another.
>
> "And you—who are you?" One of the shadows asked you. You answered, "I am in a foreign body."
>
> "Now what does that mean?"
>
> You paused. Then, "It means that I am in a foreign country." (p.61)

This visionary experience, one of many in the book, springs from a kernel of truth. Askar is in a foreign country (Ethiopia) and virtually in a foreign body (Ethiopian). Askar also feels a profound and helpless sense of guilt, a sense of responsibility for his mother's death as the price demanded by his own existence. He even asks Misra on one occasion whether death might have mistaken him for his mother. But she has absorbed enough of Islamic philosophy to reply that everyone has his time to die, and death can make no such mistakes. The adolescent "I" of the long dialogue with the "you" of childhood can identify some of these concerns in the younger boy but has certainly not shed them altogether. After all, the wound of the explusion of Somali forces from the Ogaden is still fresh, and in its turn keeps fresh all the ambiguities surrounding his own existence. Assisting in Mogadishu at a *mingis* ceremony for the expulsion of an evil spirit from a neighbor's body brings surging back all his doubts about the integrity of the individual self: "Could a good person live in an utterly bad one, you ask yourself, your imagination overwhelmed by the thought that this was possible. Could Misra hide in you? Could *another* dwell in her?" (p.205).

Another structural device used by Farah, apart from this book-long internal dialogue, is a jumping to and fro in time and space, the alternation of scenes from childhood in Kallafo and youth in Mogadishu. The reader is not suffocated by the infant Askar's virtual enclosure within the warm cosmos of Misra, because we get to breathe a bit of sea air in Mogadishu also. And this alternation leads to a kind of ping-pong between the "bad" uncle (Qorrax) in Kallafo and the "good" uncle (Hilaal) in Mogadishu. Qorrax, a brother of Askar's father, is a classic Muslim paterfamilias, ruling his large household of wives, concubines, and children with the whip. The gentle Hilaal, his mother's brother, is quite content to leave many of his expected roles to his beautiful and gifted wife Salaado. If he is happy to play cook, bottle-washer and passenger, she positively purs as eater, shopper and driver. Young Askar thus witnesses and contrasts two extreme interpretations of the husbandly role within his own family. But he has other, more poignant reasons for resentment of the domineering Qorrax. Though Askar shares Misra's bed every night, she often tip-toes off to bestow her favors upon Qorrax or upon the equally violent Koranic teacher Aw-Adan. Jealousy lends spice to every slash of the cane Aw-Adan administers to his young pupil, who is often so much in the way when he wants to monopolize Misra's attention. And this lends a strong Oedipal element to Askar's obsession with his foster-mother:

> I seem to have remained a mere extension of Misra's body for years—you saw me when you set eyes on her. I was part of the shadow she cast—in a sense, I was her extended self. I was, you might even say, the space surrounding the geography of her body. (p.75)

Some of these switches between the two worlds of the novel are modulated through dreams. When Askar begins his journey from the Ogaden and crosses the official frontier into Somalia, the action slides smoothly into a dream-sequence, in which he meets a girl who claims that she is no real person, only a shadow standing in a borrowed skin, but that he, though real enough, is too easily content with the smooth surface of things, turning them into a mirror in which he sees only his own features. He awakes to a shout from the bus passengers that they are in the first Somali town, but the unresolved dream has entered his consciousness. The nameless girl; the skull from which they drink; the two horses, one of which drops its rider; the luxuriant garden of full fruits; these will recur in all his musing. Much of the book's lyricism springs from this gliding between dream and reality. Somali culture would certainly not discount the significance of dreams, but the sophisticated Hilaal and Salaado probably would. In any case, Askar, caught between tradition and modernity, never seeks help in interpreting them. They seem only to add to the bafflement produced by maps and mirrors, which refuse to yield back what he demands of them. The dreams provide a sort of subtext in which many elements from his waking life recur, but oddly sequenced and arranged. For instance, during Misra's funeral he lies in a fever (he seems often to retreat into fever at times of crisis). His feverish dreams mingle elements from his past, present and imaginative life, but are also preparations for the news of her death, which his aunt and uncle have kept from him. Askar dreams that he is in the usual lush Edenic garden, sitting in the shade of the tree which was planted on the day of his birth and eating its fruits. All these images of sweetness and innocence are marred by the taste of blood in his mouth, always a signal of guilt in him. But a moment later the scene changes; he is naming the trees and plants like Adam and all the burden of guilt is lifted from him. Suddenly he sees a vulture and a dog racing each other for a piece of meat. He sees the Adenese who was accused of fornicating with a hen walking along with a shoe in his mouth, while Uncle Qorrax hobbles shoelessly behind him. Then he sees Misra throned in a kind of glory and she asks whether after her death she will live on in his mind or only in those of her murderers. This dream mingles everything from his earliest memories to the unknown events accompanying it in time. His only happy association of Uncle Qorrax is with his bright and elegant shoes, bound to attract the attention of a crawling infant. What can be the meaning of his shoelessness, or of the odd mouthful carried by the Adenese? Even while he is wondering, he is awoken to the news of Misra's murder, mutilation, and burial. He has at least glimpsed Misra in his dream as "the ruler of this land of games, of maps telling one's past and future" (p.237), before learning the news of her brutal end. He has witnessed her elevation upon a throne and heard her flat denial of any betrayal of the Somali fighters. In another dream he has embraced her beside a stream of water, in contrast with the cold formality with which he has treated her in reality since her arrival in Mogadishu. These dreams seem to have prepared him both for the news of her death and for the posthumous reconciliation which will enable him finally to bury her in his heart.

The dream sequences are thus both corrective of his behavior and a means of stimulating his highly selective memory. The girl he dreamed of at the frontier has warned him against his superficiality. Later he recognizes her features in those of his Mogadishu girlfriend Riyo. The dreamed-of features seem to have "gone before" the actual encounter in time. But such repeated dream encounters can also be a means of explanation, as well as correction. Askar has often dreamed of an old man coming towards him with a young girl's face on his shoulders. Towards the end of the book he dreams of a boy washing a skull in a stream, who tells him that it is of a man who raped his daughter and who died haunted by the sense that he was wearing her face. Perhaps Askar had once known the story, and in self-protection had stored it among his repertoire of dream-images. But equally, Askar has sometimes felt a sense of the interchangeability of bodies and identities:

> "I was once a young man—but I lost my identity. I meta-morphosed into an old man in his seventies, then a young woman. I am a septuagenarian wearing the face, and thinking with the brain, of a young woman" (p.61)

But dreams are not just explanations or illuminations of experience; they may also serve as heralds of coming knowledge or events, both personal and public. Ben Okri has recently written brilliantly of dreams performing just such an active role in the struggle for the soul of the nation:

> A nation was being born in our area. Somewhere else an avatar was dying, and another one was ready to take her place, in an endless secret chain of dream worlds which, at the right time, explodes into a new way...and the dreamers are often unaware of the forces they are bringing into our lower world of the earth, for great truths take time to manifest in our leaden reality. And when they do manifest, their effect through time

is never entirely pure...We read our omens as prophe-
cies, which become facts.[2]

Two phrases here stand out for their relevance to Farah's use of
dream. A Somali nation is certainly struggling to be born in the
events surrounding the action of the novel, and that struggle cannot
be separated from the saga of Askar and Misra. Also, "their effect
through time" is precisely what we seem to see in their recurrence in
the hero's consciousness. But whatever their significance is as
omens, dreams also serve an essential structural purpose. They complement Askar's fragmentary way of telling his story, reminding his
reluctant memory of all that he would rather omit or forget. The closing words of the novel carry us straight back to its beginning. On the
first page Askar had admitted: "You are a question to yourself. It is
true" (p.3). And, after telling the story of Misra and Askar to successive groups of policemen, lawyers, judges and juries, he concludes
his book with the words, "Askar told it to himself." The dreams are a
major voice in that telling, often one that the waking, narrating voice
can neither understand nor control. But in the telling, they often add
unsuspected dimensions to the tale. In his reveries Askar likes to
believe that he sprang living from the dead body of his mother. This
would make his birth extraordinary and epic, like those of other
African epic heroes such as Mwindo and Sundiata, far transcending
the apparently obscure fate of the orphan. Thus he treasures the egg
found in the body of a slaughtered foul; something living drawn from
the bowels of the dead. And he dreams of the humble Misra as a kind
of sea-goddess, wading through the waves and feeding the fishes
with her menstrual blood. Dreams can thus liberate and enlarge our
perceptions, yet he reflects that they can also divide. As a child he
was separated from Misra only in dreams, when they lay side by side
but each locked in their visions. This contrasts interestingly with
Okri's views on dreaming. Both writers agree that there is no hard
edge around personality, that others can invade or inhabit our identities. But Farah sees dream as a refuge from invasions, as a private

realm; whereas for Okri the dreams of the powerful can grow like nightmares in the minds of their victims, riding through their nights just as they ride through their days. Thus for Azaro there is no refuge from deadly dreaming of Madame Koto or "the blind old man."

Anglophone African fiction has perhaps taken a long time to recover from the shock of the untutored genius of Amos Tutuola. Overreacting to his freewheeling style, with its use of visions, block-letters, exclamatory headlines, and other devices to direct the pace and meaning of narrative, it retreated into a kind of stylistic realism, which involved sacrificing some of the key techniques of oral art. Meanwhile the Mande novelists Camara Laye and Ahmadou Kourouma, writing in French, had made essential use of dream as an alternative voice of experience and narrative. Novels like Laye's *Le regard du Roi* (1954) and *Dramouss* (1966), or Kourouma's *Les soleils des indépendances* (1970), are inseparable from this dimension. Not until the early work of Ben Okri, beginning with *The Landscapes Within* (1981), and Farah's employment of dream in *Maps* does it begin to enjoy a comparable importance in anglophone fiction. Okri's short chapters and annunciatory headlines in the Azaro sequence of novels also take the reader straight back to Tutuola and his uninhibited prose. The forest returns as the abode of voices, spirits, and weird manifestations which often flow through and transform the diurnal life of the streets. The thinning of the forests is a thinning of life itself. And it is Azarao's formidable Dad who offers this insight into the real significance of dream: "sometimes we are more awake in our dreams: we hear what the spirits are whispering...we become what we really are."[3] Askar's retreats into feverish dreams at all moments of crisis (the loss of the Ogaden, the finding and burial of Misra's body) might be seen as a kind of equivalent for the forest in the nomadic imagination of the savannah. It is perhaps then that he sees himself as he really is, and that troublesome memories insist upon a hearing. The world of dream is no mere supplement to that of waking, but that which illuminates it and lends it meaning.

It is time to return to maps and mirrors, which haunt Askar's dreams as much as his waking. It is Salaado who tries to bring them into a relation in which they may draw meaning from each other:

> And so, nailed next to the map which indicated where you were born, there was a calendar. There, if you wished, you could follow the progress of the war in the Ogaden. Nailed next to the calendar was a mirror. Here you could register your bodily changes...(p.145)

Arranged like this, they finally stop dancing round and querying each other. But Askar is clearly a young man who will never stop challenging enigmas.

NOTES

1. Nuruddin Farah, *Maps* (New York: Pantheon, 1986), p.3. Further page references are given in parentheses in the essay.

2. Ben Okri, *Infinite Riches* (London: Vintage, 1998), pp.222, 223.

3. ibid., p.329.

FARAH'S *MAPS*:
Deterritorialization and "The Postmodern"
Charles Sugnet

Nuruddin Farah's *Maps* has been widely appreciated for its brilliant exploration of the connections between national partition, gender identity, and narrative form, and the book has been fortunate enough to receive criticism worthy of its complexity.[1] There remains, however, a certain critical unease and uncertainty about *Maps*, about the novel's "difficulty" for readers, about why Farah chose to alternate among first, second, and third-person narrations, and about what it means for an African novelist to be what Derek Wright calls "a thoroughgoing postmodernist."[2]

Operating on Borges' principle that each writer chooses his own predecessors,[3] I want to examine certain affinities that Farah has expressed for specific "postmodern" writers, rather than addressing him as a generic case of the "postmodern." Such a tracing will reveal that the European postmodernists Farah alludes to are often those writing from situations of exile, deterritorialization, and national par-

521

tition, and that the postmodern in Farah's work is not a case of metropolitan insight flowing from the center to the less developed
peripheries, nor of a peripheral writer imitating the center, but a case
of affinity between writers confronting analogous situations.
Understanding Farah's work may help us better appreciate what is at
stake in Beckett's trilogy, as well as the other way around. Such a
tracing may also offer some insight about the logic behind Farah's
shifting pronouns in *Maps*. And it may confirm Farah's importance in
opening up new possibilities for African writing in an era when post-
independence nationalism has long seemed threadbare. (For the last
word on relations between postmodern and postcolonial, see Kwame
Anthony Appiah's "Is the 'Post-" in 'Postcolonial" the 'Post-' in
'Postmodern?"[4])

Sand Children: "The Only Way to Talk About Yourself is to Talk About Somebody Else"

In the autumn of 1988, two years after the publication of *Maps*,
Nuruddin Farah came from Khartoum to the University of Minnesota
to teach a course called "Postcolonial Fictions." Many of the books
he assigned were familiar ones: Achebe's *Arrow of God,* Ngugi's *A
Grain of Wheat*, Paule Marshall's *Praisesong for the Widow*, and
George Lamming's *In the Castle of My Skin*. Free of the ghettoizing
boundaries the academy inflicts on itself, he had no hesitation about
moving Toni Morrison's *Beloved* from its "Afro-American" category,
and teaching it under the sign of the "postcolonial" with African and
Caribbean writings. But the book on his syllabus that most of his students had not heard of was Tahar ben Jelloun's *The Sand Child*. The
English translation had just appeared, was available only in an expensive hardback edition, and was difficult to get, but Nuruddin was
determined to include in his course this story of a female Moroccan
child raised as male by a father who insists on a son after having
seven daughters in a row.

There are many points of connection between *The Sand Child* and *Maps*: both describe the violent mapping of the body through practices like circumcision; both explore the movement from oral to written and the way culture writes the body; both expose the artifice of gender construction by following an ambiguous case of gender formation; and both are interested in the analogies and disjunctures between gender formation and the formation of national identity. The Moroccan father, Haji Ahmed Suleyman, decides in desperation that his next child will be a boy no matter what: he sticks part of his index finger between the baby's legs to be circumcized, and young Ahmed is given men's clothing, a man's education, and male privilege. Like Saint Jean Genet, Ahmed figures out what is being done to him and consciously decides to will it, to make it his existential project.

Nuruddin suggested to his class that the "misgendered" young Ahmed is very like the "native" described by Fanon—a product of cultural violence. He treated the whole episode as an allegory of colonialism, in which the midwife could be called a collaborator, the daughters compared to those who accept the leftovers of the French regime, etc. The tormented young Ahmed keeps a journal in the Beckettian hope of recording that he has ceased to be, and one of the things he wants to cease being is a colonial subject. This kind of loose analogy between colonialism and sexism is not surprising, but Nuruddin typically complicated his allegory by calling attention to Haji Ahmed's newspaper announcement of the birth, which concludes "Long live Ahmed! Long live Morocco!" and frightens the French police, who don't want such an influential man to be a nationalist patriot. At one and the same moment, in the same newspaper announcement, Nuruddin suggested, Ahmed's father is announcing in a patriarchal-nationalist way that he wants to be free of French colonial violence and distortion, *and* is imposing on his eighth daughter the kind of coercive, distorting identity formation the French would impose on all Moroccans. Colonialism may be analogous to sexism, but anti-colonial nationalism is not necessarily good for women! (Both evidence and theory on this point have been accumulating rapidly since Nuruddin taught this class: see, for example Kumari Jayawardeena's *Feminism and Nationalism in the Third World*, Ann McClintock's "'No Longer in a Future Heaven': Women and Nationalism in South Africa," Andrew Parker et alia's *Nationalisms and Sexualities*, and Anne McClintock et alia's *Dangerous Liasons*.[5])

Both in his trilogy on dictatorship and in various interviews and conversations, Nuruddin Farah has been fairly explicit about his theory of dictatorship: he believes that the patriarchal family is the microcosmic model and school of dictatorship. In a country where fathers rule their families despotically, where women are treated as property, and children can be beaten on a whim, enlightened government is unlikely. Changes of government which simply change the name of the big man at the top will fail until family relations in the society have changed sufficiently, and especially until gender construction and the treatment of women have changed. This has been evident since his first novel, *From a Crooked Rib*, which synchronized a young woman's quest for freedom with the moment of Somali national independence. *The Sand Child*'s Ahmed takes a similar position: "no, my friend, the family as it exists in our countries, with the all-powerful father and the women relegated to domesticity...that family I reject, wrap up in mist, and no longer recognize."[6]

The analogy between family and nation is much easier to trace, of course, if both its terms can be imagined as stable. This has never been true in Farah's work, with its proliferation of doubled siblings and its complex inquiry into the nature of family bonds on one side, and a politically divided Greater Somalia on the other. But the death of Deeryie, who could be called the last honest patriarch, at the end of Farah's first trilogy, and the Ogaden wars, which mutilate the body of the nation, render both family and nation drastically unstable as Farah begins *Maps* with a series of questions. And these instabilities disrupt the form as well as the content of the novel.

Borges Makes a Cameo Appearance in Nuruddin's Classroom

The events of *The Sand Child*, which I summarized above as though it were formally a simple narrative, are in fact narrated in the most inconclusive manner possible. Portions of the story are told by an oral storyteller who appears on different dates in front of different gates to the city of Marrakesh. This storyteller carries a large notebook which is supposed to be Ahmed's journal, and the text contains verbatim quotes from it, but the storyteller admits sometimes that the pages are blank—washed out by exposure to moonlight, burned by the authorities, etc—and that he is inventing the passages from the journal. No textual stabilization of his narrative is possible. (There is also the problem of Ahmed's grammatical gender, which the French original sometimes renders as masculine, sometimes as feminine.) After only a few installments of Ahmed's story, the storyteller is "eaten by his words" (perhaps because he has distorted a passage from the Koran) and disappears. Young technocratic town planners clean up the public space where his auditors gathered and install a musical fountain that will play Beethoven's Fifth in jets of water. (Naturally a Club Med is also in place.) Three of the auditors meet for tea and attempt to finish the story in what Farah called in class "a collective, corrective retelling," but they only succeed in articulating three different versions of it, three more paths in what Jorge Luis Borges would call the infinite garden of forking paths. (My ten-year old class notes tell me that Nuruddin compared ben Jelloun's narrative technique favorably with that of African realist writers who believe "there is only one correct version" of a story.)

In a chapter called "The Blind Troubador," Borges himself makes an appearance in *The Sand Child*. Ben Jelloun does not name him, but the physical description is unmistakeable, and the chapter is full of references to his work, including a verbatim paragraph from Borges' "The Circular Ruins." One of Borges' favorite notions, given memorable expression in a story called "Tlon, Uqbar, Orbis Tertius," is that life imitates art, in spite of what mimetic theorists from Aristotle to

Stendhal have claimed. This makes storytelling a serious business; as ben Jelloun's public storyteller says: "I do not tell stories simply to pass the time. My stories come to me, inhabit me, and transform me."[7] And in ben Jelloun's tale, stories have visible effects on the bodies of those who tell them and those who hear them.

But where do those stories come from? The narrator of *The Sand Child* concludes as follows: "When the book was emptied of its writing by the full moon, I was afraid at first. But these were the first signs of my deliverance...If any of you really wants to know how this story really ended, he will have to ask the moon when it is full. I now lay down before you the book, the inkwell, and the pens. I shall now go away and read the Koran on the tomb of the dead."[8] This last may seem an abnegation, just as in some Borges stories where the narrator retires to an apparently obscure textual pursuit such as translating the works of Sir Thomas Browne in the style of Quevedo. But rereading the Koran may be a form of rewriting, and this storyteller may in fact be making a big claim. Nuruddin stressed to the class that *The Sand Child* was a kind of wicked copy of the patchwork quilt that sacred books like the Bible or the Koran usually are, that ben Jelloun's novel was an invitation to a secular rereading (=a vernacular retelling?) of the Sacred Book. Rushdie's *The Satanic Verses* had been published by this time—Nuruddin had seen Rushdie in London in August or September of 1988 and arrived in Minneapolis with a signed copy of the book under his arm—but the worst of the Rushdie persecution had not yet occurred when the class was discussing *The Sand Child*. Later, when the Rushdie affair was at its worst, it was clear that Nuruddin thought of his own work as similarly inviting rereadings of holy books.

National Partition, Narrative Instability

The sacred text that *Maps* most scandalously violates, however, is the sacred text of nationalism, with its mobilization of subjects for a triumphal linear progress toward national consolidation. Askar, the novel's central figure, born in the Ogaden, with a father who died in prison for the cause of the Western Somali Liberation Front, should certainly grow up to join the Front himself if the novel were following a nationalist trajectory. And indeed, as Rhonda Cobham points out, Askar begins to separate from the female world of Misra, his surrogate mother, by playing guerrilla warfare games with a band of young male companions.[9]

But that narrative direction is interrupted: by the end of the novel, Askar has menstruated (or hallucinated that he menstruated, or...?), and repeatedly dreams of his identity merging with those of a young girl and an old woman. He has neither joined the Liberation Front nor enrolled at the university to help liberate his people with knowledge and a pen, but has instead become a kind of artist-criminal, subverter of authority, enemy of the state, and perpetual asker of questions. Askar has not achieved a stable personal and sexual identity, nor has he been able to stabilize the notion of national identity. On the second last page of the novel, he is still asking "Who is Askar?" And the case of Misra, Askar's Somali-speaking Oromo surrogate mother, has confounded his best attempts to define national identity. It's impossible to know whether she is Somali kin, as Askar's aunt and uncle claim on her Mogdishu residence papers, or a treacherous Ethiopian betrayer of Somalis. Even the terms in which this question might have been asked have themselves become questions. "The point is," says Askar's uncle Hilaal, "who's an Ethiopian?"[10] (In "Childhood of my Schizophrenia," a wonderful one-page autobiography published in *The Times Literary Supplement*, Farah points out that the "Ethiopian" soldiers in the Ogaden of his childhood were miserably underpaid and often forcibly recruited from other colonized parts of the Ethiopian empire.[11])

By this point, narration itself has also become problematic: Farah's narrator notoriously refers to himself in all three persons, as "you," "I," and "he." (As we shall see, pronouns sometimes come unstuck from their referents in Paris or Dublin or Nazareth as well as in Mogadishu.) If the production and publication of the second trilogy (*Maps, Gifts,* and *Secrets*) has sometimes stuttered a bit, it may be because the end of *Maps*, with all the tools for production of meaning lying in ruins, is such a difficult starting point for anything; the actual collapse of Somalia as a state during this period must have complicated the writing as well.

"Postmodern" Affinities: Apprehending Yourself Elsewhere

If the critics find Askar's instabilities very "postmodern," well, Farah has chosen to be influenced by several "postmodern" writers. His first novel, *From a Crooked Rib*, begins with a quotation from Beckett. In "Why I Write," Farah says that Beckett, Joyce, and Virginia Woolf were his favorite writers for a long time, and Beckett's superb trilogy was almost certainly one of the models that encouraged Farah to produce his work in trilogies.[12] The opening of *Maps*, like the room where Beckett's Molloy is confined with a pencil and a few sheets of paper, suggests the novelist at work, a "scene of writing": "You sit, in contemplative posture, your features agonized and your expressions pained . . ." (p.3). And part of that first page echoes Borges' fascination with the idea, expressed in "The Circular Ruins" and elsewhere, that we are dreamed into being by others: "It appears as though you were a creature given birth to by notions formulated in heads, a creature brought into being by ideas . . ." (p.3).

Farah's *Maps*, like *Midnight's Children*, has a close relationship with Gunter Grass' *The Tin Drum*. Farah's Askar is only a grapheme away from Grass' Oskar, and Farah even manages to slip Gunter Grass' name and the phrase "tin drum" into his novel. In an essay first published in *Granta* and reprinted (along with his favorable review of *Maps*) in his essay collection, *Imaginary Homelands*, Rushdie acknowledges the inspiration of Gunter Grass for him, Grass as the immigre and exile, Grass as the excessive writer saying "go for broke," Grass as a retriever and reinventor of lost realities.[13] *The Tin*

Drum, Midnight's Children, and *Maps* all have frankly unreliable narrators who take an excessive interest in their mothers' sexuality, and who have disturbed sexual identities of their own. All three novels have plots that foil any search for definitive paternal/national origin. Askar's father may be the handsome young freedom fighter standing in front of the "liberated" Ethiopian tank; or he may be Askar's horrible Uncle Qorrax, tyrant, rapist, and collaborator with the Ethiopians. Rushdie's narrator, born at the moment of Indian independence, may be descended from a Kashmiri doctor, an Englishman with a toupee, or any of several other choices. And the paternity of Oskar in *The Tin Drum* is equally in doubt. Moreover, all three novels are written by men whose countries have been partitioned, and who believe they have irretrievably lost the geographical spaces of their childhood. (One lesson Rushdie draws is the imperative to "pickle" lost territories in writing, and the scene of writing in *Midnight's Children* is a pickle factory. When Farah's Askar speaks of why he draws maps, he says it is to "pickle" truth, and *Maps* is pungent with the flavors and smells of Askar's lost Ogaden childhood.)

Writing about Deleuze and Guattari's notion of "deterritorialization" in the minority discourse issue of *Cultural Critique,* David Lloyd describes some of the cultural consequences of such geographic loss:

> Minority groups are so defined in consequence of a dislocation or deterritorialization which calls their collective identity in question and leads to their categorization as instances of 'underdevelopment': whether a minority group is defined in terms of gender, ethnicity, or any other typology, its status is never merely statistically established, but involves the aspersion of 'minority' exactly in the sense of the common legal usage of the term for those too young to be out of 'tutelage.' To enumerate them all too briefly and all too schematically, the characteristics of a minor literature would involve the questioning or destruction

529

of the concepts of identity and identification, the rejection of representations of developing autonomy and authenticity, if not the concept of development itself, and accordingly a profound suspicion of narratives of reconciliation and unification.[14]

For Lloyd, one other important characteristic of such literatures is that they are written in a "major" language from a "minor" position; their minority status is thus defined in relation to an established canon. *The Tin Drum, Midnight's Children*, and *Maps* are all responding to deterritorialization, and it's interesting in light of Lloyd's remarks about legal minority, that they all have narrators who are in some way dwarfed or stunted, born with adult sensibilities, but unable to grow up. Lloyd's remarks about writing in a "major" language from a "minor" position might also shed some light on Farah's particular brand of English, which is very expressive but abstracted, not centered as the authentic or colloquial speech of a particular time and place. (Deleuze and Guattari's example is of course Kafka, the Czech Jew writing in a German that doesn't belong to him, that feels like the language of his oppressor.[15])

Lloyd is himself an Irishman from a partitioned country who writes about Irish literature through the lens of the postcolonial. Beckett is also Irish, and may not be as metropolitan as his French location would indicate. He too comes from a partitioned country, and is triply deterritorialized, first by the English colonialism which took Ireland from the Irish, then by his own exile in Paris, and finally by his exile in the French language, a "major" one, but not his own. Ireland, which suffered for certuries as the proving-ground for English colonialism, is in many ways at the margins of Europe; it used to be referred to as the only Third World country where the exploited labor happens to be white. Just as Achebe and Yeats shared an interest in uprisings against the British, so Farah and Beckett may share a sense of deterritorialization and failure of national consolidation. For Irish writers, the English language can never have the same solid social reference it has for the English. After Joyce filled English like a helium baloon until it nearly floated away, Beckett had little choice but to deflate it and then to flee altogether into a decomposing French.

Thinking back to Borges' appearance in *The Sand Child*, it's obvious that "postmodern" connects with "premodern," and that Borges' narrative tricks aren't the property of the metropole either. Borges was a Spanish-speaking Anglophilic writer who lived in Buenos Aires, a peripheral and culturally hybrid place. He was fascinated with the Kabbalah, with the *1001 Nights*, with the Koran, with Averroes, with all the philosophy and literature exchanged between Islam and Christendom through Spain. No wonder he turns up in ben Jelloun's fictional Marrakesh; this is not a metropolitan intrusion—just part of Borges' nomadic peregrinations around Europe's peripheries. If there ever was a "subject of the enlightenment," a believer in rationality, progress, and stable political identity, it's unlikely that he—and it would have been a he—would have come from Dublin, the Ogaden, or Buenos Aires. I do not speak Somali and am not qualified to trace the influence of Somali oral poetry on Farah's work, but it seems clear from what is available in English on the subject that the poetry makes use of veiled allusions, complex metaphors of ambiguous application, etc. The favorite example one hears over and over is of the oral poet compelled to praise the tyrant, who produces a scathing denunciation of the tyrant, veiled in such a way that the tyrant does not hear it, but other auditors do. This is the kind of text famously produced by Borgesian tricksters like Pierre Menard. It seems likely that Farah's Somali literary inheritance did not contradict, but worked in synergy with, the examples of Beckett, Borges, and the *1001 Nights* as he moved toward a complex, multi-layered, self-conscious form of the novel, in which every "truth" gets interrogated by another.[16]

Deterritorialization: It's the Fault of the Pronouns

"Decomposition" is Beckett's word for the process that reduces authoritative Western discourses to a single, frail, fluctuating voice that can't go on but does go on. Beckett means this word "decomposition" in at least two senses. While the talkers of his trilogy chatter on, their bodies literally decompose, rot, disappear. And their identities decompose in the sense opposite to that of "composition course" or "composition book"—that is, insofar as identity is a matter of linguistic composition, it is coming unravelled in Beckett's trilogy, where the language does not progress or consolidate, but comes undone. Both Farah's *Maps* and Beckett's *The Unnameable* (third of the trilogy) start from a radical scepticism. Farah: "You question, you challenge every thought which crosses your mind" (p.3). Beckett: "What should I do, in my situation, how proceed? By aporia pure and simple? Or by affirmations and negations invalidated as uttered, or sooner or later?"[17] From here, it doesn't take the Unnameable (or Askar, for that matter) long to get into trouble with pronouns: "I never spoke, I seem to speak, that's because he says I as if he were I...perhaps it's not he, perhaps it's a multitude, one after another, what confusion...you don't know whose, someone says you, it's the fault of the pronouns, there is no name for me, no pronoun for me, all the trouble comes from that, it's a kind of a pronoun too, it isn't that either, I'm not that either..."[18] As Beckett's Molloy says, "The only way to talk about yourself is to talk about someone else." The person the pronouns are talking about is always somebody other than the person speaking. Borges' short, paranoid, and undecidable story of his double, "Borges and I," is another version of the same problem. (Just as in the Borges story, Nuruddin has the habit of referring to his public self by the last name, so that he might say, for example: "Did you see the interview with Farah in *The Village Voice*?" And the signature Farah signs in the fronts of books is different from the legal signature Nuruddin uses for checks or contracts.)

This is the instability Farah has let into his writing with the shifting pronouns of *Maps*. Roland Barthes, a shrewd theorist who has read Beckett's writing carefully, introduces a spatial dimension into his discussion of shifty pronouns:

> "An American (or positivist, or disputatious: I cannot disentangle) student identifies, as if it were self-evident, *subjectivity* and *narcisssism*; no doubt he thinks that subjectivity consists in talking about oneself, and speaking well of oneself. This is because he is a victim of the old couple *subjectivity/objectivity.* Yet today the subject apprehends himself *elsewhere,* and subjectivity can return at another place on the spiral: deconstructed, taken apart, shifted, without anchorage: why should I not speak of "myself" since this "my" is no longer "the self"? The so-called personal pronouns: everything happens here: I am forever enclosed within the pronomial lists: "I" mobilize the image-repertoire, "you" and "he" mobilize paranoia."[19]

I have heard Farah say, when pressed in public by Chinua Achebe, that he used the three different pronouns in an effort to build up a complete African subject from its fragmented parts.[20] But Nuruddin, like Borges' Pierre Menard, is a notorious trickster, and I'm going to argue that the pronouns function exactly opposite to what he said, that Askar remains fragmented at the end of *Maps*. Rhonda Cobham tries gamely to stabilize Farah's fluctuating pronouns by tying them to the three functions of judge, witness, and audience Askar offers on the novel's last page, as he undergoes police interrogation about Misra's death. Nuruddin is a reader of whodunits, and Cobham correctly points out the intertextual relations between *Maps* and Ngugi's political thriller *Petals of Blood.*[21] To this Derek Wright adds the shrewd suggestion that *Maps* may be structured like Graham Swift's *Waterland* (a novel Nuruddin very much admires) where the narrator is trying to hide his guilt from himself and the reader.[22] But these analogues are too conservative and realistic to fully explain what Farah is doing. I think it may be more appropriate to evoke those postmodern detective stories (like the second part of *Molloy* or Michel Butor's *L'emploi du Temps*) where the question is not "Who done it?" but rather "Has a crime been committed? Has anything 'happened' at all?" In such books, the narrator feels guilty, but the crime can never be precisely specified. Note how the epistemological anchors of policing and judging to which Cobham appeals suggest territorialization, how they almost require a state and a state apparatus. Can a man without a country be tried and convicted? Would such a process finally provide the convict with a stable identity? After trying hard to organize the pronouns into a reasonable scheme, Cobham concedes that "the lines between these three perspectives are not always reliably indicated by the pronouns used."[23]

Derek Wright, in his book length-study of Farah, also tries to stabilize certain elements of Askar's fluctuating identity. On the question of Askar's menstruation, for example, Wright opts for a univocal, realistic, "scientific," narrative explanation: "When Askar, as a result of a urinary infection, imagines himself to have menstruated . . . ."[24] This seems to me a reduction of the rich novel that Farah has offered us, recuperating him to the very form of realist/nationalist fiction that he has rejected. Similarly, Wright correctly observes that Farah has written a great novel of the body, but then tries to suggest that the body can serve as a transcendental ground for identity, avoiding all the problems of cartography the book raises: "The body seems in the novel to be an alternative way of constituting identity, more reliable than maps."[25] But the body is itself mapped by culture, and the way it gets mapped depends partly on the cartography of the national territory at hand. As a male who menstruates, Askar certainly confounds any easy schematizing of bodily identities. Misra's body is found with one breast missing and the heart cut out, mirroring the mutilation of the national territory in the Ogaden war. And the book is full of other characters with missing body parts, wooden legs, etc. One such passage detailing horrific bodily mutilations in war (penises cut off, fetuses ripped from wombs) culminates with the phrases "Stories with fragmented bodies! Bodies which told fragmented stories!" (p.154) (Wright's book is on the whole good and useful, but as Jacqueline Bardolph observed in her favorable review for *Research in African Literatures*,[26] Wright's habit of beginning each chapter with a summary of the novel sometimes leads him to sound as though the novels have a straightforward content that can be summarized; in the chapter on *Maps*, he sometimes sounds as though Askar is a unitary subject, even though he knows this is not true.)

I suspect there is nothing "reliable" about Farah's narrative, so that Askar's gender and national identity continue to fluctuate in a stream of words. But perhaps there was a slight inaccuracy in the way I described Farah above as "letting in" that instability, because perhaps he had no choice. Note that Barthes identifies the student as"American (or positivist)" implying that certain attitudes come with certain national locations. And Beckett's *The Unnameable* laughably uses the word "situation" ("What to do in my situation") when he has nowhere to sit and is not sure if he has a body, if he even has an ass to sit on. His situation is that he is unsituated; thus aporia pure and simple. And how is Farah situated? Does he have a location, or is he a nomad of the pronouns?

Someone Was Speaking Nationalist Rhetorics

David Lloyd suggests that it is perfectly possible for a literature of minorities to fulfill a "major" function. "One notable case in point," he says, "would be the literature of nationalism which adopts the same aesthetic terms [same as the 'major' literature or the canon] in order to forge an oppositional national identity." Such a move, Lloyd observes, places the young, underdeveloped nation on the narrative path to "development" and adulthood, but at the enormous cost of accepting the imperial power's hegemonic right to define adulthood, development, aesthetic standards, etc. "Nationalisms reterritorialize dislocated identities historically, and, despite their initially progressive intents, continue thereby to acquiesce in imperial hegemony even after 'independence.' An alternative response is that represented by what we are terming minor literature, which refuses to reterritorialize identity, preferring to extend the critique of those developmental narratives which perpetuate hegemonic culture."[27]

A careful application of these sentences to Nuruddin Farah's career would show that they describe the trajectory that he has lived through and written about, from the nascent national allegory of Ebla's quest in *From a Crooked Rib*, through Koschin's uneasy attraction to the General's apparently progressive national revolution in *A Naked Needle*, to the end of *Maps*, where a nationalist reterritorialization has become impossible. But Farah was never willing to grant the exclusive masculinity of the national subject, and perhaps his gender politics made it inevitable from the start that he would not or could not perform a nationalist reterritorialization. All of these issues connect back to the question of language choice as well. Farah has stayed very close to his Somali subject matter and has taken a great deal of trouble to keep a Somali passport, but unlike, for example, a nationalist like Ngugi, Farah has written very little in any African language, and has chosen a European language that was not uniformly taught in his country. Instead of speaking for, or even necessarily to, the people of Somalia, he has sought a transnational or international audience.

Another way of expressing why Farah avoids a nationalist move that would stabilize his narrative is to say that he knows the high price of nationalism. At one point in *Maps*, as a group gathers around a bus about to depart, the narrator says "Someone was speaking nationalist rhetorics, in which plenty of Somali as well as enemy blood was shed" (p.126). While some critics emphasize a negative side to the confusion and indeterminacy of Askar's narrative, there are huge advantages to avoiding a clear-cut nationalism, a clear-cut masculine identity, and so on. In a book filled with nationalist brutalities culminating in the horrible mutilation of Misra's body (women bear a disproportionate share of the cost of nationalism) deferring a nationalist re-territorialization seems like a good thing. Thus Farah can't situate himself firmly on home territory, and perhaps isn't comfortably seated anywhere at all. But he's not just floating free either—he is in some kind of inescapable relation to the Somalia that doesn't exist, to the Somalias that he imagines into being. His most recent book, the nonfiction *Yesterday, Tomorrow: Voices from the Somali Diaspora*, continues the project by pursuing the scattered fragments of a deterritorialized Somalia across Europe.[28] Not surprisingly, it often focuses on the way gender and power are reconfigured under the pressures of exile.

"My stories come to me, inhabit me, and transform me."

I'd like to express more fully what the nature of this inescapable relation might be like by referring to a passage from Edward Said, another writer from a partitioned country who is consciously anti-colonial and anti-imperialist, but who nonetheless works hard to avoid narrating a triumphal nationalism. In a remarkable moment of *After the Last Sky*, Said, whose tone and demeanor do not suggest the "postmodern," confesses that he too has trouble with the pronouns:

> This is not an 'objective' book. Our intention was to show Palestinians through Palestinian eyes without minimizing the extent to which even to themselves they feel different, or 'other.' Many Palestinian friends who saw Jean Mohr's pictures thought he saw us as no one else has. But we also felt that he saw us as we would have seen ourselves—at once inside and outside our world. The same double vision informs my text. *As I wrote, I found myself switching pronouns, from 'we' to 'you' to 'they,' to designate Palestinians. As abrupt as these shifts are, I feel they reproduce the way 'we' experience ourselves, the way 'you' sense that others look at*

*you, the way, in your solitude, you feel the distance
between where 'you' are and where 'they' are.*

The multifaceted vision is essential to any representation of us. Stateless, dispossessed, de-centered, we
are frequently unable to speak the 'truth' of our experience or to make it heard. We do not usually control
the images that represent us; we have been confined
to spaces designed to reduce or stunt us; and we have
often been distorted by pressures and powers that
have been too much for us."[29] (My emphasis)

Less directly philosophical or linguistic than Beckett or Barthes,
Said's formulation contains more of the burden of history, emphasizing the political and geographic causes of pronoun instability, of a
subject who apprehends himself literally *elsewhere*. If we think about
the farcical superpower politics that determined the Ogaden wars,
"pressures and powers that have been too much for us" has a
poignant application to *Maps*, and "stunt" is exactly the right word for
what has happened to Askar-Oskar-Saleem. At another moment in
After the Last Sky, Said confronts a photo of his mother's home town:
"Even a picture of an Arab town—like Nazareth where my mother was
born and grew up—may express this alienating perspective. Because
it is taken from outside Nazareth (in fact, from Upper Nazareth, a totally Jewish addition to the town, built on the surrounding hills), the
photograph renders Palestine as 'other.' I never knew Nazareth, so
this is my only image of it, an image of the 'other,' from the 'outside,'
Upper Nazareth."[30] Said certainly has a "situation," even if he no
longer has a homeland and is standing in a purely imaginary place.
This situation, a permanent but alienated and undetermined relation
to a place you did not create, cannot control, and can never get back
to, is similar to Farah's (and to Grass' and to Rushdie's—hence the
poignancy of "pickling" that which is already lost).

In a recent essay on Farah and the postmodern, Derek Wright
observes that "it would be perverse to claim Farah as a thoroughgo-

ing postmodernist," and in his book-length study he observes that "After reading *Maps* four times, I must confess that I am still undecided whether psychological realism or postmodern experimentalism is the dominant mode of the novel."[31] But perhaps the choice is not such a stark binary choice between two predetermined, off-the-shelf modes of writing, and perhaps Farah's artistic freedom is not the kind of liberty implied by "experimentalism." Farah is certainly formally daring and innovative, but his innovations seem ultimately responsible to the gravity of his situation. *Maps* is certainly a complex book, an intellectual book, but what I find striking about it is how emotionally moving it is to read—so much bodily closeness, so much pain, so much loss, is detailed and *felt* in its prose. Over and over in its pages, the ideas of the nation and masculinity cause bodies to be rent, often by the very people who love those bodies. As Partha Chatterjee and others have pointed out in the debates over Anderson's *Imagined Communities*, the nation may well be imaginary, but it manifests itself in practices and institutions which have a heavy weight.[32]

I doubt that Farah set out to be a thoroughgoing postmodernist or any other kind of "ist." Instead, he used whatever literary precedents he could find, both in Africa and in Europe, to help him invent a scrupulously felt and thought account of the weight of nationalism and national partition, an account that challenges ideas and practices that have been so costly. Even at this late date, there is still a widespread assumption that African novels are under a special obligation to be both realist and nationalist. Certain critics, syllabi, and even departments still demand the reterritorializing maneuvers that David Lloyd so rightly interrogated nearly fifteen years ago, and still insist that African fiction demonstate an "Africannness" (through authentic oral sources, avoidance or modification of European models, etc.) that separates it from fiction produced elsewhere. One part of Farah's great contribution has been to break free of these limitations and invent another way for fictions by African writers to be responsible to the pains and pleasures they have witnessed. It is therefore important to avoid either recuperating Farah's work to the realist/nationalist model from which he has deliberately escaped, or making too much of his perceived "postmodernism," thereby implying that narrative indeterminacy is somehow the property of the West and is anomalous in African writing.

NOTES

1. See, for example, Rhonda Cobham, "Boundaries of the Nation: Boundaries of the Self: African Nationalist Fictions and Nuruddin Farah's *Maps*," *Research in African Literatures* 22, 2 (1991), 83-98; reprinted in *Nationalisms and Sexualities*, ed. Andrew Parker et al (London & New York: Routledge, 1992), pp.42-59.

2. Derek Wright, "Nations as Fictions: Postmodernism in the Novels of Nuruddin Farah," *Critique* 38, 3 (1997), 194.

3. Jorge Luis Borges, *Ficciones* (New York: Grove Press, 1962).

4. Kwame Anthony Appiah, "Is the 'Post-' in 'Postcolonial" the 'Post' in 'Postmodern?'" In *Dangerous Liaisons*, eds. Anne McClintock, Aamir Mufti, & Ella Shohat (Minneapolis: University of Minnesota Press, 1997).

5. Kumari Jayawardeena, *Feminism and Nationalism in the Third World* (London: Zed Books, 1986); Anne McClintock, "'No Longer in a Future Heaven': Women and Nationalism in South Africa," *Transition* 51 (Fall 1991), 104-124 (reprinted in *Dangerous Liaisons*); Andrew Parker ed., *Nationalisms and Sexualities*.

6. Tahar ben Jelloun, *The Sand Child*, translated by Alan Sheridan (New York: Harcourt Brace Jovanovich, 1987), p.64.

7. ben Jelloun, p.8.

8. ibid., p.164.

9. Cobham, 93.

10. Nuruddin Farah, *Maps* (New York: Pantheon, 1986), p.147. Further references are given in parentheses in the essay.

11. Nuruddin Farah, "Childhood of My Schizophrenia," *The Times Literary Supplement*, 23-29 (November, 1990), p.1264.

12. Nuruddin Farah, "Why I Write," *Third World Quarterly* 10, 4 (1988), 1595; Samuel Beckett, *Three Novels by Samuel Beckett: Molloy, Malone Dies, The Unnameable* (New York: Grove Press, 1965).

13. Salman Rushdie, *Imaginary Homelands* (New York: Viking Penguin, 1991), pp.273- 81, and *Midnight's Children* (New York: Alfred A. Knopf, 1981); Gunter Grass, *The Tin Drum*, translated by Ralph Manheim (New York: Random House, 1961).

14. David Lloyd, "Genet's Genealogy: European Minorities and the Ends of the Canon." *Cultural Critique* 6 (Spring 1987), 173.

15. Gilles Deleuze and Felix Guattari, *Kafka: Toward a Minor Literature*, translated by Dana Polan (Minneapolis: University of Minnesota Press, 1986).

16. Derek Wright, *The Novels of Nuruddin Farah* (Bayreuth: Eckhard Breitinger, 1994), pp.16-20.

17. Beckett, p.291.

18. ibid., pp.403-04.

19. Roland Barthes, *Roland Barthes by Roland Barthes* (Berkeley: University of California Press, 1994), p.168.

20. At University of Minnesota, Minneapolis, 16 April 1989.

21. Cobham, 91; Ngugi wa Thiong'o, *Petals of Blood* (New York: E.P.Dutton, 1978).

22. Wright, *The Novels of Nuruddin Farah*, p.112; Graham Swift, *Waterland* (London: William Heinemann, 1983).

23. Cobham, 88.

24. Wright, *The Novels of Nuruddin Farah*, p.122.

25. ibid., p.118.

26. Jacqueline Bardolph, "Review of *The Novels of Nuruddin Farah* by Derek Wright," *Research in African Literatures* 26, 2 (1995), 226.

27. Lloyd, 173, 174.

28. Nuruddin Farah, *Yesterday, Tomorrow: Voices from the Somali Diaspora* (London and New York: Cassell 2000).

29. Edward Said, with photographs by Jean Mohr, *After the Last Sky: Palestinian Lives* (New York: Pantheon, 1986), p.6.

30. Said, p.40.

31. Wright, "Nations as Fictions," 195; *The Novels of Nuruddin Farah*, p.122.

32. Partha Chatterjee, *The Nation and its Fragments* (Princeton; Princeton University Press, 1993); Benedict Anderson, *Imagined Communities* (London: Verso, 1983).

"ALAS, NO ANSWER"?
Structure as Theme in Nuruddin Farah's *Maps*
Julie Phelps Dietche

To read a novel such as *Maps* is not easy and many potential readers may fall by the wayside. It is not a pleasant experience to be dragged into the center of an ongoing war, a spinning inquisition, to be offered up snips and fragments of memories set down in random sequence, punctuated by an endless barrage of questions, dreams, letters (unwritten and unposted), scenes cut sort with a snap, disembodied voices, shadows, and a single voice that barks commands—"Tell me all! and so? And then?"—and also cries out in weakness and confusion—"Who am I?" and "Dearest Misra, why did you have to do this?" Nuruddin Farah's sixth novel *Maps* (1986)[1] tells the story of Askar Cali- Xamari, a young man who at 18 sees himself as at a crossroads. There is a war going on and Askar is trying to decide whether to register to attend the National University in Mogadiscio or whether to join the men of the Western Somali Liberation Front (WSLF) fighting to reclaim the Ogaden. Askar, a precocious, highly intelligent young man, has done well in his studies under the careful guidance of various priests, maids, a private tutor, and his uncle and aunt (both of whom are academics).

As Askar is facing the decision of what to do next, a figure from out of his past suddenly appears; this person is Misra. Askar being an orphan, Misra has been the person who raised him; for the first seven years of his life, Askar has called her "Mother." The ongoing war between the Somali people and the Ethiopians looms large in this novel. Askar has not seen Misra for ten years. She being an "Ethiopian" (Oromo) has remained in Kallafo. Misra now travels to Mogadiscio and enters the city in disguise, using an assumed name. She seeks out Askar and his adopted parents for protection, arrives at their doorstep, on the run from the war and from the rumours spread about her. Askar has been told, just recently, that Misra has betrayed the Somali people and as a result over 600 freedom fighters have been killed. The people in Kallafo, including many of Askar's relatives, have turned against Misra, accused her of treason, and have driven her out.

Askar feels torn, caught up in a horrible dilemma: should he welcome (or even see) Misra, his "mother," when she may have betrayed that other mother—the Somali "motherland"? Misra's impending visit unleashes a storm of emotion in him; his mind, his heart fill with memories of the past, of Misra, of his relatives, of his childhood growing up in Kallafo. This unleashing of memory and emotion *is* what the novel is about. To deal with the present (Misra has arrived), Askar must circle back; he must confront the past and his past selves. He must know who he is and what he stands for in order to go on.

The reader must join the character in his search. The early pages of the novel are particularly difficult because when we join him on page one, we cannot get our bearings; we don't know who he is or what kind of a story this is or who Misra is or what is going to happen or what *is* happening. Neither does Askar! The difficulty the reader may feel mirrors the protagonist's own dilemma. *He* is not sure exactly who he is or who Misra is or if in truth he can separate himself from her. "And you question, you challenge every thought which crosses your mind. Yes. You are a question to yourself....You doubt, at times, if you exist outside your own thought, outside your own head, Misra's or your own" (p.1).

Since the very mind (Askar's) that we are forced to enter on the first page of the novel is so uncertain, many elements of the structure which throw the reader off-balance can be seen as integral parts of the story, indeed as the story itself. The bulk of the novel re-enacts in mind time Askar's struggle to remember, to confront and to know. The story cannot be told in a neat tidy timeline because this is not the way Askar is experiencing it. We must as readers share Askar's hesitant and disjointed search; we must go *through* the experience as Askar does. Structure is the key that unlocks the meaning of this dense and clotted tale.

If we look at the "events" of the story and how these events are unfolded chronologically, we can see that there are two stories: there is the story that begins on page 181 with Misra's arrival in Mogadiscio (Askar is 18) and what happens after Misra's arrival, what happens to *her*. This story takes up a mere 65 pages, the last one- quarter of the novel, which runs to 246 pages in all. This part of the novel is actually told in the future which in terms of the "story" has not yet arrived. Askar was born in 1970, moves to Mogadiscio in 1977 at age seven, and yet Askar is 18 at the end (and at the beginning) of the novel, which puts him floating somewhere in the as yet unlived future; *Maps* was published in 1986.

But what about the first 181 pages? This other story occurs in Askar's mind; once he hears that Misra is in Mogadiscio, he is instantly caught up in a whirl of doubt and questions as he undergoes a kind of mental rehearsal for his first meeting in ten years with the woman who is both his "enemy" and his "mother." The events and the scenes in pages 1-181 can be seen as occurring in a time warp or a mental bubble. The story told in the first three-quarters of the novel loops backwards and then later connects with the second story (Misra's arrival in Mogadiscio and the events that follow). Although the events that occur after Misra's arrival are related, by and large, in a straight-forward chronological order (that is, Misra arrives, enters the hospital for surgery, then disappears, etc.), in the bulk of the story chronology is shattered.

Thus, on the first page, the reader is pulled into the enormous bubble (the mental maelstrom) of Askar's mind, Askar as he stands before a mirror in his uncle's house in Mogadiscio (p.181), preparing to meet Misra. The story gets told by leaps and bounds, regressions, flashbacks and flashforwards. For example, on the opening pages, Askar is 18 and is living with his uncle in Mogadiscio; there follow memories and scenes from his boyhood in Kallafo: another uncle, Qorrox, is described and Askar shares the same bed with Misra and Aw-Adan (pp.11-12). On page 17, the text leaps ahead to Mogadiscio and a vague appraisal of Hilaal and Salaado, then slips back to Askar at age seven just newly arrived in Mogadiscio and trying to write a letter to Misra. A long (three-page) letter cuts into the text (pp.19-22), a letter written by Hilaal to Askar when Askar was 14 and considering running away to Kallafo to join the fight. In Chapter 2, the story dwells at length and longingly on some of Askar's memories as a boy: Misra is bathing Askar; they are playing. She is rinsing soap from him, tickling him, and squeezing his "uff," making him laugh (p.35). Chapter 3 begins with a long dream (five pages long, pp.42-46); the time is dream-time; events and images are obscure and can't be understood until more of the novel is read. Then at the conclusion of the dream Askar becomes 17 again ("Awake and washed, handsome, shaven and 17 years old . . ."[p.47]) and we learn that Misra has arrived in Mogadiscio. On the next page (p.48), Askar has heard that she has become a traitor. Five chapters and 126 pages later we reconnect with this same moment in time, Askar waiting for Misra to arrive. Askar and Misra finally actually do meet and the second story begins in the middle of Chapter 9.

Between these two points (pages 47 and 181) time in the novel is askew: events, scenes from the past, conversations, dreams occur at random just as Askar remembers them. In one scene, Askar may suddenly recall snatches of a conversation he had with Misra or the intensity of his hate for Uncle Qorrox when Askar was six and this will suddenly cut to something someone said when Askar was 17; or a dream is described; or Askar recalls crossing the border from Ethiopia to Somalia and overhearing a stranger comparing unburied corpses to the collective memories of a nation (pp.122-23). All is chaos; all is jumble.

Repetition plays a significant part in breaking apart the chronology in the story. A scene, a remembered image, a feeling may be so strong that it persists and is repeated as Askar's mind whirls obsessively. For example, memories of being bathed by Misra break through, occur and reoccur, as does Askar's memory of feeling ill, dizzy and of tasting blood in his mouth. The broken stream of Askar's thoughts reflects the struggle he has to remember. Contradiction lies at the heart of the novel. The different sides of Askar struggle and do battle. The war is on within. If part of Askar wants to remember and wants to try to figure out his roots and his past, another part of Askar may not want to know. One Askar is weak and afraid; the other fights to recover the past. Right down the middle of the novel there is this split. Askar's mind works by confrontation, by opposition, seems to spin in opposite directions, never at one. A feeling of integration, of unity is missing. On a structural level, chronology must be shattered and broken because that is the way it is in Askar's mind.

Point of view in the novel also adds to the stress and uncertainty that the reader may feel. The narrative is divided into three parts and within these parts, 12 chapters, each of approximately 18 pages. There is a brief Interlude between Chapters 6 and 7, marking the ends of Parts 1 and 2. Within this basic structure, there is a carefully controlled pattern of alternating points of view: Chapters 1, 4, 7, 10 are told as "you"; Chapters 2, 5, 8, 11 as "I"; Chapters 3, 6, 9, 12 as "he." In the Interlude, all three points of view are used. However, what appears to be a shifting point of view here is not really that at all, but is a trick of technique for the "you," "I," and "he" are all Askar. For example, from Chapter 1 (narrated as "you"): "If you touched someone other than Misra, you burst instantly into the wildest and most furious convulsive cry. But if Misra were there, you fell silent...." (p.5). From Chapter 2 (narrated as "I"): "I crouched in the *baaf*, my eyes half-closed, in concentration and anxiety, waiting for the water to descend...I would shake, I would shiver" (p.35). From Chapter 3 (narrated as "he"): "He remembered how she used to lavish limitless love on him when sick; how she took care of him with the attentiveness of a child mending a broken toy" (p.47). We can see that the points of view are just superficially different ways to move in and out and about a single mind, the mind of Askar. In addition, the point of view within the chapters does not always remain constant. For example, in a chapter told as "I," a "you" will break through (see pp.24, 75); or in some passages an omniscient author (a fourth point of view) weaves in and out, seeming to be privy to thoughts that Askar (as the novel's governing point of view) could not know (see p.108).

This mixing of points of view reflects on a structural level one of the central themes of the novel, that is, Askar's uncertainty as to who he is. For Askar, nothing is simple. He does not trust appearances. He wants to know the deepest truth about himself and about his people and his country, but the truth that he finds is filled with contradictions. Askar's mind moves through clouds of doubt to further shadows of uncertainty. Is he himself? Is there another who speaks through him? Is the very skin he inhabits his own? Is he truly a man, or could he be a woman? His identification with Misra is intense and at times complete; he also sees himself as a young girl, an old man, and a shadow. Askar's uncertainty in a sense *defines* Askar.

Farah's use of multiple points of view serves the theme by forcing the reader to go through the uncertainty that Askar does. Just as the reader begins to get a sense of the "he" of a certain chapter, the "he" suddenly becomes a "you" and then slips into "I." With the "he" there seems to be a pretense of distance and of objectivity, with the "you" an engaged, accusatory stance, the "I" being the most intimate and leading the narrator deeper and deeper into the interior. On a structural level, the mixing of points of view re-enacts Askar's sense of being divided and torments the reader just as Askar himself is tormented by his sense of being split apart into different selves. Askar must try on different faces; the reader must try on these different faces, too.

Farah's use of different kinds of material in the text is closely related to the use of multiple points of view. Askar in his struggle to recover, to re-know his past discovers information in a variety of ways. For example, a disembodied voice speaks (in italics, pp.179-80); letters by Askar are written (and unwritten) to Misra and not posted; a journal kept by Askar's real (birth) mother, written in Italian, offers tantalizing hints, but remains undeciphered by Askar; a long (two and one half pages) letter from Hilaal to Askar is quoted in total (pp.19-22); drawings by Askar are described carefully. A number of dreams, some as long as four pages, weave in and out of the narrative and are described in minute detail; vignettes, glimpses (a paragraph or two), parts of dreams are remembered and other parts forgotten, the images in the dreams recounted in raw harrowing detail. Askar leaving home for the first time, traveling by bus to Mogadiscio, overhears a man talking; the man becomes a voice, but is Askar asleep or awake? Did the man really speak these words? How can Askar know for sure, how can he remember the truth about all these voices and dreams which happened ten years before? He remembers a maid down on all fours washing the floor and "sees" her raped, but did this really happen? Askar is trying to piece together the story of his life and his story lies hidden in a number of different places. He must search through the rubble, must leave no stone unturned; if a "voice" speaks, Askar must listen, must remember. The inclusion of this disparate material—letters, dreams, drawings, an untranslated journal, disembodied voices—underscores on a structural level the fragmented nature of Askar's search. The novel itself gets told in bits and pieces, in fragments unearthed from the past. Whether a particular chapter is told as "I," "you," or "he" scarcely matters because within each chapter there is such a raucous cacophony of disparate voices emitting from such a wide variety of sources.

The text is littered with questions: questions about self, questions about the past, questions about the on-going war. On page after page, the questions rage on as if a river had broken its banks and was running off in all directions at the same time. The questions asked are clearly Askar's search for answers but the questions can also be seen as part of Farah's technique and as an important structural device. Indeed, the asking of questions is the engine that propels the story forward. Whether asked by Misra, Cusmaan, Hilaal, or by some shadowy creature in a dream, all of the questions belong to Askar because it is his memory, his effort to reconstruct the past which governs the whole. This novel tells the story of Askar's mind thinking.

A cursory review of the many questions helps us to see on another level the basic split in Askar's personality. There are basically two contrasting selves: Firstly, there is Askar, the weak one, uncertain, filled with doubt, seeming to be paralyzed by his endless questions. This Askar hesitates to take anything at face value including himself, who he is, what people have told him, Misra and who she is. This Askar questions, too, the value, even the possibility of succeeding in his efforts to uncover the truth, to know himself. For example, Askar (to himself): "[Am I] not the rememberer but the remembered?" (p.39); "Is your own memory untrustworthy?" (p.70); "Who was Misra? A woman, or more than just a woman?" (p.243) In awaiting Misra's arrival Askar's mind whirls with questions (there are eleven on a single page): "Will I have to touch her?...The body speaks, the soul obeys—is that not so?" (p.55) In a later passage: "Did she exist as I remembered her?...Misra? Masra? Misrat? Massar?" (p.243). And then, secondly, there is Askar, the strong one, aggressive, filled with determination; this Askar is a fighter on the attack and he uses his questions both to goad himself, to force himself not to give up and also to force others to give him the answers he seeks. For example, Askar (to himself): "Do you remember?" (pp.18, 205); "What else did I notice when I first got there?" (p.159); "Well?" (p.179); "At least you remember this. You don't?" (p.207) In a passage when Misra is telling him the story of her childhood abduction, Askar is pushy and persistent: "'Yes, yes, but did the girl have a half-brother or a half-sister?...And then what happened?...And then?'" (p.70) And with Karin: "'Get on with it and quick too...Tell me the worst. What're you waiting for?'" (p.175) In a later scene, Misra lies recovering from surgery in her hospital bed: Askar insists: "'Did you or did you not do it? Be truthful...Who was it that accused you of being a traitor?...His name?...His name?'" (pp.209-10) Still later, with Hilaal and Salaado: "'Tell me everything that you know'" (p.239). We can hear the voice of a prosecuting attorney here; many passages become scenes of inquisition with Askar being at times the accuser and at other times the accused.

The questions asked in Askar's dreams reflect this same basic dichotomy; both the hesitant unsure voice of Askar and the harsh accusatory voice can be heard. For example, in the first long dream of the novel, Askar wonders "Was it conceivable...that he had lost whatever knowledge he had gained about himself through the years?" and a few lines later, the "nagging 'Who am I?' or 'Where am I?'" (p.44) In a later dream Askar and a young girl banter back and forth in questions but when she suggests "'All will be well with you,'" Askar's voice turns hard: "'How do you know?'" When she says "'You're going back to *yourself*,'" Askar responds "'And so?'" (pp.129-30) In a long dream near the end of the book, Misra asks who will remember her—"'In whose [head] will I reside?'" Askar responds by continuing the questions: "'But do these notions...of death and a memory of me...come together in your head like keys come with locks in our thoughts?'" The dream is cut short, "Alas, no answer." Askar wakes up (pp.237-38).

The questions punctuate the story and seem to tear apart the text giving the reader no rest: What is an Ethiopian? "Hasn't Misra chosen to be one of us?" "'Your people, my people—what or who are these?'" (pp.94-95), and on and on. But even as the questions seem to impede, to prevent the story from getting told, this is not true entirely. Although they momentarily force Askar to pause, to think, these same questions lead him on to discovery and to further questions.

The questions *are* Askar's story: they force the reader to participate in Askar's quest. The structure of the novel can be seen as a whirling circle filled with fragments, bits and pieces of information. These fragments must be gathered together somehow and it is through the questions that Askar poses that the past is recovered. Without the questions, there would be no Askar, there would be no discovery and there would be no novel called *Maps*.

In studying *how* the story of Askar gets told, we can notice one additional technique and that is explosions or the sudden cutting off of the narrative. There are a number of scenes that are cut off just as if a curtain suddenly dropped from the sky or as if a guillotine fell upon the narrator's (Askar's) neck and cut off his thinking. Perhaps the most dramatic example of this occurs in Chapter 10 when Askar is interviewing Misra in the hospital, trying to force her first to admit whether or not she is guilty and then to tell him the name of the person who betrayed *her*. Misra is hesitant to say and he has to bore into her repeatedly asking "'His name?...His name?'" When Misra at last finds the strength to tell him—"'Aw-Adan'"—the scene ends at that point. "There was a sudden power cut...you could not think of anything to say. Neither could she" (p.210). Cut.

In a very touching scene, Misra and Askar have been talking about an Adenese man who seduces young boys; Misra is down on all fours scrubbing the floor and being quiet while Askar (only six) is asking grown-up questions about "human dignity." The scene suddenly dissolves: "You heard Misra's chest explode in a convulsive cry...and you fell silent" (pp.67-68). In another dream, Askar remembers Misra with great love and emotion—"I was utterly in love with her." He imagines Misra standing in the sea feeding the fish with her menstrual blood and remembers the sea wearing a "blue gown," a moon reflected in the water, and he and Misra embrace. He breaks in: "No, I do not remember anything else! I remember no flood! I recall nothing else either!" (pp.214-15). The scene is cut instantly and finally as if Askar himself fears he might explode with the potency of the image (and with its forbidden joy). The scene ends: he can bear no more!

The frequency of scenes such as these, scenes that end abruptly, prematurely and that seem to explode, suggests the heavy burden the narrator carries as he both seeks to remember and recoils from the potency of his memories. Askar's feelings are strong. He wishes to know who he is but in his search he seems to be in danger of bursting under the strain. (He acknowledges this stress [p.40]: "My head, I feel sometimes, will explode..."). Askar must feel the fullness of his love for Misra and at the same time he must feel the fullness of his revulsion, his need to reject just such an image of dependence and of love—"we embraced." But even putting Misra aside, what of the 600 men killed, the men of the WSLF? The Ogaden—the land (also beloved) which these men were fighting to recover—now lies littered with arms without bodies, legs without feet, bodies without heads. The road that Askar travels goes directly through this landscape littered with dismembered corpses.

The novel cannot be told in all its fullness. A structural device such as the cutting short of scenes reflects the cutting short of lives, the dismemberment of war: Hilaal decides to burn his research and further conversation is cut (p.152). Askar suddenly becomes ill, ending the interview with Karin (p.177); a light bulb goes "pop" (p.196); Askar and Hilaal are left stranded in a car whose ignition cuts off (p.221). Throughout the novel (especially in the dreams) guns explode, bodies are blown to bits; a real bomb lands between Misra and Askar as the war accelerates (p.110). Once again, we can see that the structure, the *way* the novel is told reflects the theme, or even *is* the theme. Askar has grown up with war; his mind is a war-zone. It is only natural that his dreams and his memories should be torn, scattered by the winds. The novel as a whole can be seen as mutilated. Once Askar learns the last grim details of Misra's death, the novel continues for only a few feeble tattered pages (pp.242-46). Hilaal and Salaado plan to slaughter a goat to thank the gods for their protection, but the meal remains unprepared, uneaten; the police arrive suddenly and take the three off for questioning. The story remains unfinished, cut short; we never learn, for example, whether Askar decides to attend the university or to fight in the Ogaden. There is at the same time no conclusion, no resolution to the whirling nightmare of his quest. He explains in the final paragraph that he will tell the story again and again. The end of the novel points both forward and backward to the first page. The narrative begins where it ends; its structure spins in a circle. Askar's search does not end. Misra is gone, but he cannot forget her.

With the news of Misra's abduction and murder, it is as if a hole had been blown right through the heart of the novel; the novel explodes, loses its center, and ends quickly. So powerful is the impact upon Askar of Misra's death, so haunted is he by her, so obsessed by his memories of her warmth, her joy, that for him it almost seems to be more painful to live than to die. Certainly, he is filled with guilt, just the guilt of being alive. But so large does Misra loom, so great to him is her loss and so deeply does he feel it (and so too does the reader) that this calls into question all that has caused it: the war. Many of Askar's questions in the novel have concerned the war. Both Hilaal and Cusmaan have spent many long hours teaching Askar about the history, the complexities, the politics of war. Askar as a Somali shares the dream of a unified country for the disparate Somali people. As has been noted, at various points in his life, he seriously considers joining the front in the Ogaden to fight, even to give his life if he must for the Somali dream of one nation. But war kills and maims. Misra's heart is cut out before her mutilated body is tossed like refuse into the sea. For 246 pages Askar's mind whirls backwards and forwards over this nightmare landscape of pain, betrayal, and death. He lives, finally, suffused with guilt and suffering, attempting at once to choke down his memories of Misra and her murder and all that she meant to him, to forget and never to forget.

The structure of the novel forces the reader to dream the dreams, to share the nightmare, to ask the questions with Askar: man must fight for what he believes in, but at what cost? The lines on the map grow dim, the map itself crumbles, curls up, grows dark at its edges as the flames of war rise up, killing the very young men—the believers—who would create the Somali nation. The reader must love and adore Misra as Askar does and must feel the horror of her death and the meaninglessness of it. Askar's father has died in prison, 600 Somali freedom fighters have died, each one as mourned and as beloved as Misra.

Askar's obsession with Misra's guilt (her betrayal) in some ways is a false issue, and his outrage might be better directed at those in command. The point is: Askar has been close to Misra; he feels he *is* her. The closeness, the identity, is what he struggles with. The horror of war is brought home to the reader as it lies deep in Askar's psyche for in many ways Askar *is* both Somali and Ethiopian. The lines drawn on the maps go right through him. But it is not maps that make war, not bombs, planes, or nuclear devices, but man, and it is man who must stop it by struggling to know himself. The questions of identity raised in this novel are not the idle sophisms of a young man temporarily living a cushy privileged existence in Mogadiscio. Farah goes beyond this. Man *must* ask these questions. Askar must keep digging, looking in the mirror, forcing himself to remember his past and the people who raised him. It's not an easy job. It's not an easy novel, but we as readers must also forever struggle with the question Farah asks—Is the price of war too high?—and must tear up our maps and never cease our inquiry. The questions raised here are not the concern only of the Horn of Africa. Questions of identity, of manhood, and of national aspirations are questions that all people have. We must tell and retell the story as Farah does here. To know yourself is to know everything and to know nothing, and to draw a line on a map (or in the sand) and to fight over that line is to fight over everything and nothing. To ask questions is to presume there are answers. The answers in this novel beckon, always and never within reach. Farah both maps and mocks man's effort to know himself and the ideals he holds most dear, and to make a place for himself and for his people in the world.

The novel threatens to self-destruct under the burden of its theme. Must man, in the name of "home," "country," and all that he loves most, forever kill his mother, his brothers, destroying what he would preserve? The story even as it is being told must seem to stagger, to choke, to drown in its own blood and the congestion of its questions even as disparate voices cry out for calm, for clarity and for coherence. Structure is theme in Nuruddin Farah's brilliant novel. "Alas, no answer" *is* the answer but it can never *be* the answer. The stakes are too high to write an easy book or to read one.

NOTES

1. Nuruddin Farah, *Maps* (New York: Pantheon Books, 1986). All page references are to this edition and are given in parentheses in the essay.

This paper was originally presented at the 33rd Annual Meeting of the African Studies Association in Baltimore, Maryland, on November 1, 1990.

NURUDDIN FARAH'S *MAPS:* The Faint Borderland of a Warrior of Words

Rossana Ruggiero

My current obsession is one in which, as though in a reflected vision, I see the rest of the world in a broken mirror and discern the distorted truth of the things which I behold. Then I spot the fractured quality of the souls deflected in the looking-glass: I see amputated limbs and am consequently overwhelmed with images suggesting Guernica. Since I am speaking in the tongue of images, my most recurrent vision remains one full of rifts: the rift between the text and its author, the rift between the text and its interpreter, the rift, ultimately, between my self and my country![1]

Nuruddin Farah has not lived in Somalia for more than twenty years, and during this long exile he has tirelessly travelled all over the world, always coming back to a base in Africa, living, as he has declared, "in the dubious details of a territory I often refer to as the country of my imagination."[2] The writer has compared this imaginary country to the tangle of a web he has had to weave during his forced remoteness from home. Before his exile, as a child, he experienced being banished from the places in which he had grown up. The dramatic conditions of the Somali people who reside in the Ogaden territories occupied and annexed by Ethiopia after the Second World War had already compelled the writer to face the tragedy of a people who realised that their country did not exist any more, either as a physical reality or as an idea:

> I've always considered countries to be no more than
> working hypotheses, portals opening on assumptions
> of loyalty to an idea, allegiance to the notion of a
> nation...I ask what becomes of a person, indeed what
> becomes of a people when their country-as-a-hypothe-
> sis ceases to function?[3]

Published in 1986, *Maps* tries to answer this question. Set in the 1977 Ogaden war, *Maps* has been described as "a sojourn into a land of pain...a venture into the unexplored geography of domination in the Horn of Africa."[4]

In this novel Farah focuses his attention on analysing—as through a magnifying glass—the complex and multiform components of Somali society, depicted in a parallel "body-territory" through which he expands his investigation of the relation between gender and national identity, and asserts his "refusal to accept the categories of gender and nation as sacrosant or independent of each other."[5] He challenges conventional dichotomies and taboos in the culture of his country, representing its intrinsic contradictions and deeply rooted abuses and examining what is perhaps the most vulnerable of its assumptions: that of the cultural and ethnic uniformity of the Somali people.

Maps provides us with a further tile in a mosaic that is often explicit in Farah's fiction in the shape of a maze the exit of which is never possible to find, there being only innumerable and different entrances that merge into one another, thus creating a complex and intricate narrative whirl. The novel tells the story of Askar, a boy endowed with prodigous insight, whose name means "warrior." The child is found, at birth, near the corpse of his mother by Misra, a young Ethiopian woman of Oromo and Amharic origins, who looks after him with compassionate love and devotion. The two characters combine the different human and cultural realities of the Ogaden, a border territory of mixed ethnic populations, a painful piece of the "sacred" body of mother-land-Somalia, disputed by Ethiopian and Somali armies.

Maps is a symbolic and sorrowful journey into deep fears rooted in the core of the concepts of sexual and national identities, which assert themselves in juxtaposition with the 'other'. The *leit-motif* of menstrual and circumcisional blood is used to dramatise sexual diversity and becomes symbolic of the deep rift between the two sexes in a culture which imposes on them different roles and strictly codified behavioral norms. In dealing with this controversial subject, the writer is aware of touching hitherto unquestionable canons but, as Rhonda Cobham has argued: "The destabilization of national and sexual boundaries forces a remapping of the terrain that would take into account the complexity of the modern nation state in Africa."[6] Farah considers this step as an inevitable process of individual and collective growth and rebirth. The multi-cultural and multi-ethnic web of Somali society is metaphorically expressed by the androgynous element—a symbol of both the undefined and the ambivalent—which determines the ambiguity that is the hallmark of the whole story told in the novel. There is in the work a persistent parallel between the human dimensions of bodies and the geographical features of territory. During his childhood, Askar feels part of Misra's body: "Misra who eventually tucked me into the oozy warmth between her breast...so much so I became a third breast...and I would find myself somewhere between her open legs as though I was a third leg."[7] This physical fusion allows Askar to move freely between maleness and femaleness, a movement which is interrupted by circumcision—the act of ritual separation, the passage from the surrogate maternal body to the mother-country:

> Now he was at last a man, that he was totally detached
> from his mother-figure Misra...In the process of look-
> ing for a substitute, he had found another— Somalia,
> his mother country...A generous mother...who gave
> plenty of herself and demanded loyalty of one, loyalty
> to an ideal, allegiance to an idea, the notion of a
> nationhood. (p.96)

This 'passage' has its geographical equivalent in the Interlude, in which the young protagonist crosses the Ogaden border towards Mogadiscio, and it sanctions his entry into the world of maps and books by which Askar, in Patricia Alden's words, tries to "map his psyche, to draw a portrait of himself and, in doing so, simultaneously, to map a terrain in which that self must act, to map the nation."[8]

As the critic Graham Huggan argues:

> The prevalence of the map topos in contemporary
> post-colonial literary texts, and the frequence of its
> ironic and/or parodic usage in these texts, suggests a
> link between a de-reconstructive reading of maps and
> a revisioning of the history of European
> colonialism...The reassessment of cartography in
> many of their most recent literary texts indicates a
> shift of emphasis away from the desire for homogene-
> ity towards an acceptance of diversity reflected in the
> interpretation of the map, not as a mean of spatial con-
> tainment or systematic organization, but as a medium
> of spatial perception which allows for the reformula-
> tion of links both within and between cultures.[9]

Misra is the figure Farah uses to explore the hybrid cultural reality of the Ogaden and to symbolize its multi-ethnic and plurilingual
border territory. Derek Wright observes that: "Misra is not a unitary
being who can be comprehensively enclosed and defined by maps
but represents the various parts of cultures and countries—Oromo,
Ethiopian, Somali—which are to be found in mongrelized, migration-
prone areas like the Ogaden."[10] This process of hybridization clashes
with the exasperated ethnocentrism of Askar, who at first—through
Misra—shares the vital contribution of the ethnic mixture: "Misra,
who had been for me the end-all and cosmos of my affections...for me
life began in her hands and it was in her touch that I began to exist"
(p.96). Then, after the circumcision, there emerges the 'other', the
stranger, the enemy: "I felt that the mood which prevailed was one of
hostility towards her...Was she not from the highlands?...How could
she be trusted?" (p.178). His entrance into the adult world carries all
those prejudices which are often linked with ethnic fanaticism,
strengthened and supported by religion, and these mingle with each
other and become weapons with which to fight the fear of being
invaded by the 'other' in a territorial fetishism celebrating and
defending the purity of one's own race against the contamination of
the 'different'.

Maps, as Hilarie Kelly has argued,[11] is a tragedy of separation,
telling a long story of parental losses, wounds, sterility and mutilations experienced by all of the characters. We find continual references to mutilated bodies: "Stories of fragmented bodies! Bodies
which told fragmented stories! Tales about hearts and fractured
souls!" (p.154). The physical mutilations become metaphors of the
characters' deprivations and symbolize the dismemberment of motherland Somalia. Misra's mastectomy matches the defeat of the Somali
army and the final loss of the Ogaden. Her breast cancer is simultaneous with the loss of the contested territory; the mutilation of her
body mirrors that of the land, the mastectomy becoming a metaphor
for the loss of part of "the milky breast of a common mother" with
which Askar identifies Greater Somalia. When Misra is murdered and

her heart is cut out by members of the Western Somali Liberation Front, Askar's moral responsibility is called upon, as he is a supporter of the partisan movement.

However, the mutilations could also refer to a version of the Yoruba myth of the *abiku*, believed to be an embodied evil spirit that returns to life through a prodigious child, destined to cause sorrow and affliction to his family. The child is usually afflicted with infirmities that cause his death, after which his body is slashed, cut in pieces and buried in different places to prevent further reincarnations. Askar himself is considered an "epic child" like Sundiata and Mwendo, and he repeatedly falls ill in the most crucial moments of his life. But, contrary to his name, he does not accomplish any of the heroic deeds the reader would have expected him to. Askar is mainly absent from the history of his country, his contribution to the destiny of the Somali nation non-existent. His almost paranoid attempt to draw personal and political maps turns into a vain, unfruitful sequence of Hamletic questions: "He floated...suspended between numerous undefinied states of reality and unreality...dreaming (was he), sleeping (was he)" (p.178). Askar's name could have been chosen, ironically, by the writer also for the English verb it contains, in one of those semantic polyvalences so frequent in Farah's fiction. In Mogadiscio the young protagonist is taken care of by another surrogate family. In the maternal uncle's house he finds another body to plunge in: the body of knowledge, made up of maps and books which he devours in a mad, omnivorous hunger for knowledge, searching, in Cobham's words, for a "notional truth that will map out a way for him once and for all to be one with Misra as well as his separate self; that will allow the Ogaden to live out of its generic identity as a place of mixed ethnic populations as well as its specific destiny as part of Somalia."[12]

The truth Askar searches for in his reading, far from being achieved, makes his psychological equilibrium even more unstable and precarious. His intricate historico-geographical arguments do not lead him to any active choice; he remains essentially a warrior of words that do not turn into any responsible deed. Having to face the dilemma of defending or betraying one of his two mothers, Misra or Somalia, he is unable to come to any decision, and in such a way is destined to betray both. On the last page of the novel, as Felix Mnthali observes:

> We come face to face with those indelible scars which in the end leave us with an Askar who remains an unfulfilled dream, a 'soldier' whose emotional and spiritual paralysis render him ineligible for the great mission of liberation for which both his name and the extraordinary circumstances of his birth have prepared us. Askar does not complete his quest for identity and the most haunting question he leaves with us is: "Who is Askar?"[13]

The final question is left to the reader like a blank map, containing, however, numerous imaginary routes that everyone can freely follow in the attempt to define the border of a territory that escapes every attempt at representation.

NOTES

1. Nuruddin Farah, "A Country in Exile," *Transition* 57 (1992), 6.

2. Nuruddin Farah, "Homing in on the Pigeon," lecture given by the author at Oxford University in November 1991, pp. 1-2.; later published in *Index on Censorship* 22, 5-6 (1993), 16-20.

3. Farah, ibid., p.1.

4. Hussein A. Bulham, "Maps," *Africa Events* (July 1987), 78.

5. Rhonda Cobham, "Boundaries of the Nation, Boundaries of the Self: African Nationalist Fictions and Nuruddin Farah's *Maps*," *Research in African Literatures* 22, 2 (1991), 84.

6. Cobham, 95.

7. Nuruddin Farah, *Maps* (London, Picador, 1986), p.24. Further references are given in parentheses in the text.

8. Patricia Alden, "Mapping the Personal and the Political: the Child-Geographer in Nuruddin Farah's *Maps*," *African Literature—1988: New Masks*, eds. Hal Wylie, Dennis Brutus and Juris Silenieks (Washington, D.C.: Three Continents Press, 1990), p.124.

9. Graham Huggan, "Decolonizing the Map," *The Post-Colonial Studies Reader*, eds. Bill Ashcroft, Gareth Griffiths and Helen Tiffin (London, Routledge, 1995), pp. 407-08.

10. Derek Wright, *The Novels of Nuruddin Farah* (Bayreuth University: Bayreuth African Studies, 1994), p.113.

11. Hilarie Kelly, "A Somali Tragedy of Political and Sexual Confusion: A Critical Analysis of Nuruddin Farah's *Maps*," *Ufahamu* 16, 2 (1988), 33.

12. Cobham, 94.

13. Felix Mnthali, "Autocracy and the Limits of Identity: A Reading of the Novels of Nuruddin Farah," *Ufahamu* 17, 2 (1989), 64.

DIMENSIONS OF GIFT GIVING IN NURUDDIN FARAH'S *GIFTS*

Francis Ngaboh-Smart

Nuruddin Farah has emerged as one of Africa's "finest" writers, probably because of the almost unsurpassable quality of his numerous works. The Dictatorship trilogy, for example, show both Farah's concern with artistry and his humane orientation, as he attacks the depredations of the Barre regime. In *Maps*, while Farah's subtle criticism of the disaster inherent in the Somali quest for a univocal identity reveals his commitment to life, the meticulously crafted work seems to have extended the stylistic boundary of the African novel, which, to me, accounts for his current global reputation.

It seems, however, as if after the overt concern with the politics of dictatorship in *Variations* and the disavowal of an atavistic sense of identity in *Maps,* Farah has at last decided to give us a respite from such absorbing issues in *Gifts.* At least this is how Derek Wright has described *Gifts*: "the most sunny and radiant, albeit not the most profound, of Farah's novels. Its...disciplined clarity of style [is] refreshing after the somewhat mannered esoterics of *Maps.*"[1] But the simplicity of the novel, stylistic and thematic, could easily be exaggerated. It is, for example, possible to argue that Farah's appropriation of

567

Marcel Mauss's *The Gift* broadens the thematic scope of his own work in two significant respects. First, Farah's use of Mauss indicates that he may be aware of, if not foregrounding, the complexity of the moral and political implications of gift giving, generally. Second, but more specifically, Farah's sustained use of Mauss seeks to show how gifts from developed to so-called developing countries function as part of a complex array of asymmetrical discourses that articulate the vision of donor countries. Such gifts, Farah may be arguing, help the affluent countries either to incorporate the poorer nations into their sphere of influence or to construct the identity of the impoverished recipients.

Of course, this hardly suggests that *Gifts* is not slender on plot and characterization, concentrating, as it does, on two characters, Duniya and Bosaaso. The gradual unfolding of the love relationship between the two is what in fact provides the plot with a unifying thread. For example, we learn that, married at an early age to a blind man the age of her grandfather, Duniya has two children as reminders of her loveless relationship, Nasiiba and Mataan. When the husband, Zubair, dies, Duniya leaves her village for the city, Mogadiscio, where she again falls in love with the journalist Taariq, with whom she has another child, Yarey. But by the beginning of the novel, Duniya admits that although she has been married twice, she has never been in love, and she feels that Bosaaso would at last provide such a love: "When she had accepted to...marry Zubair, she had said it was an aberration...and Taariq only a stop-gap, could Bosaaso be the conflux of their river of souls, flowing into one another, together, for ever?"[2] Duniya reflects on her relationship with Bosaaso. And they eventually marry at a climactic moment when Abshir, Duniya's full-brother who lives in Italy, visits her in Mogadiscio.

Nevertheless, Duniya and Bosaaso's relationship not only gives the novel a human dimension, but it also disguises Farah's ambitious attempt to link giving and identity. For the love between Duniya and Bosaaso, a gift from one disinterested human being to another, becomes an ironic commenting device on ideologically motivated gifts from developed countries. The political and social dimensions of gift giving, therefore, remain Farah's primary focus in the novel, and he foregrounds this concern in numerous ways. For example, in an article in which Farah assesses his role and reasons for writing, he emphatically described *Gifts* as a "novel...about foreign aid."[3] Second, in the author's preface, Farah grounds the novel in a tradition of sociological and philosophical speculation on gift giving by evoking the authority of Mauss: "In writing this novel I have incurred many debts, the most important of which is owed to Marcel Mauss, author of *The Gift*." In acknowledging his debt to Mauss, Farah thus extends the universe of reference for his novel. Therefore, to understand the sophistication of Farah's thought, we must talk about patterns of gift giving in the novel in relation to Mauss's concept of "the gift" on which Farah draws for his theme in *Gifts*.

References to various forms of gifts do indeed resonate in most episodes in the novel. Gift giving is, in fact, so important to Farah that at times the novel becomes a catalog of various gift situations. For example, in the face of the fuel shortage that paralyzes life in Mogadiscio, there is talk of a government delegation to the "oil-producing Arab countries in the hope of returning with tankerfuls of petrol" (p.2). In addition, the newsprints at the end of most of the chapters give us an indication of the inundating flow of foreign gifts into the country: "the governments of the USA and the Netherlands" promise to help eradicate the plague of locusts in Somalia (p.7). Furthermore, the Somali head of state appeals to the "Federal Republic of Germany, Britain, France, and Italy" for help (p.7). Also, there is the gloomy revelation from Reuters about the imminent starvation of poorer nations because of their dependence on the richer countries "whose debts they are unable to service, let alone repay" (p.31). Finally, there are references to Liv Ullman's "mission of mercy" in "countries in Africa South of the Sahara"; the effort of "aid agencies" in minimizing the deforestation of the "Third World"; the Italian government's help in completing an Italian-Somali dictionary; and many more.

With these numerous references to gift giving, the question, then, is: what is a gift? Mauss, investigating the form of exchange mainly among Indians of the American Northwest, describes their gift system as a potlatch—"total services of an agonistic type," or an extravagant destruction of property.[4] For Mauss, the potlatch was closely "tied up with the notion of honor and prestige," although wealth seemed to be "lavishly expended." Furthermore, although exchange was voluntary, the "give and take" was marked by three interdependent obligations: "The obligations: to give, to receive, to reciprocate." A chief who failed in any of the obligations was bound to incur the loss of honor, suffer social humiliation, and, at times, lose his identity, or "lose the weight attached to his name." It was thus a system that was bound up with "the duty of returning with interest gifts received in such a way that the creditor becomes the debtor." Underlying this "struggle of wealth," it would seem, was an understanding of the "collective nature of the contract."[5] That is, the potlatch was intended to construct the boundaries of the social groups involved in the exchange: "It was indeed the whole clan that contracts on behalf of all, for all that it possesses and for all that it does, through the person of the chief...It is a struggle between nobles to establish a hierarchy among themselves from which their clan will benefit at a later date."[6] It would seem that Farah is against the destruction of this "archaic" system of gift giving "in which persons and things merge" harmoniously.[7]

Thus, although the novel uses a wide variety of terms such as aid, assistance, donation, relief, and present to cover its notion of gift, the terms generate and redefine issues of personal and national identity. That is, the novel's examination of the political, economic, and cultural implications of gift giving depicts the oppositions among hostility, charity, obligation, condescension, and patronage inherent in the relationship between the wealthier and poorer nations. With this background in mind, Farah's criticism of modern gift exchange, therefore, demands closer analysis—first, from the perspective of the richer nations, and second, from that of the poorer nations.

As a criticism of the richer nations, the novel shows that what are normally perceived as kind gestures to the poorer nations are not really "disinterested." Like the gift exchanges in a potlatch, gifts from richer to poorer nations are actually compulsory or self-interested exchanges. The main motivation behind such gifts is to ensure that the poorer nations buy the goods or accept the ideologies of the wealthier nations. Third-World recipients of gifts must, therefore, "recognize" the donors or their children and become "grateful" to them. The novel makes reference to this obligation in numerous instances. First, Bosaaso and another important character, Dr. Mire, one of Farah's most articulate creations, engage in an elaborate discussion of the nature of gifts from the wealthier nations, and they come to an important conclusion about what such gifts amount to. They see donors as "traders...wandering the African continent, propagating their faith, making gifts of their deities and beliefs...presents that Africans accept with little question" (p.93). Similarly, Taariq, a character whose articles often double or amplify the voice of the omniscient narrator, writes:

> Every gift has a personality—that of its giver. On every sack of rice donated by a foreign government to a starving people in Africa, the characteristics and mentality of the donor, name and country are stamped on its rib. A quintal of wheat donated by a charity based in the Bible Belt of the USA tastes different from one grown in and donated by a member of the European Community....One has, as its basis, the theological notion of charity; the other, the temporal philosophical economic credo of creating a future generation of potential consumers of this high quality wheat. (p.195)

For Taariq and, perhaps, Farah, too, whereas the typical potlatch is a circulation of "honor" through "equivalent" exchanges, modern foreign gifts aim at "turning the African into a person that is forever dependent" (p.195). In short, the imposition of a feeling of obligation or indebtedness in the receivers has become the motive force for most foreign givers. When Africa accepts gifts, it is expected to reciprocate by buying several things from the West, material, spiritual, and conceptual. Africa's loss is, therefore, generally greater than the value of the gift it receives. For instance, the notion of an "Allah-created cosmos," *Dunya*, from which Duniya's name derives, could be construed as a gift, a symbolic displacement of the traditional Somali belief in the "ending of life, a termination of this existence" for "the Judaeo-Christian and Islamic systems...reward-offering, life-after-death rationalization, a credo in which you are guaranteed paradisiacal delights after death" (p.93).

In Farah's presentation of foreign gifts as a network of obligation, he seems to be engaging in a Nietzschean reading of the gift as "debt," which imposes a memory of duty and perpetual servitude on the receivers. Nietzsche's second essay in *On the Genealogy of Morals* states that the concept of "mercy" "remains the privilege of the most powerful man," who "by winking and letting those incapable of discharging their debt go free" demonstrates his power or his will for self-preservation, what Nietzsche calls "overcoming."[8] The creditor-debtor relationship that Nietzsche talks about can, therefore, be seen as a perversion of the potlatch, which allows the free flow and commingling of things and people. The terrifying aspect of the creditor-debtor relationship is obvious in the way Nietzsche talks about the indebtedness of the living to the dead, which ultimately demands of the debtor "a wholesale sacrifice, something tremendous in the way of repayment to the 'creditor.'"[9] For Nietzsche as well as for the Farah of *Gifts*, then, the powerful nation as "the creditor always become[s] more humane to the extent that he has grown richer; finally how much injury he can endure without suffering from it becomes the actual measure of his wealth."[10] Thus by adapting Mauss's essay on the potlatch, Farah, like Nietzsche, may be aware that the "feeling of personal obligation [is] the oldest and most primitive personal relationship, that between buyer and seller, creditor and debtor."[11]

This is the concept of gift that Ingrid, the character who symbol-ically articulates the Western point of view in the novel, clings to. Ingrid has lived in Somalia for three years, and at the end of her stay, she sells her "china set" to Bosaaso and his wife, Yussur, for "ten US dollars." Yussur reminds Ingrid that a Somali senior civil servant's monthly salary is equivalent to ten US dollars (p.46). But Ingrid insists that she is selling the set "dirt cheap, more or less giving it away" (p.45). This is Ingrid's idea of a gift, and when Yussur cavils at such a perverse notion of gift, Ingrid is outraged and blurts out the Westerner's conception of the African's attitude to foreign aid:

> This china, for instance, has survived for almost ten years in the caring hands of Europeans who knew how to appreciate such treasure...It makes me sad to think that you, Yussur, may behave like these *Apfricans* all over the place who have no idea how to take care of sensitive gadgets with souls, like a car, a computer with software sensibilities or a set of china with as fragile an animal as a bird's. To my mind *Apfricans* haven't got what it takes to appreciate the cultural and technological gifts that are given to them. (pp.45-46).

What Ingrid is saying is that "the notion of giving for its own sake is alien" to the West. Like the foreign donors, whose point of view she encodes, for her, "[a]id is aid, good or bad, whether there are strings attached and whatever its terms of reference" (p.46). One would assume that Ingrid and the West believe that when the United States, "the world's richest country," gives "ninety million dollars to Somalia," but spends "twenty millions" of the money on food grown in the "USA by American farmers" and on "the salaries of Americans working...and living like lords in luxury they are not used to at home" (p.47), Africans must accept that the West has "certain things that [we] Africans need" (p.46). With such a logic, what Westerners seem to have dispensed with in the gift situation is what the novel probably expresses in the Somali proverb *Quebiya Qada*: "he who distributes the offerings of fortune receives little as part of his personal share" (p.47).

Also, significant for Farah's adaptation of Mauss's model is the fact that the gift exchanges in potlatch ceremonies are usually sublimated "warfare." Although potlatch gifts seem "disinterested," the "sumptuary destruction of wealth...takes on an extremely marked agonistic character." It is, therefore, "essentially usurious," the intention being to "outdo the rival chief."[12] Thus, like the extravagant exchanges of the potlatch, foreign donations, the novel seems to imply, in their magnitude and unrelenting avalanche, are distortions of reciprocity, often motivated by competition and antagonism among donor countries. Or, furthermore, foreign gifts are what Pierre Bourdieu, following in the footsteps of Mauss and Nietzsche, has called "symbolic taxes" by which groups mobilize the loyalties of their members[13] and "play simultaneously in the registers of unavowed self-interest and publicly declared honour [while] the agents strive to conceal the objective truth of the exchange."[14] Consequently, while many African countries may see the competitive game of foreign donation as an opportunity for earning free gifts, they fail to realize that they are the real losers in a seductive game in which gifts surreptitiously ask them to gamble everything, whereas the foreign donors, who seem to be ostensibly motivated by reckless spending, really create bonds of camaraderie among themselves and, in the process, extend their influence in the Third World. Therefore, foreign gifts, as important elements in modern international economic practice, emerge in the narrative as modes of marginalization. Deprived of the means for economic and political self-determination, Farah's Third World countries respond by uncritically embracing their British, American, Russian, and Italian masters. In analyzing present global economic and political relationships, *Gifts* is thus unique in presenting gifts as tools that disenfranchise the poorer nations.

Farah's criticism of the perversion of gift giving in the modern world is, however, equally directed against the receivers of gifts, the poorer nations, since they discard one fundamental component of the gift economy: the "obligation to reciprocate." "The punishment for failure to reciprocate is slavery for debt," Mauss tells us. "The individual unable to repay the loan or reciprocate the potlatch loses his rank and even his status as a free man."[15] The poorer nations, by refusing to reciprocate, seem to indulge in a "profane" abrogation of this basic element of the gift. Thus Farah shows how in Somalia and, undoubtedly, other Third World countries, spending lavishly has become the established pattern of governance. The economically impoverished nations enact a perverted version of the potlatch by engaging in an orgy of wealth destruction.

As such, while Taariq, for example, is aware of the psychological and moral dangers of foreign gifts, he is also critical of the actions of leaders of the poorer nations, whose extravagant consumption of wealth causes them to be seen as participants in a degraded potlatch. To criticize leaders of the poorer nations for their unprincipled destruction of the gifts they receive, Taariq draws our attention to a TV documentary on the "Ethiopian famine" in which there are "alternative shots of starving masses and pictures of the world's powerful politicians attending the emperor's lavish feast at which delicacies like caviar had been served" (p.193). Duniya also observes that "both as individuals and as governments, we Somalis, better still, we Africans, tend to live beyond our means" (p.169). Finally, in the scene where Bosaaso withdraws his gifts from his spendthrift sister-in-law, Waaberi, Duniya accurately compares Bosaaso's admonishment of Waaberi to the stern rebuke of representatives of African countries by a "donor" country for "being immodest in the number of Mercedes and similar extravagances and in the show-pieces they display to the rest of the world" (p.220). The novel further shows how, interestingly, the poorer nations, especially in Africa, demand gifts as if they have "a proprietary right over the properties of others" (p.195).

Farah's criticism of the orgy of sumptuous feasting on foreign aid by independent nations is what perhaps brings him close to Frantz Fanon. If anything, Farah's unprincipled consumers are Fanon's nationalist bourgeois criticized in *The Wretched of the Earth*. According to Fanon, during this period in the history of independent nations, there is often a "scandalous enrichment." The middle class spends "large sums...on cars, country houses, and all those things which have been justly described by economists as characterizing an underdeveloped bourgeoisie."[16] The conduct of Fanon's nationalists is similar to Farah's leaders: both pervert the gift system because, whereas in the potlatch spending is "a phenomenon of social structure, the gathering of tribes, clans, and families,"[17] or an activity through which a chief creates social bonds and solidifies the community, for Third World leaders, this dimension of the gift is lost, since they spend without any intention of creating solidarity. The depressing outcome is evident in Mogasdiscio: "No electricity, no bread baked, no paper" (p.17).

Thus, Farah has misgivings about the Third World propensity to spend unproductively. Third World extravagance, therefore, demonstrates the negative aspect of uncritical spending, since it makes the poorer countries helpless; in short, through extravagant spending, Third World nations only further the effects of imperialism. Farah's opposition to both foreign and Third World perversion of the original spirit of the potlatch is therefore obvious. As a result of the above deviations from the potlatch system, Farah creates characters whose behaviors are symbolically opposed to the perversion of the spirit of gift giving—Duniya and Bosaaso, Nasiiba, and Mataan with his numerous folktales about reciprocity.

The behaviors of Nasiiba and Duniya as gift givers manifest striking similarities to Georges Bataille's notion of "expenditure." Bataille, using Mauss's *The Gift* and, presumably, Nietzsche's observations on the genealogy of "bad conscience" respectively, seeks an alternative to "classical" economic practice, which he calls "restricted economy." This economic model, according to Bataille, is based on "utility," "acquisition," and "conservation." In contrast to such a rational commercial exchange, Bataille proposes a model of "loss," or "unconditional expenditure" free from the quest for "balance":

> Human life cannot in any way be limited to the closed systems assigned to it by reasonable conceptions. The immense travail of recklessness, discharge, and upheaval that constitutes life could be expressed by stating that life starts only with the deficit of these systems; at least what it allows in the way of order and reserve has meaning only from the moment when the ordered and reserved forces liberate and lose themselves for ends that cannot be subordinated to anything one can account for.[18]

The principle of "unconditional expenditure" as opposed to that of "balanced accounts" or compensation is represented in the behaviors of Nasiiba and Duniya; their actions must, therefore, constitute an alternative configuration of human relationship in *Gifts*.

Nasiiba, Duniya's daughter from her first marriage, is a character who, among other things, functions as a symbolic donor in the novel. She has a friend, Fariida, who is pregnant by a married man, Qaasim. Fariida never really wanted the man to marry her, and had indulged him only for diversion: "I had lost my virginity to a boy my age, and was anxious to experiment with older men just for fun" (p.190), Fariida explains. Accordingly, Fariida "enjoyed the illicit affair," allowing Qaasim to finance their expensive trips. In an unguarded moment, though, Fariida conceives. As the time of her delivery gets closer, a doctor advises her that the delivery will be risky in her anemic condition. This is when Nasiiba, who has already sacrificed a great deal by cutting classes to see her friend, decides to donate her blood. In recounting the circumstances of the pregnancy to Duniya, Fariida says, "Since my blood is the same rare group as Nasiiba's, you might say I owe my life to her...Nasiiba was an angel" (p.188). Nasiiba's gift of blood to Fariida is set against the recuperative gift giving of foreign donors. She freely expends her most precious resource without any hope of a return. Asked by her mother, "[W]hy did you donate blood you can ill afford?" Nasiiba replies, "I felt like giving blood...the blood bank was short of it and, being in a generous mood, I felt like donating mine" (p.25). As such, her prodigality is a donation that goes against any notion of the compensation or restitution that marks foreign gifts.

The ethics of expenditure, however, is most evident in the love between Duniya and Bosaaso. Their relationship demonstrates aspects of unasked-for generosity. On the eve of the consummation of their protracted courtship, Duniya unabashedly declares: "Tomorrow evening, Duniya will spend the night at Bosaaso's to make of her body a gift to him" (p.198). But before Duniya and Bosaaso can move towards this model of emotional expenditure, the novel explores instances of relationship based on negative reciprocity. The most immediate example of such a love relationship is Duniya's marriage to Zubair. Her marriage to the blind, old man was part of an informal exchange between her father and Zubair, the most important company and visitor Duniya's father had during his last days. As a compensation for Zubair's devoted friendship, it would seem, the dying father decided to give his friend a gift, Duniya: "As he put it then, Duniya was 'a gesture of kind violence' to his friend and peer Zubair. Would Duniya please take him as her lawful husband" (p.36)? It turned out that Duniya never had a say in her transfer to Zubair, and to avoid "her parents' malediction," she consented to the marriage. It is obvious that the novel is against this bondage to a contractual relationship; it is a relationship concerned with the preservation of the family, without any feeling for Duniya's happiness. As such, Duniya married Zubair not because she freely gave herself, but because she was oppressed by a sense of duty and obligation, or almost ensnared and bound over to Zubair. After Zubair's death, Duniya is determined to start afresh; hence her flight to Mogadiscio.

After her first experience, one would expect that Duniya could now make a more independent and reasoned choice in marriage. Indeed, she does make an independent choice by marrying Taariq. But how free is her choice of Taariq from a feeling of duty and obligation? When Duniya falls in love with Taariq, she is under a heavy obligation to repay Taariq for his kindness to the children, especially

Mataan. Years later, she would regret not properly knowing Taariq before giving herself to him. Thus Duniya in this second marriage failed to discern one of the fundamental principles of the gift, which is to understand and interpret the other. After all, gift giving is primarily a hermeneutical project; one must interpret the character of the other to ensure that gift giving does not become a violence, or a degradation of the other. Duniya's father, as we have seen, failed to interpret the other; and Duniya herself, in giving her body to Taariq, misinterpreted him. Her relationship with Bosaaso is supposed to rectify this oversight. Thus in her third venture into marriage, Duniya seeks a conception of love as "twin ideas united in their pursuit to be separable and linked at the same time" (p.148). This she can achieve by first establishing her independence, that is, by rejecting gifts or overtures from Bosaaso that she sees as "a way of making one feel obliged, trapped in a labyrinth of dependence" (p.20). Accordingly, one of the informal rules of behavior she establishes for even her children is to avoid "unauthorized gifts of food...ill-gained presents and cash" (p.24). In her own personal conduct or response to Bosaaso, Duniya, aware of the force of a gift, shows her "reluctance to accept [Bosaaso's] gifts" (p.150), perhaps to protect her space and to give herself time to understand him. Thus, when Bosaaso gives her the first lift that brings them together, Duniya is determined to pay for the ride. Another time, Duniya rejects Bosaaso's lift by riding a motor scooter Mataan borrows from his friend "to make the point to Bosaaso that she had alternative ways of getting to work, wasn't totally reliant on his good-will and kind gestures" (p.169). For Duniya, the open-air ride constitutes "a new-found freedom...more fun than the humiliation of being in the company of somebody one didn't know" (pp.168-69). In a country where other women "dressed in...exquisitely tailored clothes," apparently to attract "offers," Duniya's conduct demonstrates the prudence of a woman moving away from a space "owned by men, run and dominated by men" to one where she is a "free tenant" (p.171). Once Duniya succeeds in establishing such a space, she is prepared to accept, and also force

Bosaaso to accept, that she is an independent being. As such, Bosaaso, who all along seems to cling to a notion of generosity that is not marked by reciprocity, learns to reexamine the nature of the gifts he has made thus far. For example, Bosaaso eventually stands up against the persistent demands of his late wife's relatives, especially Waaberi. It is Waaberi herself whom Bosaaso asks to recount his renunciation of the perverted gift system: "You [Bosaaso] described yourself as an exploited man, who was being socially blackmailed into giving what he didn't wish to give any more" (p.219). Therefore, Duniya and Bosaaso's love blooms as they establish a mutual ground of understanding.

This self-respect is what the novel denies characters such as Muraayo, Shiriye, and Kaahin who, as foils, enhance the structural and thematic centrality of Duniya and Bosaaso in the novel. Muraayo is Qaasim's wife, who consciously flaunts her body. Her favorite pastimes are visiting the coiffeuse, the tailor, the silversmiths, and the goldsmiths. She is obviously aware that her ample size has the power to "fill the sex-starved fantasies of Somali men" (p.105). Mataan says that she "pampers her huge body with an overdose of self-adulation" (p.105). Mataan's statement is proved to be true when we later learn that not only is Muraayo unfaithful to her husband, but even their "primal scream" during "love making" is not "love making but acting" (p.105). No wonder Taariq describes Muraayo as a woman with "little in-depth understanding of symbols...what she does is to live on the surface of things, in the glitter of false beauties, easily contented with the superficiality of things" (p.121). As such, Muraayo's concept of gifts is severely limited to "give, buy, receive."

Shiriye, a character often described in animal images, has never known the "meaning of a kind gesture" (p.80). Not only did he accept a gift from Zubair that sold Duniya into bondage, but when Duniya and the children stayed with him in Mogadiscio, he failed to provide them with the protection and kindness that the tradition he so avidly respects demands of him as elder brother, making Duniya and the children "live in virtual terror and humiliation" (p.171). But the most reprehensible of all three characters is Kaahin. He is an embarrass-ment to his friend, Bosaaso. He carries a sticker on his car that reads: "Kaahin: women's Cain" (p.152). He thus has a perverted under-standing of love as the exchange of gifts. He disguises himself "behind fancy-looking cars and mountains of laundered money" and "seduces [women] with handouts of cash" (p.152). Kaahin is typical-ly a man after sensual pleasure, and he does not believe in love as the exchange of equivalent emotions.

In contrast to the above foils, Bosaaso and Duniya know the real nature of gifts, so they are able to move away from a world that con-flates giving with goods. Through their actions and especially through the gradual development of their love, Duniya and Bosaaso show a refusal to participate in the perverted gift system peddled by both foreign powers and their countrymen. In the process, a novel that may otherwise be construed as mainly concerned with foreign aid also becomes an articulation of the positive view of love as gift giving. That is, love becomes a non-compulsory gift giving, through which, as Mauss would say, "people learn how to create mutual inter-ests, give mutual satisfaction" rather than "sacrificing themselves to one another" (p.82).

In the unfolding of the love, we see Duniya, for example, move from a relation of entrapment and seduction by tradition (Zubair) through giving her body as compensation for kindness (Taariq) to finally opening her soul to Bosaaso. Her movement is symbolically captured in images of freedom and renewal. This freedom is what Duniya's disrobing and redressing on her first night out with Bosaaso demonstrates. On this night, the roles of mother and young daughter are symbolically reversed as Duniya, helpless as a baby, allows Nasiiba to transform her into a new woman. Nasiiba insists that her mother step "out of her puritanical robe" and that she desist from considering herself a "shrine" (pp.134,135). Transformed into a new radiance, Duniya is no longer worried about "flying away," and she is certain that she and "Bosaaso would once again be united— and in love" (p.135). The bounty of her new relationship figures in the generosity of nature, which functions as a repeated motif for rendering the reciprocity between man and nature. For example, from the time Duniya's thoughts focus on the relationship with Bosaaso, there is a symbolic link between her and the natural forces, such as the "pollinating butterfly," dragonfly, and birds—all, presumably, images that are used to describe how nature provides a model for man's relationship with man. These natural images culminate in the scene where we witness the unreserved exchange of emotions during Bosaaso and Duniya's first love making. We are told that in the frenzy of that love making, "they were seeing each other's body not by feel alone but by the moon shining in as well," and Duniya calls herself "the shooting-star...by-passing all known and unknown planets of the celestial system" (p.207). Theirs is therefore a gift in which the self ecstatically abandons itself in an unjustified passion without concern for self-preservation.

In Bosaaso and Duniya, then, Farah advocates the freely given gift associated with love. Here are two isolated and self-sufficient people. They meet and engage in a play with the exchange of gifts of the emotions, in which giving or receiving becomes an equivalent exchange. Their conduct, therefore, provides a view of a social relation that prioritizes disinterestedness. As such, they not only attempt to interpret each other correctly, but they also believe that the self is not an isolated unit, but a force that allows for conversation, what Duniya calls, in reference to Fariida's child, "a compulsory set of grammatical oppositions...a we of hybrid necessities" (p.132). The exorbitant nature of this exchange is also evident in the novel's evocation of the angels, which, I presume, are a metaphor for the expansion of the self. We must therefore constantly oppose their exchange of gifts to that of both the foreign donors and the degradation of the spirit of reciprocity by leaders of poorer nations. Through them, Farah criticizes the exchange of gifts that implicitly demeans the poor, or ambiguous terms such as donation, aid, help, and mercy, which obscure the values these terms disguise as signifiers of power.

However, in order not to be naive about love as a panacea for all problems, the novel shows the difficulty of carrying out the ideal of love in an economically oppressed world such as Somalia. As a result, Duniya's oscillation between free-gift and shrewdness, in some instances, may perhaps testify to the precariousness of the ideal of love. Therefore, one must finally insist that Farah's conception of the gift may not be so simple, after all. He knows that because foreign aid has often impeded the postcolonial stride toward national and self-definition, it may be necessary to probe such gifts to reveal the hidden agenda of the donors.

The above analysis shows that even the simplicity of the novel's style may be deliberately deceptive, since Farah makes the content of the novel inextricably dependent on its form. This is to say that although *Gifts* deals with love, its complex treatment of gift giving, which subtly actuates hierarchies of meaning, also extends to its imaginative structure. This is most evident in the novel's compositional and narrative methods, marked, as they are, by a formal excess and a drama of intertextuality similar to the extravagance and antagonism peculiar to the potlatch on which Farah draws for his political reading.

The formal excess is evident in the proliferation of narrators, the insertion of a long catalog of gifts from foreign newscasts and, generally, the embedding of oral narratives within the novel, all indicative of vying narrators and narrative conventions. First, there is the public narrator, the omniscient narrator, who provides us with the plot of actions. Second, there are oral transcribers—for example, Dr. Mire, who tells a Somali anecdote during Nameless's funeral; Tariiq, who narrates a Somali creation myth as well as the story about a cow; and above all there is Mataan, who transcribes numerous Somali folktales and embeds them within the main narrative. These mini- narratives, it should be noted, are still marked by their oral conventions, and even where they supplement the theme of the main narrative, they are in competition with the plot and conventions of the omniscient or main narrator. Third, there are the newscasts from foreign papers and Mogadiscio dailies, such as Taariq's feature article, "Giving and Receiving: The Notion of Donations." These journal articles and newscasts, like the embedded folktales, are also marked by a stylistic protocol that differs from that of the fundamental narrative. Finally, there is a fictional editorial text in the form of epigraphs for each of the chapters, presumably by Farah.

These insertions signify the novel's explosion of conventional novelistic boundaries, and one is inclined to say that despite the careful arrangement of events, the meaning of *Gifts* is dependent on its formal excess. *Gifts* is, therefore, unlike the typical realistic novel where, more often than not, inserted documents validate a work's universe of reference. *Gifts*' borrowed materials function differently; they create a collage of texts. The result is that the multiple texts produce tension through overlap or intersections, which structurally undermine a symmetrical narrative logic. In this regard, the competition among the different narrative conventions is, in a way, similar to the antagonism inherent in the potlatch. For example, Taariq's folklore appropriations, but more especially Mataan's adaptations, are borrowed discourses that inflate the story and call attention to the novel's textual economy. Indeed, most of Mataan's stories such as those about Juxaa and his neighbor, or Juxaa and the hunter, extend the theme of negative reciprocity, but generally they create verbal abundance in what would otherwise remain a schematically organized novel. Therefore, Farah's subversion of traditional novelistic practice, it must be emphasized, generates a discourse of "expenditure" that, among other things, replicates the emotional "expenditure" manifested by Duniya and Bosaaso.

Farah's pronouncements on writing will make such a reading plausible. His reflections on writing and language have increasingly attempted to show that he defies any conception of art or writing that seeks to substitute a single truth for the openness that both literature and life demand. For example, in "Why I Write," Farah tells us that whereas for the dictatorial regime of Sayid Barre "the truth that matters" is the "unity of the Somali nation," a "groomed truth, the nursed truth...a truth plastered with a 'cured' cloth," an otherwise "monologic" discourse, he seeks to present truth as "the breath that someone somewhere in the world will inhale."[19] Such a conception of truth is obviously a means of pulverizing the idea of a "home-grown truth."[20] Thus, in both the Dictatorship trilogy and *Maps*, but especially in *Maps*, Farah tended to be stylistically concerned with language and narrative strategies, as well as with the theme of "Africa's upheaval and societal disorganisation."[21] About language, Farah also says, "I will use any languages that I choose to write in...I find that not only are Somalis my people, but the whole continent of Africa; India, where I grew up intellectually...the Arab world, which has influenced me culturally."[22] This expanded notion of culture and language has, I argue, influenced Farah's compositional method by the time he comes to *Gifts*. His style has become a verbal potlatch, challenging the existing limits of the narrative conventions that would see the African novel as self-contained. He now sees narrative as intersections and borrowings, which for Farah would more faithfully represent the problematic of being heir to diverse traditions. After all, in "Why I Write," Farah insists on the need to search for his "missing half."[23] For such a quest, one would assume, the writer has to replace the single tradition with inclusive signifiers, which is at once both "a sacrifice and a challenge," as Derrida would say about writing.[24]

Writing as "a sacrifice and a challenge" is how, at some moments, *Gifts*, as a reflexive text, talks about itself. Describing Taariq's method of writing, Duniya tells Nasiiba that "there was pain on his face when he wrote, every word leaving its mark somewhere on his body" (p.27). But it is in taking up such a challenge that Farah tries to reconceptualize postcolonial identity discourse. That is, although in *Gifts* there is the impulse to organize and tell the story of the colonized people, which is what the omniscient narrator does, on the other hand, Farah seems to have slowly moved to an acceptance of the global exchange of people and discourses. The lists from journalistic discourse, the imported folktales, the framing epigraphs, and the traditional poetics of the omniscient narrator all show Farah's awareness of a "polyphonic" universe of discourse. Or better still, for

Farah, the issue has become how the Third World writer can deal with the proliferation of languages and narrative conventions that govern his or her world.

After the disintegration and upheaval that Farah writes about in *Maps*, the idea that it is possible to make sense of the world from the perspective of a single language or narrative tradition, or from the perspective of a non-circulating conception of knowledge, seemed to have become increasingly impossible in *Gifts*. As a result, stylistically, *Gifts* does not refer us back to a restricted economic of language. Through the novel's narrative largesse, Farah seems to be throwing the challenge evident in the potlatch to his implied readers in their configuration of identity, probably urging them to generate an identity as flexible as the range of dIscourses he appropriates.

Consequently, no matter how one interprets *Gifts,* it is difficult to avoid the conclusion that for Farah, narrative and identity have become mediums of exchange, which is perhaps what the Foundling symbolizes. Throughout the novel, the child gathers a number of identities: the Foundling, the Nameless One, and the Offspring of Jinns. However, our conception of the child's identity remains fluid. Like most "colonial formations" that Farah refers to in his interview with Feroza Jussawalla and Reed Way Dasenbrock,[25] the child's identity has been "invented": "everybody had turned the Foundling into what they thought they wanted, or lacked" (p.128). However, if as Duniya appropriately remarks, the Foundling shall continue to "live on," he will do so as an allegory of a living dialogue, and as the novel's conception of existence as a prism through which traditions, attitudes, and discourses percolate. The Foundling therefore extends the novel as a surfeit of signification in which discourses, as attitudes to the world, coalesce to enable a cooperative dialogue of opposing points of view. On the whole, through the Nameless One, Farah implies that the postcolonial subject is not yet dead. "He[she] is still living," but like the Foundling, he or she has the distinction of collecting gifts from the chorus of voices or discourses in the world (p.128). Here is the movement away from insularity that the emphasis on homelessness at the end of *Maps* seems to have symbolically anticipated. For rather than the politics of containment that most people associate with postcolonial literature, *Gifts* foregrounds the appropriation of discourses as another condition for writing and even identity. Thus, while extensively improvising on Mauss, Farah does not support Mauss's conviction that "we can and must return to archaic society."[26] Rather, like other African writers who are slowly being referred to as postmodern (Ben Okri and Kojo B. Laing are examples), Farah seems to privilege an "impure" conception of identity and writing: "a living...concrete thing...on the borderline between oneself and the other."[27] However, the sustained attack on neocolonial forms of domination as well as the exposure of the disastrous miscarriage of the ideals of nationalism in *Gifts* would indicate that Farah's postmodernism may be an attempt to rescue the radical moment in the anti-colonial revolt.

NOTES

1. Derek Wright, *The Novels of Nuruddin Farah* (Bayreuth: Bayreuth University, 1994), p.136.

2. Nuruddin Farah, *Gifts* (London: Serif, 1993), p.76. Further references are given in parentheses in the text.

3. Nuruddin Farah, "Why I Write," *Third World Quarterly* 10, 4 (1988), 1599.

4. Marcel Mauss, *The Gift*, trans. W.D.Halls (New York: Norton, 1990), p.7.

5. ibid., pp.33, 35, 39, 41.

6. ibid., p.6.

7. ibid., p.48.

8. Friedrich Nietzsche, *On the Genealogy of Morals* and *Ecce Homo*, trans. Walter Kaufman (New York: Vintage, 1967), p.73.

9. ibid., p.89.

10. ibid., p.72.

11. ibid., 70.

12. Mauss, p.6.

13. Pierre Bourdieu, *Outline of a Theory of Practice*, trans. Richard Rice (Cambridge: Cambridge University Press, 1977), p.95.

14. Pierre Bourdieu, *Algeria 1960*, trans. Richard Rice (Cambridge: Cambridge University Press, 1979), p.22.

15. Mauss, p.42.

16. Frantz Fanon, *The Wretched of the Earth*, trans. Constance Farrington (New York: Grove Weidenfeld, 1991), pp.167, 155.

17. ibid., p.38.

18. Georges Bataille, "The Notion of Expenditure," in *Critical Theory since Plato*, ed. Hazard Adams (New York: Harcourt, 1992), pp.863.

19. Farah, "Why I Write," 1597, 1599.

20. ibid., 1597.

21. ibid., 1599.

22. Feroza Jussawalla and Reed Way Dasenbrock. *Interview with Writers of the Post-Colonial World* (Jackson: University Press of Mississippi, 1992), p.45.

23. Farah, "Why I Write," 1599.

24. Jacques Derrida, *Writing and Difference*, trans. Allan Bass (Chicago: University of Chicago Press, 1978), pp.274.

25. Jussawalla et al, p.45.

26. Mauss, p.69.

27. Mikhail M. Bakhtin, *The Dialogic Imagination*, trans. Caryl Emerson and Michael Holquist, ed. Michael Holquist (Austin: University of Texas Press, 1990), p.293.

CHARITY WOUNDS
HIM WHO RECEIVES:
Nuruddin Farah's *Gifts*

Kirsten Holst Petersen

A quick way to get to the center of the concerns and discussions of Nuruddin Farah's novel *Gifts* (1992) is to listen to what he himself says about it. He is uncharacteristically brief and to-the-point regarding the theme: "I moved to Africa and have since written...another novel set in present-day Somalia, about foreign aid, entitled *Gifts*."[1] The stage of foreign aid has two main factors, the donor and the receiver, and Farah has clear opinions on their relative roles: "We cannot but condemn outside interest, because these outsiders do not have anything new for us, and their interest is generally unhealthy. But then again, we must condemn both our own people and our heads of state for encouraging that interest."[2] He castigates Africans for a series of perceived shortcomings: "I think our people are sick, too: they are ill-informed, uneducated, unwilling to learn, prey to bourgeois tastes, they love the most fashionable car, the most fashionable clothes, and so on"; and this

591

shows him the way towards a solution to the problem: "In my opinion, the explanation for all the ills of Somalia, as of Africa, need not be sought elsewhere, but must be found within the country and the continent, and the cure must also be found within."[3]

With the theme, the problem and possibilities for a solution settled, Farah turns to the literary aspects of the novel, its form and language. "As my point of departure I usually propose a topic, a theme, and then I pursue the ideas as they might occur to anyone else. I don't imagine that there is any single voice, so this is why my novels are multi-voiced and, hopefully, multi-layered."[4] This commitment to a multiply-voiced form amounts to an ideological stance: "What I like to do, in telling a story, is to study the numerous facets of a tale and to allow very many different competing views to be heard, which in a sense points to the democratic drift of my writing, the drift of *tolerance*."[5] This commitment leads Farah to "give even the people I disapprove of a chance for their words to be heard. It is only through a debate that we can reach an acceptable logical conclusion."[6] This "tolerance," as Farah calls it, raises the question of the status of the concepts of reality and truth: Farah maintains that "I cannot tell others how things are, I can only tell them how I perceive things to be."[7] This, however, does not prevent him from stating his overall theme as "Truth versus Untruth," and claiming that he is writing, for the sake of posterity, "the true history of a nation." Yet, he maintains, "I am not one of those people who live in the confines of their own conception of truths."[8] That he does have an opinion, however, is evident from such statements as "I seldom insist on imposing my interpretation of the text on other readers. I usually like readers to make up their own opinions."[9] The inconsistency of these somewhat contradictory opinions is, however, an active and important part of Farah's art, as he invites the reader to join him in his "thinking aloud" in the form of his novels: "If I use myths, and if I repeat things and oblique ways of answering these, I would also like the reader to come with me and to experience my self-doubting."[10] This invitation to the reader to engage in a dialogue with the author through the medium of his novel constructs the novel as a site of discussion. The form of the novel supports this intention.

In *Gifts* Farah sets out to explore the theme of development aid by offering a series of different responses, each framed in its own discourse. In the structure of the novel the narrative is a conventional love story in which a man and a woman fall in love, overcome their fears and reservations, and are finally united. Surrounding this narrative is a bricolage of other forms: press releases, oral tales, proverbs, letters, an article, and news on the radio. A pattern of relationships of opposition or analogy or explication exists between the different discourses, and much of the discussion in the novel is situated in the tension between these different discourses.

The turning point of the discussion is the contradictory and dangerous nature of gifts. The terms of the discussion owe a debt to Marcel Mauss's seminal study *The Gift: Forms and Functions of Exchange in Archaic Societies* (1954) which Farah acknowledges on the dedication page of the novel. Mauss makes the point that "The danger represented by the thing given or transmitted is possibly nowhere better expressed than in very ancient German languages. This explains the double meaning of the word *gift* as gift and poison."[11] In the narrative part of the novel this double nature of the gift is explored in terms of venereal disease. A woman with gonorrhoea says: "You see, doctor...it's my husband who brings things into the house, good and bad things. Please help me and my baby."[12] In this case the gift of life turns into the poison of disease or disfigurement, and in another instance a woman poisons her husband for giving her the same gift. It is perhaps not a sheer coincidence that the word *gift* in modern Danish means both poison and to be married. On the development aid scene "tinned milk to Poland after the Chernobyl disaster" (p.172) is an obvious example of the poisoned gift. In the novel Farah makes a sharp distinction between gifts that are good and gifts that are bad: the good gifts operate within the confines of a modern gift economy in which the motives for giving range from altruism to varying degrees of reciprocity, but they never cross the line from gifts to commodities which can be traded in the market-place of hearts or hungry mouths. The novel's moral discussion explores the fine line between gift and commodity, the limits of com-modification. Most things can be either gifts or commodities, depending on the circumstances of the exchange, but despite the fact that most things can be bought and sold in the market economy of the modern world, the encroachment of market mechanisms and terms into areas of human relations raises questions of a moral nature. In a recent article Margaret Radin uses the term "market-inalienability," by which she means those things or rights which can be given away but not sold. She includes "personal attributes and the integrity of the body, sacred objects, and kinship relations."[13] The motivating force in the narrative of *Gifts* is the characters' battle to keep their love life, family relations, friendships, and personal integri-ty out of the commodification of human relations which character-izes the development aid scene. The distinction between the two spheres of morality is made explicit in the different linguistic regis-ters associated with them. Ebla, the main character in Farah's first novel *From a Crooked Rib*, knows that girls were "just like objects...sold and bought as shepherds sold their goats,"[14] and she refers to her sex as her "bank." The use of market rhetoric here is an obvious transgression of morality: Ebla talks like a prostitute. She is, however, also a symbol of Somalia which in that novel is seen to pros-titute itself to the big powers. In *Gifts* Somalia is also seen as prosti-tuting itself, this time to the international aid organizations, and here this act is also underlined by a linguistic register which commodifies human relations. The difference is that in this novel it is the actual register of journalism and UNICEF reports. The development aid scene, which in theory is a gift situation, is shown by its very lan-guage to have moved into the economics of human relations. In the following I take up Farah's invitation to discuss the issues of gifts and development aid with him through a debate about and with *Gifts*.

My intuitive understanding of *gift* corresponds to definition no.3 in the *Oxford English Dictionary*: "something, the possession of which is transferred to another without the expectation or receipt of an equivalent"; and it connotes the ideas of goodness, selflessness, and pleasure, carrying with it a value beyond its commercial or aesthetic worth. It is, in Lewis Hyde's words, the gift "that, when it comes, speaks commandingly to the soul and irresistibly moves us."[15] Sceptics, not to speak of cynics, would doubt the possibility of a pure gift, untainted by self-interest, and Derrida sets out to prove its impossibility with a set of logical deductions which rely on ethical imperatives for their strength. Taking as his starting point the same gift situation as the OED definition, he proposes that "there is gift, if there is any,...in a partition without return and without division, without being-with-self of the gift-counter-gift." Defining the basic gift definition as "someone giving something to some one other," he maintains that "[t]hese conditions of the possibility of the gift designate simultaneously the conditions of the impossibility of the gift," and thereby "define or produce the annulment, the annihilation, the destruction of the gift." This is because, as there must be no return of the gift, the donor must not count on restitution and the receiver must not contemplate it, and to be certain that this is the case, "[i]t is thus necessary, at the limit, that he [the donor] not *recognize* the gift as gift. If he recognizes it *as* gift...this simple recognition suffices to annul the gift." The reason for this is that it gives him back "a symbolic equivalent."[16] Therefore it will also make the gift impossible as gift if it is recognized as such by the receiver, even "before *recognition* becomes *gratitude*. The simple identification of the gift seems to destroy it." Thus "*the gift as gift* ought *not to appear as gift: either to the donor or the donee.*"[17] This is because the donor will start to congratulate himself and the recipient will start to feel gratitude, both of which will annul the pure gift situation. To Derrida the essence of the gift is that "it appears and that it not appears" simultaneously,[18] and this puts it into the same category as time and being. However, to a writer of a novel about gifts this logical annihilation of his subject does constitute a problem.

Farah faces this problem by making Derrida's position the starting point of a continuum of possible gift situations, ranging from the altruistic to the deliberately destructive. Clothing the simultaneous being and non-being in the physical garb of a social/realist narrative is obviously impossible, but Farah gets very close to the ideal gift situation in the story of the old woman who helped Taariq when he had been thrown out of the house one night, drunk and sleepy. "I fell asleep in the shade of a tree...when out of the silver brightness of a full moon the figure of an old woman bearing the gift of a blanket emerged. She covered me with it, tucking me in like a motherless baby. But she didn't leave me all that night. She sat by me, on a low stool, guarding me against thieves and dogs whom she shooed away whenever they approached" (p.119). She had gone when he woke up, so in some sense he was unaware of being given a gift and certainly unable to reciprocate, even with a show of gratitude.

For it to be possible for him to relate the incident at all, however, he had to be semi-awake on and off, and in that state he heard the old woman mention the name Marilyn. This identifies the old woman as a neighbor, thus leading to an accidental meeting of Taariq and his rescuer. When he thanks her she first denies her act of giving, and when that becomes impossible in the face of the evidence she gets angry and scolds Taariq: "why devalue the significance of the act by mentioning it in public? Why must you speak of it?" (p.124). His speaking of it destroys its aspect of pure gift, in Derrida's terms, but it gives Farah the opportunity to show that her attitude would allow for the possibility of a moment of the pure gift, with her not conceiving of her act as a gift and Taariq asleep. Duniya, the main character and "chronicler" (p.242), approves of the old woman's sentiments, and although she cannot be unproblematically seen as the author's mouthpiece she is nevertheless portrayed with enough sympathy to carry some of the novel's moral burden. Unselfish and unobtrusive giving is represented as a good thing through characters of whom the author clearly approves.

Duniya is also the center of another of the novel's attempted fictionalizations of Derrida's ideal gift model, in which one half of the giver/receiver unit acts in accordance with the pure gift situation. She takes in the foundling baby and defends her action against her thoroughly mercenary half-brother by saying "*we* are keeping him out of pure kind-heartedness, motivated by goodwill, an act of mercy such as one might extend towards a blind man crossing a dangerous road" (p.80). Whilst this justification reveals no lack of knowledge of the gift as gift on the part of the donor, the receiver, being a new-born baby, compared to a blind man, keeps his side of the equation: he is truly ignorant of the gift. Again, the description of the two characters involved in the discussion leaves little doubt about the author's approval of this action. Duniya's act of generosity is set against the bribe-taking, woman-denigrating Shiriye's objections to the baby's likely bastard status and the cost involved in feeding it. The approval is wrapped up in the Somali proverb, "He who distributes the offerings of fortune receives little as his personal share" (p.47). This is used to clinch the argument against the grossly insensitive foreign aid worker Ingrid and can thus be taken to carry some of the book's moral burden.

This search for possible approximations to the scenarios of Derrida's pure gift has one more instance: that of the giving of blood, but here the moral implications are different. Duniya's daughter Nasiiba is discovered to have been secretly giving blood at the hospital, and Duniya's response is a blank "but why?" On receiving a reply which is the idealistic answer to that question—"The blood bank was short of it and, being in a generous mood, I felt like donating some of mine" (p.25)—she "shifted in discomfort" (p.26). The point is related to Nasiiba's waywardness and is considered under the same heading as her receiving unwanted gifts and not settling the family's bill at the grocery store: all these acts are disturbing and secretive and form part of the (slight) suspense built into the plot. The real reason for the blood donation is revealed when the plot is resolved: the foundling's mother is identified as a friend of Nasiiba, and because of the circumstances of the clandestine birth and a shared rare blood group Nasiiba gives blood to save her friend's life.

This answer to Duniya's repeated question of "why?" is satisfactory in terms of the novel's plot, but it passes up a very good opportunity for exploring the nature and possibility of the ideal gift situation.

In a book which is a passionate plea for voluntary blood donations (the British system) as opposed to payment for blood (the American system), Richard M.Tittmuss describes the voluntary community donor as "the closest approximation in social reality to the abstract reality of a free human gift." The primary characteristics of such donations are: "the absence of tangible immediate rewards in monetary or non-monetary forms; the absence of penalties, financial or otherwise; the knowledge among donors that their donations are for unnamed strangers without distinction of age, sex, medical condition, income, class, religion or ethnic group."[19] Whilst accepting that most donors have personal reasons for donating blood, Tittmuss still hopes that the altruism in giving to strangers, which is part of the blood-giving situation, may "touch every aspect of life and affect the whole fabric of values."[20] He sees it as an aspect of modern social welfare, and he supports his view by quoting Wilensky and Lebeaux: "The social welfare system has really been thought of as help given to a stranger, not to the person who by reason of personal bond commands it without asking. It assumes a degree of social distance between helped and helper."[21] This ideal is in fact implied in Nasiiba's answer, but it is deemed too suspect to be trusted, and this is borne out by the plot in which the acceptable reason is a personal gift to a friend in need. The ideal is approached in terms of individual and personal relationships, but not on a social level. The extended family is at one point compared to a trade union where the unemployed members receive "unemployment benefit" from family members with employment (p.196). Nevertheless, this equation is wrong, precisely because the family members are personally known and connected to the giver. The same personalized relationship is part of the tradition of the *Qur'an* which, as it is described in *Gifts*, has aspects of the pure gift situation mixed with a ritualized set of conditions (p.194).

The notion of giving to strangers without any possibility of return, which is the essence of blood donation, seems unknown and somewhat incomprehensible in the moral universe of the book. In a heavily biased discussion between the insensitive aid worker Ingrid and the thoughtful Somali woman Yussur, the latter asks, "Why give, Ingrid?...What's in it for your people to give my people things?" Ingrid's answer is that there are some things the Africans need, to which Yussur replies "but that is ridiculous...Surely you don't give something of value to yourself simply because someone else does not have it or is in need of it?" (p.46). Ingrid's answer is a catalogue of everything that is wrong with the development aid and food relief situation. The implication is very clear: the development aid situation does not include even a theoretical possibility of an approximation to Derrida's pure gift model. This I see as a lacuna in the novel's careful strategy of outlining every possible attitude in the development aid scenario. From the point of view of an ordinary citizen in a donor country, aid to the Third World surely closely resembles giving to strangers without expecting any return. The fact that governments, aid organizations, the World Bank, and the IMF do not see it that way and do not implement it in that spirit is a different matter. Behind the ugly scene of development aid as it is exposed and discussed in the novel lies at least a theoretical possibility of intentions to approximate the ideal gift situation. In the pattern of the novel this lacuna is overlaid with representations of the actuality of development aid, and this is based on a different premise.

The cynical answer to the challenge of Derrida's ideal gift paradigm is given by Marcel Mauss in his study *The Gift: Forms and Functions of Exchange in Archaic Society*. In his enquiry into "primitive and archaic types of society" Mauss is concerned with a gift exchange phenomenon which he calls "prestations." He defines them as "in theory voluntary, disinterested and spontaneous, but in fact obligatory and interested. The form usually taken is that of the gift generously offered; but the accompanying behaviour is formal pretence and social deception, while the transaction itself is based on obligation and economic self-interest." Mauss's investigation is comparative. He finds that "the same morality and economy are at work, albeit less noticeably, in our own societies," and this enables him to draw moral conclusions about present day behavior.[22] In the world of Farah's novel the negative end of the gift situation continuum is represented by development aid, and the discussion is carried out in Mauss's terms: It is seen to be in theory generously offered, but in reality based on economic self-interest and ego-boosting.

In the bricolage of the novel this level is represented by a series of press releases. The novel is tightly constructed, and each chapter follows roughly the same pattern: starting with a dream sequence, it moves into the plot and ends with a section of factual writing, most often a press release, but it also includes news on the radio, an article, a letter, and some oral tales which are companion pieces or answers to the press releases. This progression from symbol to a developing love story to a series of stark statements moves the novel from the personal to the political and sets up a discussion between the two. In the dream sections Duniya fights a battle with herself to overcome her resistance to accepting gifts and thereby giving in to the love offered her by Bosaaso who in his dreams works up the courage to take the necessary risks to dare to love. This subconscious emotional maturing process is described in a series of fluid dream images, centering on birds and butterflies, colors and movements. It naturally precedes the development of the plot in which the two protagonists reach the same goal, but through interaction with each other and other characters and through discussions and debate. The press releases which end the chapters contradict the development and maturing aspect of the dream and plot sections by their stark and uncompromising finality. Their technical and economic vocabulary does not leave room for emotions or change; its neutral prose simply gives information about facts and figures from the development aid world: 300 to 500 people dying daily, food aid worth 260 dollars etc. The press releases are meant to condemn themselves, but at first sight they seem simply neutral or objective.

However, although they offer seemingly random snippets of information, they do in fact outline the very areas which critics of development aid highlight in their assessments. In his article to the newspaper Taariq suggests that his readers "walk this well-trodden path in the company of Susan George and Teresa Hayter" (p.196). Farah chooses to take a knowledge of these views for granted because he wants to concentrate on the situation of the receivers, so I shall briefly outline them.

The topics under discussion are aid in the form of agricultural reforms, leading to ecological disaster, famine, and debt; food relief aid leading to famine; educational and research aid, leading to psychological dependence; the West's political complicity in creating starvation situations; and the vulgarity of turning Africa's mass starvation into media events.

Agricultural high technology and the cash crop imperative are seen as the main causes of disaster. High technology creates unemployment, is expensive and therefore leads to dependence on loans. It also creates ecological disasters. The first press release, a UNICEF bulletin, describes the efforts to eradicate locusts by spraying insecticides from the air. In a discussion of the battle against the tsetse fly, Marcus Linear outlines a similar scenario. Poisons which are banned in the West are dumped on the Third World, mainly helping Western chemical manufacturers, and the need for such drastic action is not thoroughly investigated or is found to be artificial. Such "aid" is thus destructive of the environment, both native plants and animals, and "the use of hard chemical pesticides to open up new lands also opens the door to further, and much more intensive, deployment of chemicals to keep subsequent crops pest-free."[23] It can also cause sterility in both men and women, and the truly cynical view among some development aid workers is that this is not a bad thing. The cash crops grown are often luxury items, aimed at rich consumer markets in the West. They take up land which could grow essential food, and worse, the Third World countries have no influence on the prices, which fluctuate wildly. As Susan George states: "A country cannot be independent when it depends on the goodwill of rich consumers to keep on buying its coffee or its fresh strawberries even in periods of economic crises and spending cutbacks."[24] This leads to debt and dependency, and Farah, like Teresa Hayter, quotes Hubert Humphrey: "And if you are looking for a way to get people to lean on you and be dependent on you...it seems to me that food dependence would be terrific" (pp.194-95).

Educational and research aid forms the subject of another of the press releases which informs its readers of a "number of professors on secondment from Italian institutes of higher learning" (p.96), helping to complete an Italian-Somali dictionary to aid research. The cultural dependency set up by indoctrination in the educational system, and its detrimental effect on development, is eloquently described by Susan George: "Research...is not a luxury good but an important input to control: it helps to strengthen the power of those who exercise it while simultaneously contributing to thickening the ideological smokescreen behind which this power is exercised."[25] Farah's insistence on the complicity of language in the alienating relationship between North and South is indicated in his reporting on language professors and dictionary writing. "Language is a product of a people's attitude to the world in which they find themselves" (p.47) says Yussur. The translation of traditional names into the names of American actresses and of starvation into the clinical language of press releases represents a debasement of human values.

The Reuter release on the European community forcing President Mengistu to accept the monitoring by EEC officials of food distribution to Tigray and Eritrea contains two possible but oppositional messages. One is that development aid, particularly through the IMF, has politically unacceptable strings attached, and the other is that it often helps to prop up corrupt goverments.

Central to the whole discussion as it is carried out in the novel is the article which Taariq, Duniya's former husband and ex-alcoholic journalist, writes for his Mogadishu newspaper. The genre is that of the essay, a logical but also emotional exploration of a particular problem, often of a moral or ethical nature. This factual, non-fictional genre is, however, made fiction in the structure of the novel by its being written by a fictional character. Thus, to assess the degree to which it accords with the author's views, it is necessary to establish the credibility given to the character. At the plot level of the novel he is unstable and somewhat inconsistent. He starts off as the accidental savior of Duniya, particularly good as a father-figure for her son; it then transpires that he is an alcoholic, for which reason Duniya leaves him, but at the time of the action in the novel he has reformed and resumed his passionate writing. Duniya, who is the chronicler and moral center of the novel, is "delighted that Taariq could still have lucid moments of virtuosity" (p.198). This is a typically non-committal conclusion to a discussion, which is what gives the novel its multi-voiced and inconclusive appearance, but at the same time the discussions themselves are often heavily biased, both in terms of the argument itself and in terms of the characterization and physical descriptions of the characters expressing the views. The final impression of Taariq is that of a sensitive and intelligent man, and it is tempting to see his article "Giving and Receiving: The Notion of Donations" as the author's endorsed perspective. A further indication of this is its strategic position in the novel. It is placed at the end of Part Three which is titled "Duniya Loves" and which charts the maturing of her love for Bosaaso. As a result of reading the article she decides to "make of her body a gift" (p.198) to him, and this leads on to the fourth and final part of the book, provocatively called "Duniya Gives," in which her giving as an act of love is juxtaposed with the ugly giving of the development aid scene.

In the article Taariq repeatedly expresses the opinion that "foreign food donations create a buffer zone between corrupt leaderships and the starving masses" (p.194); he puts the somewhat rhetorical question, "Can we conclude that if foreign governments stop aiding the African dictators with food hand-outs, then their people will rise against them?" (p.193); and he answers it himself with the words, "Famines awaken a people from an economical, social or political lethargy" (p.194). This is an uncharacteristically cynical view, advocating as it does starvation and revolt as a better solution than survival and no revolt. It is an idealistic solution which, however, works best in practice if one knows that the starving and revolting are going to be undertaken by people other than oneself. The reason for this harsh view is evident in every sentence in the article. It is suffused by a deep sense of humiliation, caused by the situation of begging. "Empty brass bowls make excellent photographs...to starve is to be of media interest these days...he who begs has no self-pride" (pp.193-94).

The essence of the ideal gift situation was that there should be no return, but the essence of the gift situation as Mauss defines it is that the gift implies, indeed demands, a return. Development aid is described as a gift situation in Mauss's terms, but without a return gift. Taariq cannot foresee a situation in which the Africans will be in a position to return the gifts, and therefore they are condemning themselves to being "forever dependent" (p.195). The dependency which is the result of an unreturned gift is explored by Mauss in his study in which he sets out to enquire into the principle whereby the gift has to be repaid.

Mauss is describing a system he calls total prestation, in which groups and tribes, not individuals, carry out exchanges, and the things exchanged are not only goods and property but "courtesies, entertainments, ritual, military assistance, women, children, dances and feasts."[26] He calls this kind of total exchange "potlatch," and he sees it as "a struggle among nobles to determine their position in the hierarchy to the ultimate benefit, if they are successful, of their own clans."[27] It takes the form of excessive showering of gifts on your exchange partner or even wilful destruction of wealth. The purpose of this seemingly insane generosity is, however, to humiliate your gift partner. He has an absolute obligation to return the gift, and if he cannot match it he loses the authority, honor, and prestige which an extravagant show or deliberate destruction of wealth confers. Although giving is losing, yet "the loss seems to profit the one who suffers it."[28] In the novel, Nasiiba and Bosaaso enjoy a vicarious victory from Poland's humiliation of America when, in return for contaminated milk, the Poles sent blankets for the homeless of New York.

Claude Lévi-Strauss sees the potlatch as the logical outcome of a situation in which "goods are not only economic commodities, but vehicles and instruments for realities of another order, such as power, influence, sympathy, status and emotion."[29] Looked at in this way, the increase on the gift is not profit in a capitalist sense but represents gains of a symbolic order. It establishes a hierarchy and confers power and honor on the winner. Sanctions against non-reciprocation included not only loss of dignity but also enslavement for debt. In this way gifts were dangerous and double-edged: they could easily turn into their opposite, showing the poisoned side of the coin. At this level the potlatch is an extreme version of the gift-as-power competition, and its parallel to the development aid situation is not hard to see. Today, as well, wealth translates itself into power, even when it is given away, and unreciprocated gifts create dependency and powerlessness.

In the ancient gift societies there was another component of the transaction: the *hau* or spirit of a person was transmitted to his possessions. Therefore some of the spirit of the owner went with the thing exchanged, and through it he held power over the receiver until he was presented with a counter-prestation. The power resided in both the thing given and the person, and there was not a strict separation between the two. "To give something was to give part of oneself."[30] The gifts themselves had a history and a personality, and people could be named after them. In the novel a young girl is ironically named Marilyn after "a famous actress who is now dead" (p.67), and this causes real pain to her grandmother after whom the girl was originally named Maryam: she complains about the immorality of half-naked actresses and then says enigmatically, "besides, I will not live forever" (p.68). She is obviously concerned that this particular aspect of the gift from the West will obliterate the power of her own spirit. What one gives away in this system is part of oneself, of one's nature and substance, whilst "to receive something is to receive a part of someone's spiritual essence." The pattern of exchange creates a spiritual bond between things "which are to some extent the parts of persons," and this close relationship gives rise to the concept of inalienable things in which there exists an indissoluble bond between a thing and its original owner.[31] Annette B.Weiner defines the concept in the following way: "What makes a possession inalienable is its exclusive and cumulative identity with a particular series of owners through time. Its history is authenticated by fictive or true genealogies, origin myths, sacred ancestors, and gods."[32] The exchange of inalienable possessions was a transaction not of goods but between people, and the purpose—to produce friendly relations between two people or groups—was a moral one. The economic definition of gift (non-commodity) exchange is "an exchange of inalienable things between transactors in a state of reciprocal dependence," and this is set against market capitalism's buying and selling which in Marx's terms is described as an exchange of alienable things between transactors who are in a state of reciprocal independence.[33] Mauss's comparative perspective is between these two modes of being, in which he sees the first as the better system because it is based on community feelings and because it carries out transactions between people rather than things. Most importantly, he finds traces of it buried in modern, seemingly soulless transactions, like selling homes rather than houses and in the sharing aspects of Friendly Societies and Trade Unions.

As property in modern societies is indisputably privately owned and disposed of to strangers, the concept of inalienability is not directly transferable, but the modified concept of market-inalienability is important in this context. In terms of the novel's plot, the strivings, doubts and difficulties of the main characters are centered on keeping these aspects of their lives untainted by commodity exchange: Duniya is pathologically afraid of receiving any form of gift, particularly from Bosaaso, as she fears that it will turn the giving of love into a bargain and deprive her of the possibility of giving "the gift of her body" freely. Her daughter Yarey is "decommodified" in the course of the novel: she moves from being placed with her uncle, in return for cheap rent for her mother, to living with her mother. Bosaaso ends an authentic donor situation in which he has supported the lavish and unproductive life style of his former mother-in-law and her daughter, and Taariq is able to write again, despite censorship and ominous threats.

On the level of development aid this concept can perhaps help explain some of the deep sense of humiliation mixed with anger which is expressed in Taariq's article. Mauss quotes from Emerson's essay "On Gifts and Presents": "Charity wounds him who receives, and our whole moral effort is directed towards suppressing the unconscious harmful patronage of the rich almoner."[34] These are sentiments which modernity shares with the ancient gift societies, but in the development aid situation the "harmful patronage" is not likely to be unconscious. Apart from eminently alienable goods like money and food, development aid brings inalienable gifts with their own genealogies, myths, and gods. In the novel the crass Danish voluntary worker gives voice to a sense of relinquishing inalienable gifts to unworthy recipients. She talks about Africans "who have no idea how to take care of sensitive gadgets with souls, like a car, a computer with software sensibilities or a set of china with as fragile an anima as a bird's." To her mind, Africans "haven't got what it takes to appreciate the cultural and technological gifts that are given to them" (p.46). The implications are that the cultural and technological gifts of the West contain an inalienable essence which is the secret of their/our power. In her study of inalienable possessions Weiner discusses the paradox of keeping-while-giving. She maintains that the essence of the potlatch was to keep the most valuable possessions out of circulation while at the same time making sure that the fact that you have them is kept uppermost in people's minds, because "the authority and esteem embedded in inalienable wealth was far greater than its exchange value."[35] It was the "being in possession" that conferred power and prestige. This phenomenon of keeping-while-giving does seem to be part of the development aid scene insofar as the large transfer of alienable goods does not appear to have any effect. Something is kept back, causing the ugly situation of ostentatious givers and humiliated, angry receivers.

This is not a problem which Nuruddin Farah's novel can solve. It can, in fact, not even suggest a solution. In terms of the debate which takes place in the novel it does offer a solution—"stop the aid and go home"—but in terms of the narrative itself, where otherwise the positive values of Farah's humanistic and intensely moral universe prevail, the problem of the economic dependence of the main character is solved by the arrival on the scene of an expatriate brother who flies in and showers green dollar notes onto his grateful sister.

Some problems are just too hard to solve.

NOTES

1. Nuruddin Farah, "Why I Write," *Third World Quarterly* 10, 4 (1998), 1599.

2. Maya Jaggi, "A Combining of Gifts: An Interview with Nuruddin Farah," *Third World Quarterly* 11, 3 (1989), 1599.

3. Jaggi, 198.

4. Armando Pajalich, "Nuruddin Farah Interviewed by Armando Pajalich," *Kunapipi* 15, 1 (1993), 64.

5. Pajalich, 63.

6. Pajalich, 64.

7. Farah, "Why I Write," 1598.

8. Jaggi, 196.

9. Pajalich, 67.

10. Pajalich, 64.

11. Marcel Mauss, *The Gift: Forms and Functions of Exchange in Archaic Societies* (London: Cohen & West, 1954), p.62.

12. Nuruddin Farah, *Gifts* (London: Serif, 1992), p.14. Further page references are given in parentheses in the text of the essay.

13. Quoted in John Frow, *Time and Commodity Culture: Essays in Cultural Theory and Postmodernity* (Oxford: Clarendon Press, 1997), p.148.

14. Nuruddin Farah, *From A Crooked Rib* (London: Heinemann, 1970), p.84.

15. Lewis Hyde, *The Gift: Imagination and the Erotic Life of Property* (New York: Vintage, 1979), p.xvii.

16. Jacques Derrida, *Given Time: 1. Counterfeit Money* (Chicago: University of Chicago Press, 1992), pp.12-13.

17. Derrida, p.14.

18. Derrida, p.27.

19. Richard M.Tittmuss, *The Gift Relationship: From Human Blood to Social Policy* (London: Allen & Unwin, 1970), p.88.

20. Tittmuss, p.198.

21. Titmuss, p.216.

22. Mauss, pp.1, 2.

23. Marcus Linear, *Zapping the Third World: The Disaster of Development Aid* (London: Pluto Press, 1985), p.59.

24. Susan George, *Ill Fares the Land: Essays on Food, Hunger and Power* (Washington, D.C.: Institute for Policy Studies, 1984), p.12.

25. George, p.60.

26. Mauss, p.3.

27. Mauss, p.5.

28. Bataille, quoted in Frow, p.118.

29. Levi-Strauss, quoted in Frow, p.115.

30. Mauss, p.10.

31. Mauss, pp.10-11.

32. Annette B.Weiner, *Inalienable Possessions: The Paradox of Keeping-While Giving* (Oxford: University of California Press, 1992), p.33.

33. Chris Gregory, *Gifts and Commodities* (London: Academic Press, 1982), p.12.

34. Mauss, p.63.

35. Weiner, p.36.

NURUDDIN FARAH'S *GIFTS*

Abdulrazak Gurnah

ifts[1] is Nuruddin Farah's seventh novel, and it has the distinction of having been available in translation before its publication in the language in which it was written. It appeared in 1992 as the inaugural book for a new British publisher, Serif, just after its publication in Zimbabwe by Baobab Press. The structuring theme of the novel is the giving and receiving of gifts, and implications of authority and dependence which follow from it. The political dimension of this is aid, which is figured in the narrative in a variety of ways: news items that caption the end of chapters; the crass European and American aid-workers who despise the people they have come to succour, and among whom they "live like lords"; the clinic where Duniya works as a midwife which was built by the Chinese and is partly staffed by Chinese doctors. The political argument is found most fully in a long journalistic piece by Taariq deep into the novel, analysing the degradation of African societies as a consequence of dependence. But gifts also figure in relations between individuals, especially at a time when hardship and disorder have become unavoidable. The Mogadiscio of *Gifts* is not the bullet-riddled wasteland of today, but it is still a city full of dangers and shortages, where lone women are

611

stalked by motorists and bread is unobtainable.

The central figure of the novel is Duniya, a twice-married single mother of three, living in "a flat" which belongs to Qaasim, the elder brother of her divorced second husband. She pays only a nominal rent for the flat, and receives regular donations of dollars from her brother in Rome—dollars from various sources figure as a concrete image of domination in the novel—but Duniya is sensitive about gifts because she fears the kind of dependence that will put her completely in the hands of men. It is familiar territory for Farah, whose women are, more often than not, aggressively obsessed with their vulnerability. Duniya means "the world." The irony of the name lies in the multitudinous possibilities it suggests, and the impoverished outcomes that are Duniya's reality. Her story demonstrates the powerlessness of women and children, and demonstrates how women are forced to remain children in Somali culture. Duniya's father died when she was seventeen. On his death-bed he had asked that she should be given as a wife to his good friend and neighbour Zubair, who was then seventy and blind. The only person present when Duniya's father gasped these cruel final words was Duniya's mother, who was hard of hearing. None the less, a father's death-bed wishes have an irresistible potency and Duniya was married. To make the point about the commodification of women, Duniya's half-brother Shiriye comes to protest her oppression, but goes away when Zubair gives him the bride-wealth. Shiriye and Qaasim are the predatory representatives of the patriarchy, and they are both figured as self-indulgent, greedy and physically unattractive—though in the case of Qaasim, not unattractive enough to deter Fariida who sacrificed herself on the altar of his vanity in return for trips to Nairobi and elsewhere.

Duniya's first husband, who despite appearances turned out to be a vigorous and affectionate man, lived long enough to provide Duniya with twins, Nasiiba and Maatan. She meets her second husband Taariq when she rents a room from him, but the marriage so casually contracted does not last. She comes home from work to find Taariq feeding her ten-year old son whisky, and that was that. This is more or less where we find Duniya at the beginning of the novel, and Farah sets out the interwoven and proliferating domestic arrangements with great skill to demonstrate how trapped everyone is by their circumstances, but above all how trapped women are by dependence.

Bosaaso, who becomes Duniya's lover, also has his own story. Abandoned by his father, Bosaaso's mother at first feeds them by singing at functions and taking payment in kind. Later she attends classes and becomes a teacher, while her son struggles through school and eventually becomes an economist working in New York for the UN—acquiring a Green Card and amassing dollars. He returns to Somalia with his friend Mire, both of them taking no payment and asking only that they be provided with somewhere to live. As with the story of Duniya, Bosaaso's is a story of survival. His domestic arrangements, the death of his wife, and his past are once again used to great effect by Farah to demonstrate how encumbered their lives are. At the beginning of the novel Bosaaso offers a lift to Duniya who is on her way to work at Dr Mire's clinic. The lift is a gift that is also the beginning of his wooing of her. If Duniya represents unfulfilled possibilities, she is also an inner world whose dreaming is displaced by the waking world. At the opening she dreams of a butterfly, a fragile, colourful image that we later understand to be the love which first came to her in her sleep. For *Gifts* is above all a story of the discovery and acceptance of love, and the theme of gifts as dependence is transformed before the end to acceptance as an act of generosity. The most surprising gift that Duniya is offered is that of the foundling. Her daughter Nasiiba brings home a baby she claims to have found in the rubbish, and Duniya agrees to keep it. The attention this act receives has some implications. The baby found in rubbish suggests how much the community is in decline, and the discovery of the baby's parentage intensifies this. The baby was the result of the vain and egotistical affair between Qaasim and Fariida, an unwanted embarrassment which the young mother was happy to have taken off her hands. But more importantly, Duniya's acceptance of the gift of the foundling is unequivocal. Despite the burdens she can anticipate, and the complications which begin to accumulate around her, she comes to understand that it is a gift which opens rather than closes possibilities. By becoming joint guardians of the foundling, Duniya and Bosaaso also become "co-responsible" for their lives.

Gifts is written with greater tolerance, affection and humour than any other Farah novel. Even the villains of the patriarchal oppression, Shiriye and Qaasim, escape utter demonisation. The security apparatus so evident in Farah's recent books is absent here. Despite the degradations and deprivations of the community, individuals act with surprising generosity to each other: the old woman who covers Taariq with a blanket and later comes to put her family at Duniya's disposal after she accepts the foundling, the shopkeeper Aw-Cumar and so on. The love affair between Duniya and Bosaaso is rendered with poetry and control, and the language of the novel is Farah's habitual lyricism.

NOTES

1. Nuruddin Farah, *Gifts* (Harare: Baobab Books; London: Serif, 1992).

SECRETS:
The Somali Dispersal and Reinvented Identities

Alamin Mazrui

The Somali have often been regarded as one of the most homogenous peoples of the African continent. There is first the claim to a common ancestor, Samaal, to whom all the six clan families trace their origins: Even if it has less than sufficient evidence of authenticity, this "myth" of common origin features quite strongly in the collective imagination of Somali identity. Secondly, in spite of dialectal differences—some of which border on mutual unintelligibility—the Somali perceive themselves as speakers of a common language. Thirdly, virtually all Somalis are followers of some brand of Islam, if not in actual religious practice then at least in cultural orientation. Even though the face of Islam is almost absent in *Secrets,* the religion has been at the defining core of Somali identity. Finally, the vast majority of Somalis are nomadic-pastoralists with a shared relational universe vis-à-vis the environment around them. Precisely because of its potential threat to this seeming "oneness" of the people, nomadism has paradoxically fostered a strong attachment to custom and collective being often rooted in one of the most resilient

615

oral traditions. At the same time, however, by bringing the Somali into constant contact with other peoples of the region, nomadic mobility has served as a source of great dynamism in Somali identity. Between the pole of the "others" who have become Somalized in time (e.g. the Wardei, an Oromo people turned Somali), to the Somali "self" that has been "otherized" (e.g. the Garre, a linguistically Oromized Somali people), there is a whole range of intercultural experiences that are constantly (re)shaped by new contacts and environments. Under the influence of the (Bantu) Pokomo, for example, an increasing number of Somali are learning to combine pastoral activity with agricultural enterprise, leading to an entire conceptual revolution, with all the attendant cultural implications, in how they relate to land and water resources.

The diasporization of the Somali, traditionally fostered by nomadic movement, became compounded by the encounter with Europe that began in the nineteenth century. European colonial experience and its aftermath left a Somali people divided and forced to imagine a variety of national identities/citizenships—including Somalia, Kenya, Djibouti, Ogaden/Ethiopia. Nuruddin Farah's *Maps* is partly a story of this dual process of dislocation and compounding of identities, leading eventually to an irredentism that took both an ideological and military form. For a while, the Somali people were a divided nation in search of a common state where all *Somalis* can also claim to be *Somalians*. With Somalia as the core, *Maps* reveals the challenges and struggles, trials and tribulations of being and becoming citizens of a multiplicity of new nations while continuing to adhere to a trans-national identitarian space of longing and belonging.

What state there was in the imaginary enclosure of Somalia, however, eventually collapsed with the eruption of the civil war in the 1990s. It is partly this moment of rupture that *Secrets* seeks to capture. The divided Somali now saw themselves dispersed to various parts of the world, a dispersal catalysed in part by the apparent hostility towards them by the neighbouring government of Kenya. To the Somali Diaspora in Italy and the Arab world stimulated by political and economic conditions at home, was now added the Diaspora of the civil war—in Canada, in the USA, and in other parts of the world.

In their new immigrant spaces, these refugee Somali(an)s have sometimes been regarded as cultural enclaves needing integration into "the mainstream." In Columbus, Ohio, with a Somali(an) community of more than eleven thousand people, which is more than double what it was two years earlier, even the census exercise by the US Census Monitoring Board was difficult to conduct supposedly due to the linguistic and cultural gap. A Somali-language radio program had to be launched to reach this community more effectively. In the words of the Ohio Secretary of State J.Kenneth Blackwell, "Somalians are the only linguistically isolated minority group. Now, for the first time, we have the Islamic and African American communities… reaching out in a concentrated effort to get them involved"[1] But how have these immigrants responded to these efforts to get them "involved"? How have they been reinventing themselves anew in their global setting? How have they been inscribing themselves in the dynamics of their new yet unfamiliar homes? How have they continued to relate to their former homeland of Somalia and how have those in dislocated Somalia continued to relate to them? These are some of the questions that constitute part of the saga of *Secrets* and which this essay intends to explore.

The civil war and the consequent collapse of the state of Somalia generated two seemingly contradictory processes within the Somali(an) body politic: clannization, on the one hand, and globalization, on the other hand. As a political trajectory, clannism, of course, was itself partly triggered by colonial politics. Nonno, a key character in *Secrets*, who represents the Somali(an) historical consciousness, was once detained because he refused to have the name of his clan in his identity card, then a requirement of the Italian colony. After his release he was issued with a card that identified him as British because he hailed from the part of the Somalia protectorate ruled by the British. Asked why he preferred being "British" to having his clan identity, Nonno responded as follows:

> Because "British" is a political notion, alluding to the
> state, the Crown et cetera...whereas being English,
> Welsh, Irish, or Scottish points to one's tribal prove-
> nance. One's "Somaliness," as opposed to being iden-
> tified as belonging to a particular clan, defines a polit-
> ical entity. The clan is non-political, based as it is on
> one's primordial blood identity.[2]

But, by the very act of making it a mandatory expression of a national identity card, the colonial authorities politicised the clan by inserting it more rigidly into the political space of the new formation of Somalia.

The struggle in post-colonial Somalia, then, was partly to eradicate the clan face of Somaliness and foster only its national imaginary. There was genuine enthusiasm at independence in the 1960s that the unification of the southern and northern regions of what had become Somalia and which had been colonised by Italy and Britain, respectively, would herald a new era of Somali nationhood capable of conquering all internal differences. The Somali were being encouraged to forget that they were Darood or Hawiyye, and to remember only their Somaliness in the nation-state terms of Somalia. But the civil war had now cast Somaliness asunder, fracturing and splitting it into its politicized pieces of clanhood. In the process:

> We were being made to rethink our relationships, what
> Somalia meant to each of us, the smaller unit succeed-
> ing where the larger unit, that of nationhood, had
> failed. Peace has flown away, I thought, peace is in
> fright. (p.227)

And the struggle for one Somalia for all Somalis, indivisible, under one flag, had now given place to attrition, where "jaw-breaking wars are going on, mutinous communities taking on one another" (p.227).

As indicated earlier, one of the most important factors that supposedly forged a sense of common identity among the Somali(ans) was in fact their common language, Somali. Where most other African nation-states were "bedevilled" by a myriad of tongues, often accused of promoting a divisive consciousness among its native speakers, Somalia was seen as endowed with a natural linguistic glue that made its people cohesive and relatively insulated from internal ethno-nationalist confrontations: The Somalians needed only to guard themselves against the external enemy.

This myth of a Somalia(an) people united by a common language was shattered by the civil war. What mattered now was no longer the fact of speaking a common tongue, but one's particular regional or clan accent in Somali. One's accent became an asset in one context and a liability in another. Damac, Kalaman's mother, was able to save her life partly because she was able to determine the Somali accent of her attackers in a moment in those turbulent times (p.22). And Kalaman could feel comfortable conversing with a strange interlocutor partly because he noticed from her accent that she was from the Central Region, which is where his own mother hailed from (p.81). And it is on account of their Somali accent or intonation that some men were stopped for questioning, having been suspected of sympathizing with "the local armed militia grouping, with vigilantes who infiltrated the city nightly" (p.93). By accident of dialect and accent, therefore, many an innocent person fell "victim to this head-on confrontation between the dictator, as the head of his Red Berets and his army thugs, and the leaders of the vigilantes, who claimed to be fighting for the overthrow of the regime, though they were bearing arms with a view to advancing not the interests of the nation but their own" (pp.93-94).

As the society was being split up into smaller units of clans and sub-clans, however, it was also getting increasingly globalized as some of its members found their way to parts of Africa, Asia, Europe, and the Americas. And as much as this dispersal was geographic, it also involved new political performances of citizenship, and increasingly new forms of cultural hybridization at the juncture of other minority and majority cultural histories and identities—forging, in turn, new types of connections and responses to the motherland. The isolationism of the clan at "home" was now running parallel with its mongrelization on the global stage. How was this identitarian "crisis" to resolve itself?

Kalaman, the main character of *Secrets*, is in fact a metaphoric representation of these competing extremes of the challenge of Somali identity precipitated by the civil war. The name Kalaman itself is a mystery, evoking curious debate with "some arguing it was Islamic, others that it was a pre-Islamic Somali name" (p.163). According to Patricia Alden and Louis Tremaine, this untraditional name that his grandfather bestowed on him at birth is an incorrect prediction that, "like himself, Kalaman will be an orator, which is one of the meanings of the word *kalaman* in Arabic."[3] To Said Samatar, on the other hand, the name Kalaman metaphorically refers to the character's "split" frame of mind.[4] But could the name also be a *dual* form of the Arabic *kalam* (Word), as in *kalamu-llah* (the Word of God)? *Kalaman*, then, would symbolize duality—two words, standing for different meanings—and ambiguity—one word standing for two or more meanings. In Kalaman's case, the duality or ambiguity relates to the uncertainty of who his father actually is. Is he the son of one father, Yaqut, who brought him up from birth—alluding to the biological "oneness" of the clan—or is he an offspring of a multiplicity of fathers who participated in the gang-rape of his mother, alluding to the mongrelization of the Somali precipitated by colonial—Italian, British, Ethiopian—and postcolonial conditions of existence?

The collective act of gang rape is, in fact, seen to be a negation of clan identity. As Kalaman himself wonders, "How would people react to the news that I was the issue of a gang-rape?...Naturally, it would confound a lot of simpleminded, clan-obsessed persons who might feel cheated of their right to know the name of the rapist, my biological father, if only to assign me to the one of the clans. If they pitied me, it would be because I was the poor sod who hadn't a blood family to be loyal to, to kill and die for, in this epoch of clan-kill-clan" (pp.236-37). This lack of clear, unambiguous clan identity leads Nonno to describe Kalaman as a citizen "at the crossroads where several worlds meet" and his path as one that forks "in all sorts of directions" with signposts giving "confusing directions to where there is no return" (p.236). Within the framework of a modern Somali consciousness, clanhood is perceived to provide identitarian rootedness and stability: But it has also become a pawn in the hands of warlords eager to fan fratricidal wars. Yet without it, Somalia and, indeed, Somalihood is an indeterminate vortex of confusion.

Kalaman's global, multicultural self is symbolized in various other ways. His kitchen cupboard is a display of jars of imported honey from the West, Zairois *pilipili*, Ethiopian *bereberre*, Indian spices, and so forth (p.42). The company he runs is engaged in, among other things, translation work across several languages, including Somali, Arabic, English, and Italian (p.48)—all very much a part of the historical construction of Somalia's identity, but also of its linguistic globalization in the here and now. With Somali, it symbolizes its "national self"; with Arabic, its historical connection with the Arabo-Islamic heritage that goes back to antiquity; with Italian, its continuing links with an ex-colonial metropolis; and with English, its membership in a new global constellation. As much as Kalaman's name invokes a certain "twoness," therefore, it is the trans-national that is eventually privileged over the clanic.

To some extent, this interplay between language and identity reflects Farah's own position with regard to the choice of the language of composition of the African writer. Farah regards Ngugi's view that he chose to write in his native Gikuyu because "he felt he could reach more of his own people through his mother tongue" as tantamount to linguistic clannism. He takes particular issue with Ngugi's definition of "my people." In his own case, Farah argues :

> ...when I come to define who my people are, and I ask
> myself, really and truly, who I feel closest to, I find that
> not only are Somalis my people, but the whole of the

621

continent of Africa; India, where I grew up intellectually, and where I wrote my first novel; the Arab world,
which has also influenced me culturally; all these are
my people. My people are the people in any part of the
world who have been colonized and have been
deprived of their own pride.[5]

Farah, then, seeks to define his own identity in terms of conver-
gent and concentric circles of interacting communities, ranging from
the clan to the global. In spite of himself, however, the tension
between clannization and globalization, between the one and the
many, between the "pure" and the hybrid, endures throughout
Secrets, raising doubts not only about the meaning of Somaliness, but
also about its very *raison de être*. Does a Somaliness based on the
nation-state make any sense at all in view of the total collapse of
Somalia and the sweeping hand of globalization, or must Somaliness
be reconfigured along some different parameters? Y.M.I., the initials
of Kalaman's putative father (p.230), actually translates into a question that Somalia poses for its children: *Why (Y) Am (M) I (I)*? For
what reason need I exist as a nation-state? As indicated elsewhere,
"Most African states are fundamentally without roots in the societies
in which they find themselves. Institutional collapse abounds and, in
its bid to survive, the failed state sometimes devours its own citizens—the rage of the castrated."[6] Things fall apart; the center can no
longer hold! At the same time, the forces of globalization are said to
be pushing national sovereignty gradually towards extinction. Is
there a reason, then, for the very existence of Somalia as a *state*?

The globalization of Somali(an) identity and its peculiar relationship with the "motherland" is explored in *Secrets* through characters
like Sholoongo, Timir and Waliya. The word "sholoongo" refers to
women's groups in which the membership contributes money on a
regular basis to meet the financial needs of individual members on a
rotational basis—a phenomenon sometimes dubbed "merry-go-
round." Sholoongo, therefore, may be a representation of the collec-

tive being of the Somali(an) woman. She "assumes the different personae an actress assumes, while representing the full spectrum of human and animal possibilities...She is there, in *others*. As such, she will live forever, because she will be remembered by others, for whatever motive" (p.200). Sholoongo is, in fact, Somalia the *motherland.* Her seeming obsession with sex, which has led to "mean men badmouthing [her] a bitch, a witch, a whore" (p.55), is intended to feed the perverted image of the woman, the Eve of patriarchal imagination. This image, in the case of Somalia, has partly led to the horrors of infibulation of which Sholoongo herself is a victim.

As significant is Sholoongo's *duugan* origins, "delivered of her mother when the stars were bivouacking at a most inauspicious station," a baby born only to be buried alive (p.2). The *duugan* metaphor is perhaps in reference to the *jahiliyya*, the supposed pre-Islamic era of ignorance in Arabia during which people supposedly treated female children as undesirables and sometimes took the drastic step of burying them alive. As a *duugan* child, therefore, Sholoongo also represents the Somali(an) woman in her repressed and marginalized state under the patriarchal dispensation. Of course, the abandonment of baby Sholoongo also contributes to the apocalyptic vision of Somalia, of Africa, as one state after another continues to devour its own children.

Once a childhood friend and "secret lover" of Kalaman, Sholoongo reappears in *Secrets* as a full-grown woman, having just returned from the USA. She is now a US citizen serving as "the chairperson of the New York branch of the All-America Shape-shifters' Union, a body as powerful as the Artists Guild of the USA" (p.54)—demonstrating the extent to which, as the "collective womb" of a dynamic Somaliness, she continues to influence individual identity. She is a Somali-born American—in citizenship and also, to some extent, in culture—married to a Moroccan-born fire-eater whom she met in New York "where a progeny of scandals are reared in every adult's imaginings" (p.114). For all practical purposes, the adult Sholoongo is an embodiment of a confluence of cultures from Africa, the Middle East and the West, a continuing mystery "come from America, a *duugan* originally from the Ogaden, empowered to use the white man's juju to supplement [her] powers" (p.273).

As a shape-shifter/actress, Sholoongo is, of course, engaged in the act of performance. This role invokes the idea of citizenship as performative negotiation in the new public space of one's immigration. Citizenship becomes as much a question of legal documentation as of cultural consumption, production and, more importantly perhaps, display. In the words of May Joseph, "Socially and politically produced conceptions of participatory democracy inform the phenomenological experience of performance as they conjoin with available and imagined vehicles for constructing contemporary citizenships. The multiply structured and structuring arena of performance as a lived and invented practice of social relations involves a self-conscious realization of citizen as subject."[7] And it is this new self-consciousness of being American that Sholoongo displays with the "flaunting of her US passport" which, in according her a new identity, even conceals her real age (p.34).

In spite of her new-found American citizenship, and in spite of having a husband in the USA, however, it is to Somalia that Sholoongo returns in search of a progeny. The nostalgia for and sense of belonging to the "motherland" has not been dampened by the many years of separation from Somalia. "I am here to bear a baby," she tells Kalaman. She wants Kalaman to be the father, perhaps with the anticipation that the expected offspring would be Somali(an) with the legacy of multiple, ambiguous identities. But when Kalaman turns down her request to serve as the biological father of the preconceived baby, Sholoongo seeks to achieve her objective by engaging Nonno in *hor-gur*, a word of her creation to mean "rape" not from behind (or *daba-gur*) as practised by men, but from the front. But can a woman rape a man? The act of *hor-gur* is itself a symbolic challenge to the patriarchal dispensation within which Somali(an) identity is framed. It is also an attempt to reappraise and perhaps celebrate the matriarchal face of Somaliland that has been eradicated by Islamic and European colonial intrusions.

Nonno, of course, reminds one of Ngugi wa Thiongo'o's *Matigari*, an ageless character who has lived the entire span of Somalia's life, from the precolonial to the postcolonial, and who means different things to different people. As a young man "Nonno had replaced the letters *s* and *b* in his name Misbaax with the letter *f* and *t*, a journey long and short at the same time, Misbaax, "light" in Arabic, becoming Miftaah, "a key"! (p.241). Even as Somalia now becomes clouded by the war, Nonno remains the key that can release the light onto its history, consciousness and psyche. It is this historical consciousness of Somalia—even though there is nothing particularly Somali about Nonno—that Sholoongo, the collective representation of the Somali(an) woman turned-American, rapes in order to reproduce Somalia in its new globalized womb.

But even in this act of engaging Nonno sexually, the objective of producing a Somali(an) child of ambiguous identity is never lost. While Sholoongo and Nonno are in Nonno's house, the sexual act itself takes place on a bed traditionally used by Kalaman since childhood: It is Kalaman's bed. And beds, as it turns out, "have a place of juridical importance in Islam when it comes to determining paternity," in disentangling "the knots in the blood of a baby under dispute between two claimant fathers" (p.266). Here we are reminded of a saying by the Prophet Muhammad to the effect that "The baby is the bed's." Some Muslim jurists have interpreted this saying to refer to the "matrimonial bed" which establishes the baby as the "legal" product of the two parents in a wedlock. But Sholoongo gives the saying a more literal meaning: Since the bed is Kalaman's, the child she hopes to bear in this sexual union with Nonno would also be Kalaman's. As a symbol of future Somaliness, therefore, the baby's identity is one of even greater complexity—a product of an Americanized collective Somali(an) mother and an ageless and multiple Somali(an) biological father, who happens to be the grandfather of the baby's "legal" father, Kalaman, himself of complex identity.

But, alas, the conception does not take place. The old and the new are no longer in harmony partly because Somalia is no more, having been contaminated and eventually destroyed by clan politics. Nonno is quite aware of this impending rejection as he tells Sholongoo, "I would rather I didn't come in you...I contain waste," he explained, "as if my spermal sense has gone awry, infected with germicide. In point of fact you wouldn't want to have anything to do with me, if you knew" (p.271). But Sholoongo does not heed Nonno's warning: She pleads with him, "Please, come in me" (p.271). And soon after he obliges her, she begins to drip and itch. "I dripped like a faucet with a slow leak. Then itched much more ferociously than before, a hairy scratch at the inside of my groin, as though an insect had found its way into my clothes" (p.281). She washes and washes with hot water, scrubs herself repeatedly, oils every crevice and cranny of her body, and holds her legs close together "and tighter in the uncomfortable posture of a young girl sore from a recent infibulation," but all in vain (p.281)—Sholoongo herself had, of course, undergone infibulation in keeping with the Somali definition of womanhood (p.272). And so the love affair between Somalia and its Diaspora comes to a painful, itching, oozing end, like a body that has rejected its transplanted part.

Sholoongo's half-brother, Timir, offers yet another dimension of the globalization of the Somali and their nostalgic relationship to Somalia. Like Sholoongo he too had just returned from the USA where he is now a citizen. Kalaman immediately notices how America had changed Timir as he seeks to perform his newly acquired cultural citizenship of his new domicile. His conversation with Kalaman took the form of "paying homage to a yoga-practising latter-day hippie with arty pretensions, the kind of thing you might say at a party in California" (p.53) where Timir now resides. He is alienated from the Somaliness of his Somalia, and can now relate to it only through the tinted glasses of his globalization. He finds it difficult to believe that Kalaman's mother once used to make him wear an amulet on his upper arm folded in leather on which was inscribed the numerical power of his names. To Timir, such claims can only be understood

626

when mediated through his jet-lagged brain—the jet being a material facilitator of globalization—and *performance* of "magic and taboo" by circus hands on television screens—yet another instrument of globalization (p.57).

Timir is also now openly wearing his out-of-the-closet colors, having become an active member of the American gay movement (pp.36-37). His gay orientation is not, of course, exclusively a product of his American experience. There is evidence of it even in his childhood in Somalia. In one such Somalia scene he is seen with another character, Fidow, "at it" in the river "assuming that no one would see them. It was very early in the morning. Their bodies clinched together like dogs, Fidow behind, Timir in front and half-bent, Fidow in in-and-out motion. Timir submissive...Timir then took his turn mounting Fidow from behind" (pp.61-62). In spite of the hostility of Presidents Robert Mugabe of Zimbabwe and Yoweri Museveni of Uganda towards homosexuality, which they regard as un-African, Farah seeks to project it as a thriving reality of African sexuality. But the cultural milieu in Somalia did not allow an open expression of this sexual preference: It was only in the USA that Timir could come out of the closet and campaign actively for gay rights.

In this typically American way of expressing sexual orientation, there is also an act of performance. Timir describes himself as an all-round theater person. "I teach the theory of theater," he says, "I act semiprofessionally in plays whenever I have the time or the opportunity. I review now and then under a pen name for one of the local weeklies" (p.56). And with Wayne, his African American lover, they sometimes "swap roles and call each other by the other's name, and now and then stand in for one another. Wayne loves to pass himself off as an African, Timir as African-American" (p.65). They even exchange roles and wear each other's clothes. Finding himself at the cultural juncture of African American history that relates to the African continent in its own peculiar way, then, Timir seeks to acquire an American cultural citizenship by coming to new terms with his Somali(an) origins.

This redefined relationship with Somalia manifests itself in his attempt to secure a Somali wife while at "home" in Somalia. Perhaps partly in an attempt to maintain a facade of heterosexuality for the benefit of his Somali(an) kith and kin, we are told that "he's come to buy a woman, preferably one with an infant and who, out of gratitude for his wealth and his American passport, is prepared to slave for him and his artsy boyfriend in San Francisco in a threesome setup" (p.37). And just as Sholoongo had come initially to ask Kalaman to father a child with her, Timir now seeks to have this same man on the global cultural crossroads as a witness and best man in his marriage.

Again, however, as in the case of his sister Sholoongo, Timir's attempted reconnection with Somalia fails. Somalia is too diseased and localized into clanhood and Timir too "hybridized" and "global-ized" to make a harmonious consummation between them possible. There is news of a tragedy that "a man whose description matches Timir's...has been blown up sky-high as he drove his rental car. The rumour is that he is dead" (p.285). And, as readers, we never come to witness the planned marriage between Timir and a local Somali woman, preferably with an infant baby. On the European side of the Somali Diaspora is Waliya, "one of Somalia's most up-and-coming fashion models" residing in Italy and whose name was a recurrent feature of Italian tabloids. In particular, readers would repeatedly be fed with "a fantastic diet about a young Somali woman growing up in abject poverty in a mud hut in darkest Africa" (p.211). One cannot miss the allusion to Iman here, the popular Somali model in America whose initial entry into the USA performance scene was surrounded by all sorts of exotic stories about her background. Waliya maintains a villa of a house in Somalia which she visits once in a while, "staying fussily for a day or at most two" (p.219) and within which precincts she is known as Her Majesty—refusing to wake up in a house "that didn't cater for her dependency" (p.221). The place is fully stocked with radio and television sets, video players and "a clutter of latter-day gadgets" (p.218) as well as a full range of alcoholic drinks not permitted by the religion, Islam, of which the Somalis are members.

628

Her lifestyle is reminiscent of many a western star in the entertainment world, perhaps addicted to some drug, having "more liquor in her body than blood" (p.221), and staying "in bed all day, up all night partying, showing off" (p.219). Waliya's dis-Somalization appears complete.

In addition to the villa and the mother who occupies it throughout much of the year, Waliya's connection with Somalia is the hefty contributions she makes "in cash and in hard currency, to uplift the morale of our clan's armed militia. We have politicians of all manner knocking at our door, when she comes. She is a key contributor, as important to the clan as the hotelier who finances the running of the local wing of the USC, our militia grouping" (p.219). But this kind of financial obligation is by no means peculiar to Waliya. Elsewhere Timir explains how their own clanspeople "want us to contribute toward the arming of the militia which is to fight in the interests of our people. They have the weapons, not the ammunition. Since we come from America, we are being asked to make our contribution in dollars" (p.53). The dispersed Somali who are increasingly getting "dis-clanised" in culture and life-style, therefore, are now ironically expected to demonstrate their allegiance to Somalia through the material and deadly reinforcement of clan identities and clan politics.

Waliya is claimed to have been a Nureyev fan from infancy. A photograph of this ballet dancer, suspended between a legendary act of leaping and a flamboyant pirouette finale, supposedly hung on the mud wall of Waliya's home throughout her childhood. The fixed presence of the image of Nureyev in the house was deemed to have brought great joy to baby Waliya (p.211). In reality, however, the Nureyev claim was nothing but an invention of a young adult troubled perhaps by her "pedestrian beginnings." Nureyev, in other words, became part of the "young model's construction of an imagined identity" (p.211). By embracing the ballet idol Waliya was seeking to locate herself in a trans-Somali(an) cultural space that can serve as a foundation for new identitarian performance(s).

It is significant that the Nureyev "myth" in Waliya's life is directly connected with an African American, for it is in African America that many of the dispersed Somali(an)s in the USA have found their refuge and within which identities are being reimagined and reshaped. How will African America eventually transform Diaspora Somalia? This first generation of Somali(an)s in the West has continued to maintain linguistic, cultural and kinship linkages with Somalia. At this historical juncture they are *American Somali(an)s*. Future generations may lose their ancestral language, cutting the linguistic umbilical chord with wider Somalia. At that point, they will have become *Somali(an) Americans*. And a good portion of this transformation is likely to take place within the cultural and demographic borders of African America. It is partly this pan-African space that is projected in the African American initiated cultural migration of new kinds of western performances in the image of Nureyev. Kathy, the African American who inadvertently introduces Waliya to Nureyev, is herself a Nureyev fan and, but for a spinal condition, had "once dreamt of making it to the big time as a ballet dancer" (p.212). While serving as a Peace Corps volunteer in Somalia Kathy had a poster of Nureyev on one of the walls of her residence. It was from this picture, introduced by an African American, that Arfaco and her daughter Waliya later came to develop the idea of inscribing Nureyev into Waliya's new imagined identity.

More important than Nureyev (as performance culture) in this pan-African connection, is Kathy's role as a teacher of English—a linguistic product of enslavement in African America and of colonialism in much of Africa. Much debate has taken place on the place of English in pan-African identity: Is it a boon or a curse? According to Alexander Crummell, perhaps one of the earliest pan-Africanists, Africans exiled in slavery to the "New World" had inherited "at least this one item of compensation, namely, the possession of the Anglo-Saxon tongue."[8] Crummell wished for the rest of the black race, therefore, this same divine providence given to African Americans: In the English language Crummell saw a medium superior, in form and substance, to "the various tongues and dialects" of the indigenous populations of Africa. In Crummell's conception, then, the Anglicization of the black race, Africa included, was a necessary phase in its (linguistic) civilization.

More pragmatic in his views than Crummell was another early pan-African giant, Edward W.Blyden. Ngugi wa Thiong'o has suggested that Blyden "wanted a system of education which rejected all the errors and falsehoods about the African and, while he wanted the Greek and Latin classics as part of the curriculum for his visions of an African university, he also wanted African languages to be an integral part of it."[9] In reality, however, Blyden regarded the multiplicity of "tribal languages" in Africa as divisive in its effects, and felt that this linguistic gulf could best be bridged by English more than by any other European language partly because English itself was a product of diverse cultures. In the words of Blyden:

> English is, undoubtedly, the most suitable of the European languages for bridging over the numerous gulfs between the tribes caused by the great diversity of languages and dialects among them. It is a composite language, not the product of any one people. It is made up of contributions by Celts, Danes, Normans, Saxons, Greeks and Romans, gathering to itself elements...from the Ganges to the Atlantic.[10]

As history would have it, however, English became a potential tool of communication not only between Africans across the ethnic divide, but also between people of African descent across the oceans. And the language came to play an important role in the growth of the movement that came to be known as Pan-Africanism.[11] Through her instruction of English, therefore, Kathy becomes a continuing embodiment of the dialectics of linguistic pan-Africanity.

The link between African America and Somalia is further explored through a love affair between Kathy and Nonno. As a Peace Corps volunteer Kathy is Nonno's tenant. But in time the two became intimately involved in a sexual relationship. Kalaman, then a child, once

witnessed them in a romantic moment, showering together, scrubbing each other's backs until Nonno's "residues of youth" resurfaced.
"They were good for each other," we are told. Is Kathy the personifi-
cation of the African American romance with Africa? And just as
Kathy "took in" Nonno as they made love to each other, it is African
America that has "taken in" sections of the dispersed Somali(an)s in
parts of the USA. One can be sure that African Americanization will
be one strand in the reinvention of Diaspora Somalia.

After spending several years alone as a depressed widower,
Nonno found that his "fragmented spirits" were perked up by Kathy.
This is a romantic engagement that alludes to the possible role of
African America in the reconstruction of Africa following the fragmentation of its state structures. Will African Americans, through ini-
tiatives like the National Summit concluded in February 2000, be to
Africa what Jews in the USA have been to Israel—beacons of hope
and support? Will African American concerns with Africa help re-
inspire African renewal?

As members of the first generation of Diaspora Somali(an)s continue to retain strong familial, linguistic and cultural ties with the
"homeland," they are bound to affect the lives of those who did not
get the opportunity to leave or who simply decided not to leave. It
was mentioned earlier how members of the Somali(an) Diaspora,
especially the more successful ones among them, were expected to
feed the clan-war machine at home. And those who failed to do so
were likely to have been considered betrayers of the clan cause and
clan interests. But the reinvented Somali(an)s abroad touched the
lives of fellow Somali(an)s at "home" not only in this collective sense,
but also at the more individual level. And for some at "home" the
experience was a dream; for others it was a nightmare.

For Arbaco, Waliya's mother, her daughter's success as a model
was indeed a dream come true. It was a vicarious maturation of her
own life as one of the floaters in urban Somalia—i.e. "cynical women,
divorcees or widowers, women on the margins of respectability,
courtesans with loyalty only to their self-interest" (p.213). They have

little faith in the future and provide manifold services for immediate self-aggrandizement in the here and now. Now Waliya's lucrative income from modelling provides her with the lavish life she always wanted. Waliya's villa in Somalia is, for all practical purposes, Arbaco's villa. Waliya's reinvented and imagined identity had certainly turned out to be a blessing for Arbaco.

On the other hand, there is the case of the mother in Somalia who commits suicide—an abomination in Islam—because of the "artificial" manner in which her daughter decides to conceive a child. The Somali-born daughter, now residing in the USA as an American citizen, "had borne a test-tube child" (p.196). How was the mother to relate to the identity of a grandchild born of a test tube? For the suicide victim, her daughter's life in America had taken a trajectory that, morally, she could no longer bear living with. Science in the West was beginning to test and challenge the certainty of Somali identity in new ways and to push its fragile borders to new frontiers.

These tensions and accommodations between the dispersed and the "stayees" are also played out in the arena of the global equalizer, AIDS. Timir and Sholoongo came home to attend the funeral of their father who, in his last hour, had wasted away like an AIDS victim (p.53). On the other hand, it is those who have been in contact with the West, returnees like Timir and Sholoongo, who are suspected of being the likely carriers of the AIDS virus (p.119). The West sees AIDS as a disease that originated in Africa. Africans see it as a Western-borne disease. Each perception inscribes a particular identitarian quality in the "other."

It is only Sholoongo who recognizes AIDS as a trans-national, global phenomenon. As she entertains the possibility that Nonno (with whom she is engaged in a sexual union) may be HIV positive, she reminds herself that her own Maghreb husband in the USA is also HIV positive. For her the AIDS virus is no more than a part of her continuing struggle to survive and reproduce:

...it's been my ill luck to keep courting men on the

verge of extinction, myself a returnee from the
precipice of death, surviving it thanks to the kindness
of a wolf, the maternal instinct of a lioness, the protective motherliness of an ostrich. (p.221)

But Sholoongo is a returnee not only from Somalia's wilderness of
demoralization which led to her abandonment as a child, but also
from the wilderness of America where parts of Somalia are being
recreated. And like Sholoongo, Somalia will survive and reproduce
itself, both at "home" and abroad, against all odds.

Yet in this very act of reproduction, the problematic of identity
continues to pose a challenge to the Somali(an) "organism." The
uncertainty of Kalaman's paternity, of his biological father, makes it
impossible to assign him a Somali clan identity: The confusion surrounding Kalaman's personal identity is also the crisis of identity
that now bedevils Somalia. Kalaman compares his own experience
grappling with the problem of identity

...to learning that X, a friend, had AIDS. We didn't know
what to do, at least I didn't. So what do you say to
someone afflicted with an identity crisis like mine, akin
to AIDS in that it points to a kind of death? (p.237).

Yet, in the final analysis, Kalaman comes to terms with "himself,"
accepting Yaqut and Nonno as his legitimate father and grandfather,
notwithstanding the biological fact of being an issue of a gang rape
with an indeterminate biological father. And like Kalaman, Somalia
will no doubt discover itself anew under the wings of new "parental"
experiences in Africa itself, in America, Italy, the Middle East, and
elsewhere in the world. There is hope for Somalia, both at "home"
and abroad.

NOTES

1. J.Kenneth Blackwell in *The Columbia Dispatch*, Saturday 6 May 2000, p.B4.

2. Nuruddin Farah, *Secrets* (New York: Arcade, 1998), p.193. Further references are given in parentheses in the essay.

3. Patricia Alden and Louis Tremaine, *Nuruddin Farah* (New York: Twayne, 1999), p.74.

4. Said S.Samatar, "Are There Secrets in *Secrets?*" *Research in African Literatures* 31, 1 (2000), 141.

5. "Nuruddin Farah," in *Interviews with Writers of the Post-Colonial World*, eds. Feroza Jussawalla and Reed Way Dasenbrock (Jackson and London: University Press of Mississippi, 1992), p.45.

6. Ousseina Alidou and Alamin Mazrui, "*Secrets:* Farah's Things Fall Apart," *Research in African Literatures* 31, 1 (2000), 122.

7. May Joseph, *Nomadic Identities: The Performance of Citizenship* (Minneapolis: University of Minnesota Press, 1999), p.13.

8. Quoted in Kwame Anthony Appiah, *In My Father's House: Africa in the Philosophy of Culture* (Oxford: Oxford University Press, 1992), p.3.

9. Ngugi wa Thiong'o, "Europhonism, Universities and the Magic Fountain: The Future of African Literature and Scholarship," *Research in African Literatures* 31, 1 (2000), 2.

10. Edward W.Blyden, *Christianity, Islam and the Negro Race* (London: W.B. Whittingham, 1888), pp.243-44.

11. Alamin Mazrui, "Pan-Africanism in the Age of Globalization: The Linguistic Agenda," *The Literary Griot: International Journal of Black Expressive Culture Studies* 11, 1 (1999), 71.

OUT OF THE CLOSET:
Farah's *Secrets*
Michael Eldridge

I am afraid I might wake up and find Somalia totally
obliterated from the map of my unconscious.
—NONNO (*Secrets*)

Cidlaan Dareemaya (I Feel Alone)

The directions to Somalia through Nonno's cryptic unconscious must be elliptical at best, and one dimly suspects, as the American folk adage has it, that You Can't Get There From Here. Indeed, on even the more reputable American mental maps, Somalia lies merely in the rough vicinity of Recurrent Famine and Interethnic Feud—which is how its neighbors Sudan and Eritrea appeared on that royal road to the American psyche, the front page of the *New York Times*, throughout the turbulent early summer of 1998. Somalia, Somalia (shadows of starving skeletons give way absent-mindedly to specters of khat-crazed clansmen)...wasn't there some nasty business about Marines getting killed there a while back? Weeks later, when the stuck collective memory was jarred loose by two resounding blasts, the bewildered protestations of Kenyans and Tanzanians that theirs were peaceful countries could only ring hollow. For our vague recollection was now clarified and confirmed: East Africa? An altogether treacherous place. Regardless of how pitiful and helpless its inhabitants might appear, no matter how selflessly and heroically we might try to Restore their Hope, those ingrates over there just hate us. (To think that those Kenyans had the nerve to carp about the FBI's disregard for *African* victims of the embassy bombings!) And that's why, in the case of our deadly, ill-begotten peacekeeping adventure half a decade before, we jumped in our troop-carriers and fled back home, leaving Somalia, one more backwater basket-case we'd never tour again, to drop off the map of our consciousness.

Yet it's in the nature of the repressed to return. More recently, that ragged memory of a nation has strayed back into the subliminal reaches of the American mind—not through the well-rutted routes of the front-page news, but over the secluded backroads of the Arts and Culture section. The celebrity supermodel Iman—in whose glamorous gauntness famine morphed, mollified, into famine-*chic*—was the pioneer foremother. But years down the pike she has become merely Somali-in-quotes, her allegiance now belonging more properly to some bizarre Republic of Benetton, on the distant Planet Hollywood, in the Galaxy of Fashion Café. A more down-to-earth candidate for Somali cultural ambassador might be the veteran singer (or, as her CD packaging hopefully identifies her, "Afro-Pop diva") Maryam Mursal. Mursal made her North American début during that same explosive summer of 1998, opening for the high-visibility "Africa Fête" tour in support of not one but two albums (one folkloric, the other high-tech) that she'd recorded for English rock star Peter Gabriel.[1] In liner notes and web-site hype, the label's publicists mythologized Mursal's harrowing seven-month exodus through the desert (travelling on donkeys, five children in tow) to eventual refuge in Denmark. Journalists covering her shows had obviously read their press kits, and dutifully played up the generic human pathos and the special "indominability" of her case, sentimentalizing her into an iconic Mama Afrika, beleaguered but surviving.

The particular lesson that the *Christian Science Monitor* drew from Mursal's example (with words borrowed from a festival organizer) was that "African countries who are known only for their political turmoil can produce 'beautiful and wonderfully danceable music as well.'"[2] One despairs of the tiresome regularity with which the American media dress up doleful boilerplate as late-breaking bulletin, each lurid citation of political chaos and public-health crisis meant to reconfirm Africa as an eternal river of rebellion and coup, butchery and genocide, plague and virus. But here is the sunny flipside of that benighted view, a type of well-meaningness that's just a hair's-breadth away from condescension—as if to say: "isn't it inspiring how those plucky Africans manage to make beauty even amid misery and squalor," or, less charitably, "they may have made a mess of things, but they sure can dance." Even the indomitable Mursal was temporarily powerless against such facile representations. In a backstage interview with the same reporter on the second night of the tour—her first real opportunity to speak to the American public, she must have thought—Mursal anxiously apologized on behalf of her country for those dead U.S. soldiers, railing against the "bandits" who now run Somalia. Yet she spoke those words (just as she spoke all *onstage* words but "thank you") through a ventriloquist: her Danish bassist-bandleader/producer-arranger/publicist-translator, Søren Jensen. Indeed, despite being irresistibly genial, despite having the ebullient presence of a seasoned performer, Mursal seemed palpably stymied on stage that night, upstaged by her polyglot sideman, unable to establish a rapport with her largely indifferent, monolingual audience. Non-Anglophone, she was effectively mute: the eager, befuddled foreigner who for the moment could only nod and smile enthusiastically.

But there is of course another Somali exile, five years Mursal's senior and professionally active just as long as she, himself wandering (and celebrated) around the world for over twenty-five years

now, who suffers from no such linguistic handicap: Nuruddin Farah
has been writing in playfully punctilious, sinuously circuitous, elegantly idiosyncratic English—the prose equivalent of Mursal's
"Somali jazz"³—since 1970. But with no Peter Gabriel to sponsor him,
no archangelic doorman to usher him into the gated community of
the American literary establishment (which had seemingly filled its
quota of exotics, never mind Africans, until very recently), Farah was
stalled for years on its waiting list, languishing of late in small-press
purgatory. His first brush with the American A-list, *Maps*, had barely
reached bookstore shelves in 1986 when it and the rest of Pantheon's
"Modern Writers" were dumped unceremoniously into the remainder
bins, just after editor Andre Schiffrin was shown the Random House
door. *Maps* received one or two polite reviews in the U.S. press, as did
Farah's acknowledged masterpiece, the trilogy *Variations on the
Theme of an African Dictatorship*, upon its reissue by the tiny but well-
regarded Graywolf Press in 1992. But even though *Variations* reap-
peared shortly after its putative subject, the loathesome Siyad Barre,
had been despatched to oblivion, and shortly before U.S. Marines
staged a telegenic hoopla on the beaches of Mogadishu (two fortuitous marketing tie-ins beyond Graywolf's wildest dreams, one would
have thought), Farah remained unheralded and unheard-of—but for
fifteen minutes of notoriety from a sardonic Op-Ed piece he penned
for the *New York Times*.⁴ That eloquent essay was grudgingly equivocal about looking gift- horses in the mouth, but his next novel *Gifts*
emphatically was not, and it couldn't find a stateside publisher. For
all that American readers learned of him between then and 1998,
Farah may as well have been preaching in the wilderness. Like his
mother tongue (which quietly achieved a written script only in 1972),
like his creation Nonno (at whom the epithet is hurled in an enigmatic obloquy), Farah remained in the U.S. a kind of "closet literate."

In the more exclusive confines of American academia, his profile
was only slightly higher. Though Farah has been an itinerant professor and writer-in-residence at several American universities, and
while *Maps* has appeared on not a few syllabi over the years, his sub-

tle, cosmopolitan novels aren't easily slotted into the crude national nooks and ethnic crannies of undergraduate literature curricula. And where scholarly publishing is concerned, though Farah himself has been a semi-regular contributor to the stylishly rehabilitated *Transition*, the handful of critics writing *about* him are mainly habitués of the comparatively dowdy Commonwealth (in America, "World") Literature club, where the estimable Australian Derek Wright years ago built a cottage industry in Farah criticism and now has a near-lock on the franchise. Still, it was such loyal and enthusiastic chroniclers of Farah's career as these who could most fully appreciate the extra-academic consequence of the appearance of his latest novel, *Secrets*.[5] Not only would it mark the completion of an important *new* trilogy, the definitive pronouncement by the sage of Somalia on the state of things since the demise of his nemesis Siyad Barre (and since his own first *retour au pays natal* in over twenty years). Here in America, lowly Arcade's bold commitment to bring out all three of those novels—cannily timed to capitalize upon Farah's awarding of the Neustadt Prize—would further represent a renewed bid for the wider visibility and recognition that was so long overdue. For their part, the academics planned a *festschrift* issue of *World Literature Today*. All that remained was for their counterparts in the popular press to shoulder a share of the burden.

As it happened, the bag that the journalists hefted was decidedly mixed, and any judge, professorial or otherwise, would be obliged to give them low collective marks for their performance. Between the start of May and the end of July 1998 (a period nearly coincidental with Mursal's tour, as it happened), fourteen reviews of *Secrets*, some lengthy, most brief, appeared in American national or regional newspapers and popular magazines. (One more showed up on middlebrow tastemaker NPR's *All Things Considered*.[6]) A few were strewn with downright embarrassing colonialist howlers: for the *Orlando Sentinel*, the book's exotic setting (a place where birds and animals have totemic significance "totally alien to our urban plastic civilization" and where "the spirits" constantly intrude on human affairs) reminds us that "this is an African novel."[7] Similarly, the *Seattle Times* reviewer opined that *Secrets* "teems with the earthy physicality of Africa" and depicts Somalia as "a place of primitive ritual and taboo, shape-shifting and witchcraft, jumbled with computers, automobiles and European clothing."[8] Even a more sensitive judge, however, could show symptoms of this latter critical affliction—what we might name, mindful of Conrad's Marlow, Dog-In-Breeches Syndrome—a perceptual neurosis whereby a presumedly barbarous subject clothed in, even brushing against, "civilized" costume strikes one as troublingly incongruous. In New York *Newsday*, for example, novelist Valerie Miner reckoned that Farah was largely concerned in *Secrets* with "chart[ing] the tensions between cultural traditions and modern pressures." How, she misguidedly wondered on behalf of the novel's protagonist, could one "live as an educated, urbane sexual free agent in a poor country shaped by fundamentalist Islamic codes and pre-Islamic mysticism"?[9] Those with a milder strain of the syndrome, notably George Packer in the *New York Times* and Scott Malcomson in *The New Yorker*, tended to have "magical realism" on the brain. Inordinately impressed by the book's bits of casual impossibility, they were solemnly determined to see them not as the muted wallpaper Farah intended, but as garish posters crying out loud to be noticed. As the Minneapolis *Star Tribune* (a relatively benign case) put it: *Secrets* "takes the reader to a place where the real and fantastic comfortably co- exist."[10] But when Argentina, Columbia, Germany, India and Pakistan, even far-off Ohio, are by now such fantastically familar pieces of real estate on the contemporary literary landscape, should Americans really imagine that Farah was proposing Somalia as some brilliant new development?

Several reviewers cast patronizing aspersions upon Farah's linguistic competence, as though he were a bright ESL student who had nevertheless overreached a bit on a final essay. George Packer was circumspect enough to be equivocal, contenting himself, for the most part, with backhanded praise: Farah's voice is "lush" and "urbane," he allowed—yet "collisions of folkloric, academic and realist prose" produce startling sentences that "would not survive a writers' workshop in America" (is that a good or a bad thing, one wonders?), and that seem "at times wildly improbable in a way few native speakers would permit themselves." Other, dimmer, less diplomatic critics were by turns more ingenuous (the *Orlando Sentinel*'s Richard Crepeau, in what is itself often marginally grammatical English, marvelled that Farah writes so well for a foreigner!) or more obtuse: the *Seattle Times*' Sheila Farr, who also found Farah's narrative technique "odd" and "distracting," pronounced his English flawed, "straight from the dictionary," unwittingly clichéd, stilted and overblown. "Like Somalia itself," she concluded, "Farah's voice is still struggling toward harmony."

In fact, nearly all reviewers were resolved (one or two quite self-satisfiedly so) to read *Secrets* as some such national allegory. The story is a "painful metaphor for civic strife in contemporary Somalia" (*Newsday*), Kalaman's family a microcosm of "the chaotic East African nation" (*Seattle Times*) and his "confused self-identity...a metaphor for his strife-torn homeland" (Minneapolis *Star Tribune*). "Both the country and Kalaman's life are on the brink of collapse" (*Orlando Sentinel*); his genealogical research "uncovers the brutal circumstances of both his own origins and his country's" (*The New Yorker*); his case-history "dare[s]to be read as a prophecy of Somalian apocalypse" (*VLS*).[11] To fall back on this allegorical prop is neither wholly unjustifiable nor entirely misguided, as I hope to explain below, but for the majority of popular reviewers, hobbled more by critical laziness than by genuine disability, it was a crutch that helped no one to walk. Having raised allegorical possibilities mainly to cluck their tongues about the unsettled state of things over there (yet having forgotten, like an unpleasant vacation, the details of "our" own disastrous involvement in those things), they left the allegory unexamined. One nibbled again at the title of the work, another mumbled something more about the book's mystical lyricism, then most everyone excused themselves from the table, implicitly sated with the chestnut that Somalia, like all of Africa, remained a "haunting," insoluble riddle.

The popular book review isn't ordinarily a venue for profound or even conclusive thinking, of course, so it's doubtless somewhat churlish of me to treat these few so snidely. They did give Farah's work visibility, after all, and some, like the canny and clear-sighted Greg Tate, provided a genuine public service, offering readers a near-perfect example of critical acumen and sympathy.[12] But picking through the crumbs of that first serving of notices of *Secrets*, one can't help feeling as though the reason the diners excused themselves so hastily was that they had gagged on a gristly, unuttered question, spit it out into their napkins, and found it (upon surreptitious examination) so unappetizing that it couldn't be asked frankly in polite company, at least not without a great deal of mortified embarassment. Indulge me, then, as I brazenly exercise in their stead the American prerogative, adopting for the remainder of this essay the narcissistic assumption that all stories are either about "us" (Vietnam, *our* national tragedy; Nairobi and Dar es Salaam, reminders of *American* vulnerability; Somalia, a cautionary tale on the dangers of sticking *our* necks out) or *for* "us"— as if Farah's novel were intended to answer, at last, that indelicate, indigestible question; to penetrate, once and for good, the Heart of Darkness; to unveil for our eyes the secret of *Secrets* that has so doggedly held its silence. Namely (to rephrase reviewer Sheila Farr's conclusion in the form of a question): why is Somalia "still struggling toward harmony"? Why are Things forever Falling Apart over there? Why, four decades up the putatively postcolonial river, do the brutes seem quite intent upon exterminating themselves, saving Kurtz the trouble? If, according to the insistent allegory, family indeed stands for nation, and nation is forever degenerating into chaos, then does this family just have bad genes?

Sometimes I feel like a fatherless child...

A novel which, on its face, is concerned with cutting to the heart of sinister secrets would appear on some level to be compatible with, if

not altogether sympathetic to, such uncouth questions. Its protagonist, preoccupied with origin-myths and primal scenes, determines
early on to unlock the family skeleton-closet—and hints soon follow
that his probe will simultaneously sound the unfathomable, clan-
deepened chasm into which his country is rushing headlong. A tex-
tualist, he suspects that a key may be hidden in the deceptively simple riddle of his unorthodox *name*, whose mirage-like meaning is said
to materialize with only a nudge.[13] Yes, we fellow literary sleuths
concur, responding to his interpretive cue: "Kalaman," a mother-
obsessed Hamlet "ridden with uncertainties" (p.110), is at the same
time not-quite-K, trapped in the guilty web of an increasingly
Kafkaesque plot. Or he's well-nigh-Christ, at age thirty-three a reluctant savior, agonizing over the implications of his immaculate conception. Or he's quasi-Caliban, somehow robbed of his birthright,
engrossed by the memory of what he repeatedly names his "calf-
love," and in thrall to a grandfatherly Prospero who, after one last
dramatic reprise, casts off clandestine books and the mantle of Sufi
sorcery for the sake of the domestic well-being of the next generation. What materializes from such fervent free-association, however,
is a whole lot of heat but not much light; as governing metaphors,
notions such as Kalaman-*cum*-Kaliban have a limited reign. One is
tempted to yield to Nonno's early explication (as disingenous, possibly, as Beckett's directive to see no symbols where none intended)
that Kalaman is in fact "a cul-de-sac of a name" (p.4): a decoy, a red
herring, that, like so many of the supposed secrets insinuated in this
book, leads nowhere and signifies nothing—or at least nothing you
could put your finger on. Indeed, the virtue of the name Kalaman,
Nonno explains, is precisely that it's *free* of associations, meant to
"stand on its own, independent of your father's name or mine" (p.5).
Yet if it's a floating signifier, then it drifts into a dead-end, where with
the very same father-free explanation Nonno has anchored its meaning securely and unmistakably. That is, while Kalaman suspects
Nonno of continuing to withhold some shameful intelligence regarding his given name, the secret is actually as plain as the nose on his

face—or rather, as the other proboscis in his pants—and Kalaman, suddenly mindful of his mother's friend Arbaco's bawdy remarks about the hereditary family schlong, knows it. Though Nonno has a reputation for "evasive waffle" (p.173), in this instance his meaning has become perfectly obvious (just as Kalaman said) with only a nudge. The handle signifies exactly what Nonno as good as announced it did, and what Kalaman's undersized penis confirms: he is not in fact "of that line"; he is, to speak plainly, a bastard.

What apparently drives the plot of *Secrets*, then, is one of the oldest engines in the world. Like some nineteenth-century English novel, the story hinges on the question of doubtful paternity: did X really sire Y? (Later, like that novel's own eighteenth-century forebear, it titillates and teases, offering and deferring a lifting of skirts and a climactic money-shot: will X ever bed Y?) The whole thing seems to boil down, in short, to "sperm-and-blood"—and if pornographic traces of such intimate fluids are what Kalaman thinks he's sniffing for, then they are precisely what Farah will rub his nose (and ours) in at staggered intervals, in a prurient pageant of obscene ostentation. The short Prologue dishes out a condensed soup of Kalaman's precocious sexual initiations; it gives off powerful whiffs and mouth-watering smacks of incest, bestiality and voyeurism; homo- and bisexuality; masturbation orgies and libations of menstrual blood. The remainder of the novel is suffused with a pungent sexual funk that turns from sweet to sickening in a post-arousal olfactory instant, wafting across species and generations via pederasty, buggery, and gang-rape, not to mention jailbait blowjobs (on ample cocks) and father-son suckling (on auxiliary breasts). Some of this is laid forth with the ennobling solemnity of myth, some with the outrageous flagrance of camp. Yet Farah's purpose is on the whole quite serious: like the young Kalaman, like Sholoongo, he means—casually, wantonly—to shock, to provoke, to break taboos (a subject on which the book conducts a running, complicated debate). Still, if Farah's plan is to get his readers in one way or another hot and bothered, it is also to douse us with a cold shower: for after all, the awful mystery thought to lie at the heart of the novel (Kalaman's bastardy) has curiously been divulged in its very first pages; the darkest of the book's sexual secrets is already an open one. Consequently it's hard to understand why, near the book's end, the formal acknowledgment of Kalaman's bastardy—by comparison with the rest of the book's outsized sexual secrets a rather mundane bit of intelligence—creates such a fuss, why it's at the center of such gauzy, earth-shaking melodrama and intrigue. Nonno has insisted that "there is nothing special about [Kalaman's] beginnings" (p.190), that a Dickensian revelation of his paternity can neither shatter nor settle a thing. And indeed, the elaborate disclosure of the gruesome circumstances of his doubtful genesis doesn't constitute a revelation, much less a resolution. That is, it doesn't bring narrative closure, and it most certainly doesn't explain why people are killing one another over who begat whom. Just as in the recurring, enigmatic parable of the "poor sod" who raised his finger in a specially darkened room, everyone here already knows what Kalaman's been doing when he "emerges" (p.186). The meaning of the fool's gesture is understood to be vaguely shameful, but beyond that, utterly uncertain: what does it indicate? Or, as Kalaman asks querulously at another point: "What will we learn? And to what end?" (p.197). These are not mere rhetorical questions. Later, Kalaman is unaccountably puzzled by his inability to "put [his *own*] forefinger" on the outcome of his calculations (p.235). In short, the novel conducts an awful lot of business around his beginnings, without showing much profit at the end of the business day. "Open secret" may be a misleading metaphor, then. Better—as befits a novel whose characters off-handedly allude to Hitchcock: the problem of his bastardy (and all the sexual extravagance it entails) is, like Kalaman's cul-de-sac of a name, a MacGuffin, a kind of arbitrary diversion important mainly as a pretext for moving things along. Like the raised finger of the proverbial man in the darkened room, it points upward, but elsewhere.

"I am a person, a clan is a mob."

Although Kalaman's long meditation on his own name ends with a veiled disclosure of lineal transgression, it begins, as it were, with an open vow of filial subversion. Narratively speaking, that is, the first taboo that young Kalaman would break is one associated with the patriarchal significance of naming: if his father's name is such a dead-end, he reasons, why not adopt his mother's (p.6)? Nonno steers him off such an "ill advised" course with a mixture of amusement and genuine concern; for a variety of reasons, he intimates, it would be imprudent to draw such "anomalous attention" to one's doubtful beginnings. It seems that the nominal independence Nonno bestowed upon his grandson at christening ought not to be declared, then. Yet if that autonomy is without voice, it's not without value. For it eventually emerges that the name "Kalaman" was also meant as a cryptic token of salvation, a "secret of survival" (p.138): Nonno was uttering a charm, a juju, whereby his grandson might achieve not just euphemistic "independence" from his father and grandfather's line, but spiritual independence from *any* line—liberation from the onerous burden of clan membership. He might be marked as a bastard, a fatherless child, yet his tainted conception was paradoxically immaculate, keeping him unsullied (or unsulliable) by what this book sees as a more stubborn stain. In that hopeful, utopian anointing—by which Kalaman might be free of, might *flout*, an ideology that reduces one's identity to a series of "begats"—lies the kernel of a much subtler critique.[14]

Throughout this latest trilogy, Farah has consistently promoted a notion of family based on something more fluid than blood or semen, just as he's argued for a nation with borders more porous than those it inherited from its colonial past. Nonno's caution that Somali culture may not yet be ready to accept, let alone adopt, such liberal views—that it is still impolitic in such an orthodox place to call attention to one's "genetic" anomalies—seems implicitly to reprise this argument (as does his approval of Sholoongo's fine disregard of taboo, her "out-

648

rageous defiance of the ethos of the very society which castigated her at birth"). Yet I want to insist on a third register of meaning to Nonno's discourse. That is, his admonition to Kalaman to avoid making too much of fatherlessness (like his earlier intimation about naming inquiries leading down dead ends) must not be taken primarily as a warning against uncovering hurtful truths best left buried, or even against unwittingly courting persecution from "simpleminded, clan-obsessed persons" (p.236). Rather, it should be read as a clue that, in the lifelong game of blindman's buff that young Kalaman has barely begun, to grope, to point one's finger, to thumb one's nose at "clans" is to pursue a path that's already cold—that has (as Shakespeare might have put it, in all its multiple meanings) "no issue."

This, of course, flies in the face of orthodox American explanation. For U.S. foreign correspondents and policy "experts" have since 1992 knowingly assured us that the real secret, the hidden key, to understanding Somalia is *precisely* clan politics, which are so thoroughly arcane and so bizarrely alien to our sensibility as to be thrillingly incomprehensible. (Never mind that the concept comes to us most immediately through the Scots, whose American descendants take exaggerated pride in concocting elaborate, pseudo-"clan" identities.) Soon after Sholoongo's unexpected return, Kalaman cursorily repudiates just such an argument-from-clan-politics as a lazy and ignorant one—then wearies of disproving it even before he's begun (p.43). Yet readers would do well to attend to his throwaway remark, as an early injunction against indulging all variations of what we might name the Allegorical Fallacy.

Though Farah has arguably been partial to such allegory in the past, crossing the lines of familial allegiance with those of colonial maps, charting the dynamics of personal beholdenness over those of international aid, in *Secrets* he has it play hide and seek. He floats allegorical possibilities only to sink them; offers, then withholds. The sometime, sleight-of-hand metaphor can be reluctant and forward at the same time—more intimate than familial, for instance, when "the lay of our bodies" is metonymically equated with "the territories of our pain" (p.174). It's undeniable, however, that family troubles and civil strife are frequently apposed, even that the latter (in the unsettling forms of shots in the night, smoke in the distance, checkpoints on the road, corpses in ditches) regularly invades the preoccupied domain of the former. The impending national descent into anarchy, hanging like thunderheads from Damac's first worry-prone premonition (p.22), is indeed the brooding backdrop for every stage of the deepening familial intrigue. Even the characters remark upon, and sometimes reinforce, the coincidence, as if they themselves were overtly, tantalizingly, *asking* for their story to be treated figuratively: "two young people had set a history in motion, in canny prediction not only of what might happen to them but of what might happen to the nation in its hour of imminent dissolution," reflects Nonno (p.112). "I doubt there is a way of explaining these incidents in isolation from the tension all around," Kalaman adds; ". . . [t]hey are all connected" (p.118). Yet if, as Greg Tate avers, there are indeed "dots between Kalaman's trauma and that of his politically scarred nation," then one must insist on reading those dots as ellipses. When connected they don't produce a clear picture—or rather they produce a picture that, like Sholoongo (who is scapegoated as an outside agitator precipitating *both* family havoc and national apocalypse), continually shifts its shape. For just as often Farah, mindful of both Aijiz Ahmad and Derek Walcott ("No nation now but the imagination"), cagily dismisses any easy analogy between domicile and nation: "I doubt," Nonno coyly demurs, "that local scandals have earth-shattering proportions to them" (p.114). By the end of the Interlude, Nonno openly mocks the possibility, mischievously threatening to "put on a vaudeville show" starring a menagerie of beasts with talismanic significance in the family saga. "To portray the tragedy that is Somalia!" he crows (p.208). As commentary on the paranoid ramblings of the preceding pages, his hyperbolic wit seems sensible and cool: the elements of the intermittent allegory are after all uncertain and confused, its structure is obscure and incoherent, its sums don't quite add up—and yet (as with our persistent suspicion that the shifty Sholoongo really *is* the catalyst of all this turmoil, after all) nig-gling doubts remain. "We were being made to rethink our relation-ships," Kalaman thinks later, in strung-out despair, "what Somalia meant to each of us, the smaller unit succeeding where the larger unit, that of nationhood, had failed" (p.227). It's as if Farah finds the allegory distasteful but inevitable, an unsavory, and unedifying, fig-ure which must nevertheless be eaten, digested—and shat out.

Or rather (to return to the other end of the critical digestive tract): Farah gamely, if perversely, undertakes to retrieve from the recesses of their crumpled napkins that chewed-up piece of gristle about which his American reviewers were so squeamish. If they thought they tasted national allegory, then by god he'll serve them up national allegory. But under his supervision, they'll be required to eye it up close, breathe it deeply, caress it with their lips and finally take the spit-sodden scrap back into their mouths and swallow hard. They may think the secret of Somalia is hidden in an allegory where-in clan stands for nation—but the *real* secret, Farah insists, is that this notion of clan really doesn't explain anything about Somalia at all. It's not clans *per se* but rather "clan logic," the received wisdom about the role of clan in Somalia, that is closest to the dark heart of his novel. *That* is the spurious secret he will patiently, persistently, expose; the empty conceit he will adamantly (if imperfectly) debunk; the stinking blanket-explanation he will air out and de-louse. Clan is merely another MacGuffin, to which neither this novel nor Somalia "boils down."[15]

The book's serpentine unravelling of clan logic takes a number of twists and turns (particularly throughout the "Interlude" comprising Kalaman and Nonno's duelling soliloquies) that I won't follow here. But perhaps its kinky thread can be neatly, if arbitrarily, tied off in a Kalamanic rumination inspired by his father's own circumlocutious go at unveiling the family secret. "[W]hat makes one kill another because [an] ancestor is different from one's own," reflects Kalaman, ". . . has little do with blood, more with a history of the perversion of justice" (pp.76-7). This historical perversion, this fatal failure of understanding, is itself of obscure ancestry. Tracing its murky lineage across various points (and parables) in the book, we infer that such contorted thinking was begat by secrecy, paranoia, and vengefulness; which were begat by colonialism, dictatorship and famine; which were begat by...nothing, no one, in particular? A "supreme being not begotten and who Himself does not beget" (p.76)? Surely that's an unsatisfactory explanation, deriving as it does from Kalaman's childhood fantasies of fatherless, semi-divine children. If there's any progenitor at all, then it's more likely a flesh-and-blood one, a pathetic little figure hiding behind the terrible face of the great Oz. And indeed, the origin of clan logic turns out to be a pale imitation of original sin: little more than cowering egotism, self-serving narcissism. "Clan," Farah has repeatedly asserted, in this novel and elsewhere, is merely a fig leaf, a thin shred of kinship allegiance covering over naked opportunism and egomaniacal thuggery, a man-made perversion masquerading as a natural phenomenon. The lesson of *Secrets* is not, as several reviewers would have it, that had those primitive Somalis only cast off their bafflingly backward notion of clan (as the author, evidently an improved specimen, did), they might have had a healthy nation founded in more heterogeneous kinds of community (like ours!) and saved their country from ruin.[16] No: Somalia did not crumble because of some ancient, fundamental notion of "clan" or "tribe." On the contrary: as in Rwanda, the Balkans, Nazi Germany and elsewhere, the late Somali incarnation of the idea is thoroughly, regrettably, modern. Moreover, "clan"—"a notion difficult to locate, slippery, contradictory, temperamental, testing one's capacity to remain patient during trying times" (p.294)—is itself a category no more intrinsic to Somalia than to the rest of the world. Like some sort of flesh-eating staph bacterium, it's endemic to all human societies, living right there on their skin. Furthermore, it has no innate connection with militias, let alone fratricide—though it has a latent potential, if cultured under the wrong circumstances, to mutate into any number of malevolently antibiotic-resistant, egocentric disorders: paranoia, xenophobia, suicidal tendencies, general bad-mindedness. In short, Somalia's chronic clan-riddenness (like Africa's "anarchy") is a condition that's not congenital, the product of begats, but political, the product of maneuvers and machinations. That it represents itself otherwise is why Nonno, "no longer content with allegories" (p.204), favors a political identity—even one of foreign origin, *Britannico*—over one that claims to be primordial. Nations, for him, are not analogous to kin, but *preferable*. Political categories, openly man-made conceits, may at least be contested, but there is little recourse against such would-be transcendental signifiers as "blood" (p.193).

"I itch."

"Clan," then, didn't sire Somalia, however much its aberrant deployment may have fostered it. And if we still insist on reading family history allegorically, then from a forensic examination of the traumas that produced a depressive, distrustful Damac and her callow Kalaman, we might conclude that the calamitous Somali predicament was engendered in the commonest of crimes, the most banal of evils: brutal (colonial?) rape and venal (postcolonial?) extortion—with the support of a transhistorical misogyny abetted by generations of ministers both religious and civil. But even more important than the crime, perhaps, was the cover-up—by its victims: the inwardly-directed shame and reticence, the false pretense of normality, all resolutely calculated to yield an adult who (no matter how extravagant his childhood) might live, like Kalaman, in quiet, button-down, bourgeois oblivion. There, the stench of the putrid crimes festered, but both family and neighbors studiously ignored it, like decorous dinner guests in the presence of some fetid smell emanating from an indeterminate corner of the table. In a collectively failed test of will, the entire body politic could not find the strength of character even to *acknowledge* its own body odor, let alone bathe its slowly decaying flesh. If you can't exactly fault a people for succumbing to an infection, you can at least indict them—and Farah does—for not washing their hands or cleaning between their legs.

Such an explanation, such a distribution of blame, may seem oddly individualist: like the ecotopian canard that faults consumers before chemical companies for fouling the planet, it traces the root cause of national collapse to the dark heart of each Somali. But that is the clearest explanation we'll get. ("Our challenge," offers Nonno, in language that's lexically and syntactically polyvalent, the slipperiest articulation of our elusive non-analogy, "is to locate the metaphor for the collapse of the collective, following that of the individual" (p.191).) "Independence" was meant to be Kalaman's potential salvation, but in this irredeemably fallen, clan-ridden country, there is only damnation left, and at some point he has to face squarely his own independent part in the collective culpability. Clannishness may be a cover for selfishness, but the blame for allowing "clans" to emerge is on the head of every member of the community. Each individual—especially the oblivious, middle-class, cosmopolitan, intellectual individual—is an "accomplice" in the country's ruin (p.190), a "sharer in the censure" (p.192). "No one innocent," raves Nonno. "No one of us" (p.108). Such summary judgments, such rituals of self-blame, are openly, if equivocally, contested (in the parable of the frenzied locust-eaters, for example), yet they resonate with pronouncements we have heard before. In *Close Sesame*, the intelligentsia's collective passivity is what allowed Siyad Barre to happen ("What I could never have predicted," Deeriye grieves, "is how easily governable we are");[17] here in *Secrets*, its soulless egoism is what allows *clans* to happen ("what a small-minded, mean people we were," laments Kalaman, after the fact). For a people in such sleepy oblivion, Sholoongo's return is a belated olfactory wake-up call, her animal smell a redolent reminder of beastly Somalia's rotting corpse. After a time, Kalaman can no longer distinguish this odor from that of his *own* body; at Nonno's rural retreat, he compulsively showers, as if Sholoongo's stench—or Somalia's—were emanating from his own armpits.

654

At the book's end, having battled each other to an epic draw, Nonno and Sholoongo, two shamans with atavistic links to a pre-Islamic, "pre-tribal" Somalia, abandon the field, leaving the somber stage strewn as in some Shakespearean tragedy with the surviving generation (who are by contrast, dull, diminished, unimaginative). But narratively speaking, Kalaman's weepy vow to wed the bland Talaado and dutifully sire a grandchild is parodically fulfilled by Nonno and Sholoongo's "simulated rape in reverse" (p.294). Far from setting the world aright, cleansing it of *nabsi*, the doubtful issue of *that* coupling is nothing but an itchy, putrid ooze. As a resolution to family crisis, then, the huggy, tearful melodrama of Chapter Eleven is pure Douglas Sirk: for just under the syrupy surface, in the same subconscious out of which Nonno cloudily conjures his Somalia, persist roiling secrets which even a mystical mind-fuck cannot resolve. The road to catastrophe on Nonno's subliminal map is still dotted with armed checkpoints (manned, perhaps, by mothers with guns); beyond that there is no legend, no set of magical codes. "As a citizen of the crossroads where several worlds meet," Nonno offers Kalaman, "you will...come upon footpaths forking in all sorts of directions, signposts giving you confusing directions to where there is no return" (236). "Our country is as good as gone," he adds on his deathbed. "Make of your life what you may" (p.296). Kalaman may be "confident that [Nonno] will live on in me," but in the face of such bleak nihilism, this forced self-assurance is so much whistling through the graveyard.

Still, while Nonno leaves no interpretive guide, it's worth paying attention to where he—and Sholoongo—go. Nonno slips off to the afterworld, leaving Kalaman existentially stranded. But Sholoongo, presumably, withdraws to America, from whose impressionable unconscious she seemingly sprang, to resume her role as flim-flam woman peddling spiritual mumbo-jumbo to gullible "yoga-practicing latter-day hippie[s]" (p.53). If individual Somalis and their African neighbors snag a proportionately larger share of blame for the country's annihilation, then here is an indication that America will not be let off the hook entirely. To begin with, Sholoongo's mere presence tweaks our nose for deciding to peer into the closet of Somali letters only after the body politic we were determined to see there has become a skeleton.[18] But beyond that, her return reminds us that in the wake of all imperial adventures comes a stream of refugees; in that sense, and not just in our narcissistic imaginations, the Somali story really *is* part of America now. Interestingly, the majority of Somalis in the United States have settled not on its coastal peripheries (like Sholoongo in New York and her half-brother in San Francisco), but, like Vietnamese and Hmong before them, in the mid-west—in Minnesota, to be exact. Quite literally, then, Somalia now resides deep in the American heartland.

In a way, Sholoongo lives there too, wandering amid the stereotypically stolid, repressed, and complacent descendents of Scandinavian pioneers. This is fertile ground for tricksters, whose primary function, after all, is to shock the self-satisfied into a more troubling kind of self-recognition. *Secrets*, it turns out, is an intimate agent of such self- consciousness. If literary imagery ordinarily privileges sight and sound, then Farah's novel, as we have seen, persistently asserts two more underprivileged senses, repeatedly embarassing all of us spiritual Nordics by dwelling on the disgusting and the funky. But at the last, it also exercises—or irritates, perhaps—our tactile sense: like Sholoongo's lice smuggled through U.S. customs, like the mysterious secretion crawling down her thighs, *Secrets* aims to settle in the crotch of our unconscious, and make us itch.

NOTES

1. Since the early 1980s, when Gabriel became involved in anti-apartheid efforts, he's become justly famous as a promoter of "world music" in the West. Though the name of his label ("Real World") makes a slightly presumptuous claim of "authenticity," it's generally acknowledged that Gabriel's own integrity and good

faith are impeccable. Maryam Mursal, *The Journey*, CD, Real World CAR 2370-2, 1998; [Maryam Mursal and] Waaberi, *New Dawn*, CD, Real World CAROL 2365-2, 1997.

2. Gloria Goodale, "Dancing to the Global Beat of Africa Fete '98," *Christian Science Monitor* 26 June 1998, B6.

3. As Mursal explains it (and performs it), "Somali jazz" is a cosmopolitan gumbo of imported American soul and R&B, liberally seasoned with local (Afro-Arab) melody, rhythm and vocal inflection.

4. Nuruddin Farah, "Praise the Marines? I Suppose So," *New York Times* 28 December 1992, late ed., A15.

5. Nuruddin Farah, *Secrets* (New York: Arcade, 1998).

6. Alan Cheuse, rev. of *Secrets*, by Nuruddin Farah, *All Things Considered*, Natl. Public Radio, 24 June 1998.

7. Richard Crepeau, "'Secrets' rich with revelation," *Orlando Sentinel* 26 July 1998, metro ed., F6.

8. Sheila Farr, rev. of *Secrets* by Nuruddin Farah, "Briefly," *Seattle Times* 24 May 1998, M2.

9. Valerie Miner, "Sholoongo's Web," *Newsday* [New York] 3 May 1998, B14.

10. David Rathbun, "Telling 'Secrets,'" *Star Tribune* [Minneapolis] 5 July 1998, metro ed., 14F. See also George Packer, "Somali Shapeshifters," *New York Times* 19 July 1998, late ed., sec. 7, 11; and Scott L. Malcomson, "Family Plot," *The New Yorker* 74:16 (15 June 1998), 78-79.

11. Greg Tate, "Bawdy Politic," *Voice Literary Supplement* 2 June 1998, 140.

12. Other more-or-less judicious reviews include Cheuse (*op cit.*) and Lisa Meyer, "Family Tensions Mirror Somalia's Clan Warfare," *San Francisco Chronicle* 5 July 1998. Popular reviews from the same period not directly cited in this essay are as follows, in chronological order of appearance: Susan Salter Reynolds, rev. of *Secrets* by Nuruddin Farah, "Discoveries," *Los Angeles Times* 21 June 1998, home ed., 11; Wes Davis, "Torn Between the Past and Present in Somalia," *Newark Star-Ledger* 21 June 1998, final ed., 9; Bruce Allen, "It isn't easy knowing who you are, wherever you are," *Raleigh* [N. Carolina] *News & Observer* 28 June 1998, final ed., G5; Elizabeth Bukowski, rev. of *Secrets* by Nuruddin Farah, "Bookmarks," *Wall Street Journal* 17 July 1998, natl. ed., W10; T. Obinkaram Echewa, "'Secrets': The Sexual Obsessions of a Somali Middle-Class Family," *Philadelphia Inquirer* 19 July 1998, Q7; and Abdel Abdi, "The 'secrets' of a forgotten people," *Washington Times* 26 July 1998, final ed., B7. One or two (such as Echewa and Abdi) are relatively inoffensive, but most are of a piece with those already discussed. The trade journals *Kirkus Reviews*, *Booklist*, and *Publishers Weekly* also gave *Secrets* favorable (though not especially perceptive) notices.

13. Farah, *Secrets*, p.1. Further references are given in parentheses in the text of the essay.

14. This critique may not be reduced to a cliché such as "family is what you make it," however—or as George Packer has it, "Love...matters more than blood." To such hackneyed homiletics we must counterpose Kalaman's dry sardonicism: "Love...is a mother armed" (p.150).

15. It's worth remembering that on his wild goose chase into the

Heart of Darkness, all that Marlow-the-proleptic-postmodern discovered was the absence of "presence." Kalaman, too, like that other searcher after transcendental truth, discovers that it is not Out There—or even in here. That is: there is no elaborate, *X-Files* conspiracy to obscure The Truth, despite Kalaman's dogged, Mulder-like efforts to construct one (p.235). Moreover, anatomizing the secrets and dysfunctions of one family won't tell him anything about himself, much less about the tragedy of a nation that's "fragmenting in family fiefdoms." The devolution of the two units is at best coincidental, not allegorical. Still, if one *X-Files* slogan ("The Truth is Out There") doesn't bear up under scrutiny, another ("Trust No One") may, with a slight modification. "[M]istrust your kin," Kalaman wisely concludes early on (p.77).

16. "[Farah's] Somalia," Laura Demanski blithely asserts, "longs to be freed of ancient antagonisms and delivered into stable nationhood built on reason." ("Families suffer together—artfully," *Baltimore Sun* 10 May 1998, final ed., 13E.)

17. Nuruddin Farah, *Close Sesame* (Minneapolis: Graywolf, 1992).

18. Since receiving the Neustadt, and especially since the end of 1998, Farah has seen what Stephen Gray calls a "flowering of interest" in his work here on U.S. soil. (Stephen Gray, "Nuruddin Farah: The Novelist and the Nomad," *Publishers Weekly* 246:34, 23 August 1999, 28-29.) Indeed, Farah's stock has risen measurably with American journalists, who speculate excitedly that the Swedes may deify him with the Nobel any day now, and so they'd better pay attention. His celebrity hasn't necessarily sharpened their critical acumen, which still tends to be blurred by primitivism and exoticism. (The indefatigable Sheila Farr, for instance, continues to delight in figuring Farah as a dog in breeches—or rather as a "shaman in a business suit": Sheila Farr, "Words from afar: Somali writer enchants with his use of language, imagery of body and mythology," rev. of *Maps* and

Gifts by Nuruddin Farah, *Seattle Times* 15 August 1999, final ed., M10.). Still, a great deal of the critical attention he's received in the past year or so is considerably more sympathetic and enlightened than that. And when the *Voice Literary Supplement* and the *Los Angeles Times* name *Secrets* among the "best novels of 1998" (the *Times* repeated that honor for *Gifts* in 1999), and when the *New York Review of Books* gushes that Farah is "the most important African novelist to emerge in the last twenty-five years" as well as "one of the most sophisticated voices in modern fiction," you don't ask questions. (Neal Ascherson, "On the Edge of Catastrophe," rev. of *Secrets* by Nuruddin Farah, *New York Review of Books* 4 March 1999, 10-11, 10.)

BOUNDARIES OF FATHERHOOD IN NURUDDIN FARAH'S *SECRETS*

Ousseina Alidou

T his paper seeks to examine how the notion of fatherhood is called into question as a viable category in *Secrets*, the latest novel by Nuruddin Farah, the 1998 laureate of the Neustadt International Prize for Literature. The problematization of fatherhood[1] is revealed first and foremost through the main character, Kalaman, himself the offspring of a gang-rape. In several of his ruminations, Kalaman comes to the conclusion that "fathers matter not, while mothers matter a lot!"[2]

Kalaman's delegitimatization of fatherhood echoes even more strongly in the consciousness of Sholoongo, another central character in the novel. Sholoongo is a child of an absentee and *de facto* father who according to popular mythology is raised by a lioness mother. Sholoongo's willingness to challenge the "traditional" Somali patriarchal understanding of fatherhood is reflected in her strong desire as a woman to exercise her reproductive right by choosing to bear a child with a man other than her "legitimate" husband. And when her expected sperm donor expresses his worries about fathering her child, she assures him that "the way I [Sholoongo] see it, fathers are an outdated irrelevance" (p.66).

661

However, as the novel progresses in its treatment of the notion of fatherhood through the multiple identities of both Kalaman and Sholoongo, we see that, in fact, what both characters are rejecting is the legitimacy of paternity—biological fatherhood, so much taken for granted in conservative patriarchal cultures. Both Kalaman and Sholoongo are, after all, rejects of their biological fathers. On the contrary, through a process of gradual maturation of their consciousness born out of their own personal experiences, they come to recognize and appreciate that geniune fatherhood is ultimately a social and individual private commitment rather than a biological phenomenon. It is this refocusing that eventually leads Kalaman to acknowledge that "mothers matter a lot, [but] Yaqut [the social surrogate father] matters too" (p.262). In fact, throughout their mysterious and intertwined lives both Kalaman and Sholoongo develop affectionate bonding with individuals who are not their biological kin.

In addition to privileging "social fatherhood," however, Farah makes an even more radical departure as an African writer by questioning the socially constructed gender boundaries of fatherhood and motherhood. Kalaman's father and mother, therefore, virtually play inverse parenthood roles to those ascribed by Somali society. The novel begins with a prologue in which the narrator, Kalaman, reveals to the reader his psychological struggle to understand the intriguing identity of his childhood friend Sholoongo as a multiple—half human, and half animal with supernatural powers—as well as his own name. The psychological quest for belonging within a culture which determines one's identification through a paternal lineage becomes a pursuit which projects Kalaman, the protagonist, and Sholoongo as mirror entities whose tragic births metaphorically account for the current state of Somalia as a raped nation-state. From his grandfather, Nonno, Kalaman learns:

> Sholoongo was delivered of her mother when the stars were bivouacking at a most inauspicious station. She was born a *duugan*, that is to say, a baby to be buried.

And that was what her mother tried to do: she carried the infant out into the bush and abandoned her there. But Sholoongo survived, and lived to haunt the villagers' conscience, especially her mother. (p.2)

Sholoongo's mother foresees the social stigma directed at the female child in general, and of *duugan* birth in particular, and the subjugation of women in the Somali patriarchal social order which vindicates absentee husbands and fathers like Madoobe. This awareness triggers in Sholoongo's mother a kind of consciousness tied to the determination to free (or liberate) her female child, Sholoongo, from the shackles of patriarchy. Sholoongo's mother, therefore, chooses infanticide as an act of freeing her *duugan* child who is expected to be buried alive according to Somali tradition.

But, further we learn of the failure of the infanticide. As Nonno puts it:

I cannot vouch for the truth, but in the version I heard, a lioness adopted and raised her [Sholoongo] together with her cubs, then abandoned her at a crossroads, where some travelers found her. These took her to the nearest settlement, which happened to be her mother's hamlet. You might think this far-fetched, but this is the stuff of which some people's misfortune is made, myth galore! (p.2)

Unexpectedly, then, as a biologically and socially parentless child, Sholoongo survives both her mother's attempted infanticide, thanks to a mother lioness, and her neglect and abandonment by her biological father.

With Sholoongo turned innocent victim by her procreators, *Secrets*, thus, interrogates the legitimacy of "fatherhood" through the character Madoobe, a seaman, who is supposedly the biological father of Sholoongo. More preoccupied by his profession as a seaman,

Madoobe is presented in *Secrets* as a *de facto* husband who deserted his matrimonial home after the consummation of their marriage: He sporadically comes home, fulfills his manly "obligation," inadvertently impregnating his wife during his visits and takes off without maintaining any contact with her. Thus, Madoobe is aware neither of the welfare of his wife nor of her pregnancy, her delivery, her attempted infanticide, her suicide, and the fate of the orphan child left behind. In Nonno's account:

> The girl's father [Madoobe] turned up...a seaman on leave. Bizarre though it may seem, the villagers did not tell him the whole truth. Only that he had to slaughter several goats as part of a sacrificial ceremony for his own safe return, nothing about suicide. Nor did anyone bother to inform him that his daughter was born *duugan*. Remember, he was away, at sea, when she came into this world. (p.3)

Indeed, Madoobe was never told anything by the community—but there is no evidence that Madoobe himself ever asked.

But *Secrets* also shows further that Madoobe's long lasting abandonment of his matrimonial home and the responsibilities associated with his status as a husband and father is vindicted by Somali "tradition." His actions are licenced by his privileged position within patriarchy. As a result, the community does not feel any need to scold him or call him to reason. In fact, the entire community is more concerned about his safety against his *duugan*-born child against whom he should seek protection. Furthermore, Madoobe's abandonment of his family is rewarded by the community with a new bride whose relatives also seek protection from the *duugan*-child (p.3).

There is a feminist bio-cultural view that patriarchy derives its power through the appropriation of the woman's body—both in its sexual and labor functions—and the claiming of the offspring. As Ruth Ginsberg suggests:

Male historical praxis is necessarily directed at solving both alienation [from his seed from the moment of ejaculation] and uncertainty [resulting from the intellectual apprehension of the ascertainty of paternity]. Thus, the organizing steps of patriarchy, that is the appropriation of the children from their mothers and their naming after the father, serve the same purpose where marriage is not an agreement between man and woman but a social contract concerning the ownership of women and their offspring, guaranteeing certainty and continuity.[3]

But Madoobe's life is the very negation of this understanding of patriarchal praxis. For he is a man who is content to enjoy the privileges of patriarchy without assuming its responsibilities. Owning his offspring, therefore, features little in his consciousness. He develops no anxiety about fatherhood, nor alienation; instead Madoobe merely feels relieved in his sexual discharge.

Through the fate of both Sholoongo and her mother, Farah invites the reader to a careful examination of the objectification of Somali womanhood in a society where patriarchal privileges strip the female of human agency. The birth of a female-child within such a cultural dispensation represents a case of misfortune since patriarchal lineage is guaranteed only through the male heirs. As a victim of these cruel patriarchal values that cause the dehumanization of her mother and violate her right to live, Sholoongo overtly argues against the necessity of fatherhood which she describes as "an outdated irrelevance" (p.66).

Farah's position is not a simplistic indictment of individuals like Madoobe. It is rather a meticulous critique of patriarchal cultures that impose an anxiety of gender performance on the individual by requiring a set of behaviors and assigning roles for males and females by which they must abide. For Sholoongo's parents, parenthood becomes an act of performance of social responsibility forced upon them by Somali patriarchal values. Consequently, biological notions of parent-child, father-child, and mother-child are relational ties which individuals, especially females, experience through tremendous agony, while the patriarchal male looks at them as simply a ritualistic performance devoid of fundamental moral and material responsibility. This social imposition creates a set of contradictory outcomes whereby, instead of the anxiety of fatherhood in the father's claiming of the offspring, we witness the anxiety of the offspring seeking a paternal identification.

Unlike Sholoongo's mother, the lioness that discovered Sholoongo in the wildeness uses her maternal instincts to nurse and nurture Sholoongo together with her cubs which she has just delivered. The maternal instincts of the lioness, in other words, prevail over its cannibalistic instincts with which its species is normally associated by humans. In the quest to escape the cruelties of Somalia's patriarchal order, therefore, Farah elevates the more humanistic choice of the lioness to nurture over the murderous drive of her biological mother based on wanton violence (infanticide and suicide). Both Madoobe's disclaiming of family and his wife's resorting to murder lead Farah, through the voice of Kalaman, to interrogate the biological relevance of notions such as parenthood, fatherhood and motherhood, in addition to the traditionally accepted uncertainty of fatherhood in Somali patriarchal culture. If fatherhood was considered uncertain, actions like that of Sholoongo's mother has now put motherhood in serious doubt. As Kalaman puts it:

> There is a Somali proverb that says that mothers are
> certainty...if there is a parent of which we tend to be
> certain, it is the mother. But we are in an epoch in
> which mother-as-certainity no longer holds true:
> babies are abandoned in garbage bins. I read in a local
> paper the other day about the casualty of uncertainty,
> a mother committing suicide because her Somali-born
> daughter, now an American citizen, had borne a test-

tube child. Why did the mother take her own life? Is it
because she couldn't bear living any longer in a world
where the mother-as-certainty was questioned, undermined as it was by the secret-derived science of
today? (p.196)

Somalia has become an orphan, a child that is, for all practical
purposes, both fatherless and motherless, partly because of the
uncertainty of both fatherhood and motherhood. The state of par-
entlessness has been contrasted with animal violence. While violence in humans can be perpetrated against the vulnerable innocent
without any rational basis, the violence of animals is often triggered
by the need to stop excessive aggression against their kind. Thus, the
animal violence against human beings is symbolised by the elephant's deadly search for Fidow, which should be read as a vengeful
but founded act of condemnation of human unfairness. Unlike in
Somali culture where patrilineage seems to represent the fundamental criteria for belonging or rejection, the elephant operates on the
certainty of biological kinship. Farah introduces the tale of the vengeful elephant against the ruthless hunter, Fidow, to point out the fundamental difference between animal responses to kinship versus the
Somali's. If for the elephant kinship is established inclusively as a
matter of identification with a biological species, for the Somali clan
ties are determined through primordial paternal bloodlines. In the
words of Kalaman: "One's 'Somaliness' as opposed to being identified
as belonging to a given clan defines a political entity. The clan is non-
political based as it is on one's primordial blood identity" (p.193).
Allegiance to paternally determined members of a clan and rejection of other Somalis not affiliated to one's clan can account for deadly animosity among the Somalis:

Intimate friends betrayed one another on account of
narcissistic differences, a man raping his sister-in-law
and emptying her of her fetus just because the woman

667

belonged to a different bloodline from his. Someone
had earlier beaten a drum, a mob walking behind him
as they marched through the thoroughfares of the
metropolis. They were chanting a nursery rhyme,
invoking the sentiments of hatred against the clans
from elsewhere. (p.193)

The fact that they are all members of one species requiring allegiance to each other by virtue of their shared "humanness" is a reality that has been erased by the face of patriarchy. The patrilineal order
in Somali society creates conditions in which paternity becomes a
source of anxiety for individuals such as Kalaman, born out of a gang-
rape, an offspring with no single identifiable father. The narrator in
the interlude of *Secrets* attempts to capture Kalaman's psyche regarding the implication of the uncertainty of his biological father:

He [Kalaman] was a prisoner in the whale's all inclusiveness, a newt-man with no recognizable identity.
His wish to reclaim his deracinated, not-clan-based
identity was denied. He was given the choice of dying
at the hands of a nonmember of his mother's clan or
his father's, or to roam in the belly of the whale as a
newt. He chose to be a newt, preferring this to allying
himself with the murderers. (pp.192-93)

Under these brutal clan-like conditions and an ostentatious display of inhumanity, the uncertainty of Kalaman's biological fatherhood then becomes an asset rather than a liability. At the very least
it frees him from any moral pressure to participate in the bloody orgy
of "clanicide."

Nonno, Yaqut's father and Kalaman's adoptive social grandfather,
seems well aware of the power of being a "Somali without a clan." In
order to protect Kalaman against the social stigma associated with
his 'beginning' as a product of a gang rape whose paternity is uncer-

tain, Nonno gives him a name that implies no paternal or maternal lineage. Nonno justifies his action as necessary for establishing Kalaman's autonomous selfhood and by the same token tries to dispel the memory of the brutal event by which he came into being. Thus, the meaning of Kalaman implies 'reflexivity':

> Name a child Mohammed, and everybody is bound to
> ask 'Mohammed Who?'...I had the foresight to call you
> Kalaman because I knew it would stand on its own,
> independent of your father's name or mine. (p.5)

Nonno is interrogating the necessity of naming a child by association with another human being, be that person a biological parent or a religious figure like the Prophet Muhammad. In his view, naming by association—by association to a clan, to religion, etc —is one of the factors that leads to human violence, one against another.

In spite of Nonno's attempt to spare Kalaman from the agonies of his birth history, however, intruders prompt Kalaman's curiosity to question the certainty of Yaqut, his mother's husband, as his biological father. A female friend of Kalaman's mother who, it seems, has internalized Somali patrilineal ideology, is the first to plant this seed of doubt in Kalaman's mind:

> A friend of my mother's [Qalin] had the crude habit of
> alluding to the sameness or largeness of manhoods,
> Nonno's, and my father's, both of whom, according to
> her, "hung down a ton!" Why was it that I didn't? Was I
> or was I not of that line, the son of my father, Nonno's
> grandson? (p.5)

This doubt is reinforced by Sholoongo who has a sexual encounter with both Yaqut and Nonno. Her disregard for the necessity of biological parenthood leads her to use her knowledge of both Yaqut's and his father's genital sizes to raise Kalaman's awareness about his relationship with Yaqut and Nonno: "Yours is no bigger than a navel button. Are you sure you are your father's son? Because he hangs down like a leather strop" (p.8).

None of these promptings, however, manage to get Kalaman to question the nature of his relationship to Yaqut and Nonno. On the contrary, even when he discovers that his biological father may be other than Yaqut, he treats the news with disdain. After all, the rape of his mother by sexual predators whose action goes unpunished by a phallocentric patriarchal society remains a violation of his mother and himself. Kalaman thus writes off any potential biological father and this decision gives further weight to his statement that "...[*rapist*] fathers matter not, while mothers matter a lot!" (p.66).

Under the circumstances of the experiences, Kalaman embraces Sholoongo's position, herself an offspring of an *absentee* father, that questions the absurdity of societal privileging of a mythical and disfunctional notion of father/fatherhood and the processes of its affirmation to the detriment of mother/motherhood. Through the unravelling of the tragedy and the myth of both his birth and that of his lover, Sholoongo, Kalaman demonstrates a new level of consciousness that calls for children's right to choose a matrilineal affiliation as opposed to patrilineage as commonly recognised by the "conservative traditional" and patriarchal Somali culture. Thus, he posits to his beloved adopted grandfather, Nonno, the words of Sholoongo, suggesting that

> since Nonno's and my father's and my name were all dead ends, would it harm anyone if I added my mother's name to this odd mix? Because not only was this fair to the woman who carried me for nine months, but in more than one sense it was also a daring thing to do in a country where nobody contemplated such a step. I put this across as though it were my own idea, not Sholoongo's. (p.6)

670

But Nonno warns Kalaman against an individualistic course of action. Given the prevailing system of values in the society at large, action that is so individuated, radical and progressive as it may appear, is bound to lead to negative outcomes.

> ...I'm sure I needn't remind you that children of unknown male parentage are, in our part of the world, referred to as the 'misfortunates.' Quite often they are burdened with nicknames bearing association with their mother. You know of the one exception to this: the Somali prefix *bah* indicates a mother's name with which a woman ancestor is identified, in the context of house-name siblings in a polygamous situation. This does not apply to you. After all, you are an only child of a monogamous union. And surely you do not want anyone to think you are an illegitimate child? (p.7)

The old man's warning to Kalaman must be read as a warning that the success of a revolutionary act within a society is most often the product not of an individualistic act but arises from a society's readiness to transform itself. In other words, a transformation of the cultural practices of a society must be galvanized by an internal cataclysm—the rise of consciousness of the entire society through a social movement. But in his response, however, Kalaman reminds the old man that what is often required—the cataclysm—to transform Somali culture in its patriarchal assault on women and children is the breaking of silence against sexual violence against the women with consequences for children and the entire society. After all, the only certain parent following Damac's gang-rape is Damac herself. So on what basis should she be effaced from Kalaman's identity?

> The adult in me took over with unprecedented punctilliousness as I retorted that our society was unfair to women, this being a view I had often heard Nonno

671

advance, and with eloquence. I went on, "Fancy the unfairness of it all! Imagine the outrageousness of it, not to be allowed to take one's own mother's name!"..."He [Nonno] nodded his head but said nothing..." (p.7)

Could the adding of Damac's name to his own be Kalaman's way of challenging the concience of his community in its acquiescence with the sexual violence of its women folks? At this juncture, Kalaman sees himself as finding greater identitarian stability by association with the mother than to maintain a name that seemingly leaves him unconnected to either parent.

As an adult, however, Kalaman himself comes to the realization that the valuation of motherhood need not always be independent of fatherhood. We may remember that as the question unfolds of who his biological father is, he stumbles on an old letter kept in secret by Nonno. As he reads it, he learns about the shameful secret of the gang rape of his mother and the possibility that he might originate as an offspring of Y.M.I, the author of the anonymous letter left as a reminder of the brutal act. Y.M.I could be read in English as "why am I?" Could this existential question be left deliberately as Kalaman's heritage?

Under different circumstances, the fact of gang-rape would have reduced Kalaman and his mother to virtual outcasts. But Yaqut and Nonno come to Damac's rescue. They embrace her fully and help her to heal. And they extend their love to Kalaman and bond with him unconditionally. Their love and concern for him is partly reflected in Nonno's determination to give Kalaman a name that is independent of theirs as the paternal link or of Damac as the maternal link—to protect him from potential victimization by a society obsessed with lineage. All this elevates the two men in Kalaman's eyes and they become his true love. Thus, Kalaman recasts his understanding of fatherhood in the sociological sense and concludes, "Mothers matter a lot! Yaqut matters too!" (p.264). In the process, Kalaman expresses his closeness to Yaqut and challenges the traditional understanding of sex-based notions of motherhood and fatherhood. In this reconfiguration of gender identity as it relates to parenthood, Damac represents both the biological mother and the breadwinner, a role traditionally associated with the male head of the household, that is the father. Yaqut becomes responsible for Kalaman's mothering, contrary to conventional Somali practice. Kalaman decribes his secured conditions as follows:

> As an infant I was physically inseparable from my father. I would fall asleep with his finger in the tight clasp of my fist. My mother wasn't around a lot. He was often indoors, often practicing a profession with greater flexibility than my mother's. She went out daily, busy running the family business, including my father's souvenir stall, a shelf of assorted items, the product of the magic wonders. She made more money than he. It was just as well, he would comment, because she was always running around, a scorpion without a tail. But he was more content doing what he did, prolonging the lives of objects. When he was praised, my father's eyes lit up, like formidable flames. (p.78)

Kalaman goes further in his appraisal of his surrogate father by showing how Yaqut, in his commitment to assume a natural bonding with his beloved son [Kalaman], develops a natural spontaneity as a child care-giver, a role that is traditionally performed by a mother. Yaqut's geniune disposition to mothering is presented through Kalaman's recollection of childhood memories:

> He would strap me to his back as he lettered the head-stones he had been commisioned to etch, as he engraved names on slabs of marble. He fed me, washed me. On occasion, my mother's friend Arbaco looked after me when he was, for some reason, unavailable. When I couldn't breathe because my

673

nasal passages clogged, my father took my nose in his
mouth and, at a single drag, sucked the unease out of
me, phlegm and mucus and all. (p.78)

A mother usually is not repulsed by anything which comes out of
the body of her child. She regards her child as an extension of her
own body which reflects her maternalness—as a biological continuation of herself. Thus, Yaqut's total lack of uneasiness in clearing
Kalaman's clogged nostrils by sucking his nasals clearly symbolizes
his embodiment of a desexualized-motherhood. This is confirmed by
Kalaman's following comments:

> With the radio off and my mother's high-pitched voice
> on the run, I would cry until my weeping dislodged all
> they had in the way of nerves...We would play at his
> being my mother, and I would pretend as if he were
> breast-feeding me. We dwelt in a world of make-
> believe, my father and I, pleased with each other until
> my mother returned. (p.79)

Kalaman's depiction of his mother's seeming tyrannical behavior
once at home after a long busy day outside the family home reminds
us of the stereotypical attitude of most patriarchal men. These
assume the right to be comforted and to be aggressive as a result of
their outgoing role as breadwinners. Upon returning home from work
they take their frustrations out on the women and children and
demand from them complete silence as they seek their "right" to rest.
As Kalaman puts it:

> On returning home in the evenings, my mother
> imposed a curfew of silence upon us [Kalaman and
> Yaqut]. She would switch it off. Stone silent, he [Yaqut]
> would stare at her. Vexed, she would try to outstare
> him, and would fail. No maid ever stayed in my

674

parents' employ for more than a week, because my mother's tempers chased them away. (pp.78-79)

Damac remains the unconventional woman within the Somali patriarchal order for she remains officially unmarried and the provider to the two men in her intimate life—her son, Kalaman, and her husband, Yaqut. Her status as the provider is also symbolically illustrated by her four nipples—like a cow—with both Kalaman and Yaqut feeding on them. Damac recounts:

> You see, I had two dwarf additional breasts way down on my abdomen. How it excited me to have them sucked, an indulgence my husband Yaqut was forever prepared to grant me. To suck, he would go down on his knees, and take my Tinies in his mouth, one at a time, in virtuous performance of a private ritual which we delighted in together. It was a divine pleasure to have Kalaman at my breast feeding, and at my feet my husband prostrated in worshipful adulation of my Dwarfines...It was as if I had been blessed with a set of twins, one at each of my breasts, suckling. (p.168)

Thus, Kalaman and Yaqut are depicted as twins who are totally dependent on their breadwinning mother for their subsistence and their basic survival.

By depicting Damac as the breadwinner, the provider and the head of the household, Farah challenges the conventional portrayal and understanding in patriarchal culture which depicts the woman only as care-giver, nurturer, dependent-wife, and mother. But he is also interrogating the gender boundaries of motherhood and father-hood. In spite of Damac's unconventionality with his family, however, Kalaman proudly presents it as a viable and harmonious unit: "When my mother was in an agreeable mood, then all three of us showered together, jets of shivery water, with me standing between them, playful, full of rejoicing" (p.79). The three-some and Nonno symbolize a new possibility that a new social order based on a totally new understanding and reconstruction of the politics of lineage and gender relations for a better Somali is indeed achievable. The question is whether the Somalis themselves are ready for this challenge.

Somalia as a postcolonial nation-state is partly a product of the colonial gang-rape of Somaliland by foreign imperial patriarchal powers including the Ethiopians, Italians, British, French, and—more recently—the Americans. Somalia's current violent quest for nationhood within one state evolves out of Somalis' deliberate amnesia about the gang-rape of their motherland. It seems that what the Somalis retain from that historical memory is the very mechanisms of appropriation that were used by the imperial powers to fragment their collective consciousness and identity. These are the strategies of indiscriminate violence employed by the Somali warlords towards their own people in their quest for power and self aggrandisement. As Nonno observes:

> ...let's for a change talk about the entire country, and its impending collapse into blood-letting anarchy. And let's agree for what it is worth that our nation's predicament is our own predicament too, collectively and individually, each of us an accomplice in its ruin. Can anything be done to stop the country from fragmenting into family fiefdoms? I doubt that this is feasible at this stage. Because what is happening to the collective identity of the nation and in the individual lives of its people is not tiddlywinks, a game played with pieces of plastic made to jump into a container. What is happening is a life-and-death matter. The games are becoming more deadly on a daily basis. (p.190)

In the final analysis the devaluation of biological fatherhood-paternity, in the case of both Sholoongo and Kalaman, is also a metaphor about the superficiality of clanhood upon which the Somali psyche is supposedly based. As Kalaman suggests:

> But what makes one kill another because this mythical ancestor is different from one's own: this has little to do with blood, more with a history of the perversion of justice. What makes one refuse to intermarry with a given community has to do with the politics of inclusion and exclusion. Forming a political allegiance with people just because their begats are identical to one's own—judging from the way in which clan-based militia groupings were arming themselves—is as foolish as trusting one's blood brother. Only the unwise trust those close to them, a brother, a sister, or an in-law. Ask anyone in power, ask a king, and he will advise you to mistrust your kin. (pp.76-77)

Clanhood presumes the certainty of the biological father. If the biological father is, in fact, uncertain, as in the case of Kalaman, or totally irrelevant, as in the case of both Sholoongo and Kalaman, what becomes the moral basis of the clan's existence? Y.M.I (Why Am I?), then, is a symbolic allusion not only to Kalaman's heritage, but to Somalia's and indeed Africa's entire existential future and crisis of identity.

NOTES

1. Throughout *Secrets* Farah uses fatherhood to imply both paternity that is biological fathering and fathering in the social sense. My contention is that paternity is the contested notion of fatherhood in the novel. I maintain the same argument with regard to the distinction between maternity and motherhood.

2. Nuruddin Farah, *Secrets* (New York: Arcade Publishing, 1998), p.66. Further references are given in parentheses in the essay.

3. Ruth Ginsburg, "The Anxiety of Fatherhood," *Modern Language Quarterly* 52, 4 (1991), 360-61.

PART SIX

Non-Fiction

BROTHERS AND OTHERS IN
YUSSUF AND HIS BROTHERS
Betty Oliver

"Satan set at variance me and my brethren"
(Koran 12: 100)

Farah's play *Yussuf and His Brothers* has been produced once, in July 1982 at the University of Jos in Nigeria, and Gerald Moore, who attended this premier, described it as "an absorbing, yet elusive and mystifying experience."[1] The play has not, at the time of writing, been published and perhaps this is understandable as it is not an easy play, being full of allusions and innuendo which a non-African, and specifically a non-Somali, may find problematic; but, more importantly, a play relies almost entirely upon the spoken word and there are times when Farah does not appear to be completely comfortable with unsupported conversation. Koschin in *A Naked Needle* is a more fluent character in his internalised introspection than in his conversations with Nancy, just as in the play both Yussuf and Aynaba appear to converse in a stilted artificial manner, unlikely between man and wife. Nevertheless, Farah produces the impression

681

that within each of them lies a furnace of emotion and doubt. Aynaba's jealousy of the known love which Yussuf holds for her son, Raageh, and the suspected desire he has for Siraad is coupled with her doubt as to the exact part he played in the death of her first husband and the extent of his complicity in Hussen's arrest. After four years of marriage she asks herself "Who is Yussuf and, equally, who are his brothers?" The play, like most of Farah's work, asks the questions, but provides no answers. While Yussuf is solely the centre of interest and action, his background, indeed his philosophy, remain an unravelled mystery. Is he the overt nationalist who is apparent, or is he the covert traitor who condemns his brother to death only to claim the widow for himself? Or is he even a mortal being? Aynaba asks him "Who are you really? Are you not like us?" Perhaps he does not fully understand himself, for his reply is uncertain; "I wish I knew" (p.4).

Although the play is set in no particular country and no particular enemy is defined, there are obvious analogies with the political situation in Somalia: an amorphous threat hangs like a veil over the people and it is apparent that death awaits any who question the rightness of the status quo and of whatever undefined authority is currently empowered. However, reference to the apparent permanency of the colonial masters and their Zulkifl collaborators suggests a nationalistic uprising rather than a rebellion against an internally imposed regime, but this is not explicit and complaints about colonialism could be used to obscure the true target at which the play is aimed, as the situation in Somalia and in many other parts of Africa would preclude an overt declaration against authority. The Narrator states that geographically we are in a peninsula (euphemism for Horn?) of Africa where one region is rebelling against the central power of the Empire. The indigenous people are repressed, living in temporary shelters and nomadic huts while the rulers and their sycophants, the Zulkifls, control government and business, entrenching their power and permanence. This could relate to many parts of postEuropean colonial Africa, but reference to "nomadic huts" and the "central power of the Empire" strongly suggests Somalia with its large population of nomads and its attenuated war against the Ethiopian empire for control of the Ogaden.

The role of the Narrator who guides us through *Yussuf* has similarities to the Greek chorus, but he offers very little explanation and his implications and suggestions in no way provide answers to the reader's questions. He is himself a questioner, reminding his audience of Islamic values and truths, promising not to intrude unduly but to let the rhythm and fluidity of the tale determine its own pace. Jacqueline Bardolph, whose article "Yussuf and His Brothers" is the only critical material written about the play to date, explains that the theatre in Somalia continues to flourish in the oral tradition of the culture and that a play always contains a message, "relayed explicitly by the chorus which extracts meanings and lessons."[2] In the case of *Yussuf* these are somewhat obscure and one is left to supply details from one's own knowledge and imagination, particularly as much of the background to the general theme takes place off stage and the reader is reliant upon the Narrator for this concomitant information. In this respect *Yussuf* is probably, of all Farah's work, the closest to the oral message of traditional Somali poetry, relying heavily upon the personal images which the reader can empirically conjure.

The setting has a timelessness which could fit most periods of history but certain properties bring it firmly into modernity. Although Yussuf's symbols are those of Islam, the rosary and the prayer mat, the young Kulmie introduces materialism with the watch which Zulkifl has given him and which so obsesses him that he neglects to attend the mosque to pray publicly. His sister, Aynabo, avers that Kulmie has turned traitor for rings, wrist watches and dreams of worldly comforts, but as the play unfolds we are forced to doubt his betrayal; the precious watch is lent to Hussen so that he may know the exact time he is to meet his wife and Yussuf during the staged escape plan, and this inadvertently costs Kulmie his life. In some respects he is a farcical character, a "tamer and feeder of lions" (p.12) who forgets to lock the gate of their cage as he belatedly prepares their food: the outcome is inevitable. He is apolitical, having no interest in the local polemics, living for present pleasures, but showing an unexpected courage as he helps Hussen to escape from the mob following the debacle of his execution. Is he reacting instinctively to the emotional pressures of the mob; was his fortuitous presence a pure coincidence, or had he planned a part in the rescue? He had made enormous efforts to ascertain advance details of the execution, thrashing Raageh and attempting to bribe Gheddie and his wife, but for what—betrayal of the rebels or betrayal of authority? Kulmie remains one of the question marks of the play and the fact that he is eaten by his own ravenous lions does nothing to mollify the reader. Farah uses Kulmie to express one symptom of the obfuscatory malaise which presently exists in Somalia: Aynabo seeks the return of Kulmie's body but is told by the Zulkifl that nothing remains to bury; the lions have eaten him. This is parallelled in *Sweet and Sour Milk* where the regime refuses to provide a death certificate for the murdered Soyaan, despite his twin's attempts to obtain this vital written document. Thus for posterity there will be no evidence that Soyaan had ever existed, he will soon be an illusion remembered only in the minds of those he loved.

In contrast, Raageh is an open character, a lad of thirteen who adores his stepfather and emulates his every action, sharing his prayers, his clothes, his love, his political hopes; he becomes Yussuf's second self, the future hope not only for the man but for the country; the bridge, the double that exists in all of us, Yussuf's "other head" (p.76), his country's "Future-Man" (p.21). As Yussuf says, Raageh's future is tied to that of the nation. The boy has courage and withstands Kulmie's beating without revealing any vital information; and he is honest, refusing to accept the much-proferred watch as a bribe since he can offer nothing in return: at the same time he is a typical boy who proudly fights the Zulkifl louts to defend the honour of Hussen. For Raageh, if Hussen is to die it must be in defence of the rebellion with the full honours of a martyr, the world knowing that it was he alone who blew up the bridge.

Yussuf's wife, Aynabo, suffers a deep jealousy of the bonds and affection which Yussuf shares with Raageh: she feels herself to be exiled within her own home, shut out from their mutuality, and her jealousy extends to Siraad, Hussen's wife. Aynabo recalls how four years ago *her* husband, Yussuf's cousin and also one of his band of brothers, similarly should have faced a firing squad and how Yussuf had plotted to rescue him also, first taking her and Raageh into his home for protection; but the scheme had misfired when the husband (who remains unnamed) took his own life, either not knowing of the scheme for his rescue or preferring his personal solution to the ignominy of that rescue, thus robbing the rebels of a martyr-figure. Aynabo remained with Yussuf, now as his wife, but she has harboured secret doubts that Yussuf may have connived at her husband's death in order to acquire her for himself, just as she now fears that he may be manoeuvring Siraad into a similar position. She claims that it was only after she became Yussuf's wife that she learned he had sent his first wife away. Yussuf is later to admit to Gheddi that he had sent his family away to safety as he was unsure of his own fate.

Aynabo's fears that she is about to be replaced are proven unfounded: Hussen faces his executioners convinced that he will die, unbelieving that they have saved him by deliberately firing into the air on all three commands to shoot. In the ensuing melee, as the spectators erupt into a tumult, he escapes with Kulmie's aid, but Gheddi and his twelve-man firing squad are trapped; unable to make their way through the mob, they are arrested. From the point of view of the rebel cause this is irrelevant: the plan had been not merely to save one life, but to make of that life a *cause celebre* on which to focus public support and to demonstrate the strength of the rebel underground. Hussen, however, is faced with the dilemma of living on with the knowledge that, although he may be free, thirteen men will have been sacrificed for his one life and the martyrdom which he was seeking will still be denied him. Gheddi meantime has accepted his own predicament: he is damned whatever he does. He has sworn on the Koran to be a servant of the regime, but he is also a true believer in the rebellion. If he permits his soldiers to execute Hussen he is damned in the eyes of his own people; if he abets an escape plot the regime will exact retribution but, more importantly, his Islamic vow will be violated. He makes the pragmatic secular decision and plans to escape immediately after the aborted execution.

Hussen's confrontation with death has changed his perspective. He realises that he cannot live as a hero-figure; his honour, his whole identity, has been lost in those terrifying moments when he believed he was dead. His only recourse is to surrender, thus achieving his freedom and restoring his honour through the reality of death. He also suspects that Yussuf has manipulated not only his escape but also his initial arrest. While Hussen has consistently denied his own guilt in the blowing up of the bridge, he knows that an equal declaimer of his innocence has been Yussuf, but Yussuf has never been willing to produce evidence to substantiate this innocence. The saboteur was identified by his raincoat—Hussen's raincoat—but we know that Yussuf owns an identical garment; Aynabo accosts him with this fact, and with his having been seen near the bridge on the night of the bombing. The emphasis given to the raincoats may appear rather contrived, but Farah frequently adopts the detective mode and drops clues for his readers which may be recalled later. Thus in one text there may be brief mention of characters and incidents to which we are introduced in depth in subsequent works.

Exactly who planted the bomb remains one of the imponderables of the play. For Yussuf it is an unimportant detail; it is not an individual who "plants a bomb which blows up a bridge, he does so not as a person but as though he were the nation: and he is the nation...we're all one person" (p.72). Yussuf sees Hussen not as a man but as a symbol of struggle, one who has no right to make restitution of himself, but who must take the place of Aynabo's husband, he who lacked the courage to be martyred for his people. Hussen also sees himself as a symbol, but for him that symbolism is not of one who has been dragged back from the abyss of death but of the man who planted the explosive which blew up the bridge. He will be the eter-

686

nal light of the unknown warrior, the one who gave his life that others might live. If he is to die, let it be as a martyr; he will then be credited with the explosion, whether or not he is innocent. He decides to greet death willingly, restoring his own identity and simultaneously eluding Yussuf's puppetry.

Yussuf's power and leadership abilities seem to evaporate with Hussen's decision and, as Bardolph says, he appears to be caught in a double-bind, unable to give decisive answers to questions, diminished by Hussen's transformation.[3] Hussen's rebirth has undermined his own. In the final scene we learn of Yussuf's having arisen from the dead; Banana, the African condottiere who has flown in with his personal army of mercenaries to restore order for the regime, had years previously rescued Yussuf, drowned and apparently dead. To Yussuf, Banana is the man who gave him this gift of life, the biological father-figure whom the adolescent child meets again after many years, having glimpsed him briefly only once or twice before. To Banana this return to life is "a gift of the divine" (p.69); "Our help came down to them, delivering whom We pleased" (*Koran* 12: 110). Banana is to remain an enigma until the final moments of the play. Has he come to uphold the regime or has he assumed the legendary mantle of Shaka who will lead the oppressed and oust the oppressors? He is a figure larger than life, who can command men (and women); a big, handsome man; a man of appetites who gives hints of his political affiliations but leaves us guessing. It is not until the Epilogue that Farah offers hope: Raageh reads that they live, but in exile—as did Farah—waiting to return. Meantime, there are bridges, which join not themselves but other objects, just as a man serves not only himself but others as well. Raageh is the future, the as-yet uncommitted, but the one who will share the treasure left behind. He must grow and be cared for, as Yussuf cared for his garden, for the Koran states that kindness must be shown to widows and orphans, who must be dealt with justly: "remember they [orphans] are your brothers" (*Koran* 2: 219). The hope, however, may be challenged by doubt, for the responsibility for this care will now fall upon the shoulders of a boy barely into his teens.

The play is entirely oral, the only evidence of written material being Yussuf's letter to Raaageh which comprises the Epilogue; this at least will remain as proof that Yussuf existed, just as, in *Sweet and Sour Milk*, Soyaan's Memorandum and his piece on Clowns, Cowards and Upstarts proclaims his existence, unlike Kulmie who leaves no memorial and will inevitably become a non-person. Is Farah analogizing Somalia's transition from a purely oral culture to one which has belatedly been given its own script, or does Yussuf now feel free to put into writing what none had previously dared to commit to paper? As Soyaan understood the dangers of his written Memorandum, so would Yussuf have realized that oral reporting can be denied as rumor, but paper and the written word are irrefutably damning. All governments are adept at utilizing rumor; in more "developed" societies where the written word is the accepted mode of communication, politicians well appreciate that journalists can be fed a rumor of an impending action which is likely to be publicly detrimental; this then becomes a governmental possibility which is allowed to "float" through the media to enable the people's reaction to be assessed. At this junction it is only rumor, but it rapidly becomes fact if reaction is either indifferently favorable or non-existent. But Yussuf must rely upon the spread of information by oral means only, and this is in part why Aynabo's husband was uncertain whether or not he would be rescued; the brothers had been unable to gain access to speak to him directly. It is not until Yussuf has physically left the country that he dares to communicate with Raageh in written form, and this makes his letter all the more symbolically important in the life of the boy.

Is Yussuf the metaphor for Farah, the one who has left his people, but persists in their consciousness as a bridge to the outside world, an exile in body but not in spirit? The bridge symbol is significant throughout the play. In the first scene Aynabo watches the man and boy as they walk towards the bridge, the boy's eyes raised admiringly to his stepfather "like a drawbridge"; they part, the child to cross the bridge and the man to turn back and take a different road. Raageh is Yussuf's bridge to the nation: the Zulkfils live on the other side of the bridge in an area removed from the country's proletariat, and the sabotage of the bridge is the pivot around which all action rotates. Farah, in writing of his early childhood in Kallafo, has stressed the importance of the town bridge which it was necessary to cross in order to reach the schools which lay on the other side, the side of Government Hill, the seat of authority. This was a bridge guarded by Ethiopian soldiers who enjoyed inflicting upon their subject people intimidation, humiliation, interrogation, and even rumored rape. At the same time he was aware of the cultural bridge which his genera-tion had crossed in its educational absorption of a worldview alien to that of his parents, a view in which his people's history and ancestry were notably absent "from the rollcall of world history."[4] Bardolph questions whether Yussuf is a symbol for the elite, the "artist or visionary, the man who has been singled out because he could read the present and forecast the future" and who subsequently arouses the suspicions of his brothers.[5] But is the exiled writer regarded with suspicion by his peers or only by authority? Is resentment of the exile only present when it is whipped up and inculcated by authori-ty? Few British resented W.H.Auden's 1939 departure from a Britain embarking upon the horrors of war until considerable adverse pub-licity suggested that his exile was a matter of self-preservation and a betrayal of those who remained. I suspect it is more likely that Farah sees Yussuf as an analogy for himself, a seeker after truth. In his inter-view with Maya Jaggi he said:

> Truth in all its contexts is what finally leads you to comprehend the first and most important questions that all human beings ask themselves. 'Who am I?' 'Why am I who I am?' 'What is my place in this world?' And it is in answer to these questions that I have been writing, coming to the same questions from different angles, using different characters.[6]

Yussuf is presumed to have died twice, first by drowning and later in a cholera epidemic, of which he was the sole survivor. Banana recounts dragging him dead from the water, watching life flutter softly back into the inert body and feeling convinced that a miracle has happened. As one who has tasted of the Lethe and has experienced what lies on the other side of life, is Yussuf now no longer mortal but a symbol, a spirit of the true soul of his people? As he looks into his hand mirror, his major leitmotif, could it be that he is seeking a reflection which no longer exists? Is he now truly a man or has he transcended mortality? Borges reminds us that "killing or engendering are divine or magical acts which notably transcend the human condition"[7] and Yussuf is a man who is prepared to kill for his cause. Aynabo accuses him of sitting huddled in a corner clutching his mirror, "seeing I know not what" (p.20). has it that ghosts have no reflections: as he says, he knows death and his funeral rites have been conducted. His first act on returning to life in Banana's grasp is to ask for a mirror. Does he need assurance that what has returned from that brief encounter with eternity is indeed Yussuf? He is obsessively interested in Hussen's reaction to facing death while waiting in the prison cell, with time like a crucifix bearing heavily upon his shoulders. Yussuf wishes to experience vicariously the anticipation of death, his drowning having given him no time for the ceremony and ritual of its approach. Banana hints that he may have undergone a Biblical resurrection.

The Narrator tells us that Yussuf has been likened to the "mirror's splintered and wounded soul" (p.14). If he is only a reflection of the others outside himself, he has undergone a transubstantiation where his own mutable soul can migrate to Raageh so that he is the boy in the same way that the boy is the nation, thus establishing his duality with Raageh and through Raageh with the country. Yussuf is accused variously of being simultaneously the man he once was and the one he has become, one the sum of whose fragments exceeds the total, a miracle of a man whose disappearances have become legendary, yet who has the saintly strength of one who believes in the eternal. He remains unmoved and says he is prepared to make do with his faulty soul. In his final message to Raageh, Yussuf says that the mask is no longer necessary, "nor do I need any other prop." Now that he has established his oneness with Raageh, the "Futureman," he can physically disappear; no need remains for the mirror, as none remains for his presence in the physical body. He is the instigator, the invisible one who cannot be identified as the perpetrator, about whom the others, the Brothers who are also believers, orbit (*Koran* 49: 10). It is he who, like the Biblical Joseph, monitors the situation from a distance of objectivity.

There are strong Biblical analogies in *Yussuf and His Brothers*, Farah drawing upon both the twelfth Surah of the Koran and upon Genesis in the Bible in basing the character of his protagonist. Like his namesake, Yussuf is a man who sees a dreamful future; this earns him the animosity of his brothers, just as Joseph was envied by the sons of Bil'hah and Zilpah (*Genesis* 37: 2) who saw him as the favorite child of their father Jacob. The Koran remains silent on the naming of the brothers, although Farah permits Raageh to name four "uncles" who may or may not be brothers in the rebellion. But one brother is named, Hussen, just as the Bible (although not the Koran) names Reuben, and both are uniquely men of compassion: Reuben is he who returns to the well attempting to save the young Joseph (*Genesis* 37: 29); Hussen intends to surrender, knowing that he cannot live with the death of thirteen innocent men on his conscience, that he must make restitution of himself. Yussuf's shirt is one of his major stage properties, a Biblical symbol which figures prominently in his association with Raageh. The boy angers his mother by insisting upon wearing his stepfather's "dirty shirt that smelt of [his] filth and sweat" (p.7) in his desire to become part of the man he respects and loves; so too does the shirt, or coat, feature frequently in Joseph's life. His beloved father Jacob "had made for him a coat of many colours" (*Genesis* 37: 3), and it was this shirt that the brothers returned bloodstained to the old man as proof that the boy had been eaten by the wolf: "'The wolf devoured him. But you will not believe

691

us, though we speak the truth.' And they showed him their brother's shirt, stained with false blood" (*Koran* 12: 18). As a parallel, a mud-stained raincoat is identified as proof of guilt: but of whose guilt?— Hussen's or Yussuf's? In the Koran the shirt, torn from behind, proves Joseph's innocence of seduction of the Egyptian's wife, and lastly it miraculously cures Jacob's blindness: "And when the bearer of good news arrived, he threw Joseph's shirt over the old man's face, and he regained his sight: 'Did I not tell you, God has made known to me what you know not'" (*Koran* 12: 96). Abandoned by his brothers, Joseph is presumed to have died; so too does Yussuf apparently die and, like his Biblical brother, he returns after many years from the dead, and each man knows he is not free from sin and that his soul is prone to evil, but that the Lord is forgiving and merciful, all-knowing and wise (*Koran* 12: 52; 12: 100) and that he is placed here on earth to fulfil the wishes of the Lord. Raageh, like Jacob, is "brought out of the desert [into manhood]...after Satan had stirred up strife between [Yussuf] and his brothers" (*Koran* 12: 100). For Raageh the shirt stained from his stepfather's body has absorbed the very essence of the man, and as the boy feels the cloth touching his flesh he becomes less the thirteen-year-old boy and more the man to whom the future of the nation may be entrusted, until in the final scene he is asked to assume the mantle of that man, "his future...tied to that of the nation." His duality with his stepfather on the one hand and his country on the other is affirmed.

Duality plays an important part in *Yussuf and His Brothers*, the Castor and Pollux syndrome[8] of twinnings, groupings and the mirror-technique being frequently used. Farah also touches upon Jean-Paul Sartre's existentialist ideas of the 1950s—his theory of *the other*. Farah's concept of his own divided personality is emphasized in his childhood memories, a time when he was constantly aware of learning in languages other than his own, of utilizing paradigms other than his own people's, of receiving other nations' wisdoms, and of being himself, as a Somali child in the Ogaden, "the unnamed *other*...the child of contradictory inadequacies."[9] Hussen wonders if Yussuf is listening or if his mind is elsewhere. "The posture he strikes invariably suggests to me as though he were a twin-brother in Manichean communication with *the other* who had died young" (p.13), a spiritual twin with whom he is exploring a dualistic theology. Yussuf's monozygotism is reflected in many of the characters, none of whom is ambiguous. Farah frequently uses twinning as a metaphor. In his novel *Sweet and Sour Milk* there are the twin brothers Soyaan and Loyaan who suffer violence at the hands of Somalia's hostile military regime; *Sardines* pairs the protagonist women into ages, social strata, and religious convictions; *A Naked Needle* joins the women who are voyeurs in their various associations with Somali men. But Yussuf and his brothers appear to be more than twinned; they are the multifaceted perspective of one entity, each containing all. Yussuf is a hologram of the entire band of brothers which is the people of the nation, divided yet indivisible, perhaps anarchic but determined to wrest power from those who have abused it. In his symbolic relationship with the brothers he has become less an individual and more a codetta in a fugue, even in his periodic disappearances underlining this transformation: "I keep telling them that we're all one person: that if one of the brothers plants a bomb which blows up a bridge, he does so not as a person but as though he were the nation: and he is the nation" (p.72). Yussuf is portrayed generally as the "manifold manifestations of the many-facedness of a mirror" (p.14), but specifically he enjoys a duality with his stepson, Raageh, whom he has endowed with his revolutionary soul and who will be the bridge to the future for his country. Banana dreams of a Yussuf with two heads, one his own and one that of Raageh. At the same time, Farah twins Yussuf and Hussen, whose raincoats are identical and appear to be one. Banana asks if there was ever a time "when they looked so much alike [that] it was possible for one to be taken for the other" (p.68), and Hussen, in turn, is paired with Aynabo's former husband, each refusing rescue and preferring death, albeit in a manner of their individual choosing. Both Yussuf and Hussen have faced certain death and have drawn aside the veil to return to life, or have been restored by God for a time ordained (*Koran* 39: 42), but during this experience Hussen has found within himself a twin, *the other*, the subjugated self, and his dilemma is to choose which of the two halves shall survive—the one who has indulged in the secret sacrilegious thoughts or the one whom the gods have blessed, the good Hussen who is descended in a direct line from the Prophet's daughter Fatima. He appears to have chosen the former as he later flouts his infidelity before his wife, Siraad. His schismatic experience contrasts with that of Yussuf, who fears himself to be not merely bifurcated but fragmented. Banana also has reflections and doubles. It is only in the Epilogue that there is revealed that which Banana has spoken to Yussuf, the self or the double who is Banana's stand-in in many situations; and he has a reflection in the ill-fated Kulmie. Both are creatures of doubtful alliances. Do they align themselves with authority or with rebellion? Can they be trusted or are they among those basest creatures, the faithless, who violate their treaties and have no fear of God? (*Koran* 8:57). Aynabo believes that she shares a destiny with Siraad, a destiny which is being determined by Yussuf. Each woman's husband has been condemned to execution before a firing squad; Yussuf insists that each is innocent but refuses to offer evidence in defence of either. Each woman understands that Yussuf will fulfil his Islamic obligations to widows and orphans by taking her into his home, yet each ponders the possibility that he has been the *agent provocateur* in the arrest of her husband.

Although Farah has experimented with dyadism in his other novels, it is most pronounced in *Yussuf*, where the counterpoints of light and darkness, life and death, the sacred and the profane, are complementary to one another and are delicately balanced. As Yussuf's final letter tells Raageh, "nothing exists unless its double exists too, life has no meaning unless death exists to complement it...I am a man and...at the same time a woman and child...there is God in man and the devil in a saint" (p.77). The play questions how we face life and death; is it with the conviction that to die for a cause is worthwhile, hoping that we leave a better world for our children? Should we follow Hussen and confront death head-on, convinced that by so doing we remain morally intact, am individual whole and integral, not shattered to the point of disintegration as Yussuf has become, a man divided within his soul? Should we leave the conflict, hoping to live to fight another day, as Farah himself did, believing that we can influence our country's destiny from beyond its borders? *Yussuf and His Brothers* presents questions which extend far beyond the traditional Somali mores, moving the reader into universal metaphysics. The poetic serenity of Yussuf's final letter, accepting as it does the multiplicity of roles and choices which permeate man's life, leaves us with what is perhaps Farah's personal philosophy: "There is a universe of doubt and man drowns in it unless he finds a cause for which he must die" (p.77).

NOTES

Yussuf and His Brothers remains unpublished at the time of writing. Page references are to the typescript which was kindly sent to me by Professor Jacqueline Bardolph.

1. Gerald Moore, "Personality and Heroism" (review of *Yussuf and His Brothers*), *West Africa*, 16 August 1982, 2113.

2. Jacqueline Bardolph, "*Yussuf and His Brothers* by Nuruddin Farah," *Commonwealth: Essays and Studies* 7, 1 (1984), 58.

3. ibid., 61.

4. Nuruddin Farah, "Childhood of My Schizophrenia," *Times Literary Supplement* 23-29 November 1990, 1264.

5. Bardolph, 64.

6. Nuruddin Farah, "A Combining of Gifts: An Interview" (with Maya Jaggi), *Third World Quarterly* 11, 3 (1989), 184.

7. Jorge Luis Borges, *Labyrinths* (Harmondsworth: Penguin, 1987), p.281.

8. Karl Miller, *Doubles* (Oxford: Oxford University Press, 1985), p.402.

9. Farah, "Childhood of My Schizophrenia," 1264.

TESTING IDEAS:
Nuruddin Farah's Radio Plays
Eckhard Breitinger

N uruddin Farah's renown as a writer rests exclusively on his work as a novelist. With the exception of Jacqueline Bardolph's article "Yussuf and his Brothers"[1] and a four-page section in Patricia Alden and Louis Tremaine's *Nuruddin Farah*,[2] the quite voluminous body of criticism on Farah has completely neglected his excursions into the field of drama and theatre. Even Farah himself seems to have conceived his dramatic pieces as only of secondary importance compared to his prose writings. While he has been over-conscientious as regards how his novels were to be published, translated and republished, there seems to have been no effort to make the scripts of his radio plays *A Spread of Butter* and *Tartar Delight* and his stage play *Yussuf and his Brothers* available in a print publication.[3]

The two radio plays in particular sound as if they came from the "sketch book" of the novelist, where he was experimenting with situations of psychological conflict, exploring character constellations, and testing atmospheric settings and topics, which he then further developed in his dictatorship trilogy. This is particularly obvious in

A Spread of Butter, a 35-minutes two-hander play, broadly based on a 1976 stage version with the title *The Offering*. It is one of the limitations of the form of the (non- experimental) radio play, with its clearly defined time slot and the need to communicate plot, atmosphere and character through invisible voices only, that it requires a clear structuring and a strict concentration on the plot situation and characterisation. In a way, *A Spread of Butter* reminds us of the structure of the short story as it is laid down in many theoretical statements: the unique situation based on one single event and narrated without side-stepping into parallel plots or sub-plots.

A Spread of Butter is situated in the closed space of a prison cell in an unnamed African country, ruled by an exploitative dictator. The Professor, one of the leading intellectuals of the country with an international reputation as a political scientist and philosopher, teaches at the only national university, where he is almost idolatrously venerated by his students. He has been detained after students' riots demanding freedom of expression and democratic elections, as the master mind behind the students' unrest and as the leading brain of a circle of coup-plotters who have allegedly attempted to overthrow the President. The Professor's counterpart in the play is a bright young military officer of junior rank, who appears in the prison cell to interrogate him. In the beginning, the obvious assumption is that the interrogation should establish the guilt of the Professor, independent of what the questioning will really reveal: "Anyone found guilty of one or more of these [accusations] is punishable minimally with death" (p.13). The charge is high treason, and it is expected that the military tribunal specially established for this case will find the Professor guilty, sentence him to death and have him executed immediately. This is the logical assessment of the situation on which the Professor bases his reaction to the young officer's interrogation. He is fully aware that the sole purpose of any interrogation of a political prisoner in this country is not to uncover the truth or to ascertain the innocence of the accused, but to serve as a "ritualistic ceremony" that demonstrates the unrestricted power of the President and his regime of henchmen. Knowing full well that he is mainly required to play his role in a foreclosed scenario, the Professor tactically designs his responses in the two areas of, on the one hand, individual psychology or personality, and, on the other, broad general statements on the moral qualities of the polity and society in the country.

The Professor does not strike us as a particularly strong, heroic or even likeable person. His reaction in the beginning veers from arrogance to fear and self-exculpation. Though hesitantly, he makes the interrogator understand that he is a person of international standing, "tutoring the offspring of the President," and feels under-rated or even insulted at being interrogated by a junior officer only: "Oh my God, high treason and a sub-lieutenant" (p.1). And he responds to the tenacity of the questioning by denying any causal connection between his lecturing the students on the principles of democracy or its perversion through "deification," and the students' taking to the streets in rioting:

> ...an academic article addressed specifically to my anaemic set of intellectual friends, an article about concepts...the concept of deification, that of personal-ity cults...the use and abuse of isms. (Pause) I named no names. (p.7)

The Professor denies the political responsibility of the role model which he should assume or actually did assume as a teacher and intel-lectual leader of the younger generation. The young officer very natu-rally feels offended by the Professor's arrogance and uses his position of superior power in the interrogation process to remind the Professor of his status as a member of the priviligentsia. He reminds him that his academic distinction, with his degrees from the top American univer-sities, was extracted from the sweat of the common people: "... fed on tax-payer's money, tax levied on a woman's bundle of fire wood, a sack of coal, or a man's sale of his goat. Your salary is from there as well" (p.3). He thus shifts the tone of the interrogation from the original questions of the Professor's involvement in coup-plotting and his responsibility for the students' riots to the broader issue of the role of the intellectual and political elite in Third World countries, and the wide-spread tendency of the elitists to become oblivious of the grass-roots that alone made their rise to the top possible in the first place.

> "Must the faceless, nameless and anonymous men of our masses work and sweat in order to have you earn more titles? How many of our people can read or write? What percentage use their thumb to sign a loan sheet from a money-lender?...Must the poor peasant sweat away to enable you and the like of you to soar higher and higher?" (pp.14-15)

The Officer tries to make the Professor understand that he is not in the least interested in proving his guilt for one particular incident in the political development in their country, but that he is interested in testing the credibility and moral integrity of the Professor. He thus also reveals that the purpose of the interrogation is completely different from what the Professor must have assumed in the beginning. The Officer came to the prison as the representative of the new military junta that had overthrown the President immediately after the imprisonment of the Professor and he is now trying to win over the Professor to become part of a government of national redemption. With this disclosure or revelation, the power balance of the interrogation is tilted and shifts from the Officer to the Professor, who suddenly and unexpectedly finds himself in the position of dictating the terms of the conversation. He immediately starts to pay back the Officer in the same kind. As a repartee to the reproaches of parasitical elitism, he questions the Officer about the seriousness and the social responsibility of the military by referring to the many instances of national redemption committees that proclaim with tremendous verbal bombast the "ethical revolution" of the new regime, only to camouflage its political essence.

He questions the nature of the intended changes—whether it was only a change of power into different hands or whether it would really be a change of political structures and essence.

> "You will name the governing organ the National Revolutionary Command and you will nominate yourselves ministers and ambassadors. You'll promote yourselves colonels and generals ...The former President ...came to power in an army coup. He said the same things you are saying now. I am not easily convinced." (p.20)

In the end, it appears as if the Professor is on top again as the winner in the intellectual debate—albeit by a small margin. The question of winning or losing, however, seems to be marginal in this dispute, because the essence of the play touches, rather, on the basic structural problems of newly independent nations, where different groups of the privileged elite can either end up in a clear confrontation—the military and the civilians—or come together in a shaky compromise of co-operation. As in his novels, Farah does not bring the plot to a clear-cut ending, but rather suggests an open and quite unstable balance between the involved parties.

> *Professor:* I won't help you bury your smelly waste in the clean sand of my laundered shore. No way. (He opens door) I won't help you bury your smelly waste, like a cat. I will not.
> *Officer:* See you in the evening. (p.23)

Farah implicitly suggests his own structural analysis of the two extreme poles in the socio-political structure: the common people appear only as a rhetorical device in the political pronouncements of the elitists or as the masses who can be manipulated into rioting or violent uprisings. The idolatrous dictators, who are so addicted to the personality cult, are also a creation of the political elite; only they, more often than the masses, escape manipulation and thereby create havoc in their societies.

A Spread of Butter parallels the political debates of the dictatorship trilogy, particularly those of *Close Sesame* and *Sweet and Sour Milk*; it complements the arguments put forward in the novels. In terms of radio drama, the play is rather conventional as practically most of the BBC African Theatre plays are. It is obvious that the purpose of the BBC African Theatre radio series is not to compete aesthetically with the John Cage style of experimental acoustic art.

Farah's second radio play, *Tartar Delight*, sounds in the first instance like an autobiographical sketch of an episode in the writer's exiled life in London. A kind of continuation of Soyinka's famous poem "Telephone Conversation," where a black writer tries to rent a room from a white landlady, Farah's *Tartar Delight* deals with what might happen once the black writer actually moves in. Like *A Spread of Butter, Tartar Delight* is a two-hander of 30 minutes, during the course of which the power relations between the two counterparts— dialoguers or adversaries in argumentation—change drastically and undergo complete inversion. In the beginning, we witness how Saleh, a budding Somali writer in exile, moves into Anita's flat with a small bag of belongings and a mechanical typewriter. He is in search of a quiet place where he can complete the script of a novel, unmolested and undistracted by the social demands of the community-in-exile, the fellow writers, or his girlfriend. He occupies the room of Anita's twelve-year-old son, who is away on holiday. Saleh presents himself as seclusive, stand-offish and even conceited. He keeps talking about the tasks of the artist in general and the writer in particular, his commitment to aesthetic principles, the responsibility of the writer in exile, and the basics of the creative process, which reminds us in a way of the Wordsworthian principle of "recollection in tranquillity." He wards off all of Anita's attempts to establish a personal relationship with her tenant. Saleh's refusal to get in any way involved with, or even tolerate a basic relationship on personal terms with, his land-lady only stimulates Anita's ambition to crack the hard shell of his seclusion and wilful isolation. With the natural instinct of the landla-dy, she wants to find out who her new tenant is, why he is hiding, and from whom or what he appears to be running away. After all, he might even be involved in the politicking of rival exile groups or be wanted by the police. Since Saleh is absolutely unco-operative, she rings a friend in a bookshop to find out about his reputation as a writer, what kind of books he has published, how they are selling, or if they are selling at all. Once she has established Saleh's "innocence" concerning what might worry her as a landlady, she grows deter-mined, as a woman, to find out about his innocence or seductability as a male. She starts making passes at him, telling him that she—as a woman—takes him as a challenge, and that unlocked doors are an irresistible temptation for her. Saleh tries to ward off her advances by being extremely unresponsive, even rude. But within a week, Anita succeeds in sneaking into Saleh's bed, celebrating her successful conquest of the male as "other," and an exotic male at that.

As in *A Spread of Butter*, we witness a dramatic change in who controls the situation, who assumes the hegemonic role in social interaction. While Saleh, at least in the beginning, seems to be in total control of the situation and demonstrates the extent of his control by his conceitedness, by being so ostentatiously full of himself, and by claiming to be absolutely uninterested in any kind of social interac-tion, not to speak of sexual interaction, it is Anita who opens the bat-tle of the sexes and scores a clear win when she tells Saleh, after their first night, that she will leave that same day to go on holiday with her lover. She explicitly challenges Saleh's male stance when she con-fronts him with her analysis of gender relations: Saleh, like any other male, finds it impossible to accept that a woman like Anita should take the initiative in starting a sexual relationship and also remain in control of how that relationship should develop, how far it should go, how long it should last, and how and when it will end.

In *A Spread of Butter*'s psychological analysis of the effects of dictatorship on individual behavior, the links with the intellectual framework of the dictatorship trilogy, written shortly afterwards, are quite obvious. In *Tartar Delight* Farah seems to provide test-tube conditions for another issue that keeps recurring in his novels: the ascribed role of women in society and the exercise of power within sexual relationships. Most of Farah's female protagonists have something of Anita's independence in thinking and behavior, but most of them are placed in a social setting that would never allow them to exercise this kind of freedom. Misra in *Maps* might be Anita's closest relative.

Similar affinities to Nuruddin Farah's prose writing can be discerned in his stage play *Yussuf and his Brothers*. The characters and the major plot line (if there is any) bear similarities to the koranic/biblical story of Yussuf/Joseph, son of Jacob and Rachel. It is not only Yussuf's alleged death and his coming back to prominence that invite comparisons; it is rather Yussuf/Joseph's powerful position and his relationship to women in his Egyptian exile that bear on Farah's play. Like his biblical/koranic forbear, Yussuf has advanced into an important position of political power from which he can control the life-lines of his society. But he does so from an unspectacular and almost informal managerial position, and not as a political front-stage character like a minister or party chairman. Joseph/Yussuf in Egypt managed to organise and control in a period of famine the distribution of "essential commodities" in his own community, and he also decided on the supply of relief goods to the equally suffering neighboring countries (the grain he sold to his half-brothers as relief for Jacob's clan in neighboring Kanaan/Israel). Farah's Yussuf controls the public transport system and thereby the essential physical mobility of the people; implicitly, he herewith also controls the movement of ideas. Joseph/Yussuf became a great success as businessman and manager in his Egyptian community, whose amenities he put to use for his own operations without fully identifying with Egypt as "fatherland." Farah's Yussuf, on his African peninsula, does not suffer from physical exile; under the colonialist/neocolonialist regime he feels the pressures of a psychological and intellectual exile. He also uses the structures of an alien regime to pursue his own agenda of liberation and his search for a national and individual identity. The koranic/biblical model of the Joseph/Yussuf story is in itself extremely complex, contradictory, and in no way conclusive. As is to be expected with Farah, he enlarges or even maximises these ambiguities and the obliqueness of his model. In a way, the overall affinities of Farah's play seem to be more with Thomas Mann's famous tetralogy *Joseph und seine Brüder* which "marks the transition from middle-class individualism to mythical archetypes...and descends into the deepest well of humanity where myths are generated from the original norms grounded in the original forms of human life."[4]

Central to the plot-line is the planting of a bomb under the bridge that links the civilian town to the government quarters and the palace of the governor. Farah does not even spell out clearly whether the bridge was actually destroyed, and whether the link between the governing and the governed was thus, effectively, broken. Hussen is suspected of having planted the bomb and is arrested, tried, and sentenced to death. Yussuf arranges with the commanding officer of the firing squad to shoot into the air and let Hussen escape, rather than turning him into an easily usable martyr for the liberation movement. Yussuf had already engineered a similar strategem on an earlier occasion, but the man failed the project by committing suicide after escaping execution. Yussuf married the widow Aynaba, and this time there seems to be a similar attraction to Hussen's wife Siraad. In the course of the plot, the suspicions that Yussuf was the one who planted the bomb, and was his own double/twin brother, doubling up other members of the nationalist movement, grow stronger, but they are never fully established or substantiated. In the end, Yussuf is saved by his old friend Banana, who is both a loyal servant and a soldier of the colonial regime, and a fairly independent military commander who tends to operate in the manner of the Somali warlords of the 90s. As we would expect with Farah, the play is open-ended. None of the conflicts or the questions raised during the play are really resolved; everything remains in a limbo of undecidedness and ambiguity.

Yussuf and his Brothers differs substantially from all the African plays that we have seen since the early 60s. There is nothing in the direction of "total theatre" or "integrated theatre," where music, dance, song, and mime are merged into a dynamic performance abounding with physical action. Farah's play is a *drame à thèse,* a theatre of ideas and verbal exchange, rather than a physical stage action. The play has a strong epic quality, but not in the sense of the Brechtian epic theatre with its *Verfremdungseffekt* that puts the spectator into a distanced position of rational reflection. Farah's play is epic in the sense that practically the entire plot remains unrepresented on stage. The plot action is not transformed into and presented as visible stage action; the events that constitute something like a plot-line are recorded in the dialogues between Yussuf and the various other characters. They are always presented in the epic praeteritum as a dialogical exchange between two figures on what had happened beyond the stage space and beyond the time of dramatic representation on stage. The dialogic partners whom the spectators see on the stage always refer to the events that happened elsewhere at another time. Cutting the continuity of narration into short "takes" of Yussuf dialoguing consecutively with other characters, reveals splintered scraps of information only. Farah deliberately interrupts dramatic continuity, fragmenting the plot- line and providing practically no clues on how the fragments could be pieced together, or be assembled in a unifying structure that generates and conveys "meaning." Farah's *Verfremdungseffekt* builds on continually emphasising the distance and difference between the stage action in the theatre space and the recorded dramatic action of the play. He points to the difference between the characters seen on the stage dialoguing and the implied dramatic plot that consists of the events which the characters are talking about. This distancing between the presentation on stage and what this presentation re-presents in political and dramatic terms, is where we experience the typical Farah effect of mystification. The plays and the prose writings seem to concentrate on the construction of a patterned system of enigmas.

706

NOTES

1. Jacqueline Bardolph, "*Yussuf and his Brothers* by Nuruddin Farah," *Commonwealth* 7, 1 (1984), 57-70.

2. Patricia Alden and Louis Tremaine, *Nuruddin Farah* (New York: Twayne, 1999), pp.60-64.

3. The plays by Farah discussed in this essay are: *A Spread of Butter* (BBC Radio, African Service, 24 December 1978; German translation Saarlaendischer Rundfunk SR, 16 October 1984; based on a stage version titled *The Offering*, produced at the University of Essex, 1976); *Tartar Delight* (submitted to BBC Radio, 1984); and the stage play *Yussuf and his Brothers* (premiered at the University of Jos, Nigeria, 2-4 July 1982).

4. Thomas Mann, *Freud und die Zukunft*, 1936.

ALL OUR TOMORROWS:
Farah's Refugee Book
Derek Wright

W hat causes Africa's only culturally and linguistically homogeneous nation to collapse into a madness that has made its name a byword for man-made famine, anarchy, and mindless carnage? In *Yesterday, Tomorrow: Voices from the Somali Diaspora* Nuruddin Farah does not attempt to identify ultimate causes. The Somali refugees whom he interviewed in Kenya, Italy, Britain, Switzerland and Sweden between 1991 and 1998 do, however, point accusatory fingers in a number of directions.

The gangsterism of the warlords, says a doctor now working in a Florence hospital, represents the Somalis' loss of touch with the moral tenets of age-old kinship and lineage traditions, while an ex-film documentarist in a Mombasa camp attributes it to the political perversion of justice along the same inveterately tribal lines. A Swedish-based Somali scholar traces the terror to the Somali people's failure to unite against a humiliating dictatorship. Less abstractly, a former public servant and female relative of Aideed, encountered in Mombasa, places the blame on "Siyad's children," a dictatorship-generated subproletariat of illiterate layabouts and vicious street urchins who swelled the ranks of the militias. One such Swiss-bound ex-*Muuryaan* (armed thug), whose professed crimes include the rape of a five-year-old girl, puts his derangements down to a mind-bending mix of drink, dope and *qaat* fed to him by Aideed's militia and its induction of a robotic state beyond fear and morality. One of his typical victims, a former science lecturer who was tortured by enemy clan vigilantes and made to witness the rape of his wife and daughters, traces the catastrophe to ignorance of the nation's history, Mogadiscio's cowboy film culture, and the demonic avarice of neighbors and colleagues (a sometime bodyguard of the dictator admits that he switched to the service of a warlord-cousin to increase his supply of loot and fled only when losing out to bigger looters with better guns).

A former high school principal, now a housemaid, explains that Somalia is in a mess for the same reason as her Milan apartment, where her shiftless brothers and male cousins sponge on her bread-winning labor and, without lifting a finger to cook, clean or earn, are maintained in the style to which they were accustomed back home: What is at fault is a tradition that keeps women minors all their lives while glorifying boys as men from an early age, thus sanctioning self-righteous indolence, gunslinging irresponsibility, and petulant egomania (her septuagenarian father back in Somalia expects her to fund his "irrational lust" for an extra, teenage wife).

But the refugees do not hold Somalia solely responsible for its ruin. The inmates of the Mombasa camp, where the author is briefly reunited with his own father and sister, implicate foreign elements, including Kenyan business men and even Sudanese peace delegations, in the plundering and auctioning off of the capital's treasures (gold statues are melted down in return for supplies of arms). Then, in an authorial interlude, Farah turns the spotlight on Europe's sudden loss of interest in the colonies once looted by itself and its tendency to barricade itself against their refugees and blame them for its own socio-economic ills, just as they, during the post-independ-

710

ence period, continue to blame Europe for theirs.

Almost everyone, at some time, mentions the clans and the destruction of political infrastructures and social justice by Barre's feudal nepotism—a Machiavellian system which, according to a British-based former civil engineer, was so expertly managed that the militia groups which overthrew him directed their retaliatory action not against his tyranny but against unarmed civilians of other clans. Yet Farah is at pains throughout his book to challenge both the mistaken opinion (and convenient United Nations myth) that the civil war was an organized conflict between two major confederal clan families and the hold-all, wrap-around concept of clan loyalty as the evil common denominator and explicator of all actions. In the general mayhem of a nation in anarchy it is not long before the "undefined violences" become indistinguishable, as do good and evil, innocence and sin, and, as the sole survivor of a family massacre puts it, "life and death, truth and falsehood."[1] "Civil wars," adds the film documentarist, "do not wait for reasons" (p.45) and none are given by Farah's book. Most of its interviewees do not trace causes or seek out explanations; rather, they assign blame. The Somalis—runs the gist of Farah's Epilogue—are a nation of "blamocrats." For the mess to which all have contributed their fair share, they blame the dictator, the failed fledgling democracy, or the warlords whose sole desire is for power, if only over the rubble of a country that no longer exists. The Mahdists blame the Aideeists, who in turn blame the Americans, who blame the starving Somalis for shooting at them. The individual blames the nation, the nation its leaders, the leaders their followers, and this general shying away from personal responsibility, this inability of individuals to place themselves in the territory of the collective collapse, is a testament to the collective failure. In a blamocracy each group disavows itself of the havoc wreaked in its name, the favorite target for the buck in this case being the clan. As a Gothenburg refugee puts it, "we were not Somalis when we were in Somalia," only members of a clan family (p.190). Through generic references to clan identities and the attribution of failure to the working of clan structures, individual personalities and actions are subsumed into the larger unit and escape censure: the self is never to blame.

This history of evaded responsibility is borne out by the individual testimony of some of the refugees. An ex-academic in Naples describes his countrymen as "egregiously unrepentant" and the manager of a Kenyan hotel accommodating wealthy Somali refugees is shocked to discover that a people who have brought chaos down on their heads "do not appear to have been humbled by the experience in any way" (p.33). In the place of breast-beating and soul-searching, and in the absence of any self-analysis, there is only the crass self-importance of "a nobility in exile" and the proud blazoning of racial identity which, for the hotelier, constitute "an attitude problem towards other Africans" (p.32). The principal-turned-housemaid remarks that her pampered brothers and cousins show no regrets and refuse to admit to any wrongs or to the utter failure of their lives. Everyone blames someone else: at the multi-national Gersau refuge in Switzerland it is only the Somalis who, because of the rancours and rivalries within their rank and file, fail to set up a community centre for their people. Farah observes, during his Kenyan sojourn, that Somalis seen huddling together "speaking in conspiratorial whispers" would, at the next encounter, be "sworn enemies, shunning one another like needles" (p.37).

In the Mombasa refugee camp Farah's father explains that "we fled because we met the beasts in us, face to face" (p.3). His son, an exile who has never been a refugee, is shocked by the venom of the inmates' clan hatreds and insists that he belongs "neither to *us* nor to *them*," but the aim of his book is to seek out the "us" in the "them," so that all accept and bear their share of the blame for the collective disaster. A recent arrival, fresh from the horrors of Mogadiscio, observes that in a city where virtually every family has a relative in one of the armed gangs, no one enjoys immunity from or innocence of the prevailing thuggery. A London refugee, smuggled out of the country by a brother-in-law vigilante who has murdered, tortured and raped, is so tormented by guilt and self-hatred that he cannot expunge the stench of unburied corpses from his hair and clothes. Farah admits in the Preface to his book that he himself was so "plagued with doubts, and...dismayed by the sorrow which has been of a piece with being a Somali" (p.viii) that he more than once almost abandoned the project in despair. Nevertheless, in the face of many obstacles, and never losing sight of the suffering of innocents in the midst of collective guilt, he forces himself to remain loyal to the idea of imposing order on the years of misrule and anarchy that have shattered his nation and scattered his family (his father died in the Mombasa camp and siblings have been dispersed to Canada, Ethiopia, Holland, and the United States).

During his many arduous travels to gather material for the book, Farah repeatedly—in an unflagging spirit of solidarity with the refugees—puts himself through the harassments and humiliations endured by them at the hands of immigration, embassy, camp and UN Refugee Commission officials. Thus the refuges receive as much attention in his narrative as the refugees and they fare no better, offering in some cases only a choice of horrors. In Milan he is informed by a biochemistry-professor-turned "carrier" (people smuggler) that Somalis routinely flee persecution by both officials and citizens in their first (African) country of asylum. In the "halfway house" of Kenya they face daily extortion at the hands of immigration officers, while in Yemen they are beaten up and raped by the locals and robbed by the police. That the Somalis are no safer in these places than in Mogadiscio is ignored by European immigration authorities who heartlessly invoke the letter of the Geneva Convention on first-country asylum: "He is a refugee all right...but not *our* refugee" (p.146). The peculiarly Swiss Catch-22 is to refuse asylum on the grounds that the Somalis cannot prove persecution or torture by their government because there *is* no government, and then to regard them as "safe" in the area which, in lieu of a government, is deemed to be controlled by their clan militia (for official purposes, mere anarchy gives way to the fiction of the clearly-delineated clan war). In Sweden the refugees are housed in isolated, noisy, overcrowded camps where they are prey to arson attacks, shootings and the campaign of a racist serial killer, and where, in a period of economic crisis and cultural exclusivism, they become the focus of a once-welcoming country's growing distaste for its relationship with Africa.

Somalis, Farah observes in his Epilogue, are locked in "a dialogue with a tomorrow that is ensconced in a yesterday" (p.192), and it is in this dialogue, in which both "yesterday" and "tomorrow" have become equally unreal, that the novelist finds aspects of the refugee trauma in his own exiled condition. The country of the imagination, the yesterday-world long dwelled in by the itinerant literary exile— more a working hypothesis than a real place—becomes also the mental domicile of the displaced fugitive. But what happens when, as a result of tumultuous upheavals like the Somali holocaust, the home country ceases to exist, either as an idea or as a physical reality? What happens to a people for whom there is neither a hypothetical home nor an actual residence to return to? While the writer has grown accustomed, over a twenty-five year period, to handling imaginatively the depressions and neuroses of exile and making them feed his creativity, the refugees are plunged into a radically altered state in which they become "other" to themselves and cannot reconcile themselves to their new self-images or their host country's perception of them. If the refugee ever gets to return home it will be, as the cineaste languishing in the Mombasa camp points out, to somewhere that has changed beyond recognition, while he himself will have become another person altogether.

This malaise is the mental condition of most of the refugees in Farah's book. A few thrive and make good in their new lives in other parts of the world (the women are the most adaptable and resourceful), but the majority fail to cope with their disorientation and estrangement or with the occupational displacements that reinforce the geographical ones (lieutenant-colonels and teachers become factory laborers and dockers). Many are irreparably wounded and marked for life by their experiences, both in their own and in other people's minds. Some lead lives of unending anxiety and depression, others of hopeless, abject misery.

Farah has much to say about the peculiarities of the volatile national temperament and he insists on holding Somalis—not excluding himself— collectively accountable for the death of their country, but he does not single them out as a special case and leaves no loopholes for complacency. The presence in the Mombasa camp of the former director of a Somali refugee camp, now himself a refugee, is a timely reminder that between 1981 and 1989 Somalia itself was host to one of Africa's largest-ever refugee influxes, its famine-struck Ethiopian "guests" accounting for more than a quarter of its population. The Kenyan camp director pauses to reflect, at his interviewer's prompting, that political turmoil in his own country could just as easily have led him to seek refuge in Somalia, reversing their situations. The final flourish of a century of pogrom and mass migration was, moreover, a traumatic decade of universal displacement—Rwanda, Bosnia, Kosovo, Chechniya, East Timor—in which the national and continental borders between the sources and the sanctuaries of refugees shifted unpredictably, resisting any idea of an African monopoly. Farah's courageous and unflinchingly honest book, sparing neither himself nor his subjects, helps us to understand not only Somalis but the experiences of all peoples, from all parts of the world, who are forced from their homelands to places where they have to begin life all over again. In their ordeals lie, potentially, all our destinies. Somalia's yesterday could be anyone's tomorrow.

NOTES

1. Nuruddin Farah, *Yesterday, Tomorrow: Voices from the Somali Diaspora* (London: Cassell, 2000), pp.9, 129, 152. Further references are given in parentheses in the text.

CHRONOLOGY

1945	Born 24th November in Baidoa in Italian-occupied part of Somalia.
1947	Family moves to Kallafo in the Ogaden, soon to be handed over by Britain to Ethiopia. Attends Qur'anic school.
1960	Somali independence from Britain and Italy.
1963	War in the Ogaden. Family moves to Mogadishu where Farah completes his secondary schooling.
1965	Publication of first story, "Why Dead So Soon?," in *Somali News*.
1966-69	Studies Literature and Philosophy at Punjab University, Chandigarh, India.
1969	Receives B.A. degree. Marries Chitra Muliyil, an Indian student in Delhi. Military coup in Somalia brings Siyad Barre to power. Farah returns to Somalia but is refused a government licence to produce his play *A Dagger in Vacuum*.
1969-73	Teaches at National University of Somalia and Dhagaxtur and Ward-higley Secondary Schools in Mogadishu.
1970	Publishes *From a Crooked Rib*. Birth of son, Koschin.
1972	First marriage ends. Somali language receives written orthography.
1973	Serialization of Farah's Somali-language novel in *Somali News* halted by government censors.
1974	Departs for England on UNESCO fellowship: start of 22-year absence from Somalia. Postgraduate in Theatre Studies at University of London, attached to Royal Court Theatre for eight months.
1975	Postgraduate studies continued at University of Essex. His play *The Offering*, written in lieu of M.A. thesis, produced at Essex.

1976   Leaves Essex without completing requirements for M.A. Drama degree. Publishes *A Naked Needle* which incurs the wrath of the Barre regime. While in transit in Rome in July he is warned by phone by his brother not to return to Somalia and remains in Italy.

1976-79 English-language teacher and translator in Rome and Milan.

1978   *A Spread of Butter* broadcast by BBC African Service.

1979   Publishes *Sweet and Sour Milk*. Moves to Los Angeles. Works on film scripts and is Visiting Scholar at African Studies Center, UCLA.

1980   English-Speaking Union Literary Award for *Sweet and Sour Milk*.

1981   Publishes *Sardines*. Six months as Guest Professor in Department of Comparative Literature at University of Bayreuth, West Germany. Moves to Jos, Nigeria.

1982   Visiting Reader at University of Jos where his play *Yussuf and His Brothers* is written and produced.

1983   Publishes *Close Sesame*.

1984   Moves to the Gambia.

1986   Publishes *Maps*. Moves to Khartoum, Sudan. Teaches at University of Khartoum.

1989   Moves to Kampala, Uganda.

1990   First publication of *Gifts* in Swedish (as *Gåvor*) in Stockholm. Teaches at Makerere University. Meets Amina Mama, Nigerian sociology professor. Mother dies in Mogadishu.

1991   Resigns position at Makerere after criticism by Ugandan President and moves to Ethiopia. Receives Tucholsky Literary Award in Stockholm. Gives lectures in Oxford on plight of Somali refugees. Brief reunion with father in Kenyan refugee camp. Siyad Barre falls from power in Somalia.

1992   *Gifts* published in English. Marries Amina Mama in July and moves to Kaduna, Nigeria.

1993   *Gifts* wins Best Novel Award in Zimbabwe. Father dies in Mombasa, Kenya. Birth of daughter, Abyan.

1994   Awarded Premio Cavour for Italian edition of *Close Sesame*.

1995   Birth of son, Kaahiye. Siyad Barre dies in exile in Abuja, Nigeria.

1996   Return visit to Somalia after 22 years in exile.

1998   Publication of *Secrets*. Wins Neustadt International Prize for Literature. French edition of *Gifts* wins St Malo Literary Festival award.

1999   Moves to Cape Town, South Africa.

2000   Publishes *Yesterday, Tomorrow: Voices from the Somali Diaspora*.

BIBLIOGRAPHY

I. Primary Works

NOVELS

From A Crooked Rib. London: Heinemann, 1970.

A Naked Needle. London: Heinemann, 1976.

Sweet and Sour Milk. London: Allison & Busby, 1979; London: Heinemann, 1980; Saint Paul, Minnesota: Graywolf Press, 1992.

Sardines. London: Allison & Busby, 1981; London: Heinemann, 1982; Saint Paul, Minnesota: Graywolf Press, 1992.

Close Sesame. London: Allison & Busby, 1983; Saint Paul, Minnesota: Graywolf Press, 1992.

Maps. London: Picador; New York: Pantheon, 1986.

Gifts. Harare: Baobab Books; London: Serif Publishers, 1992.

Secrets. New York: Arcade, 1998.

STORY

"Why Dead So Soon?" Mogadishu: Somali News, 1965.

PLAY

The Offering. Lotus (Afro-Asian Writings) 30, 4 (1976), 77-93.

Produced at University of Essex, 1975.

OTHER WORKS

Yesterday, Tomorrow: Voices from the Somali Diaspora. London: Cassell, 2000.

ESSAYS

"Do You Speak German?" *Okike* 22 (1982), 33-38.

"Do Fences Have Sides?" *The Commonwealth in Canada: Proceedings of the Second Triennial Conference of CACLALS, Part Two*, ed. Uma Parameswaran (Conference held at University of Winnepeg, 1-4 October 1981). Calcutta: Writers' Workshop, 1983, pp.174-82.

"The Creative Writer and the African Politician." *Nigerian Guardian* 7 September 1983: 11; *Classic* 1 (1984), 27-30.

"The Life and Death of Words." *South* (April 1984), 54.

"A Tale of Tyranny" (review of Chinua Achebe's *Anthills of the Savannah*). *West Africa* 21 September 1987, 1828-31.

"Why I Write." *Third World Quarterly* 10, 4 (1988), 1591-99.

"In Praise of Exile." *Third World Affairs* (1988), 181-82. Reprinted in *Literature in Exile*, ed. John Glad. Durham, N.C.: Duke University Press, 1990, pp.64-67.

"Teutonic Aggro." *West Africa* 7-13 August 1989, 1292.

"Haunted Beauty of the New Uganda." *Weekend Guardian* 21-22 October 1989, 5.

"Childhood of My Schizophrenia." *Times Literary Supplement* 23-29 November 1990, 1264.

"The World as a Writer's Home." *African Commentary* 2, 1-2 (1990), 57-58.

"Fear is a Goat." *The Guardian* (Lagos) 1 June 1990, 9.

"A Country in Exile." *Transition* 57 (1992), 4-8. Reprinted in *World Literature Today* 72, 4 (1998), 713-15.

"Savaging the Soul of a Nation." *In These Times* 28 December 1992, 14-17.

"Praise the Marines? I Suppose So." *New York Times* 28 December 1992, A15.

"Homing in on the Pigeon." *Index on Censorship* 22, 5-6 (1993), 16-20. Reprinted as "Bastards of Empire: Writing and the Politics of Exile." *Transition* 5, 1 (1995), 26-35.

"False Accounting." *Granta* 49 (1994), 171-81.

"Travellers' Tales." *Observer Magazine* 27 February 1994, 44.

"People of a Half-Way House." *London Review of Books* 21 March 1996, 19-20.

"The Women of Kismayo: Power and Protest in Somalia." *Times Literary Supplement* 15 November 1996, 18.

"My Father, the Englishman, and I." *Under African Skies*, ed. Charles Larson. New York: Farrar Straus Giroux, 1997, pp.288-92.

"Country Cousins." *London Review of Books* 3 September 1998, 19-20.

"Celebrating Differences: The 1998 Neustadt Lecture." *World Literature Today* 72, 4 (1998), 709-12.

INTERVIEWS

Anon. "Nuruddin Farah—Committed Writer." *New African* (January 1979), 85.

Anon. "Close Sesame: The End of a Trilogy." *Africa Now* (December 1983), 82-83.

Anon. "Just Talking: Chinua Achebe and Nuruddin Farah." *Artrage* 14 (Autumn 1986), 4-8.

Aiyejina, Funso, and Bob Fox. "Nuruddin Farah in Conversation with Funso Aiyejina and Bob Fox." *Ife Studies in African Literature and the Arts* 2 2 (1984), 24-37.

Caulker, Elaine. "Interview with Nuruddin Farah about his Writing." *BBC Arts and Africa* radio transcript 47 (1974), 3-4.

Fox, Robert Elliot. "Art Personality: Nuruddin Farah." *Daily Times* 19 August 1989, 12; 2 September 1989, 10; 9 September 1989, 10-11; 16 September 1989, 15. Reprinted in *Masters of the Drum: Black Literatures Across the Curriculum*, ed. Robert Elliot Fox. Westport, CT: Greenwood Press, 1995, pp.157-70.

Frederikse, Julie. "Interview with Nuruddin Farah." *BBC Arts and Africa* radio transcript 506 (1983), 1-5.

Gray, Stephen. "Nuruddin Farah: The Novelist and the Nomad." *Publishers Weekly* 23 August 1999, 28-29.

—————. "The 'Mover-About.'" *Mail & Guardian* (Johannesburg), 27 August-2 September 1999, 31.

Imfeld, Al. "Nuruddin Farah." *African Writers On the Air.* Cologne: DW Dokumente, Deutschlandfunk Dokumentation & Archive, 1983-84, pp.112-19.

Jaggi, Maya. "Bitter Crumbs, Sweet and Sour Milk." *Guardian* (London) 3 April 1993, 29

—————. "A Combining of Gifts: An Interview." *Third World Quarterly* 11, 3 (1989), 171-87.

Jonas, Maggie. "Living in a Country of the Mind." *New African* (December 1987), 60-61.

Jussawalla, Feroza and Reed Way Dasenbrock. *Interviews with Writers of the Post-colonial World.* Jackson: University Press of Mississippi, 1992, pp.42-62.

Kitchener, Julie. "Author in Search of an Identity." *New African* (December 1981), 61.

Lampley, James. "A View of Home from the Outside." *Africa* (December 1981), 81-82.

Langille, Mary. "Coming Out of Oral Tradition to Write about Dictatorship." *The Varsity* (University of Toronto) 26 November 1987, S7.

Marioghae, Veno and Gloria Anozie. "Nuruddin Farah: Nomad par Excellence." *Classique* (Lagos) 26 March 1990, 38.

Marshall, Julian. "Interview with Nuruddin Farah about his play *The Offering.*" *BBC Arts and Africa* radio transcript 109 (1976), 4-5.

Momodu, Dele. "Farah's Gains in Exile." *Weekend Concord* (Lagos) 12 August 1989, 6. Reprinted *Weekend Concord* (Lagos) 19 December 1992, 2.

Morris, Patricia. "Interview: Nuruddin Farah in London." *African Concord* 24 April 1986, 40.

—————. "Wretched Life." *Africa Events* (September 1986), 54-55.

Moss, Robert. "Mapping the Psyche." *West Africa* 1 September 1986, 1827-28.

Nazareth, H.O. "In the Land of the General." *City Limits* 11 November 1983.

Nucci, Giovanni. "Somalia, dittature e braciole di maiale: Saggio—intervista sulla letteratura di Nuruddin Farah." *Africa e Mediterraneo* 19 (1996), 77- 79.

Okezie, Emmanuel. "The Novel Form is not African: Nuruddin Farah Speaks on Writing in Africa in a Common Language." *This Week* 13 October 1986, 39.

Pajalich, Armando. "Nuruddin Farah Interviewed by Armando Pajalich." *Kunapipi* 15, 1 (1993), 61-71.

Presson, Rebekah. "Nuruddin Farah." *New Letters on the Air.* Kansas City: University of Missouri, 1993 (tape cassette).

Ryle, John. "Writer Against the Warlords." *Mail & Guardian* (Johannesburg) 14 June 1996, 38.

Smith, Martha. "Marty's People: Nuruddin Farah." *Providence Journal Sunday Magazine* (Providence, Rhode Island) 3 November 1991.

Sweetman, David. "Interview with Nuruddin Farah." *BBC Arts and Africa* radio transcript 355 (1980), 1-6.

Tetteh-Lartey, Alex. "Interview with Nuruddin Farah about BBC Somali Short Competition he adjudicated." *BBC Arts and Africa* radio transcript 67 (1975), 1-3.

——————. "Interview with Nuruddin Farah." *BBC Arts and Africa* radio transcript 100 (1975), 1-6.

——————. "Interview with Nuruddin Farah about *Sweet and Sour Milk.*" *BBC Arts and Africa* radio transcript 305 (1979), 1-5.

——————. "Interview with Nuruddin Farah about his Trilogy of Novels, especially *Close Sesame.*" *BBC Arts and Africa* radio transcript 519 (1983), 3-5.

Vaughan, P. & R.Wells. "Kaleidoscope." *BBC Arts and Africa* radio discussion of Farah's works, especially *Maps.* Radio transcript, 13 March 1986, 5-7.

Versi, Anver. "Farah—A Complex Simplicity." *New African* (November 1991), 47-48.

Vincent, Theo. "Nuruddin Farah, Somalia." *Seventeen Black And African Writers on Literature and Life*, ed. Theo Vincent. Lagos: Centre for Black and African Arts and Civilization, 1981, pp.46-53.

Vivan, Itala. "Letteratura Somala: Anatomia di una dittatura." *Nigrizia* (December 1984), 42-43.

Williams, Trish. "My Country in Mind." *BBC World Service* broadcast, 13-14 March 1986.

UNPUBLISHED WORKS

A Man in the Hand (novel), 1966.

To Make a Deal (novel), 1967.

Doctor and Physicist (revue), broadcast by Indian radio, 1968.

A Dagger in Vaccuum (play), broadcast by German radio, 1969.

Tolow Waa Talee Ma (extract from novel in Somali), printed in *Somali News*, Mogadiscio, 1973; serial publication censored and discontinued.

A Spread of Butter (play), broadcast by BBC African Service, 24 December 1978.

Yussuf and His Brothers (play), produced at University of Jos, Nigeria, 2-4 July 1982.

Tartar Delight (play), 1984

II. Secondary Works

BOOKS, ESSAYS & REVIEWS

Adam, Ian. "Aesthetically Radical Fiction" (review of *Sardines*). *CRNLE Reviews Journal* 1 (1983), 91-93.

—————. "Nuruddin Farah and James Joyce: Some Issues of Intertextuality." *World Literature Written in English* 24, 1 (1984), 34-42.

—————. Review of *Close Sesame*. *World Literature Written in English* 24, 2 (1984), 250-52.

—————. "The Murder of Soyaan Keynaan." *World Literature Written in English* 26, 2 (1986), 203-11.

Abdi, Abdel. "The 'secrets' of a forgotten people." (review of *Secrets*) *Washington Times* 26 July 1998, B7.

Ahmed, Ali Jimale. "Farah and the (Re)Writing of Somali Historiography: Narrative as a Politically Symbolic Act." *Daybreak is Near: Literature, Clans, and the Nation-State in Somalia*. Lawrenceville, NJ: Red Sea Press, 1996, pp.75-99.

Alden, Patricia. "Mapping the Personal and the Political: The Child-Geographer in Nuruddin Farah's *Maps*." *African Literature 1988: New Masks*. eds. Hal Wylie, Dennis Brutus, and Juris Silenieks. Washington, D.C.: Three Continents Press, 1990, pp.119-24.

—————. "New Women and Old Myths: Chinua Achebe's *Anthills of the Savannah* and Nuruddin Farah's *Sardines*." *Matatu* 8 (1991), 67-80.

Alden, Patricia and Louis Tremaine. "Reinventing Family in the Second Trilogy of Nuruddin Farah." *World Literature Today* 72, 4 (1998), 759-66.

——————. *Nuruddin Farah*. New York: Twayne, 1999.

Alidou, Ousseina and Alamin Mazrui. "*Secrets*: Farah's 'Things Fall Apart.'" *Research in African Literatures* 31, 1 (2000), 122-28.

Alrawi, Karim. "Nuruddin Farah: Webs of Intrigue." *New African* (June 1987), 12-13.

Appiah, Kwame Anthony. "For Nuruddin Farah." *World Literature Today* 72, 4 (1998), 703-05.

Balogun, Francoise. "Promenade a travers les romans de Nuruddin Farah." *Presence Africaine* 145 (1988), 157-64.

Bardolph, Jacqueline. "Women and Metaphors in Nuruddin Farah's *Sweet and Sour Milk* and *Sardines*." *Proceedings of the Second International Conference of Somali Studies 1-6 August 1983*, ed. Thomas Labahn. Hamburg: Buske, 1984, pp.429-45.

——————. "Yussuf and His Brothers by Nuruddin Farah." *Commonwealth: Essays and Studies* 7, 1 (1984), 57-70.

——————. "Un cas singulier: Nuruddin Farah, ecrivain somali." *Notre Librairie* 85 (1986), 61-64.

——————. "L'evolution de l'ecriture dans la trilogie de Nuruddin Farah: Variations sur le theme d'une dictature africaine." *Nouvelles du Sud* 6-7 (1986-87), 79-91.

——————. "*Maps* de Nuruddin Farah et l'Identite Somalie." *Bulletin des Etudes Africaines de l'INALCO* 7, 13-14 (1987), 249-66.

—————. "The Literary Treatment of History in Nuruddin Farah's *Close Sesame*." *Proceedings of the Third International Congress of Somali Studies*. ed. Annarita Puglielli. Rome: Il Pensiero Scientifico Editore, 1988, pp.133-38.

—————. "Time and History in Nuruddin Farah's *Close Sesame*." *Journal of Commonwealth Literature* 24, 1 (1989), 193-206.

—————. "Nuruddin Farah: L'ecriture du nomade." *Politique Africaine* 35 (1989), 121-26.

—————. "Ideologie et fiction chez Ngugi Wa Thiong'o et Nuruddin Farah." *Notre Librairie* 98 (1989), 88-92.

—————. "Azaro, Saleem and Askar: Brothers in Allegory." *Commonwealth: Essays and Studies* 15, 1 (1992), 45-51.

—————. "Nuruddin Farah." *Dictionary of Literary Biography: Twentieth Century Caribbean & Black African Writers*, Vol.123. eds. Bernth Lindfors & Reinhard Sander. Detroit: Gale Research, 1993, pp.35-40.

—————. "Dreams and Identity in the Novels of Nuruddin Farah." *Research in African Literatures* 29, 1 (1998), 163-73.

—————. "Brothers and Sisters in Nuruddin Farah's Two Trilogies." *World Literature Today* 72, 4 (1998), 729-732.

—————. "On Nuruddin Farah." *Research in African Literatures* 31, 1 (2000), 119-21.

Beer, David. "Aspects of Somali Literature in European Languages." *Horn of Africa* 2, 4 (1979), 27-35; reprinted as "Somalia" in *European Language Writing in Sub-Saharan Africa, Vol.2.* ed. Albert Gerard. Budapest: Akademiai Kiado, 1986, pp.999-1010.

——————. "Nuruddin Farah." *Encyclopedia of World Literature in the Twentieth Century.* ed. Leonard S.Klein. New York: Frederick Ungar, 1982, pp.76- 77.

Breitinger, Eckhard. "Experiments in the Novel Form: Soyinka, Farah, Ngugi, Fugard." *Studies in Commonwealth Literature: Papers Presented at the Commonwealth Literature & Language Conference at Bayreuth University, June 16-19, 1983.* eds. Eckhard Breitinger & Reinhard Sander. Tubingen: Gunter Narr, 1985, pp.95-104.

Bulham, Hussein A. Review of *Maps. Africa Events* (July 1987), 78-79.

Calder, Angus. "Sweet and Sour" (review of *Sweet and Sour Milk*). *The Literary Review* 8-21 March 1980, 13.

——————. "Nachbemerkung." Nuruddin Farah, *Aus Einer Rippe Gebaut (From A Crooked Rib).* Translated by Gunter Bohnke. Bonnheim-Merten: Lamuv, 1986, pp.134-38.

Cobham, Rhonda. "Boundaries of the Nation, Boundaries of the Self: African Nationalist Fictions and Nuruddin Farah's *Maps*." *Research in African Literatures* 22, 2 (1991), 83-98. Reprinted in expanded form as "Misgendering the Nation: African Nationalist Fictions and Nuruddin Farah's *Maps*" in *Nationalisms and Sexualities.* ed. Andrew Parker. New York: Routledge, 1992, pp.42-59.

Cochrane, Judith. "The Theme of Sacrifice in the Novels of Nuruddin Farah." *World Literature Written in English* 18 (1979), 69-77.

Colmer, Rosemary. "Nuruddin Farah: Territories of Pain." *International Literature in English*. ed. Robert Ross. New York: Garland, 1991, pp.131-42.

Crace, Jim. "Drowning in Style" (review of *Close Sesame*). *South* 50 (April 1984).

Dasenbrock, Reed Way. Review of *Close Sesame*. *World Literature Today* 59, 1(1985), 147.

—————. "Creating a Past: Achebe, Naipaul, Soyinka, Farah." *Salmagundi* 68-69 (Fall/Winter 1985-86), 312-32.

Dietche, Julie Phelps. "Child of War: Askar in Nuruddin Farah's *Maps*." *Children and Literature in Africa*. eds. Chidi Ikonne, Emelia Oko, and Peter Onwudinjo. Ibadan: Heinemann, 1992, pp.199-214.

Durix, Jean-Pierre. "Through to Action" (review of *Close Sesame*). *Times Literary Supplement* 16 December 1983, 1413.

—————. "Nuruddin Farah ou l'enigme de la liberte." *L'Afrique Litteraire et Artistique* 67 (1983, 175-89.

Eldridge, Michael. "Out of the Closet." *World Literature Today* 72, 4 (1998), 767-74.

—————. "Remapping the Motherland: *Maps*." *Third World Quarterly* 10, 4 (1988), 1628-31.

Ekwe, Herbert. "A Weekend of African Literature." *Nigerian Guardian* 17 August 1986, 88.

Ewen, D.R. Review of *Sweet and Sour Milk. World Literature Written in English* 20, 2 (1981), 221-24.

——————. "Nuruddin Farah." *The Writing of East and Central Africa*. ed. G.D. Killam. London: Heinemann, 1984, pp.192-210.

Garscha, Karsten & Dieter Riemenschneider, eds., *Afrikanischer Schriftsteller im Gesprach: Die Funktion Moderner Afrikanischer Literaturen*. Wuppertal: Hammer, 1983.

Gerard, Albert S. *African Language Literatures: An Introduction to the Literary History of Sub-Sahara Africa*. Washington, D.C.: Three Continents Press, 1981, pp.155-60.

Gikandi, Simon. "The Politics and Poetics of National Formation: Recent African Writing." *From Commonwealth to Post-Colonial*. ed. Anna Rutherford. Sydney: Dangaroo Press, 1992, pp.377-89.

——————. "Nuruddin Farah and Postcolonial Textuality." *World Literature Today* 72, 4 (1998), 753-58.

Gorlier, Claudio. "The Italian Dimension of Nuruddin Farah's Fiction." *Africa-America-Asia-Australia 2*. Rome: Bulzoni, 1986, pp.7-16. Revised and reprinted as "Nuruddin Farah's Italian Domain," *World Literature Today* 72, 4 (1998), 781-85.

Gray, Stephen. "The West's Ambivalent Gifts." (review of *Gifts*) *Weekly Mail & Guardian Supplements* 30 July-5 August 1993, 4.

——————. Review of *Gifts. London Magazine* June/July 1994, 156-58.

—————. "Family Secrets." (review of *Secrets*) *Worldview* 12, 1 (1999), 68-69.

Gugler, Josef. "African Commentary on Dictators: Wole Soyinka's Plays and Nuruddin Farah's Novels." *Journal of Modern African Studies* 26, 1 (1988), 171-77.

Gurnah, Abdulrazak. "Islam and Literature." *CRNLE Reviews Journal* 2 (1994), 71-76.

Hawley, John C. "Nuruddin Farah: Tribalism, Orality and Postcolonial Ultimate Reality and Meaning in Contemporary Somalia." *Ultimate Reality & Meaning* 19, 3 (1996), 189-205.

Herdeck, Donald E. "Nuruddin Farah." *African Authors: A Companion to Black African Writing Vol.1*. Washington, D.C.: Black Orpheus Press, 1973, p.137.

Hinde, Thomas. "The Walls of Dawn" (review of *Sardines*). *Sunday Telegraph* 29 November 1981.

Hope, Christopher. "Boundaries of Desire: *Maps* by Nuruddin Farah." *New York Times Book Review* 15 November 1987, 40.

Imfeld, Al & G.Meuer. "Nuruddin Farah: A Modern Nomad." *Afrika* 21, 9 (1980), 23-25.

Juraga, Dubravka. "Nuruddin Farah's *Variations on the Theme of an African Dictatorship*: Patriarchy, Gender and Political Oppression in Somalia." *Critique* 38 (1997), 205-20.

Kazan, Francesca. "Recalling the Other Third World: Nuruddin Farah's *Maps*."*Novel* 26 (Spring 1993), 253-67.

Kelly, Hilarie. "A Somali Tragedy of Political and Sexual Confusion: A Critical Analysis of Nuruddin Farah's *Maps.*" *Ufahamu* 16, 2 (1988), 21-37.

—————. "Commentary on Felix Mnthali 'Autocracy and the Limits of Identity.'" *Ufahamu* 17, 2 (1989), 70-73.

Kidwai, S.Ahmed. "The Two Novels of Nuruddin Farah." *Somalia and the World: Proceedings of International Symposium held in Mogadishu,October 15-21, 1979.* ed. Hussein M.Adam. Mogadishu: HALGAN, 1980, pp.191-201.

Kindred, Wendy. "Ethiopia and Somalia: Factions and Fiction." *Maine Scholar* 2 (1989), 47-54.

Kitchener, Julie. "Variations on a Theme" (review of *Close Sesame*). *New African* (December 1983), 52.

Larson, Charles. "Third World Writing in English." *World Literature Today* 57, 1 (1983), 58-59.

—————. "The Precarious State of the African Writer." *World Literature Today* 60, 3 (1986), 409-13.

Lessing, Doris. "Oppressors" (review of *Close Sesame*). *New Society* 10 November 1983.

Lewis, Peter, "Closing the Cave" (review of *Close Sesame*). *London Magazine* 23, 11 (February 1984), 101-05.

Lindfors, Bernth. "A Basic Anatomy of East African Literature." *Design and Intent in African Literature.* eds. David Dorsey, P.A.Egejunu and Stephen Arnold. Washington, D.C.: Three Continents Press, 1982, pp.51-57.

Lowe, Collean. "The Politician and the Writer Fuel Debate." *Kenya Times* 9 September 1983, 14.

Malcolmson, Scott L. "Family Plot." (review of *Secrets*) *New Yorker* 15 June 1998, 78-79.

Mazrui, Alamin. "Mapping Islam in Farah's *Maps*." *The Marabout and the Muse: New Approaches to Islam in African Literature*. ed. Kenneth W.Harrow. Portsmouth, NH: Heinemann; London: James Currey, 1996, 205-17.

Mbosowo, Mary D. "Rural-Urban Migration of Young African Women in Nuruddin Farah's *Née de la côte de Adam*." *Journal of African Children's and Youth Literature* 7-8 (1995-97), 51-63.

McDowell, Robert. "Nuruddin Farah." *African Writers* Vol.1. ed. C.Brian Cox. New York: Scribner's, 1997, pp.249-62.

McEwan, Neil. *Africa and the Novel*. Atlantic Highlands: Humanities Press; London: Macmillan, 1983, pp.117-21.

Miner, Valerie. "Sholoongo's Web." (review of *Secrets*) *Newsday* (New York) 3 May 1998, B14.

Mnthali, Felix. "Autocracy and the Limits of Identity: A Reading of the Novels of Nuruddin Farah." *Ufahamu* 17, 2 (1989), 53-69.

——————. "A Reply." *Ufahamu* 17, 2 (1989), 74.

Momodu, Dele. "Somalian Writer Nuruddin Farah Paints African Women in Colours of Gold." *National Concord* (Lagos) 5 December 1988, 5.

Moore, Gerald. "Personality and Heroism." (review of *Yussuf and His Brothers*) *West Africa* 16 August 1982, 2113.

——————. "Nomads and Feminists: The Novels of Nuruddin Farah." *International Fiction Review* 11, 1 (1984), 3-12.

Morris, Patricia. "The Politics of Language." *African Concord* 14 August 1986, 19-21.

Ngaboh-Smart, Francis. "Dimensions of Gift Giving in Nuruddin Farah's *Gifts*." *Research in African Literatures* 27, 4 (1996), 144-58.

——————. "*Secrets* and a New Civic Consciousness." *Research in African Literatures* 31, 1 (2000), 129-36.

Ngugi wa Thiong'o. "Nuruddin Farah: A Statement of Nomination." *World Literature Today* 72, 4 (1998), 716.

Ntalindwa, Raymond. "Colonialism and Dictatorship." *West Africa* 6 March 1995, 335-36.

"Nuruddin Farah." *Contemporary Literary Criticism*. eds. Daniel G.Marowski & Roger Matuz Detroit: Gale Research, 1989, pp.131-41.

"Nuruddin Farah." *A New Reader's Guide to African Literature*. eds. Hans Zell, Carol Bundy & Virginia Coulon. London: Heinemann, 1983, pp.386-88.

"Nuruddin Farah." *Black Literature Criticism*, vol.2. ed. James P.Draper. Detroit: Gale Research, 1992, pp.757-70.

Oboe, Annalisa. "Dall'esilio una voce." *Nigrizia* 110, 6 (1992), 64-66.

Oguibe, Olu. "Love in the City of Blood: Nuruddin Farah's *Gifts*." *Africa World Review* November 1993-April 1994, 37-38.

Okomilo, Ikhememho. "Power Game in Somalia" (review of *Sweet and Sour Milk*). *Africa* 101 (January 1980), 72-73.

Okonkwo, Juliet I. "The Art of Nuruddin Farah's Novels." *Nigerian Journal of the Humanities* 5-6 (1981-82), 32-39.

——————. "Nuruddin Farah and the Changing Roles of Women." *World Literature Today* 58, 2 (1984), 215-21.

——————. "Nuruddin Farah and the Politics of Somalia." *Présence Africaine* 132 (1984), 44-53. Reprinted as "Literature and Politics in Somalia: The Case of Nuruddin Farah." *Africa Today* 32, 3 (1985), 57-65.

——————. "Farah and the Individual's Quest for Self-Fulfilment." *Okike* 29 (1989), 66-74.

——————. "The Novelist as Artist: The Case of Nuruddin Farah." *Commonwealth Novel in English* 5, 1 (1992), 46-58.

Oriere, Oje. "Politicians and Artists: Mouse Cat Relationship." *Sunday Standard* (Nairobi) 10 November 1985, 11.

Packer, George. "Somali Shapeshifters." (review of *Secrets*) *New York Times Review* 19 July 1998, 11.

Pajalich, Armando. *Filiazioni e affiliazioni (nel testo periferico africano)*. Venice: Supernova, 1995.

Palmer. Eustace. "Two Views of Urban Life: Meja Mwangi, *Going Down River Road*; Nuruddin Farah, *A Naked Needle*." *African Literature Today* 9 (1978), 104-08.

Petersen, Kirsten Holst. "The Personal and the Political: The Case of Nuruddin Farah." *ARIEL* 12, 3 (1981), 93-101.

——————. "First Things Last: Problems of a Feminist Approach to African Literature." *Kunapipi* 6, 3 (1984), 35-47.

Phillips, Maggi. "The View from a Mosque of Words: Nuruddin Farah's *Close Sesame* and the *Holy Qu'ran*." *The Marabout and the Muse: New Approaches to Islam in African Literature.* Portsmouth, NH: Heinemann; London: James Currey, 1996, pp.191-204.

Pilling, Jane. Review of *Sardines. Time Out* 4 December 1981.

Pullin, Faith. Review of *Sardines. British Book News* (Spring 1982), 320.

Rathbun, David. "Telling 'Secrets.'" (review of *Secrets*) *Star Tribune* (Minneapolis), 5 July 1998, 14F.

Riesz, Janos. "Nuruddin Farah: Somalia's Literary Light." *World Press Review* (September 1981), 60.

——————. "Ein Kosmopolit aus Somalia: Das Werk des Schriftstellers Nuruddin Farah." *BAOBAB* 2 (1982), 14-21.

——————. "Nachwort" to Nuruddin Farah, *Wie Eine Nackte Nadel (A Naked Needle)*. Translated by Barbara Hillgen. Frankfurt: Lembeck, 1984, pp.322-27.

Riggan, William. "Nuruddin Farah's Indelible Country of the Imagination: The 1998 Neustadt International Prize for Literature." *World Literature Today* 72, 4 (1998), 701-02.

Ruggiero, Rossana. *Lo Specchio infranto: L'opera di Nuruddin Farah*. Pasian di Prato, Italy: Campanotto Editore, 1997.

Rushdie, Salman. "Nuruddin Farah." *Imaginary Homelands*. London: Granta, 1991, pp.201-02.

Said, A.N. Review of *Sweet and Sour Milk*. *Horn of Africa* 4, 3 (1981), 38-40.

Samater, Said S. "Are There Secrets in *Secrets*?" *Research in African Literatures* 31, 1 (2000), 137-43.

Shrapnell, Norman. "In a Hell of a State" (review of *Sardines*). *Guardian* (London), December 1981.

Sander, Reinhard. Review of *A Naked Needle*. *World Literature Today* 53, 4(1979).

Schraeder, Peter. "The Novels of Nuruddin Farah: The Socio-Political Evolution of a Somali Writer." *Northeast African Studies* 10, 2-3 (1988), 15-26.

Smith, Angela. "Nuruddin Farah." *Contemporary Novelists*. eds. D.L.Kirkpatrick & James Vinson. London & New York: St Martin's Press, 1986, pp.278-79.

——————. *East African Writing in English*. London: Macmillan, 1989, pp.27-41.

Sparrow, Fiona. "Telling the Story Yet Again: Oral Traditions in Nuruddin Farah's Fiction." *Journal of Commonwealth Literature* 24, 1 (1989),164-72.

Stratton, Florence. "The Novels of Nuruddin Farah." *World Literature Written in English* 25, 1 (1985), 16-30.

Sugnet, Charles. "Nuruddin Farah's *Maps*: Deterritorialization and 'The Post-Modern.'" *World Literature Today* 72, 4 (1998), 739-46.

Tate, Greg. "Bawdy Politic." *Voice Literary Supplement* (review of *Secrets*) 2 June 1998, 140.

Troughear, Tony. Review of *Sardines*. *Horn of Africa* 6, 1 (1983), 50-52.

Turfan, Barbara. "Opposing Dictatorship: A Comment on Nuruddin Farah's *Variations on the Theme of an African Dictatorship*." *Journal of Commonwealth Literature* 24, 1 (1989), 173-84.

Versi, Anver. "Farah's Mindscapes" (review of *Maps*). *New African* (May 1986), 65.

Vivan, Itala. "Chi e." *Nigrizia* (December 1984), 43.

—————. "Nuruddin Farah: il primo romanziere somalo." *Tessere per un mosaico africano*. Verona: Morelli Editore, 1984, pp.41-67.

—————. "Nuruddin Farah's Beautiful Mat and its Italian Plot." *Culture* (Milan) 9 (1994), 137-48. Reprinted in *A Talent(ed) Digger: Creations, Cameos, and Essays in Honour of Anna Rutherford*. eds. Hena Maes-Jelinek, Gordon Collier, and Geoffrey Davis. Amsterdam: Rodopi, 1996, pp.378-86; and in *World Literature Today* 72, 4 (1998), 786-90.

Waaberi, Cabdiraxmaan A. "Nuruddin Farah's *Gifts*: Webs of Intimacy." *Hal-Abuur* 1, 4 (1995), 44-46.

Waberi, Abdourahman A. "Organic Metaphor in Two Novels by Nuruddin Farah." *World Literature Today* 72, 4 (1998), 775-80.

Walmsley, Anne. "Nuruddin Farah and Somalia." *Index on Censorship* 10, 1-3 (1981), 17-19.

Whiteman, Kaye. "Of Imagery and Language." (review of *Gifts*) *West Africa* 6-12 September 1993, 1600.

Woolfson, Karen. "Writers in Conversation." *African Concord* 14 August 1986, 18-19.

Wright, Derek. "Requiems for Revolutions: Race-Sex Archetypes in Two African Novels." *Modern Fiction Studies* 35, 1 (1989), 55-68.

—————. "Parents and Power in Nuruddin Farah's *Dictatorship* Trilogy." *Kunapipi* 11, 2 (1989), 94-106.

—————. "Unwritable Realities: The Orality of Power in Nuruddin Farah's *Sweet and Sour Milk*." *Journal of Commonwealth Literature* 24, 1 (1989), 185-92.

—————. "Somali Powerscapes: Mapping Farah's Fiction." *Research in African Literatures* 21, 2 (1990), 21-34.

—————. "Zero Zones: Nuruddin Farah's Fiction." *ARIEL* 21, 2 (1990), 21-42.

—————. "Oligarchy and Orature in the Novels of Nuruddin Farah." *Studies in Twentieth Century Literature* 15, 1 (1991), 87-99.

—————. "Ethics and Ethnics in Nuruddin Farah's *Maps*." *New Researcher* 1 & 2 (1992), 104-11.

—————. "Parenting the Nation: Some Observations on

Nuruddin Farah's *Maps.*" *College Literature* 19, 3 (1992)/ 20, 1 (1993), 176-84. Reprinted in *Order and Partialities: Theory, Pedagogy and the Postcolonial.* eds. Kostas Myrsiades and Jerry McGuire. Albany: State University of New York Press, 1995, pp.377-389.

——————. "Fabling the Feminine in Nuruddin Farah's Novels." *Essays on African Writing: A Re-Evaluation.* ed. Abdulrazak Gurnah. Oxford: Heinemann, 1993, pp.70-87.

——————. "Nuruddin Farah." *Routledge Encyclopaedia of Post-Colonial Literature.* eds. Eugene Benson & G.W.Connolly. London: Routledge, 1993, pp.481-83.

——————. *The Novels of Nuruddin Farah.* Bayreuth: Bayreuth African Studies, Breitinger, 1994.

——————. "Going to Meet the General: Deeriye's Death in *Close Sesame.*" *Journal of Commonwealth Literature* 24, 2 (1994), 23-30.

——————. "Illness as Metaphor in Nuruddin Farah's Novels." *New Literatures Review* 30 (Winter 1995), 31-46.

——————. "Nations as Fictions: Postmodernism in the Novels of Nuruddin Farah." *Critique* 38, 2 (1997), 193-204.

——————. Review of *Gifts. International Fiction Review* 20, 2 (1993), 151-52.

——————. Review of *Gifts. World Literature Today* 68, 1 (1994), 195-96.

——————. "Orality and Dictatorship: Ngugi wa Thiong'o's *Matigari* and Nuruddin Farah's *Sweet and Sour Milk.*" *New*

Directions in African Fiction. New York: Twayne, 1997, pp.60-79.

—————. "Orature into Literature in Two East African Novelists." *Contemporary African Fiction*. ed. Derek Wright. Bayreuth: Bayreuth African Studies, Breitinger, 1994, pp.139-53.

—————. "History's Illuminated Prints: Negative Power in Nuruddin Farah's *Close Sesame*." *World Literature Today* 72, 4 (1998), 733-38.

—————. "Nuruddin Farah." *The Companion to African Literature in English*, eds. Douglas Killam & Ruth Rowe. London: James Currey; Bloomington: Indiana University Press, 2000, pp.95-96.

—————."The New Realism: Post-Independence Disillusionment in African Fiction." *The Cambridge History of African and Caribbean Literature*. ed. Abiola Irele. Cambridge: Cambridge University Press, 2002.

—————. "Nuruddin Farah." *Encyclopedia of Postcolonial Studies*, ed. John Hawley. Westport, CT: Greenwood Press, 2001, pp. 168-70

—————. Review of *Yesterday, Tomorrow: Voices from the Somali Diaspora. World Literature Today* 74, 3 (2000), pp. 574-75.

SELECTED THESES AND DISSERTATIONS

Ahmed, Ali Jimale. "Tradition, Anomaly and the Wave for the Future: Somali Oral Literature, Nuruddin Farah and Written Somali Prose Fiction." Ph.D., Queens College, City University of New York, 1990. *DAI* 50: 12 (1990): 3948A.

Gozzi, Claudio. "Variazioni sul tema di una dittatura africana: La trilogia di Nuruddin Farah." Ph.D., University of Verona, Italy, 1986.

Mixon, Gloria. "The Social and Political Status of Women in the Novels of Nuruddin Farah." M.A., University of Wisconsin, Madison, 1983.

Olagunji, John O. "The Role of Interior Monologue, Dialogue and Narrative in Selected Novels of Nuruddin Farah and Ayi Kwei Armah." M.A., University of Ibadan, Ibadan, Nigeria, 1985.

Oliver, Betty. "Patriarchy and Power: The Political Susceptibility of Islam in the Writing of Nuruddin Farah, with Particular Regard to the Position of Women." M.A., Northern Territory University, Darwin, Australia, 1992.

Phillips, Maggi. "Storytellers, Shamans and Clowns: Postcolonial Engagement with the Supra-Human in the Novels of R.K.Narayan, Nuruddin Farah, Bessie Head, Ben Okri and Salman Rushdie." Ph.D., Northern Territory University, Darwin, Australia, 1996.

NOTES ON CONTRIBUTORS

Ian Adam is a member of the English department at the University of Calgary, Canada. He has published widely on Post-Colonial literatures. From 1980 to 1990 he edited the journal *ARIEL: A Review of International English Literature*. In 1990 he edited (with Helen Tiffin) *Past the Last Post*, an exploration of postcolonialism's relations with postmodernism.

Ali Jimale Ahmed is Associate Professor in the Department of Comparative Literature at Queens College and at the Graduate Center of the City University of New York. He is the author of *Daybreak is Near: Literature, Clans and the Nation-State in Somalia* (1996) and has edited *The Invention of Somalia* (1995) and co-edited *Silence is Not Golden* (1995). He is also president of the Somali Studies Association of North America.

Patricia Alden is professor of English at St Lawrence University, where she is also on the faculty of the African Studies Program. She is the co-author, with Louis Tremaine, of *Nuruddin Farah* (1999) and the co-editor of *African Studies and the Undergraduate Curriculum* (1994). She currently writes on Zimbabwean literature.

Ousseina Alidou is Assistant Professor of African linguistics and literature in the Department of Africana Studies at Rutgers University. Her research focuses on gender and discourse and the politics of cultural production in Afro-Islamic societies. Her publications include *A Thousand Flowers: Students' Struggle for Education in Africa* (2000), co-edited with Silvia Federici and George Caffentzis.

Jacqueline Bardolph, who died in 1999, was Professor Emerita at the University of Nice, France. Her published works include *Le roman de langue anglaise en Afrique de l'est 1964-1976* (1981), *Ngugi wa*

747

Thiong'o, l'homme et l'oeuvre (1981), and many articles on postcolonial literatures. She edited *Oppression et expression dans le littérature et la cinéma: Afrique, Amérique, Asie* (1981), *Short Fiction in the New Literatures in English* (1989), and *Littérature et maladie en Afrique* (1991).

Eckhard Breitinger is the publisher of Bayreuth African Studies and is professor in the African Studies Institute at Bayreuth University. He has taught in the Caribbean and at several African universities and has published on African, Caribbean, American and African-American literatures, including American Radio Drama. He has translated plays and poems into German and has exhibited his theatre photographs in Africa, Europe and the United States.

Guillaume Cingal was born in 1974. A former member of the Ecole Normale Supérieure, Paris, he currently teaches English at the Université-de-Paris-10 and is working on a doctoral thesis. He has published articles on the South African poet Breyten Breytenbach as well as on Nuruddin Farah.

Rosemary Colmer is Senior Lecturer in English at Macquarie University, Sydney, where she teaches drama and post-colonial literature. Her publications include essays on Nuruddin Farah, Ayi Kwei Armah, and Alex La Guma in *International Literature in English* (1991) and *African Writers* (1997), and journal articles on Achebe, Armah, and Awoonor.

Reed Way Dasenbrock was educated at McGill, Oxford and Johns Hopkins Universities, receiving his Ph.D. from the latter in 1982. Since then he has taught at New Mexico State University, where he is now Professor of English and Associate Dean of the College of Arts and Sciences. He is the author or editor of eight books, including *Interviews with Writers of the Post-Colonial World* (1992), which included an interview with Nuruddin Farah.

748

Julie Phelps Dietche is Professor in the Department of English at the University of Wisconsin, Stevens Point. She has taught in the People's Republic of China and Burkina Faso, and worked as a teacher trainer in Senegal. Her publications include "Child of War: Askar in Nuruddin Farah's *Maps*," in *Calabar Studies in African Literature* (1992), and "Voyaging Toward Freedom: New Voices from South Africa" in *Research in African Literatures* (1995).

Michael Eldridge teaches literature and culture at Humboldt State University in Arcata, northern California. His essays and reviews have appeared in *Diaspora*, *Transition*, *World Literature Today*, the *Utne Reader*, and *In These Times*. He is currently at work on a book about Calypso fads, race, and American cultural identity.

Simon Gikandi is the Robert Hayden Professor of English Language and Literature at the University of Michigan, Ann Arbor. He was born in Kenya and educated at the Universities of Nairobi, Edinburgh, and Northwestern. His works include *Reading the African Novel* (1987), *Reading Chinua Achebe* (1991), *Writing in Limbo: Modernism and Caribbean Literature* (1992), and, most recently, *Maps of Englishness: Writing Identity in the Culture of Colonialism* (1996) and *Ngugi wa Thiong'o* (2000).

Claudio Gorlier is Professor of Literature in English at the University of Turin and has previously taught at the University of Venice, Bocconi University, Milan, and the University of Indiana. He has published books and essays in Italian on English, American and Commonwealth literatures, and has contributed essays in English to critical anthologies and to *World Literature Written in English*, *Research in African Literatures* and *World Literature Today*. He is co-editor of *Commonwealth Literary Cultures: New Voices, New Approaches* (1993).

Abdulrazak Gurnah was born in Zanzibar, Tanzania, and was educated there and in England. He is the author of five novels, including
Paradise, which was shortlisted for the 1994 Booker Prize, and, most
recently, *Admiring Silence* (1996). He has also edited two collections
of criticism, *Essays on African Writing 1 & 2* (1993, 1995). He teaches
literature at the University of Kent at Canterbury, England.

John C. Hawley, Associate Professor of English at Santa Clara
University, has edited seven books, including *Cross-Addressing:
Resistance Literature and Cultural Borders*; *Christian Encounters with
the Other*; and *The Postcolonial Crescent: Islam's Impact on
Contemporary Literature*. Forthcoming are *Divine Aporia* and the
Encyclopedia of Postcolonial Studies. His articles on Victorian and
African literatures have appeared in *Research in African Literatures*,
ARIEL, *The Literary Griot*, and elsewhere.

Dubravka Juraga has published essays on postcolonial, Russian and
East European literature. She is the co-author of *Bakhtin, Stalin and
Modern Russian Fiction: Carnival, Dialogism and History* and *The
Caribbean Novel in English: An Introduction*, and is currently editing a
collection of essays titled *Foundations of Modern Caribbean
Literature*. She teaches at the University of Arkansas.

Francesca Kazan teaches British Literature and Autobiography in
the English Department at the University of Alabama in Tuscaloosa,
dividing her time between there and London, where she was born
and raised. She has published academic essays on Charlotte Bronte,
Forster, Woolf, and Farah. These days she focuses on creative non-
fiction, which has been published in *The Gettysburg Review*.

Alamin Mazrui is Associate Professor in the Department of African
American and African Studies at Ohio State University, where he
teaches courses in linguistics and literature. He is author of five
books, including a play and an anthology of poetry in Swahili, and

(with Ali A.Mazrui) *The Power of Babel: Language and Governance in the African Experience* (1998).

Felix Mnthali is Professor of English at the University of Botswana. He has also taught at the University of Malawi and at the University of Ibadan. His poetry has appeared in anthologies in Africa, Europe, New Zealand, Canada, and the USA. He has also published a novel, a play, and critical essays on African literature.

Gerald Moore is the author of some of the earliest works in African and Caribbean literary studies, such as *Seven African Writers* (1962) and *The Chosen Tongue* (1969), as well as joint editor of the first major anthology of African poetry (Penguin, 1963). He has also published *Wole Soyinka* (1971; revised 1978), *Twelve African Writers* (1980), translations of novels by Mongo Beti and Henri Lopez, and the fourth edition of the Penguin Anthology of Modern African Poetry (1998). He has taught at Sussex University, in Hong Kong, and at various African universities, and is about to take up a research fellowship at the University of Texas. He lives in Italy with his wife and younger son.

Francis Ngaboh-Smart, a Sierra Leonian, is an assistant professor of English and postcolonial theory at the University of Wisconsin, Oshkosh. His articles on Nuruddin Farah and Kojo Laing have appeared in *Research in African Literatures* and *Connotations.*

Betty Oliver, born in London, lived for many years in Islamic countries in the Middle East and Africa. She holds degrees from Queensland and the Northern Territory Universities and wrote her M.A. thesis on the works of Nuruddin Farah. She has published stories, poems, and reviews. She and her husband now live on Queensland's Sunshine Coast.

Armando Pajalich is Associate Professor of New Literatures in

English at the University of Venice, Italy. He has published several books on African literatures in English and on British Modernism, many Italian translations of African classics (by Fugard, Cronin, Okigbo, and Soyinka), and six books of poetry and short stories.

Kirsten Holst Petersen is a graduate of Aarhus University, the School of Oriental and African Studies at the University of London, and Copenhagen University. She is currently Associate Professor at Roskilde University, Denmark. She is associate editor of *Kunapipi*, the international journal of postcolonial literature, and has published widely in the field of postcolonial studies, particularly in African literature, including *John Pepper Clark* (1981), *Criticism and Ideology* (edited, 1988), and numerous co-edited works.

Maggi Phillips lectures in Dance History and Contemporary Performance Theory as well as co-ordinating faculty research and the M.A. Creative Arts degree at the Western Australian Academy of Performing Arts at Edith Cowan University, Perth. She has published essays on Nuruddin Farah, Bessie Head, Ben Okri and other African authors in books and journals and has co-authored an article on dance in the Australian dance journal *Brolga*.

Rossana Ruggiero lectures in Italian language in the Faculty of Languages and Linguistics at the University of Malaya, Kuala Lumpur, and has contributed for many years to Adult Learning and Multiculturalism programs in Italian secondary schools. She has a Ph.D. in Postcolonial Literature and Culture and has published essays for the literary review *Africa America Asia Australia* and a book on Nuruddin Farah, *Lo specchio infranto: L'opera di Nuruddin Farah* (1997).

Peter J. Schraeder is Associate Professor in the Department of Political Science at Loyola University, Chicago, where he is a specialist in African politics and international relations. He is the author of

United States Foreign Policy Toward Africa: Incrementalism, Crisis and Change (1994) and *African Politics and Society: A Mosaic in Transformation* (2000). He is currently completing a book entitled *African Foreign Policy: The Impact of Democratization on Policy Formulation and Implementation.*

Florence Stratton teaches in the Department of English at the University of Regina, Canada. Her main areas of interest are African literature and Canadian literature. She is the author of *Contemporary African Literature and the Politics of Gender* (1994).

Charles Sugnet teaches literature and African cinema at the University of Minnesota in Minneapolis. His essays have appeared in *The Nation,* the *Utne Reader, The Village Voice, In These Times,* and *Transition.* His current research is on West African popular culture, including Senegalese music videos. He is co-editor, with Alan Burns, of *The Imagination on Trial.*

Louis Tremaine is associate professor of English and International Studies at the University of Richmond. He is the co-author, with Patricia Alden, of *Nuruddin Farah* (1999), has written on a number of African and African-American novelists, and is a translator of the work of the Algerian novelist Mohammed Dib.

Barbara Turfan has been the African Studies Librarian at the School of Oriental and African Studies, University of London, since 1984. Already a historian, she developed a stronger interest in African literature while studying for a Masters degree in African Area Studies.

Derek Wright, the editor of this volume, retired from academic life in 2000 after teaching for 30 years at colleges and universities in Britain, Africa, and Australia, most recently at the University of Queensland. He is the author of over a hundred articles on literatures in English and has published ten books, including *Ayi Kwei Armah's Africa: The*

Sources of His Fiction (1989); *Wole Soyinka Revisited* (1993); *The Novels of Nuruddin Farah* (1994); *New Directions in African Fiction* (1997); and *Contemporary African Fiction* (edited, 1997).

Farah with University of Oklahoma President (and former Oklahoma
Governor and U. S. Senator) David L. Boren, following Farah's Neustadt
lecture, University of Oklahoma, 29 October 1998
Photo by Gil Jain

Nuruddin Farah accepting the 1998 Neustadt International Prize for
Literature, University of Oklahoma, 29 October 1998
Photo by Robert H. Taylor

Nuruddin Farah, Wendy Keitner, Bruce Bennett, Marion Fraser, Diana Brydon,
Lorraine McMullen
Winnipeg, October 1981
Photo by Helen Tiffin

Glenda Adams, Pat Monk, Nuruddin Farah,
Winnipeg Airport, October 1981
Photo by Helen Tiffin

Farah at *Fruehjahrsbuchwoche*
Munich, 1993
Photo by Eckhard Breitinger

Farah with his wife, Amina Mama, following the Neustadt award ceremony
University of Oklahoma, 29 October 1998
Photo by Robert H. Taylor

Farah with the Neustadt Silver Eagle feather symbol of the Neustadt Prize
University of Oklahoma, 29 October 1998
Photo by Robert H. Taylor

Nuruddin Farah
Jos, 1983
Photo by Eckhard Breitinger

INDEX

Lewis, I.M. 149
Lloyd, David 529, 535, 539, 541
Lopes, Henri 290
Lukacs, Georg 377

M

Machiavelli 176, 337, 711
MacKinnon, Catharine 302, 307
Mad Mullah 408, 409, 410, 491
madness (in *Close Sesame*) 100,
    295, 375, 407, 409, 410, 421,
    424, 425, 433
Mann, Thomas 705, 707
marriage
    arranged 199
    mixed 102, 256
Marxism xvii, xx, 152, 307, 420
Mauss, Marcel 568, 569, 587, 593,
    599, 609
Mazrui, Alamin vi, 615, 617, 619,
    621, 623, 625, 627, 629, 631,
    633, 635-636, 730, 737, 750
McHale, Brian 127
menstruation (in *Maps*) 190,
    471, 488, 534
Mercator 121, 470, 513
Miller, Arthur 219
motherland 88, 192, 483, 502,
    506, 546, 563, 620, 622-624,
    676, 733
mothers 46, 59, 127, 307, 318,
    372, 382, 391, 394, 444-445,
    529, 565, 655, 661-662, 665-
    666, 670, 672

Mudimbe, V.Y. 304, 450, 465
Mugo, M.M.G. 81-83, 93
murderers, in detective novel
    335-336, 516, 668
Mursal, Maryam 638-641, 657
Mussolini, Benito 347, 351
Muuryaan 710

N

names 2, 4-5, 26-27, 29-30, 75,
    138, 167, 169, 176, 179, 362,
    413, 511, 602, 626, 645, 673,
    691, 699
naming 96, 367, 413, 425, 470,
    479, 516, 648-649, 665, 669,
    691
Nasr, Seyyed Hossein 395, 398
national identity (in *Maps*) 68,
    87, 108, 123, 200, 449, 457-
    458, 463, 477, 479, 502, 523,
    527, 535, 560, 570, 618
National Security Service, Somali
    (NSS) 7, 202
nationalism, Somali 62, 210, 409,
    487, 491-492
Negritude 450
neocolonialism 77, 103
Ngugi wa Thiong'o 144, 325, 329,
    414, 420, 451, 465, 542, 631,
    635, 731, 738, 744, 747, 749
Nietzsche 102, 193, 257-258, 323,
    572, 574, 576, 588
nomads iv, xii, 155, 157, 159,
    161, 163, 165, 167, 169, 171,

, 536, 540, 579, 581, 601,
4, 611-613, 622, 632, 663,
665, 671-672, 674, 687, 693,
704, 710, 714, 723, 729-730,
737, 739, 746

Wright, Derek i, iii-v, vii, xii-xiii,
80, 88-89, 93-95, 97, 99, 101,
103, 105, 107, 109, 111, 113,
115, 117, 119, 121, 123, 125,
127-129, 253, 255, 257, 259,
261, 286, 288, 290, 305, 329,
345, 347, 349, 351, 353, 355,
357, 370, 372-374, 378, 488-
489, 508, 521, 533-535, 538,
540-542, 563, 566-567, 587,
641, 709, 711, 713, 715, 743,
745, 753

Y

Yates, Francis 480, 492